Tł

1 0 w m

The Official 'Biography'

of

The Swans

Town & City

by

David Farmer

with contributions from

Brian Lile & Colin Jones

Foreword by John Hollins, MBE

Published by

South Wales Evening Post

For our long-suffering wives
Pat, Judy and Glynis

Copyright © 2000 David Farmer, Brian Lile & Colin Jones

First Impression: September 2000

Published in 2000 by
Evening Post
Adelaide Street, Swansea SA1 1QT

The right of David Farmer, Brian Lile & Colin Jones
to be identified as the Authors of the Work has been
asserted to them in accordance with the
Copyright, Designs and Patents Act 1988.

A CIP catalogue record for this book is
available from the British Library.

ISBN 0 9539191 0 2

Printed and bound in Wales by
Dinefwr Press Ltd.
Rawlings Road, Llandybïe
Carmarthenshire SA18 3YD.

Contents

Foreword

JOHN HOLLINS, MBE

I am pleased to be given the opportunity of writing the foreword for this book, which, following our championship promotion last season, is a very timely publication. My job, of course, is concerned with taking the club forward in the short and medium term and not directly with its story. Yet, I am well aware of the importance of the club's history in the eyes of our supporters. Since I have been at the Vetch I have been regaled with stories of the 1948-9 promotion side, of the remarkable squad of talented local boys who thrilled the crowds in the fifties and, of course, of the excitement of the surging charge up the tables of the Toshack era.

Reading this book, I have also become more aware of the darker periods in the club's history; when it was obliged to apply for re-election and when it was in the hands of the receiver. There are lessons in both the positive and the negative of which we should be aware.

It has given me great pleasure, too, to note the number of new club records which our squad set last season, for I am extremely proud of my players and their dedication and application to the Swansea City cause! They deserve to be able to enjoy seeing the marks which they have set writ large in the club's records.

No Swans fan should be without this book, which I am sure will give great pleasure to readers. Certainly it is the most comprehensive 'bible' of all things to do with the Swans which has ever been published. Like all who care about this club, I am grateful to Professor David Farmer and his colleagues for the time and trouble they have taken in preparing the book for publication.

Preface

GEORGE EDWARDS
(Editor, *South Wales Evening Post*)

As someone who has been closely involved with football and football clubs since the early 1960s (they started sports reporters young in those days) it has been a pleasure to have become associated with Swansea City since assuming the editorship of the *South Wales Evening Post.*

This association in not always a straight-forward one. The issue of balance and of reconciling the interests of the club with those of readers and supporters is a tricky one. Directors, managers and players are sensitive to criticism as well they might be. So are we all when our skill or commitment is brought into question, and inevitably relationships between clubs and newspapers are not always smooth.

Papers think clubs get thousands of pounds worth of free publicity every week (which they do), while clubs claim that some people buy the paper only to read about the football team, which is equally true. So the two have to rub along together, each defending its own position, sometimes falling out but invariably making up.

The *Evening Post*, of course, would have no credibility at all if our reporters made excuses for poor Swans performances – not only no credibility with supporters, but none with the club, but it goes without saying that an affection develops and a reporter is pleased when his team wins, disappointed when a match is lost.

My first contact with the Swans came back in the days when Trevor Morris was manager. I would call him from the Midlands for team news every now and then and he was always happy to chat and find out the team news from my end. He was considerate, too. If a player dropped out on the morning of a game for some reason or other he would always phone to tell me.

Happy days. Soccer was different then – more homely and less cynical. Players, even the best players, would sometimes travel to the ground by bus (few could afford cars) and one I knew in the old Second Division actually arrived by bicycle. Hardly David Beckham. These days players get a much better deal and I don't begrudge those in the lower divisions a penny, because it is a short career. If players have a problem it is with coping with their status and handling the spotlight. In this sense managers are now keener than ever, to encourage players to be level-headed, to keep their feet on the ground, and it strikes me that, in this respect, John Hollins and Alan Curtis are doing an extremely good job.

There is a good feel about Swansea City at the moment, not simply because they have just won the Third Division championship, but because the club appears to have discovered focus and direction.

Professor David Farmer's splendid book, especially the chapters covering the early and middle 1990s, serves to emphasise the importance of this, providing as it does a sharp reminder of the trials and tribulations the Swans and their fans have suffered. Drama after drama, manager after manager, abortive take-overs, even humiliation.

The stability the Swans have craved seems finally to have arrived with a forward-looking but realistic board and an experienced and talented manager who believes in the fundamental values of the game.

What will the future hold, I wonder?

Author's Introduction

I find it difficult to believe, yet my calendar confirms the fact, that it is almost twenty years since I began writing the first version of the history of the Swans. During that time a new generation of supporters has emerged and much has happened, not only at the Vetch but in the wider world of football. For example, the Bosman ruling, and the establishment of the Premier League have had a major influence on soccer in general, as has the greater emphasis which has been placed on European and world-wide competition. Who would have forecast twenty years ago that one of England's leading clubs would voluntarily 'scratch' from the prestigious FA Cup in order to play in a short tournament in South America?

The all-pervading influence of television companies on kick-off times, on fixture lists and on the incomes of clubs has become ever more apparent, while the salaries of some players in the top echelons of soccer and the transfer fees which are paid for them have increased, seemingly exponentially. In turn, together with the activities of players' agents, these changes have also influenced the level of payment made to footballers in the Nationwide League. Paradoxically, perhaps because of the pressures on Premier League clubs to maintain their station in the top echelon of English soccer, they have tended to purchase players with a proven record in the top flight, rather than for development from a club in the Nationwide League. One result of this is that the selling market upon which many smaller clubs relied to boost their incomes has been adversely affected to their detriment. Meanwhile, in Wales, the reorganisation of Welsh football has resulted in the Principality's three Football League clubs being excluded from the nation's cup competition, which, since the inception of the European Cup Winners' Cup, provided them with a route into Europe. Not surprisingly, all these changes have had a major influence on the fortunes of Swansea City and need to be borne in mind when reading the account in this book of the last twenty years at the Vetch. As John Donne put it: 'No man is an island, entire of itself; every man is a piece of the Continent, a part of the main.' The same might be said of a football club.

Thanks

It is inevitable that a project which has necessitated extensive research over a period of twenty months will have involved many people other than the author. Consequently, in this introduction it is appropriate for me to thank those who have given me assistance over this period. Space does not allow me to name every person who has assisted, but I wish to place on record my appreciation of all the help I have been given. Taken together that assistance has made a significant contribution to the writing of the book which is in the reader's hands. I am very grateful for that support.

As the cover of the book indicates, both COLIN JONES and BRIAN LILE made important contributions to its development. Both are enthusiastic Swans supporters who have compiled extensive records of the club and its history. Brian's knowledge of soccer in Swansea, particularly before the advent of the professional game in the town, is second to none. Colin's records are computerised, which has enabled him to develop the detailed grids which relate to each football season since 1920, and from which the data on appearances in the statistical section of the volume has been extrapolated. In addition, Colin's extensive library of programmes of Swans matches proved to be a very useful source of illustrations for this book. For his part, apart from writing the introductory chapter, Brian also acted as proof-reader/joint editor which proved to be extremely helpful for me, particularly in the later stages of the book's development. My warm thanks to both.

I am pleased to be able to thank my publisher, the editor of the *South Wales Evening Post*, GEORGE EDWARDS, for his support and guidance, and his colleagues, sports editor, DAVID EVANS, sports photograph archivist, BARBARA POWELL, chief photographer, ALAN TRETHEWY and PHIL DAVIES of his staff, for their assistance in the compilation of material for this book. I am grateful, too, to LEN PITSON, a former senior photographer at the *Post* for his assistance in locating prints of earlier times in the Swans' history. Thanks are due, too, to JOHN BURGUM and RICHARD SHEPHERD, both of whom gave me access to their photograph libraries.

Once again, I have the pleasure of thanking Professor Sir GLANMOR WILLIAMS, Swansea's premier historian, for the sage advice and warm friendship, which he provided throughout the development of this book. His dedication in reading the material and commenting on it, always in a manner which motivated me, has been greatly appreciated. My thanks go, too, to the staff of the West Glamorgan Archive Service, particularly GWYN DAVIES for providing me with willing service whenever I used that facility. My thanks, too, to MARILYN JONES and the staff of the Central Reference Library in Alexandra Road, particularly CLAIRE TRANTER, for their willing asistance. GWYN REES, another Swans fanatic, provided us with a comprehensive record of the club's involvement in the Welsh and FA cups, which proved to be very useful in cross-checking the listings which we had developed from our own records. I am grateful to him.

I am pleased, too, to thank my daughter, JILL ISAAC, for her expert conversion of my typing into disks ready for the printer. As before, her work was meticulous.

EMYR, EDDIE and STEPHEN at Dinefwr Press, once again, showed great enthusiasm for the project and fine professional expertise in turning the material which they received into a finished product. I am indebted to them and to artist ROG who painted the excellent front cover panel, which depicts Swans of each decade since the club came into being. Diolch yn fawr iawn.

I would also like to thank the many people at the Vetch who, over the last twenty years have allowed me the privilege of association with the club which I have followed for many years. In writing this book I have been able to utilise the extensive records which I have collated over the last twenty-five years. However, many individuals have augmented those records with insights and information which helped place my material into context. Among them were former directors, MALCOLM STRUEL, BOBBY JONES, HARRY HYDE and MEL NURSE, former managers FRANK BURROWS and ALAN CORK, and former players such as TERRY MEDWIN, LEN ALLCHURCH, MEL CHARLES, COLIN WEBSTER and TOM KILEY. I am grateful to them all. I should like to thank my current colleagues, too: Chairman STEVE HAMER, NEIL McCLURE, who has been the prime mover for the club in liaison with the council regarding Morfa, JOHN HOLLINS, ALAN CURTIS and RON WALTON, all of whom have been of considerable assistance to me in a variety of ways. Finally, I thank my wife for putting up with me being wrapped up in another production schedule for the best part of two years. Usual message.

The book

The story which you are about to read is, as far as I have been able to make it, an accurate and, I hope, an objective account of the life and times of the Swans. In writing it, whilst recording 'facts' I have attempted to capture the club's ethos as well as the ambition, character and successes and failures of the various 'actors' who have populated the Vetch Field since 1912 when the club was formed. Furthermore, I have attempted to do this whilst producing a book which is as attractive to look at as it is to read.

Whatever the shortcomings of the finished product – and I accept responsibility for them all – I offer it as an honest attempt to present a complex story in a form which will be attractive to the reader and which reflects the subject in the most appropriate way. If my colleagues and I have succeeded in that then we shall be delighted.

The structure of the book

As will be seen from the contents page, following this introduction are twenty-four chapters each of which recounts the story of two or more seasons. From 1920, at the end of each chapter a grid relating to the seasons which are covered in the particular chapter is included. These grids include results, teams, scorers and appropriate totals for the campaign in question. Following the final chapter there is a comprehensive statistical section which includes data relating to a wide variety of Swans matters, particularly club records. Owners of the original version of this book will find that the new edition contains a great deal more material, both text and illustration, than its predecessor and, whilst based upon my previous book, its earlier part has been rewritten, while errors have been corrected and, of course, the happenings of the last two decades covered for the first time. I trust that readers will enjoy the finished product, and that someone in the not too distant future will be able to write a sequel telling the story of the climb of the Swans to a significant place in England's football hierarchy.

Up the Swans!

DAVID FARMER
Swansea
September 2000

Chapter 1

Prelude

Although Swansea Town AFC was not formed as a professional club until 1912, football of some kind was played in the town for at least half a century before that. As elsewhere, the game was probably brought to the town by young men returning home from public schools in England, where it was born. Typical of these were the sons of the gentry and the schoolmasters presumably involved in the first recorded game in Swansea, which was played at Maesteg House in February 1865, when the Grenfell family's Kilvey team drew with Swansea Grammar School after several hours play. It is not clear whether the game which they played resembled rugby or 'Association' as the two codes were only then becoming distinct, although the Sunday schools and the borough police were probably kicking a round ball on their respective Whitmonday outings in the late 1860s and early 1870s, when football was one of their favourite games.

It appears that there were two town soccer teams as early as 1870, one of them known as Blue Star, who played each other at Bryn-y-mor Field or on the sands – sometimes by moonlight! The first contemporary reference to a town team dates from December 1871, when 'twelve gentlemen of the town' lost to the Grammar School, but, again, the rules adopted were not specified. Nine months later, however, on 26 September 1872, a town association football club was formed by members of Swansea Cricket Club seeking a winter diversion, and it played its first game, against Neath, on 23 November. Had they stuck to soccer they might now have been the eighth oldest Football League club, but in October 1874 they switched to rugby to form Swansea RFC. This club would hold sway for the next forty years and gain an international reputation as 'Association' struggled to acquire even local popularity.

There are but scant references to 'the dribbling code' in the press during the 1870s and 1880s. A team called Swansea, possibly the rugby club, entered the inaugural Welsh Cup in November 1877, only to promptly scratch from the first round, while the first Swansea-born international, J. R. Morgan, of Cambridge University and Derby School, captained Wales between 1877 and 1882.

In the only reported game of the decade, played on the sands in April 1878, Blue Star drew with Mr. Dogget's XI, and there were only two matches in the 1880s: the Grammar School's 7-0 victory over Merthyr Proprietary School in December 1881, and Swansea Albion's 0-0 draw with the YMCA at the Recreation Ground in December 1889. When the South Wales Football League was formed in 1890, no west Wales clubs were included. In September of that year Swansea AFC was formed at the YMCA, to be succeeded by a second club of that name at a meeting at the Longlands Hotel (the site of the present YMCA) on 25 January 1893. This club only survived for six seasons, but there have been teams upholding the name of Swansea virtually ever since.

The team played its football at the Vetch Field, which had been transformed from neglected waste ground two years earlier. After an opening game at Neath, they made their home debut on 17 March against an XI captained by Billy Bancroft, the Swansea and Wales rugby player. Very few came to watch, but the crowd of 10,000 which turned up at St. Helens rugby ground when Wales played Ireland in February 1874, suggested that there was a future for soccer in the town. A month later Preston North End

THE ORIGINAL SWANSEA TOWN – AN AMATEUR SIDE FORMED IN 1906

Top row: H. Evans, H. Smart, P. Jones, S. Labbett, F. Hemming, C. Turner, A. Savage, C. Strothers, P. J. Potter, D. Ll. Hughes (Secretary), W. E. Johns, S. Palmer (President). Bottom row: W. F. Clark, F. Wynne, R. Sheppard, R. Brunt, S. Rees, S. Clark, G. Rees (Referee).

drew 3,000 to the same venue and showed a Swansea and District XI how the game should be played while defeating them 6-1.

After losing most of their games in their first full season, Swansea, playing in their new colours of black-and-white stripes, broke even in the 1894-5 campaign, recording their first victory over Cardiff, and making their debut in the Welsh Cup. In the second round they beat Knighton 2-1 at the Vetch, only for the visitors to successfully protest over the dimensions of the Vetch Field and to win the replay at Knighton 3-0. A change of name to Swansea Villa for the 1895-6 season only, did not attract any more spectators in spite of the goal-scoring feats of Father Kelly, who hit seven in a 15-0 trouncing of Burry Port. It was the following season, however, which saw their finest hour, when they reached the final of the South Wales Cup, unluckily losing 2-1 to Rogerstone, south Wales' leading club, before a crowd of 3,000 at Cardiff Arms Park in March 1897. They also lost at Rogerstone in the Welsh Cup.

With the game growing in popularity in the town (the Swansea and District League had been formed in 1896), Swansea reached their peak in the 1897-8 season, their record reading: played 30, won 22, drawn 2, lost 6. They lost 4-1 to Aberystwyth in the first round of the South Wales Cup, but had the audacity to beat Aberdare (South Wales League runners-up that season) 6-0 at the same stage in the Welsh Cup, only to be disqualified for fielding a professional, which was illegal before 1900. By this time the club was, at last, beginning to attract support, and over 2,000 lined the ropes in April for 'the best game ever seen at the Vetch Field', when F A Cup semi-finalists Derby County only managed to win 2-1 after Swansea had done most of the attacking in the second half.

Swansea became the first west Wales club to join the South Wales League in 1898-9 for their one and only season. Disappointingly, they finished bottom-but-one, and lost to Pontardawe, who would replace them, in the second round of the South Wales Cup. In the April they were banished from the Vetch Field, which, it was rumoured, was to be built over, though fortunately the

Swansea Gaslight Company bought it for storage space. Later that month Swansea, undaunted, brought West Bromwich Albion to St. Helens but could not repeat the heroics of the game with Derby, losing 13-1. Small crowds, shortage of money and the impossibility of keeping a settled side added to the club's misfortune and they were forced to disband, their swansong being a 7-0 victory at Llandeilo the following week. Curiously, a team called Swansea Wanderers played on at the Vetch Field for a while.

For the next seven seasons there was no town team, interest at senior level being maintained only by the district league. The leading team in that competition was East Side, sometimes styled Swansea East Side, who occasionally ventured further afield to keep the town's football name alive. A new enthusiasm was kindled, however, in September 1906 with the formation of Swansea Town, amateur precursors of the professional club. They wore blue, played their home games at Victoria Park, and won the championship of the district league in their first season. One of their rivals played under the revived name of Swansea Villa, but they would only survive two seasons. Swansea Town beat East Side 5-3 in a South Wales Cup first-round tie in the 1907-8 season before losing to Ebbw Vale in round two.

It was East Side, however, who brought Bristol City Reserves to St. Thomas Athletic Ground in March 1908, when a crowd of 1,600 saw the visitors win 3-2 after 'a splendid fight' by the local men. Swansea Town retained the district title, but their application to join the South Wales League for the 1908-9 season was rejected for the lack of a suitable ground. East Side, who changed their name to Swansea United and played in amber and black, were accepted and now became the town's premier club. They were, however, out of their depth. They lost to Merthyr in the quarter-finals of the South Wales Cup, while Swansea Town, now in decline, were defeated 7-1 by Maerdy Corinthians on their new ground at Cwmbwrla in the previous round. In April, Town and United joined forces to take on Bristol Rovers at Dan-y-graig, the visitors strolling to an 8-1 victory.

When the Swansea and District

League requested the Southern League to send some of their best teams to the town to play exhibition matches at the start of the 1909-10 season, a Crystal Palace XI duly obliged. They came to Dan-y-graig in January and defeated a Swansea team, which was more representative of the town than that which had faced Bristol Rovers, 3-2. More importantly, they were accompanied by Harry Bradshaw, the secretary of the Southern League, who urged district league officials to form a town club with a view to joining that competition. That there was sufficient enthusiasm in the town for this was demonstrated by the appearance of a crowd of over 4,000 at Morriston in April 1911 to see the home side play Swansea United, now back in the district league as champions, in the final of the Swansea Challenge Cup.

United's return to the South Wales League for the 1911-12 season brought no greater success than their earlier foray, while their aspirations in the Welsh Cup were cut short by Llanelli in a preliminary round. Developments of greater import were afoot, however. 'Big Soccer Boom: Swansea to join the Southern League' ran a headline in January 1912, when Harry Bradshaw returned to the town for discussions with local club secretaries and supporters. Eight south Wales teams, including Cardiff and Merthyr, and several small-town clubs, had joined in the previous two seasons, and it was felt that if the latter could succeed, then Swansea could do even better. A committee was elected which included J. W. (Jack) Thorpe, the future club's first chairman, and S. B. Williams, its secretary for many years. On 2 May Swansea Town was admitted to the Southern League Division Two, and at the end of June the club was registered as a limited company with a capital of £2,000. In the same month the Vetch Field was leased from the Swansea Gaslight Company. Swansea's soccer pioneers had set the scene for the coming of the professional game to the town.

Brian Lile

Chapter 2

A Professional Club is Born

The next step in establishing a professional soccer club in Swansea involved the new committee in formally applying to the Southern League for membership. In parallel they were negotiating with the Swansea Gaslight Company for a viable lease on the Vetch Field. Those who had supported the development of soccer in Swansea must have been very pleased.

On 14 June, a public meeting was held at which J. W. Thorpe told his audience that agreement had been reached with the Gaslight Company and that other matters were in hand. Thorpe also asked for financial support, saying that if the committee could be assured of a sum of £75 that night they would proceed with setting up the club. At the end of what proved to be a busy meeting, Jack Thorpe left the hall having been formally appointed as chairman of the new company and having obtained promises which more than covered the club's financial requirements. 'I had,' he said, 'hardly hoped for such a positive result.'

Thorpe and his colleagues now had to move fast. The Vetch Field had to be prepared as an enclosed stadium, banks had to be established to house spectators, changing facilities had to be built, a manager recruited, kit purchased and a team found. Since the new season was to start in the following September, all this work had to be completed in just eleven weeks.

By 13 July the board announced its shortlist for the post of manager, from which it selected Walter Whittaker, who had been Exeter City's player-manager and goalkeeper. Whittaker, with less than eight weeks to go before the club's first match, cast his net far and wide to find a team. Billy Ball, who was destined to become Swansea's first professional soccer hero, came from Stoke, Coleman from Brighton and what was to turn out to be an extremely important signing, W. Jack Nicholas from Derby County. Two amateurs, Willie Messer and W. T. Havard (at the time a clergyman in Swansea), were also signed following a trial match at Morriston. Messer, and Fisher, who signed later, and

Some former Chairmen, Managers and Secretaries

Chairmen

J.W.THORPE
the father of Swansea Town A.F.C.

B. WATTS JONES

P.E. HOLDEN

O. EVANS
the first "promotion" chairman

Secretaries

S.B. WILLIAMS
who served the club from its inception in 1912 until 1946

TREVOR HOSKINS

Managers

JOE BRADSHAW
the first "promotion" manager

BILLY McCANDLESS
who did the South Wales 'hat trick' by taking the Swans to Division Two

W. Jack Nicholas

'The cry "Give it to Ballie" [was] a popular one . . . even on the stage, for there was a play at the old Star Theatre in which an artiste inquired what she should do . . . The reply came from the "gods".'

Letter to 'South Wales Evening Post', 7 October 1937.

Billy Ball

secretary S. B. Williams had been members of the old Swansea Utd. Then, in between overseeing the construction work which was going on at the Vetch, the manager recruited several other players, including Hamilton from Leeds and Cleverley from Brentford.

By the middle of August the frenetic work at the Vetch was beginning to show results, but a great deal still needed to be done. In those days of picks and shovels, the proper levelling of a pitch, development of the banks and so on represented a significant task in the time available. Such was the interest in the work that the *Cambria Daily Leader* published a photograph showing men at work on the development of the Vetch Field under the direction of Whittaker. The manager, it seems, had wide ranging responsibilities. On the field, by that time his hastily gathered team of itinerant soccer players had provided him with some idea of their talents. In addition, the would-be fans had had their appetite whetted. Two thousand 'lined the ropes' at the Recreation Ground to watch the club's second public trial. 'Play,' it was reported, 'was bright and open.' Whittaker, from the unlikely vantage point of his goal, expressed himself pleased with developments.

1912-13

Two days before the club's first Southern League game, against Cardiff City, the team played a match at Merthyr. This was to give the new combination a thorough test, for the Merthyr club had won the championship of the Second Division of the Southern League in the previous season. Although the home side won the match 2-1, Whittaker felt that it had been a useful exercise.

In their first season (1912-13) the Swans won the Welsh League Championship and the Welsh Cup: no mean achievement for a newly-established club.

At least it had given his players another opportunity to improve their understanding. Interestingly, the Swansea goal was scored by one of the amateurs, clergyman W. T. Havard, who would go on to win the M.C. in the Great War, become a Welsh rugby international and a bishop. Not only Catholic priests could play football!

On 7 September 1912, when Cardiff City came to the Vetch for the inaugural professional league match, the ground was *en fête*. 'Both elevens,' it was reported, 'underwent the ordeal of an army of

photographers' and His Worship the Mayor of Swansea was there to kick off. Given that this was the first match in the club's history, the board was delighted to find that 8,000 people crowded the ground. Such support augured well for the viability of the fledgling club, though only time would tell in that regard. One novel feature of the Vetch at that time was that the playing surface was rolled clinker.

The match ended in a 1-1 draw and the name on the lips of the crowd as they streamed away from the Vetch after the game was Billy Ball. The diminutive centre-forward had endeared himself to his new fans as a result of his bustling play. His distinction was to score the first ever Swans goal in the Southern League. He went on to have a brief but exciting career in Swansea colours.

Yet Ball was not the only success of the afternoon. The board, the manager and the supporters were all of a mind that the whole team had shown its potential. Cardiff, after all, had had two seasons experience of professional football in the Southern League. Once they find their feet, the popular argument ran, Swansea Town would do well. As events at the end of the season were to show, that confidence was justified.

The draw with Cardiff, a win against Leicester Fosse in a friendly at the Vetch, and the club's first Southern League victory at Tonpentre, caught the imagination of the public. Reflecting this, 'Pendragon' in the *Leader*, was moved to write:

> Folks who treated the new movement with something like contempt at the start, are becoming reconciled to the fact that Association has taken such a firm root that it constitutes a menace to the supremacy of rugby.

He concluded prophetically, however:

> Rugby may lose its supremacy, but it will continue to hold a large section of the public.

As soccer became more established, two factions appeared in the town, each championing their favoured game and the press became embroiled in the process. For example, controversy developed about the size of gates at St. Helens and the Vetch. The two papers were caught up in this argument, each accusing the other of being less than truthful regarding the attendance data which they published. Not that this was helpful to either cause. However, an objective commentator would have noted that most sources showed that more than double the number watched matches at the Vetch than were at St. Helens for rugby games, This, of course, was hardly surprising given that soccer had a novelty advantage, was easier to understand and that rugby at the time was in the doldrums. Logic, though, plays a minor part when those involved in a dispute are fired by emotion. Nonetheless, as the arguments indicated, the concerns of the rugby fraternity were becoming more real as the season progressed.

By the end of October the Swans Supporters' Club could boast three hundred members; the management at the Vetch announced that they were going to build a grandstand capable of seating a thousand people; and gate income was more than justifying the confidence of those who had promoted the club. The town's tradespeople were also beginning to see the potential of the new movement in advertising terms. Stewarts, 'The king tailors', for example, offered one of their famous overcoats to any Swansea Town player who could score two goals in a home league match. It was Billy Ball who claimed the first coat; he also scored the club's first hat-trick in a match against Aberdare.

Prior to that game the Swans found that having a clinker surface had disadvantages, among them was the fact that wet grass pitches at away venues were both heavier and more slippery than the unturfed Vetch. Of course, the converse was true for sides who came to play the Swans, because the surface there was hard and practically dry at all times. Nevertheless, the 'cons' outweighed the 'pros'; grassing the Vetch was to be a priority during the close season.

Overall, the Swans gained considerable success in their first season. In the Welsh Cup they created a surprise by beating Wrexham on their own pitch and followed this by winning at Merthyr's ground, beating the home side 3-0. As a result of that victory, the Swans found themselves in the semi-final of the competition at the first time of asking. There they were to play Cardiff City, who were running away with the championship of the Southern League's Second Division. The venue was Ninian Park, which provided the Taffsiders with a significant advantage. Yet, in front of the largest crowd (over 20,000) the team had entertained they outplayed the home side to win 4-2. Ball scored two, Coleman one, while Cardiff's Cassidy was credited with the first own-goal recorded in the Swans' favour. It was a remarkable victory

The 1912-13 squad and directors with the Welsh Cup and the Welsh League trophy.

and was well-deserved. Incredibly, the team was in the final of the Welsh Cup in the first season of its existence. Swansea could be justifiably proud of its soccer team, and indeed it was. When the team arrived at High Street Station they were welcomed by a large crowd. An outsider might have been forgiven for thinking that they had actually won the cup, but the size and the good humour of the throng showed that professional soccer had a well-established bridgehead in the old borough. The town had a new set of heroes.

By the end of March the Swans were on target for three prizes. They were top of the Welsh League, in the final of the Welsh Cup and well-placed in the Southern League. Whilst promotion was missed, they won the Welsh League title and, in due course, the Welsh Cup. It was a remarkable achievement for a club in its first year of existence. Even the rugby fraternity joined in the eulogies as squabbles between supporters of the two codes were forgotten, and the whole town basked in the team's reflected glory.

When the Welsh Cup winners returned to Swansea East Dock Station at 10 p.m. on 25 April 1913 – after beating Pontypridd 1-0 in a replay at Tonypandy – there was a huge crowd to welcome them. Players and officials stood on a brake which was pulled by ardent enthusiasts in place of horses. Then, at the town's Royal Hotel, speeches were made from the balcony 'and the crowd cheered every word'. The chairman, Jack Thorpe, thanked Walter Whittaker for all he had done, and the manager, with every justification, must have felt pleased with himself and with his players. Yet, as he was to find, opinions in football are sometimes shorter-lived than memories in politics.

1913-14

It seemed as if the whole of Swansea was awaiting with relish the start of the new season. Committed soccer followers and the uncommitted alike were borne along on a tide of enthusiasm. The talking point around the town was, will the Swans gain promotion this time? Surely, the argument went, if the club can finish

> *In their second season the Swans became the first club from south Wales to reach the second round proper of the FA Cup.*

third at its first attempt, promotion to Division One should be assured. That the heady target was simply the first division of the Southern League might seem insignificant today; at that time it represented a worthy goal for the young club.

For the new campaign, the Vetch Field was grassed. Groundsman George Hart, according to the *Nottingham Evening Post*, had guaranteed that grass would grow there, despite the fact that a visiting 'expert' had said that it was impossible.

George was proved to be right and on 13 September for the club's first home match (against Barry) the players enjoyed the feel of turf underfoot. Kneepads, which had been *de rigeur* on the old clinker pitch, were left in the dressing room.

Several new faces appeared in the Swans side for the early games of the season. Among them were Jock Weir, a big centre-forward who, in due course scored in six matches in a row and who represented the Southern League in a game against the Irish League, and Jack Williams who was to play over 100 games for the club up to 1923.

One innovation for the club's second season was that, in addition to the competitions in which it had been involved during the previous campaign, it entered the FA Cup, which meant that the club could be required to play many more matches. Not that this had ever been done by a club from south Wales. Yet, at the time, to those buoyant supporters anything seemed possible.

Results early in the season encouraged the supporters in that belief. The defence was frugal and many goals were scored; Grier, for example, scored a hat-trick in a match against Barry Town. With the

side doing so well the crowds flocked to the Vetch; twelve thousand were in attendance when the Swans beat Newport 3-0, and ten thousand came to see the side win its second qualifying round in the FA Cup. Unlike the previous season's Welsh Cup run, when every match had been played on an 'away' ground, this time every round was at the Vetch. In due course, after victory in the final qualifying round, they were drawn to play Merthyr at home. Whilst Merthyr had also qualified for the first round proper of the FA Cup, they had done so only after a replay. Consequently, technically at least, the Swans were the first south Wales club to reach the first round. It was another achievement for the club to register in its records.

After Merthyr had been beaten on that historic day, the crowd, the directors, players and supporters were in high spirits. A record gate of eighteen thousand had paid £450 for the privilege of watching the match and that income was three times that which a Merthyr director had indicated as being possible at the inaugural meeting eighteen months before. Furthermore, the Swans were now in the second round of the English competition. That they were the first Welsh team to reach the last thirty-two was enough in itself, but the possibility of another large gate added to the directors' joy.

Meantime, 'Ajax' in the *Post* was waxing lyrical about the feats of the Vetch club:

> They (the Saxon teams [*sic*]) can no longer afford to be contemptuous when an eighteen-month-old Welsh club can win a place at the first attempt among the . . . best sides of the season.

If 'Ajax' was suggesting through his use of the epithet 'Saxon', that this was to be the Welsh against the English, then his knowledge of the make-up of the Swans team must have been slight. There were no Welshmen in the side duly selected to play against Queens Park Rangers, the team drawn against the Swans for the round. The match was to be played at the Vetch, which some interpreted as reinforcing the hypothesis that God must be a Welshman. At the Vetch, the management and the team welcomed the draw, for, whilst QPR were playing in the First Division of the Southern League, a higher station than the Swans, so were Cardiff and Merthyr, both of whom had been beaten *en route* by the men in white.

On hearing the draw, officials of the London club offered the home directors a financial incentive to play the tie on their ground, but the Swansea board refused. Quite apart from any question of ground advantage and acknowledgement of their responsibility to the club's supporters, the Swansea directors had another card up their collective sleeve. They doubled admission prices from 6*d.* (2.5*p*) to 1*s.* (5*p*). This caused controversy in the town and both local papers carried angry letters from irate fans, but that anger fell on deaf ears. The directors judged that their supporters would 'stump up' because of the importance of the match; they were proved to be right. Their judgement proved to be less sound, however. as regards team selection. Inexplicably, the committee changed a winning side for the match; QPR won 2-1 in front of a crowd of over 18,000.

Unfortunately, after the euphoria of the FA Cup run, the spirit of the team appeared to be affected to its detriment. Games were lost in the Southern League at Croydon, Barry and Luton. Given the backlog of matches in the league, which arose as a result of the cup games, plus the fact that the club was in the semi-final of the Welsh Cup, promotion seemed a less likely possibility than it had at the same time in the previous campaign. Then, in attempting to play off outstanding games, on 7 March the club played a league match and the Welsh Cup semi-final. The result of this ridiculous decision was that both matches were lost; promotion was missed and the club fell at the final hurdle in the cup.

In the face of these setbacks, the directors signed Ivor Brown from Reading and Joe Bulcock from Crystal Palace. It is interesting to note that a director, Abe Freedman, was said to have signed Bulcock. The manager, it seems was not involved in the process. Unfortunately, in the time remaining, neither player could provide the necessary stimulus to improve performance. At the end of its second season the club had nothing more tangible to reflect its endeavours then a new stand. The team finished fourth in the Southern League, and were runners-up in the Welsh League and in the Welsh Cup. Nevertheless, despite these disappointments, no one doubted that Association was firmly established in the town and that it had developed a secure and viable niche in Swansea's sporting life.

Sadly, the man who had built the original side in such a short time and from a standing start did not gain from his efforts. The *Sporting News* reported that the sacking of Walter Whittaker, 'came as a great shock to all Swansea'. Whether the sacking was to do with the club's failure to improve upon its performances in its first season, or whether it reflected changes in the attitude of the board (chairman Thorpe had been replaced by Frank Newcombe) we shall never know. No statement was made to the press at the time, while both local papers, presumably reflecting popular opinion, paid tribute to Whittaker's work, although that would have been small consolation to the former goalkeeper.

On a more cheerful note, 'Cygnet' in the *Sporting News* was able to point to 'the great headway which has been made in fostering soccer in Swansea'. The club had not been slow in 'spreading the gospel'. Apart from assisting the amateur game in the town, it had worked to re-establish the soccer game in Swansea schools. Twenty-five years later Swansea Town was to reap a rich harvest from the seeds which were planted at the time.

Chapter 3

Then Came the War

> *For the first year of the Great War conscription was not enforced. Whereas rugby was 'abandoned for the duration', the soccer authorities claimed that their contractual arrangements made it necessary for them to continue playing during the 1914-15 season.*

With the departure of Whittaker, a new manager J.William Bartlett was appointed in his place on 8 May 1914. Bartlett had turned down an offer from the German FA to take charge of the whole of southern Germany on their behalf. In view of what was to happen a few months later, it is interesting to speculate whether the new manager had some premonition about the coming of war with that country. Bartlett had been manager at Leicester Fosse (who had played a friendly at the Vetch in 1913). Perhaps he had impressed members of the Swansea board at that time. Other newcomers included Tom Hewitt, a Welsh international from Chelsea who became a great favourite at the Vetch, and Amos Lloyd, a winger who could operate on either flank. Meanwhile, Allman and Cubberley, both talented players, had been transferred to Manchester United.

By mid-July, only four members of the original board remained. Frank Newcombe was chairman, while three of the other directors had been elected the previous season: Abe Freedman would serve until 1922 and from 1935 to the early fifties, becoming chairman in 1939; B. Watts-Jones would serve until 1934, succeeding Newcombe as chairman on his death in 1915, and acting as the club's Southern League representative, as well as being a member of the I.F.A. Board on behalf of Wales; and John Barclay Owen, who would become chairman in 1929 and continue on the board until his death in 1935. They were joined by several newcomers, including Owen Evans, who would become chairman in 1923 and remain associated with the club until 1939; William Messer, who was intriguingly described as 'dealer and bird fancier', whose son played for the club from 1912-14; and Thomas White, who would serve the club until 1941. While players and managers figure most prominently in this history, it is only proper that the contribution made by these pioneer directors should be noted.

1914-15

The news of the outbreak of war came as pre-season training plans were being made. The directors had signed twenty-one professionals, who, together with other staff represented a significant outgoing for a newly established business.

Rugby convert Ben Beynon played rugby union, rugby league and soccer.

Consequently, the board was extremely relieved to learn that the Association authorities had decided to carry on for the coming season as planned. Since conscription was not then in force, apart from registered reservists, the players were required to honour their contracts. With a jingoistic atmosphere prevailing at the time, these men faced many pressures, particularly having to live with the implication that they and their masters were unpatriotic.

In Swansea the problem was exacerbated by the fact that all amateur rugby had been cancelled immediately war was declared. One result of this was that the local papers featured photographs of leading 'All Whites' who had volunteered for Kitchener's army. In London, at the end of October, a *Times* editorial thundered that it was a national scandal that professional footballers, 'in the prime of their manhood,' should be 'bribed away from their country's service by the managers of their clubs.' But, whatever pressures they were facing, the players had to carry on. Coincidentally, they were joined by a Swansea rugby player, Benny Beynon, who played for the Swans as an amateur, which, the player believed, would allow him to return to the fifteen-a side game after the war.

Despite many difficulties, including almost losing the Vetch for military use, the club set out upon the third season of its existence. Whatever happened in the league, the management was praying for another good cup run, both to stimulate interest and improve the club's financial position. In that regard, the gods were to smile on them again and, in due course, the club and its players were to be involved in the biggest game of their short history.

Because of its success in the FA Cup during the previous season, the club was exempt from competition until the fourth qualifying round. Newport were disposed of at that stage, as were Port Vale and Leicester Fosse in subsequent rounds. The crowds for these games were not as large as they had been for the previous season, but they lacked nothing in enthusiasm, and were enjoying two new heroes: Ivor Brown, a skilful inside-forward and

Swansea players in the casual dress of the day before the FA Cup tie against Blackburn Rovers in January 1915. From left to right: Ivor Brown; Owen Evans (Director); Bert Gilboy; Ben Beynon; David Anderson; Jack Duffy; Amos Lloyd; Ben Hurst; Harry Read; Joe Bulcock; Jack Hewitt; manager of the Langland Bay Hotel; Charlie Lock and W. Wishart (Trainer).

Amos Lloyd who could not only cross the ball with precision but could score goals from either wing. As a result of these victories, for the second season in succession, the club found itself in the first round proper of the FA Cup. Incredibly it was drawn home again, the twelfth successive occasion over two seasons that the club had been favoured in that way. However, it was the name of the club which was to oppose them which really set the town alight. Kitchener, the Kaiser and more local controversies were all forgotten in the excitement. The opponents were to be Blackburn Rovers – champions of the Football League. The Manchester United of their day, they had won the 1913-14 First Division by seven clear points and were now lying second in that competition. The pundits declared the result to be a foregone conclusion. As the *Athletic News* put it after the event:

> If there was one team expected to enter the second round without much trouble, that was Blackburn Rovers.

Despite a tempting offer from the Lancashire club to play the tie at Blackburn, the Swans directors decided to stay at the Vetch. Sixteen thousand people showed their appreciation of the decision and gate receipts were £737. No one queried the increase in ticket price this time.

On that historic day, to the concern of the Swansea supporters in the crowd, Blackburn attacked from the first whistle. Their skilful football stretched the home side to its limits. Club captain Joe Bulcock at left back was a tremendous inspiration as

When Blackburn came to the Vetch for the FA Cup tie in Jan. 1915, they played against a Swansea side which had been drawn at home on twelve successive occasions in that competition. The Swans won and astounded the football world: Blackburn were Football League champions, the Swans in the Second Division of the Southern League.

wave after wave of Blackburn attacks were repelled. Hewitt at right back, Hurst in goal and Duffy at centre-half completed the final wall which the Lancastrians could not penetrate. After twenty minutes, when Blackburn's attacking pressure eased, the Swans broke away and, in their first real attack, took the lead. Amos Lloyd took a pass from Benny Beynon, tore down the wing and crossed to find Beynon. As the *Post* put it, 'Beynon sent the ball into the right hand corner of the net with a lightening shot.' Beynon, the only

amateur on the field and a rugby player to boot, had breached the visitor's defence. Half time arrived with the score unchanged. Could the Swans hold out? Whatever was said in the two dressing-rooms during the break, the greater effect was evident in the display of the home side. They grew in confidence, but then the expectant crowd was silenced as a Blackburn man went down in the Swansea penalty area. The shrill blast of the referee's whistle cut the air like a knife. Penalty! Hurst crouched as Blackburn's Bradshaw approached to take the kick. Bradshaw, though it is doubtful whether any of the Swansea camp knew at the time, had scored with thirty-six consecutive penalties before the Vetch match. That sequence and Blackburn's interest in the FA Cup for that season ended when the player shot wide. When the final whistle blew to the cheers of the exultant home fans, it signalled one of the biggest upsets in the history of Association football up to that time. If English football had not had cause to note little Swansea Town before that event, they had every reason to be aware of them afterwards.

The Blackburn match ended another sequence, for, drawn away in the next round, the team was required to travel to Newcastle. At that time, the home side was a powerful combination in the First Division with an excellent home record. Consequently, the omens did not seem bright for the men in white. They had never travelled so far, never played on the ground of a first-division club, nor performed in front of such a large crowd – 30,000 were there to see the home side defeat the 'Welshmen'. The match programme demonstrated the confidence of the Tynesiders: 'Swansea, after all, are just a plucky persistent team – that's all.' How wrong they were! Not only did the Swans hold the Magpies to a draw, necessitating a replay at the Vetch, they were applauded from the field at the end of the game by a sporting Geordie crowd.

Prior to the home match against Blackburn, the players had attended a special service at St Nicholas's Church. Then the curate had told the players that if they played a straight game their opponents would 'rove no more'. Given the apparent success of that intercession with the Almighty, they tried again before the replay with Newcastle. It was, it was said, a service of thanksgiving for the Newcastle result. The manager read the lesson. Was this further proof that God was a Welshman? Sadly, no. The team lost the replay 2-0, although Joe Bulcock was a passenger for most of the game.

That cup run produced considerable income for the club, which was just as well. Many thousands of fans were in the forces, which, with trains and other forms of

> *When Leyton resigned from the Southern League during the 1914-15 season, the Swans' record win (9-0) had to be expunged from the records.*

transport curtailed, meant that gate receipts from league matches were far lower than they had been in previous seasons. The FA Cup defeat allowed the team to concentrate on its other competitions and, for the second time in three years they fought their way to the Welsh Cup final. Their opponents were Wrexham and, because of travel restrictions, the game had to be played either at the Racecourse or the Vetch. It was agreed that the venue would be decided by the toss of a coin; Wrexham called correctly and claimed home advantage. After holding the Robins to a draw, the

Swans, not unreasonably, assumed that the replay would be at the Vetch, but Wrexham wished to toss again. Following a heated impasse, the Welsh FA had to step in and declared Cardiff as the venue, which seemed rough justice for the Swans. In the event, Wrexham won the replay 1-0 and S. B. Williams had learned an expensive lesson about the vagaries of human nature. The time to negotiate such matters was before, not after, the first match was played.

On the league front, poor gates had resulted in many resignations. Abertillery, Brentford, Barry, Maerdy and Leyton had all fallen by the wayside and the Swans suffered more than most from the deduction of points won against these sides. In addition, Leyton's resignation meant that the Swans' record 9-0 victory over them had to be expunged from the records. At the end of the season, yet again, the club was fourth in the Second Division of the Southern League. Despite their excellent cup run, which demonstrated the potential of the side, the elusive First Division seemed as far away as ever.

Chapter 4

War, Post-War and First Division Football

Whilst there were no players under contract during the 1915-18 war period, the company which was Swansea Town still had to protect its physical assets. The lease for the ground still applied, the landlords had to be paid and the stadium maintained. In short, the club had to carry on in some measure purely to maintain itself and survive.

On the death of Frank Newcombe, B. Watts-Jones became chairman and he and his board colleagues determined to keep the club solvent whilst contributing to local war funds through staging matches at the Vetch. By astutely encouraging local leagues (which included teams from factories making munitions), promoting charity matches between select sides, and arranging games with Army and Navy sides the club was kept afloat. By this means, too, soccer was kept in the public eye, for the last thing the board wished to do was to lose the momentum which had taken the infant club so far in such a short time. Watts-Jones recognised that they also needed to consider longer term issues. What was going to happen after the war?

As time passed, the reality of the club's position became clearer. The effects of *anno domini* played a part, for many of the men who had played before the war were too old when it finished. Then three Swans, A. Cleverley, Ted Mitchell and Joe Bulcock had been killed in action, W. Y. Brown wounded and Jock Hamilton given the Military Medal. Meantime, manager Bartlett, not having a job at the end of the 1914-15 season had moved on to pastures new. As a result, when the Armistice was eventually signed in November 1918, the board found itself in need

When the First Division of the Southern League was enlarged in 1919, the Swans gained most votes in the ballot to select additional clubs for the competition.

Ivor Brown

of a new manager and new players. The parallels with 1912 were evident, although, this time the club had a ground, a board and an administrative structure.

Chairman, B. Watts-Jones, who had been the club's representative with the Southern League, was given the task of ensuring its continuing participation in that competition. Astutely he went beyond his brief, because he noted that there was

continuing concern regarding the viability of the league's second division. Many clubs in it (and some in the first division) had gone out of existence during the war. At its worst this could mean that the Swans would not have a competition in which to play. Watts-Jones had no doubt that his task was to ensure that his club was included in a revamped first division. He was to succeed in no small measure.

As the troops were returning home at the beginning of 1919, the directors strove to put their house in best order. If the club was to become a member of the First Division of the Southern League, they would have to persuade the powers-that-be with evidence of their viability as an ongoing business. Meantime, Swansea Town was earning its revenue by providing fine entertainment for the Swansea public to enjoy. Jock Weir helped himself to several hat-tricks and scored four on two occasions, while Ivor Brown was thrilling the crowds as a 'manipulator of the ball'.

On 6 January 1919 the Southern League announced that it was to extend its first division to twenty-two clubs. No decision was taken at the time as to which additional clubs would be elected, although there was a widely held view that the Swans were among the favourites for such recognition. On the other hand, there was a lobby group which argued that Swansea was inconveniently situated as far as clubs from London and the south east were concerned. Happily, that 'location' group was soundly defeated. On 3 April 1919 it was announced that the club which had attracted most votes (48) was Swansea Town. The size of Swansea gates and the effective lobbying of Watts-Jones had won the day for the Swans.

On hearing the news, Abe Freedman announced that, 'The success of the soccer code in Swansea is now assured.' He then paid tribute to the 'wonderful spadework' of Watts-Jones over the previous eighteen months. In their confidence, the Vetch board also held out an olive branch to the town's rugby club, wishing that it 'might be as successful in the future as it was in its palmy days.' The men at St. Helens took that gesture gladly and, at their AGM, the chairman spoke about 'working amicably with those in charge of our sister code.'

From the playing point of view, despite a considerable amount of experimentation, the club had a successful half-season in 1919. Several new faces appeared in the white shirt at that time, including Billy Hole, who was to become the club's first Swansea-born international. Twenty games in all were played, with the Swans winning sixteen and drawing one. Among the club's opponents during this period were Brentford, Reading, Bristol Rovers and Swindon. Many fine games ensued which, given the club's success, provided Association with a welcome fillip. As a result, the supporters 'couldn't wait for the season to come'.

Billy Hole

Letter from the new Swansea Town chairman confirming the Vetch lease.

1919-20

In mid-June of 1919, the directors of Swansea Town made a decision which was to have a considerable bearing on the future of the club. Joe Bradshaw, who was the son of the secretary of the Southern League, agreed to be manager of the Swans. Since the club did not advertise the post, and Bradshaw was still in the army at that point, it is reasonable to conclude that the appointment stemmed from Watts-Jones's relationships. If the director had so impressed members of the Southern League that the club's application to join its first division was so warmly received, it is quite likely that he influenced the league's secretary as well. If that was the case,

no doubt father told son about the promise of the club and the opportunity which it represented.

Bradshaw came to the Vetch with experience of the job – he had been manager at Southend before the war, but presumably, saw the Swansea job as providing a new challenge. Whatever the circumstances, when he arrived home from France, he was welcomed in London by Watts-Jones and immediately began his search for players. 'Demob' leave, it seemed, was very short for Bradshaw. With just six weeks to the start of the season he had to appraise his staff and acquire others. One early appointment was that of trainer Ernie Edwards, who had a fine reputation in the field, for, under his charge the Burnley team had won the FA Cup.

At the club's AGM and that of the Supporters' Club, Watts-Jones and H. Dodd respectively, urged supporters to take up the additional shares which were being offered. Both argued that while the club was in a sound financial position, additional capital was necessary to ensure its continuing development. The shareholders were told that the club was facing difficulties with the Gaslight Company, which was demanding a considerable increase in its charges. Presumably, this meant that the gas men, when granting the original lease, had little idea of the business potential of their tenant club, and that it had turned out to be far bigger than they had assumed.

On 12 August it was announced that Jack Nicholas, the club's pre-war captain, had been re-engaged as player-coach. The news of the appointment was received with great enthusiasm by all concerned. Nicholas had been a popular figure, a skillful footballer and an effective leader of men. With Ernie Edwards being concerned with fitness, the coach's role was to be more akin to the modern track-suited manager. The idea might not have been original, but it was certainly progressive. As for Nicholas, it is arguable that the playing ethos of the Swansea club evolved from the pattern set by him in that first post-war season.

In the meantime, several new players had been added to the club's strength. Among them were men who were to be members of the famous 'promotion' side five years later. Three of them made an immediate impact: Jock Denoon, a beanpole of a goalkeeper, came from QPR, Jimmy Collins was signed whilst with the army in mid-Wales and F. Robson, a full back, came from the manager's old club, Southend. As is ever the case, news of these signings fuelled the enthusiasm of the club's supporters and, by the middle of August, 'Cygnet' in the *Leader* was warning against over-optimism. He believed that the first division of the Southern League was extremely competitive, that there would be few, if any, easy games and the team would have to travel considerable distances. But, with their memories of the victory over Blackburn, of a successful half-season, and the new signings to sustain them, there was an air of optimism among the Swans supporters as the new season began.

The club's first game in the First Division was played at Luton on the 'Strawplaiters' ground. Ten thousand people were present to see the game, which ended in a 1-1 draw. Evan Jones scored the Swans' goal and Luton had to convert a penalty to save a point. The Swansea team which played in that historic match was: Denoon; Hewitt, Robson, Collins, Ogley, Durnin; Harris, Jones, Birch, Brown (I.) and 'Tich' Evans. Evans, a diminutive winger whom the Swans had signed from Barry, was to make tragic headlines before the season was very old.

Although the Swans won their next match, at Southampton, after six games had been played the side had just three points to its credit.

W. Y. Brown

Confidence ebbed and criticism mounted. One obvious detrimental factor was the inability of the forwards to score many goals, and amateur selectors began writing to the papers to make this and other points. Even club captain, Evan Jones, was criticised. Manager Bradshaw's response was to drop newcomer Birch and replace him with old favourite Jock Weir. In addition, following defeat at Exeter in the club's sixth match, the manager made another signing in the shape of the intriguingly named W. Y. Brown. Whilst the fans were delighted to see a new face, they were puzzled by the fact that the player was a centre-half when the team's problems appeared to be in the forward line. Nevertheless, when Brown made his debut in a Vetch match against Cardiff, there were fifteen thousand people in the ground.

One interesting feature of this game was that it was refereed by D. J. Sambrook, who was a well-known Swansea official. The league ruling that referees had to be from 'neutral' towns had to be ignored

because of the rail strike which was in being at the time. It was a compliment to his excellence that the visitors should allow a Swansea man to referee a local derby. Sambrook's performance must have satisfied the visitors, for there were no complaints, even in defeat. To the delight of the home supporters, the Swans won 2-1.

But, still the critics wrote to the local papers. 'Cygnet', for example, throughout October, was commenting on the number of letters which he had received criticising the selection committee, though he did some criticising of his own, too. His target was a section of the crowd who 'ruined what might have been several enjoyable games by . . . barracking players.' He also noted that Swansea pessimists had been 'waxing eloquent on the probability of relegation at the end of the season.' Yet, as the journalist pointed out, there was no provision for relegation that season. He went on to comment that such was the mindset of these gloom merchants that they saw greater dangers in a situation than could possibly exist.

For the home match against Brighton at the end of October, Billy Hole, who was a £3 per week part-time professional, appeared on the right wing for his home league debut. Harris, who had joined the club from Nottingham Forest, moved inside to accommodate him. The new pairing did well and the local press praised their performances. In an adjoining column to the report of that match in the *Leader,* an item on the 'All Whites' game that afternoon had the headline 'BEYNON PROMINENT AND DROPS GOAL'. This, of course was none other than the hero of the Blackburn FA Cup match. Given their goal-scoring problems, the Vetch camp must have wished he was playing for them.

Despite several wins in early November, the barrackers must have still been in evidence. In that month at a Supporters Club 'Smoker', Watts-Jones spoke about the serious consequences of 'this negative practice'. According to the chairman, more than one Swans player had confessed to him that he suffered from nerves every time he played at the Vetch. Watts-Jones appealed to supporters to 'Get behind the team'. He also commented on the difficulty of signing new men. The board was willing to 'dip down . . . but only for better players than they had'.

Subsequent to that meeting, the team put together a run of six games without defeat, which, of course, was the best means of all of silencing the barrackers. The star of the sixth of these matches was 'Tich' Evans, but the player was not available for the following match because his wife was seriously ill. By that time the club was in mid-table position with seventeen points from the same number of games.

Part of the reason for the improvement in the form of the team was the influence of W. Y. Brown, who had moved to centre-forward and was demonstrating his versatility. Another outstanding figure was Ivor Jones at inside-forward. Jones had joined the club from Caerphilly after showing up in a match against the Swans reserve side. His partner was Billy Hole, now a regular in the first team. Both men were outstanding in a game against Brentford in mid-December, whereas 'Tich' Evans had a relatively quiet match, though this was hardly surprising since his wife had died only two weeks before. An interesting feature of that Brentford game was that, apart from W. Y. Brown, the forwards were all Welshmen. It was the start of a trend which was to develop even further in years to come.

With the team now occupying a more comfortable position in the league table, the interest of supporters in the FA Cup was stimulated by a tie against Gillingham. The old confidence had returned and the optimists, at least, were forecasting another good run. Gillingham, however, would not be coming to the Vetch to make up the party. They would have to be beaten. By the Thursday, two days before the match, preparation was well underway, when Ernie Edwards, the

Ivor Jones

trainer, noticed that 'Tich' Evans was missing. Jack Nicholas, who had taken a fatherly interest in Evans since his wife had died, went to look for him. What Nicholas found was to cast gloom over the whole club. Poor Evans was lying under the stand with his throat cut. One newspaper reported that 'the player's head was almost severed from his body'. There was an open razor in his hand. Not surprisingly, the players and staff were shocked. The diminutive winger had been extremely popular with his colleagues and with the crowd. The black arm bands worn by the players during the match at Gillingham were an inadequate token of the sorrow which the players felt. W. Y. Brown's rallying call, 'Let's win it for Tich' was to be of no avail. After drawing in Kent and again at the Vetch, they lost the third game by the odd goal in three. For the first time in its history in the competition, the Swans had failed to enter the first round proper of the FA Cup.

In January 1920, The *Sporting News* included 'pen pictures' of the Welsh rugby team to play England in the first post-war rugby international. Among those listed was Benny Beynon, who was described as:

'The most consistent outside-half in the Principality . . . Benny made history . . . playing centre-forward for the Swans when he scored the goal which enabled them to gain their sensational win over Blackburn. He is probably the best centre-forward the Swans have. Still, rugby is his game.'

The fact that the Swans did not have him was to the benefit of the Welsh rugby XV who defeated England in front of a forty-thousand gate. Beynon went on to win a further cap against Scotland, then, almost immediately, he astounded the rugby world by signing as a professional with the Swans. Some said that Beynon had signed in a fit of pique at the selfish play of Shea who had partnered him in the Scottish match. Most, however, recognised the basic dilemma of a man with a talent which allowed him to play both codes exceptionally well. They also understood, even if they didn't admire, the economic pressures which had taken so many rugby union players north to the professional game. Benny had taken a shorter route, at least for the time being.

Prior to Beynon's signing, the board had 'dipped down' again to buy Joe Spottiswoode, an outside-left of considerable ability from Chelsea. The Swans paid £500, a significant sum at the time, to bring the player to the Vetch. As the seasons ahead were to show, the club had made a sound investment. Around the same time, Ivor Jones was capped by Wales for a match against Ireland and, according to the *Leader*, Billy Hole was also under scrutiny. Jones, who had played just fourteen Southern League games prior to his selection, thus became the first Swansea Town player to represent Wales whilst with the club. He was to be the first of many.

During the final two months of the season the side was successful enough to draw large crowds to the Vetch. For example, on 5 April a crowd of over 20,000 saw the Swans play Reading. Then, only five days later, when Brentford came to play a league match, 15,000 watched the game and saw Ivor Jones and Billy Hole each score two goals. Finally, for the last match of the campaign, versus Plymouth, 18,000 crowded the ground. Overall, despite the FA Cup disappointment and a poor start, the club had enjoyed a reasonably successful season, finishing ninth in what transpired to be its only season in the first division of the Southern League. Joe Bradshaw must have felt reasonably satisfied with his season's work.

Chapter 5

The Football League

The prospect of a third division for the Football League was first considered by that body in 1908. However, the idea was not pursued because there had 'not been an adequate number of applicants of sufficient stature'. A year later, the Southern League requested a joint conference with the senior body to discuss a possible merger. Had that conference been successful, the history of professional soccer in Swansea might have been completely changed.

The decision of May 1920 to form a third division of the Football League came as a surprise to many English clubs. The president of the league referred to the scheme as 'an extraordinary movement'; so it was, because the soundness of the scheme and the speed with which it was introduced suggest a great deal of behind-the-scenes activity. The tightly framed schedule and scheme were put to members of the Football League at their AGM in 1920, and although an amendment was tabled calling for the decision to be deferred, the proposal was carried by a large majority. The first division of the Southern League was to become the basis for the new third division of the Football League.

As a result of that decision, Swansea Town found itself in a position where, theoretically, at least, it could win its way to the top flight of English association football. Yet, twelve short months before, the club's major concern had been whether or not it was possible to gain admission to the first division of the Southern League. Thus, in retrospect, B. Watts-Jones's achievement in negotiating that entry can be seen to have been even more important than it appeared in May 1919.

Overall, the progress of the club must have been as unbelievable to those early Swans supporters as the

Joe Bradshaw

Wilfie Milne

rise to the first division of the Football League was to become sixty years later to their grandchildren. After only four seasons of competitive professional soccer, Swansea Town was an (associate) member of the Football League. The Swans, along with Merthyr and Newport, were to carry the hopes of

Wales in the new Third Division. Cardiff, meanwhile, had stolen a march on their compatriot clubs by making an independent application for admission direct to the second division of the Football League. Their success in this application must have been a bitter pill for the Portsmouth club, which had won the championship of the Southern League at the end of the previous season. Nonetheless, Cardiff (who finished fourth), clearly had presented their case extremely well. By that action, Cardiff regained the lead in terms of status over Swansea Town which they had held, first in 1910-11 and then in 1913-14. It was to be some time before the roles were reversed.

Now that the Swans were members of the Football League, they were bound by certain rules. One of these required the club to charge men 9*d.* (4*p*) and ladies and boys 6*d.* (2½*p*) for admission to matches. There was also the important principle that visiting clubs should be paid twenty per cent of the admission money based upon these figures. Increased charges for admission to a stand or enclosure were not included in the 'pooling' scheme. Another rule related to the amount of money which a club could pay to its players. There was a strict scale of wages which was common to every club; a starting wage for new Football League players was £5 per week, increasing by annual increments of £1 to a maximum of £9 per week. Most players were paid their appropriate amount during the season and a lower figure during the summer.

Manager Bradshaw, relishing the challenge which he now faced, lost little time in making further signings. In one respect, membership of the Football League made his task easier, for men who might not have been prepared to move outside it now saw Swansea as a *bone fide* club. Among the manager's early signings was a stalwart who was to make club history by playing a record 585 league matches. His name was Wilfred Milne. Milne stood 5'8" and weighed 11st. 7lbs. but was a giant in many respects. The only other June signing to make any impact was Jimmy Edmundson, a centre-forward from Sheffield Wednesday, for whom the Swans had paid a fee of £500. An interesting fact about Edmundson

Swansea Town staff for the 1920-21 season.

was that he had been on the books of Leeds City when they became bankrupt. Subsequently, along with other Leeds assets, he was auctioned in order to meet the demands of creditors. At the Vetch, at the end of his first season, he finished top scorer with twenty goals.

Before the historic first season started. 'Cygnet' was able to report that, 'the optimists are having a field day at present . . . The Swans directors have sufficient faith . . . to rest confident that Swansea Town at the end of May next will be somewhere near the top.' Unfortunately, though, early results were disappointing and by 11 September five matches had been played and three lost. When October ended the side had lost all five away games and had not scored a single goal in the process. Predictably, criticism mounted among fans and in the press. 'Cygnet' went so far as to say that the Swans were mediocre, though he was quick to defend Bradshaw from the 'flailing tongues and acid pens'. 'The manager,' he argued, 'has not been given a free hand.'

By the end of October the club was fifth from the bottom of the league table and the supporters were plunged into gloom. Rumours were circulating about players who wanted to leave and, during one match, there was crowd trouble which abated only

when Watts-Jones and a police sergeant went to speak to the supporters involved. Modern association football administrators would be delighted to know what magic was conjured up then, for the problem was solved almost at once.

Ivor Jones was the first Swansea Town player to be selected for Wales at professional level and Billy Hole was the first Swansea-born man to be capped while with the club. However, J. R. Morgan, who was captain of Wales for their second match, was born near Swansea and A. T. Jones, who played in the club's first match was a Welsh amateur international.

Despite the depressing form, the crowds still flocked to the Vetch. Fourteen thousand attended a match against Portsmouth, a thousand more saw Northampton and sixteen thousand came to watch Grimsby.

Grimsby, however, were something of a novelty, since they were the only club in the Third Division which did not originate from the Southern League. They had finished bottom of the second division at the end of the previous season and had lost their place to Cardiff in the last re-election voting for Division Two. As a result, they could not have felt very amicably disposed towards Welsh clubs. Nevertheless, in their first match with Grimsby the Swans won 3-1 and, a week later beat them 2-0 on their own ground. Happily for the Vetch men, these two games were the beginning of a run of fifteen matches without defeat – a record for the new third division.

During that period, the right wing pair of Ivor Jones and Billy Hole proved to be outstanding. Thus in April 1921, when both were selected to play for Wales against Ireland at the Vetch, no one was surprised. During that match, Hole had the distinction of scoring the first international goal registered at the Vetch. He could also claim to be the first Swansea-born man to be selected by his country while playing for his home-town club.

By the end of 1920, the club's fortunes had improved to the extent that it had won twenty-one points from the same number of games. Elsewhere, in November, the Millwall and Crystal Palace grounds had both been closed for two weeks as a result of crowd disturbances. In Swansea, 'Cygnet' was pointing out to the 'very few roughs in the Swansea crowd who hurl disgusting epithets at players', that, unless they mended their ways, similar action might be taken against the Swans. On the field, Benny Beynon was leading scorer with nine goals from nine matches, but, disappointingly, he was badly injured in the final match of the year and was never such a force again.

In January, Bury, a Second Division side , were drawn to play at the Vetch in the first round of the FA Cup. Such was the interest in the game that a new ground attendance record of 21,300 was set on the day. The gate of £1,470 was also a record, which might have made S. B. Williams think back to the first budget figure which had been suggested at the club's inaugural meeting: it was just £30 more for the whole season. There was another piece of history made that day, for a newsreel camera captured a few moments of the game as the Swans, playing excellent football, beat the Lancashire men with something to spare. 'Cygnet' was so excited by the play that he contended: 'It was, without doubt, the best game ever played by the Swans.'

One feature of the Bury match which was repeated at the Vetch for many years, was the singing of 'Bubbles', with the crowd on the big bank swaying back and forth in unison as they sang. The same choir was in evidence three weeks later in the second round against Plymouth. Yet again, a new ground record was set, as 23,808 people were there to sing the songs. Sadly, though, the visitors won the match 3-2 and W. Y. Brown had a penalty attempt saved by the Argyle goalie.

In the league, the tremendous success of the team from November to February had converted the fickle pessimists into rabid optimists. Promotion was being talked about around the town, but it was Plymouth, again, who were to dash such hopes by winning at Home Park. Even though the next eight

> *The Swans set a record for the new division during their first season when they remained unbeaten for fifteen matches from 23 October 1920 to 26 February 1921.*

S. B. Williams

Swans matches provided the team with a further unbeaten sequence, it was not enough to clinch promotion. At that time, only the champion club was promoted; the Swans finished the campaign in a creditable fifth position in the new league which, in itself, was gratifying. If only they had had a better start!

As the season came to a close there was one distasteful note to remind sportsmen of the pettiness of some minds of the period. Benny Beynon had not received his caps for either of the matches which he had played for the Welsh Rugby XV. 'Ajax' had taken up the matter with the secretary of the Welsh Rugby Union, who declared that a cap was a gift 'from the Union. It did not follow,' he said, 'that it must be given to every player who assists.' Perhaps realising the lameness of his argument, he added that a cap would not be given to a player,who during the season has joined the Northern Union or any other professional footballing organisation. Beynon, it seemed, was regarded as a defector – outside the pale – as far as the

honour which he had earned was concerned, even though the ball which he now used was a different shape.

At the club's AGM an attempt was made to bring J. W. Thorpe back onto the board. However, he declined to stand, saying that he felt that other members of the board would not welcome him. The meeting proved to be lively enough, with the chairman declaring a gross income for the year of £30,000 – a significant amount of money at the time. When pressed by questioners about new players, the chairman, B. Watts-Jones set the meeting back on its heels by declaring that they should 'bear in mind that it took some time for new players to be acclimatised to the town, as Swansea was a most depressing town for strangers to live in.' The newspaper reports did not carry any reaction to the comment. However, bearing in mind the fierce pride in his home town of the average Swanseaite, such a comment must have aroused indignation not only among Swans followers but among the population at large.

1921-22

Despite the economic depression which gripped the country, there was tremendous enthusiasm for soccer in south Wales as the new season opened.

Cardiff City had won promotion to the first division and fifty thousand people watched their opening match, while in the Eastern Valley sixteen thousand saw newly elected Aberdare Athletic's first Football League match on that same day.

At the Vetch, notwithstanding rumours which had been circulating that he was retiring, W. Y. Brown was still club captain. He found himself with two new colleagues: Ernie Morley, a full-back from Swansea's Sketty district and Willie Davies, who came from Rumney. Davies had been signed in exchange for a donation of 10s. 6d. (52.5p) to his old club. Both he and Morley were to become internationals. Unfortunately, once again, the side started the season badly. Not only were early results unfavourable (the team picked up just six points from the first nine games) but the rigours of economic depression reduced the size of gates as the season progressed. Eighteen thousand had come to the Vetch to see the opening match of the season, but, apart from two crowds of fifteen thousand, the remaining attendances averaged little more than ten thousand.

By the beginning of October 'Cygnet' was reporting that some members of the Swans team were being 'booed and howled at and greeted with derisive shouts'. Some of the Swans, he went on to argue, preferred playing in away matches rather than at the Vetch, and the writer was moved to describe the villain who perpetuated such 'base deeds':

> Generally he is short of stature, anaemic looking, with a head too big to suggest it contains only brains, a high shrieking voice, reminiscent of a rusty saw in quick staccato action. He is blind to every good move initiated by Swansea Town players, but his attention to a faulty clearance or badly placed transfer is microscopic . . . He is heard . . . in the grandstand week after week and the marvel is that he has been allowed unchecked to disturb the players. Verb sap.

Commentators over the years might have wondered if this character had ever left the stands during difficult times in the club's history. Nonetheless, throughout this period, 'Cygnet' himself was constructively critical of the team's performances. It seemed that the marvels of the Bury match of the previous season had been forgotten. Happily, though, the agonies for the Swans' fans of the mediocre league results were assuaged, yet again, by success in the FA Cup. During December, Bournemouth and Bristol Rovers were disposed of, following which the fates decreed that the Vetch men should play West Ham at home. Notwithstanding the team's poor league form and the economic difficulties, twenty-six thousand were at the match to create yet another attendance record; they saw the teams battle out a goalless draw. This necessitated a replay at West Ham four days later, when the Swans surprised the critics by holding the Hammers to another draw.

The consequence of that was that, for the second time in the club's history, it was required to play a third game to settle a tie. This time, at Bristol City's ground, they won by the only goal of the game.

The success of the club in the FA Cup was, clearly, an important financial factor for the Swansea club. It was also an extremely valuable confidence booster for the team. However, its importance in allowing the possibility of major English clubs

---

In April 1922 the Swans beat Bristol Rovers 8-1 to set a club record. This was more than the total number of goals scored by the team in its previous eleven matches.

---

coming to play at the Vetch was of even greater moment. These were among the reasons why a leaflet had been delivered to the English FA in January 1922 by the Swans Supporters' Club. The document related to the deliberations of the English body concerning a proposal to ban Welsh clubs from their cup competition. The lucid appeal of the chairman of the Supporters' Club, H. C. Dodd and his secretary R. J. Wiltshire, had the desired effect. In mid-February 1922, the *Athletic News* reported that 'Rule four has been changed to allow Welsh senior clubs not exceeding fourteen in number to enter competitions'.

By that time, as if in recognition of their security of tenure, the Swans had won their way into the third round of the cup for the first time. Their opponents for this historic match were Millwall, a side from whom the Swans had taken three points during their own poor spell. Consequently, management, players and supporters in Swansea were confident of success, but Milllwall, living up to their nickname, 'The Lions', tore the Swans apart. Keen, their centre-forward, scored all four goals in an emphatic victory on their own ground in front of 30,000 people. After the excitement of the cup, the drabness of the side's league performances must have been a considerable disappointment to

Swansea supporters. And this was reflected in the gate for an evening match at the Vetch against Charlton: only two thousand people watched the game – the lowest attendance there since the club was formed.

One reason for the poor crowds was probably the team's lack of ability to score. For example, during February and March, in nine league matches, the side scored just nine goals and, in the first three games in April they did not add to that total. Given the lack of goals, the economic situation and the poor form of the side, plus the fact that Ivor Jones had been sold to West Bromwich the week before, when Bristol Rovers came to play at the Vetch on 15 April 1922, no one expected a large crowd. Indeed there were only three thousand in the ground to see what turned out to be an historic Swans victory. The team scored as many goals (eight) as they had done during their previous eleven matches. It was a remarkable result, with W. Y. Brown and Jimmy Collins each scoring hat-tricks.

Unfortunately, the huge win did not presage a return to scoring form. Indeed, in the bizarre game against Brentford, which was the final home fixture of the season, the team scored just one goal against nine men. Three Brentford players had missed their connection at Cardiff and did not arrive at the Vetch until the second half of the game. Meantime, the visitors had taken to the field ,the nine including their manager, who played in goal.

When the season ended, the directors were faced with a set of gloomy indicators relating to the business which was Swansea Town. Widespread unemployment throughout the Welsh coalfields had decimated the Welsh League and, as a result, Swans reserve matches were costing the club money instead of contributing to its income. With poor first-team gates exacerbating the problem, there seemed little prospect of improvement in the seasons immediately ahead.

One victim of the recession was B. Watts-Jones, the club's chairman. In mid-March he had resigned from the board following the closure of his own business.

Some said that he had given so much time to the affairs of Swansea Town that he had neglected his own. In his stead, J. W. Thorpe, the club's original chairman, was elected to a place on the board. Thorpe had been campaigning for improvements in the running of the club over the previous two years and his ideas had captured the imagination of the public. Now he had the opportunity to help put them into practice. Meantime, manager Bradshaw must have been looking over his shoulder: his major ally, the man who had brought him to the club, had gone, whilst the club's supporters had suffered the poorest season since its inception.

At the club's AGM, Abe Freedman, who had stepped into the position of chairman following Watts-Jones's departure, found himself having to deal with a highly critical meeting. After moving the adoption of the report and balance sheet for the previous season, Freedman praised Watts-Jones for the tremendous work which he had done for the club. These well-deserved comments were delivered and accepted in a mood of genuine appreciation of the former director's efforts. However, the meeting was clearly awaiting the opportunity to voice criticism.

After reporting a twenty-five per cent fall in income, Freedman stated that the directors were determined to secure promotion, 'not only to the second division, but eventually to division one'. He went on to say that he and his colleagues had carefully considered the purchase of new men, but given the industrial slump, they had concluded that the time was not ripe for 'lavish expenditure'. Nonetheless, if they could not get promotion with the present players they would go further afield to secure new talent. The spirit and the sentiment behind the statement drew applause which was both loud and long. Nevertheless, that applause masked the true feelings of the bulk of those in attendance. Everyone there wanted to achieve the stated objectives; the problem was that they did not feel that the present board could make it happen. Cassius, it seemed, was lurking in the wings.

In due course, a notice of motion was moved from the floor to the effect that the board should be reduced to seven. 'Too many cooks . . .' said the seconder of the motion. In the event, the meeting was adjourned until the following Friday, when a ballot for a seven-man board produced several shocks.

Swans cup-tie team, November 1922.
Top, right to left: E. Edwards (trainer), E. Morley, J. Denoon, W. Milne, Joe Bradshaw.
Middle: W. Hole, H. Deacon, J. Smith, L. Thompson, J. Spottiswoode.
Bottom: J. Harwood, J. Roulson (Captain), J. Williams.

The most remarkable was the omission of acting-chairman Abe Freedman. The new board consisted of J. W. Thorpe (chairman), D. J. Bassett, Thomas White, Owen Evans, James Saunders, David Rees and Trevor Evans. Thorpe must have looked back on that moment ten years before when he became chairman of a completely new club. Now, he was in charge of a sizeable business, considerable assets, and a reasonably well-established Football League club. His return was widely approved by the fans, particularly those who had fond memories of the exciting days when the club was first formed. As so often happens with human memory, the past, when recalled, was endowed with brighter hues than those which it had, in reality, been coloured. Nevertheless, whilst being flattered by the popular recognition which he had received, Thorpe must have realised that the expectations which that brought with it could make the coming season a testing time.

1922–23

At the beginning of the new season, it became clear that manager Bradshaw had been given a freer hand than hitherto. Despite the economic situation Bradshaw had

signed twelve new men. Among these was the former Portsmouth player, John Harwood, and two young Birmingham men, Harry Deacon and Len Thompson. £250 had been paid for centre-forward, John Smith from QPR, whilst Birmingham had received £500 for Joe Roulson. With few players leaving in exchange for fees, Thorpe must have leaned heavily on the club's bankers for money to trade.

One poignant departure was Ben Beynon. The erstwhile rugby international severed his connections with both the club and soccer and returned to the rugby fold. This time, having been a professional soccer player, it was to join the Oldham Rugby League club. Many men have played both rugby codes, some have played soccer and rugby, but very few have played both rugby and soccer at a high level. Benny thus carved a special niche for himself in the sporting history of his home town as well as the games which he graced.

For the opening match of the new campaign – against Merthyr – more than twenty-thousand crowded the Vetch. Despite the economic difficulties of south Wales at the time, there was a large contingent from Merthyr. Since the Swansea side included seven new men, it was hardly surprising that the new combination did not gel immediately. Merthyr had a strong side and if the tackling of full-back Langford had been described as 'uncompromising', it would have been something of an understatement. The player not only made his mark on the Swansea outside-left's legs, but also on the mind of the Swansea manager.

After a reasonable start to the season (the side had earned ten points from as many games) the team's performances were beginning to catch the imagination of the public. Despite the economic situation, Thorpe's willingness to back his manager resulted in gates averaging fifteen thousand for the first five home matches, which was a considerable improvement on the previous season. By 11 November the Swans were one of only twelve league clubs which could boast an unbeaten home record. In addition, they were second top scorers in the Football League. Such was the spirit of Swansea supporters at this time, that, after beating Portsmouth on their own ground, promotion was being spoken of with confidence. On 30 December, just before the final match of 1922, manager Bradshaw was engaged for a further period. After the problems of the previous season he must have been delighted. His team seemed to have shared his mood, for in that game they hammered Aberdare Athletic 5-1 as if in celebration.

By this time, Deacon and Thompson were established at inside-forward, with Hole and Spottiswoode on the flanks. Had the Swans fans of the period been able to see into the future, they would have noted that the promotion side was beginning to take shape. As it was, during the first half of the season, the team had done exceptionally well at the Vetch, scoring five goals on four occasions. Overall, they had gained thirty-one points from twenty-three matches and scored fifty times. They were in the kind of form of which managers dream. Centre-forward John Smith, with sixteen goals, was the leading scorer, while Billy Hole had nine to his credit. The one disappointment was an early exit from the FA Cup, but with promotion a possibility, that seemed of little consequence.

The new year started with another win – a 1-0 victory at Aberdare, but the next result was something of a shock: Luton, on their own ground, beat the Swans 6-1. Since the team had been virtually unchanged for sixteen matches and had done so well, the reason for such a defeat was difficult to establish. Bradshaw said that it was a 'freak result', which, given that the team won the next five games, seemed to be a reasonable conclusion. In January, the *Athletic News*, when comparing the Swans' performance with that of the previous season, headed the item, 'WARNING TO SWANSEA TOWN'. After complimenting the team on its performance thus far, it stated: 'Swansea must conserve their stamina . . . the testing time comes after the middle of March'. At the end of February, after a fine run of results, the team was to find that the warning was worthy of careful consideration.

At the beginning of March the Swans were second in the division, only two points behind Bristol City. In the middle of the month they lost at Watford, then, after drawing that return at the Vetch, they lost twice in succession to QPR and Charlton. The prize of promotion, which had looked to have been within their grasp, now seemed to be slipping away. Two fine wins at the Vetch against the two London sides renewed hope again, and with four matches left to play, the optimists felt that there was still a possibility that their team could close the gap between them and Bristol City, the leaders. It was not to be: they finished third in the division, having scored 78 goals. Overall, it had been a commendable performance, but not good enough, for in those days, only the champions were promoted from each of the two third divisions. Naturally, all concerned with the Vetch were disappointed, but even then, there was something of a silver lining to the cloud. One of the final four games had been against Plymouth away. That day, the home centre-forward was outstanding, scoring twice and making a big impression on manager Bradshaw. The player was to become one of the final acquisitions of the Swansea manager's team-building process. His name was Jack Fowler.

In May 1923, Swansea Town became the first Welsh side to play abroad when they toured Denmark. It was an interesting innovation and, in due course, was to result in another important signing by Bradshaw. The chairman, J. W. Thorpe, accompanied the players on the tour, giving the manager the opportunity to reflect on the previous season's experiences. Both local papers had commented on the success of the seven-man board, but it was clear that there had been some lobbying on behalf of the men who had been deposed at the previous AGM. Thorpe must have wondered whether their relative success would be sufficient to ensure that he and his colleagues continued in office. He would have been right to be concerned, for at the June AGM, a former director, T. M. Martin, had withdrawn a motion to restore the board to its former size. Presumably, he had judged it to be prudent to do so after weighing up his chances of success. From this distance it is reasonable to argue that he was right – given the club's success in the season which had recently ended; but he was not finished yet.

At the meeting, Thorpe opened his report with the words, 'I think that you will agree with me that last year's side was the best we have possessed since the formation of the club.' It was a statement which no one was prepared to contradict and one which ensured that the meeting began in a positive manner.

Later in the evening, however, there was a note of criticism which serves to provide another example of the Swansea pessimist. In response to an innuendo from the floor, Thorpe rounded on the individual concerned. He said, 'If ever you hear the old story that they don't want promotion (which is trotted out whenever we drop a point or two), tell them the truth.' To applause from the floor, the chairman went on to firmly refute the rumour. According to the *Leader*, 'the meeting ended in a warm glow', though as far as Thorpe was concerned that warmth was illusory. At a subsequent meeting of the board he found himself relieved of the chair, being replaced by Owen Evans. The reason given for the change was that the post was to 'go around'. Since, subsequently it did not, it would appear that Thorpe, despite his success, had more enemies than friends within the club. Whatever the reason for the change, it was to mark the beginning of the end of his involvement with Swansea Town.

Swansea Town FC Season 1920/21 Division 3

#	Date	V	Opponents	Score	Scorers	Att.	Crumley J	Robson ER	Evans F	Smith F	Holdsworth E	Williams J	Hole WJ	Jones I	Edmundson J	Rigsby H	Spottiswoode J	Ogley W	Collins J	Brown WY	Prentice JH	Durnin J	Beynon B	Milne W	Gray GR	Stapleton W	Catlow T	Slater J	Denoon J	McCullum D	Jackson S	Hoyland F	Gough C	Jennings W	Messer B
1	Aug-28	A	Portsmouth	0 3		20,232	1	2	3	4	5	6	7	8	9	10	11																		
2	Sep-02	H	Watford	2 1	Ogley, Jones I	12,000	1	2			4	6	7	8	9	10	11	3	5																
3	Sep-04	H	Portsmouth	0 0		14,000	1	2			4	6	7	8	9	10	11	3	5																
4	Sep-08	A	Watford	0 3		10,000	1	2			4	6	7	8	9	10	11	3	5																
5	Sep-11	A	Luton Town	0 3		9,000	1	2			4	6	7	8	9			3	5	10	11													
6	Sep-16	H	Norwich City	5 2	Ogley 2(1pen), Beynon 3	11,000	1	2				6	7	8		10		3	5		11	4	9												
7	Sep-18	H	Luton Town	1 1	Jones I	14,000	1	2				6	7	8		10		3	5		11	4	9												
8	Sep-25	A	Northampton Town	0 2		8,000	1	2				6	7			10	11		5	8			9	3		4									
9	Oct-02	H	Northampton Town	2 2	Beynon, Brown	15,000	1	2				6	7			10	11		5	8			9	3		4									
10	Oct-09	A	Southampton	0 3		12,000	1				5	4	7	8	9		11			10				3	6	2									
11	Oct-16	H	Southampton	1 1	Jones I	12,000	1					6	7	8	9		11		5	10				3	4	2									
12	Oct-23	H	QPR	1 3	Jones I	16,000					5	6	7	8	9		11			10				3	4				1	2					
13	Oct-30	A	QPR	1 1	Edmundson	8,000							7	8	9		11		5	10				3	6				1	2	4				
14	Nov-06	H	Grimsby Town	3 1	Gray, Beynon, Brown (pen)	16,000							7	8			11		5	10			9	3	6				1	2	4				
15	Nov-13	A	Grimsby Town	2 0	Beynon 2	6,000		2					7	8			11		5	10			9	3	6				1		4				
16	Nov-20	H	Brighton & H A	0 0		14,000		2					7	8			11		5	10			9	3	6				1		4				
17	Nov-27	A	Brighton & H A	1 1	Beynon	9,000		2					7	8			11		5	10			9	3	6				1		4				
18	Dec-04	H	Crystal Palace	0 0		15,000		2					7	8			11		5	10			9	3	6				1		4				
19	Dec-11	A	Crystal Palace	1 0	Brown	7,500		2					7	8			11		5	10			9	3	6				1		4				
20	Dec-25	A	Bristol Rovers	2 1	Beynon, Edmundson	14,000		2					7		8		11		5	10			9	3	6				1		4				
21	Dec-27	H	Bristol Rovers	2 2	Brown 2	20,000		2					7	8			11		5	10			9	3	6				1		4				
22	Jan-01	A	Norwich City	1 1	Edmundson	8,000		2				4	7	8	9		11		5	10				3	6				1						
23	Jan-15	A	Southend United	2 1	Jones, Edmundson	6,500		2				4	7	8	9		11		5	10				3	6				1						
24	Jan-22	H	Southend United	2 0	Edmundson, Brown	15,000		2				4	7	8	9		11		5	10				3	6				1						
25	Feb-05	A	Brentford	2 1	Spottiswoode, Collins	5,000		2					7	8	9		11		5	10				3	6				1		4				
26	Feb-12	A	Merthyr Town	3 0	Edmundson 2, Spottiswoode	18,000		2					7	8	9		11		5	10				3	6				1		4				
27	Feb-19	H	Merthyr Town	1 0	Spottiswoode	20,000		2					7	8	9		11		5	10				3	6				1		4				
28	Feb-26	A	Plymouth Argyle	0 1		14,000							7	8	9		11		5	10				3	6	2			1		4				
29	Mar-05	H	Plymouth Argyle	3 0	Edmundson 2, Jones	16,000		2					7	8	9		11		5	10				3	6				1		4				
30	Mar-12	A	Exeter City	2 1	Edmundson 2	6,000		2					7	8	9		11		5	10				3	6				1		4				
31	Mar-19	H	Exeter City	2 1	Edmundson 2 (1 pen)	9,000		2					7	8	9		11		5	10				3	6				1		4				
32	Mar-25	H	Reading	2 1	Hole, Edmundson	15,000		2					7	8	9		11		5	10				3	6				1		4				
33	Mar-26	H	Millwall	0 0		16,000		2					7	8	9				5	10		11		3	6				1		4				
34	Mar-28	A	Reading	3 1	Jackson, Brown, Edmundson	10,000		2					7	8	9				5	10		11		3	6				1		4				
35	Apr-02	A	Millwall	2 0	Edmundson 2	25,000		2					7	8	9				5	10		11		3	6				1		4				
36	Apr-09	A	Newport County	1 1	Edmundson	9,000		2						8	9				5	10				3	6				1	7	4	11			
37	Apr-16	H	Newport County	1 2	Edmundson (pen)	13,000		2					7	8	9		11		5	10				3	6				1		4				
38	Apr-23	H	Gillingham	2 0	Jones, Spottiswoode	10,000		2					7	8	9		11		5	10				3	6				1		4				
39	Apr-28	H	Brentford	1 1	Edmundson	12,000		2				6	7		9		11		5	10				3					1		4		8		
40	Apr-30	A	Gillingham	1 2	Hole	15,000		2				6	7	8	9		11		5	10				3					1		4				
41	May-02	H	Swindon Town	1 1	Gough	7,000	1						7		9				5	10				3	6	2		4		11			8		
42	May-07	A	Swindon Town	0 0		9,000		2					7	8	9		11		5	10				3				4						1	6
					Apps		12	35	1	1	7	17	40	36	32	10	34	6	36	35	3	12	12	35	32	7	1	2	29	17	5	1	2	1	1
					Gls								2	7	20		4	3	1	6			9		2						1		1		

#	Date	V	Opponents	Score	Scorers	Att.	Crumley J	Robson ER	Evans F	Smith F	Holdsworth E	Williams J	Hole WJ	Jones I	Edmundson J	Rigsby H	Spottiswoode J	Ogley W	Collins J	Brown WY	Prentice JH	Durnin J	Beynon B	Milne W	Gray GR	Stapleton W	Catlow T	Slater J	Denoon J	McCullum D	Jackson S	Hoyland F	Gough C	Jennings W	Messer B
1	Dec-18	H	Hartlepool, FAC-Q	3 0	Edmundson, Hole, Beynon	18,000		2			4		7		8		11		5	10			9	3	6				1						
2	Jan-08	H	Bury, FAC-1	3 0	Edmundson 2, Brown	21,310		2			4		7	8	9		11		5	10				3	6				1						
3	Jan-15	A	Mid-Rhondda, WC-4	0 1	played on same day as league game																														
4	Jan-29	H	Plymouth A, FAC-2	1 2	Edmundson	23,808		2			4		7	8	9		11		5	10				3	6				1						

Swansea Town FC Season 1921/22 Division 3(South)

#	Date	V	Opponents	Score	Scorers	Att.	Denoon J	Robson ER	Milne W	Durnin J	Collins J	McCullum	Hole WJ	Jones I	Edmundson J	Brown WY	Spottiswoode J	Morley EJ	Slater J	Hoyland J	Williams J	Crumley J	Beynon B	Jennings W	Gray GR	Davies W	Jackson S	McDevitt W	Stapleton W
1	Aug-27	A	Watford	0 0		7,000	1	2	3	4	5	6	7	8	9	10	11												
2	Aug-29	H	Aberdare Athletic	1 2	Edmundson	18,000	1	2	3	4	5	6	7	8	9	10	11												
3	Sep-03	H	Watford	3 0	Edmundson, Jones 2	15,000	1	2		4	5	6	7	8	9	10	11	3											
4	Sep-05	A	Aberdare Athletic	1 2	Brown	16,000	1	2		4	5	6	7	8	9	10	11	3											
5	Sep-10	H	Southend United	1 1	Edmundson	13,000	1	2		4	5	6	7	8	9		11	3	10										
6	Sep-12	H	Brighton & H A	2 1	Jones, Edmundson	12,000	1	2	3	4	5	6		8	9	10	11			7									
7	Sep-17	A	Southend United	0 1		5,500	1	2	3	4	5	6	7	8	9	10	11												
8	Sep-24	H	Swindon Town	1 3	Edmundson	14,000	1	2	3		5	6	7	8	9	10	11				4								
9	Oct-01	A	Swindon Town	0 1		9,000	1	2	3		5	6	7	8	9	10	11				4								
10	Oct-08	H	Exeter City	2 1	Brown, Edmundson	9,000		2	3		5	6	7	8	9	10	11				4	1							
11	Oct-15	A	Exeter City	1 1	McCullum	7,000		2	3		5	6	11	10		8	7				4	1	9						
12	Oct-22	H	Millwall	3 0	O/Goal, Brown 2	8,000		2	3		5	6	7	8		10	11				4	1	9						
13	Oct-29	A	Millwall	0 0		15,000		2	3		5	6	7	8		10	11				4	1	9						
14	Nov-05	H	Gillingham	2 0	Edmundson, Brown	11,000		2	3		5	6	7	8	9	10	11				4	1							
15	Nov-12	A	Gillingham	0 0		10,000		2	3		5	6	7	8	9	10	11				4	1							
16	Nov-19	A	Luton Town	0 3		10,000		2	3		5	6	7	8		10	11				4	1	9						
17	Nov-26	H	Luton Town	1 1	Hole	12,000		2	3		5	6	7	8		10	11				4	1	9						
18	Dec-10	A	Brighton & H A	0 0		9,000		2	3		5	6	7	8	9	10	11				4	1							
19	Dec-24	H	Newport County	2 2	Edmundson, Brown	10,000		2	3	6	5		7	8	9	10	11				4	1							
20	Dec-26	A	Merthyr	0 1		14,000		2	3		5	6	7	8	9	10	11				4	1							
21	Dec-27	H	Merthyr	3 2	Williams, Jones, Hole	20,000		2			5	6	7	8	9	10	11	3			4			1					
22	Dec-31	A	Plymouth Argyle	1 3	Jones	14,000		2		5		6	7	8	9		11	3	10		4	1							
23	Jan-02	A	Newport County	3 2	Jones, Slater 2	9,000	1	2		5		6	7	8	9		11	3	10		4								
24	Jan-14	H	Plymouth Argyle	3 0	Edmundson 2, Davies	16,000	1	2	3		5		7	10	8		11				4				6	9			
25	Jan-21	A	Charlton Athletic	0 1		8,000	1	2			5	6	7	8		10		3	11		4					9			
26	Feb-04	A	Northampton Town	1 0	Davies	3,000	1	2	3		5		7	8		10	11				4				6	9			
27	Feb-11	H	Northampton Town	2 2	Edmundson, Davies	12,000	1	2	3		5		7	10	8		11				4				6	9			
28	Feb-20	A	Southampton	1 1	Beynon	7,000	1	2	3		5	4					11			7	8		9		6	10			
29	Feb-25	H	Southampton	1 0	Beynon	15,000	1	2	3		5	6		8			11			7	4		9			10			
30	Mar-04	A	QPR	0 1		6,000	1		3		5	6	7				11	2	10		4		9			8			
31	Mar-09	H	Charlton Athletic	0 0		2,000		2	3		5	6	7	8			11		10		4		9	1					
32	Mar-11	H	QPR	1 0	Davies	13,000		2	3		5	6	7	8			11		10		4	1				9			
33	Mar-18	H	Norwich City	1 1	Slater	11,000		2	3		5	4	7	8			11		10			1			6	9			
34	Mar-25	A	Norwich City	2 3	Hole, Spottiswoode	8,000	1	2	3		5	6	7	10	8		11				4					9			
35	Apr-01	H	Reading	0 0		7,000	1	2			6	5	4	8		10		3		7						9	11		
36	Apr-08	A	Reading	0 2		8,000	1	2			5	6		8		10	11	3		7	4					9			
37	Apr-14	A	Portsmouth	0 3		17,000	1	2	3		5	6		8		10	11			7	4					9			
38	Apr-15	H	Bristol Rovers	8 1	Brown 3, Collins 3, Beynon, Spottiswoode	3,000	1	2	3		8	6	7			10	11				4		9					5	
39	Apr-17	H	Portsmouth	2 2	Brown, Williams	15,000	1	2	3		8	6	7			10	11				4		9					5	
40	Apr-22	A	Bristol Rovers	0 0		10,000	1	2	3		9	4		8		10	11			7	6							5	
41	Apr-29	H	Brentford	1 0	Collins	5,000	1	2	3		9	4				10	11			7					6	8		5	
42	May-06	A	Brentford	0 3		10,000	1	2			8	4	7			10	11	3							6	9		5	
					Apps		26	41	32	12	39	38	38	29	24	30	40	11	8	8	31	14	13	2	7	13	1	5	
					Gls						5	1	4	7	11	10	2		3		2		2			2			

#	Date	V	Opponents	Score	Scorers	Att.	Denoon J	Robson ER	Milne W	Durnin J	Collins J	McCullum	Hole WJ	Jones I	Edmundson J	Brown WY	Spottiswoode J	Morley EJ	Slater J	Hoyland J	Williams J	Crumley J	Beynon B	Jennings W	Gray GR	Davies W	Jackson S	McDevitt W	Stapleton W
1	Dec-03	H	Bournemouth, FAC-Pre	4 0	Edmundson 2, Jones 2	10,000			3		5	6	7	8	9	10	11				4	1							2
2	Dec-17	H	Bristol Rovers, FAC-Pre	2 0	Hole, Edmundson	15,000		2	3	6	5		7	8	9	10	11				4	1							
3	Jan-07	H	West Ham Utd, FAC-1	0 0		26,000	1	2	3		5	6	7	8	9	10	11				4								
4	Jan-11	A	West Ham Utd, FAC-1 Rep	1 1	Hole	20,000	1	2	3		5		7	8	9	10	11				4				6				
5	Jan-16	N	West Ham Utd, FAC-1 Rep 2	1 0	Spottiswoode	7,000	1	2	3		5		7	10	8		11				4				6	9			
6	Jan-23	A	Aberdare Ath, WC-4	3 2	Jones, Edmundson, Davies				3		5	4		10	8		11	2		7		1			6	9			
7	Jan-28	A	Southend Utd, FAC-2	1 0	Jones	10,000	1	2	3		5		7	10	8		11				4				6		9		
8	Feb-18	A	Millwall, FAC-3	0 4		30,700	1	2	3		5			8	9	10	11			7	4				6				
9	Feb-27	A	Ton Pentre, WC-5	0 1		2,500	1	2	3		4			8	9	10	11			7	4				6				

N – Neutral Ground: Ashton Gate

Swansea Town Season 1922/23 Division 3(South)

#	Date	V	Opponents	Score	Scorers	Att	Denoon J	Cook AF	Milne W	Roulson J	Harwood J	Ward J	Hole WJ	Deacon H	Smith JW	Campbell AF	Spottiswoode J	Collins J	Morley EJ	Greaves E	McCullum D	Edmundson J	Gough CWM	Williams J	Thompson L	Bennett E	Davies W	Crumley J	Johnson GH
1	Aug-26	H	Merthyr T	1 1	Smith	20,500	1	2	3	4	5	6	7	8	9	10	11												
2	Aug-30	A	Reading	4 4	Spo'woode, Campbell 2, Deacon	4,200	1	2	3	4	5		7	8	9	10	11	6											
3	Sep-02	A	Merthyr T	1 2	Smith	13,500	1	2			5		7	8	9	10	11		3	4	6								
4	Sep-04	H	Reading	2 2	McCullum, Edmundson	12,000	1	2		4	5		7	8					3		6	9	11						
5	Sep-09	H	Southend Utd	1 0	Hole	12,200	1	2			5		7	8		10			3		6	9	11	4					
6	Sep-16	A	Southend Utd	1 0	Edmundson	10,000	1	2			5		7	8		10			3		6	9	11	4					
7	Sep-23	H	Gillingham	1 0	Deacon	11,200	1	2		4	5		7	8		10			3		6	9	11						
8	Sep-30	A	Gillingham	2 2	Hole, Thompson(pen)	4,700	1		3	4	5		7	8	9				2				11	6	10				
9	Oct-02	H	Swindon T	5 0	Gough 3, Hole, Smith	11,000	1		3	4	5		7	8	9				2				11	6	10				
10	Oct-07	H	Bristol C	4 1	Williams,Roulson,Smith,Thompson	16,500	1		3	4	5		7	8	9				2				11	6	10				
11	Oct-11	A	Bristol C	0 1		14,000	1		3	4	5		7	8	9				2				11	6	10				
12	Oct-21	A	Exeter C	5 1	Hole 2,Smith 2, Thompson	12,400	1		3	4	5		7	8	9				2				11	6	10				
13	Oct-28	A	Exeter C	0 1		5,200	1		3	4	5		7	8	9				2				11	6	10				
14	Nov-04	A	Brighton	3 1	Smith, Hole, Spottiswoode	10,500	1		3	4	5		7	8	9		11		2					6	10				
15	Nov-11	H	Brighton	0 0		13,000	1		3	4	5		7	8	9		11		2					6	10				
16	Nov-18	A	Portsmouth	3 0	Smith 3	13,790	1		3	4	5		7	8	9		11		2					6	10				
17	Nov-25	H	Portsmouth	2 1	Deacon 2	11,607	1		3	4	5		7	8	9		11		2					6	10				
18	Dec-09	A	Swindon T	1 2	Deacon	5,000	1		3	4	5		7	8	9		11		2					6	10				
19	Dec-16	H	Millwall	0 1		10,500	1		3	4	5		7	8	9		11		2					6	10				
20	Dec-23	A	Millwall	2 0	Smith , Hole	14,000	1		3	4	5		7	8	9		11		2					6	10				
21	Dec-26	H	Newport C	5 1	Harwood,Thompson,Smith 2,Deacon	16,300	1		3	4	5		7	8	9		11		2					6	10				
22	Dec-27	A	Newport C	2 1	Hole,Deacon	3,000	1		3	4	5		7	8	9		11		2					6	10				
23	Dec-30	H	Aberdare Ath	5 1	Thompson,Smith 2,Hole,Harwood	12,300	1		3	4	5		7	8	9		11		2					6	10				
24	Jan-06	A	Aberdare Ath	1 0	Smith	7,000	1		3	4	5		7		9	8	11		2					6	10				
25	Jan-20	A	Luton T	1 6	Thompson	6,500	1		3	4	5		7	8	9		11		2					6	10				
26	Jan-27	H	Luton T	1 0	Hole	15,500	1		3		5		7	8	9		11	4	2					6	10				
27	Feb-03	H	Northampton T	4 0	Smith,Harwood,Thompson,Deacon	14,000	1	2	3		5		7	8	9		11	4						6	10				
28	Feb-10	A	Northampton T	3 1	Smith,Williams,Hole	4,600	1	2	3	4	5		7	8	9		11							6	10				
29	Feb-17	H	Norwich C	3 1	Smith , Deacon 2	14,000	1	2	3		5		7	8	9		11	4						6	10				
30	Feb-24	A	Norwich C	4 1	Smith2 (1 pen),Thompson,Deacon	6,000	1	2	3	4	5		7	8	9		11							6	10				
31	Mar-03	H	Brentford	0 0		14,200	1	2	3	4	5		7	8	9		11							6	10				
32	Mar-10	A	Brentford	1 0	Hole	5,000	1	2	3	4	5		7	8	9		11							6	10				
33	Mar-17	A	Watford	1 2	Deacon	7,000	1		3	2	5		7	8	9		11	4						6	10				
34	Mar-24	H	Watford	0 0		16,000	1		3	4	5		7	8	9		11							6	10	2			
35	Mar-30	A	QPR	1 2	Hole	15,000	1	2		4	5		7	8	9		11							6	10	3			
36	Mar-31	A	Charlton Ath	1 3	Hole	9,000	1			4	3		7	8			11		5					6	10	2	9		
37	Apr-02	H	QPR	3 0	Deacon,Davies,Thompson	17,000				4	3		9	8			11	5	2					6	10		7	1	
38	Apr-07	H	Charlton Ath	3 2	Deacon,Smith,Thompson	15,000				4	3		7	8	9		11	5	2					6	10			1	
39	Apr-14	A	Plymouth A	0 2		9,000	1			4	5			8	9		11		2					6	10	3			7
40	Apr-21	H	Plymouth A	1 1	Hole	15,200	1	2		4	5		7	8	9		11							6	10	3			
41	Apr-28	A	Bristol Rovers	0 0		10,500	1			4	5		7	8	9		11							6	10	2			
42	May-05	H	Bristol Rovers	0 1		10,200	1		3	4	5		7	8	9		11							6		2	10		
			Apps				40	17	29	36	42	1	41	41	37	7	32	8	27	1	5	4	10	37	34	7	3	2	1
			Gls							1	3		15	15	21	2	2				1	2	3	2	10		1		

#	Date	V	Opponents	Score	Scorers	Att	Denoon J	Cook AF	Milne W	Roulson J	Harwood J	Ward J	Hole WJ	Deacon H	Smith JW	Campbell AF	Spottiswoode J	Collins J	Morley EJ	Greaves E	McCullum D	Edmundson J	Gough CWM	Williams J	Thompson L	Bennett E	Davies W	Crumley J	Johnson GH
1	Dec-02	A	Merthyr T FAC Qual	0 0		9000	1		3	4	5		7	8	9		11		2					6	10				
2	Dec-07	H	Merthyr T FAC Rep	0 1		15,000	1		3	4	5		7	8	9		11		2					6	10				
3	Mar-12	H	Llanelli WC 6	2 1	Deacon, Smith	15,000	1	2	3	4	5		7	8	9		11							6	10				
4	Mar-19	H	Newport Co. WC7	4 2	Smith 3, Thompson	8,000	1	2	3	4	5		7	8	9		11							6	10				
5	Apr-11	A	Cardiff C WC S-F	2 3	Smith, Thompson	12,000	1			4	5		7	8	9		11		3					6	10	2			

Chapter 6

Division Two in Sight

Things were somewhat brighter on the economic front as the season began. At the end of July the *Leader* announced that 'for the first time since 1921 the Swansea area has less than three thousand people unemployed'. As a consequence of this the directors hoped that a successful season would result in larger home gates at the Vetch. They were certainly not disappointed when eighteen thousand people attended the opening match, with Luton, particularly since considerable controversy had surrounded the board's decision to increase season ticket prices to £3.10s. (£3.50p.). When Harry Deacon scored to take the points for the Swans, any lingering doubts about the size of gates or the price of tickets were dispelled.

By 8 September, with five successive victories behind the team, 'Rolande' in the *Leader* was maintaining that Swansea Town players had enhanced their reputations. They were, it seemed, particularly popular in London and could be relied upon to play attractive football wherever they went. Even though the team lost its sixth match, an unchanged side, captained by centre-half Collins, was retained for a total of twelve matches. Unfortunately, though, in the last of these, Billy Hole suffered a severe injury which kept him out for the remainder of the season. Fortunately for the Swans, they had an able deputy to replace him – Willie Davies, who had cost the club a 10s.6d. transfer fee.

By early November the Swans sat at the top of the table and, on the tenth of that month they thrashed Merthyr 5-1, with centre-forward Smith scoring a fine hat-trick. It was his way of responding to criticism in the local press that he was 'not the man he was'. Not surprisingly,

throughout this early part of the season confidence at the Vetch and among supporters was at a high level and, yet again, promotion was a regular topic of conversation in the old borough. Manager Bradshaw, however, appeared to believe that he needed to strengthen his squad. On 16 November a new outside-left, Corkingdale, joined the club from Wellington Town. Then, in the last week of the month, the unceremonious Merthyr tackler, Langford, came to the Vetch in exchange for a substantial fee, although, according to the the vendors, it was 'half the asking price'. The collapse of the endangered steam coal economy was, clearly, beginning to leave its mark on the finances of the formerly prosperous iron-town club.

On his arrival, Langford immediately struck up a sound relationship with left-back, Milne and, with the whole team playing well as 1923 came to an end,

Swansea Town led their division by four points from Portsmouth. They had dropped only ten points in twenty-two games, which represented an improvement on the previous season for the second campaign in succession. The question remained, however, could the team maintain its form over the next twenty matches and achieve promotion? It was not necessary for the *Athletic News* to warn the club this time.

The first match of 1924, at Swindon, was lost by the only goal of the game, but Swansea spirits were still high. Apart from holding on to the top position in the table, the side was unbeaten at home. For the first time, the FA had granted the Swans exemption until the first round proper of their cup competition. Their opponents at that stage were Clapton Orient, a second-division side. Once again, the Vetch crowd swayed to 'Bubbles' but, with the pitch in a bad state because of rain, the teams could only draw. Two replays were again needed to provide a result, the prize for which was a home tie with mighty Aston Villa. Happily for the Swans they won the second replay at White Hart Lane. Thus it was that Villa became the third First Division club to play a competitive match at the Vetch Field.

In awaiting the day, the town was agog with excitement, while both the *Leader* and the *Post* indulged

1923-24 new signings – flat caps being the order of the day!
Left to right: Sykes, McPherson, Miller, Wood, Logie and Robson.

themselves in earnest discussion about the game. Whilst welcoming the thrills of the cup, both papers believed that it was important to keep in mind what, they argued, was the main objective of the club – promotion. But, even though supporters wanted league success as much as ever, with the town in the grip of a virulent strain of cup-fever, the short term took preference over the longer. As far as the board was concerned, there was another issue at the front of their minds: in difficult financial times, the expectation of a big crowd and the gate income which went with it, was a considerable attraction. Furthermore, what gave comfort to all Vetch parties was the fact that the team was still two points clear at the top of Division Three (South) with just seventeen games to be played.

On the day of the Villa match the whole town appeared to be in festive mood. The previous evening the Villa team and directors had been met at High Street station by Owen Evans, S. B. Williams and a large body of supporters. The visitors were lodged at the Osborne Hotel, while the Swans had gone to Llandrindod Wells. In the event, it was the sea air rather than the spa water, coupled with highly controversial refereeing decisions, which won the day. Despite the thousands of Swans supporters in the ground, countless others on the rooftops at Gam Street, William Street and elsewhere, a packed bank, 'Bubbles' and the whole repertoire, the Midlanders returned home with their ticket into the next round. Most reports suggested that the Swans had four-fifths of the game territorially, but that counted for little against Capewell's two goals.

For the Swans and their supporters the result was disappointing, but the club, now somewhat richer, could concentrate, as the saying goes, upon their promotion drive. Their confidence was boosted, too, when Willie Davies was selected to play for Wales. Davies, who was twenty-two and had played just a handful of league matches, took his chance well, scoring on his debut. Unfortunately, 'concentrating on the league' did not produce the desired result: between the game with Villa and 1 March, the side lost all three of the matches it played. Manager Bradshaw was

clearly concerned, for he acted immediately by signing Jack Fowler from Plymouth. He had admired Fowler's play for some time and must have been extremely persuasive, for the directors 'coughed up' a club record £1,250 for the centre-forward.

Incongruously, the Swans directors failed to capitalise on the news of the purchase with a view to boosting the size of the gate for Fowler's debut. 'Rolande' complained at this lack of co-operation between the directors and the press. He described their attitude as 'an inane policy', which hardly endeared him to the Swansea board, but he certainly had a point! Fowler, though, was unmoved by the controversy, scoring in his first match and leaving the field to an ovation. Was this man to be the leader of the goal-scoring force which would achieve the longed-for promotion for the Swans? Davies, Deacon, Fowler, Thompson, Spottiswoode; the line-up was almost right but the timing was wrong.

At the time of Fowler's signing the team still led the table, but, sadly, it won only one of its next seven games and slipped down to fifth. Nevertheless, when that unhappy sequence ended, Fowler was firmly entrenched as the crowd's favourite and scored the first hat-trick of his Swans career in a game against Brentford. In that match, 'Reynard' in the *Post*, declared that the Swans played 'in irresistible fashion'. Unfortunately, during the next three games, Newport, Bristol Rovers and Norwich all found ways of resisting. The club's victory in the final match of the campaign was but a token gesture. Portsmouth were promoted, Plymouth the bridesmaid, and Swansea Town fourth.

As the club made its final arrangements for a second Danish tour, 'Rolande' reflected on another season of partial success. He did not pull his punches:

Things went smoothly until just after Christmas when the rot set in. From that time on it can be said that the team was never twice in the same spirit . . . [There arose] a number of petty jealousies which boded ill for the future . . . With the reduction of the board to seven members it was hoped that there would be greater unanimity, a better spirit

. . . but regrettably . . . this has not been the case . . . There is room for a distinct improvement in the composition of the body that controls the Swans.

It seemed that the seven men who comprised that governing body were, once more, on trial.

Joe Sykes

1924-25

Before the new campaign began, Willie Davies had been sold to Cardiff for a 'substantial fee' and a Scot, Lachlan McPherson had signed for the Swans from Notts County. Bradshaw had noted the the latter playing for County in Denmark (when they were on tour there at the same time as the Swans). The player was stated to be a 'ball-artist' who was equally at home at wing-half or inside-forward. Another signing, which was to prove to be of significant importance to the Vetch club, was Joe Sykes, who came from Sheffield Wednesday. A Sheffield spokesman told the *Post* that his club had refused to sell Sykes to Liverpool, who once offered £3,000 for his signature. No one indicated what the Swans had paid, but, whatever the amount, it was to pale into insignificance when measured against the monumental service which the young man subsequently gave to the Vetch club.

At a poorly attended AGM, despite a flawed attempt from the floor to force all seven directors to resign, things were comparatively

Joe Sykes watched by a young Abe Freedman makes his way to address the crowd after the Swans had won the championship of Division Three (South).

quiet. There were even happy moments: the re-election of B. Watts-Jones to the board and a resolution to congratulate Cardiff City on finishing second in the first division. Watts-Jones was to be involved with Cardiff in less happy circumstances before many years were to pass. The chairman also announced that 749 members had been enrolled by the club for the coming season. This terminology, now more frequently associated with cricket, related to the number of season tickets which had been sold. The effect of this money in advance on the club's cash flow was significant and timely, for, whilst Willie Davies had been sold, four new men had been signed and Billy Hole, Jock Denoon and Jimmy Collins were all due for benefits during the coming season. Whatever the strength of the fans' desire for promotion, it would have needed to be great indeed, to equal that of the directors for business success. But then, in professional soccer, the two

objectives frequently go hand in hand.

In front of a crowd of 20,000 people, the season started well: Swindon were beaten 2-0, with Fowler scoring both goals and McPherson prominent. However, after five matches had been played only three points had been gained. In response to this, Bradshaw made an adjustment to his defence for the next match, which was against Merthyr. It was to prove to be a master-stroke. Joe Sykes was drafted in at centre-half in place of the injured Collins. The Swans won with a further brace of goals from Fowler, and Sykes had begun a long association with Swansea's first team.

After drawing with QPR and losing to Exeter, the directors must have been worried, for gates were beginning to fall and there was growing pessimism among supporters. On 27 September, with the 'All Blacks' at St. Helens, less than ten thousand turned up to see the game with Charlton, whilst

double that number had attended the opening game of the season. Nevertheless, those who were there left the ground in high spirits, for the London club was crushed 6-1, with Fowler hitting the net five times, a new club record. With wins in the next two matches, things looked brighter for the team which, by then, had earned twelve points from ten matches. Although this record was nothing like as impressive as their performance during the previous season, at least the sequence of wins had given supporters hope.

Two further wins followed, including a decisive 3-1 victory over Watford. Since that game was watched by a crowd of 18,000, hope among supporters must have quickly turned to belief. As far as the directors were concerned, the improvement in both performances and gates must have given them comfort that their investment in players had not been in vain. On that same day, Billy Hole played his first game for the reserves after a long convalescence. Miller, who had been signed from Bournemouth, had been filling his place, but, as 'Rolande' put it, 'he isn't Billy Hole'.

Just when supporters were beginning to feel that Bradshaw had found the right blend of players, inconsistency struck again. The next three matches produced only one point. 'Alarch', writing in the *Post*, believed that the poor form could be traced to defensive errors, though he might have noted that with respect to the team's away form, it was the attack which was lacking in effectiveness. Only three goals had been scored in the seven away matches which had been played. Whereas 'Alarch', in his analysis of the situation accused McPherson of over-elaborating and Sykes of lack of consistency, 'Rolande' in the *Leader* was clearly a Sykes fan. Even in the middle of what was a difficult spell for the team, he was describing Sykes as 'brainy', 'given to clever anticipation', and 'carpet passes are a feature of his play'. There was little doubt, too, that Sykes was a great favourite with the fans. Despite his relative lack of height he seemed able to out-jump the big centre-forwards of his day. In addition, he was a natural leader of men.

On 1 November after losing at Norwich, the club languished in mid-table. It was an extremely poor start compared with the previous two seasons, yet support was still strong. Vetch Field league matches were attracting an average of sixteen thousand people, whilst away matches were well-supported too. The *Leader*, for example, ran a 'non-stop corridor express' excursion to Paddington for a game against Southend. The charge was *16s.* (80*p.*) and seven hundred people booked tickets for the trip. As ever, the loyal following made themselves heard wherever they went with the ever-popular 'Bubbles' and well-loved hymns like 'Cwm Rhondda'.

With the weather not helping the Swansea cause, by the middle of November fewer people were coming to the Vetch as the start of one of the wettest winters in living memory made standing on the open bank a less than attractive proposition. Nonetheless, at the end of the match with Brentford, it must have seemed like a bright summer's day to the ten thousand or so who braved the lashing rain and stood on the open

'Tanner Bank'. Wet they might have been, but they glowed inside. With Collins and Bennett suspended for 'a serious breach of club discipline', Joe Sykes was made captain and Ernie Morley returned to right back. These men were part of a team which overwhelmed the London side, scoring seven without reply. Every press report commented on the Swansea forward line. 'Superb', 'outstanding' and 'irrepressible' were among the superlatives used to describe the play of the front five. Thompson, who scored four, and Deacon, with a hat-trick, were in tremendous form. Paradoxically, leading-scorer, Jack Fowler failed to find the net.

When the news of the victory spread through the town, the optimists were released from their stupor. So, it seemed, was the team, for, on the back of that victory, a winning run began to develop and confidence grew with it. Millwall were defeated in London, while Luton and Bournemouth were beaten in successive games at the Vetch. In the Luton match, watched by three Arsenal directors, Thompson was outstanding and it did not take long before the tongues were wagging around the town: Thompson was being sold to Arsenal. A press statement refuted this, stating that the Arsenal men were there to watch a Luton player. Whether that was true or not, the London directors must have been impressed with the play of the talented Thompson, for the 'Gunners' were to secure his services before many seasons passed. For the Bournemouth match, a 'new' face appeared in the Swans forward line: he was Dai Nicholas, whom the club had signed from Stoke. Actually Nicholas had played for the Swans, as an amateur, just after the war and before signing as a professional for Merthyr. His first match as a Swans professional was at inside-left, replacing Thompson who was injured.

After seventeen matches had been played the Swans had climbed to fourth place in the league table. Plymouth were top, followed by Swindon and Bristol City. (It is interesting to note that Bristol had been relegated at the end of the previous season. At the end of the 1979-80 campaign they were, also, to join the Vetch men as a result of

relegation. Was this the long arm of coincidence, or is there some pre-arranged order of events which affect the fortunes of football clubs?).

On 12 December, Swansea's own radio station was opened. The local papers were full of comment on this momentous event and of the exciting prospects for this new marvel of modern science. The town's mayor spoke the first words after the Reithian announcer had intoned, 'Swansea Relay Station calling the British Isles'. Association football was not yet part of the 'feast of programmmes' which were promised but, in due course, Swansea Town was to play a part in the earliest attempts to report soccer on radio 'as it happened'.

As a prelude to Christmas, division leaders Plymouth Argyle were soundly beaten at the Vetch by a Swans side which played outstanding football. At the end of the game, according to the *Post*, Moses Russsell, who had guested for the Swans during the war, 'was drained of all energy'. It was a significant victory, for the Argyle were a fine side (by then the Swans were third) and the game was a dress-rehearsal for the first-round FA Cup tie which the sides were to play at the Vetch in January.

After sharing the points twice with Bristol City on Christmas Day and Boxing Day, the Swans were required to travel to Swindon on 27 December. Three games in three successive days put a considerable strain on players, a problem which was exacerbated by the state of the Swindon pitch, which was very heavy after incessant rain. With heavy boots and a leather ball, given to absorbing water, the players on both sides must have been very tired. Happily for the Swans, they dealt with these problems more effectively than the home side and came away from the Wiltshire town with both points. Tired as they were, when they opened their newspapers the following morning they were elated. Swansea Town sat proudly at the top of the league table! Whilst they held that lofty position simply on goal average (Plymouth had the same number of points), in the midst of the gloomy weather which seemed to envelop the whole country, they must have looked forward to the second half of the season with a warm glow of confidence.

Champions three times over – Third (South), Southern League and Welsh League.

The first match of 1925 was postponed because of the effects of the continually heavy rain which, some locals maintained, was the result of the big guns being fired during the Great War. Whatever the cause, it seemed to be an unfortunate interruption at the time when things were going so well for the team. However, as if to prove that clouds have a silver lining, Plymouth's game went ahead and the 'Pilgrims' lost, and even though Bristol won and went to the top, they had played more games than the Swans.

More than 21,000 people were at the Vetch for the next match to be played, which was the FA Cup tie with Plymouth. On the day, the Swans were in outstanding form and brushed aside the Devon men, winning 3-0. Apart from the quality of the victory, it was a result which gave the team an extra psychological advantage over the Plymouth side, who were perceived to be their greatest rivals for promotion. The Swans fans were in confident mood. Why not a cup and league double? Bradshaw tried to take the pressure off his men, but with the cup virus rampant again and promotion a

distinct possiblity it was a difficult task.

For the second year in succession their opponents in the second round of the cup were Aston Villa.

Before that match, however, there was an important league match to be played for, in order to regain first place, the Swans had to beat QPR. To the delight of their supporters they did that and found themselves at the top with a one point lead, two games in hand and a superior goal average. At that, not only the optimists were counting their chickens, though, given the fact that the team had stumbled twice in previous seasons after being well-placed, there was a certain caution in most minds.

Any lingering doubts, of course, were pushed to the back of supporters' minds as they contemplated the cup tie with Villa. Could the Swans beat them this time? It was the question which attracted over 20,000 people to the ground for the game, even though the directors had doubled admission prices to 10s. (50p) for the stand and 2s. (10p) for the ground. After the game, which Villa won 3-1 despite 'Bubbles', the other choral aids and a

fighting display by the home team: the directors counted a handsome income record for a single match of £2,800, a soothing balm for the defeated club. Yet, the defeat had another effect: in the two previous seasons, a cup defeat had been followed by poor performances in the league. Naturally, the resident gloom-mongers seized upon this, while even the positive thinkers had their doubts.

Northampton Town, who were the next opponents, did their best to ensure that the unhappy sequence would continue, but, fortunately a Swans side showing six changes from the cup game, snatched victory in the final minute. Then, after drawing at Charlton the Swans registered two wins, against Southend and Norwich. In the latter game, Harry Deacon outwitted five men in an amazing dribble to score. By now the side was bubbling with confidence, which was boosted by the selection of Fowler and Morley to play for Wales against England on 27 February.

On 14 March, with just thirteen games to play, the Swans travelled to London to play lowly placed Brentford. Most commentators felt that the two points were safely in Swansea hands, but the home side had other ideas: they won 3-1. The shock waves caused by this defeat seemed to hit Swans fans and players alike. Confidence began to ebb and only three points were gained from the next four matches. This led 'Rolande' to assert gloomily that 'history is repeating itself'. 'About this time last year,' he recalled, 'the form of the team slumped . . . a similar thing happened about the same time in the previous season.' The directors, he reported, had sent the team to Southend for brine baths. Whilst that must have seemed like taking Newcastle to the coals, it appears to have had the desired effect, for the Swans gained a point at Luton in the next match. After that game, with rival clubs having faired poorly too, the Swans still held a slender lead at the top of the table.

They held that position until 11 April, when, with six matches to go, Plymouth climbed above them. With Len Thompson out through injury, Billy Whitehead was brought in to replace him. The newcomer duly obliged by scoring twice at Bournemouth, but the positions remained unchanged. At that stage Plymouth had a one point advantage and a slightly better goal average, but, after the next two matches, the position was reversed. The Swans had won two games, whilst Plymouth had lost one of theirs. The table read:

	P	W	L	D	F	A	Pts
Swansea Town	39	21	8	10	64	33	52
Plymouth Argyle	39	21	9	9	68	37	51

No one needed to be told that the remaining matches were crucial, particularly since the gods responsible for setting the fixture list must have designed it with malicious amusement in mind. The next Swans fixture was against Plymouth on their own turf. Both sets of fans envisaged the game as the decider and 35,000 people packed Home Park, including an estimated 5,000 from Swansea. The GWR did well that day.

To the delight of the home supporters, Plymouth took an early lead, but, with Ernie Morley outstanding, the Vetch men began to get back into the game. After considerable pressure on the home goal, Billy Hole was fouled on the edge of the penalty area. Harry

The **South Wales Daily Post** *of 29 May 1924, commenting on the forthcoming second Danish tour, included a quotation from the Danish sports paper* **Athletic News:**

'[The Swans] play beautiful football, stylish and elegant; their style is reminiscent of Aston Villa, a team identified with the most classic football.'

Deacon took the kick and 'the visiting fans leaped into the air as the ball flew into the net'. At that, Plymouth shoulders drooped and, despite a hearty battle, at the final whistle honours were even. For Plymouth it was a point lost, for the Swans it was one gained. The unfortunate Plymouth supporters were inconsolable. Would they finish second for the fourth time in succession? In their penultimate match, a mid-week fixture, the Argyle did all they could by winning and moving above the Swans in the league table. At that stage they led by one point, though the Swans had a game in hand.

When the Swans won their own mid-week match – against Reading – while Plymouth were also victorious in their last game, a *Boys' Own* finish to the league campaign was assured. Plymouth had completed their quota of games and had amassed fifty-six points. Since the Devon men had a superior goal average, it was necessary for the Swans to win their final game to ensure that the championship came to the Vetch. Everyone, it seemed wanted to be there as the whole town was caught up in the excitement. On the day, 24,000 people created

another new ground record for the Vetch. The opponents were Exeter City, a sound side lying seventh in the table. On paper, the Swans were thought to be too skilful to fail against the men from Devon. Yet, many a slip . . . Two onlookers with more than a passing interest in the outcome of the match, sat in the stand, no doubt, supporting their fellow Devonians, they were the manager and captain of Plymouth Argyle.

Those who were there that day said that the tension in the air was unbearable. Many Swansea hearts pounded as the home side strove to settle into its normal pattern of play, but it needed a goal to begin that process. It was left to Harry Deacon to break the deadlock. Picking up the ball in his own half, he cut through the Exeter defence and, after beating two men passed inside to Fowler who, 'catching the ball in full stride, with a first-time ground drive sent the ball into the corner of the net'. The joy of the Swans fans was tinged with relief, though there was a long way to go yet. Picking up their game, the Swansea men kept pressing for a second goal, but the visiting custodian was in outstanding form and denied every one of the forwards at one time or another. Indeed, it took a further twenty minutes before a second Swansea goal was scored, this time by Thompson. Exeter, however, refused to give up the ghost and, ten minutes from the end, with the Swansea forwards searching for a third goal, Smelt broke away and virtually walked the ball into the Swansea net. The Swansea hearts in the ground at that moment were transmitted into Swansea mouths. Clocks and watches seemed to stop as the 'Grecians' pressed towards the home goal. Exeter, with hope of a point when none had existed before, found new life and confidence and surged forward in search of an equaliser. Indeed, such was the pressure that, in the final minute, the Swansea goalkeeper was forced to make a nervous save. The roars of the home crowd when the final whistle was blown were preceded by gasps of relief. For the Vetch men and their supporters, the second division was, at last, a reality. For Plymouth, the agony of finishing in second place again was, as it was to be on three further occasions, renewed.

Swansea Town Season 1923/24 Division 3(South)

#	Date	V	Opponents	Score	Scorers	Att	Brookes GH	Morley EJ	Milne W	Bellamy H	Collins J	Booth R	Hole WJ	Deacon H	Smith JW	Thompson L	Spottiswoode J	Davies W	Holland J	Langford AE	Corkingdale WJ	Roulson J	Harwood J	Whitehead WT	Fowler J	Denoon J	Lamb WC	Crapper J	Bennett E	Sullivan C
1	Aug-25	H	Luton Town	1 0	Deacon	18,000	1	2	3	4	5	6	7	8	9	10	11													
2	Aug-29	A	Reading	4 3	Smith,Thompson,Deacon,Collins	4,000	1	2	3	4	5	6	7	8	9	10	11													
3	Sep-01	A	Luton Town	2 1	Deacon 2	9,500	1	2	3	4	5	6	7	8	9	10	11													
4	Sep-03	H	Reading	5 1	Deacon 2,Thompson 2,Smith	18,800	1	2	3	4	5	6	7	8	9	10	11													
5	Sep-08	H	Northampton T	2 1	Smith,Thompson	17,000	1	2	3	4	5	6	7	8	9	10	11													
6	Sep-15	A	Northampton T	0 2		11,500	1	2	3	4	5	6	7	8	9	10	11													
7	Sep-22	H	Gillingham	3 1	Thompson,Smith,Deacon(pen)	15,500	1	2	3	4	5	6	7	8	9	10	11													
8	Sep-29	A	Gillingham	1 0	Thompson	7,000	1	2	3	4	5	6	7	8	9	10	11													
9	Oct-06	H	QPR	2 0	Deacon 2	17,000	1	2	3	4	5	6	7	8	9	10	11													
10	Oct-13	A	QPR	2 2	Booth,Deacon	11,500	1	2	3	4	5	6	7	8	9	10	11													
11	Oct-20	A	Plymouth A	0 2		16,000	1	2	3	4	5	6	7	8	9	10	11													
12	Oct-27	H	Plymouth A	1 0	Hole	15,000	1	2	3	4	5	6	7	8	9	10	11													
13	Nov-03	A	Merthyr	0 0		15,000	1	2	3	4	5	6		8	9	10	11	7												
14	Nov-10	H	Merthyr	5 1	Thompson 2,Smith 3	16,500	1	2	3	4	5	6			9	10	11	7	8											
15	Nov-17	H	Brighton	1 0	Thompson	16,000	1	2	3	4	5	6		8	9	10	11	7												
16	Nov-24	A	Brighton	1 4	Smith	9,500	1	2	3	4	5	6		8	9	10	11	7												
17	Dec-01	H	Charlton Ath	1 0	Deacon	15,000	1		3	4	5	6		8	9	10	11	7		2										
18	Dec-08	A	Charlton Ath	3 1	Thompson,Smith,Deacon	6,000	1		3	4	5	6		8	9	10	11	7		2										
19	Dec-22	H	Norwich C	1 0	Thompson	11,200	1		3	4	5	6		8	9	10		7		2	11									
20	Dec-25	H	Watford	1 0	Deacon	12,000	1		3		5	6		8	9	10		7		2	11	4								
21	Dec-26	A	Watford	2 2	Smith,Deacon	10,500	1		3		5	6		8	9	10		7		2	11	4								
22	Dec-29	H	Swindon T	1 1	own goal	16,000	1		3		5	6		8	9	10		7		2	11	4								
23	Jan-05	A	Swindon T	0 1		8,200	1		3			6		8	9	10		7		2	11	4	5							
24	Jan-19	A	Bournemouth	0 0		4,500	1		3		5	6		8		10	11	7		2		4		9						
25	Jan-26	H	Bournemouth	1 0	Smith	15,300	1		3		5	6		8	9		11	7	10	2		4								
26	Feb-09	A	Millwall	1 2	own goal	10,000	1		3		5	6		8	9		11	7	10	2		4								
27	Feb-16	A	Aberdare Ath	1 0	Smith	14,500	1		3		5	6		8	9	10	11	7		2		4								
28	Feb-23	A	Aberdare Ath	2 4	Collins,Deacon	13,500	1		3	4	5	6		8	9		11	7	10	2										
29	Mar-01	H	Southend Utd	2 1	Booth(pen),Fowler	14,300	1		3		5	6		8		10	11	7		2		4			9					
30	Mar-08	A	Southend Utd	0 0		6,700		2		4	5	6				10	11	7	8	3					9	1				
31	Mar-13	H	Millwall	1 2	Booth	15,000		2		4	5	6				10	11	7	8	3					9	1				
32	Mar-15	A	Exeter C	0 1		6,500	1	2			5	6		8		10	11	7		3		4			9					
33	Mar-22	H	Exeter C	1 0	Roulson	11,500	1					6		8		10		7		2		4	5		9			3	11	
34	Mar-29	A	Portsmouth	0 3		20,000	1		3	4		6					10	7	8	2			5		9		11			
35	Apr-05	H	Portsmouth	0 0		16,700	1		3	4	5	6					10	7	8	2					9			11		
36	Apr-12	A	Brentford	2 2	Bellamy,Fowler	9,800	1		3	4	5	6					10	7	8	2	11				9					
37	Apr-18	H	Newport Co	2 1	Fowler,Thompson	14,000	1		3	4	5	6					10	7	8		11				9			2		
38	Apr-19	H	Brentford	4 0	Fowler 3,Holland	12,000	1		3	4	5	6					10	7	8	2	11				9					
39	Apr-21	A	Newport Co	1 4	Holland	9,000	1		3	4	5	6					10	7	8	2	11				9					
40	Apr-26	A	Bristol Rovers	0 2		8,000		2	3	4	5	6					10	7	8		11				9	1				
41	Apr-28	A	Norwich C	0 2		5,000		2	3		5	6		8		10		7			11	4			9	1				
42	May-03	H	Bristol Rovers	3 1	Davies,Deacon,Thompson	10,000		2	3		5	6		8		10		7			11	4			9	1				
						Apps	37	22	38	36	39	35	12	32	29	39	27	27	16	22	10	13	3	1	14	5	1	3	1	
						Gls				1	2	3	1	16	12	13		1	2			1			6					

#	Date	V	Opponents	Score	Scorers	Att	Brookes GH	Morley EJ	Milne W	Bellamy H	Collins J	Booth R	Hole WJ	Deacon H	Smith JW	Thompson L	Spottiswoode J	Davies W	Holland J	Langford AE	Corkingdale WJ	Roulson J	Harwood J	Whitehead WT	Fowler J	Denoon J	Lamb WC	Crapper J	Bennett E	Sullivan C
1	Jan-12	H	Clapton Orient FAC 1	1 1	Smith	14,800	1		3		5	6		8	9	10	11	7		2		4								
2	Jan-17	A	Clapton Orient FAC Rep	0 0		5,000	1		3		5	6		8	9	10	11	7		2		4								
3	Jan-21	N	Clapton Orient FAC 2 Rep	2 1	Deacon,Smith	12,824	1		3		5	6		8	9		11	7	10	2		4								
4	Feb-02	H	Aston Villa FAC 2	0 2		19,035	1		3		5	6		8	9	10	11	7		2		4								
5	Feb-14	H	Ebbw Vale WC 4	1 0	Holland		1		3		5	6		8			11	7	10	2		4			9					
6	Mar-06	H	Wrexham WC 5	0 0		6,000	1		3		5	6		8			11	7	10	2		4			9					
7	Mar-19	A	Wrexham WC Rep	0 1		9,115	1		3			6		8	9	10	11			2			5					7		4

N – Neutral Ground: White Hart Lane

Swansea Town FC Season 1924/25 Division 3(South)

#	Date	V	Opponents	Score	Scorers	Att.	Robson ER	Morley EJ	Milne W	McPherson L	Collins J	Bellamy H	Miller J	Deacon H	Fowler F	Thompson L	Spottiswoode J	Langford AE	Lamb WC	Sykes J	Holland J	Denoon J	Bennett E	Nicholas DS	Booth R	Hole WJ	Logie J	Whitehead WT	Corkingdale WJ	Davies W
1	Aug-30	H	Swindon Town	2 0	Fowler 2	20,000	1	2	3	4	5	6	7	8	9	10	11													
2	Sep-01	H	Bristol Rovers	2 2	Fowler, Thompson	14,500	1	2	3	4	5	6	7	8	9	10	11													
3	Sep-06	A	Reading	0 2		9,000	1			4	5	6	7	8	9	10	11	2	3											
4	Sep-08	A	Bristol Rovers	0 3		11,000	1	2		4	5	6	7	8	9	10	11		3											
5	Sep-13	H	Merthyr	2 0	Fowler 2	14,000	1	2		4	8	6	7		9	10	11	3		5										
6	Sep-20	A	QPR	0 0		9,800	1		3	4	5	6	7	8	9	10	11	2												
7	Sep-24	A	Exeter City	0 2		5,000	1		3	4		6	7		9	10	11	2		5	8									
8	Sep-27	H	Charlton Athletic	6 1	Thompson, Fowler 5 (1pen)	9,500		2	3	4		6	7	8	9	10	11			5		1								
9	Oct-04	A	Northampton Town	3 1	Thompson 2, O/Goal	8,400		2	3	4		6	7	8	9	10	11			5		1								
10	Oct-11	H	Watford	3 1	Deacon, Thompson, Fowler	16,000		2	3	4		6	7	8	9	10	11			5		1								
11	Oct-18	A	Southend United	0 1		8,250		2	3	4		6	7	8	9	10	11			5		1								
12	Oct-25	H	Aberdare Athletic	2 2	Fowler, Thompson	15,000		2	3	4		6	7	8	9	10	11			5		1								
13	Nov-01	A	Norwich City	0 2		7,500			3	4	5	6	7	8	9	10	11					1	2							
14	Nov-08	H	Brentford	7 0	Deacon 3, Thompson 4	11,500		2	3	4		6	7	8	9	10	11			5		1								
15	Nov-15	A	Millwall	2 1	Thompson, Fowler	14,500		2	3	4		6	7	8	9	10	11			5		1								
16	Nov-22	H	Luton Town	4 1	Fowler 3, Spottiswoode	15,000		2	3	4		6	7	8	9	10	11			5		1								
17	Dec-06	H	Bournemouth	1 0	Miller	15,500		2	3	4		6	7	8	9		11			5		1		10						
18	Dec-13	A	Brighton & H A	0 0		7,950		2	3	4		6	7	8	9	10	11			5		1								
19	Dec-20	H	Plymouth Argyle	2 0	Fowler, Deacon	18,000		2	3	4		6	7	8	9	10	11			5		1								
20	Dec-25	H	Bristol City	1 1	Fowler	16,500		2	3	4		6	7	8	9	10	11			5		1								
21	Dec-26	A	Bristol City	0 0		24,000		2	3	4		6	7		9	10	11			5	8	1								
22	Dec-27	A	Swindon Town	2 0	Fowler 2	9,000		2	3		5	6	7	8	9		11					1		10	4					
23	Jan-17	A	Merthyr	2 0	Deacon, Fowler (pen)	8,500		2	3	4		6	7	8	9	10	11			5		1								
24	Jan-24	H	QPR	2 0	Fowler, Nicholas	12,000		2	3		6	4	7	8	9		11			5		1		10						
25	Feb-07	H	Northampton Town	2 1	Hole, Thompson	15,600		2	3		5	6		8	9	10				4		1		11		7				
26	Feb-14	A	Watford	3 1	Deacon, Fowler 2	8,000		2	3	4		6		8	9	10				5		1		11		7				
27	Feb-16	A	Charlton Athletic	0 0		5,400		2	3	4		6		8	9	10				5		1		11		7				
28	Feb-21	H	Southend United	4 0	Thompson, Fowler 2, Deacon	11,500		2	3	4		6		8	9	10				5		1		11		7				
29	Mar-07	H	Norwich City	2 0	Deacon 2	15,250		2	3	4		6		8	9	10				5		1		11		7				
30	Mar-14	A	Brentford	1 3	Thompson	8,500		2	3	4		6		8	9	10				5		1		11		7				
31	Mar-18	A	Gillingham	0 0		3,800		2	3	4		6		8	9	10	11			5		1				7				
32	Mar-21	H	Millwall	2 2	Bellamy, Deacon	14,800		2	3	4		6		8	9	10				5		1		11		7				
33	Mar-28	A	Luton Town	0 0		7,000	1	2			5	6		8	9	10		3		4				11		7				
34	Apr-02	A	Aberdare Athletic	1 3	Deacon	12,000	1	2			5	6		8	9	10		3		4				11		7				
35	Apr-04	H	Gillingham	2 0	Nicholas, Logie	11,300	1				5	6		8	9			3		4			2	11		7	10			
36	Apr-10	A	Newport County	0 3		13,000	1			4		6		8	9			3		5			2	11		7	10			
37	Apr-11	A	Bournemouth	2 0	Whitehead, Deacon (pen)	8,500		2		4		6	7	8	10			3		5		1		11				9		
38	Apr-13	H	Newport County	1 0	Deacon (pen)	19,000		2		4		6		8	10		11	3		5		1						9	7	
39	Apr-18	H	Brighton & H A	1 0	Fowler	15,800		2		4		6		8	10			3		5		1		11				9	7	
40	Apr-25	A	Plymouth Argyle	1 1	Deacon	30,000	1	2		4		6		8	9	10		3		5				11		7				
41	Apr-30	H	Reading	1 0	Thompson	17,500	1	2		4		6		8	9	10		3		5				11		7				
42	May-02	H	Exeter City	2 1	Fowler, Thompson	25,000	1	2		4		6		8	9	10		3		5				11		7				
						Apps	14	36	29	28	21	42	25	39	42	34	26	14	2	32	5	28	3	19	1	15	2	3	2	
						Gls						1	1	15	28	16	1							2		1	1	1		

#	Date	V	Opponents	Score	Scorers	Att.	Robson ER	Morley EJ	Milne W	McPherson L	Collins J	Bellamy H	Miller J	Deacon H	Fowler F	Thompson L	Spottiswoode J	Langford AE	Lamb WC	Sykes J	Holland J	Denoon J	Bennett E	Nicholas DS	Booth R	Hole WJ	Logie J	Whitehead WT	Corkingdale WJ	Davies W
1	Jan-10	H	Plymouth A, FAC-1	3 0	Deacon, Thompson 2	21,000			3	4		6	7	8	9	10	11			5		1	2							
2	Jan-31	H	Aston Villa, FAC-2	1 3	O/Goal	19,909			3	4		6	7	8	9	10	11			5		1	2							
3	Mar-02	H	Cardiff C, WC-5	4 0	Thompson 2, Whitehead 2	15,000			3	4		6		8		10	11			5		1	2			7		9		
4	Mar-23	H	Aberdare Ath, WC-6	1 0					3	4		6	7		9		11			5	10	1	2					8		
5	Apr-20	H	Wrexham, WCSF	1 3	Deacon	6,000			3	4				8	9			2		5		1				7	10		11	6

Chapter 7

First Semi-final

1925-26

At the beginning of the new season the Arsenal had recruited the eminently successful manager, Herbert Chapman, from Huddersfield Town. As a result, the northern club was seeking a replacement and, despite having received many applications, decided that the man for the job was Bradshaw of Swansea. Happily for Swansea fans, their manager refused Huddersfield's offer and continued with his work at the Vetch.

There were changes at the Vetch, though: J. W. Thorpe was ousted in a boardroom coup, but took the decision with dignity, promising his continued support. At the AGM where that announcement was made, it was also stated that the club's gross receipts for the previous season amounted to £31,353, which was just £600 short of the record which had been set in 1921. Members were told that work was in hand to increase the ground capacity to accommodate 31,000 people. 'Eventually,' the chairman continued, 'our scheme will allow for attendances of 58,000.' The meeting was also told that S. B. Williams had been appointed full-time secretary, whilst Joe Bradshaw had been engaged for a further period. Each of these statements was greeted with long and loud applause. At least in the day-to-day management of the club, continuity seemed to be assured.

The club's first match in the Second Division of the Football League took place at the Vetch on 29 August 1925. South Shields provided the opposition. Joe Sykes was the Swans' skipper, and his team took an early lead with a Harry Deacon goal. The visitors, however, were not prepared to let the home side have a fairy-tale start and scored one more than the Swans, the last in the final minute of the game. The Swans had played well, but lost both points and their ground record at one fell swoop. In the games which

followed, they won at Fulham, lost at Preston, then scored fourteen goals without replay over four matches. Such was the form of the side that 'Alarch' and 'Rolande' in the town's two papers were sufficiently stirred to mention promotion. Meanwhile, a minor sensation occurred when the medals and cups which the players had won during the previous season were stolen from the shop window of J. B. Owen. The *Athletic News* noted that 'a thousand posters containing the announcement of a reward of £20 have been circulated'. The tokens of what it had taken so long to achieve had been lost in a few minutes.

By the time the first FA Cup tie of the season came to be played, the side had gained seventeen points from fifteen matches. It was a respectable start to life in their new station and the team was developing a fine understanding. Denoon was back in goal, Milne was partnering Langford at full-back, the half-back line comprised Collins, Sykes and McPherson, while Hole, Deacon, Fowler, Thompson and Nicholas were the forwards. It was that side

which faced Exeter in the first-round match on the Grecians' own turf. According to 'Rolande', there was no evidence of a cup-tie atmosphere at the game. Not that the Swans were concerned, they won 3-1.

Two weeks later, in the second round, Watford came to the Vetch to play what was described as a 'robust, bustling game which threw the Swans out of their stride'. Nonetheless, despite missing a penalty, the Swans won by the odd goal in five. Given that they were thirteenth in the league table, progress in the cup was of considerable importance to the club and its supporters. Consequently, it came as something of a disappointment when the Swans were drawn away in the next round. The match was to be played on 9 January at Bloomfield Road, Blackpool, where the home side had not lost since early September. Happily for the Swans, when the final whistle blew, that record had been broken. Swansea Town, unchanged for the third cup match running, had won 2-0. For the first time in their history the Swans awaited news of their fourth-round opponents.

Two good wins in the league, including a superb display against Preston, provided the prelude for the next cup tie, which, the fates decreed, should take place at the Vetch. The opponents were Stoke City, a side with whom the Swans

Jack Fowler heads for goal in the Swans' first match in Division Two.

had drawn twice over Christmas. The cup, of course, was another matter, though the prevailing attitude in the town was one of confidence. Twenty-one thousand were present when Joe Sykes led his men out 'to a great roar'. 'Alarch' was to write later that the fans were seeking excitement, and the cup, with its sudden-death appeal, provided such experience and fed their 'fever', which he described as 'an unconquerable passion; a mixture of parochial pride, native effervescence and a desire for distinction.'

If the various contemporary accounts are anything to go by, that passion was in evidence from the start. After some preliminary fencing, Deacon, Fowler and Thompson began to make their mark. Such was the quality of their play that the Swans scored six, and even though the team relaxed somewhat to allow Stoke to net three times themselves, the home side were outstanding victors. Jack Fowler was the hero, scoring four, no doubt being motivated by the crowd singing a parody of a contemporary song, 'Fow-Fow-Fow-Fowler, score a little goal for me!'

Astonishingly, the side was now in the draw for the fifth round of the FA Cup and all the talk was about the Swans emulating Cardiff, who had played at Wembley the previous season. It was heady stuff for the newly promoted side. The reality was, though, that there were three more hurdles to clear before that could be possible. Nonetheless, the symptoms of the fever which 'Alarch' had identified were so intense that the ability of the patients to think objectively was marred by a rosy haze. That haze became even more dense after two further wins in the league took the club to eighth place. For the next cup-tie, the now obligatory special train service was provided by the GWR. Indeed, five specials left Swansea packed with fans, while every available motor bus had been booked. The opponents, this time, were Millwall, old adversaries of the town team, at The Den. Thousands of people were reported as having been 'locked out' as over 42,000 crammed into the Millwall ground to create a new attendance record for the London club.

For eighty-seven minutes neither defence gave an inch, but, with three

> *The name of the referee for the March 1926 FA Cup tie against Arsenal at the Vetch was Mr Caswell. Given that this is the name of one of Swansea's beaches, there were those who regarded the fact as a favourable omen.*

minutes left, Thompson pushed a delightful ball through to Nicholas, who lost little time in crossing to Fowler, who, 'though closely marked, shot hard and true just inside the upright'. At that, according to 'Alarch', 'the Swans fans went delirious with excitement . . . and cheered for a full five minutes.' If that was true then the cheering went on long after the final whistle had been blown. In 1981, octogenarian, Billy Hole, remembering that day, recalled 'We had no doubts in our minds. We felt that we could beat anyone!'

On the following Monday, when the draw for the quarter-finals was made, 'anyone' was given an identity. The Swans opponents, at the Vetch, were to be the mighty Arsenal. When an Arsenal official heard where the tie was to be played, he thought that it would be a big disadvantage to his team: 'We are not used to cockpits,' he said, 'nor are we used to having the crowd within kissing and hissing distance of the players.' Yet, as 'Alarch' pointed out, 'the Vetch could not beat the Gunners, the Swans would need to do that.'

The Arsenal match was to be played on 6 March. In the meantime, the league battle diverted the attention of the fans, at least to some degree. During this period, Blackpool were thrashed 6-1, with Thompson scoring three, and Nottingham Forest were beaten on their own ground. Suddenly, it seemed, the Swans were fourth in the Second Division. At that, heady talk of a league and cup double swept through Swansea. On the morning of

the Arsenal match, however, the cup was the focus of attention. By 11 a.m. queues started to form at the Vetch turnstiles and by the time Joe Sykes led out his warriors-in-white the ground was packed. The crowd roared its welcome and the scene was set for a memorable match. Manager Bradshaw, however, was not there; he was at home recovering from influenza.

The Arsenal kicked off against strong sunshine and an early confidence-booster for the Swans and their fans was a fine tackle on Charles Buchan by Milne. The crowd had been warned about this expensive buy; was this tackle a good omen? As the game wore on, it seemed to be, for the Swans were more than holding their own. Nicholas, and Hole on the flanks were causing the Arsenal defenders considerable trouble. Yet it was the 'Gunners' who came closest to opening the scoring; Brain, with only Denoon to beat, hesitated and Joe Sykes, recovering brilliantly, took the ball off his toe. Home supporters breathed again and, minutes later, roared with joy. McPherson, Nicholas and Thompson combined well before the last named cleverly beat a defender, pivoted and crashed the ball into the Arsenal net.

As the second half developed, Lachlan McPherson's grip on Charles Buchan became tighter. At the other end, the Swans wingers were pressing home their advantage. It was after good work by Hole that Fowler received the ball and, cutting between two backs, he left Harper helpless in the Arsenal goal with a piledriver of a shot. The roar of the home crowd had hardly died down before Arsenal were back in the game. Denoon fumbled and the ball was in the net. Buchan urged his men to greater effort and the Swans became more desperate in defence. With seconds to go, every Swan was in his own half defending. Billy Hole, remembering the tension of those moments, said that he received the ball in his own penalty area and, looking up, kicked it as far as he could into the Arsenal half. There was no time for the throw to be taken. To the huge delight of the Swansea faithful, the final whistle sounded. Swansea Town had won another famous victory. Surely, to reach the final was now a foregone conclusion. Unfortunately, that was

Len Thompson scores the first goal against Arsenal in the FA Cup on 6th March 1926.

not the ending which the fates had in mind. In the semi-final, against Bolton, the team 'froze' and were beaten by an experienced side which went on to win the cup.

As far as the Division Two competition was concerned, the backlog of games, a spate of injuries and the disappointment of losing in the semi-final, resulted in the Swans finishing in fifth place. Whilst manager Bradshaw could look back on a job well done in the club's first season in Division Two, the fans had scented greater things. They wanted more!

1926-27

The 1926 AGM heard the chairman declare a record income for the previous season of £33,769.6s.4d. Given the economic conditions in the country, it was a remarkable figure. The members heard a report of a successful tour of Denmark and Sweden and were told that there was great harmony amongst the players. Joe Bradshaw, enjoying the glow of congratulations, emphasised that team-spirit and predicted, 'I think that we shall give as good, if not better, next time.' Sadly, four weeks later, 'we' did not include Bradshaw. 'Purely on account of domestic reasons', he severed his connection with the club and joined Fulham. His departure was a tremendous loss to the Vetch club, and one which, as history was to show, was to have a markedly detrimental effect on the club's progress.

A quotation from an article by Charles Buchan, the captain of the Arsenal side which had been defeated by the Swans in the FA Cup, was included in the **Cambria Daily Leader** *of 17 March 1926: 'Our boys did their best, but we were up against one of the cleverest sides we have met for many a long day.'*

It is part of Swansea's folklore, that the untimely injury to Tom Kiley in 1955 cost the club promotion to division one. Most fans believe that, apart from the events of 1981, that was the only occasion when the side might have achieved promotion to England's premier division. As will be seen, however, there was another occasion when the cherished prize might have been won. Although, it was the lack of a manager rather than a key player which was to be the reason for the opportunity being missed.

After Bradshaw left, it appears that

the directors decided that they could run the club without the services of a professional manager. It is difficult to interpret their action in any other way, for it was eight months after Bradshaw left before they recruited a replacement. It is interesting to contrast their behaviour with that of Huddersfield Town, who recruited their new man within two weeks of Chapman leaving them. Huddersfield, after winning the championship three seasons in succession under Chapman, finished runners-up in their next two campaigns. Conversely, Swansea Town, after starting well at the beginning of the 1926-27 season faded to a disappointing twelfth by the time it ended. In retrospect, the decline in the club's fortunes which was to become evident in the years ahead, may be seen to stem from the failure of the directors to act in time. The momentum of success had been lost. The window of opportunity slammed shut.

Reading, newly promoted, were the first visitors to the Vetch for the new season and, despite having only ten men for most of the game, the Swans took both points. On 18 September after a Fowler hat-trick had floored Barnsley, the Vetch men were unbeaten. By 30 October the side was in second place in the league table, and first place was achieved on the following Saturday. Without question it was an auspicious start. At right back, young Ben Williams was playing well, Joe Sykes' cultured play was being appreciated by the fans, while Thompson (15) and

Fowler (11) were the leading goal scorers in the Second Division. With only two matches out of fourteen being lost, the lack of a manager appeared to concern very few. With the club so well-placed, it is probable that the directors were lulled into a false sense of security.

The Swans were still on top on 13 November, but 'Rolande', in the *Sporting News* that evening, sounded a warning. Perhaps he felt moved to challenge what he saw as a surfeit of optimism. Whatever his reasoning, he declared, 'Watch Middlesbrough, they have been doing consistently well for weeks'. On 18 December the journalist's warning was shown to have been particularly pertinent: the Swans lost 7-1 in the north-eastern town (Camsell scored four). It is true that the Vetch men finished with just nine players, but the defeat was a shattering psychological blow to the team. What was worse, there was no manager to lift their sagging morale. It was the beginning of the end of promotion hopes for that season.

On the economic front, gates were being adversely affected around the country by the continuing depression. Indeed, at the end of the season, Aberdare Athletic, the newest of the Welsh clubs in the Football League, was the victim of the cold hand of depression. At the Vetch, apart from one crowd of around 25,000 for a game just after Christmas, the season's average attendance was down as against the previous year. At that time, the *Athletic News* was the most influential paper of its kind in the country. Just before the Middlesbrough debacle, the paper printed an item querying the lack of action at the Vetch in appointing a new manager. In mid-January, the paper returned to the topic and, in a rather scolding tone, implied that the club should act without further delay. The Vetch directors might have bridled about this, but they still did not act.

In January, the first round of the FA Cup brought with it the now-familiar excitement. Could the club get to Wembley this time? After the resounding defeat of First Division Bury, the overwhelming opinion in Swansea was 'yes'. For the moment, the lack of a manager was forgotten and the old confidence returned. Nonetheless, a persistent concern of the supporters related to the many scouts who had been reported as

Commenting on the new stand at the Vetch, the **Cambria Daily Leader** *of 26 April 1927 noted: 'It is a double-decker stand, and the first of its kind in Wales. It will accommodate: standing (on the Richardson Street terrace under cover) about 4,000; seated (new stand above) 2,120. [In all] 9,517 people will be able to witness matches at the Vetch under shelter.'*

watching the Swans. At the time emphatic denials were issued from the Vetch, stating that no players were to be sold, though, in the months ahead, those denials proved to be hollow. In the league, successive away defeats saw the Swans slip to eighth place in the table. However, a second-round cup win at Barnsley was something of a salve for the anxieties of supporters.

By mid-January the directors were using the local press to respond to the continuing comments about the lack of a manager. London papers had carried stories of dissatisfaction among the players because of the delay. Even though the chairman, Owen Evans, denied this, rumours persisted. On 14 February the *Athletic News* noted that J. H. Thomson, the manager of Bury, had resigned. 'Here,' trumpeted the paper, 'is a new candidate for the [Swansea] field.' The paper's journalistic 'nose' was unerring. Thomson was to come to the Vetch, but not at that time. One new face did appear during that week, however, when Ferguson, a goalkeeper, came from Gillingham. He was to give the club outstanding service. The fans were encouraged, too, by the form of Wilf Lewis, who, after playing but a handful of matches for the Swans made a fine international debut.

Despite poor league form, the Swans won their third-round FA Cup tie with South Shields, although a replay was necessary following a draw on Tyneside. In the second division, matters left a great deal to be desired and gates were badly affected. Only 9,000 watched a match against Portsmouth, although it was raining heavily. To make matters worse, in the next round of the cup, Reading beat the Swans at the Vetch. The arguments that Langford had been injured in the warm-up before the match and was a passenger throughout, Thompson did not play and the incessant torrential rain made for a heavy pitch which did not favour the 'ten men', did little to dispel the gloom which seemed to descend upon the town. The season continued amid accompanying greyness. It was as though the spark had gone out of Swansea soccer.

At the end of March the club was like a ship without a captain. 'Waverley', now writing in the *Post*, was of the opinion that a new manager would soon be appointed. He thought that the news would come as a relief to all supporters, for: 'the club has lacked the guiding influence of a manager of merit.' On 4 April both local papers announced the appointment of James Hunter Thomson. Was this the manager of merit which the club needed?

The new man commenced his duties immediately, and whilst little could be done about the outcome of the current season, at least he could plan for the club's extensive close-season tour of Spain and Portugal. The itinerary for this excursion involved the Swans playing the unknown local sides, including Real Madrid and Benfica. The real challenge, however, was thought to come from two Scottish teams, Motherwell and Celtic, both of whom were to be involved in the tournament. Thomson must have relished this opportunity, for the trip gave him a chance to get to know his players and their strengths and weaknesses. Before the party sailed, there was a sad moment as Jock Denoon was released and left the Vetch for the last time. The big goalkeeper had played almost 200 games for the Swans, starting in Southern League days, and had been part of the famous promotion side.

Swansea Town FC Season 1925/26 Division 2

#	Date	V	Opponents	Score	Scorers	Att	Robson ER	Morley EJ	Langford AE	Collins J	Sykes J	Bellamy H	Hole WJ	Deacon H	Fowler J	Thompson L	Nicholas DS	Corkingdale WJ	Evans JH	Humphries B	Denoon J	Milne W	McPherson L	Edwards EJ	Morris DH	Thomas G	Rouse VA	Lewis WL	Williams BD	Handley CHJ	Davies W	Rathmore
1	Aug-29	H	South Shields	1 2	Deacon	20,505	1	2	3	4	5	6	7	8	9	10	11															
2	Aug-31	A	Fulham	1 0	Thompson	13,757	1	2	3	4	5	6	7	8	9	10	11															
3	Sep-05	A	Preston	2 4	Own Goal,Thompson	15,131	1	2	3	4	5	6	7	8	9	10			11													
4	Sep-12	H	Middlesbrough	4 0	Deacon,Nicholas,Fowler 2	20,289	1	2		4	5	6	7	8	9	10	11			3												
5	Sep-14	H	Stockport Co	4 0	Fowler,Nicholas 2,Thompson	17,123	1	2		4	5	6	7	8	9	10	11			3												
6	Sep-19	A	Portsmouth	0 0		11,057	1	2		4	5	6	7	8	9	10	11			3												
7	Sep-21	H	Fulham	6 0	C'dale,Deacon,Thompson2,Fowler2	16,629	1	2		4	5	6	7	8	9	10		11		3												
8	Sep-26	H	Wolverhampton W	2 4	Fowler,Hole	22,624	1	2		4	5	6	7	8	9	10		11		3												
9	Oct-03	A	Derby Co	0 5		16,609	1	2		4		6	7	8	9	10		11		3	5											
10	Oct-10	H	Sheff. Wednesday	1 3	Thompson	27,992			2	4	5		7	8	9	10						1	3	6	11							
11	Oct-17	H	Nottm. Forest	3 0	Thompson,Deacon 2	16,845			2	4	5		7	8		10						1	3	6	11	9						
12	Oct-24	A	Southampton	1 4	Deacon	11,739			2	4	5		7	8	9	10						1	3	6	11							
13	Oct-31	H	Port Vale	1 0	Edwards	15,612			2	4	5		7	8	9	10						1	3	6	11							
14	Nov-14	H	Hull City	2 0	Fowler 2	15,947			2	4	5		7	8	9	10						1	3	6	11							
15	Nov-21	A	Chelsea	3 1	Thompson,Fowler,Hole	43,827			2	4	5		7	8	9	10						1	3	6	11							
16	Dec-05	A	Barnsley	0 2		4,786			2	4	5		7	8	9	10						1	3	6	11							
17	Dec-19	A	Darlington	3 3	Fowler 3	3,813		2		4	5		7	8	9	10						1	3	6	11							
18	Dec-25	H	Stoke City	1 1	Deacon	15,069			2	4	5		7	8	9	10	11					1	3	6								
19	Dec-26	A	Stoke City	1 1	Fowler	19,866			2	4	5		7	8	9	10	11					1	3	6								
20	Jan-01	A	Stockport Co.	3 1	Own Goal,Fowler 2	8,651			2	4	5		7	8	9	10	11					1	3	6								
21	Jan-02	A	South Shields	1 3		9,319			2	4	5		7	8	9	10	11					1	3	6								
22	Jan-16	H	Preston	4 1	Fowler 3,Thompson(pen)	18,180			2	4				8	9	10	11				5	1	3	6			7					
23	Jan-20	A	Bradford City	1 3	Fowler	6,012			2	4			7	8	9	10					5	1	3	6	11							
24	Jan-23	A	Middlesbrough	3 0	Fowler 2,Thompson(pen)	12,134			2	4	5		7	8	9	10	11					1	3	6								
25	Feb-06	A	Wolverhampton W	3 2	Thompson2(1 pen),Fowler	12,411			2	4	5		7	8	9	10	11					1	3	6								
26	Feb-13	H	Derby Co	2 0	Morris	21,237			2	4	5		7	8		10	11					1	3	6	9							
27	Feb-25	H	Blackpool	6 1	Thompson3,Fowler2,Deacon	16,998			2	4	5		7	8	9	10	11					1	3	6								
28	Feb-27	A	Nottm. Forest	2 0	Thompson 2	13,354			2		5		7	8	9	10	11					1	3	6		4						
29	Mar-11	H	Sheff. Wednesday	2 2	Lewis 2	17,086			2	4	5		7		9	10						1	3	6	11			8				
30	Mar-13	A	Port Vale	0 3		19,030			2	4	5		7		9			11				1	3		8		6	10				
31	Mar-18	H	Portsmouth	1 0	Humphries	11,207			3	2	4		7		9					5		1			11	8	6	10				
32	Mar-20	H	Bradford City	1 0	Morris	13,965							7	8					3	5		1		6	9		4	10	2			
33	Mar-29	H	Southampton	3 1	Fowler 3	10,581			2	4	5			8	9	10			11			1	3	6			7					
34	Apr-02	A	Oldham	0 0		18,858			3	4	5			8	9	10	11					1		6			7		2			
35	Apr-03	H	Chelsea	0 0		20,933			3	4	5			8	9	10	11					1		6			7		2			
36	Apr-05	H	Oldham	3 3	Lewis,Morris,Own Goal	18,669			3	4						10	11				5	1		6	9		7	8	2			
37	Apr-10	A	Clapton Orient	0 2		14,863	1		2		5	4	7	8		10	11						3	6	9							
38	Apr-12	H	Clapton Orient	0 0		8,378	1		2		5	4	7	8		10	11						3	6	9							
39	Apr-17	H	Barnsley	3 0	Nicholas,Thompson,Deacon	10,343	1		2	4	5			8		10	11					9	3	6			7					
40	Apr-24	A	Blackpool	0 0		9,949	1		3	4	5		7	8		10	11							6					9	2		
41	Apr-26	A	Hull City	2 4	Corkingdale,Morris	4,146	1		2		5	4	7			10		11					3	6	8				9			
42	May-01	H	Darlington	1 1	Thompson(pen)	10,219	1		2	4	5		7	8		10	11						3	6					9			
						Apps	15	11	34	38	35	12	36	37	32	39	25	6	7	7	27	27	31	11	9	6	4	8	5			
						Gls							2	9	28	19	4	2		1					1			5	3			

#	Date	V	Opponents	Score	Scorers	Att	Robson ER	Morley EJ	Langford AE	Collins J	Sykes J	Bellamy H	Hole WJ	Deacon H	Fowler J	Thompson L	Nicholas DS	Corkingdale WJ	Evans JH	Humphries B	Denoon J	Milne W	McPherson L	Edwards EJ	Morris DH	Thomas G	Rouse VA	Lewis WL	Williams BD	Handley CHJ	Davies W	Rathmore
1	Nov-28	A	Exeter C FAC-1	3 1	Thompson,Deacon,Nicholas	9,500			2	4	5		7	8	9	10	11					1	3	6								
2	Dec-12	H	Watford FAC-2	3 2	Nicholas,Fowler,Thompson	18,000			2	4	5		7	8	9	10	11					1	3	6								
3	Jan-09	A	Blackpool FAC-3	2 0	Fowler,Deacon	13,520			2	4	5		7	8	9	10	11					1	3	6								
4	Jan-30	H	Stoke C FAC-4	6 3	Thompson,Hole,Fowler 4	21,000			2	4	5		7	8	9	10	11					1	3	6								
5	Feb-20	A	Millwall FAC-5	1 0	Fowler,Deacon	42,250			2	4	5		7	8	9	10	11					1	3	6								
6	Mar-06	H	Arsenal FAC-6	2 1	Thompson,Fowler	25,158			2	4	5		7	8	9	10	11					1	3	6								
7	Mar-27	N	Bolton W FAC-SF	0 3		25,476			2	4	5		7	8	9	10	11					1	3	6								
8	Feb-24	A	Colwyn Bay WC-4	1 1	Lewis		1		2										11		5					8	9	7	10	3	4	6
9	Mar-04	H	Colwyn Bay WC-4 Rep																													
10	Apr-06	A	Wrexham WC-5	1 0	Morris	9,367	1		2	4	5	6	7	8						11									9	10	3	
11	Apr-22		Rhyl WC SF	3 1			1		2	4	5		7	8		10			11				3	6					9			
12	Apr-29	A	Ebbw Vale WC F	2 3	Thompson 2		1		2	4	5		7	8		10			11				3	6					9			

N – Neutral Ground: White Hart Lane

Swansea Town FC Season 1926/27 Division 2

#	Date	V	Opponents	Score	Scorers	Att	Denoon J	Williams BD	Milne W	Collins J	Sykes J	McPherson L	Hole WJ	Deacon H	Fowler F	Thompson L	Nicholas DS	Woodward T	Carr JEC	Lewis WL	Hills JJ	Langford AE	Humphries B	Marlow O	Steele A	Thomas G	Ferguson A	Morley EJ	Sampy WE	Reid EJ
1	Aug-28	H	Reading	3 0	Thompson 2,Nicholas	16,559	1	2	3	4	5	6	7	8	9	10	11													
2	Aug-30	A	Grimsby T	1 0	Fowler	14,926	1	2	3		5	6	7	8	9	10		4	11											
3	Sep-04	A	Wolverhampton W	2 2	Thompson 2	18,405	1	2	3		5	6	7	8	9	10	11	4												
4	Sep-11	A	Nottm. Forest	2 2	Fowler,Thompson	10,716	1	2	3		5	6	7	8	9	10	11	4												
5	Sep-13	H	Grimsby T	1 1	Thompson	14,229	1	2	3		5	6	7	8	9	10	11	4												
6	Sep-18	H	Barnsley	5 2	Fowler 3,Thompson 2	18,006	1	2	3		5	6	7	8	9	10	11	4												
7	Sep-20	H	Blackpool	2 0	Thompson 2	14,264	1	2	3		5	6	7	8	9	10		4	11											
8	Sep-25	A	Man. City	1 3	Fowler	24,314	1	2	3		5	6	7	8	9	10		4	11											
9	Oct-02	H	Darlington	5 1	Thompson 2,Fowler 3	15,377	1	2	3		5	6	7	8	9	10	11	4												
10	Oct-09	A	Portsmouth	0 1		17,021	1	2	3		5	6	7	8	9	10	11	4												
11	Oct-16	H	Clapton Orient	3 2	Thompson 2,Fowler	14,242	1	2	3		5	6	7	8	9	10	11	4												
12	Oct-23	A	Notts. Co	3 1	Thompson(pen),Fowler,Deacon	11,634	1	2	3		5	6	7	8	9	10	11	4												
13	Oct-30	H	Hull City	1 0	Thompson	20,772	1	2	3		5	6	7	8		10	11	4		9										
14	Nov-06	A	South Shields	1 0	Deacon	4,422		2	3		5	6	7	8	9	10	11	4			1									
15	Nov-13	H	Preston NE	0 0		17,199		2	3		5	6	7	8	9	10	11	4			1									
16	Nov-20	A	Chelsea	2 2	Thompson,Fowler	18,140		2	3		5	6	7	8	9	10	11	4			1									
17	Nov-27	H	Bradford City	1 0	Fowler	14,842		2	3		5	6	7	8	9	10	11	4			1									
18	Dec-04	A	Southampton	1 1	Fowler	15,002		2	3		5	6	7	8	9	10	11	4			1									
19	Dec-11	H	Port Vale	2 2	Thompson 2	16,344		2	3		5	6	7	8	9	10	11	4			1									
20	Dec-18	A	Middlesbrough	1 7	McPherson	27,804		2	3		5	6	7	8	9	10	11	4			1									
21	Dec-25	A	Oldham Ath	2 5	Deacon,Thompson	20,820			3	4		6	7	8	9	10	11				1	2	5							
22	Dec-27	H	Oldham Ath	3 0	Lewis 3	24,239			3	4		6	7	8		10	11			9		2	5	1						
23	Jan-01	A	Blackpool	1 3	Lewis	13,754			3	4	5	6	7	8		10	11			9		2		1						
24	Jan-15	A	Reading	0 3		14,372	1		3	4	5	6	7	8	9	10	11					2								
25	Jan-22	H	Wolverhampton W	4 1	Thompson,Hole,Collins,Nicholas	14,204	1		3	4	5		7	8	9	10	11					2			6					
26	Feb-05	A	Barnsley	1 1		8,308	1		3	4	5	6	7	8	9	10	11					2								
27	Feb-12	H	Man. City	1 3	Thompson	20,345	1		3	4	5	6		8	9	10			11			2					7			
28	Feb-26	H	Portsmouth	1 1	McPherson	9,054	1		3	4	5	6	7	8	9				11	10		2								
29	Mar-10	H	Nottm. Forest	2 1	Lewis,Fowler	8,935			3	4	5	6	7	8	9	10				11							1	2		
30	Mar-12	H	Notts. Co	0 1		13,026			3			6	7	8	9	10	11	4					5				1	2		
31	Mar-19	A	Hull City	1 2	Lewis	13,143			3	4	5	6	7	8	9	10				11							1	2		
32	Mar-21	A	Clapton Orient	0 1		8,241			3	4	5	6	11	8	9	10										7	1	2		
33	Mar-26	H	South Shields	2 0	McPherson 2	9,380			3	4	5	10	7	8	9				11						6		1	2		
34	Apr-02	A	Preston NE	0 4		13,534			3	4	5	6	7	8	9				11							10	1	2		
35	Apr-09	H	Chelsea	2 1	Fowler,Thompson	10,435			3	4	5	6	7	8	9	10			11								1	2		
36	Apr-15	A	Fulham	3 4	Deacon,Fowler 2	24,555			3	4	5	6	7	8	9	10	11										1	2		
37	Apr-16	A	Bradford City	0 5		17,679			3	4	5	6	7	8	9	10	11										1	2		
38	Apr-18	H	Fulham	4 2	Deacon 2,Thompson 2	11,312				4	5	6	7	8	9	10	11										1	2	3	
39	Apr-23	H	Southampton	2 2	Deacon,McPherson(pen)	8,523				4	5	6	7	8	9	10	11										1	2	3	
40	Apr-30	A	Port Vale	1 1	Thompson	7,483				4	5	6	7	8	9	10	11										1	2	3	
41	May-02	A	Darlington	1 3	Carr	8,704			3	4	5	6	7	8	9	10			11								1	2		
42	May-07	H	Middlesbrough	0 1		11,913				4	5	6	7	8	9	10	11										1	2	3	
			Apps				18	20	38	22	39	41	41	42	39	35	34	20	7	8	8	8	4	2	2	2	14	14	4	
			Gls							1		5	1	7	19	26	2		1	6										

#	Date	V	Opponents	Score	Scorers	Att	Denoon J	Williams BD	Milne W	Collins J	Sykes J	McPherson L	Hole WJ	Deacon H	Fowler F	Thompson L	Nicholas DS	Woodward T	Carr JEC	Lewis WL	Hills JJ	Langford AE	Humphries B	Marlow O	Steele A	Thomas G	Ferguson A	Morley EJ	Sampy WE	Reid EJ
1	Jan-08	H	Bury FAC-3	4 1	Thompson 3,Deacon	21,843	1		3	4	5	6	7	8	9	10	11					2								
2	Jan-29	A	Barnsley FAC-4	3 1	Fowler 2,Hole	28,902	1		3	4	5	6	7	8	9	10	11					2								
3	Feb-19	A	S. Shields FAC-5	2 2	Fowler,Deacon	24,384	1		3	4	5	6	7	8	9	10	11					2								
4	Feb-24	H	S.Shields FAC-5 Rep	2 1	Deacon,Thompson	24,000	1		3	4	5	6	7	8	9	10	11					2								
5	Mar-05	H	Reading FAC-6	1 3	McPherson	20,000	1		3	4	5	6	7	8	9				11	10		2								
6	Mar-28	A	Aberdare WC-5	1 3	Nicholas			2		4	5	6			9	10	11		8			3					1			7

Chapter 8

The End of an Eventful Decade

1927-28

'The Swans' Annual', as the club's AGM was referred to in the local press, proved to be a muted affair. There was no doubt that everyone was disappointed with the outcome of the previous campaign. Nevertheless, new manager Thomson was warmly welcomed and the directors gave details of the new 'double-decker' stand which was being built over the terracing at the Richardson Street end of the ground. It was to be capable of seating 2,120 people, but the pessimists were wondering whether it would be needed.

In the close-season, following a successful Iberian tour, Thomson's activity in the transfer market was on a diminished scale. A goalkeeper and centre-half were recruited from Bury and a winger, Hiles, from Newport. Meantime, Langford and Steele were among those who left. Thomson, it appeared, was happy with the players which he had, and early results seemed to confirm his judgement. Although the opening result, a 7-4 defeat at Manchester City, was something of a shock, when the Swans won the return 5-3, the smiles of their fans began to reappear. On 17 September, when the new stand was used for the first time, 16,000 people were at the Vetch to see the game. Only one hundred, though, were in the new stand, but what a game they saw from their unique vantage point! The Swans beat Wolves 6-0. By 1 October, after another amazing victory, 6-3 over South Shields, the Swans lay in sixth place in the table, it must have seemed like old times.

One encouraging factor behind this revival was that the team was playing well without the benefit of the presence of key-man, Len Thompson. The player had undergone an operation on his left

Manager, James H. Thomson

knee. Despite the fact that the defence was leaking goals, the team was scoring more, which, from the viewpoint of the average fan, made for considerable excitement. In the process, Lewis, McPherson and Fowler were among the six highest scorers in the Football League. Winger Billy Hole, who provided many of the crosses for these goals, had a goal of his own, too. In the middle of October he opened a confectionery and tobacco shop in Swansea. Happily his business flourished and, at the time of writing, his sons continue to run the several businesses which emerged from that shop.

At the same time, it seemed that the *Post* was searching for its right team, for a new name appeared at the head of the paper's soccer column. 'Olympian', was his chosen *nom de plume*, and, even though he was not to last long, he did his best to find positive things about which to write. In mid-October he was praising Joe Sykes for his work on

and off the field, and young Ferguson, the goalkeeper, for his play. Meanwhile, 'Rolande' in the rival *Sporting News*, was more secure in his appointment; he had seen three of his contemporaries come and go. Consequently, when the depression eventually forced the amalgamation of the *Post* and *Leader*, 'Rolande', the senior, more experienced man became the new newspaper's football writer. Such was his security of tenure that he was to survive in that role until the late forties, at which time it was commonly held by the wags that the journalist wrote his pieces without ever being at the matches. In mid-November, though, he was deeply concerned about the startling inconsistency of the side and its dismal away record: they had drawn three games and lost five on their travels. The *Athletic News* was baffled by this form: 'Given the club's excellent home record, this is one of the mysteries of present day football.'

On Christmas Eve the mystery shifted its focus, for the Swans surrendered their home record to Reading. While Sykes and Thompson were absent that day, it was reported that, following the game a 'gloomy attitude was prevalent'. This depression also spread into the new year, when, after a defeat at Fulham on 7 January, the side dropped to twelfth place in the league. Worse was to follow, for in the first round of the FA Cup the Swans were beaten by Wrexham, at the time a mediocre Third Division (North) side.

At the end of January the board were in discussions with a body called the Welsh Racing and Athletic Association. The topic was the establishment of a greyhound track at the Vetch. No details were provided for the public, but a group of shareholders demanded that they should have the opportunity to put forward their views on the matter. Professional football was one thing, but the powerful chapel lobby did not wish to have anything to do with a sport overtly associated with gambling. In the event they need not have worried. As was made clear following an unofficial approach to the appropriate officer, the local authority was just as concerned. Any such application would have little chance of succeeding. One of the

Manager Thomson with the Swans at West Bromwich, 1927-28.

reasons given was that a particularly influential body was of the opinion that such a sport would not be in the interests of those who administered the adjacent gaol. The prisoners, it seemed, would be adversely affected by such activities; though no one explained precisely how that could come about.

Playing at Clapton Orient on 10 March, the team earned a draw with Len Thompson scoring – not that there was anything unusual about that. What was unusual was the presence of the Arsenal manager, Herbert Chapman, at the game. He must have been impressed, for, six days later, Thompson exchanged the white shirt of Swansea for the red and white of Arsenal. The fee, not announced at the time, was £4,000. Thompson, who had played almost two hundred games for the Swans, scoring eighty-six goals in the process, was to be the first of several key departures. It seemed that manager Thomson or the directors were intent on breaking up the promotion side.

Thompson was to be missed, but ten days later his fellow Sheffielder, Harry Deacon took his benefit. 9,000 people turned up in his support to see Heart of Midlothian, the first Scottish side to appear at the Vetch, play the Swans. A week later another link with the club's past was broken when director D. J. Bassett died. The board acted quickly to replace him:

> **Heart of Midlothian were the first Scottish side to play at the Vetch.**

J. W. Thorpe was restored to the board. This time, however, his presence did not produce the kind of result which had come about following his previous return from exile.

With little to play for, during the last two weeks of the season manager Thomson experimented with his side. Wilf Lewis, a local boy, became a fixture at centre-forward; Lloyd, another local, was at left-half, and Gunn, a Scottish junior, took Thompson's place at inside-left. So successful was this combination that the team was unbeaten in its last eight matches and finished a creditable sixth in the league table. The fans, however, were beginning to fret. Lewis was attracting attention wherever he played and, with Thompson having been transferred, they were concerned that the club's better players would be sold for large sums. Despite denials from the Vetch, their fears could not be assuaged.

Presumably heartened by the run of results towards the end of the

season, chairman Owen Evans was reasonably confident at the club's 'Annual'. Even though he was obliged to report a decrease in revenue of some £4,000, he strongly affirmed that 'It is not our policy to transfer players'. Later on, though, he pointed out that retaining players meant that the club was obliged to pay benefits regularly. In addition, £5,540.15s had been spent on the new stand. Apparently forgetting the statements made at a previous meeting about increasing the capacity of the ground, he now thought that additional seating would not be needed for many years to come. Time was to prove his 'second thought' to be right. No further seating was added until fifty years had passed.

1928-29

Few new faces were evident as the season commenced. Ernie Morley had been sold to Clapton Orient and the only senior player to arrive was W. Black, a Scot from Hearts. Manager Thomson was, clearly using his connections in Scotland to spot talent. Among the young local boys who were vying for first team positions were Hanford and Tabram. Both were to make their mark at the Vetch while Black, who had cost the club £450, was to play only a handful of games.

The first match of the season was away to Chelsea, where 47,000 watched the game. The metropolis, it appeared, was not as badly affected by economic conditions as were other parts of the country. The home side won the match 4-0, which was hardly a boost to Swansea confidence. Perhaps the Swans were adversely affected by the historic nature of the game, for, in accordance with a decision made by the league authorities in the previous week, 'by way of experiment' the Chelsea team wore numbers. The Swans, however, retained their numerical anonymity, which some wag claimed was in keeping with their inability to score.

After an amazing 5-5 draw with Blackpool at the Vetch (Harry Deacon scored four), results were far from satisfactory. By the end of September, eight matches had been played, only one of which had been won; fourteen goals had been scored

Harry Deacon

by the Swans, while opponents had registered twenty-five. After a 5-0 defeat at Stoke, the club was second from the bottom of the table. The pessimists were having a field day. Injuries to key players and the lack of adequate reserve cover exacerbated the situation. Then, as if to rub salt into an open wound, the team was beaten by a Clapton Orient side which contained three former Swans. One of them, Ernie Morley, was selected to play for Wales during the following week.

There appeared to be a ray of hope in November when the Swans found some form, beating Tottenham 4-0 at the Vetch. Apart from the welcome victory, this game provided two points of interest. It was the London club's first visit to the Vetch and, in the final minute, Jack Fowler scored his hundredth league goal for the club. Although he only added one more goal to his Swans tally, Fow-Fow-Fowler had richly repaid his record transfer fee. Whilst the supporters were cheered by that victory, their joy receded when they learned that Wilf Lewis had been sold to Huddersfield for £6,500, the highest fee the club had received for a player up to that point. With Fowler's form falling away, the directors had sold his natural successor.

Selling Lewis after promising not to transfer key players hardly endeared Owen Evans to the fans. The size of Vetch gates soon began to reflect a growing disenchantment with the board and with the team's performances. Only 10,000 turned

up to see a match with Notts County, even though former-Swan, Willie Davies, was in the County side, and the visitor's custodian was the brother of the Swans' goalkeeper. Those who were there went home happy, though, for the Swans won the match: it was only the side's fourth win in sixteen games. Fortunately for the Swans, however, other sides had performed even more poorly. As a result, the modest success of the men in white allowed them to improve their league position to seventh from the bottom.

At the year end, both local papers were critical of the Vetch management. 'Olympian', in the *Post,* after pointing out that large fees had been received for players who had left the Vetch, added that 'No outstanding move had been made to remedy weaknesses.' The pattern, which was to become familiar to Swans fans in ensuing years, had begun to be established. It involved a syndrome in which key players were transferred for short-term financial reasons, while crowds diminished in the face of poor performances. In turn, this phenomenon led to the necessity for further sales in order to boost failing finances. Meantime, the supporters were beginning to lose heart.

Even the FA Cup failed to stir the imagination of the Swansea public, although a win at Nottingham Forest did something to restore spirits. But even that was short-lived encouragement for, in the next round, the side lost to Leicester City by a single goal. At that, in accordance with the received wisdom, the Swans could concentrate on the league. In the next match that concentration appeared to be beneficial.

On the morning of 2 February 1929, Lachlan McPherson was married in a Swansea church. In the afternoon, he appeared at the Vetch in a match against WBA along with a newcomer from the Cheshire League, called Cheetham. The combination of the bridegroom and the recruit brought excitement to the Vetch for the first time for several months. The Swans scored six while conceding just one. The joy of the fans, however, was tempered by a strong rumour that Huddersfield were about to sign the newly married Scot. The fans were downcast, for the paucity of top-class talent at the

Vetch at the time was illustrated by Cheetham's debut. The player had been signed from non-league football just ten days before and had had only one game for the reserves. Furthermore, he was to leave the club within eighteen months with the comment on his transfer form that 'he did not show improvement'. Nor, for that matter, did the Swans.

By the middle of April the side was in some danger of relegation. Although lying eighth from the bottom with three matches to play, they were by no means safe. As 'Olympian' put it, 'There can be no question that the threat of relegation is a real one for Swansea Town.' Although the club avoided that ignominy, when the final game had been played, it was third from the bottom, its poorest position since gaining promotion to the Second Division. It had been an extremely disappointing season which, sadly, reflected the position of all south Wales clubs of that period. Cardiff had finished bottom of Division One and were relegated, while both Merthyr and Newport ended their campaigns among the bottom eight of the Third Division (South).

In the town, the strength of feeling regarding the team's poor performance was reflected by a journalist using the pen-name 'Athos'. Writing in the *Post* after the season ended, he unsheathed his sword with a vengeance: 'It has been,' he noted, 'the worst season in the club's history . . . They have never finished so low in the league . . . have never lost so many games . . . nor created so much dissatisfaction.' He went on to express the very strong opinion that the deficiencies evident within the club, had arisen as a result of 'the inability of the club's directors to achieve unanimity in the hundred-and-one questions concerned with running it.'

Chairman Owen Evans was not at the AGM to respond to this and other criticisms. T. M. Martin, who deputised, had to report a further decline in gate receipts – to £14,229, the lowest since the war. The club, he argued, had to sell players to survive, for the depression had continued for longer than expected. As if seeking light in the gloom he praised the sterling work of club captain, Joe Sykes, on and off the field. It was a quality of service which the popular Sykes was to continue to provide for many years to come. One incident towards the end of the meeting served to throw some light on the manager's position at the club. Former director D. C. Rees claimed that the club's failure during the recent season had been due to the directors picking the team. In his opinion, and that of the assembled shareholders, it seemed, the manager should do so. It was an echo of the cry from earlier seasons, 'Let the manager manage!'

1929-30

The final season of the decade was greeted with muted interest, which was reflected by the sad jokes in currency around the town at the time. For example:

> Man to friend: 'Have you been to see the Swans lately?'
> Friend: 'No, they don't come to see me when I'm bad.'*

In the face of this apathy, the directors gave permission for some new faces to be brought in, but the fees which were paid for them were indicative of their perceived quality. While the sale of Wilf Lewis had created yet another transfer-out record, the £1,240 paid for Jack Fowler still remained intact as the club's record purchase. The new players cost hundreds rather than thousands of pounds, and, as time was to show, generally speaking you get what you pay for. Among the newcomers were Handley, a winger from Spurs, Armand, an inside forward from Leeds, and Hindley, a goalkeeper from non-league football. Another local youngster joined at the same time; he was Ronnie Williams, a strong, bustling forward.

After six games of the new season the gloom had intensified at the Vetch. Four of these matches had been lost, including one at home, and the club had picked up just two points. 'Rambler', in the *Post*, felt that the problem lay with the inside-forwards. Since the whole of the back division remained unchanged during this period, it appeared that the manager was of a similar opinion. Not once in the six games had the team fielded the same forward line.

As if to confound the critics, on

21 September the team scored a fine 5-0 victory over Bradford City, but then failed to score in the next two matches. The latter of these was the first Football League game played between the Swans and the newly relegated Cardiff City. The poverty of the fare provided for the crowd in a goalless draw at Ninian Park was enlivened only by a fire which broke out in the main stand. After that event, the Swans were fourth from the bottom of the league table. At that point in the season, it looked to the supporters as if the new term was going to create in them as much heartache as had the previous season.

As the campaign wore on the picture changed very little. An

> *In February 1929, Lachlan McPherson was married at a Swansea church in the morning. That afternoon he turned out for the Swans against West Bromwich Albion.*

excellent 4-0 win over Preston at the beginning of October proved to be a single 'swallow'. There followed two heavy defeats and a series of matches in which nine were lost out of ten played. After twenty games the club had gathered a meagre ten points and was bottom of the table. In the following game, on Christmas Day, young Ronnie Williams was given a chance at centre-forward. He was the sixth player to be tried in that position during the season and proved to be a great success – scoring a hat-trick on his league debut. The crowd, badly in need of a new hero, grasped him to their collective bosom like a long-lost brother. With three points from the next two matches, things looked brighter, but the hopes of the supporters were severely bruised when it was announced that Lachlan McPherson and Ben Williams had both signed for Everton for substantial fees. The old 'promotion' side had been denuded of its stars, while those who sought to replace them were of lesser stature. The supporters must have asked, if

the side was struggling with men of this calibre in its ranks, what chance did it have without them?

In analysing the club's performance, both local papers pointed to its awful away record. During the first half of the season the side had picked up only two points from eleven games played away from the Vetch. Coupled with indifferent home form, as 1929 came to a close, this resulted in the Swans being in twenty-first place in the Second Division. 'Rolande's' conclusion that this was 'worrying' seemed to the beleagured supporters to be the understatement of 1929.

With the January games completed, the worry must have got to the directors, for two new men were signed: Easton from Everton (£850) and Lindsay (£575) from Liverpool. A week later, Len Williams, a full-back from Wolves, joined them. The first match in which all three appeared was against Cardiff City at the Vetch. Happily, the Swans won 1-0, but relegation remained a real threat, for, by the middle of March the club was still in the bottom-but-one place in the table. Then, as if some metamorphosis had taken place, the team put together a series of performances of note. They won six of the last eight matches, beating second-placed Oldham as well as champions-to-be, Blackpool. Given that Blackpool conceded three without scoring, the shrinking band of optimists in Swansea, whose position had hardly been tenable for two seasons, began to stretch themselves in anticipation. When the season ended the Swans were in what appeared to be a healthy fifteenth position in the table. In fact, though, they were only three points clear of relegation.

The supporters and the Vetch management breathed a collective sigh of relief and tried to look at the late revival in form as an encouraging omen for the next season. However, their thinking must have been coloured by happenings elsewhere in south Wales. Merthyr Town, the club whose officials had encouraged the Swans at the time when the club was formed, finished bottom of the Third Division (South) and were not re-elected. The unrelenting hand of the depression had struck its second Welsh victim. It waited in the wings ready to claim a third.

---

* *'Bad' is sometimes used in Swansea parlance to mean 'ill'.*

Swansea Town FC Season 1927/28 Division 2

#	Date	V	Opponents	Score	Scorers	Att	Ferguson A	Williams BD	Milne W	Collins J	Sykes J	McPherson L	Hole WJ	Deacon H	Fowler J	Lewis WL	Nicholas DS	Hiles B	Woodward T	Thomas G	Morley EJ	Hanford H	Sampy WE	Thompson L	Lloyd C	Gunn K
1	Aug-27	A	Blackpool	2 2	Fowler 2	15,771	1	2	3	4	5	6	7	8	9	10	11									
2	Aug-29	A	Man. City	4 7	Lewis 2,Deacon,Hiles(pen)	34,316	1	2	3	4	5	6	7	8	9	10		11								
3	Sep-03	H	Fulham	2 1	Lewis,Hole	14,617	1	2	3	4	5	10	7	8		9	11		6							
4	Sep-05	H	Man. City	5 3	McPherson 3 (1 pen),Lewis 2	17,554	1	2	3	4	5	10	7	8		9	11		6							
5	Sep-10	A	Barnsley	3 3	Lewis, Thomas,Nicholas	13,647	1	2	3	4	5	10		8		9	11		6	7						
6	Sep-17	H	Wolverhampton W	6 0	McPherson 3(1 pen),Fowler 3	16,672	1	2	3	4	5	10	7		9	8	11		6							
7	Sep-24	A	Port Vale	0 2		10,197	1	2	3	4	5	10	7		9	8	11		6							
8	Oct-01	H	South Shields	6 3	McPherson,Lewis 3,Fowler 2	13,697	1	2	3	4	5	10	7		9	8	11		6							
9	Oct-08	A	Leeds United	0 5		18,097	1	2	3	4	5	10	7		9	8	11		6							
10	Oct-15	H	Nottm. Forest	2 0	Fowler, Deacon	14,844	1	2		4	5	6	7	8	9	10	11				3					
11	Oct-22	A	WBA	2 5	Deacon, Lewis	15,245	1	2		4	5	6	7	8	9	10	11				3					
12	Oct-29	H	Clapton Orient	5 0	Lewis 2,Deacon 2,McPherson	12,562	1	2	3	4	5	10		8		9	11		6	7						
13	Nov-05	A	Chelsea	0 4		41,220	1	2	3	4	5	10	7	8	9		11		6							
14	Nov-12	H	Bristol City	1 1	McPherson	13,600	1	2	3	4	5	10	7	8	9		11		6							
15	Nov-19	A	Stoke City	1 1	Fowler	9,938	1	2	3	4	5	6	7	8	10	9	11									
16	Nov-26	H	Oldham Ath	0 0		12,469	1	2	3	4	5	6	7	8	10	9	11									
17	Dec-03	A	Notts. County	0 2		11,618	1	2	3		5	6	7	8	10	9	11		4							
18	Dec-10	H	Southampton	2 0	McPherson,Fowler	10,676	1	2	3	4	5	6		8	10	9	11			7						
19	Dec-17	A	Grimsby T	2 1	Deacon, Hiles	9,581	1	2	3		5	6		8	9	10		11	4	7						
20	Dec-24	H	Reading	0 1		9,034	1	2	3		5	6	7	10	9	8	11		4							
21	Dec-26	A	Preston NE	2 4	Deacon,Lewis	26,206	1	2	3			6	7	8	9	10	11		4			5				
22	Dec-27	H	Preston NE	0 1		15,264	1	2	3			6	7	8	9	10	11		4			5				
23	Dec-31	H	Blackpool	1 0	Lewis	9,185	1	2	3			6	7	10	9	8	11		4				5			
24	Jan-07	A	Fulham	2 3	Fowler, Lewis	15,008	1	2	3			6	7	10	9	8	11		4				5			
25	Jan-21	H	Barnsley	3 0	Thompson 2,Lewis	6,429	1	2	3			6	7	4	9	8	11		5					10		
26	Feb-04	H	Port Vale	2 0	Fowler 2	6,745	1		3			6		8	9		11		5	7			2	10		4
27	Feb-11	A	South Shields	1 3	Hole	3,572	1	2	3			6	7		9	8	11		5					10		4
28	Feb-18	H	Leeds United	1 1	Thompson	13,444	1	2	3			6	7	4	9	8	11		5					10		
29	Feb-25	A	Nottm. Forest	2 0	Lewis ,Fowler	11,687	1	2	3			6	7	4	9	8	11		5					10		
30	Mar-03	H	WBA	3 2	McPherson,Thompson,Lewis	15,355	1	2	3			6	7	4	9	8	11		5					10		
31	Mar-10	A	Clapton Orient	1 1	Thompson	11,508	1	2	3			6	7	4	9	8	11		5					10		
32	Mar-17	H	Chelsea	0 0		15,653	1	2	3		5	6	7	10	9	8	11		4							
33	Mar-24	A	Bristol City	1 2	Lewis	17,123	1	2	3		5	6	7	10	9	8	11		4							
34	Mar-31	H	Stoke City	1 1	Fowler	10,893	1	2	3		5	6	7	10	9	8	11		4							
35	Apr-06	A	Hull City	2 0	Gunn ,McPherson(pen)	8,877	1	2	3		5	6	7	8	9		11		4							10
36	Apr-07	A	Oldham Ath	1 0	Gunn	14,860	1	2	3		5	6	7	8	9		11		4							10
37	Apr-09	H	Hull City	2 0	Lewis, Nicholas	15,732	1	2	3		5	6	7	8		9	11		4							10
38	Apr-14	H	Notts. Co	1 1	Lewis	11,566	1	2	3	4	5	6	7	8		9	11									10
39	Apr-21	A	Southampton	2 0	Lewis, Gunn	8,820	1	2	3			5	7	8		9	11		4						6	10
40	Apr-28	H	Grimsby T	3 2	Lewis 2,Deacon	9,208	1	2	3			5	7	8		9	11		4						6	10
41	Apr-30	A	Wolverhampton W	1 1	Lewis	8,972	1	2	3			5	7	8		9	11		4						6	10
42	May-05	A	Reading	0 0		7,771	1	2	3			5	7	8		9	11		4						6	10
					Apps		42	41	40	21	24	42	37	37	28	39	37	7	34	5	2	2	3	7	6	8
					Gls							12	2	8	15	25	2	2		1				5		3

#	Date	V	Opponents	Score	Scorers	Att	Ferguson A	Williams BD	Milne W	Collins J	Sykes J	McPherson L	Hole WJ	Deacon H	Fowler J	Lewis WL	Nicholas DS	Hiles B	Woodward T	Thomas G	Morley EJ	Hanford H	Sampy WE	Thompson L	Lloyd C	Gunn K
1	Jan-14	A	Wrexham FAC-3	1 2	Hole	12,000	1	2	3			6	7	4	9	8	11		5					10		
2	Feb-28	A	Holyhead WC-5	8 1			1	2	3			6	11	4	9	8			5	7				10		
3	Apr-02	A	Cardiff C WC-6	0 1		10,000	1		3	4	5	10	11		9				8	7			2		6	

Swansea Town FC Season 1928/29 Division 2

#	Date	V	Opponents	Score	Scorers	Att	Ferguson A	Williams BD	Milne W	Collins J	Sykes J	McPherson L	Hole WJ	Deacon H	Lewis WL	Black W	Nicholas DS	Woodward T	Davies J	Sampy WE	Lloyd C	Marson F	Gunn K	Fowler J	Pattimore H	Thomas G	Whitehouse JF	Cheetham J	Caldwell T	Hanford H	Livingstone
1	Aug-25	A	Chelsea	0 4		47,264	1	2	3	4	5	6	7	8	9	10	11	6													
2	Aug-27	H	Blackpool	5 5	Deacon 4,Lewis	12,152	1	2	3	4	5		7	8	9	10	11	6													
3	Sep-01	H	Barnsley	2 1	Lewis 2	12,005			3	4	5		7	8	9	10	11		1	2	6										
4	Sep-03	A	Blackpool	2 2	Marson, Lewis	12,899			3	4	5		7	8	9	10			1	2	6	11									
5	Sep-08	A	Bristol C	1 2	Lewis	15,608			3	4	5		7	8	9	10	11		1	2	6										
6	Sep-15	H	Nottm. Forest	3 5	Deacon,McPherson(pen),Hole	12,204			3	4	5	6	7	8	9	10	11		1	2											
7	Sep-22	A	WBA	1 5	Lewis	14,751			3	4	5	6	7	8	9		11		1	2				10							
8	Sep-29	H	Clapton Orient	0 1		10,412	1		3	4		5	7	8			11			2	6			10	9						
9	Oct-06	A	Stoke C	0 5		12,787	1			4		5	7	8			11			2	6			10	9	3					
10	Oct-13	H	Grimsby T	2 1	Lewis,Lloyd(pen)	10,443	1			4	5		7	8	9	10	11			2	6					3					
11	Oct-20	A	Preston NE	2 2	McPherson(pen),Lewis	14,484	1		3	4	5		7	8	9	10	11			2	6										
12	Oct-27	A	Middlesbrough	2 0	Fowler 2	12,026	1		3	4	5			8		10	11			2	6			9		7					
13	Nov-03	A	Oldham Ath.	1 2	Lewis	10,876	1		3	4	5		7	8	9	10	11			2	6										
14	Nov-10	H	Tottenham H	4 0	Hole,Fowler2, Deacon	6,906	1	2	3	4	5		7	8		10	11				6			9							
15	Nov-17	A	Wolverhampton W	0 0		16,911	1	2	3	4	5			8		10	11				6					7	9				
16	Nov-24	H	Notts. Co.	1 0	Black	10,498	1	2	3	4	5					8	11				6			10		7	9				
17	Dec-01	A	Millwall	0 3		19,781	1	2	3	4	5		7	8			11				6			10		9					
18	Dec-08	H	Port Vale	2 0	Nicholas, McPherson	8,968	1	2	3	4	5		7	8		10	11				6			9							
19	Dec-15	A	Hull C	1 1	Fowler	10,702	1	2	3	4	5	6	7			8	11						9	10							
20	Dec-22	H	Southampton	1 1	Nicholas	7,681	1	2	3		5	6	7	8			11	4					9	10							
21	Dec-24	A	Bradford PA	1 3	Fowler	26,925	1	2	3		5		7	8		10	11	4			6			9							
22	Dec-26	H	Bradford PA	3 1	McPherson 2,Deacon	15,197	1		3	4	5		7	8		10	11			2	6			9							
23	Dec-29	H	Chelsea	0 1		12,659	1		3	4	5		7	8		10	11			2	6			9							
24	Jan-05	A	Barnsley	1 2	Hole	3,848	1		3	4	5		7	8		10	11			2	6			9							
25	Jan-19	H	Bristol C	0 2		9,787	1	2	3	4	5		7	8		10	11				6			9							
26	Feb-02	H	WBA	6 1	Ch'ham,Gunn2,McP'son,Marson,Hole	8,695	1	2	3	4	5	6	7	8								11	10					9			
27	Feb-09	A	Clapton Orient	2 1	Cheetham,Thomas	10,330	1	2	3	4	5	6		8								11	10			7		9			
28	Feb-16	H	Stoke C	3 3	Cheetham 2,Gunn	8,987	1	2	3	4	5	6				8						11	10			7		9			
29	Feb-20	A	Nottm. Forest	1 2	Cheetham	5,872	1	2	3	4	5	6				8						11	10			7		9			
30	Feb-23	A	Grimsby T	1 4	Marson	9,422	1		3	4	5	6				8				2		11	10			7		9			
31	Mar-02	H	Preston NE	5 0	Gunn3, Cheetham 2	13,133	1		3		5	6				8		7	4	2		11	10					9			
32	Mar-09	A	Middlesbrough	0 0		18,430	1		3	4	5					8				2		6	11	10		7		9			
33	Mar-16	H	Oldham Ath.	3 2	Marson,Gunn,Deacon	11,442	1		3	4	5	10		8						2		6	11			7		9			
34	Mar-23	A	Tottenham H	1 1	Deacon	25,107	1		3	4	5	10		8						2		6	11			7		9			
35	Mar-29	A	Reading	0 2		13,579	1		3	4	5			8				10		2		6				7		9			
36	Mar-30	H	Wolverhampton W	2 0	Deacon,Cheetham	4,234	1			4	5	6		8				10		2		11				7		9	3		
37	Apr-01	H	Reading	0 1		16,843	1				5	6		8				4		2		11				7		9	3		
38	Apr-06	A	Notts. Co.	1 5	Cheetham	9,429	1			4		6	7	8						2		11	10					9	3	5	
39	Apr-13	H	Millwall	2 0	Deacon 2	11,502	1		3	4		6	7	8						2			10					9		5	
40	Apr-20	A	Port Vale	0 0		8,587	1		3	4	5	6	7	8			11			2			10					9			
41	Apr-27	H	Hull C	0 1		11,242	1		3	4	5	6	7	8			11			2			10					9			
42	May-04	A	Southampton	0 3		6,344	1		3	4	5	6	7	8			11			2			10					9			
	Apps						37	15	37	36	37	36	28	37	10	11	31	5	5	27	24	14	24	11	2	13	2	15	3	2	
	Gls											6	4	12	9	1	2					4	8	6		1		9			

#	Date	V	Opponents	Score	Scorers	Att	Ferguson A	Williams BD	Milne W	Collins J	Sykes J	McPherson L	Hole WJ	Deacon H	Lewis WL	Black W	Nicholas DS	Woodward T	Davies J	Sampy WE	Lloyd C	Marson F	Gunn K	Fowler J	Pattimore H	Thomas G	Whitehouse JF	Cheetham J	Caldwell T	Hanford H	Livingstone
1	Jan-12	A	Nottm.Forest FAC-3	2 1	Own Goal ,Deacon	16,188	1	2	3	4	5		7	8		10	11				6			9							
2	Jan-26	A	Leicester C FAC-4	0 1		40,000	1	2	3	4	5	6	7	8			11					10	9								
3	Feb-28	A	Newport Co. WC-5	1 5			1		3					8		10			4	2		11				7		9		5	6

Swansea Town FC Season 1929/30 Division 2

#	Date	V	Opponents	Score	Scorers	Att	Ferguson A	Williams BD	Milne W	Collins J	Sykes J	McPherson L	Hole WJ	Deacon H	Cheetham J	Freeman A	Handley CHJ	Nicholas DS	Armand JE	Gunn K	Thomas G	Hanford H	Davies G	Sampy WE	Lloyd C	Fowler J	Craig A	Williams R	Middleton J	Lindsay J	Easton WC	Williams L	Caldwell T	Tabram WD	Ranson JG
1	Aug-31	A	Hull C	0-1		10,068	1	2	3	4	5	6	7	8	9	10	11																		
2	Sep-02	H	Bristol C	1-1	Nicholas	16,315	1	2	3	4	5	6	7	8	9	10		11																	
3	Sep-07	H	Stoke C	2-2	Gunn 2	13,316	1	2	3	4	5	6	7		9			11	8	10															
4	Sep-11	A	Bristol C	1-2	Thomas	12,925	1	2	3	4	5	6	11		9				8	10	7														
5	Sep-14	A	Wolverhampton W	1-4	Thomas	14,662	1	2	3	4	5	6	11	8	9					10	7														
6	Sep-16	H	Reading	0-1		11,101	1	2	3	4	5	6		8	9					10	7	11													
7	Sep-21	H	Bradford C	5-0	Gunn2,Armand,Thomas,M'Phson (p)	11,779	1	2	3	4	5	6	11	8					9	10	7														
8	Sep-28	A	Barnsley	0-1		7,961	1	2	3	4	5	6	11	8					9	10	7														
9	Oct-05	A	Cardiff C	0-0		29,093	1	2	3	4	5	6	7			10			9				11												
10	Oct-12	H	Preston NE	4-0	Gunn2,Armand,McPherson(pen)	14,636	1	2	3	4	5	6	7	8				11	9	10															
11	Oct-19	H	Bradford PA	2-4	Hole, Armand	13,215	1	2	3	4	5	6	7	8				11	9	10															
12	Oct-26	A	WBA	2-6	Cheetham 2	19,596	1		3	4	5	6	7		9			11	8	10				2											
13	Nov-02	H	Tottenham H	0-1		8,961	1	2	3		5	10	7		9	4	11		8						6										
14	Nov-09	A	Southampton	1-2	Hole	16,387	1	2	3		5	10	7		9	4	11		8						6										
15	Nov-16	H	Millwall	3-1	McPherson(pen),Hole, Handley	9,413	1	2	3		5	10	7	8		4	11			9					6										
16	Nov-23	A	Oldham Ath	1-4	Gunn	14,417	1		3	6	5	10	7	8		4	11			9				2											
17	Nov-30	H	Nottm. Forest	1-1	McPherson	9,297	1	2	3		5	10	7	8		4	11			9					6										
18	Dec-07	A	Chelsea	0-1		16,548	1	2	3		5	4	7	8			11		9	10					6										
19	Dec-14	A	Bury	2-4	Handley,Gunn	7,627	1	2	3		5		7	8			4		11	10					6	9									
20	Dec-21	A	Blackpool	0-3		10,139	1	2	3	4					9	10	11		8		7				6		5								
21	Dec-25	H	Notts. Co	3-2	Williams 3	7,148	1	2	3		5	4	11	8		6				10	7							9							
22	Dec-26	A	Notts. Co	0-0		19,284	1	2	3		5	4	11	8		6				10	7							9							
23	Dec-28	H	Hull C	2-0	Deacon,McPherson(pen)	4,555	1		3		5	4	11	8		6				10	7			2				9							
24	Jan-04	A	Stoke C	1-0	Williams	9,431	1		3	4	5		11	8		6				10	7			2				9							
25	Jan-18	H	Wolverhampton W	2-2	Gunn,Williams	9,984	1		3	4	5					6	11		8	10	7			2				9							
26	Jan-25	A	Reading	1-3	Sykes	8,597	1		3		5		11			4			6	10	7			2				9				8			
27	Feb-01	H	Barnsley	0-2		9,955	1		3		5		11			4					7			2	6			9			8	10			
28	Feb-08	H	Cardiff C	1-0	Lindsay	22,121	1		3		5					4	6		11	9	7									8	10	2			
29	Feb-15	A	Preston NE	0-0		9,032	1		3		5					4	6		11	9	7									8	10	2			
30	Feb-19	A	Bradford C	3-3	Handley,Deacon,Lindsay	8,240	1				5					4			11	9	7									8	10	2		3	6
31	Feb-22	A	Bradford PA	0-3		13,489	1				5					4			11	9	7									8	10	2		3	6
32	Mar-01	H	WBA	1-0	Handley	12,976	1				5					4			11	9	7									8	10	2		3	6
33	Mar-08	A	Tottenham H	0-3		30,331	1				5					4			11	9	7									8	10	2		3	6
34	Mar-15	H	Southampton	2-2	Easton,Williams Ron	8,821	1		3		5		7			4			11								6	9			8	10	2		
35	Mar-22	A	Millwall	2-0	Nicholas,Williams Ron	19,937	1		3	6			7			4	10		11						5			9			8	2			
36	Mar-29	H	Oldham Ath	3-0	Williams Ron 2,Thomas	13,503	1		3	6						4	10		11		7			5				9			8	2			
37	Apr-05	A	Nottm. Forest	0-1		6,604	1		3	6						4	10		11		7			5				9			8	2			
38	Apr-12	A	Chelsea	3-0	Hole,Williams R,Armand	14,944	1		3	6			11			4			10		7			5				9			8	2			
39	Apr-18	A	Charlton Ath	2-0	Williams R, Thomas	9,904	1		3	6			11			4			10		7			5				9			8	2			
40	Apr-19	A	Bury	0-1		5,573	1		3	6			11			4			10		7			5				9			8	2			
41	Apr-21	H	Charlton Ath	2-0	Armand 2	18,051	1		3	6			11			4			10		7			5				9			8	2			
42	Apr-26	H	Blackpool	3-0	Thomas,Williams R,Armand	16,433	1		3	6			11			4			10		7			5				9			8	2			
					Apps		42	20	38	15	42	21	32	34	10	23	19	5	25	18	26	9	1	7	9	1	1	16	1	8	16	16	15	4	4
					Gls						1	5	4	2	2				4	2	7	9		6				12		2	1				

#	Date	V	Opponents	Score	Scorers	Att	Ferguson A	Williams BD	Milne W	Collins J	Sykes J	McPherson L	Hole WJ	Deacon H	Cheetham J	Freeman A	Handley CHJ	Nicholas DS	Armand JE	Gunn K	Thomas G	Hanford H	Davies G	Sampy WE	Lloyd C	Fowler J	Craig A	Williams R	Middleton J	Lindsay J	Easton WC	Williams L	Caldwell T	Tabram WD	Ranson JG
1	Jan-11	A	Walsall FAC-3	0-2		12,715	1		3	4	5		11	8		6				10	7			2				9							
2	Mar-13	H	Merthyr WC-5	4-2	Easton2, Thomas,Williams Ron		1						11								7	5						9		10	8	2	3		
3	Apr-02	A	Cardiff C WC-6	0-4		8,000	1		3				7	4			11					5						9		8		2		6	10

Chapter 9

The Thirties – Disappointment and Cyril Pearce

The 1930s started and ended with disappointment for Swans fans. At the end of the 1930-1 season the team was twentieth in the league, while in the final campaign before the war it finished in nineteenth position. Indeed, on only two occasions during the decade did the club manage to finish outside the bottom eight teams in the division. In addition, relegation was a worrying threat right up to the final games of three seasons. It was a time when the old promotion side was finally disbanded, and one during which two managers failed in their attempts to restore Swansea soccer to its former glory. Nonetheless, it is not a period which can be ignored in setting down the chronicle of Swansea soccer. Several talented players emerged during the decade, and many hundreds of people were involved during difficult times in raising funds to help ensure that the Vetch club continued to exist.

1930-31

After an indifferent start, by the turn of the year the club had gained a comfortable mid-table position. Ferguson, Sykes, Hanford and Ronnie Williams all did well during this period, while the same defence appeared in twelve successive games. In January, the largest gate of the season (19,604) came to the Vetch to watch Everton play the Swans. The general opinion was that, with the defence operating so effectively the 'Toffee-men' could be given a good run for their money. The reality was that the Mersysiders carried too many big guns for the Swans; they scored five goals, including a brace

Cyril Pearce

for the famous 'Dixie' Dean. Two former Swans, Ben Williams and Lachlan McPherson were also outstanding for the visitors. The home hero was Ronnie Williams who helped to salvage a little pride by scoring for the Swans.

With three matches left to play, the team found themselves in danger of relegation, as were Cardiff City, who were bottom. The position of the two clubs reflected the impact of the depression upon the whole of south Wales. It struck, too, in other sectors. The last edition of the *South Wales Daily Post* was published on 15 March 1930. Two days later, it was absorbed by its rival, the *Leader* and re-emerged as the *South Wales Evening Post*. 'Rolande', it was who chronicled drama of the final weeks of the season for that paper.

When the Wolves drew at the Vetch on 18 April and the Swans were heavily beaten at Bradford, relegation appeared to be highly likely. It was not surprising, therefore, that there were fewer than

6,000 at the Vetch for the final match. Those who came saw a patchwork team win the game by 1-0, which, given what was happening elsewhere, was sufficient to save the club from demotion. While Swansea supporters sighed with relief, those of Cardiff were obliged to face life back in the Third Division (South) only two seasons after their team had been playing in the First Division. Further east, Newport supporters were required to swallow an even more bitter pill. Their side finished bottom of the Third Division (South) and were not re-elected. Consequently, they became the third casualty of south Wales soccer. Of the original five, only two remained. For the first time in its history, Swansea Town was the premier club, at least in the southern part of the Principality. That crown, however, was balanced uneasily upon the brow of a sickly king.

During the close-season, two players who had given the club outstanding service left the Vetch. They were Billy Hole and Harry Deacon. Between them they had played almost seven hundred games for the Swans and scored over 120 goals. Both men had been extremely popular with the fans. They left along with several recent signings, all of whom had failed to make an impression at the Vetch. Then in August, without warning, manager Thomson resigned his position. Once again, the directors made no move to find a replacement. They had not, it seemed, learned from their previous experience of trying to run as a managerless club.

1931-32

The cold hand of recession which had been a major cause of the ejection of Newport County from the Football League, had the converse effect on Swansea Town. When County became a non-league club, Cyril Pearce, who had been on their books, became available and the Vetch club signed the centre-forward just before the new season began. Pearce, who had not had an outstanding career, was joining a mediocre side, but, within a matter of weeks, Swansea supporters realised that they had found a player with that special talent of scoring goals regularly. Not since Jack

Fowler had they had such a hero to adore. By the end of October the side had gathered a mere twelve points from thirteen games, yet Pearce had scored seventeen times. When only half the season had passed, the centre-forward was a mere four short of Fowler's record of twenty-eight league goals in a season. It was a remarkable tally, particularly since no other Swansea player could boast more than five goals. Sadly, despite Pearce's goal-scoring prowess, the inconsistency of the remainder of the side meant that results were poor. Pearce, however, was unperturbed and carried on scoring regularly. With sixteen matches still to play, he created a new scoring record for the Swans. Almost seven decades later, his eventual total – thirty-five – has still to be beaten.

Satisfaction with the Pearce goal-machine apart, having been knocked out of the FA Cup at the first time of asking, and making little progress in the league, the sole competition upon which players could focus was the Welsh Cup. After victories over Newport and Chester and others in earlier rounds, the club was paired with Wrexham in the final of the competition. In view of the circumstances which had prevailed on an earlier occasion when the clubs had met in the final tie, both parties agreed that, should there be a drawn game at the first venue, any replay would be on the other club's ground. In the event, Wrexham won the toss to host, what turned out to be the first match of two, for it was drawn. That game was played on 5 May, and even though the Swans had their vital final league match on 7 May, the replay was fixed for 6 May. This time, the Swans won by two clear goals. Nine of the Swans played in both cup ties and in the final league match. It was a remarkable, if foolhardy, feat of endurance.

Happily, enough points were gained to avoid relegation and, with the club winning the Welsh Cup, the season ended on a more positive note than might have been the case. Whilst that was true of results on the field, the financial implications of the team's poor performances were worrying for the board. For example, the lowest gate ever recorded for a Swans Second Division match up to that time (3,393) had watched a game in November, whilst only

> *During the 1931-32 season, Cyril Pearce set a club record by scoring 35 times.*

4,281 were at the Vetch to see Pearce score twice in the club's final fixture. For those who were running the club, these statistics made grim reading. It was hardly surprising, therefore that, during the close-season, the board felt it to be necessary to transfer Cyril Pearce to Charlton. Unfortunately, the centre-forward's goal-scoring ability was to be badly missed. Whilst the directors must have rued their decision in the seasons ahead, they could at least point to the fact that the club was still in business.

> *The Swans' 500th match in the Football League was against Burnley (away) on 9.4.32*

1932-33

When the side was announced for the first game of the season, only Lewis remained of the forward line which had completed the previous campaign. Initially, of the newcomers, Martin, who had joined the club from Wolves, proved to be the most effective, scoring three times in four games. After a fine win against Chesterfield, in which Ronnie Williams replaced an injured Martin, the side was ninth in the table, a considerable improvement on the previous season. Then, when the team gained a point at the expense of Bradford City, who were leading the division, they improved their position to a heady fifth. They were still in that position at the turn of the year and the optimists among Swansea supporters were expecting even better in the second half of the season, for apart from Martin's goal-scoring, the form of two young Swans, Harry Hanford and Sid Lawrence, suggested bright futures

for both players. There was some apprehension, though. Given the small gates which the team was attracting, and the number of scouts from other clubs who were following the Swans, the supporters feared the worst. Meantime, however, there was the FA Cup to divert their attention. Could another cup-run bring in sufficient money to ensure that the best players were retained at the Vetch? Certainly, the club's third-round opponents were attractive enough.

They were Sheffield United, then a prominent first division side, whom the Swans had never previously played. Although the 'Blades' ran out winners by 3-2, it was only after the home side had been reduced to ten men following an injury to Ronnie Williams that they took the lead. Once again, the club's flirtation with the FA Cup had been brief, however, at least it had been reasonably lucrative: 23,281 people watched the match.

With the *Post* predicting a 'brighter new year for west Wales' on the economic front, and the team having done quite well against Sheffield, the directors were said to be 'reasonably confident' about the remainder of the campaign. They also stressed the need for the crowds to come back and support the club. By the middle of February, that confidence looked to be reasonably justified. However, in March, Ronnie Williams was badly injured; then, as unpredictable as ever, the side lost five matches in succession. Following that unhappy run, they won only three of their remaining seven games. Nevertheless, they were still tenth at the end, their best position for five years. Ferguson, Lawrence, Sykes and Hanford had been outstanding in defence, which was just as well, since the team had scored only fifty goals during the entire season. At the AGM, chairman Owen Evans emphasised that the board had had to be prudent with expenditure. 'They had,' he reported, 'given consideration as to whether to appoint a manager . . . Money was tight . . . [and] things had not gone as we would have wished.' He also said that if the public were not satisfied, then the directors would be prepared to stand down. No one in the hall moved or spoke: Owen Evan and his colleagues were re-elected *en bloc*.

Alex Ferguson

1933-34

At the end of the 1933-4 season the club's league position was considerably worse than it had been for the previous term. The side was nineteenth in the table and had been in grave danger of relegation right up to the final match of the campaign. Indeed, as in 1930-1, they needed to win their last game in order to survive. In itself, that dismal fight had been enough of a disappointment for the fans. What added to their chagrin was the transfer of Ronnie Williams to Newcastle half way through the season. The return of former-Swan, Willie Davies, had done little to diminish the feeling amongst the club's loyal supporters that its better players were always going to be sold. In reality, of course, the directors of the day were making sure that their books balanced, for, in an economy which was only coming out of recession very slowly, few bankers would countenance continuing losses. When gate income was reduced and cash flow a problem, they felt that there was little else they could do.

On the field, away form continued to be a problem. For the first time in its history, the team failed to win a single game at an away venue. The major bright spot in a gloomy season was the FA cup, in which the team progressed to the fifth round only to lose to First Division Portsmouth. That match was of considerable importance from the financial point of view, for a new Vetch attendance record was created when 27,920 people crowded the ground. The

directors noted that with some satisfaction and were encouraged that there were, still, a vast number of Swans fans in the old borough. Nevertheless, overall it had been a very disappointing season. Milne and Sykes alone remained of the old promotion team and the latter had played in only two matches. Milne had the distinction of scoring his first goal for the Swans in his 501st league game. It was from the penalty spot. He did the same thing in the final match against Plymouth; had he missed the Swans would have been relegated. There was one bright note for the future: a young half-back called Jack Warner made his debut during the season. Warner was to develop into another bright star who would be sold to help balance the books.

Among the departures from the Vetch at the end of the season was B. Watts-Jones. He resigned so that he might use his considerable influence in the football world to help save Cardiff City from extinction. Cardiff had finished bottom of the Third Division (South) and there was said to be a real danger that they might not be re-elected. That this dedicated south Wales soccer administrator helped save the 'Bluebirds' from oblivion is a story for another book. Suffice it to say here that he left Swansea Town having given many years of dedicated service both to the Swans and to Welsh football in general. His part in ensuring that the Swans would play in the First Division of the Southern League directly after the First World War, should never be forgotten.

Meanwhile, the directors decided to invest some of the revenue earned from the cup run in appointing a manager. From what was described as a 'formidable list of applicants', they chose another Scot, Neil Harris. When Harris came to the Vetch in July 1934 he had a reputation as a 'manager with sound ideas'. Unfortunately, as the future was to show, those ideas, in themselves, were not enough to ensure success. As a preamble to the club's AGM, the appointment of Harris might have been regarded as a useful stimulus of interest in Vetch matters. Sadly, if the numbers who attended the annual meeting are anything to go by, the converse might have been true. As one report put it, 'Owen Evans presided over a small

attendance of shareholders.' However, one item which was discussed at the meeting attracted wider attention. A woman living in a house adjacent to the Vetch had been summoned by the Customs and Excise authorities in conjunction with a 'stand' which had been built at the bottom of her garden, from which the Swans' matches could be viewed over the retaining wall. The problem was that the woman had been charging customers 1*s.* (5*p.*) for the privilege of seeing Swans games in comfort. Since the stand was on private property, the authorities could not prevent it being used. However, since the woman was taking money in exchange for entertainment, the Excise people claimed that she was liable to pay entertainment tax. The woman's defence was that she did not realise that she was obliged to do so. That defence was accepted with the proviso that she should pay 7*s.* (35*p*) arrears of tax and conform in the future. Naturally, the Vetch management was less than pleased with the finding, but could do little about it. As chairman Evans observed, the club was not receiving sufficient money through the gate to be viable as it was. Reporting a small surplus of £172, he said that this had only been possible because of the FA Cup run and the sale of players. The downward spiral was proceding at a rate which was to contribute to making the job facing the new manager extremely difficult.

1934-35

Yet another departure from the Vetch in August demonstrated the changing order of things. Long-serving trainer Ernie Edwards left to join Exeter City. In the same month the new manager made his first signing: Walter Bussey came to the Vetch from Blackpool. Harris was giving the general impression that he was a manager who knew what needed to be done as well as how it should be done. That the tangible results of his of his efforts throughout his time at the club were so poor in undeniable. However, the management of a football club involves a partnership of directors, management, and senior administration staff. In many ways, the results which are achieved in playing and in business terms reflect

The Swans at Port Vale, February 1935.
Back row, left to right: J. McMillan (Trainer), Sid Lawrence, Jack Warner, Joe Walton, Joe Lloyd, Wilfie Milne, Tommy Olsen.
Front: Hugh Blair, Walter Bussey, Tudor Martin, Joe Sykes, Sid Lowry, Harry Hanford.

the effectiveness of this team. In judging Harris, or any of the others who have occcupied the managerial chair at the Vetch, this fact has to be borne in mind.

As if to confirm early impressions, the Swans started the new campaign with a flourish which included a fine 5-1 win over Oldham. The captain of the side was Harry Hanford, by now an experienced and effective centre-half. By the end of September the club was thirteenth in the league table, but there followed a series of poor results and by mid-November the situation had deteriorated. 'Rolande' in the *Post* was campaigning for new men, though, Bradshaw apart, the record of the club as a buyer of players left a great deal to be desired.

While the usual crop of rumours about player departures circulated within Swansea, one of the club's players found himself in the public eye for reasons other than football. Lowry, a winger, had, 'while inebriated', threatened the conductor of a tram with a pistol. The player received a lecture on sobriety from the magistrates, was fined £6 and bound over for twelve months in the sum of £10. For his part, the conductor was commended for his bravery in the matter.

At the season's half-way stage, old

fears began to haunt the club and its supporters as, once more, relegation loomed large. Consequently everyone was pleased to welcome the diversion offered by the FA Cup. The third round opponents were Stoke City, a First Division side. On their right wing was an exciting young player by the name of Stanley Matthews, and the youngster made his presence felt by scoring for the visitors in the first minute. It was an excellent start for Stoke, but one upon which they could not capitalise. The Swans won 4-1 with a performance which belied their status. The 20,000 crowd went home happy, and a thousand of them journeyed to Derby for the next round at the Baseball Ground. There, despite special training and with Joe Sykes at inside-left, the Swans were defeated. The sparkle of the cup was gone and the gloom resulting from poor league performances descended upon the club once again.

At the end of February, 'Rolande''s column was headed: 'WHAT RELEGATION WILL MEAN'. Perhaps it was its air of inevitability which provoked a response from the Vetch, for when the season ended, the side was in a respectable mid-table position. Nonetheless, the margin of safety

was far from comfortable, while the club's financial position was even less so. In Swansea, 'Save our Soccer' became the watchword. It was a situation similar to that in which other Vetch Field personalities would find themselves in later years. There was a touch of sadness, too when the retained list was published: it was announced that Joe Sykes, the man they called 'the diminutive giant' had retired. He did not know it at the time, but ahead of him lay a long period of further service to the club which he had helped to put on the map of Football League teams.

Appeal
On June 15 1935 an appeal was launched in Swansea with the objective of 'saving the club from decline'. Almost immediately it caught the imagination of the public, and events of all kinds were mounted in aid of the appeal. The *Post* launched a 'Shilling Fund'; a heavyweight fight and even a dance took place at the Vetch; and hundreds of smaller events were held around the town. By the middle of July, Harry Sullivan, the chairman of the committee formed to manage the appeal, declared himself delighted with the progress. No doubt encouraged by the inflow of money, the directors of the club allowed Neil

Harris to trade in the transfer market. As a result, the manager bought and sold in an effort to improve his side. Walton and Lowry left, as did Irish international Blair, a new goalkeeper, S. Moore, was signed from Leeds and a winger, Jack Pears, from Sheffield United.

1935-36

Although the new side which Harris had assembled lost its first match – at Southampton, there was some encouragement for Swans supporters: they scored three times. They had not been able to do that at an away venue during the previous campaign, but on its own that was not enough. By the time 1935 came to an end, the team was in eighteenth place in the table. The team's sole significant victory had been against Bury, when Tudor Martin scored all four goals, and they had been badly beaten at Tottenham and Burnley. Yet, Warner, Hanford and Lawrence were among the most effective performers.

At the end of February, there was further unease among the supporters because of the rumours about other departures from the Vetch. 'Several managers and scouts' were said to have been following the Swans, and to the fans that could mean only one thing. On 22 February the scouts and the fans had a rare dish to digest: the club registered its second 8-1 victory, with Walter Bussey scoring four and playing well. Unfortunately, only 5,213 were in the ground to see the match, for, as had been the case when the original scoring record was set, it came during a mediocre spell. The newspapers were lavish with their praise for the football played by the Swans that day. The *Post* detected 'old-time enthusiasm' in the town when the result was known, but it was a flame of hope which was quickly extinguished. Three days later, Harry Hanford joined Sheffield Wednesday for a 'substantial fee'. For the fans, the old pattern was repeating itself. Despite the difficult position in which the club found itself, a key man in the Swans defence had been sold.

On 4 April, a sixteen-year-old centre-forward scored two goals at the Vetch for visitors Burnley. The meagre crowd were to learn in later years that they had been privileged to

Tudor Martin

> **On 22 February 1936 the Swans equalled their scoring record, beating Bradford City 8-1.**

see Tommy Lawton score his first league goals (having made his first team debut the week before). When the team played its penultimate match of the season – against Hull City – at the Vetch, the directors took the opportunity to explain the club's financial position in some detail. Clearly, they were attempting to justify their decision to sell players, Harry Hanford in particular. As a consequence of this, despite a fine 6-1 win, the supporters left the ground heavy-hearted. If all the effort which had been put into raising money through the appeal was not to be in vain, it was going to have to be reactivated. Yet the club's playing record had left much to be desired and Hanford had been sold. It seemed that the supporters had come to expect mediocrity and had voted against its influence by staying away in their thousands. That was hardly an environment in which a renewed appeal would prosper. Yet, as the 1936-7 season was to show, when there was excitement and renewed hope, even of a temporary nature, they would return in large numbers in response to the type of thrills

which once had been regular fare at the Vetch. Hope, indeed, springs eternal in the bosoms of ardent football fans.

When the retained list was posted, it was obvious that the manager had decided to clear the decks. Only sixteen players had been retained. Willie Davies, Martin, Ferguson and Pears were all shown as 'available for transfer' and several new players were signed to replace them. These included Henson and Greene (Wolves), Crowe (WBA) and Moore (Birmingham). Crowe cost £375, played one first team game and was released on a free transfer; Greene played twelve matches over two seasons, and Moore left after one season and four games. It did not take a genius to discern from this that whoever was making the buying decisions was not being successful in that task.

1936-37

The first visitors to the Vetch on the opening day of the new season were the mighty Aston Villa. The famous Birmingham club had been relegated at the end of the previous campaign and the match was to be their first in the Second Division. The Vetch administration set out to take advantage of this fact, which, in itself, gave a tremendous fillip to the pre-season promotion. 'Volunteer and paid labour' painted and renovated stands and other structures so as to have the Vetch looking at its best. The Villa side was purported to have cost transfer fees in excess of fifty thousand pounds – a huge amount at the time – and a large crowd was expected.

For the match itself, the Vetch was decorated in a variety of ways. Hoisted over the centre of the main stand was a flag bearing the club's name, while the Union Jack and the Welsh dragon flew at either end. At the small-bank end, what was described as a 'festoon' was draped along the top of the retaining wall. The management said that this was designed to welcome the new football season. The fact that it also obscured the view of those with the best-placed illicit stand may not have been accidental either. The famous Swansea choral conductor, Ivor Owen, led the massed choir of 25,180 in community singing, and

Match with Aston Villa, 1936-37 season.

the mayor was introduced to the teams, who were lined up as if it was an FA Cup final. The visitors appreciated the welcome and won 2-1 against a Swansea side which was reduced to ten men for most of the game. Whilst disappointed at the outcome, the Vetch management could at least enjoy the financial benefits of the occasion. Furthermore, the optimists argued, if the team can play so well against such formidable opponents with only ten men, they ought to do well during the rest of the season. Unfortunately, successive away matches were lost and, for the next home game, only 8,596 came to watch. At that point in the season things did not appear to be going manager Harris's way, yet, by the end of October there was a smile on the face of supporters. The team had played six consecutive games without losing and the Swans had moved up the table to thirteenth position. There was a further boost to morale too, when Jack Warner was selected to play for Wales. In his absence, young John Harris, the manager's son, came into the side. Sadly, that game marked the end of the successful run and by mid-December Vetch gates had fallen again.

As the season progressed, the old pattern of inconsistency became apparent once more. Nevertheless, despite some heavy defeats, the team was able to maintain a respectable mid-table position. It seemed that, at least, there would be a respite from what had become almost an annual fight to avoid relegation. In addition, on Boxing Day 1936 the club made history again. Their match at Villa Park became the second Football

League game to be broadcast live by the BBC. A crowd of 54,163 watched the match, whilst tens of thousands more listened to the crackling commentary in which the broadcaster used the 'eight squares' method to describe the game It was an approach which was to become familiar to football-loving wireless owners in the years to come. In mid-March the Swans were required to play two games in three days in the Midlands. On the way to Leicester for the first of these, stiffness developed in goalkeeper Moore's knee to such an extent that he was unable to play in either match. The only available substitute was long-serving full-back, Wilfie Milne, then in his seventeenth season with the club. At the end of the Leicester game, Milne was congratulated by his team mates on an excellent display. The sides had drawn 0-0 and Milne had saved several shots at

goal. It was a pity that, in the game which followed – his last for the club – he needed to pick the ball out of the net on six occasions. It was hardly a fitting finale to the career of a wonderful club servant.

The final game of the season was won 4-1 in front of a gate of just 3,620. Despite the size of the victory and its style, it could not alter the fact that yet another unimpressive campaign had ended. Away form had been poor once again, with the team winning just one match and scoring only ten goals during the season. Nevertheless, the club was still in being and there was always hope regarding the season ahead! Meantime, the last link with the old promotion side was broken when Wilfie Milne packed his bags and left the Vetch for pastures new, though not before a special benefit had been played on his behalf. More than sixty years later, Milne's club appearances record still stands. As if to mark the occasion with suitable imagery, at the time of the player's departure the Swansea transport authorities were taking up the tramlines. The old vehicles were going to be replaced by motor buses.

As had happened in previous seasons, players left and others came, though the buying policy seemed to be the same as ever. 'Three for £1,500' was still an ineffective approach to improving the calibre of the staff. The club's most expensive purchase was that of Jack Fowler, signed thirteen seasons before for £1,280 and in 1937 a player of Fowler's calibre would have cost three times that amount.

The 'eight squares' method of describing a game was developed by the BBC to assist listeners. Having not had experience of live broadcasting, it was assumed that listeners needed help in understanding where, on the pitch, the game was proceeding. As a result there was two broadcasters – one described the play, the second intoned the square (on the 'Radio Times' diagram) in which play was going on.

1937-38

The new season began with another false dawn. After five games the team was in sixth position in the league table. Fans and management alike were greatly encouraged by the start and by the progress made by players like Warner, Lawrence and young George Lowrie. By early November, though, the Swans had dropped to eleventh and there followed a disastrous series of eleven matches in which only three points were gained. In addition, the club had been ejected from the FA Cup, thus there was nothing to divert the supporters from the gloom of the team's league form. Things at the Vetch were as difficult as they had ever been: the manager's performance was being challenged, gates were falling and the team was in twenty-first position in the table. During this period, another young gem was sold: George Lowrie joined Preston for a 'substantial fee'. Although the transfer helped to assuage the financial pressures facing the board, it did little for the morale of the fans or the form of the team. It was true that two new players were recruited to replace Lowrie, but, true to form, both men were transfer-listed six months later at half their purchase cost.

Before that happened however, there was further drama for the supporters as, yet again, the Swans fought to avoid the dreaded relegation. With two matches to play the side seemed to be fixed in twenty-first position and to ensure safety they had to win both. Since they had managed to achieve two successive victories just once in the earlier part of the campaign, they were thought to have little chance of avoiding demotion. The first of these vital games was against Newcastle at the Vetch. It was a tense occasion but, as if every chapel in Swansea had held a prayer meeting to ensure a favourable result, Olsen scored in four minutes and the Swans won 2-0. The team's final league match, upon which the club's future status depended, was to take place at Bradford on 7 May.

Prior to that, though, the Swans were required to play Shrewsbury in the final of the Welsh Cup. No doubt with one eye on the survival battle, the Swans drew 2-2 with the border side, but, in view of the importance of the final match, they refused to

play extra time. After much discussion, the Welsh FA agreed that the final should be replayed early in the following season. Common sense having prevailed, the team could now concentrate upon the game at Bradford. As things stood, a draw might have been enough to save the club from relegation, but a win would make absolutely sure.

Back in Swansea, without the benefit of instant television and radio coverage, the sole source of up-to-date information on the match was the local newspaper office. Later, 'Rolande' reported that 'scores of soccer supporters waited outside the *Post* offices on tenterhooks . . . There was an excited rush as the first seller came out . . . the crowd was vastly relieved.' Almost unbelievably, Harry Lewis had scored the only goal of the game. Once more the Swans had avoided relegation; they were safe in Division Two for another season. However, the young stars were not: Jack Warner signed for Manchester United during the close season.

1938-39

Some of the money which had been received for Warner was made available to manager Harris and the Scot broke the club's buying record by paying £1,500 to Newcastle for Bill Imrie, who was coming to the end of his career but was an extremely experienced player. Another notable signing was Tommy Bamford from Manchester United. Both were big men who added stature to the team. There were departures, too, from Swansea as well as the club. Two Swansea schoolboys, Ernie Jones and Jack Roberts, joined Bolton and another pair, Tom Kiley and Bobby Daniel, went to Arsenal. The lack of attraction of the Vetch club which these departures implied was to be a detrimental factor for Swansea football for many years to come.

Despite the new acquisitions, the start of the season was hardly impressive. After eleven games, none of which had been won, the side was anchored firmly at the bottom of the league. In addition, the Welsh Cup replay with Shrewsbury had been lost. When Christmas arrived Harris appeared to have used all the alternatives which were open to him while the side had won just one of its nineteen matches. In January, the

Tommy Bamford

Swans were beaten at the first time of asking in the FA Cup and then lost four consecutive league games. The singer, Paul Robeson, in concert in Swansea in the February must have found a feeling of close brotherhood with those of his audience who were Swans supporters. Nirvana was certainly not the place in which the team found itself, though, like the negro slaves, 'that's where they longed to go'.

As the season ground on, the position hardly improved. There seemed to be no chink of light in a sullen sky and the club appeared to be anchored in twenty-first position with only six games to play. Then, as if they were playing parts in one of the serialised films then being shown in Swansea cinemas, the team transformed themselves. The immortal phrase, 'with one bound he was free', might well have been written about the team which was embroiled in the long-running Vetch saga. Three wins and two draws in the first five of the club's remaining games, provided sufficient points to ensure that Second Division football would be played at the Vetch for at least another term. At that the optimists began to think about the team continuing the next season in the manner in which they finished this time. They were also buoyed up by the fact that Swansea Schoolboys won the English Schools Shield, beating Chesterfield at the Vetch after drawing in Derbyshire. The 20,000 crowd which watched that game must have looked to the maturing of these lads as a means of restoring glory to the Vetch. Many years and a man called Adolph Hitler were to intervene before that hope became reality.

Swansea Town FC Season 1930/31 Division 2

#	Date	V	Opponents	Score	Scorers	Att	Ferguson A	Williams L	Milne W	Deacon H	Hanford H	Sykes J	Thomas G	Easton WC	Williams R	Armand JE	Hole WJ	Bell GC	McMillan WH	Rees EG	Miller J	Lindsay J	Gunn K	Craig A	Lewis DJ	Tabram WD	Davies G	Lang W	Ranson JG	Lawrence SJ	Hindley RA
1	Aug-30	H	Cardiff C	3 2	Williams R 2,Easton	20,368	1	2	3	4	5	6	7	8	9	10	11														
2	Sep-01	A	Barnsley	0 1		6,727	1	2	3	4	5	6		8	9	10	7	11													
3	Sep-06	A	Everton	1 5	Williams R	27,245	1	2	3	4	5	6		8	9	10		11	7												
4	Sep-08	H	Charlton Ath	1 1	Bell	10,363	1	2	3	4	5	6		8	9	10		11	7												
5	Sep-13	H	Bury	5 2	Easton 3(2 pens),Williams R 2	10,870	1	2	3		5			10	9		7	11		4	6	8									
6	Sep-15	A	Charlton Ath	0 3		7,125	1	2	3		5			10	9			11	7	4	6	8									
7	Sep-20	A	Plymouth A	0 0		12,688	1	2	3	8	5			10	9			11	7	4	6										
8	Sep-27	H	Reading	2 1	Easton 2	11,744	1	2	3	8	5			10	9	7		11		4	6										
9	Oct-04	H	WBA	1 1	Bell	12,497	1	2	3	8	5			10	9	7		11		4	6										
10	Oct-11	A	Port Vale	0 2		10,970	1	2	3	4	5			10	9	7		11			6		8								
11	Oct-18	A	Burnley	2 2	Armand ,Sykes	11,624	1	2	3			4		8	9	10			7		6				5	11					
12	Oct-25	H	Southampton	0 1		10,754	1	2	3			4	7	8	9	10					6				5	11					
13	Nov-01	A	Stoke C	0 5		7,094	1	2	3			4	7	8	9	10					6				11	5					
14	Nov-08	H	Milwall	4 1	Thomas,Easton 2,Own Goal	8,496	1	2	3		5	4	7	8	9	10					6						11				
15	Nov-15	A	Tottenham H	1 1	Williams R	20,211	1	2	3		5	4		8	9	10			7		6						11				
16	Nov-22	H	Nottm. Forest	3 2	Williams R 3	8,059	1	2	3		5	4		8	9	10	7	11			6										
17	Nov-29	A	Oldham Ath.	1 2	Easton	10,584	1	2	3		5	4		8	9	10	7	11			6										
18	Dec-06	H	Preston	2 1	Bell ,Easton(pen)	9,906	1	2	3		5	4		8	9	10	7	11			6										
19	Dec-13	A	Wolverhampton W	1 3	Williams R	14,202	1	2	3		5	4		8	9	10		11	7		6										
20	Dec-20	H	Bradford PA	2 1	Armand ,Williams R	9,612	1	2	3		5	4		8	9	10		11	7		6										
21	Dec-25	H	Bristol C	5 2	Williams R 2,Bell 2,Armand	11,062	1	2	3		5	4		8	9	10		11			6	7									
22	Dec-26	A	Bristol C	1 2	Bell	17,950	1	2	3	8	5	4			10	9		11			6	7									
23	Dec-27	A	Cardiff C	0 1		24,232	1	2	3		5	4		8	9			11			6	7	10								
24	Jan-03	H	Everton	2 5	Williams R ,Easton	19,604	1	2	3		5	4		8	9	10		11			6	7									
25	Jan-17	A	Bury	0 2		6,956	1	2	3		5	4		8	9		11	7			6		10								
26	Jan-24	H	Plymouth A	2 0	Easton 2	9,598	1	2	3		5	4	7	8	9	10	11				6										
27	Jan-31	A	Reading	0 1		6,858	1	2	3		5		7	8	9			11			6				4					10	
28	Feb-07	A	WBA	0 0		15,754	1		3	4	5	2		8	9		7				6		10		11						
29	Feb-14	H	Port Vale	2 1	Easton ,Gunn	8,602	1		3	4	5	2		8	9		7				6		10		11						
30	Feb-21	H	Burnley	1 1	Williams R	10,906	1		3	4	5	2		8	9	10	7				6				11						
31	Feb-28	A	Southampton	2 1	Easton ,Deacon	10,888	1		3	8	5	4		10			9	7			6				11					2	
32	Mar-07	A	Stoke City	1 2	Deacon	7,149			3	8	5	4			10		9	7			6				11					2	1
33	Mar-14	A	Millwall	1 3		17,651			3		5	4	7	8	9	10					6				11					2	1
34	Mar-21	H	Tottenham H	1 2	Easton	9,876			3		5	4	7	10	9	8	11				6									2	1
35	Mar-28	A	Nottm. Forest	0 3		6,609	1		3	4	5	6		8	9	10	7								11					2	
36	Apr-04	H	Oldham Ath.	0 0		7,959	1		3		5	4	7	8	9		11				6		10							2	
37	Apr-06	H	Bradford C	1 2	Gunn	8,309	1		3	4		5	7	8	9		11				6		10							2	
38	Apr-07	A	Bradford C	0 3		12,829	1		3	8	5	4		10	7	9	11				6									2	
39	Apr-11	A	Preston NE	0 0		7,697	1		3	8	5	4	7			10									11	6			9	2	
40	Apr-18	H	Wolverhampton W	1 1	Williams R	9,152	1		3	4		5		10	9		7				6	8			11					2	
41	Apr-25	A	Bradford PA	1 5	Williams R	4,372	1		3	8	5	4		10	9		7								11	6				2	
42	May-02	H	Barnsley	1 0	Thomas	5,752	1		3		5		7	8		10					6	9			11	4				2	
					Apps		39	27	42	20	37	34	12	40	39	29	21	19	8	5	35	8	7	2	14	4	2	1	2	12	3
					Gls					2		1	2	17	17	3		6					2								

#	Date	V	Opponents	Score	Scorers	Att	Ferguson A	Williams L	Milne W	Deacon H	Hanford H	Sykes J	Thomas G	Easton WC	Williams R	Armand JE	Hole WJ	Bell GC	McMillan WH	Rees EG	Miller J	Lindsay J	Gunn K	Craig A	Lewis DJ	Tabram WD	Davies G	Lang W	Ranson JG	Lawrence SJ	Hindley RA
1	Jan-10	A	Notts. Co FAC-3	1 3	Easton(pen)	23,802	1	2	3		5	4		8	9	10		11			6	7									
2	Feb-26	H	Llanelly WC-5	2 0																											
3	Mar-06	H	Oswestry WC-6	2 0																											
4	Apr-15	N	Wrexham WC S-F	2 5	Lewis D, Williams	4,208																									

at Chester

Swansea Town FC Season 1931/32 Division 2

#	Date	V	Opponents	Score	Scorers	Att	Ferguson A	Lawrence SJ	Milne W	Sykes J	Craven J	Miller J	Boston HJ	Williams R	Pearce C	Anstiss HA	Lewis DJ	Gunn K	Simms JL	Tabram WD	Olsen TB	Jones JL	Rees EG	Hanford H	Caldwell T
1	Aug-29	H	Leeds Utd	0 2		16,175	1	2	3	4	5	6	7	8	9	10	11								
2	Aug-31	A	Bury	1 2	Pearce	9,374	1	2	3	4	5	6	7	8	9	10	11								
3	Sep-05	A	Manchester Utd	1 2	Pearce	6,763	1	2	3	4	5	6	7	8	9	10	11								
4	Sep-07	H	Port Vale	2 3	Pearce 2	9,927	1	2	3	4	5	6	7	8	9	10	11								
5	Sep-12	A	Barnsley	3 2	Simms ,Pearce 2	5,213	1	2	3	4	5	6	7	8	9				10	11					
6	Sep-19	H	Notts. Co	5 1	Pearce 4, Simms	10,933	1	2	3	4	5	6	7	8	9				10	11					
7	Sep-21	A	Port Vale	4 0	Pearce 3, Williams R	7,969	1	2	3	4	5	6	7	8	9					11	10				
8	Sep-26	A	Plymouth A	2 4	Pearce 2	23,514	1	2	3	4	5	6	7	8	9					11	10				
9	Oct-03	H	Bristol C	2 0	Sykes(pen) ,Pearce	12,565	1	2	3	4	5	6	7		9	8	11	10							
10	Oct-10	A	Oldham Ath.	0 2		8,269	1	2	3	4	5	6	7	8	9		11	10							
11	Oct-17	H	Bradford PA	1 0	Sykes	11,279	1	2	3	4	5	6	7	8	9		11	10							
12	Oct-24	A	Wolverhampton W	0 2		14,530	1	2	3	4	5	6	7	8	9		11			10					
13	Oct-31	H	Charlton Ath	2 0	Pearce ,Williams R	9,171	1	2	3	4	5	6	7	8	9		11			10					
14	Nov-07	A	Tottenham H	2 6	Pearce 2	20,834	1	2	3	4	5	6	7	8	9		11			10					
15	Nov-14	H	Southampton	3 4	Sykes ,Pearce,Gunn	3,393	1	2	3	4	5	6	7	8	9		11	10							
16	Nov-21	A	Preston NE	0 1		6,410	1	2	3	4	5	6	7	8	9	10						11			
17	Nov-28	H	Burnley	5 1	Gunn 3,Pearce,Jones	8,051	1	2	3	4	5	6		7	9		11	10				8			
18	Dec-05	A	Chesterfield	2 1	Pearce ,Williams R	7,906	1		3	4	5	6		7	9		11	10				8	2		
19	Dec-12	H	Nottm. Forest	4 1	Pearce 2,Jones ,Gunn	9,457	1	2	3	4	5	6		7	9		11	10				8			
20	Dec-19	A	Stoke C	0 0		7,717	1	2	3	4	5	6		7	9		11	10				8			
21	Dec-25	H	Bradford C	0 1		13,737	1	2	3	4	5	6		7	9		11	10				8			
22	Dec-26	A	Bradford C	1 5	Pearce	18,059	1	2	3	4	5	6		7	9		11	10				8			
23	Jan-02	A	Leeds Utd	2 3	Gunn ,Anstiss	12,885	1	2	3	4	5	6		7	9	8	11	10							
24	Jan-16	H	Manchester Utd	3 1	Williams R,Anstiss,Miller	5,888	1	2	3		5	6		7	9	8	11	10				4			
25	Jan-23	H	Barnsley	3 0	Pearce ,Jones ,Gunn	7,998	1	2	3		5	6		7	9	8	11	10				4			
26	Jan-30	A	Notts. Co	2 1	Pearce ,Gunn	10,628	1	2	3	4	5	6		7	9	8	11	10							
27	Feb-06	H	Plymouth A	4 1	Gunn,Pearce 2,Sykes(pen)	14,191	1	2	3	4	5	6		7	9	8	11	10							
28	Feb-13	A	Bristol C	1 1	Gunn	6,547	1	2	3	4	5	6	7	8	9		11	10							
29	Feb-20	H	Oldham Ath	1 0	Lewis	9,583	1	2	3	4	5	6		7	9		11	10				8			
30	Feb-27	A	Bradford PA	1 2	Pearce	10,126	1	2			5	6			9		11	8	7		10	4	3		
31	Mar-05	H	Wolverhampton W	1 1	Williams R	12,357	1	2	3		5	6		7	9		11	8		4	10				
32	Mar-12	A	Charlton Ath	3 3	Pearce 2,Gunn	12,478	1	2	3		5	6		7	9	8	11	10		4					
33	Mar-19	H	Tottenham H	1 1	Pearce	11,357	1	2	3		5	6		7	9	8	11	10		4					
34	Mar-23	A	Millwall	1 3	Gunn	20,790	1	2	3		5	6		7	9	8	11	10		4					
35	Mar-26	A	Southampton	0 3		6,375	1	2	3		5	6		7	9	8	11	10		4					
36	Mar-28	H	Millwall	4 0	Anstiss ,Gunn ,Williams R 2	12,025	1	2	3			6		7	9	8	11	10				4		5	
37	Apr-02	H	Preston NE	0 3		9,584	1	2	3			6		7	9	8	11	10				4		5	
38	Apr-09	A	Burnley	1 4	Anstiss	5,969	1	2	3			6		7	9	8	11	10		4				5	
39	Apr-16	H	Chesterfield	1 1	Anstiss	6,849	1	2	3			6		7	9	8	11	10				4		5	
40	Apr-23	A	Nottm. Forest	1 6	Gunn	5,472	1	2	3			6		7	9	8	11	10				4		5	
41	Apr-30	H	Stoke C	1 1	Anstiss	6,040	1	2	3		5	6		7	9	8	11	10				4			
42	May-07	H	Bury	2 0	Pearce 2	4,281	1	2				6		7	9	8	11	10				4		5	3
	Apps						42	41	40	27	36	42	19	40	40	22	39	34	4	10	3	14	2	6	1
	Gls									4		1		7	35	6	1	14	2			3			

#	Date	V	Opponents	Score	Scorers	Att	Ferguson A	Lawrence SJ	Milne W	Sykes J	Craven J	Miller J	Boston HJ	Williams R	Pearce C	Anstiss HA	Lewis DJ	Gunn K	Simms JL	Tabram WD	Olsen TB	Jones JL	Rees EG	Hanford H	Caldwell T
1	Jan-09	A	Bury FAC-3	1 2	Gunn	13,268	1	2	3	4	5	6		7	9	8	11	10							
2	Feb 11	A	Merthyr WC-5	2 2	Pearce, Miller		1	2	3	4	5	6	7	8	9		11				10				
3	Feb 18	H	Merthyr WC-5 Rep	2 1	Miller, Olsen		1	2	3			6	7	8	9		11				10	4		5	
4	Mar-17	A	Newport Co WC-6	0 0			1		3			6		7	9	8	11	10		4			2	5	
5	Apr-04	H	Newport C WC-6Rep	2 0	Pearce 2		1		3			6		7	9	8	11	10		4			2	5	
6	Apr-13	A	Chester WC-SF	2 0	Pearce, Anstiss	9,000	1	2	3			6		7	9	8	11	10		4				5	
7	May-05	A	Wrexham WC-F	1 1	Lewis	8,300	1	2	3		5	6		7	9	8	11	10				4			
8	May-06	H	Wrexham WC-F	2 0	Pearce, Williams	5,000	1	2	3		5	6		7	9	8	11	10				4			

Swansea Town FC Season 1932/33 Division 2

#	Date	V	Opponents	Score	Scorers	Att.	Ferguson A	Lawrence SJ	Milne W	Sykes J	Craven J	Miller J	Blair H	Scott H	Martin TJ	Molloy W	Lewis DJ	Wilkie LH	Hanford H	Williams R	Anstiss HA	Olsen TB	Tabram WD	Caldwell T	Jones F	Jones JL	Rees EG	Gunn K	Reid EJ	Walton JW	Lowry SH
1	Aug-27	H	West Ham Utd	1 0	Martin	15,247	1	2	3	4	5	6	7	8	9	10	11														
2	Aug-29	A	Lincoln C	0 2		12,613	1	2	3	4	5	6	7	8	9	10		11													
3	Sep-03	A	Fulham	1 3	Martin	14,779	1	2	3	4	5	6	7	8	9	10		11													
4	Sep-05	H	Lincoln C	3 1	Martin, Blair 2	4,403	1	2	3	4		6	7	8	9	10		11	5												
5	Sep-10	H	Chesterfield	3 0	Molloy 2, Williams R	10,424	1	2	3	4		6	7	8		10		11	5	9											
6	Sep-17	A	Bradford C	1 1	Lewis	16,376	1	2	3	4		6	7	8		10	11		5	9											
7	Sep-24	H	Plymouth A	0 1		16,075	1	2	3	4		6	7	8		10	11		5	9											
8	Oct-01	H	Notts. Co	2 0	Williams R, Martin	9,636	1	2	3	4		6	7		9	10	11		5	8											
9	Oct-08	A	Port Vale	1 2	Blair	7,310	1	2	3	4		6	7		9	10	11		5	8											
10	Oct-15	H	Millwall	1 0	Scott	9,091	1	2	3	4		6	7	10			11		5	9	8										
11	Oct-22	A	Nottm. Forest	2 2	Williams R, Scott	7,366	1	2	3	4		6	7	10			11		5	9	8										
12	Oct-29	H	Charlton Ath	2 0	Williams R, Blair	3,503	1	2	3	4		6	7	10			11		5	9	8										
13	Nov-05	A	Stoke C	0 2		15,421	1	2	3	4		6	7	10			11		5	9	8										
14	Nov-12	H	Bradford PA	3 1	Miller, Martin, Williams R	9,668	1	2	3	4		6	7	10	9		11		5	8											
15	Nov-19	A	Oldham Ath	0 0		6,393	1	2	3	4		6	7	10	9		11		5	8											
16	Nov-26	H	Grimsby T	1 0	Scott	9,304	1	2	3	4		6	7	10	9		11		5	8											
17	Dec-03	A	Tottenham H	0 7		31,993	1	2	3	4		6	7	10	9			11	5	8											
18	Dec-10	H	Preston NE	3 1	Martin 2, Olsen	6,628	1	2	3	4		6	7	10	9				5	8		11									
19	Dec-17	A	Burnley	2 1	Williams R, Martin	6,637	1	2	3	4		6	7	10	9				5	8		11									
20	Dec-24	H	Manchester Utd	2 1	Olsen, Scott	10,727	1	2	3	4		6	7	10	9				5	8		11									
21	Dec-26	H	Southampton	2 1	Martin 2	19,752	1	2	3	4		6	7	10	9				5	8		11									
22	Dec-27	A	Southampton	0 2		17,971	1	2	3	4		6	7	10	9				5	8		11									
23	Dec-31	A	West Ham Utd	1 3	Williams R	16,876	1	2	3	4		6	7	10	9				5	8		11									
24	Jan-02	A	Bury	0 3		9,893	1	2	3	4			7	10	9				5	8		11			6						
25	Jan-07	H	Fulham	3 0	Martin 3	8,589	1	2	3	4			7	10	9				5	8		11			6						
26	Jan-21	A	Chesterfield	0 1		9,647	1	2		4			7	10	9		11		5	8					3	6					
27	Jan-28	H	Bradford C	2 0	Scott, Blair	8,242	1	2	3	4		6	7	10	9				5	8		11									
28	Feb-04	A	Plymouth A	0 1		11,135	1	2	3	4		6		10					5	8			7	11	9						
29	Feb-11	A	Notts. Co	2 1	Olsen, Blair	12,352	1		3			6	7	10	9				5	8		11					2	4			
30	Feb-18	H	Port Vale	2 0	Martin, Blair	8,049	1	2	3			6	7	10	9				5	8		11						4			
31	Feb-25	A	Millwall	1 3	Williams R	11,848	1	2	3	4		6	7	10	9				5	8		11									
32	Mar-04	H	Nottm. Forest	0 1		8,851	1	2	3	4		6	7	10	9		11		5	8											
33	Mar-11	A	Charlton Ath	1 3	Blair	13,231	1	2	3			6	7	10	9				5					8	4		11				
34	Mar-18	H	Stoke C	0 2		9,200	1	2	3			6	7	10	9				5					11	4	8					
35	Mar-25	A	Bradford PA	0 1		8,260		2	3	4		6	7	10	9				5	8		11								1	
36	Apr-01	H	Oldham Ath	2 0	Olsen, Scott	6,122		2	3	4		6	7	10	9				5	8		11								1	
37	Apr-08	A	Grimsby T	1 2	Martin	7,809		2	3	4		6		10	9				5	8		11			7					1	
38	Apr-15	H	Tottenham H	0 2		14,590		2	3	4		6	7	10	9				5	8		11								1	
39	Apr-17	H	Bury	2 1	Martin, Blair	8,941			3	4	2	6	7	10	9				5	8										1	11
40	Apr-22	A	Preston NE	0 1		8,067			3	4		6	7	8	9				5			11			10	2				1	
41	Apr-29	H	Burnley	2 0	Own Goal, Olsen	3,843		2	3	4		6	7	8	9				5			11						10		1	
42	May-06	A	Manchester Utd	1 1	Scott	9,588		2	3	4		6	7	8	9				5			11						10		1	
						Apps	34	39	41	38	4	39	40	40	34	11	13	5	39	28	6	22	2	2	6	3	2	4	1	8	1
						Gls						1	9	7	16	2	1			8		5									

#	Date	V	Opponents	Score	Scorers	Att.	Ferguson A	Lawrence SJ	Milne W	Sykes J	Craven J	Miller J	Blair H	Scott H	Martin TJ	Molloy W	Lewis DJ	Wilkie LH	Hanford H	Williams R	Anstiss HA	Olsen TB	Tabram WD	Caldwell T	Jones F	Jones JL	Rees EG	Gunn K	Reid EJ	Walton JW	Lowry SH
1	Jan-14	H	Sheff. Utd FAC-3	2 3	Martin 2	23,281	1	2	3	4			7	10	9	11			5	8			6								
2	Feb-08	A	Bristol Rovers WC-5	3 0		4,000																									
3	Mar-09	H	Cardiff C WC-6	1 1	Blair	3,000		2	3			6	7		9	8			5			11			4			10			1
4	Mar-15	A	Cardiff C WC-6Rep	1 2	Martin	5,000		2	3	4		6	7	10	9				5			11						8		1	

Swansea Town FC Season 1933/34 Division 2

#	Date	V	Opponents	Score	Scorers	Att.	Walton JW	Lawrence SJ	Milne W	Sykes J	Hanford H	Miller J	Blair H	Williams R	Martin T	Firth J	Lewis DJ	Ferguson A	Lloyd JM	Lowry SH	Olsen TB	Simons R	Morgan MM	Jones JL	Davies W	Davies RG	Craven J	Caldwell T	James J	Warner J	Nelson	Jones M	Jones F	Reid EJ	Dackins HV
1	Aug-26	A	Bury	1 4	Martin	10,228	1	2	3	4	5	6	7	8	9	10	11																		
2	Aug-28	A	Millwall	1 2	Lowry	10,144		2	3	4	5		7	8	9			1	6	10	11														
3	Sep-02	H	Hull	1 1	Martin	9,743		2	3		5			8	9			1	6	11	10	4	7												
4	Sep-04	H	Millwall	2 0	Martin, Lewis	6,892		2	3		5			8	9		11	1	6		10	4	7												
5	Sep-10	A	Fulham	0 1		19,963		2	3		5		7	9	8	11		1	6	10				4											
6	Sep-16	H	Southampton	1 0	Martin	9,842		2	3		5			8	9	10	11	1	6					4	7										
7	Sep-23	A	Blackpool	1 2	Williams	18,366		2	3		5		7	9		11		1	6	10				4	8										
8	Sep-30	H	Bradford C	2 1	Davies, Olsen	9,861		2	3		5			8	9	11		1	6	10				4	7										
9	Oct-07	A	Port Vale	0 1		9,478		2	3		5			8	9	11		1	6	10				4	7										
10	Oct-14	H	Notts. Co.	1 1	Olsen	7,715		2	3		5			8	9	11		1	6	10				4	7										
11	Oct-21	H	Nottm. Forest	1 1	Davies	8,314		2	3		5				9	8	11	1	6	10				4	7										
12	Oct-28	A	Grimsby T	1 3	Martin	6,378		2	3		5				9	8	11	1	6	10				4	7										
13	Nov-04	H	Bradford PA	5 1	Olsen2, Williams, Jones, Firth	7,402			3					9		8	11	1	6	10				4	7	2	5								
14	Nov-11	A	Preston NE	0 3		11,837		2						9		8	11	1	6	10				4	7		5	3							
15	Nov-18	H	Oldham Ath	2 2	Firth, Davies	6,245		2	3		5			9		8	11	1	6	10				4	7										
16	Nov-25	A	Burnley	1 3	Jones	8,708		2	3		5	4				8	11	1	6	10				9	7										
17	Dec-02	H	Brentford	2 3	Lowry, Olsen	4,269		2	3		5	4			9	8		1	6	11	10				7										
18	Dec-09	A	Bolton W	1 2	Firth	12,575	1	2	3		5	4			9	8			6	11	10				7										
19	Dec-16	H	Manchester Utd	2 1	Olsen 2	6,591	1	2	3		5	4			9	8			6	11	10				7										
20	Dec-23	A	Plymouth A	2 2	Lowry 2	14,872	1	2	3		5	4			9	8			6	11	10				7										
21	Dec-25	A	West Ham Utd	1 1	Davies	25,791	1	2	3		5	4			9	8			6	11	10				7										
22	Dec-26	H	West Ham Utd	1 1	Lowry	16,493	1	2	3		5	4			9	8			6	11	10				7										
23	Dec-30	H	Bury	1 1	Firth	6,024	1	2	3		5				9	8	11		6	10				4	7										
24	Jan-06	A	Hull C	0 0		9,345	1	2	3		5	4	7		9	8	11		6	10															
25	Jan-20	H	Fulham	1 0	Davies	8,311	1	2	3		5	4				8			6	11	10				7				9						
26	Feb-03	H	Blackpool	2 2	Lowry 2	8,574	1	2	3		5	6			9	8				11	10			4	7										
27	Feb-05	A	Southampton	0 1		3,396	1	2	3							8				10		6	7		11		5		9	4					
28	Feb-10	A	Bradford C	1 2	Firth	7,493	1	2	3		5	4	7		9	8			6	11	10														
29	Feb-22	H	Port Vale	4 0	Firth, Davies, Lowry, Martin	5,764	1	2	3		5	4			9	8			6	11	10				7										
30	Feb-24	A	Notts. Co.	1 1	Lowry	10,828	1	2	3		5	4	7		9	8			6	11	10														
31	Mar-03	A	Nottm. Forest	2 4	Firth Martin	8,140	1		3		5	4	7		9	8			6	11	10					2									
32	Mar-10	H	Grimsby T	1 1	Firth	10,029	1	2	3		5	4			9	8			6	11	10				7										
33	Mar-17	A	Bradford PA	1 5	Olsen	7,175	1	2	3		5	4			9				6	11	10			8	7										
34	Mar-24	H	Preston NE	1 2	James	5,968	1	2	3		5	4				8			6	11	10				7				9						
35	Mar-30	A	Lincoln C	0 1		9,353	1		3		5		10			8			6	11				2	7		4		9						
36	Mar-31	A	Oldham Ath	0 0		9,063	1		3		5		10		9	8			6	11					7	2	4								
37	Apr-02	H	Lincoln C	1 0	Milne (pen)	9,500	1	2	3		5		10		9	8			6	11					7		4								
38	Apr-07	H	Burnley	3 0	Olsen, Lowry 2	7,146	1	2	3		5		10		9	8			6	11					7		4								
39	Apr-14	A	Brentford	0 2		14,848	1	2	3		5		10		9	8			6	11					7		4								
40	Apr-21	H	Bolton W	0 0		10,569	1	2	3		5		10		9	8			6	11					7		4								
41	Apr-28	A	Manchester Utd	1 1	Firth	16,678	1	2	3		5		10		9	8			6	11				4	7										
42	May-05	H	Plymouth A	2 1	Milne(pen), Firth	7,030	1	2	3		5	4			9	8			6	11					7					10					
						Apps	26	38	41	2	39	19	14	14	32	34	16	16	39	26	31	3	3	17	33	3	9	1	4	2					
						Gls			2					2	7	10	1			11	9			2	6				1						

#	Date	V	Opponents	Score	Scorers	Att.	Walton JW	Lawrence SJ	Milne W	Sykes J	Hanford H	Miller J	Blair H	Williams R	Martin T	Firth J	Lewis DJ	Ferguson A	Lloyd JM	Lowry SH	Olsen TB	Simons R	Morgan MM	Jones JL	Davies W	Davies RG	Craven J	Caldwell T	James J	Warner J	Nelson	Jones M	Jones F	Reid EJ	Dackins HV
1	Jan-13	H	Notts. Co. FAC-3	1 0	Martin	13,500	1	2	3		5	4			9	8			6	11	10				7										
2	Jan-27	A	Bury FAC-4	1 1	Own Goal	24,368	1	2	3		5	4			9	8			6	11	10				7										
3	Feb-01	H	Bury FAC-4 Rep	3 0	Davies 2, Hanford	23,000	1	2	3		5	4			9	8			6	11	10				7										
4	Feb-17	H	Portsmouth FAC-5	0 1		27,910	1	2	3		5	4			9	8			6	11	10				7										
5	Feb-07	A	Chester WC-6	1 2	Jones M	4,300					4		7					1				6				2		3			5	8	9	10	11

Swansea Town FC Season 1934/35 Division 2

#	Date	V	Opponents	Score	Scorers	Att.	Walton JW	Lawrence SJ	Milne W	Firth J	Hanford H	Lloyd JM	Davies W	Bussey W	Martin T	Olsen TB	Lowry SH	Warner J	Lewis DJ	Davies RG	Ferguson A	Brain J	Blair H	Booth L	Sykes J	Dackins HV	Caldwell T	Harris J	Simons R
1	Aug-25	H	Notts. Co	2 1	Lowry, Olsen	11,759	1	2	3	4	5	6	7	8	9	10	11												
2	Aug-27	H	Oldham Ath	5 1	Martin,Bussey,Davies,Olsen 2	9,589	1	2	3	4	5	6	7	8	9	10	11												
3	Sep-01	A	Bradford C	0 2		7,321	1	2	3	4	5	6	7	8	9	10	11												
4	Sep-03	A	Oldham Ath	2 2	Martin 2	5,893	1	2	3	10	5	6	7	8	9			11	4										
5	Sep-08	H	Sheff. Utd	0 0		14,925	1	2	3	4	5	6	7	8	9	10		11											
6	Sep-15	A	Barnsley	0 1		10,186	1	2	3	4	5	6	7	8	9	10	11												
7	Sep-22	H	Port Vale	1 1	Bussey	5,698	1	2	3	4	5	6	7	8	9		11			10									
8	Sep-29	A	Manchester Utd	1 3	Bussey	14,865	1		3	8	5	6	7		9		11	4		10	2								
9	Oct-06	H	Newcastle	3 4	Davies W 2, Olsen	5,875	1		3		5	6	7	9	8	10		4	11		2								
10	Oct-13	H	Burnley	2 0	Davies W 2	10,076		2	3	8	5	6	7	9			10	11	4		1								
11	Oct-20	A	West Ham Utd	0 2		21,227		2	3	8	5	6	7	9			10	11	4		1								
12	Oct-27	H	Blackpool	2 1	Lowry 2	8,689		2	3	8	5	6	7	9			10	11	4		1								
13	Nov-03	A	Bury	1 2	Lowry	7,108		2	3	8	5	6	7	9			10	11	4		1								
14	Nov-10	H	Hull	2 1	Davies , Lowry	7,741		2	3		5	6	7	8			10	11	4		1	9							
15	Nov-17	A	Nottm. Forest	0 1		12,024	1	2	3	9	5	6	7	8			10	11	4										
16	Nov-24	H	Brentford	2 4	Milne 2 Pens	10,547	1	2	3		5	6	7	8			10	11	4			9							
17	Dec-01	A	Fulham	1 4	Blair	13,686		2	3		5	6			9		10	11	4		1		7	8					
18	Dec-08	H	Bradford PA	0 0		5,892			3	8	5	6	7		9		10	11	4	2	1								
19	Dec-15	A	Plymouth A	2 3	Lowry 2	13,780			3	8	5	6	7		9		10	11	4	2	1								
20	Dec-22	H	Norwich C	1 1	Lowry	3,694		2	3	8	5	6	7		9		10	11	4		1								
21	Dec-25	H	Southampton	0 1		4,062		2	3	8	5	6			9		10	11	4		1		7						
22	Dec-26	A	Southampton	0 1		18,351			3	10	5	6			8		11	7	4	2	1	9							
23	Dec-29	A	Notts. Co	0 4		13,221		2	3	10	5	6			8			11	4		1	9	7						
24	Jan-05	H	Bradford C	3 1	Firth 2, Sykes	5,921	1	2	3	8	5	6			9				4				7		10	11			
25	Jan-19	A	Sheff. Utd	1 1	Blair	14,032	1	2	3	9	5	6				8	11		4				7		10				
26	Jan-31	H	Barnsley	1 1	Olsen	4,295	1	2	3	8	5	6	7		9	10	11		4										
27	Feb-02	A	Port Vale	1 2	Martin	7,081	1	2	3		5	6		8	9		11		4				7		10				
28	Feb-09	H	Manchester Utd	1 0	Martin	8,876	1	2	3		5	6		8	9		11		4				7		10				
29	Feb-16	A	Newcastle	1 5	Bussey	9,203	1	2	3	10	5	6		8	9				4	7						11			
30	Feb-23	A	Burnley	0 3		9,452	1	2	3	10	5	6	7	8	9				4	11									
31	Mar-02	H	West Ham Utd	5 4	Martin 3,Firth, Lowry	8,380	1	2	3	10	5	6	7	8	9		11		4										
32	Mar-09	A	Blackpool	1 2	Bussey	10,979	1	2	3	10	5	6	7	8	9		11		4										
33	Mar-16	H	Bury	1 0	Martin	7,236	1	2	3	10	5	6	7	8	9		11		4										
34	Mar-23	A	Hull	1 0	Firth	4,648	1	2	3	10	5	6	7	8	9		11		4										
35	Mar-30	H	Nottm. Forest	3 0	Martin 2, Davies	8,445	1	2	3	10	5	6	7	8	9		11		4										
36	Apr-06	A	Brentford	0 1		17,212	1	2	3	10	5	6	7	8	9		11		4										
37	Apr-13	H	Fulham	2 0	Bussey, Lowry	6,738	1	2	3	10	5	6	7	8	9		11		4										
38	Apr-19	A	Bolton W	0 1		26,583	1	2	3	10	5	6	7	8	9		11		4										
39	Apr-20	A	Bradford PA	1 3	Brain	5,795	1	2		10		6						11				9	8	7			3	4	
40	Apr-22	H	Bolton W	2 1	Lewis, Brain	19,693	1	2	3	4	5	6	7	8	9				11			10							
41	Apr-27	H	Plymouth A	3 0	Olsen 2, Brain	6,562	1	2	3	4	5	6	7	8		10			11			9							
42	May-04	A	Norwich C	2 2	Own Goal , Bussey	7,415	1	2	3	4	5	6	7	8		10			11			9							
						Apps	30	37	41	36	42	42	32	37	25	23	33	32	10	5	12	8	8	1	4	2	1	1	
						Gls			2	4			7	7	11	7	10		1			3	2		1				

#	Date	V	Opponents	Score	Scorers	Att.	Walton JW	Lawrence SJ	Milne W	Firth J	Hanford H	Lloyd JM	Davies W	Bussey W	Martin T	Olsen TB	Lowry SH	Warner J	Lewis DJ	Davies RG	Ferguson A	Brain J	Blair H	Booth L	Sykes J	Dackins HV	Caldwell T	Harris J	Simons R
1	Jan-12	H	Stoke City FAC-3	4 1	Lowry 2,Blair, Bussey	20,000	1	2	3	8	5	6		9			11		4				7		10				
2	Jan-26	A	Derby Co. FAC-4	0 3		28,000	1	2	3	8	5	6		9			11		4				7		10				
3	Feb-21	A	Milford WC-5	4 1	Own Goal,Martin 2,Simons		1	2		10		6	7	8	9			11									3	4	5
4	Mar-06	H	Wrexham WC-6	6 0	Bussey 2,Firth 2,Lewis, Martin	5,000	1	2		10		6	7	8	9			11									3	4	5
5	Apr-24	N	Chester WC-SF	0 5	at Wrexham	5,300	1		3	4	5	6	7	8				11		2		9				10			

Swansea Town FC Season 1935/36 Division 2

No.	Date	V	Opponents	Score	Scorers	Att.	Moore S	Lawrence SJ	Milne W	Firth J	Hanford H	Lloyd JM	Davies W	Bussey W	Martin T	Olsen TB	Lewis DJ	Pears J	Warner J	Illingworth J	Brain J	Mackay W	Simons R	Caldwell T	Ferguson A	Lewis I	Davies RG	Leyland P	Emmanuel T
1	Aug-31	A	Southampton	3 4	Olsen, Bussey, Martin	12,528	1	2	3	4	5	6	7	8	9	10	11												
2	Sep-02	H	Leicester C	2 0	Bussey, Martin	12,530	1	2	3	4	5	6	7	8	9	10	11												
3	Sep-07	H	Norwich C	4 3	Milne 2(1 pen),Firth, Bussey	12,898	1	2	3	4	5	6	7	8	9	10	11												
4	Sep-09	A	Leicester C	1 4	Olsen	8,498	1	2	3	4	5	6	7	8	9	10	11												
5	Sep-14	A	Nottm. Forest	2 2	Davies, Martin	10,499	1	2	3	4	5	6	7	8	9	10		11											
6	Sep-16	A	Bradford PA	1 1	Bussey	7,931	1	2	3	4	5	6	7	8	9	10		11											
7	Sep-21	H	Blackpool	1 0	Olsen	13,276	1	2	3	4	5	6	7	8	9	10		11											
8	Sep-28	A	Doncaster R	1 1	Pears	16,914	1	2	3		6	5		7	8	9	10	11	4										
9	Oct-05	H	Bury	4 1	Martin 4	10,784	1		3		6	5		7	8	9	10	11	4	2									
10	Oct-12	A	West Ham Utd	0 4		23,551	1	2	3	4	5	6	7	8	9	10	11												
11	Oct-19	A	Bradford C	2 2	Brain, Martin	5,937	1	2	3	4	5	6	7		9	10	11				8								
12	Oct-26	H	Newcastle Utd	1 2	Davies	12,776	1	2	3	4	5		7	8	9	10	11		6										
13	Nov-02	A	Tottenham H	2 7	Martin, Milne(pen)	36,121	1	2	3	4	5	6	7	8	9	10						11							
14	Nov-09	H	Manchester Utd	2 1	Mackay, Davies	9,731	1	2	3	4		6	7	8	9	10						11	5						
15	Nov-16	A	Port Vale	1 0	Pears	6,541	1	2	3	4		6		8	9	10		11				7	5						
16	Nov-23	H	Barnsley	0 0		8,170	1	2	3	4		6	7	8	9	10		11					5						
17	Nov-30	A	Burnley	2 5	Davies, Bussey	6,823	1	2	3	4		6	7	8	9	10	11						5						
18	Dec-07	H	Charlton Ath	1 2	Firth	9,523	1	2	3	10	5	6	7	8	9				4		11								
19	Dec-14	A	Hull City	2 3	Brain 2	4,863	1	2		10	5	6		8				11	4		9		7	3					
20	Dec-21	H	Fulham	0 2		6,250	1	2		10	5	6	7	8				11	4		9			3					
21	Dec-25	H	Sheff. Utd	1 3	Martin	9,007		2		10	5				9		11		6		8	7	4	3	1				
22	Dec-26	A	Sheff. Utd	1 4	Lewis D	19,133		2		4					9	10	11		6		8		5	3	1	7			
23	Dec-28	H	Southampton	0 0		8,076	1	2	3	4	5				10	8		11	6		9					7			
24	Jan-04	A	Norwich C	1 0	Pears	13,148	1	2	3	8	5	6				10		11	4		9					7			
25	Jan-18	H	Nottm. Forest	2 1	Olsen, Brain	6,943	1	2	3	8	5	6				10		11	4		9					7			
26	Jan-29	A	Blackpool	1 1	Brain	7,862	1	2	3	8	5	6				10		11	4		9					7			
27	Feb-01	H	Doncaster R	2 0	Warner, Brain	7,180	1	2	3	8	5	6				10		11	4		9					7			
28	Feb-08	A	Bury	1 2	Brain	6,899	1		3	8	5	6				10		11	4		9					7	2		
29	Feb-15	H	West Ham Utd	0 1		10,378	1	2	3	8	5	6				10		11	4		9					7			
30	Feb-22	H	Bradford C	8 1	Olsen2, Bussey4,Pears,Brain	5,213	1	2	3		5	6		8		10		11	4		9					7			
31	Feb-29	A	Charlton Ath	1 4	Lawrence(pen)	14,848	1	2	3			6		8		10		11	4		9					7		5	
32	Mar-07	H	Port Vale	3 2	Martin 2, Lawrence(pen)	5,151	1	2	3			6		8	9	10		11	4							7		5	
33	Mar-14	A	Manchester Utd	0 3		27,580	1	2	3			6		8	9	10		11	4							7		5	
34	Mar-21	H	Tottenham H	1 1	Lawrence(pen)	12,498	1	2	3	10		6			9			11	4			8				7		5	
35	Mar-28	A	Barnsley	0 0		8,714	1	2	3	10		6		8	9			11	4							7		5	
36	Apr-04	H	Burnley	1 3	Olsen	5,890	1	2	3			6		8	9	10		11	4							7		5	
37	Apr-10	A	Plymouth A	2 1	Brain 2	9,975	1	2	3			6		8		10		11	4		9	7						5	
38	Apr-11	A	Newcastle Utd	0 2		12,010	1	2		4		6	7	8	9	10						11	5						3
39	Apr-13	H	Plymouth A	2 0	Bussey, Brain	20,411	1	2	3			6		8		10		11	4		9	7						5	
40	Apr-18	H	Hull C	6 1	Olsen3,Davies,Brain,Bussey	6,264	1	2	3			6	7	8		10		11	4		9							5	
41	Apr-25	A	Fulham	1 0	Lawrence(pen)	9,364	1	2				6		8		10		11	4		9					7		5	3
42	May-02	H	Bradford PA	1 2	Brain	5,471	1	2				6		8		10	11		4		9					7		5	3
						Apps	40	40	35	32	25	36	21	32	26	36	20	19	26	1	20	8	7	4	2	17	1	11	3
						Gls		4	3	2			5	11	12	10	1	4	1		13	1							

No.	Date	V	Opponents	Score	Scorers	Att.	Moore S	Lawrence SJ	Milne W	Firth J	Hanford H	Lloyd JM	Davies W	Bussey W	Martin T	Olsen TB	Lewis DJ	Pears J	Warner J	Illingworth J	Brain J	Mackay W	Simons R	Caldwell T	Ferguson A	Lewis I	Davies RG	Leyland P	Emmanuel T
1	Jan-11	A	Liverpool FAC-3	0 1		33,494	1	2	3	8	5	6				10		11	4		9					7			
2	Feb-06	H	Newport Co. WC-5	1 0	Brain	1,500	1	2				6		8		10	11		4		9		5	3		7			
3	Mar-11	A	Chester WC-6	1 4	Bussey	5,500	1	2		10		6		8	9			11	4				5	3		7			

Swansea Town FC Season 1936/37 Division 2

#	Date	V	Opponents	Score	Scorers	Att.	Moore S	Lawrence SJ	Emmanuel T	Warner J	Leyland P	Lloyd JM	Lewis DJ	Williams R	Henson GH	Bussey W	Caldwell T	Moore T	Milne W	Olsen TB	Mackay W	Simons R	Foster TC	Pears J	Brain J	Harris J	Davies RG	Williams A	Greene C	Lowrie G	Lewis I	Lewis H	Crowe E	Davies G	Bye L
1	Aug-29	H	Aston Villa	1-2	Henson	25,189	1	2	3	4	5	6	7	8	9	10	11																		
2	Aug-31	A	Coventry C	1-2	Henson	26,245	1	2	3	4	5	6	7	8	9		11		10																
3	Sep-05	A	Bradford C	0-4		7,688	1	2			5	6	7	8	9	4	3			10	11														
4	Sep-07	H	Coventry C	2-0	Foster 2	8,596	1	2		4		6	7		9		3			10	11	5	8												
5	Sep-12	H	Barnsley	3-1	Brain 2, Foster	8,072	1	2		4		6	7				3			10	11	5	8		9										
6	Sep-19	H	Southampton	5-1	Warner,Pears2,Law'nce(pen),Brain	10,458	1	2	3	4		6	7							10		5	8	11	9										
7	Sep-26	A	Burnley	0-0		12,131	1	2		4		6	7				3			10	11	5	8		9										
8	Oct-03	H	Fulham	3-0	Lawrence(pen),Brain,Williams	13,540	1	2		4		6	7	8			3			10	11	5			9										
9	Oct-10	A	Doncaster R	0-0		14,976	1	2		4		6	7				3			10	11	5	8		9										
10	Oct-17	A	Sheff. Utd	0-1		18,226	1	2				6	7	10			3					5	8	11	9	4									
11	Oct-24	H	Tottenham H	2-1	Brain 2	15,544	1	2		4		6	7				3			10		5	8	11	9										
12	Oct-31	A	Blackpool	2-3	Olsen, Williams	12,719	1	2		4		6	7	8			3			10		5		11	9										
13	Nov-07	H	Blackburn R	1-0	Brain	7,234	1	2		4		6	7	8			3			10		5		11	9										
14	Nov-14	A	Bury	0-2		9,991	1	2		4		6	7	8			3			10		5		11	9										
15	Nov-21	H	Leicester C	1-3	Brain	13,269	1	2		4		6		8			3			10	7	5		11	9										
16	Nov-28	A	West Ham Utd	0-2		16,615	1			4		6					3			10		5	8	11	9		2	7							
17	Dec-05	H	Norwich C	2-1	Olsen,Pears	7,850	1	2		4		6					3			10		5		11	9			7	8						
18	Dec-12	A	Newcastle Utd	1-5	Mackay	14,356	1			4		6			9		3		8	10	7	5		11			2								
19	Dec-19	H	Bradford PA	3-0	Olsen 2, Harris	7,193	1	2				6			9		3		8	10	7	5		11		4									
20	Dec-25	A	Plymouth A	0-0		22,246	1	2				6	7		9		3			10		5	8	11		4									
21	Dec-26	A	Aston Villa	0-4		54,163	1	2				6	7		9		3			10		5	8	11		4									
22	Dec-28	H	Plymouth A	0-1		9,248	1	2				6	7		9		3			10		5	8	11		4									
23	Jan-01	A	Chesterfield	0-4		9,217	1	2		4	5	6	7		9		3	10					8	11											
24	Jan-02	H	Bradford C	3-0	Brain, Warner 2	4,123	1	2		10		6	7	8			3					5		11	9	4									
25	Jan-09	A	Barnsley	1-0	Brain	7,690	1	2		10			7	8			3					5		11	9	4			6						
26	Jan-23	A	Southampton	1-2	Mackay	7,123	1	2		10				8	9		3				7	5		11		4			6						
27	Feb-06	A	Fulham	0-5		16,101	1			4		6	7	10	9		3					5	8				2			11					
28	Feb-11	H	Burnley	3-0	Henson,Lewis,Olsen	6,018	1	2		4	5	6	7	8	9		3			10										11					
29	Feb-13	H	Doncaster R	0-1		7,395	1	2		4	5	6	7	8	9		3			10										11					
30	Feb-25	A	Sheff. Utd	2-1	Pears, Henson	4,923	1	2		10		6	7	8	9		3					5		11		4									
31	Feb-27	A	Tottenham H	1-3	Pears	26,346	1	2		4				8	9		3			10	7	5		11					6						
32	Mar-06	H	Blackpool	1-1	Own Goal	13,686	1	2		10		6		8	9		3					5		11		4					7				
33	Mar-13	A	Blackburn R	1-2	Lewis	12,941	1	2		10		6		8	9		3					5		11		4					7				
34	Mar-20	H	Bury	2-0	Williams, Pears	10,399		2		4		6		8			3					5		11	9						7	10	1		
35	Mar-26	H	Nottm. Forest	1-0	Lewis H	11,745	1	2		4		6		8			3					5		11	9						7	10			
36	Mar-27	A	Leicester C	0-0		24,244		2		4	5	6		8			3	1						11	9						7	10			
37	Mar-29	A	Nottm. Forest	1-6	Lawrence(pen)	17,368		2				6		8			3	1				5		11	9	4					7	10			
38	Apr-03	H	West Ham Utd	0-0		10,077	1	2		4		6		8	9		3					5		11							7	10			
39	Apr-10	A	Norwich C	0-3		11,336	1	2	3			6		8	9							5		11		4					7	10			
40	Apr-17	A	Newcastle Utd	1-2	Harris	9,310	1	2		4		6			9		3					5		11		8					7	10			
41	Apr-24	A	Bradford PA	1-1	Lewis H	11,590	1	2		4		6			9		3					5		11		8					7	10			
42	May-01	H	Chesterfield	4-1	Lewis H,Henson,Lowrie,Warner	3,620	1	2		4		6			9		3					5		11						8	7	10			
				Apps			39	39	4	33	7	39	15	31	23	3	39	4	3	21	11	35	14	31	21	15	3	2	4	5	11	9	1	0	0
				Gls				3		4				3	5					5	2		3	6	10	2				1	2	3			

#	Date	V	Opponents	Score	Scorers	Att.	Moore S	Lawrence SJ	Emmanuel T	Warner J	Leyland P	Lloyd JM	Lewis DJ	Williams R	Henson GH	Bussey W	Caldwell T	Moore T	Milne W	Olsen TB	Mackay W	Simons R	Foster TC	Pears J	Brain J	Harris J	Davies RG	Williams A	Greene C	Lowrie G	Lewis I	Lewis H	Crowe E	Davies G	Bye L
1	Jan-16	H	Carlisle Utd FAC-3	1-0	Williams	8,790	1	2		10		6	7	8			3					5		11	9	4									
2	Jan-30	H	York C FAC-4	0-0		12,110	1	2		10		6	7	8	9		3					5		11		4									
3	Feb-03	A	York C FAC-4Rep	3-1	Williams, Henson 2	11,545	1	2		4		6	7	10	9		3					5	8	11											
4	Feb-20	A	Sunderland FAC-5	0-3		48,500	1	2		8	5	6	7	10			3								9	4				11					
5	Mar-03	A	Bristol C WC-6	2-1	Pears, Lowrie	2,000	1	2	3													7	8	11	9					6	10			4	5
6	Mar-15	A	Newport Co. WC-7	0-7			1		3						9						7			8			2			6	11	10		5	4

Swansea Town FC Season 1937/38 Division 2

#	Date	V	Opponents	Score	Scorers	Att.	Moore S	Lawrence SJ	Emmanuel T	Warner J	Simons R	Lloyd JM	Lewis I	Lowrie G	Pearce C	Lewis H	Lang T	Green RC	Thompson A	Olsen TB	Emmanuel L	Davies RG	Wright J	Leyland P	Williams R	Williams A	Foreman J	Millington J	Beresford J	Vernon L	John WR	Bye L	Harris J
1	Aug-28	H	Blackburn R	3 2	Pearce, Lowrie, Lang	18,577	1	2	3	4	5	6	7	8	9	10	11																
2	Aug-30	A	West Ham Utd	1 2	Lewis H	15,473	1	2	3	4	5	6	7		9	10	11	8															
3	Sep-04	A	Sheff. Wed	1 1	Green	18,750	1	2	3	4	5	6	7		9	10	11	8															
4	Sep-06	H	West Ham Utd	0 0		12,718	1	2	3	4	5	6		8			11	7	9	10													
5	Sep-11	H	Fulham	2 0	Green, Lewis H	11,647	1	2	3	4	5	6				10	11	7	9	8													
6	Sep-13	H	Bradford PA	0 1		8,268	1	2	3	4	5	6				10	11	7	9	8													
7	Sep-18	A	Plymouth A	2 2	Lewis I, Warner	18,061	1	2	3	4	5	6	7				11	8	9	10													
8	Sep-25	H	Chesterfield	1 0	Pearce	12,833	1	2	3	4	5	6	7	8	9	10	11																
9	Oct-02	A	Nottm. Forest	1 2	Emmanuel L	16,794	1	2	3	4	5	6	7	8		10	11				9												
10	Oct-09	A	Norwich C	1 1	Lewis I	17,510	1	2	3	4	5	6	7	8			11				10	9											
11	Oct-16	H	Coventry C	3 3	Warner, Pearce 2	15,233	1	2	3	4	5		7	8	9		11				10	6											
12	Oct-23	A	Bury	0 0		5,757	1	2	3	4	5		7	8	9		11				10	6											
13	Oct-30	H	Burnley	3 1	Lowrie, Pearce, Lewis H	10,111	1	2	3	4	5		7	8	9	10	11				6												
14	Nov-06	A	Tottenham H	0 2		22,328	1	2	3	4	5		7	8	9	10	11				6												
15	Nov-13	H	Sheff. Utd	3 5	Lawrence(pen), Pearce 2	13,501	1	2	3	4	5		7	8	9	10	11				6												
16	Nov-20	A	Barnsley	0 2		8,836	1	2	3	4	5		7	8	9	10	11				6												
17	Nov-27	H	Stockport Co	0 2		8,993	1	2		4	5		7	8	9	10	11					6	3										
18	Dec-04	A	Manchester Utd	1 5	Olsen	17,782	1		3	4		6	7							10		9		2		8	11						
19	Dec-11	H	Luton T	1 1	Pearce	7,454	1		3	4		6		8	9						10			2			7	11					
20	Dec-18	A	Newcastle Utd	0 1		16,322	1		3	4		6		8	9						10			2			7	11					
21	Dec-25	A	Southampton	1 1	Warner	13,583	1	2	3	4	5	6									10						7	11	8	9			
22	Dec-27	H	Southampton	0 0		20,685	1	2	3	4	5	6									10						7	11	8	9			
23	Jan-01	A	Blackburn R	1 3	Millington	19,855	1	2	3	4	5	6									10						7	11	8	9			
24	Jan-15	H	Sheff. Wed	1 1	Beresford	6,052	1	2	3	4	5	6			9						10						7	11	8				
25	Jan-22	A	Fulham	1 8	Millington	15,146	1	2	3	4	5	6									10						7	11	8	9			
26	Jan-29	H	Plymouth A	1 0	Williams R	8,729		2	3	4	5	6	7			10									9			11	8		1		
27	Feb-05	A	Chesterfield	1 4	Green	12,862		2	3	4	5	6	7					10							9			11	8		1		
28	Feb-12	H	Nottm. Forest	1 0	Green	7,974		2	3	4	5	6	7					10							9			11	8		1		
29	Feb-19	H	Norwich C	1 0	Williams R	9,404		2	3	4	5	6	7												9			11	8	10	1		
30	Feb-26	A	Coventry C	0 5		20,671		2	3	4	5	6					11								9		7		8	10	1		
31	Mar-05	H	Bury	1 0	Emmanuel T	10,267		2	9	4	5						11				10		3				7			8	1	6	
32	Mar-12	A	Burnley	0 2		9,050		2	9	4	5						11				10		3				7			8	1	6	
33	Mar-19	H	Tottenham H	3 2	Lewis H 2, Foreman	10,656		2	9	4	5	6				8	11				10		3				7				1		
34	Mar-28	A	Sheff. Utd	1 1	Foreman	10,023		2	3	4	5	6			9	8	11				10						7				1		
35	Apr-02	H	Barnsley	1 0	Lewis H	8,733		2		4	5	6				8	11				10	9	3				7				1		
36	Apr-09	A	Stockport Co	0 1		11,344		2		4	5	6				8	11				10		3				7	9			1		
37	Apr-16	H	Manchester Utd	2 2	Warner, Lawrence(pen)	13,811		2	3	4	5	6				10	11					9					7			8	1		
38	Apr-18	H	Aston Villa	2 1	Lewis H, Olsen	25,250		2	3	4	5	6	7			8	11			10							9				1		
39	Apr-19	A	Aston Villa	0 4		49,700		2	3	4	5	6				8	11			10								9		7	1		
40	Apr-23	A	Luton T	1 5	Olsen	12,433			3	4	5	6	7			8	11			10				2			9				1		
41	Apr-30	H	Newcastle Utd	2 0	Olsen, Own Goal	11,428		2	3	4	5	6	7			8	11			10							9				1		
42	May-07	A	Bradford PA	1 0	Lewis H	7,021		2		4	5	6	7			8					10	9	3					11			1		
					Apps		25	38	38	42	42	23	23	14	15	23	33	8	4	22	25	3	4	5	8	1	14	13	13	7	17	2	0
					Gls			2	1	4			2	2	8	1		4		4	1				2		2	2	2	1			

#	Date	V	Opponents	Score	Scorers	Att.	Moore S	Lawrence SJ	Emmanuel T	Warner J	Simons R	Lloyd JM	Lewis I	Lowrie G	Pearce C	Lewis H	Lang T	Green RC	Thompson A	Olsen TB	Emmanuel L	Davies RG	Wright J	Leyland P	Williams R	Williams A	Foreman J	Millington J	Beresford J	Vernon L	John WR	Bye L	Harris J
1	Jan-08	H	Wolves FAC-3	0 4		20,000	1	2	3	4	5	6				10	11							7				8	9				
2	Feb-10	H	Llanelli WC-6	8 0	Williams2, Lewis I, Vernon, Leyland 4			2	3				7				11	4			10	6		5	9					8	1		
3	Mar-31	H	Worcester WC-7	1 0	Lloyd			2			5	6	7								9	3						11	8	10	1		4
4	Apr-27	N	Rhyl WC S-F	7 2	Lang, Beresford2, Lewis, Emmanuel 2																												
5	May-04	A	Shrewsbury WC Final	2 2	Millington, Emmanuel L	14,500			3			6	7								9			2	5			11	10	8	1		4

N – Neutral Ground: Chester
Final replayed in 1938/39 season

Swansea Town FC Season 1938/39 Division 2

#	Date	V	Opponents	Score	Scorers	Att.	John R	Lawrence SJ	Emmanuel T	Rhodes RA	Simons R	Imrie JWN	Chedzoy S	Lewis I	Bamford T	Bruce W	Millington J	Davies RG	Leyland P	Lloyd JM	Richardson EW	Olsen TB	Roberts A	Moore S	Connor J	Harris J	Bye L	Paton TG	Lewis H	Tabram P	Meek J	Williams R	Edwards G	Emmanuel DL
1	Aug-27	A	Manchester C	0 5		32,514	1	2	3	4	5	6	7	8	9	10	11																	
2	Aug-29	A	Bradford PA	1 1	Rhodes	9,339	1	2		4		6	7	8	9	10	11	3	5															
3	Sep-03	H	Millwall	1 1	Bruce	15,294	1	2		4	5	6	7	8	9	10	11	3																
4	Sep-09	H	Chesterfield	1 1	Bamford	10,820	1	2			5	4		8	9	10	11	3		6	7													
5	Sep-10	A	Blackburn R	0 4		14,272	1	2		4	5			10	9	8	11	3		6	7													
6	Sep-17	H	Fulham	1 1	Olsen	6,313	1	2		4	5			8	9		11	3		6	7	10												
7	Sep-24	A	Sheff. Wed	1 1	Lewis I	22,745	1			4	5	6		8	9		11	3			7	10		2										
8	Oct-01	H	Bury	3 3	Olsen, Millington 2	11,385	1	2		4	5	6		8	9		11	3			7	10												
9	Oct-08	A	West Ham Utd	2 5	Millington, Richardson	20,992		2		4	5	6		8			11				7	10	3	1	9									
10	Oct-15	A	Norwich C	0 3		10,721		2			5				9	10	11				7			1		4	6	8						3
11	Oct-22	H	Luton T	2 3	Bamford 2	8,658		2			5				9		11			6	7	10		1		4		8						3
12	Oct-29	A	Nottm. Forest	2 1	Bamford 2	11,669	1	2		4	5				9		11			6	7		3		10	8								
13	Nov-05	H	Sheff. Utd	1 2	Bamford	11,022	1	2		4	5				9		11			6	7		3		10	8								
14	Nov-12	A	Burnley	1 1	Bamford	12,692	1	2		4	5				9		11			6	7		3		10	8								
15	Nov-19	H	Tottenham H	1 1	Millington	13,151	1	2		4	5				9		11			6	7		3		10	8								
16	Nov-26	H	Southampton	1 4	Harris(pen)	14,178	1			4	5				9		11	2		6	7		3		10	8								
17	Dec-03	H	Coventry C	2 4	Imrie, Olsen	11,022					5	6			9	8	11	2			7	10	3	1		4								
18	Dec-10	A	Plymouth A	0 0		12,692		2		4	5		7		9		11			6		10	3	1		8								
19	Dec-17	H	Newcastle Utd	0 1		11,151	1	2		4	5		7		9		11			6		10	3						8					
20	Dec-24	H	Manchester C	2 0	Bamford, Olsen	13,219	1	2		4	5		7		9		11			6		10	3			8								
21	Dec-27	H	West Brom Albion	3 2	Millington, Olsen 2	22,670	1	2		4	5		7		9		11			6		10	3			8								
22	Jan-01	A	Millwall	1 1	Chedzoy	23,808	1	2		4	5		7		9		11			6		10	3			8								
23	Jan-14	H	Blackburn R	2 1	Harris, Olsen	8,386				4	5				9		11	2		6	7	10		1		8								3
24	Jan-23	A	Fulham	0 1		3,155				4			7		9		11	2	5	6		10		1		8								3
25	Jan-28	H	Sheff. Wed	0 1		10,317				4	5		7		9		11	2		6		10		1		8								3
26	Feb-01	A	Bury	0 4		8,306		2		4	5				9		11			6		10		1				8	10					3
27	Feb-10	H	West Ham Utd	3 2	Chedzoy, Olsen, Bamford	8,711		2		4			7		9		11			6		10		1						5	8			3
28	Feb-18	H	Norwich C	0 1		11,645		2		4			7		9		11			6		10		1						5	8			3
29	Feb-25	A	Luton T	3 6	Olsen 2, Meek	11,264	1				5	4			9		11	2				10									6	8	7	3
30	Mar-04	H	Nottm. Forest	1 0	Bamford	9,002	1			4			7		9			2		6		10			11					5	8			3
31	Mar-11	A	Sheff. Utd	2 1	Bamford, Meek	26,759	1			4					9			2		6		10			11					5	8	7		3
32	Mar-18	A	Burnley	4 0	Meek, Connor, Bamford 2	10,357	1			4					9			2		6		10			11					5	8	7		3
33	Mar-25	A	Tottenham H	0 3		7,478	1	2		4					9					6		10			11					5	8	7		3
34	Apr-01	H	Southampton	1 3	Bamford	9,635	1	2		4					9		11			6		10								5	8	7		3
35	Apr-08	A	Tranmere R	0 2		9,489				4	5	6			9			2				10	3	1	11						8	7		
36	Apr-09	A	Coventry C	0 3		18,207				4					9	10		2		6				1	11					5	8	7		3
37	Apr-10	A	Tranmere R	1 0	Meek	11,075				4	5				9	7		2		6		10		1							8	11		3
38	Apr-15	H	Plymouth A	2 1	Tabram, Lloyd	6,445					5							2		6		10	3	1						4	8	7	11	9
39	Apr-17	A	West Brom Albion	0 0		5,292		2			5	4			9	11				6		10		1							8	7		3
40	Apr-22	A	Newcastle Utd	2 1	Richardson, Meek	11,705		2			5	4			9					6	7	11		1						10	8			3
41	Apr-29	H	Bradford PA	2 2	Lawrence (2pen)	7,393		2			5	4			9					6	7	11		1						10	8			3
42	May-05	A	Chesterfield	1 6	Lewis H	13,408		2												6	7	11	3	1		9			5	10	8			3
						Apps	23	28	1	25	20	27	18	9	36	13	31	20	2	32	18	30	16	19	12	13	1	6	4	11	16	9	2	20
						Gls		2		1		1	2	1	14	1	5			1	2	10			1	2			1	1	5			

#	Date	V	Opponents	Score	Scorers	Att.	John R	Lawrence SJ	Emmanuel T	Rhodes RA	Simons R	Imrie JWN	Chedzoy S	Lewis I	Bamford T	Bruce W	Millington J	Davies RG	Leyland P	Lloyd JM	Richardson EW	Olsen TB	Roberts A	Moore S	Connor J	Harris J	Bye L	Paton TG	Lewis H	Tabram P	Meek J	Williams R	Edwards G	Emmanuel DL
1	Sep-19	A	Shrewsbury WC Final	1 2	Imrie 1937/8 WC Final	8,000	1	2		4	5	6		8	9		11	3			7	10												
2	Jan-07	A	Blackburn FAC-3	0 2		17,500	1	2		4	5		7		9		11			6		10	3			8								
3	Feb-08	A	Cardiff WC-6	2 2	Olsen, Bamford	4,000		2		4			7	8	9		11			6		10	3	1						5				
4	Feb-23	H	Cardiff WC-6 Rep	1 4	Imrie	1,500				6		5			9	8	11	2				10		1						4		7		3

Chapter 10

Another War, Another Manager

As the spring of 1939 came to an end the dark shadows which were being cast by the activities of Nazi Germany were evident in every corner of the land. Nevertheless, Hitler or not, Swansea Town AFC, like its compatriot clubs, had to get on with its business. In the process, 'the old order changeth' might have been the guideline at the Vetch as the board reflected on the club's patent lack of success.

In May, trainer Percy left the club and Olsen and Lloyd were placed on the 'open to transfer' list, as well as John, Millington and Leyland. By June, manager Harris had resigned to take over at Swindon Town and Bill Irvine and Sid Lawrence had joined him. Among the group of players who were retained were some youngsters who had been signed by Harris as part of his youth policy; Roy Paul, Frank Squires and Bryn Allen were among them. All were to become fine footballers and thus help to justify Harris's longer-term management ability even if that of the shorter term left much to be desired.

Following the death of Owen Evans, a change at board level was also necessary. Abe Freedman, who had acted as chairman earlier in the club's history, assumed the role. On his appointment, Freedman announced that the club would not waste any time in appointing a successor to Harris. Presumably, the lessons so expensively learned in earlier years had been noted. True to the chairman's word, once Harris had resigned they advertised immediately for a replacement. From a total of more than a hundred applicants, on 16 June 1939, Haydn Green was appointed to the post. Green had had experience in the Football League with Lincoln City and Hull City, but had been with Southern League Guildford City

Manager, Haydn Green

immediately before coming to the Vetch.

Green was confident that he could do a great deal to improve the side. In his first public statement he spoke of developing the club's youth policy to an even greater degree. Although several new men had been signed before his arrival, Green let it be known that he was not going to buy players simply to have different faces in the team. That, he argued, would not solve his problems, for such players might not be of the type needed. He went on to hearten directors and fans alike by declaring: 'If the team is good enough we could get eighteen to twenty thousand people to follow it.' He was to be proved right, but not in the shorter term. Certainly he had ideas as to how the club should be run. At the AGM the chairman announced that 'team selection is in the hands of the manager.'

In July, Green signed John Coulter, an Irish winger from Chester, Billy Sneddon and Sam Briddon for 'substantial fees', and

the patriotically named Kitchener Fisher was recruited from Lovells Athletic. The *Post* reported 'a general recommendation of the new signings' and stated that there appeared to be a 'genuine attempt to get back to former glory'. Against this background, Abe Freedman was wise to warn supporters, 'not to expect too much in the first few games. The team will take time to bed down.'

With the newspapers filled with photographs of air-raid shelters, gas masks and other reminders of possible war, the Swans' activities were a welcome diversion for the people of Swansea. Chamberlain's attempt at appeasement, a general desire not to go to war, and a belief, held by some, that football would continue as it had in 1914 if war came, resulted in board, management and supporters looking forward to the new season with keen interest.

The new campaign started with a match at the Vetch against West Bromwich. For the first time all clubs were required to number their players in a prescribed manner; thus the WBA match made a little history of its own. Although the Swans lost the game, the home crowd was not too discouraged, for the newcomers in the team had contributed to some fine football being played. The programme for the match included the comment that the club's playing strength 'has been augmented by the acquisition of thirteen new men, to secure whom the club has spent some thousands of pounds'. The writer went on to point out that, whilst that action had resulted in a considerable addition to the club's liabilities, the board was confident that better football and more favourable results would ensue.

Haydn Green's notes included the hope that the football played at the Vetch would be 'worthy of the record support we are hoping to get'. He also called for positive vocal support, encouragement of the players and the absence of barracking. Green finished with a plea for the supporters to be patient. Without saying as much, he was implying that the team would be successful – if the supporters heeded his call.

His appeal must have struck a chord with the supporters, who no doubt hoped that a fine win at Southampton in the next match was the precursor of a successful season ahead. Then disaster struck, in the shape of a huge defeat (8-1) at Newcastle on the second Saturday. Although newspaper reports suggested that the score did not reflect the play, it was an embarrassing result. Green, however, was spared the need to face the disappointment of the fans, for, within two days of the match being played, war was declared.

Neville Chamberlain's piece of paper and whatever plans Green had to develop were consigned to the wastepaper bin. This time there was no question of league football continuing; conscription was introduced, and the Football League programme was abandoned for an indefinite period. One other change at the Vetch left S. B. Williams as the sole survivor of the original Vetch administration and ground staff. George Hart who had made grass grow when 'experts' had said it was impossible, and who guarded his beloved pitch like a mother hen, had given the club tremendous service, retired. Part of a paragraph in this history is but a small token of appreciation of his contribution to it, but he would not have asked for more.

Almost a year later, in the following August, Hitler's lack of consideration for the Swans and their affairs was spelled out in the club's annual report: it had lost £5,452 on the previous season's working, 'wholly due to the outbreak of war'. Heavy transfer commitments and a serious loss of revenue had resulted in a debit balance of £10,499.9s.8d being carried forward to the new season. The overdraft at the bank – secured on the club's assets and directors' guarantees – stood at £18,399. Not unnaturally, the directors were concerned. Yet there was little they could do. Friendlies and regional wartime football did little to capture the imagination of would-be supporters and, when coupled with travel constraints, the result was poor gates. Then, prior to the 1940-1 season, the Vetch was requisitioned for anti-aircraft purposes and the club found itself without a ground. Discussions started immediately with the rugby club and the local authority and, after prolonged negotiations, the rugby club surrendered its lease and the Swans arranged to play their matches at St. Helens.

Swans v. Villa – 'Fordy' challenges Villa goalkeeper Wakeman, watched by defenders Godfrey and Cummings.

On 25 September 1940 the *Post* published a photograph of a groundsman painting soccer markings on the hallowed turf where the Trews and Bancrofts had performed. The Swans were to pay the Corporation ten per cent of their gate money to a minimum of £10 per match. Like other clubs in the land, Swansea Town was represented by teams made up of young players as yet not old enough to be 'called up', and 'visitors'. During hostilities, such teams played in a variety of competitions without, it should be stated, a great deal of success. Nevertheless, the war period gave the club the opportunity to give experience to its younger players without the pre-war concerns of relegation affecting the matter. Paul, Squires, and Allen all had their initial games in the first team during the early years of the war, and as the conflict wore on, servicemen stationed near Swansea were given their opportunity too. Among those who were discovered in this way was Reg Weston, who was to become the keystone in the club's promotion team development in the years directly after hostilities ceased.

For the 1944-45 season, by which time the Swans had been back at the Vetch for some time, the Swans included several useful footballers among those who wore the club's strip. Leslie Jones, a Welsh international, then with Arsenal, and Ernie Jones, a former Swansea Schoolboy, who was registered by Bolton, were among them. The Swans played in League West along with Bath City, Lovells Athletic, Cardiff, Bristol City and Aberaman Athletic. Whilst there were only three

Football League teams in this grouping, the distinction was misleading. The strength of the respective sides depended in part upon the 'name' players who were stationed near to the club concerned. After the eighteen match 'season' the Swans were bottom of the table having gained just five points. There were encouraging signs in other competitions later in the season, however, not the least of which was a fine hat-trick scored by a young centre-forward called Ford. Burns, another youngster, had also performed that feat, while other names to catch the eye included a local boy, Len Comley. Swansea also had an interest in the Football League (South) cup final which was played at Wembley on 4 April 1945. Captain of the Chelsea side (playing as a guest, for he was a Wolves man) was John Harris. Harris, the son of the former Swans manager, Neil, had been transferred by his father to Tottenham.

The *Post* of 15 August 1945 carried headlines which brought rejoicing to the town: the war was over. Haydn Green and the Swansea board now had to face the huge task of rebuilding the club. In common with all other league sides the Swans had many of their staff serving in various parts of the world. Of course, the players were six years older than when hostilities had commenced and, for some, that meant that they would not play league football again. For others, like Frank Squires, the war provided an exciting opportunity to play with the top stars in the game. Indeed, Squires had played in Stan Cullis's side which provided wonderful entertainment for the troops in Italy. Another member of that team, Tom Finney, was to recall Frank's contribution to that entertainment on the afternoon when the Swans gained promotion to Division One more than thirty years later.

Because so many players were still abroad, while others were stationed far from their home clubs, the authorities decided upon an interim measure to herald in post-war football. Two leagues were formed from the clubs which made up the first and second divisions of the Football League at the start of the 1939-40 season. One of these leagues included clubs from the north, while the other constituted those from the Midlands and the south. The Swans found themselves in illustrious company, for among the First Division sides in their competition were Arsenal, Aston Villa, Derby County and Chelsea. They were the only Welsh club in the competition. The fare promised well and Swansea fans looked forward excitely to the prospect in store.

In common with most clubs during this historic season, the Swans included guest players in their teams. Stansbridge (Southampton), Hodgson (Grimsby), Corbett (West Ham) and Twigg (WBA) were among those who wore the Swans colours and added something extra for the spectators. In keeping with the nation's joy at the end of the war, and without the threat of relegation, the football was open and thrilling. After years of austerity the civilian crowds flocked to the Vetch and were joined by large numbers of demobilised service men, who were there, perhaps, to pay homage to the team which represented the home town they had longed for throughout their war service. The result, as the season progressed, was a packed Vetch Field, pre-match queues hours before the kick-off, and tremendous fervour and atmosphere. In such circumstances goals were abundant, though the Swans, particularly in the early months conceded too many. They lost in succession to WBA (4-1) and (4-2), Portsmouth (5-0) and Villa (6-3) before they gained their first victory. That occurred at the Vetch when Villa were beaten 5-4 after a tremendously exciting match. The home crowd rose as one to signal the winning goal and applaud their new hero, Trevor Ford, who

helped himself to a hat-trick in the game. The visiting officials were obviously impressed, for they made an enquiry after the match. Five days later, 'Rolande' published the first denial that Ford was to be transferred. Old fears died hard in Swansea.

Whilst the capacity crowds provided the club with healthy levels of revenue, the management were not without their troubles. At the end of September, for example, manager Green appealed to supporters for bars of soap. The commodity was still rationed and that which was allocated to the club was quickly used by twenty-two players and match officials following a game. Green was rewarded with 'the odd tablet or two' by many fans and an appeal for clothing coupons brought a similar response.

As the season progressed, demobilised players were returning to the Vetch and helped to bolster up the team. Among them were Sneddon and Briddon, the 'record signings' of the 1939 close-season, Frank Squires and Ernie Jones. In October, Squires and Jones formed the right wing of a Swans side which beat Arsenal at the Vetch and, soon after, were selected as a pair to play for Wales against Scotland in one of the Victory internationals. By the end of November, 'House Full' notices were common at the Vetch, which prompted manager Green to try to increase capacity. The terracing (railway sleepers laid on ash) was improved and extended, and an extra turnstile installed. Green was showing foresight, too, for he was planning to 'roof-over the main bank'. Building permits and material shortages were among the barriers to the achievement of the plan, but it was clear that Green and chairman Freedman believed that some of the growing revenue which was being received ought to be invested for the long-term benefit of the club and its supporters.

One item on the agenda at the club's AGM marked the severance of the final link with the original club management team. S. B. Williams, who had served Swansea Town as secretary from its inception as a limited company in 1912, resigned. Sam Williams, whose almost permanently sad expression had resulted in him being nicknamed 'Hail smiling morn', had been a

meticulous secretary/administrator/ accountant. He was to be sorely missed, not the least by Haydn Green, who adopted the title secretary/manager. Williams's meticulous record-keeping and thorough knowledge of the administrative working of the club were to be missed to the point where, eventually, lack of record-keeping at a level necessary to satisfy the board was a factor in Green's downfall.

During the second half of the season there was a novelty for British soccer fans. The Russian side, Moscow Dynamo, played in England, Wales and Scotland. The Welsh match was allocated to Cardiff since their ground could hold double that possible at the Vetch. In retrospect, the powers that be might have taken advantage of the size of Ninian Park to field a combined X1, for the Russians brushed aside Cardiff City, winning 10-1. On hearing this news, the Swansea wags seized upon the fact that three of the Dynamo goals were scored by a player called Archangelski, which suggested that God would have preferred the game to have been played at the Vetch!

About the same time, Green introduced another innovation at the Vetch – a 'broadcasting system' was installed. He also fielded a side in a match against Brentford in which Reg Weston was the only Englishman. The manager's policy with regard to youth was thus demonstrated and the idea was reinforced when Swansea Schoolboys beat Aston Boys at the Vetch in front of 20,000 people. Names to note that day were numerous and, in the event, three of the Swansea lads went on to become famous far from the Vetch. They were John Charles, Glyn Davies and Terry Medwin.

At the turn of the year Trevor Ford had scored twenty-four goals and, although the Swans were in the bottom half of the table, they were among the highest scorers. Former Swan, W. Y. Brown, was reported to have watched the team play at Fulham and to have been impressed by their display. On the administrative side, Reg Harvey was appointed assistant secretary to Haydn Green. It seemed that the tasks associated with the secretary's job were more exacting than the manager had realised.

Meantime the Fleet Street press

The Swans who played Spurs, October 1945.
Left to right: Ernie Jones, Trevor Ford, Kitch Fisher, Frank Squires, Phil Phillips, Bryn Allen, Owen (Tiger) Roberts, Gordon Davies (Captain),
Reg Weston, Frank Burns and Frank Scrine. Owen Roberts never wore a goalkeeper's jersey; instead he donned a coloured shirt.
The Bob Bankers named him 'Tiger' after the Russian goalkeeper, Fomich, who was touring the UK with Moscow Dynamo at the time.

carried many comments about the success of Swansea Town, particularly with regard to games at the Vetch against London clubs. Various hypotheses were put forward to explain these results. Among them were:

> 'It's a compact ground.'
> 'The crowd is on top of the players, giving a cramping atmosphere.'
> 'It's the Welsh fervour,' and
> 'We have to get up at six to get there.'

Why these 'reasons' were applicable only to London clubs and not to those from the Midlands, was never explained.

By mid-February 1946 hundreds of additional railway sleepers had been laid to increase the ground capacity, and on Thursday 21 February the new arrangements were put to the test. The visitors were Derby County, who fielded a side full of famous names. Their captain was Jack Nicholas, the Swansea-born son of the father of the same name who had given outstanding service to the Vetch club in its earliest years. The inside-forwards were the famous

'Raich' Carter and Irishman Peter Doherty, whilst the centre-half was Leon Leuty, an English international. It was the side which was to win the FA Cup later that season. On the morning of the match Nicholas read the lesson at the daily assembly of his old school, Dynevor. There were no floodlights at the Vetch at this time, so the match was played in the afternoon. Not surprisingly, since Nicholas's presence had been an unwitting advert for the game, the post-lunch registers marked at the school showed an epidemic of absences. To a boy those absentees braved the wrath of the following morning in order to see their heroes combat the famous Derby side. Whilst the Swans lost an exciting game 3-2, every one of those lads (the author included), and the crowd as a whole, felt that they had been well-rewarded by the standard of play. The sole concern of the afternoon revolved around the railings which collapsed at the small-bank end. 'A potential disaster was averted by good sense,' the police announced: only five people were slightly injured.

When March arrived the 'Ford is going' saga continued – with the

usual denials. Plans to cover the North Bank for a sum of £6,900 were rejected by the council, but Haydn Green maintained that he did not regard that as the final word in the matter. In addition, the manager was quoted as saying that he could have obtained £22,000 for three players, but he was not selling. Nevertheless, when a paper announced that Liverpool had offered £10,000 for Ford, the rumour-mongers had a field day. One result of this was a telegram sent to the club from 'fourteen disappointed Swansea boys' decrying the sale. Abe Freedman retorted that Ford was still a Swansea player and would not be sold.

During the penultimate match of the season – against Luton – Ford scored his fortieth goal of the term. Although it did not count strictly as a club record, since it had not been made in the Football League proper, it was a formidable total, five better than Cyril Pearce's mark. Significantly, no other Swansea player reached double figures. It was hardly surprising, therefore, that rumours about his departure continued to worry supporters during the close-season. He was, by then, an international, having played at centre-forward for Wales against Ireland.

At the end of the 1946-47 season Swansea Town were relegated to Division Three (South) along with Newport County. It was almost as if the fates, who had been defeated by Houdini-like escapes on three occasions during the thirties, had got their own back. Despite the side's lack of points, it had retained a considerable following throughout the season. Home gates had averaged over 21,000, whilst 26,584 attended the match against Coventry in April, when some fine football had been played.

The season had been eventful in several respects, one of which was probably instrumental in the downfall of manager Green. After the first five games of the campaign had been played, the team had gained only three points and had been thrashed at the Vetch by a Bradford (PA) team which included a player called Len Shackleton, who was outstanding. Green realised that he had to strengthen his team and went to Ireland to seek new men. His brief from the board was to recruit one player, but he returned with two: Norman Lockhart and Sam McCrory. Both made their debuts against Southampton on 3 October, each of them scoring to add to a brace from the ever-threatening Ford. On 11 December, Green returned to Ireland to sign Jim Feeney, a classical full-back who was to become a firm favourite at the Vetch. At the time when Feeney made his debut a youngster called Ivor Allchurch was included in the club's Welsh League team. Both he and Feeney were to grace the international scene ere long.

Green's forays into the transfer market were without precedent in the history of Swansea Town, no other manager having spent so much money on players. Green believed that the big fees would be reimbursed by more people coming through the turnstiles; his board, it seems, were not so sure. It was true that they had been able to report that they were, 'without any of the old bank overdraft', but their manager's activities were an obvious concern to them. Quite apart from the question of his exceeding his level of authority, they were perturbed to find that, in

the strictest sense, no proper accounts were being kept. Presumably in order to refill the club's coffers, on 10 January it was announced that six clubs were negotiating with Swansea Town for Trevor Ford's signature. Ford chose Aston Villa, who paid £10,000 plus a player – Tommy Dodds – for his services. Later, some said it was the fee which ensured the club's relegation, for in the nineteen games played after Ford left, the team scored more than one goal on just five occasions. More significantly, they lost by the odd goal on four occasions and had drawn twice when better finishing might have resulted in a more favourable outcome.

At the club's AGM in February, Haydn Green, responding to a question from a shareholder, asserted that 'we have too many good players on our books for us to go into the Third Division'. It was a confident statement which, in part at least, was to be shown to be true. The all-conquering side which returned to Division Two three years later was comprised of players who, with two exceptions, were under Green's command. Whatever else might be said about Haydn Green, his purchases were a testimony to his astuteness in the transfer market. It was to be more than three decades before his record in this respect was seriously challenged. Abe Freedman, speaking at the same meeting, was able to report a reduction in the club's debit balance as a result of the previous season's working from £13,000 to £5,000. In addition, he sounded an optimistic note, claiming that 'throughout the country the Swans are regarded as a team of many talents'. He underlined this statement by informing the shareholders that the size and frequency of offers which had been made to the Swans for players were, 'without precedent in the history of the club'. All these assurances were received eagerly by the shareholders and fans alike, since the team was then fourth from the bottom of Division Two.

One diversion from the worries associated with the club's lowly position occurred during the local university's Rag Week, when the students kidnapped Ernie Jones on the morning of a match. They demanded £50 as a ransom from the

club for his return. Green refused but Jones was returned in time for the game. Three months later the manager said 'yes' to Tottenham and the winger joined the London club for £7,000.

As the season progressed, Green made strenuous efforts to buy a replacement for Ford, but without success. The blizzard conditions which affected the country during the late winter did little to help Green's cause, for what looked like the beginning of a successful spell was disrupted by postponements. In the second week in April hopes were raised of a revival when the side won well at Leicester, but that was a false dawn. Consequently it became essential for the team to beat fellow-strugglers, Sheffield Wednesday on 10 May if the team was to have any chance of avoiding relegation. Although this was achieved in tense conditions, subsequent defeats by Barnsley and Millwall finally consigned the Swans to the Third Division. Haydn Green's brave words of the previous February were now remembered with sad irony by the board and the fans. Within six months the manager was to resign.

Despite the gloom of relegation, the season finished on an optimistic note. The reserves had done extremely well in their league and had won their way into the semi-final of the Football Combination Cup. They won that match by defeating Chelsea in the presence of a large crowd and progressed to the final. Their opponents in the final were Arsenal Reserves and the match was played on the 'neutral' ground of Tottenham Hotspur. Despite the disadvantage of having to play a side which was virtually at home, the Swans, including nine locals, won 2-1 and thus made a piece of football history. The Vetch club's name was the first to be etched on the base of the trophy.

In retrospect, the failure of the first team to win sufficient points in the league was something of a mystery. Throughout the season the side had played highly attractive football and had been acclaimed by opposing managers and the press wherever it went. Nevertheless, as the title of a feature in a contemporary comic had it, 'It's goals that count'. Green, as yet still in charge of the club's affairs, was well aware of that.

Swansea Town FC Season 1946/7 Division 2

#	Date	V	Opponents	Score	Scorers	Att.	Parry BJ	Briddon S	Fisher CK	Paul R	Weston R	Burns FJ	Jones E	Squires F	Ford T	Haines JTW	Comley LG	Davies RG	Jones LJ	Payne IEH	Sneddon WC	Passmore E	Emmanuel DL	McCrory S	Lockhart NH	Cunliffe R	Jones IG	Roberts OJ	Feeney J	Dodds TB	Hooper PG
1	Aug-31	H	WBA	2 3	Haines, O'Goal	24,629	1	2	3	4	5	6	7	8	9	10	11														
2	Sep-04	A	Southampton	0 4		8,262	1	2	3	4	5	6	7	8	9	10	11														
3	Sep-07	A	Newcastle Utd	1 1	Ford	54,966	1	4	3		5	6	11	8	9	10	7	2													
4	Sep-09	H	Nottm. Forest	3 2	Ford, Jones E, Haines	22,813	1		3		5	6	11	8	9	10		2	4	7											
5	Sep-14	H	Bradford PA	1 6	Comley	16,217	1			3	5	4	11	8	9	10	7	2			6										
6	Sep-21	H	Tottenham H	0 2		22,934	1	4	3	5			6	7		8	11	2				10	9								
7	Sep-28	A	Burnley	0 1		19,968	1		3	4	5		8	7			11	2		10				9	6						
8	Oct-03	H	Southampton	4 2	Lockhart,Ford(2),McCrory	21,523	1		3	4	5	6	7		9			2						10	8	11					
9	Oct-05	H	Barnsley	2 2	Payne, Ford	26,217	1		3	4	5	6	7		9			2		10				8	11						
10	Oct-12	A	Newport Co.	4 2	Lockhart,Ford(2),Payne	18,715	1		3	4	5		7		9	6		2		10				8	11						
11	Oct-19	A	Man. City	1 1	Lockhart	36,184	1	2	9	4					6	10	5							8	11	3	7				
12	Oct-26	H	West Ham Utd.	2 1	McCrory, Lockhart	22,119	1		3	4	5				9	6		2		10				8	11		7				
13	Nov-02	A	Sheff. Wed	0 3		22,793	1		3	4	5				9	6		2		10				8	11		7				
14	Nov-09	H	Fulham	0 2		21,327			3	4	5		7		9	6		2		10				8	11				1		
15	Nov-16	A	Bury	3 3	Paul, Lockhart(2)	13,352			3	9	5	4	7	8		6		2		10					11				1		
16	Nov-23	H	Luton T	2 0	Lockhart(pen),Paul	11,768			3	9	5	4	7	8		6		2		10					11				1		
17	Nov-30	A	Plymouth A	1 2	Burns	22,102			3	9	5	4	7	8		6		2		10					11				1		
18	Dec-07	H	Leicester C	3 4	Payne,McCrory,Haines	16,697			3	9	5	4	7			6		2		10				8	11				1		
19	Dec-14	A	Chesterfield	0 1		8,542			5	2		4	7	8		6				9				10	11				1	3	
20	Dec-25	A	Birmingham C	1 3	McCrory	31,309			5	2			6	9	10					7				8	11	4			1	3	
21	Dec-26	H	Birmingham C	1 0	Ford	20,003			5	2		4	7	8	9	6								10	11				1	3	
22	Dec-28	A	WBA	1 2	Squires	34,933			5	2		7		8	9					4			6	10	11				1	3	
23	Jan-04	A	Newcastle Utd.	1 2	Ford ?	22,836			5	2		7		8	9	6				4				10	11				1	3	
24	Jan-18	A	Bradford PA	0 0		14,336			2	4	5		7			6				9				10	11				1	3	8
25	Jan-27	A	Tottenham H	1 3	Paul	6,292			2	4	5		7	8		6			10	9					11				1	3	
26	Feb-01	H	Burnley	0 2		18,247			2	6	4		9	7	8		10	5							11				1	3	
27	Feb-15	H	Newport Co.	5 1	Passmore(2),Burns,Squires,Dodds	19,655			2	4			6	11	8				5	7		9						1		3	10
28	Feb-22	H	Man. City	1 2	Burns	22,497			2	4			6	7	8				5			9			11			1		3	10
29	Mar-01	A	West Ham Utd.	0 3		20,624		4		2			6	7	8				5			9			11			1		3	10
30	Mar-15	A	Fulham	0 3		17,606		4		2				7	8				5			9	6		11			1		3	10
31	Mar-22	H	Bury	1 0	Haines	22,355		4	5	2			6	7	8		9								11			1		3	10
32	Mar-29	A	Luton T	0 3		13,486		4	5	2			6	7	8		9								11			1		3	10
33	Apr-05	H	Plymouth A	3 1	Payne(2),McCrory	17,043		4	3	6	5			7	8					9				10	11			2			1
34	Apr-07	H	Coventry C	2 3	Jones E,Lockhart	26,584		4	3	6	5			7	8					9				10	11			2			1
35	Apr-08	A	Coventry C	2 3	Lockhart,Squires	16,952		4	3	6	5			7	8					9				10	11			2			1
36	Apr-12	A	Leicester C	1 0	Burns	21,515		4	3	9	5	8		7			6							10	11			2			1
37	Apr-19	H	Chesterfield	1 2	Burns	24,089		4	3	9	5	8	7	10			6								11			2			1
38	Apr-26	A	Millwall	1 1	Haines	16,079		4	3	6	5		10	7			9							8	11			2			1
39	May-03	A	Nottm. Forest	1 1	Lockhart	17,114		4	3	6	5		7	8			9			10					11			1	2		
40	May-10	H	Sheff. Wed	2 0	Haines,Jones E(pen)	22,356		4	3	6	5		7	8			9			10					11			1	2		
41	May-17	A	Barnsley	1 3	Lockhart	19,417		4	3	6	5			8			10							7	11			1	2		
42	May-26	H	Millwall	0 3		19,902		4	3	6	5		10	7										8	11			1	2		9
	Apps.						13	18	39	40	30	25	37	28	16	30	6	22	2	23	2	6	4	21	34	1	4	20	24	8	9
	Gls.									3		5	3	3	9	6	1			5		2		5	11					1	

#	Date	V	Opponents	Score	Scorers	Att.	Fisher CK	Paul R	Weston R	Burns FJ	Jones E	Squires F	Ford T	Payne IEH	Passmore E	McCrory S	Lockhart NH	Feeney J	Dodds TB	Hooper PG
1	Jan-11	H	Gillingham FAC-3	4 1	McCrory,Payne,Squires,Jones	30,000	2	4	5	6	7	8		9		10	11	1	3	
2	Jan-25	A	Luton Town FAC-4	0 2		24,327	2	4	5	6	7			9		10	11	1	3	8
3	Feb-13	H	Chester WC	1 3		10,000														

Chapter 11

Promotion and a Change of Manager

During the previous season the Swans had been acclaimed for the quality of their football wherever they went. Consequently, in the summer of 1947, sanguine fans were forecasting an early return to Division Two. One happy omen which tended to encourage such thinking, was the return of Joe Sykes as assistant trainer. The former captain had, after all, been the leading figure in the 1924-5 promotion side. Sykes was to assist Frank Barson, a former England centre-half, who came to the Vetch with a reputation as a hard man.

At the end of July, manager Green made two further signings: Jack O'Driscoll, who came from Cork for £3,000, and Frank Rawcliffe, who cost the same amount from Newport. Just before the season started, they were joined by a third newcomer, Rory Keane, another Irishman. Keane and O'Driscoll, along with Feeney, Lockhart and McCrory from the previous season, were to illustrate the effectiveness of Green's scouting connections in Ireland. All were to gain international recognition.

1947-48

The club's first season in Division Three since 1924-5 began in disappointing fashion. After five matches, only three points had been gathered. It was far from the hoped-for promotion form. At the beginning of September the new centre-forward, Rawcliffe, was dropped but responded to his critics by scoring seven goals in a reserve match at Bristol. He must have felt cold comfort, though, to read, during the following week, that the Swans

Vetch, Green's side, which thrashed Leyton Orient 5-0, read: Parry; Feeney, Keane; Paul, Weston, Burns; O'Driscoll, McCrory, James, Squires and Lockhart. Scrine was already on the club's books, and replaced Lockhart when that player was transferred to Coventry (before McCandless came to the Vetch). Thus, the promotion side of the following season differed only in the persons of Richards and Lucas. Whilst both these players made magnificent contributions to the promotion effort, the bulk of the side awaited the new manager on his

The Swans gather before the start of the 1947-48 season.

had made an offer for Tommy Lawton. It was an amazing revelation which excited supporters, who were now beginning to believe that they had a manager who actually bought good players. Whether Green's boldness in making the bid had been the 'last straw' in the eyes of the directors is difficult to establish. Whatever the reason, ten days later the manager announced his resignation.

Despite its brevity, Haydn Green's contribution to Swansea Town's history was considerable. In local folklore his tenure is often thought of as simply being the prelude to the success achieved by Billy McCandless. Yet it is was much more than this; Green bought and sold players astutely and signed several local men who were to make their names after he left. Whatever Green's failings, it is clear that Billy McCandless owed a great deal to his astuteness in finding and signing the players who made up the team which the Irishman inherited. On 27 September, for example, six weeks before McCandless came to the

arrival. Green had matched, if not surpassed, Joe Bradshaw as a successful buyer of players.

Billy McCandless, who was to become something of a legend in south Wales soccer circles, came to the Vetch in mid-November 1947, having been manager at both Cardiff and Newport when those clubs achieved promotion from Division Three (South). Thus he came with the possibility of achieving a hat-trick of promotion successes. He had the advantage of sound secretarial back-up from Trevor Hoskins and Reg Harvey, who had re-established the administrative systems which had lapsed somewhat on the retirement of S. B. Williams.

In the month before McCandlesss arrived, Norman Lockhart was transferred to Coventry for a fee three times that which Green had paid for him. Frank Squires, the pre-war schoolboy star, was also sold – for £7,000 to Plymouth, These two transactions provided the club with a considerable surplus over purchase price, emphasising Green's astuteness and providing the money

Jack O'Driscoll

Roy Paul

Billy Lucas

for McCandless to make his most successful purchase – Billy Lucas.

At the time when McCandless came to the Vetch, the club had only lost one game of its previous ten. It had twenty-one points and was in the top third of the league table. With an unchanged side, three further matches were won in succession before the team, having been reduced to ten men, was beaten in Nottingham. By the beginning of March, McCandless had tried several reserves in the first team, including Ronnie Howells, Payne, Eastham, Powell and Morris. It appeared that he was using what remained of the season to gain an insight into the calibre of his staff. Then on 16 March he signed Billy Lucas from Swindon Town for a club record fee of £11,000. Lucas would prove to be a significant purchase. When the season ended, the Swans were placed fifth in the division, which the optimists felt augured well for the coming campaign.

1948-49

During the close-season, Rawcliffe was transferred to Aldershot and was replaced by Stan Richards from Cardiff City. It was said of Richards that his knees were so bad that he could not train. It was certainly true that he did have trouble with his knees, but that did not stop him scoring twenty-six goals in only thirty-two games during his first

season at the Vetch Field. Without detracting from this excellent record however, he was part of one of the most successful sides ever to wear the white of Swansea. That was the team which lined-up for the opening match of the season, against Watford, and which did duty for most games during that memorable campaign. It was the team which had beaten Leyton during the previous season, but with Richards at number 9 and Lucas and Scrine forming the left wing.

> *In winning the 1948-49 championship of Division Three (South) the Swans of that era created many records, some of which have still not been beaten.*

On 4 September, the team, unchanged for five matches, beat Ipswich 2-0 in brilliant fashion at the Vetch. The crowd of 27,919 cheered the players to the echo. Elderly supporters were claiming that the side was a reincarnation of the old promotion team of 1925; their football flowed and thrills were commonplace. The team looked to

be unbeatable, and, indeed, they were for the first seven games. Parry was sound in goal; Feeney a classical full-back; Keane a robust and complimentary contrast; Paul a polished wing-half, while Burns on the other flank was a terrier; in the centre of the defence, like a colossus, was Reg Weston, solid, reliable and a fine leader of men. There was contrast on the wings, too: on the right was Jack O'Driscoll, lean and fast with a thunderbolt shot, while on the left was Frank Scrine, with a wicked body-swerve; at inside-right was Sam McCrory, a compact ball-player given to scoring goals; in the centre, Richards, a master of positional play and deadly with his head; and, at inside-left was Billy Lucas, the 'general' of the side. Fine individuals they were, but when they became a team the whole was greater than the sum of the parts.

After the fine win against Ipswich, the Swans were second in the league table and Swansea was buzzing with talk of their prowess. The old-time enthusiasm was back with a vengeance, as huge crowds thronged to the Vetch, and they were the people who were concerned about transfer rumours which were circulating again. When tackled by the press about the rumours, chairman Freedman felt it necessary to refute them firmly. 'We are not selling,' he stated, 'indeed we are trying to sign players to strengthen our promotion bid.' Three days later, that bid received a jolt when the then

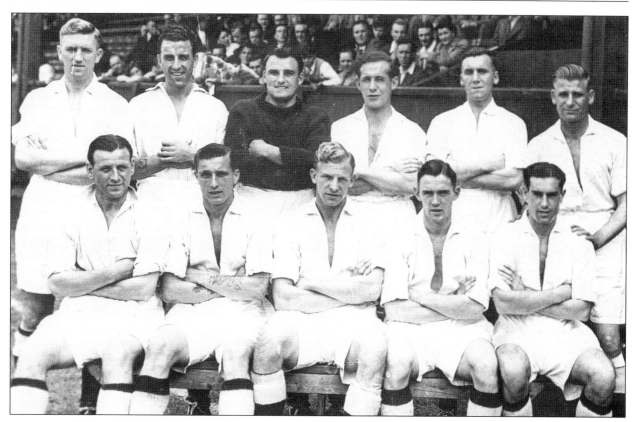

The team at the start of the second championship season.
Back row, left to right: Jim Feeney, Roy Paul, Jack Parry, Frank Burns, Rory Keane, Stan Richards.
Front: Billy Lucas, Frank Scrine, Reg Weston (Captain), Jack O'Driscoll and Sam McCrory.

top-of-the-league side lost at Leyton. There were extenuating circumstances, however: Lucas had left the field before half-time, thus requiring the team to play with only ten men for the remainder of the match. Despite not having the services of Scrine and Lucas for the next game, the team took it all in their stride. During the next six games they scored twenty goals whilst conceding only one, and in one of those matches Richards scored four. Paul was involved in an unusual scoring incident during this run. A cross from the wing found him on the edge of the penalty area, where he hurled himself forward and headed the ball into the opponents' net with tremendous force. It was a wonderful piece of skill and power.

As the season unfolded, victories came with breathtaking frequency. O'Driscoll and Keane were each selected for Ireland and Eire. At the time the sole disappointment for supporters was defeat in the FA Cup by Bristol City. The fans, though, were unperturbed; promotion was the goal, whilst the old pre-war fears of loss of form following an FA Cup defeat were forgotten. When the team faced Bournemouth on 1 January, they were comfortable leaders of the division.

Despite the team's success, there

Civic Reception at Guild Hall for the champions.

*Danny Canning punches clear, with Reg Weston (where is his head!?), Roy Paul
and Rory Keane in attendance. As the packed Bob Bank suggests,
there was a huge attendance that day at the Vetch.*

had been something of a storm-in-a-teacup during December. According to gossip, even though the team was successful, there were problems in the dressing-room. The rumours suggested that fights had taken place between Swans players. Abe Freedman, flanked by Paul and Weston, categorically denied that any such incident had taken place. The chairman, well aware of the importance of team spirit, threatened that the club would take action against rumour mongers if they persisted. His warning had the desired effect.

In February, after a fine 6-1 victory over Torquay, in which McCrory scored a hat-trick, the club was six points clear at the top of the table with a game in hand. Up to that point they had scored sixty-four goals and conceded only twenty. By the end of March they had extended their lead to seven points even though Feeney had had to have a cartilege operation during that month. Then, on 15 April, with seven games still to be played, the Swans found themselves in a position to effectively ensure promotion. Newport County were the visitors and the Vetch gates were closed an hour before the kick-off to create a new attendance record of 28,623. With former Swan Len Comley in their side, Newport showed little inclination to present the points to their neighbours. The Swans persisted, however, and won a hard-fought match 2-1, though the victory was somewhat tarnished when Newport were reduced to ten men nine minutes before the final whistle. At the end of the match the crowd swarmed onto the pitch to cheer

their heroes. As Joe Sykes had done in 1925, captain Reg Weston spoke to the throng from the directors' box. Weston said that they were not absolutely certain yet, though, as he put it, the team which was second in the table would have to score forty-nine goals in the remaining matches whilst the Swans failed to get even one point. In the event, this unlikely scenario was shown to be academic when the side took both points at Brighton. They were the champions!

On Tuesday 3 May, the team, directors, management and former players gathered at the Albert Hall restaurant. The mayor, Sir William Jenkins, paid a warm tribute to the team and to Reg Weston in particular. He was, said the mayor, a fine person, leader and sportsman. Collins, Fowler, Hole and Sykes of the old 'promotion' team added their praise, as did B. Watts-Jones. Also, as the gathering was reminded, there was still a chance of further glory. Two days later, the Swans were scheduled to play Merthyr in the final of the Welsh Cup. Unfortunately, the euphoria of the evening was not recaptured for that game. Merthyr, captained by former-Swan, Phil Tabram, beat the men-in-white 2-0. Their inside-left was a name to note for the future: it was Gilbert Beech. Even though the cup defeat was disappointing, Swans fans could look back on a remarkable season in which their favourites had set many new records which were to be cherished for many years. Among them were:

Seventeen wins in succession at home.
Six wins in succession away.

Twenty-seven victories during the season.
The best goal-difference which the club had ever registered (+53).
The most points which had ever been gained in a two-points for-a-win season.
The most 'clean sheets' in successive games which had been obtained.

With that list of achievements on their collective c.v. the side was one about which the supporters could be proud. Fifty years later, just writing about those warriors in white brings that pride to the fore.

1949-50

The man-in-the-Swansea-street was of the opinion that the club was back where it rightly belonged – in the Second Division. It was a philosophy which was to re-emerge thirty years later and which was given short shrift by John Toshack. At the time, Abe Freedman was also talking about the First Division, but, despite an outstanding season, Swansea cautiousness was still in evidence around the town. Yet the board had a vision: they were seeking planning permission for a scheme which would result in a ground with a capacity of 60,000. Alas, it was never to be. Meantime, manager McCandless had been far less adventurous than his predecessor. His only signings were Cyril and Gilbert Beech from Merthyr, and schoolboy John King, who signed amateur forms. Both Beech brothers were to give solid service to the club, while King was to set a new appearance record for Swans goalkeepers.

After beating Preston in the first match of the campaign and drawing at Sheffield United, the Swans travelled to Cardiff for their third match in Division Two. There, watched by a huge crowd of 60,855, they lost 1-0. There were extenuating circumstances, however: Rory Keane had been a passenger for most of of the game. There was a happy event after the match, too, which was something of a balm for McCandless at least. In the presence of directors from Cardiff, Newport and Swansea, the manager was presented with a gold watch to mark his achievement in taking all three south Wales clubs to promotion.

The best result in those early season matches was a fine 4-0 victory over Southampton. The win, though, was not the precursor of a successful run. By early December the side was struggling to maintain a mid-table position – not that this deterred the crowds. For the return game against Cardiff, for instance, 27,264 were in the ground to cheer a side which responded to their encouragement: the Swans won 5-1. Two days later, at West Ham, a young man called Allchurch made his debut. He was an immediate favourite with the Swansea faithful.

When December ended, the team had acquired twenty-three points from twenty-seven matches, so their position was nothing like as good as it had been at the same time in the previous season. But then, that was to be expected, the apologists argued, because they were now playing better sides. McCandless, in searching for a more effective balance, introduced Gilbert and Cyril Beech during this period. There was some comfort in the FA Cup, however, for the Swans beat Birmingham City in the third round and were then paired with Arsenal in London. For that match, the Highbury club allocated only 2,000 tickets for sale at the Vetch; not surprisingly, three times that number applied for an allocation, for memories of the 1925-6 cup victory over the 'Gunners' were still strong amongst older fans. Younger supporters, on the other hand, were fired by the enthusiasm generated by the prospect of seeing their heroes pitting their skills against famous players like Barnes, Compton, Mercer and Swindin. After the game the Arsenal manager, Tom Whittaker, confessed, 'You had us worried', but the brave effort was not enough. In a game of thrills, young Allchurch played like a veteran. He had an outstanding game, so much so that the Arsenal manager said afterwards, that he regarded him as 'the player of the century'. It was a remarkable statement in itself, but, given that he wanted to buy the player, in a negotiating sense it was doubly so.

For the first twenty minutes of the game the Swans were camped in the Arsenal half. Then in typical Arsenal style the Gunners broke away and

Watched by 57,305 people at Highbury, Frank Scrine hurtles in to head a cross from Billy Lucas which Walley Barnes is trying to reach. Other Arsenal men in the shot are Mercer, Compton, Swindin and Scott, while Swans Jack O'Driscoll, Frank Burns and Cyril Beech await developments.

Logie slammed home a fine goal. That was the only score of the first half, but when Arsenal added another, six minutes into the second period, most observers felt that the result was beyond doubt. They reckoned without the spirit of the Swans.

A well-placed free kick found Scrine on the spot to score. The Swans were back in the game and poured forward right up to the final whistle without finding the net again, at least legitimately: their second 'goal' was disallowed for off-side. The Swans supporters at Highbury that day left London proud in defeat. Their team had matched the best in the land; well almost!

They were concerned, though, to read in their Sunday papers that Arsenal were interested in three Swansea players: Paul, O'Driscoll and Allchurch were most often mentioned. Whilst the Vetch directors let it be known that they were 'not inclined to sell', the phraseology left something to be desired. Did that mean that they would sell for the right figure? As the story unfolded, however, the board did refuse the Arsenal approaches, but not before they had agreed to give the Highbury club first option on players who became available for transfer. The matter was raised again at the club's AGM, when Freedman confirmed that they had received 'numerous offers for certain players', but, he did say that the board was 'not prepared to do business in that direction'. On the other hand, he stated, just as firmly that 'extravagant expenditure on players is often a dubious form of investment, a risky

speculation.' Clearly, McCandless was having to operate in a different way from his predecessor, but then, his track record as a buyer of players was nothing like as good as that of Haydn Green.

The news in late February that John Charles had been selected for Wales was bitter-sweet for Swans supporters. Charles, as a fifteen-year-old, had been an amateur on the Vetch staff when he was spirited away by Leeds, who signed him as a professional as soon as they were able. Despite Swansea protests there was nothing that the Vetch authorities could do about the matter. Leeds had operated within the rules which existed at that time. The fact that the rules were changed as a result of the Charles case was of little consolation to the Vetch management. The incident was widely reported in the press, where credit was given to a Leeds scout for discovering Charles. The fact that John had played for the reserves at the Vetch and was an amateur on the Swans' books, suggests that he had already been discovered. Whatever the reason, whoever the instigator, Leeds' considerable gain was Swansea's marked loss.

On 23 February, Parry apart, the Swans' promotion side beat Cardiff in the quarter-finals of the Welsh Cup. It was to be the last time they were to play together. Despite the chairman's assurances at the AGM on 1 March, Feeney and McCrory joined Ipswich Town. The *Post* published a host of letters deploring the transfers. Was this, they asked, an indication of the board's desire to get to the First Division? There was no attempt to speculate in buying replacements. In retrospect, it is reasonable to argue that the board had retreated to its pre-Green policy on buying players. It was a stance which was to persist, despite the loss of key players to other clubs for large fees. Even though many exciting young players were emerging through the club's reserve sides, the future was to show that astute buying to balance homegrown talent was a necessity for success. Persistent selling without adequate replacement, on the other hand, was to have the opposite effect.

Nevertheless, despite their disappointment, the fans were able to focus upon a new hero – the tall, blond, elegant inside-left, Ivor Allchurch. After his debut at Christmas 1949 he became a regular member of the side and quickly attracted the tag 'the Golden Boy of Welsh football'. It was the beginning of an outstanding career. Before the season ended, two other significant personalities in the Vetch story appeared for the first time. The first was a tall, commanding figure, centre-half Tom Kiley, who deputised for Weston, and a nineteen-year-old winger, Harry Griffiths. The three represented the vanguard of an exciting young team, largely composed of Swansea-born players, which was to emerge within three seasons. Kiley and Allchurch won their first senior honours at the end of that season when the Swans beat Wrexham to win the Welsh Cup, another local boy, Frank Scrine, scoring a memorable hat-trick from the wing.

There were other incidents at the time, which were to have an impact upon the Vetch club. During April, Keane fractured a leg and O'Driscoll damaged an ankle. For both, the injuries were the beginning of the end of their league careers. On a more encouraging note, Swansea Schoolboys beat Manchester at Maine Road to win the English Schools Shield for the second time since the war. The captain of the side was the diminutive Cliff Jones, son of Ivor, while a certain Melvyn Charles (Manselton), was also in the side. In addition, the reserves won the Football Combination Cup for the second time. Transfers out apart, at least there were some positive signs to encourage the fans.

Sadly, whatever encouragement they felt was dealt what was described as a 'staggering blow' during the close-season. On 6 June, Roy Paul flew to Bogota to sign for the local side. Within two weeks, though, he was back home, expressing himself 'disgusted with the situation'. After a meeting with the directors on the following day, Paul was placed on the transfer list.

In June 1950, Roy Paul accepted an invitation to go to Bogota to sign for the local club. His salary would have been double that which the Football League allowed its clubs to pay and he would have received other benefits. He returned to Swansea after two weeks, but the directors decided that it would be better if he left the Vetch. Manchester City moved quickly and bought him for a modest fee.

A fortnight later he joined Manchester City for a fee 'in excess of £18,000'. Later, the Manchester manager described the deal as the best he had ever done. For Swansea it constituted the departure of another fine player, which severely weakened the team. Once again, no move was made to sign a replacement, yet, during the previous season gates had averaged over 21,000 and good fees had been received for Feeney and McCrory. In terms of income, the period was one of the most buoyant in the club's history. As the post-war euphoria for soccer receded, the lack of sensible investment by the Swansea board at that time to augment local talent, would be seen to have been a mistaken policy.

1950-51

After five games of the new season, McCandless's concern was reflected in many team changes and only one point. By the end of September, only Lucas and Weston remained of the promotion side and the team had picked up only five points from ten games. One result of this situation was that the manager was forced into the transfer market in an attempt to improve his side. Unfortunately, presumably bound by strict limits on the fees which he might pay, he did not prove to be a successful buyer. Hodges, signed from Bristol Rovers, played only two games, Howarth from Aston Villa had little more than one season with the club, and former Swansea schoolboy, Jack Roberts, played only sixteen games after signing from Bolton.

Throughout the early part of the season the team was bottom, or near bottom, of the division. It was a situation well-known to pre-war fans. Yet, as the season developed, there were signs of encouragement for supporters: Parry and Alllchurch were both capped by Wales. On 16 December a seventeen-year-old amateur appeared in goal for the Swans at Birmingham. Although the result of that match did not suggest it (Birmingham won 5-0), it was the start of another significant career – for young John King. Other debutants during that troubled time, who were to make their mark, were 'Davo' Williams, a sturdy wing-half who replaced Frank Burns, and Dai Thomas, then an inside-forward.

On 10 January the chairman expressed his concern about the club's position and hinted that they were negotiating for new players. In private, he and his colleagues criticised their manager for 'not covering enough ground' in the search for new talent. McCandlesss,

Changing faces . . . The Swans in January 1952.
Back row, left to right: Terry Elwell, Ron Turnbull, Rory Keane, John King, Kevin Clarke, Gilbert Beech.
Front: Terry Medwin, Billy Lucas, Reg Weston (Captain), Ivor Allchurch and Alf Bellis.

in response claimed that there were no players available at 'sensible prices'. Nonetheless, by the end of the month a fee of £7,500 had been agreed with Manchester City for centre-forward Ron Turnbull. He was signed and quickly made his presence felt. Indeed, it could be argued that the goals which Turnbull scored during the month of March did a great deal to save the club from relegation. By the end of the month, stemming from a fine win at Maine Road, the club had improved its position in the league to eighteenth. To the relief of all Swans supporters, that was its position at the end of the campaign.

1951–52

New wage rates for players and an increase in admission money both took effect from the beginning of the 1951-2 campaign. Admission to the field was increased to 1*s*. 6*d*. (7.5*p*.),

> **The 1,000th Football League game played by the Swans was against West Ham at Upton Park on 23 March 1951.**

while the players could receive £14 per week. There was a change, too, in the shape of the North Bank: its height had been reduced, while the front had been sunk below the level of the pitch. Other changes involved players: Ray Powell, a prolific goal scorer in reserve football, was transferred to Scunthorpe, while Andrews joined newly elected Workington, Canning went to Nottingham Forest and Parry to Ipswich. The only newcomer was Alf

Bellis, who was purchased in exchange for a small fee. One player who was not leaving, despite persistent rumours, was Ivor Allchurch. As early as 1 August the directors issued their first denial that he was to be transferred.

Despite the lack of new faces, there was a crowd of 17,905 to see the first match against Notts County. Two thousand more were there to see the next fixture against Coventry City, who included former Swan, Norman Lockhart, in their line-up. As if inspired by the noisy crowd, the team played outstanding football to score seven goals. Thereafter, the side which played in that match was unchanged for the visit of West Ham onl 13 September. Among those in the Hammers side was a centre-half whom the *Post* featured as 'Michael' Allison. But even he was not good enough to ensure a West Ham victory. The Swans won through a last-minute goal from Jack O'Driscoll, though they owed a great deal to a fine goalkeeping display by John King. At that stage, things looked a lot brighter than they had at the same time in the previous campaign: the team gained ten points from eight games. Turnbull scored six times, and the club's sole defeat was by a single goal. Unfortunately, thereafter, things did not develop as desired. Between the West Ham match and the beginning of December the side lost six games, including two in which they conceded five goals.

During this period the directors were concerned about the club's financial position. Despite large crowds, there had been a loss of £3,300 on the previous year's working; the club's debit balance was £16,000 and fees had not been received for players who had been transferred to other clubs. There was a dispute, too, with Cardiff City. The Swans had purchased a winger, who, it transpired, had a problem with his knee which resulted in his having to give up the game. The Swans claimed that he was not fit when signed. Cardiff, of course, held the opposite view. In the end, the Vetch men were obliged to pay the agreed fee of £1,000. They had forgotten a basic tenet of contract law: *caveat emptor* (let the buyer beware). As a result of that experience, the board resolved never to buy a player in the future before he had been medically examined. Unfortunately, they did not learn the lesson even then. There were other contract difficulties, too. Notttingham Forest believed that they had agreed to pay a fee of £1,500 to the Swans for Danny Canning, while McCandless thought they had agreed a sum of £2,000. In the end Nottingham, paid £1,750.

By early January, the board was so concerned about the club's lowly position that the players were called to a meeting of the directors to express their views. Whether this attempt at worker participation resulted in the players being motivated to greater effort, is difficult to establish. Whatever the reason, immediately afterwards the team put

---

The 1951-52 season Football League regulations allowed clubs to pay their players a maximum of £14 per week.

---

together a series of six wins in succession, including two FA Cup ties. The match which ended that sequence and preceded a dismal run of nine games without a win, was a fifth round FA Cup tie versus Newcastle at the Vetch.

At that time, Newcastle was the 'Bank of England' team. Players like McMichael, Brennan, the Robledo brothers and Milburn, were household names. Indeed, such was their appeal that secretary Trevor Hoskins reported a total of forty thousand applications for tickets. There were many disappointed fans that day, but those who were lucky enough to be there saw the Swans have more of the game than their illustrious opponents. Whilst Newcastle won the tie by the only goal of the game, only brilliant saves by the visiting goalkeeper, Simpson, kept the First Division team in the game.

On 11 April that form was but a memory as the side was defeated 4-1 at Bury. After that game they were nineteenth in the table, while the two clubs below them had the same number of points, one of the two having a game in hand. On 14 April, after losing at home, the Swans were twentieth. Since only two matches remained to be played, matters looked grave. They were grave off the field, too. Early in April the club's bankers informed the board that they should take action to reduce their debit balance. Even at the rate which applied at the time (five per cent) the club was finding it difficult to service the debt. In addition, chairman Freedman was unwell and was not able to attend board meetings. Thus,

in the depth of the gloom of a relegation struggle, the board was in a quandary. Feeling that there was little else which they could do, they agreed to sell their greatest asset – Ivor Allchurch. Newcastle made a firm offer of £25,000, while Liverpool and Manchester United were also interested.

Three days before the vital penultimate match against Leeds, Philip Holden, an experienced businessman, joined the board, as did D. D. Williams and J. Laidlaw-Murray. The reinforced board must have been encouraged when eighteen thousand supporters came to see the match. All the Swansea fans must have left the ground at the end of that game more than a little bemused. Their favourites put on a brilliant display to defeat the Yorkshiremen 4-1. Three days later they had further good news to enjoy. As a result of the guarantees which had been provided by the new directors, Ivor was not to be transferred.

Nevertheless, the final match – at Rotherham – had to be won if relegation was to be avoided. In the event, Allchurch, Kiley, Lucas, and young Medwin played outstandingly well and the Swans won 3-1. They had survived again! The win was not only acclaimed in Swansea. That day, as Cardifff City battled for promotion points at Ninian Park, the biggest cheer of the afternoon came when it was announced that the Swans had won. A week later, the Taffsiders won promotion to Division One, which prompted the Swans' board to send the Bluebirds a warm letter of congratulation. They were not slow in congratulating themselves either; escaping relegation by winning the last two matches of the season was no mean feat. The relief of the club and its supporters was, however, tinged with regret. Abe Freedman, who had served the club for so long, resigned because of ill health. Like S. B. Williams before him he was made a life member of the club: a fitting gesture which reflected a lifetime of service.

Swansea Town FC Season 1947/8 Division 3(S)

#	Date	V	Opponents	Score	Scorers	Att.	Parry BJ	Feeney J	Fisher CK	Paul R	Weston R	Burns FJ	O'Driscoll JF	Squires F	Rawcliffe F	Eastham G	Lockhart NH	Hopkins GG	McCrory S	James D	Payne IEH	Cunliffe R	Keane TR	Scrine FH	Comley LG	Newell E	Dodds TB	Roberts OJ	Morris WH	O'Sullivan J	Howells RG	Powell R	Lucas WH	Hooper PG
1	Aug-23	A	Bournemouth	0 1		17,474	1	2	3	4	5	6	7	8	9	10	11																	
2	Aug-28	H	Watford	3 0	o/goal, Squires, Rawcliffe	20,037	1	2	3	4	5	6		8	9	10	11	7																
3	Aug-30	H	Ipswich T	1 1	Squires	19,886	1	2	3	4	5	6		8	9	10	11	7																
4	Sep-03	A	Watford	1 4	O'Driscoll	7,674	1	2	3	4	5	6	7	8	9	10	11																	
5	Sep-06	A	Bristol City	2 3	James, Lockhart	28,068	1	2	3	4	5	6	7			10	11		8	9														
6	Sep-10	A	Southend Utd	1 1	James	8,483	1	2	3	4	5	6	7	8		10	11			9														
7	Sep-13	H	Reading	1 1	O'Driscoll	17,390	1	2	3	4	5	6	7	8		10	11			9														
8	Sep-18	H	Southend Utd	3 0	James(pen),McCrory 2	14,356	1	2	3	4	5	6	7			10	11		8	9														
9	Sep-20	A	Walsall	1 2	Burns	18,006	1	2	3	4	5	6	7				11		8	9	10													
10	Sep-22	A	Bristol Rovers	2 2	James, O'Driscoll	15,281			3	4	5	6	7			10	11		8	9	2													
11	Sep-27	H	Leyton Orient	5 0	James 2,McCrory 2, Lockhart	16,576	1	2	3	4	5	6	7			10	11		8	9			3											
12	Oct-01	A	Brighton	1 0	James(pen)	4,712	1	2	3	4	5	6	7			10	11		8	9														
13	Oct-04	A	Exeter C	1 3	O'Driscoll	8,525	1	2	3	4	5	6	7				11		8	9					10									
14	Oct-11	H	QPR	3 1	O'Driscoll, Rawcliffe 2	22,171	1		3	4	5	6	7		9	10			8				2	11										
15	Oct-18	A	Port Vale	1 1	Rawcliffe	14,355	1		3	4	5	6	7		9	10			8				2	11	8									
16	Oct-25	H	Swindon T	1 0	Comley	20,948	1	2			5	6	7		9				8				3	11	10	4								
17	Nov-01	A	Torquay Utd	1 1	Rawcliffe	8,611	1	2			5	6	7		9				8				3	11	10	4								
18	Nov-08	H	Crystal Palace	2 0	O'Driscoll 2	19,584	1	2			5	6	7		9				8				3	11	10	4								
19	Nov-15	A	Aldershot	3 0	McCrory,Rawcliffe, Comley	7,820	1	2		4	5	6	7		9				8				3	11	10									
20	Nov-22	H	Northampton T	5 1	Rawcliffe 2,McCrory 2,Scrine	13,826	1	2		4	5	6	7		9				8				3	11	10									
21	Dec-06	H	Norwich C	3 2	Rawcliffe 3	17,343	1	2		4	5	6	7		9				8				3	11	10									
22	Dec-20	H	Bournemouth	3 2	Rawcliffe 2,Comley	18,546	1	2		4	5	6	7		9				8				3	11	10									
23	Dec-26	A	Notts. Co	1 5	McCrory	42,256	1	2		4	5	6	7		9				8				3	11	10									
24	Dec-27	H	Notts. Co	1 1	Rawcliffe	23,573		2		4	5	6			9				8		7		3	11	10				1					
25	Jan-03	A	Ipswich T	2 3	McCrory 2	13,432		2		4	5	6			9				8				3	7	10				1	11				
26	Jan-17	H	Bristol City	6 1	Rawcliffe 2,Comley,McCrory 2,Scrine	15,866		2		4	5	6			9				8				3	11	10				1	7				
27	Jan-31	A	Reading	1 4	Comley	13,291		2		4	5	6			9				8				3	11	10				1	7				
28	Feb-07	H	Walsall	1 1	Powell	16,759		2		4	5	6			9				8				3	11	7				1			10		
29	Feb-14	A	Leyton Orient	0 1		16,809		2		4	5	6			9				8				3	11	7				1			10		
30	Feb-26	H	Exeter C	2 0	Powell,Scrine	12,381		2		4	5	6			9				8				3	11	7				1			10		
31	Mar-06	H	Port Vale	2 0	Rawcliffe,McCrory	18,180		2		4	5	6			9	10			8				7	3					1				11	
32	Mar-13	A	Swindon T	0 1		14,557		2		4	5	6			9	10			8				7	3					11			1		
33	Mar-20	H	Torquay Utd.	1 1	Burns	17,619		2			5	6			9	10							3				4		11			1	7	8
34	Mar-26	H	Newport Co	3 0	Scrine,Lucas,McCrory	21,861		2		4	5	6							8				3	11	7				1			9	10	
35	Mar-27	A	Crystal Palace	0 4		16,036		2		4	5	6							8				3	7					11		10	1	9	
36	Mar-29	A	Newport Co	1 1	Lucas	15,134		2		4	5	6							8					7					11	3	10		9	1
37	Apr-03	A	Aldershot	2 1	Comley,Dodds	16,884		2		4	5	6							8				3		7				11		10	1	9	
38	Apr-10	A	Northampton T	1 0	Powell	8,506		2		4	5	6							8				3		7				11		1	9	10	
39	Apr-17	H	Bristol Rovers	0 1		15,320		2		4	5	6							8				3		7				11		10	9		1
40	Apr-24	A	Norwich C	2 1	Morris,Powell	25,435	1	2		4	5	6							8	7			3	11					10			9		
41	Apr-26	A	QPR	0 0		27,757	1	2		4	5	6							8	7			3	11					10			9		
42	May-01	H	Brighton	0 0		15,918	1	2		4	5	6	7						8				3	11					10			9		
						Apps	26	26	26	39	42	42	22	8	25	15	13	2	29	12	6	1	29	22	22	5	3	4	12	2	9	13	4	3
						Gls						2	7	2	17		2		14	7				4	6		1		1			4	2	

#	Date	V	Opponents	Score	Scorers	Att.	Parry BJ	Feeney J	Fisher CK	Paul R	Weston R	Burns FJ	O'Driscoll JF	Squires F	Rawcliffe F	Eastham G	Lockhart NH	Hopkins GG	McCrory S	James D	Payne IEH	Cunliffe R	Keane TR	Scrine FH	Comley LG	Newell E	Dodds TB	Roberts OJ	Morris WH	O'Sullivan J	Howells RG	Powell R	Lucas WH	Hooper PG
1	Jan-10	A	Bristol Rovers FAC-3	0 3		25,000		2		4	5	6			9				8				3	7	10				1	11				
2	Jan-14	A	Barry T WC-5	0 2																														

Swansea Town FC Season 1948/9 Division 3(S)

#	Date	V	Opponents	Score	Scorers	Att.	Parry BJ	Feeney J	Keane TR	Paul R	Weston R	Burns FJ	O'Driscoll JF	McCrory S	Richards SV	Lucas WH	Scrine FH	Andrew M	Morris WH	Payne IEH	Powell R	Newell E	Wookey KW	Turner C	Canning LD	Clarke KN	Elwell T
1	Aug-21	H	Watford	2 0	Richards, McCrory	12,107	1	2	3	4	5	6	7	8	9	10	11										
2	Aug-25	A	Crystal Palace	1 1	McCrory	13,464	1	2	3	4	5	6	7	8	9	10	11										
3	Aug-28	A	Bournemouth	1 1	Richards	20,150	1	2	3	4	5	6	7	8	9	10	11										
4	Sep-02	H	Crystal Palace	3 0	Scrine,Richards,O'Driscoll	14,277	1	2	3	4	5	6	7	8	9	10	11										
5	Sep-04	H	Ipswich T	2 0	Richards 2	27,919	1	2	3	4	5	6	7	8	9	10	11										
6	Sep-09	H	Leyton Orient	3 1	O'Driscoll 2,McCrory	24,140	1	2	3	4	5	6	7	8	9	10	11										
7	Sep-11	A	Notts. Co	1 1	McCrory	36,316	1	2	3	4	5	6	7	8	9	10	11										
8	Sep-16	A	Leyton Orient	1 3	O'Driscoll	9,997	1		3	4	5	6	7	8	9	10	11	2									
9	Sep-18	H	Walsall	3 1	McCrory,Richards,Payne	22,597	1	2	3	4	5	6	11	8	9				10	7							
10	Sep-25	A	Torquay Utd	4 0	Payne,Richards 2,McCrory	10,459	1	2	3	4	5	6	11	8	9				10	7							
11	Sep-30	H	Swindon T	4 0	Richards 4	25,107	1	2	3	4	5	6	11	8	9	10				7							
12	Oct-02	H	Bristol Rovers	5 0	Scrine 3,Paul,Payne	27,375	1	2	3	4	5	6	11	8	9				10	7							
13	Oct-09	A	Port Vale	2 0	McCrory,Powell	17,888	1	2	3	4	5	6		8		10				11	7	9					
14	Oct-16	H	Millwall	2 0	Paul,Richards	25,155	1	2	3	4	5	6	11	8	9				10	7							
15	Oct-23	A	Norwich C	0 1		29,610	1	2	3		5	6	11	8	9	10				7			4				
16	Oct-30	H	Exeter C	6 0	Payne2,Richards2,McCrory,O'Driscol	22,767	1	2	3	4	5	6	11	8	9	10				7							
17	Nov-06	A	Southend Utd	0 0		13,503	1	2	3	4	5	6	11	8	9	10				7							
18	Nov-13	H	Northampton T	1 0	Scrine	23,095	1		3	4	5	6	7	8	9	10	11				2						
19	Nov-20	A	Aldershot	2 1	Scrine,Richards	9,644	1		3	4	5	6	11		9	8	10				2	7					
20	Dec-18	A	Watford	2 4	Scrine 2	11,469	1	2		4	5	6	11		9	8	10			7		3					
21	Dec-25	A	Reading	2 0	Lucas,Scrine	15,011		2	3	4	5	6	7	8		10	9			11					1		
22	Dec-27	H	Reading	2 1	Payne,McCrory	27,508		2	3	4	5	6	7	8		10	9			11					1		
23	Jan-01	H	Bournemouth	2 0	McCrory,Scrine	19,412	1	2	3	4	5	6	7	8		10	9			11							
24	Jan-15	A	Ipswich T	0 2		12,814	1	2	3	4	5	6	7	8		10	9			11							
25	Jan-22	H	Notts. Co	3 1	Richards,Scrine,Lucas	26,493		2	3	4	5	6	7		9	8	10			11					1		
26	Jan-29	H	Brighton	3 0	Richards 2,Payne	26,045		2	3	4	5	6	7		9	8	10			11					1		
27	Feb-05	A	Walsall	1 2	Richards	14,634			3	4	5	6			9	8	10			11		7		2	1		
28	Feb-19	H	Torquay Utd	6 1	McCrory 3,Scrine 2,Richards	23,232		2	3	4	5	6			9	8	10			11		7			1		
29	Feb-26	A	Bristol Rovers	1 1	McCrory	30,216		2	3	4	5	6	7	8	9	10	11								1		
30	Mar-05	H	Port Vale	3 1	Lucas,Payne,McCrory	13,769		2	3	4	5	6	7	8		10	9			11					1		
31	Mar-12	A	Milwall	0 2		28,169				4	5	6	7	8		10	9		11						1	2	3
32	Mar-19	H	Norwich C	2 1	Lucas,Scrine	23,676			3	2	5	6	7	8	9	10	11					4			1		
33	Mar-26	A	Exeter C	1 1	Lucas	13,157			3	4	5	6		8	9	10	11					7			1		2
34	Apr-02	H	Southend Utd	2 2	Richards 2	13,503			3	4		6	7	8	9	10	11					5			1		2
35	Apr-09	A	Northampton T	1 0	Richards	10,194			3	4	5	6	7	8	9	10	11								1		2
36	Apr-15	A	Newport Co	5 2	Lucas,McCrory2,Richards,Scrine	21,167				4	5	6	7	8	9	10	11					3			1		2
37	Apr-16	H	Aldershot	2 1	McCrory(pen),O'Driscoll	24,056				4	5	6	7	8	9	10	11					3			1		2
38	Apr-18	H	Newport Co	2 1	Scrine,Richards	28,623				4	5	6	7	8	9	10	11					3			1		2
39	Apr-23	A	Brighton	2 0	Scrine,McCrory	19,974				4	5	6		8	9	10	11			7		3			1		2
40	Apr-27	A	Bristol C	0 0		14,054			3	4	5	6	7	8		10	9			11					1		2
41	Apr-30	H	Bristol C	2 0	Scrine.O'Driscoll	18,958			3	4	5	6	7	8		10	9			11					1		2
42	May-07	A	Swindon T	0 1		21,390			3	4	5	6		8		10	11					9	7		1		2
	Apps						22	26	36	41	41	42	36	37	32	36	38	1	4	23	2	11	2	2	18	1	11
	Gls									1			7	19	26	6	18			9	1						

#	Date	V	Opponents	Score	Scorers	Att.	Parry BJ	Feeney J	Keane TR	Paul R	Weston R	Burns FJ	O'Driscoll JF	McCrory S	Richards SV	Lucas WH	Scrine FH	Andrew M	Morris WH	Payne IEH	Powell R	Newell E	Wookey KW	Turner C	Canning LD	Clarke KN	Elwell T
1	Dec-04	A	Southend FAC-1	2 1	Burns, O'Driscoll	13,000	1	2	3	4	5	6	11		9	8	10						7				
2	Dec-11	A	Bristol City FAC-2	1 3	O'Driscoll	22,136	1	2	3	4	5	6	11			8	10					9	7				
3	Jan-12	A	Barry T WC-5	7 1	O'Driscoll,Scrine3,McCrory2,Burns		1	2	3	4	5	6	7	8		10	9			11							
4	Feb-12	H	S. Liverpool WC-6	9 1	Scrine 3, Morris 4,McCrory 2	15,000	1	2	3	4	5	6		8		10	9		11				7				
5	Apr-07	W	Rhyl WC-S-F	3 0	Scrine 2, McCrory (at Wrexham)	13,000			3	4	5	6		8	9	10	11					7			1		2
6	May-05	C	Merthyr WC-Final	0 2	at Ninian Park	32,000			3	4	5	6		8		10	9			11	7				1		2

W – Wrexham
C – Cardiff

Swansea Town FC Season 1949/50 Division 2

#	Date	V	Opponents	Score	Scorers	Att.	Canning LD	Feeney J	Keane TR	Paul R	Weston R	Burns FJ	O'Driscoll JF	McCrory S	Richards SV	Lucas WH	Scrine FH	Parry BJ	Elwell T	Beech C	Newell E	Wookey KW	Andrew M	Thomas DA	Clarke KN	Allchurch I	Beech G	James WG	Kiley TJ	Griffiths H	Powell R
1	Aug-20	H	Preston NE	2 1	Richards, Lucas	26,041	1	2	3	4	5	6	7	8	9	10	11														
2	Aug-22	A	Sheff. Utd	1 1	Own Goal	21,415	1	2	3	4	5	6	7	8	9	10	11														
3	Aug-27	A	Cardiff C	0 1		60,855	1	2	3	4	5	6	7	8	9	10	11														
4	Sep-01	H	Sheff. Utd	1 0	Beech C	27,768		2		4	5	6	7	8	9	10		1	3	11											
5	Sep-03	A	Leeds Utd	2 1	Beech C, Scrine	29,767				4	5	6			9	8	10	1	2	11	3	7									
6	Sep-07	A	Grimsby T	1 2	Paul(pen)	19,465				4	5	6	7		9	8	10	1	2	11	3										
7	Sep-10	H	Southampton	4 0	Paul(2pens),Richards,O'Driscoll	24,970			3	4	5	6	7		9	8	10	1	2	11											
8	Sep-17	A	Coventry C	2 1	McCrory,O'Driscoll	25,603			3	4	5	6	7	8	9		10	1	2	11											
9	Sep-24	H	Luton T	0 0		24,297			3	4	5	6	7		9	8	10	1	2	11											
10	Oct-07	A	Barnsley	2 5	Richards, Beech C	19,662			3	4	5	6	7		9	8	10	1	2	11											
11	Oct-08	H	Blackburn R	2 0	Lucas, Beech C	20,143			3	4	5	6	7		9	8	10	1	2	11											
12	Oct-15	A	Brentford	0 0		23,871			3		5	6	7	8	9			1	2	11		4	10								
13	Oct-22	H	Hull C	1 2	Richards	22,275			3	4	5	6	7		9	8	10	1	2	11											
14	Oct-29	A	Sheff. Wed	0 3		34,604			3	4	5	6		8	9	10		1	2	11		7									
15	Nov-05	H	Plymouth A	2 2	McCrory,Paul	20,391		2	3	4		6		8	9	10	7	1		11					5						
16	Nov-12	A	Chesterfield	1 4	McCrory	11,106		2	3	4	5			8	9	10		1		11		7	6								
17	Nov-19	H	Bradford PA	2 0	Lucas, Beech C	18,729		2		4	5	6	7	8	9	10		1	3	11											
18	Nov-26	A	Leicester C	0 0		28,321			3	4	5	6	7	8	9	10		1	2	11											
19	Dec-03	H	Bury	1 2	McCrory	17,947			3	4	5	6		8	9	10	11	1	2	7											
20	Dec-10	A	Tottenham H	1 3	McCrory	50,758			3	4	5	6		8		10	9	1	2	11	7										
21	Dec-17	A	Preston NE	1 2	McCrory	28,649	1	2	3	4	5	6		8		10	9			11	7										
22	Dec-24	H	Cardiff C	5 1	Lucas 2,McCrory 2, O'Driscoll	27,264	1			4	5	6	7	8	9	10			2	11	3										
23	Dec-26	A	West Ham Utd	0 3		24,398	1		3	4	5	6	7			8	9		2	11						10					
24	Dec-27	H	West Ham Utd	1 0	McCrory	25,721	1		3	4	5	6	7	8		10	9		2	11											
25	Dec-31	H	Leeds Utd	1 2	Paul	23,192	1		3	4	5	6	7	8	9	10			2	11											
26	Jan-14	A	Southampton	2 1	Lucas, Allchurch	24,674		2	3		5	6	7			8	9	1		11						10	4				
27	Jan-21	H	Coventry C	1 2	Paul	20,320		2	3	4	5	6	7			8	9	1		11						10	11				
28	Feb-04	A	Luton T	2 1	O'Driscoll, Beech C	15,205	1		3	4	5	6	7			8				11		9				10		2			
29	Feb-18	H	Barnsley	4 0	Beech 2,Scrine, Allchurch	20,694	1	2	3	4	5	6	7			8				11		9				10					
30	Feb-25	A	Blackburn R	0 2		14,092	1	2	3	4	5	6	7			8				11		9				10					
31	Mar-04	H	Brentford	3 0	O'Goal,Lucas, O'Driscoll	21,239	1		3	4	5	6	7			8				11		9				10		2			
32	Mar-11	A	Hull C	0 0		32,873	1		3	4	5	6	7			8				11		9				10		2			
33	Mar-18	H	Sheff. Wed	1 2	Allchurch	18,917	1		3	4	5	6	7			8				11		9				10		2			
34	Mar-25	A	Plymouth A	1 0	Beech C	20,064	1		3	4	5	6	7			8				2		9				10	11				
35	Apr-01	H	Leicester C	0 0		20,591	1		3		5	6	7			8				2		9				10	4				
36	Apr-07	A	QPR	0 0		23,217	1		3	4		6				8	11			2		7				10	9		5		
37	Apr-08	A	Bury	1 1	Scrine	11,901	1		3	4		6				8	9			2		7				10	11		5		
38	Apr-10	A	QPR	0 1		18,405	1		3	4		6				8	9			2		7				10	11		5		
39	Apr-15	H	Chesterfield	0 2		18,940	1		3	4	5	6				8				2		9				10	11			7	
40	Apr-22	A	Bradford PA	2 0	Beech C,Scrine	16,169	1	2			5	6				8	11		3	9						10	4				7
41	Apr-29	H	Tottenham H	1 0	Scrine	16,417	1	2		4	5					8	11		3	9		7				10	6				
42	May-06	H	Grimsby T	2 1	Lucas, Paul(pen)	18,723	1	2		4	5					8	11		3	9		7				10	6				
	Apps						23	12	34	39	38	41	28	17	21	40	32	19	28	37	3	10	2	1	1	18	9	4	3	1	1
	Gls									7			5	9	4	8	5			10						3					

#	Date	V	Opponents	Score	Scorers	Att.	Canning LD	Feeney J	Keane TR	Paul R	Weston R	Burns FJ	O'Driscoll JF	McCrory S	Richards SV	Lucas WH	Scrine FH	Parry BJ	Elwell T	Beech C	Newell E	Wookey KW	Andrew M	Thomas DA	Clarke KN	Allchurch I	Beech G	James WG	Kiley TJ	Griffiths H	Powell R
1	Jan-07	H	Birmingham City FAC-3	3 0	Allchurch, Burns, Scrine	19,000		2	3	4	5	6	7			8	9	1		11						10					
2	Jan-28	A	Arsenal FAC-4	1 2	Scrine	57,305			3	4	5	6	7			8	9	1		11						10		2			
3			Caerau WC-5	4 1																											
4	Feb-23	H	Cardiff WC-6	3 0	Richards, Scrine 2	10,000	1	2	3	4	5	6	7	8	9	10	11														
5	Mar-30	C	Merthyr WC S-F	5 1	Lucas,Burns,Allchurch,Beech,Beech	15,000	1		3	4	5	6				8	11		2	9						10	7				
6	Apr-27	C	Wrexham WC-F	4 1	Scrine 3, Beech C	12,000	1		2			6				8	11		3	9		7				10	4		5		

C – Cardiff

Swansea Town FC Season 1950/1 Division 2

#	Date	V	Opponents	Score	Scorers	Att.	Canning LD	Elwell T	Leavy S	Burns FJ	Weston R	Beech G	Donovan FJ	Lucas WH	Scrine FH	Allchurch I	Beech C	Richards SV	Morgan AR	Huntley KSM	Williams D	Thomas DA	Parry BJ	Clarke KN	Hodges L	Barber JM	Newell E	Wilson A	Howarth S	Roberts JH	Andrew M	O'Driscoll JF	Kiley TJ	King J	Powell R	Turnbull R	Symmons I	Allchurch L
1	Aug-19	H	Birmingham C	0 1		25,012	1	2	3	4	5	6	7	8	9	10	11																					
2	Aug-24	H	Sheff. Wed	1 2	Richards	19,963	1	2	3	4	5	6	7	8		10	11	9																				
3	Aug-26	A	Hull C	1 2	Richards	35,333	1		3		5	6	7	4	10	8		9	2	11																		
4	Aug-28	A	Sheff. Utd	1 6	Richards	25,597	1				5	6	7	4		10		9	2	11	3	8																
5	Sep-02	H	Doncaster R	2 2	Lucas, Weston	20,756			3		5	6	7	4		10		9					1	2	8	11												
6	Sep-07	H	Leeds Utd	4 2	Lucas 2,Richards, Allchurch	19,501			3		5	6	7	4		10		9					1	2	8	11												
7	Sep-09	A	Brentford	1 2	Lucas	23,574					5	6	7	4		10		9					1	2	8	11	3											
8	Sep-16	H	Blackburn R	1 2	Richards	18,166					6	5	3	7	8	10		9					1			11	2	4										
9	Sep-23	A	Southampton	1 2	Howarth	22,420				6	5	3	7	4		10	11					8	1				2		9									
10	Sep-30	H	Barnsley	1 0	Donovan	19,091				6	5	3	7	4		10	11					8	1						9	2								
11	Oct-07	H	Chesterfield	2 0	Donovan, Thomas	22,005				6	5	3	7	4		10	11					8	1						9	2								
12	Oct-14	A	QPR	1 1	Beech C	19,256				6	5	3	7	4		10	11					8	1						9	2								
13	Oct-21	H	Manchester C	2 3	Thomas 2	22,762	1			6	5	3	7	4		10	11					8							9	2								
14	Oct-28	A	Leicester C	3 2	Thomas, Allchurch, Beech C	26,224					5	3				10	11				6	8	1						9	2	4	7						
15	Nov-04	H	Cardiff C	1 0	Lucas	26,393					5	3		4		10	11				6	8	1						9	2		7						
16	Nov-11	A	Coventry C	1 3	O/Goal(McDonnell)	29,672					5	3		4		10	11				6	8	1						9	2		7						
17	Nov-18	H	Bury	2 0	O'Driscoll, Howarth	18,353					5	3		4		10	11				6	8	1						9	2		7						
18	Nov-26	A	Preston NE	1 5	Thomas	25,898					5	3		4		10	11				6	8	1						9	2		7						
19	Dec-02	H	Notts. Co	2 1	O'Driscoll, Thomas	22,457						3		4		10	11				6	8	1						9	2		7	5					
20	Dec-09	A	Grimsby T	2 4	Thomas, Howarth	13,754						3		4		10	11				6	8	1						9	2		7	5					
21	Dec-16	A	Birmingham C	0 5		15,649						3		4		10	11				6	8							9	2		7	5	1				
22	Dec-23	H	Hull C	1 0	Beech C	16,371						3		4		10	11				6	8							9	2		7	5	1				
23	Dec-25	H	Luton T	0 2		16,862						3		4		10	11				6	8							9	2		7	5	1				
24	Dec-26	A	Luton T	1 3	Howarth	17,245			4			3				10	11				6	8	1						9	2		7	5					
25	Jan-13	H	Brentford	2 1	Roberts, Allchurch	15,422	1			4	5	3	7			10	11				6	8								2					9			
26	Jan-20	A	Blackburn R	0 3		17,964		2		4	5	3				10	11				6	8							7					1	9			
27	Jan-27	A	Doncaster R	0 1		21,878		2			5	3	7	4		10	11				6								8					1		9		
28	Feb-03	H	Southampton	2 1	Thomas, Turnbull	17,451		2			5	3		4		10	11				6	7							8					1		9		
29	Feb-17	A	Barnsley	0 1		8,371		2			5	3		4		10					6	7							8			11		1		9		
30	Feb-24	A	Chesterfield	1 3	Turnbull	10,549		2			5	3		4		10	11				6	7							8					1		9		
31	Mar-03	H	QPR	1 0	Howarth	18,611				4	5	3				10	11				6	7							8					1		9	2	
32	Mar-14	A	Manchester C	2 1	Turnbull 2	10,361				4	5	3				10	11				6	7							8					1		9	2	
33	Mar-17	H	Leicester C	2 1	Turnbull 2	12,914		2			5	3		4		10	11				6	7							8					1		9		
34	Mar-23	H	West Ham Utd	1 1	Turnbull	25,385		2			5	3		4		10	11				6	7							8					1		9		
35	Mar-24	A	Cardiff C	0 1		41,074				4	5	3				10	11				6	8							7					1		9	2	
36	Mar-26	H	West Ham Utd	3 2	Howarth, Turnbull, Allchurch	16,240				4	5	3				10	11				6	8							7					1		9	2	
37	Mar-31	H	Coventry C	2 1	Lucas, Allchurch	20,567				4	5	3		8		10	11				6								7					1		9	2	
38	Apr-07	A	Bury	1 1	Allchurch	11,880				4	5	3		8		10	11				6								7					1		9	2	
39	Apr-14	H	Preston NE	2 1	Turnbull, Allchurch	28,878				4	5	3		8		10	11				6								7					1		9	2	
40	Apr-21	A	Notts. Co	2 3	Allchurch, Burns	17,787				4	5	3		8		10	11				6								7					1		9	2	
41	Apr-28	H	Grimsby T	1 3	Howarth	14,585				4	5	3		8		10					6								7					1		9	2	11
42	May-05	A	Leeds Utd	0 2		11,213				4	5	3		8		10					6								7					1		9	2	11
			Apps				6	9	5	18	37	42	15	35	2	42	33	9	2	2	30	29	16	3	3	4	3	1	33	16	1	11	6	20	2	15	10	2
			Gls							1	1		2	6		8	3	5				8							7	1		2				9		

#	Date	V	Opponents	Score	Scorers	Att.	Canning LD	Elwell T	Leavy S	Burns FJ	Weston R	Beech G	Donovan FJ	Lucas WH	Scrine FH	Allchurch I	Beech C	Richards SV	Morgan AR	Huntley KSM	Williams D	Thomas DA	Parry BJ	Clarke KN	Hodges L	Barber JM	Newell E	Wilson A	Howarth S	Roberts JH	Andrew M	O'Driscoll JF	Kiley TJ	King J	Powell R	Turnbull R	Symmons I	Allchurch L
1	Jan-06	A	Mansfield T FAC-3	0 2		16,564						3		4		10	11				6	8	1						9	2		7	5					
2	Feb-10	H	Pembroke B WC-5	5 0	Howarth2,Turnbull,Allchurch,Allchurch			2		4	5	3				10				7	6								8					1		9		11
3	Mar-01	A	Newport Co. WC-6	1 2	Howarth	7,500								4					11	9		10	1					6	8	2		7	5			3		

Swansea Town FC Season 1951/2 Division 2

#	Date	V	Opponents	Score	Scorers	Att.	King J	Elwell T	Beech G	Lucas WH	Weston R	Williams D	O'Driscoll JF	Scrine FH	Turnbull R	Allchurch I	Bellis A	Howarth S	Thomas DA	Keane TR	Burns FJ	Symmons I	Clarke KN	Lamie R	Allchurch L	Kiley TJ	Beech C	Medwin T	Morgan AR	Gooderidge AE
1	Aug-18	A	Luton Town	2 2	Scrine 2	15,606	1	2	3	4	5	6	7	8	9	10	11													
2	Aug-20	A	Coventry City	2 3	Lucas, Turnbull	23,962	1	2	3	4	5	6	7	8	9	10	11													
3	Aug-25	H	Notts. County	1 1	Bellis	17,905	1	2	3	4	5	6	7	8	9	10	11													
4	Aug-30	H	Coventry City	7 1	Lucas, Scrine 2, Turnbull 2, Allchurch, Bellis	19,874	1	2	3	4	5	6	7	8	9	10	11													
5	Sep-01	A	QPR	1 1	Allchurch	18,369	1	2	3	4	5	6	7	8	9	10	11													
6	Sep-06	A	West Ham United	2 2	O'Driscoll, Bellis	16,640	1	2	3	4	5	6	7	8	9	10	11													
7	Sep-08	H	Blackburn Rovers	5 1	Turnbull 3, Allchurch, Bellis	22,047	1	2	3	4	5	6	7	8	9	10	11													
8	Sep-13	H	West Ham United	2 1	Bellis, O'Driscoll	16,135	1	2	3	4	5	6	7	8	9	10	11													
9	Sep-15	A	Hull City	2 5	Turnbull 2	27,947	1	2	3		5	6	7		9	10	11	4	8											
10	Sep-22	H	Barnsley	2 1	Allchurch 2 (1 pen)	22,335	1		3		5	6	7	8	9	10	11		4	2										
11	Sep-29	A	Sheff. United	0 5		34,173	1		3	4	5	6	7		9	10	11		8	2										
12	Oct-06	A	Birmingham City	1 1	Turnbull	28,060	1		3	4	5	6	7		9	10	11		8			2								
13	Oct-13	H	Leicester City	1 0	O'Driscoll	21,338	1		3	4	5	6	7		9	10	11		8	2										
14	Oct-20	A	Nottm. Forest	2 2	Bellis, Thomas	20,553	1		3		5	6		10	9		11		8	2	4			7						
15	Oct-27	H	Brentford	1 1	Turnbull	19,235	1		3	4	5	6			9	10	11		8	2					7					
16	Nov-03	A	Doncaster Rovers	0 3		17,797	1		3	4	5	6	7	8	9	10	11			2										
17	Nov-10	H	Everton	0 2		20,271	1		3	8		6	7		9	10	11		4	2						5				
18	Nov-17	A	Southampton	2 3	Lucas 2	15,779	1		3	8	5	6	7		9	10	11		4	2										
19	Nov-24	H	Sheff. Wed	1 2	Turnbull	9,934	1		3	8	5	6	7		9	10	11		4	2										
20	Dec-01	A	Leeds United	1 1	Allchurch	26,235	1		3	4	5	6	7	8	9	10	11			2										
21	Dec-08	H	Rotherham United	5 0	Turnbull 3, Scrine, Bellis	11,425	1		3	4	5	6	7	8	9	10	11			2										
22	Dec-15	H	Luton Town	0 3		14,896	1		3	4	5	6	7	8	9	10	11			2										
23	Dec-22	A	Notts. County	0 2		22,185	1		3	4	5	6		8	9	10	11			2							7			
24	Dec-25	H	Cardiff City	1 1	Baker (o.g.)	19,260	1		3	4	5	6		8	9	10	11			2							7			
25	Dec-26	A	Cardiff City	0 3		46,003	1		3	4	5	6		8	9	10	11			2							7			
26	Dec-29	H	QPR	2 3	Turnbull, Lucas (pen)	16,146	1		3	4	5	6			9	10	11	8		2				7						
27	Jan-05	A	Blackburn Rovers	1 3	Turnbull	27,736	1	2	6	8	5				9	10	11			3	4							7		
28	Jan-19	H	Hull City	3 0	Scrine, Turnbull 2	17,097	1	2	3	4	5	6	7	8	9	10	11													
29	Jan-26	A	Barnsley	3 2	Turnbull , Allchurch 2	13,870	1	2	3	4	5	6		8	9	10	11	7												
30	Feb-09	H	Sheff. United	3 1	Williams, Scrine, Bellis	23,160	1	2	3	4	5	6		8	9	10	11	7												
31	Feb-16	H	Birmingham City	4 0	Scrine, Allchurch, Bellis 2	24,230	1	2	3	4	5	6		8	9	10	11	7												
32	Mar-01	A	Leicester City	1 1	Beech C	31,221	1		3	4	5	6		8	9	10		7					2				11			
33	Mar-08	H	Nottm. Forest	1 2	Scrine	22,281	1		3	4	5	6		8	9	10	11	7					2							
34	Mar-15	A	Brentford	1 3	Scrine	29,753	1		3	4	5	6		8		10	11						2				9	7		
35	Mar-22	H	Doncaster Rovers	1 2	Medwin	17,150	1		3	4	5	6		8	9	10	11						2					7		
36	Mar-29	A	Everton	1 2	Lello (o.g.)	20,985	1		3		5	4		8	9	10	11					6	2					7		
37	Apr-05	H	Southampton	1 1	Bellis	15,506	1		3		5	4			9	10	11		8		6							7	2	
38	Apr-11	A	Bury	1 4	Turnbull	16,719	1		3		5	4		8	9	10										2	11	7		6
39	Apr-12	A	Sheff. Wed	1 1	Beech C	49,082	1		3		5	4		8	9	10						6				2	11	7		
40	Apr-14	H	Bury	0 2		14,264	1		3		5	4		8	9	10						6				2	11	7		
41	Apr-19	H	Leeds United	4 1	Turnbull 2, Allchurch 2,	18,206	1		3	8	5	4			9	10						6				2	11	7		
42	Apr-26	A	Rotherham United	3 1	Williams, Medwin, Beech C	14,074	1		3	8	5	4			9	10						6				2	11	7		
					Apps		42	14	42	34	41	41	21	30	40	41	37	7	11	17	3	6	5	2	1	6	9	10	1	1
					Gls					5		2	3	10	22	11	11		1								3	2		

#	Date	V	Opponents	Score	Scorers	Att.	King J	Elwell T	Beech G	Lucas WH	Weston R	Williams D	O'Driscoll JF	Scrine FH	Turnbull R	Allchurch I	Bellis A	Howarth S	Thomas DA	Keane TR	Burns FJ	Symmons I	Clarke KN	Lamie R	Allchurch L	Kiley TJ	Beech C	Medwin T	Morgan AR	Gooderidge AE
1	Jan-03	A	Merthyr (WC-5)	1 2	Scrine	5,945	1	2	6		5	4	7	10	9	8				3						11				
2	Jan-12	A	Reading (FAC-3)	3 0	Allchurch, Medwin, Bellis	28,129	1	2	6	8	5	4			9	10	11			3								7		
3	Feb-02	H	Rotherham Utd.(FAC-4)	3 0	Allchurch 2, Williams	22,246	1	2	3	6	5	4		8	9	10	11	7												
4	Feb-23	H	Newcastle Utd.(FAC-5)	0 1		27,801	1		3	6	5	4		8	9	10	11	7		2										

Chapter 12

The Young Ones

Despite the disappointments of the previous season, soccer followers in Swansea faced the new term with more than a modicum of hope. After all, the new board had refused to sell Ivor for a large fee, young Medwin was thought to be a good prospect, while outstanding schoolboys, Cliff Jones and Mel Charles, were registered as amateurs. There were some nostalgic departures, though; Billy Lucas apart, the last members of the promotion side left the Vetch: Burns joined Southend, Jack O'Driscoll went to Llanelli, and Reg Weston, not having been helped with his housing problem, signed for Derby County. Whilst Weston is not usually linked with the many names for which the Vetch Field is famous,

during his stay in Swansea he was a tower of strength. His straightforward style, coupled with his leadership abilities, complemented the many skilful players around him. He was an honest man, who never undersold himself or his colleagues.

1952-53

The only newcomer for the 1952-3 season was a goalkeeper, Gwyn Groves. He was signed from Merthyr district football as a cover for John King, who had been 'called up'. One consequence of this was that, short of the experience of the players who had left, observers thought it likely that the side might struggle. Despite

the sales which had been made, the club started the season with a debit balance of £20,000. It was a situation which reinforced the, by now, cautious board's resolve not to pay fees for new professionals. Instead, a policy evolved which was based entirely upon the development of local talent. In the event, that approach forced McCandless to blood his younger players earlier than he might otherwise have done. For example, Cliff Jones (17) made his debut in October, as did John Dewsbury (20), while Mel Charles (17) played his first game in December.

For the match against Fulham on 22 November, the side, other than Beech, was composed of Welshmen, eight of whom were Swansea-born. By the end of the season, several of these young men had matured enough to play a significant part in achieving a respectable mid-table position for the club. By then, Charles had played on twenty occasions, while Medwin and Griffiths had each turned out thirty-nine times. During the season, three sets of brothers appeared in the first

The youngsters are coming . . . The Swans at St Andrews, Birmingham, March 1953.
Back row, left to right: Billy McCandless (Manager), Billy Lucas, Rory Keane, Harry Sullivan (Director), Gwyn Groves, Dai Thomas, Davo Williams, Frank Scrine (Reserve). Front row: Harry Griffiths, Brin Jones, Terry Medwin, Ivor Allchurch, Cyril Beech and Mel Charles.

Ivor's diving header hits the post.

team: Ivor and Len Allchurch, Cyril and Gilbert Beech, and Brin and Cliff Jones. Together with the brothers Hole, they constituted a record for the club. Of the four sets of brothers, three were born in Swansea and two were sons of former players. The complicated set of circumstances which brought together this talented group of players may never be repeated. Nevertheless, in view of the board's policy on homegrown talent they can only be described as fortuitous.

During the season, the club played its first match under floodlights at the unlikely venue of Cheltenham. It was following their second such game, later in the season, that Young, the reserve goalkeeper, was to complain that they had lost through having to play against the moon in the first half. His humour was not without its irony.

With rugby's 'golden boy', Lewis Jones, 'going North' for a reputed £6,000, it was not surprising that the 'Ivor is leaving' saga continued. Indeed, he was not the only subject of such rumour: Harry Griffiths and Terry Medwin were also reported to be leaving. At the AGM, Philip Holden stated that the club's accounts did not make 'happy reading', but he issued firm denials about any impending transfers, 'To sell our better young players,' he declared, 'would mean that we would never build a good side . . . Despite tempting offers, we do not want to transfer any promising young players.' Nevertheless, he also emphasised that 'it is, clearly, impossible to find money to buy players.' It was not what the supporters wanted to hear, but, at least, the boys were safe.

A month later, the FA Cup produced some useful income, partially as a result of a quirk of nature. The Swans were drawn to play Newcastle away, in a match which attracted a gate of 63,449 and an income of almost £9,000. All that was seen by that throng was a blanket of fog. As a result, the game was replayed three days later, when only two thousand fewer were in the ground. This time they saw a fine match, Newcastle winning by three clear goals. All accounts, however, praised the Swansea performance, with Ivor, 'Davo' Williams and Tom Kiley being mentioned most of all. In February, Tom Kiley fractured a leg, which was a blow to the team, but an opportunity for young Charles, who, flanked by Billy Lucas and 'Davo' Williams, did well for the rest of the campaign. 'Rolande', indeed, was moved to predict that 'Charles will, undoubtedly be capped.'

Towards the end of the season, Billy McCandless advised the board that the young charges under his control needed careful handling if they were to develop properly. Obviously, the board felt the same way about their manager. Twice during the season, the directors had minuted an instruction to him that he should 'take a more active control of training, so that the trainer would have less influence on the style of play'. Yet the man who was to have the greatest influence on the way in which the team played was already on the staff. Joe Sykes 'the doyen of carpet passers', awaited his opportunity. At the time, Joe had signed yet another Swansea Schoolboy for the club. Mel Nurse, from the Cwmbwrla district of Swansea, which had produced so many outstanding footballers, came following the Schoolboys' victory in the final of the English Schools Shield.

1953-54

The first matches of the season were hardly encouraging. After losing at home to Doncaster, the side was heavily beaten (6-0) at Birmingham. It was a shattering experience for the young players and emphasised the manager's appeal to the board. However, the directors 'got their retaliation in first'. McCandless was given another lecture on his involvement in training, and in October, the directors were congratulating themselves. The club's debit balance had been reduced from £30,000 to £17,000. Frank Scrine had been sold to Oldham, and Arthur Morgan to Plymouth, two deals which contributed some £7,000 of the improvement. With an accountant's eye, the chairman noted that 'the club has far too many players on its books . . . No players are to be signed . . . and an attempt made to place surplus players elsewhere.'

In February, Frank Barson resigned for health reasons, and, ostensibly, the manager, who had received two further warnings about involvement in training, took control. Results, however, were indifferent. At the end of 1953 the team had gained twenty-two points. In 1954 they added only twelve points to that total, finishing just one point above Brentford, who were relegated. Most critics thought that the poor performance of the team in the second half of the season was attributable to the absence of Billy Lucas, who had been transferred to Newport in December to allow him to begin a managerial career. Whilst releasing him was a genuine attempt to reward a loyal player and help Newport, the extent of his importance to the team was only fully realised after his departure. He had been a fine footballer, an astute 'general' and a wonderful example of a ball-player from whom younger players learned a great deal. Unfortunately, in line with their stated policy, no attempt was made to replace this senior player until the club's position in the table became

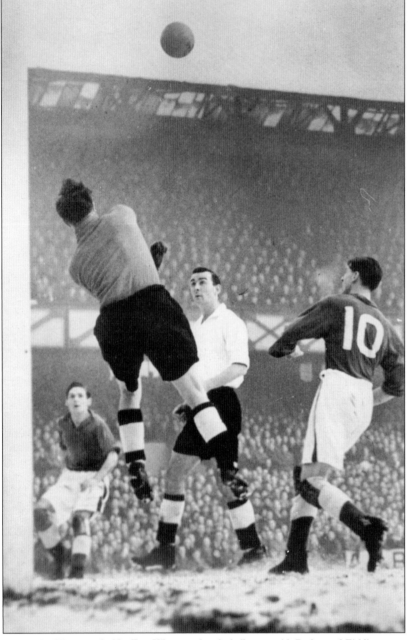

John King, watched by Tom Kiley, punches the ball away with Parker and Fielding of Everton on hand. It was during an FA Cup match at Goodison Park watched by over sixty thousand people, and played on a pitch covered with snow.

that month he was released by Spurs on a free transfer to join the Swans. Burgess's arrival coincided with the passing of an influential figure in Swansea schools football: Gabe Williams, former secretary of the Swansea Schools Football Association. It was as a result of his efforts and of those like Dai Beynon that so many excellent footballers emerged from Swansea's schools. Their selfless dedication to the task of bringing on soccer talent not only resulted in the town's schoolboy teams doing so well, but provided a rich seam of outstanding players for the Vetch club.

1954-55

For some reason the kick-off time for the Swans' opening match of the season was fifteen minutes earlier than the others in the Football League. It was an opportunity which Ivor Allchurch grasped, for he scored the first goal of the season. Percy Young, a prominent football writer of the time, recalled the goal as the opening item in his book *Football Year*:

> Within three minutes of the whistle there was a goal. It was Allchurch's goal . . . The papers were correct. Allchurch was the finest inside forward in the game . . . It had been this way. Allchurch, receiving the ball just beyond the half-way line, veered north-eastward, feinting the while. Ten yards from the corner

rather critical. Even then, the offer which they made to Cardiff for Wilf Grant was rejected by the City board as 'completely inadequate'.

Because of this policy, a situation was developing which was to be a root cause of the exacting problems which were to threaten the very existence of the club in the years ahead. Purchases were only made in desperate circumstances and, even then, for small fees; senior players were transferred for large sums and replacements were expected to appear from among the young players on the staff. As time wore on, in the face of such an approach, gates

diminished, necessitating further sales and rigorous cost-cutting. There is little doubt that strict financial controls were essential, yet money was wasted in buying cheap players, who were always a poor investment. The business adage that it is necessary to speculate astutely in order to accumulate, was not at the heart of the board's philosophy.

However, there was modest speculation in financial terms in June 1954, when the board, frustrated by McCandless's lack of desire to involve himself with training, decided to employ a coach. In July, Ron Burgess was short-listed and later

IVOR ALLCHURCH (Swansea)

A packed double-decker watches Ron Burgess tackle a visiting forward.
Tom Kiley and Mel Charles are close at hand.

flag, the position was without hope. A posse of defenders harrassed, and to contrive a neat, carefully pointed pass, appeared as impossible as to outwit, single-footed, so many claret-coloured men . . . Suddenly the right foot swung. The ball lifted and, windswept, went directly into the distant net.

Those 'claret-coloured men', included John Bond, Noel Cantwell, Malcolm Allison and Dave Sexton, for the opponents were West Ham. Ivor's goal was the first of seven which the crowd of 25,000 saw that afternoon. Burgess was an inspiration and, with Kiley and Charles, formed a formidable half-back line. It was a fine start, but results for the next two games were disappointing. The team lost at Blackburn and Doncaster despite playing fine football, but, even then, they created a club record. For the Blackburn match they fielded an all-Welsh side, nine of whom were born in the Swansea area. In that respect, at least, the founders of the club would have been distinctly proud of their successors. Meantime, the directors must have been congratulating themselves. Their 'grow-your-own' policy appeared to be working.

After the defeat of Doncaster in the following game, the directors were delighted to note that the gate for the next home match – against Fulham – was 27,000. Indeed, in three matches at the Vetch over 72,000 had paid for admission. The atmosphere created by the relative success of the team plus the

size of the crowds must have given the directors considerable comfort. Whatever the reason – probably Burgess's influence – Arthur Willis, a 34-year-old full-back was signed in time for a game against Liverpool. Willis, a stylish player, was well-used to the flowing football which the Swans were playing at the time. Whilst he cost just £3,000, he was to prove to be a fine investment.

At the end of the season the team occupied a mid-table position in their division. It had been a campaign of contrasts. They lost 7-0 to Bristol Rovers and were beaten 5-2 by Leeds, 5-3 by Stoke and 5-1 by Fulham. On the other hand, in addition to the West Ham victory, they had won convincingly against Port Vale 7-1, and Ipswich 6-1. Indeed, the style of play meant that the team had little problem in scoring; they found the net on 86 occasions. The problem was that they conceded only three fewer. From the financial point of view, the gate income for the season was considerably better than it had been for the previous term. Indeed, the average gate was only a thousand fewer than it had been during the halcyon season of 1948-9. Nonetheless, the board continued to monitor expenditure carefully and they let it be known that they were spending more money than they could afford 'given the degree of support we are getting'. Yet that support was buoyant, and the club had earned considerable income from the FA Cup. After beating Blackburn in the third round, they attracted a gate of 27,982 for the next round versus Stoke, which they

won. For the fifth round they were paired at home with Sunderland, then the big spenders in the Football League. After drawing a thrilling Vetch tie, 2-2, watched by 28,500 people, they attracted 39,671 to the replay at Sunderland, where the home side scored the only goal of the game. It was difficult to see how they could improve upon that in income-generating terms. Certainly, the Vetch could not hold many more.

On the playing front the fans were beginning to feel that they had the basis of a fine side. In particular, the young forward line (average age twenty-three) was outstanding. Harry Griffiths scored 16 goals, Mel Charles 13, Terry Medwin 12, Cliff Jones 10 and the majestic Ivor netted 20. In April, the side which took the field against Lincoln contained nine caps, while the other two, Tom Kiley and Dai Thomas, had both been Welsh reserves. There was further encouragement, too. Not only did the town's outstanding schoolboy side beat Cardiff for the Welsh Shield, but the next day, after travelling all the way to Manchester, they were victorious over the local boys to win the English Shield once again. Among the boys in that team was Herbert Williams, a player who was to give stalwart service to the Vetch club in the years to come. Others who were on the club's staff at that time, all products of the same stable as Williams, remembered their mentor at Christmas. Cliff Jones and Mel Charles presented a gift to Joe Sykes, now chief trainer, to which they attached a message: 'In appreciation of the great help you have given us'. That meant a great deal to a true gentleman of the game.

1955-56

As players and supporters were looking forward to the new season, there came the news that Billy McCandless had died. Whilst it is fair to say that the manager was hardly a dynamic figure, and that he was not comfortable with the constraints of management, he made a fine contribution to Swansea football. He marshalled the side to win the championship of Division (Three) South, and it was his introduction of Richards and Lucas into the team built by his predecessor which most clearly illustrated his

Three sets of brothers who played at Elland Road in the Leeds v. Swans league match, October 1955: John and Mel Charles, Len and Ivor Allchurch, and Cliff and Brin Jones.

perception. His sides played football with a panache which was appreciated wherever they went. Later, another stalwart, chief scout, Glyn Evans was killed in a bus crash. That accident robbed the club of another loyal and energetic servant who had made a considerable contribution to Swansea football.

Following McCandless's death, the directors decided not to replace him 'for the time being'. Instead, they gave Ron Burgess the title 'team manager', and established a three-man selection committee, with Ivor and Joe Sykes joining him for that purpose. Although the chairman was moved to say that the board looked forward to the new season with great confidence, others disagreed. Bill Paton, now the *Post's* scribe, for example, wrote in the club handbook: 'If there is to be a really serious bid to bring First Division football to the Vetch . . . I would say that the present side is not sufficiently well-balanced.' After the first five games of the new campaign, Paton appeared to be the better judge. Only four points had been gathered and the team had been thoroughly beaten at Middlesbrough. Prior to the next home game, Paton reported a conversation which he had had with the chairman regarding a rumour that Alf Sherwood was coming to the Vetch. 'We are not

after players', he was told, and, in fairness, they did not appear to need any after Bury were beaten 5-3 in a scintillating match. Two days later, Rotherham were the victims by 4-1. Following that match, the side put together an exhilarating run, including comprehensive wins at Bury (4-2) and Notts County (5-1). Every player in the forward line which did duty in the Nottingham game was a Swansea-born international.

For the match against Leeds at the Vetch on 1 October, in the middle of a run of eleven games without defeat, a new league attendance record was set: 29,477 people were in the ground and the gates closed thirty minutes prior to kick-off. Whilst that match ended in a draw, victory in the following game, against Doncaster, pushed the team into second place in the division. After winning the following match at Bristol, they were top. The young team grew in confidence with every match, with Kiley, then thirty-one, the squad's father figure and dominant force in the centre of the defence. The chemistry of the team seemed to make it irresistible. Even when three players were on international duty, reserves, Bobby Henning, Des Palmer and Dai Thomas, slotted into the side as though they were regular members.

For the sixteenth game of the season Liverpool were the visitors. By that stage confidence knew no bounds and, whilst little was said about it, the optimists were beginning to dream about promotion. Despite its indifferent start, the team had won ten of their fifteen matches and drawn two. Ron Burgess, who had played just once up to that point, waxed lyrical. He described his charges as 'the best team I have seen for many years'. The supporters had no doubt about that, either, when Liverpool, themselves a fine side, were well-beaten in a match which Bill Paton described as being 'filled with tension and high drama'. It was a game, too, in which the value of not giving up was demonstrated through Terry Medwin, who scored a superb goal to win the match. In the week which followed the whole of Swansea basked in the success of the Swans. Unfortunately, following a mid-week training session, it was announced that Tom Kiley had suffered a serious knee injury. As far as the team was concerned, had it been the stalwart's achilles heel the injury might have been more appropriate.

Without a ready-made substitute for the popular centre-half, in the next match the top-of-the-table Swans were humiliated by Leicester City, losing 6-1. That game was the beginning of dreadful sequence of eight games only one of which was won. At that, the directors did agree that a suitable player should be signed, but Burgess, within the financial constraints laid down by the board, had little success. He did sign Tom Brown from Llanelli for £3,000, but the player turned out just once during the season.

By 6 December the Swans had slipped to fourth and, after Christmas to sixth. In January morale was rock-bottom. Without Kiley the team seemed to have lost its collective confidence and its rhythm was badly disrupted. Throughout this time, Burgess strove manfully whenever he played, in particular having a wonderful game against Fulham when he was thirty-nine. Meanwhile, despite the games which had been lost, the Swans maintained a position among the leaders until well after Christmas. Indeed, as late as Easter they were still in position to challenge for promotion. It was not to be; when

Two Swansea-born Football League legends, Ivor and Fordy, with referee Mervyn Griffiths shake hands before the 1956 Welsh Cup final. It was the famous referee's final match.

the final matches had been played, they were in tenth position in the league. Not surprisingly, after the euphoria of the first third of the season, there was disappointment at this outcome among players and supporters alike. Among them was Terry Medwin, who, after discussions with Ron Burgess and certain directors, asked for a transfer on the grounds that, given the board's philosophy, he could not see the Swans achieving promotion to Division One. On 30 April the player joined Spurs for £18,000. It was the beginning of an exodus which was to take the heart out of Swansea soccer.

1956-57

The chairman's comments in the Supporters' Club handbook made interesting reading. He wrote:

'It does not make us overlook the fact that it takes quite a time to develop young players and [as a result] we may have serious gaps in our team . . . We are intending to fill the gaps with players of experience.

Later, his colleague J. Laidlaw-Murray claimed in a press interview that they were 'leaving no stone unturned to get the players we want

before the season starts'. Yet, Burgess was reporting that 'prohibitive fees were being asked for players'. It appeared that the brief given the manager was that he could spend about half the money received for Medwin on two players. It was the same ineffective approach which had dogged the pre-war activities of the club. In a market where quality players were attracting fees of £20,000, a quarter of the sum would buy little more than a 'workman', a grade of player highly unlikely to compensate for the loss of an experienced international.

On 20 August, three players joined the club. The first was Derek King, an old colleague of Burgess's at Spurs, who cost £2,000. Despite the episode with the Cardiff winger, he was signed without a medical examination. He played just five games before being forced to give up the game as a result of a knee defect. In October, Mal Morris joined the club from Pembroke. Morris, who was twenty-four, was a late entrant to league soccer and never reached the necessary standard to justify his £500 fee. A similar fee was paid for Derek Blackburn, a centre-half from Ossett Town. He, too, failed to make the grade. With due respect, all three represented the ludicrous purchasing policy which the board was adopting.

However, such considerations were far from the minds of supporters after the first match of the new season. Blackburn, admittedly reduced to ten men after thirty minutes, were soundly beaten 5-1. Mel Charles, playing at inside-right scored four. That win was followed by another at Barnsley, and with West Ham being beaten in London, the team had taken maximum points from the first three games. Even the cautious turned their thoughts to promotion. Then, inexplicably, the return match with Barnsley was lost at the Vetch and the Swans slipped to fourth place in the table. Unhappily, there followed two heavy defeats, 4-1 by Nottingham Forest at home and 7-3 at Fulham. On 11 September the *Post* reported that an offer of £12,000 had been made for Alf Stokes, which encouraged the supporters, but when neither Stokes nor anyone else arrived at the Vetch, large numbers showed their discontent by staying away. The gate for the Forest match had been 24,478. For the match

Cliff Jones

John King

but such success was short-lived. Even worse, from the supporters' point of view was the news that several other clubs were trailing the Swans wherever they went. Ivor, in particular, was said to be the target, which was not surprising, for he was in superb form, scoring a goal in each of nine successive games, including a cup-tie at Wolverhampton. In the last of these, against Bury, it was reported that he 'waltzed around five men to score' Even the home crowd applauded. After losing to Fulham in a 'nine-goal thriller', the team managed a series of six matches without defeat. Although the optimists saw this as turning the corner, their hopes were dashed yet again. Middlesbrough

against Lincoln less than half that number were in the ground.

Throughout October and November the *Post* printed critical letters from disappointed fans, urging the board to find new men. In November, Tom Kiley, who had bravely tried to shore up the defence had to have a knee operation. It was a sad ending to the career of a fine and well-liked player In that month, too, Des Palmer, Cliff Jones and Ivor all asked for transfers. In due course, all three were persuaded to stay, though it was not to be for many seasons.

There was some encouragement over the Christmas period: West Ham and Bristol City being beaten,

> *During a match against Middlesbrough in March 1957, Brin Jones, who believed that the referee had blown up for a foul, picked up the ball in his own penalty area. He was in error and a penalty was awarded which was converted by Swansea-born Harris.*

won 6-2, with a man called Clough scoring twice.

The club was tenth in Division Two when the season ended; a position which had been achieved largely as a result of the winning sequence in the new year. The team's best achievement had been to reach the final of the Welsh Cup, only to lose to Wrexham by the odd goal in three. With John Charles having gone to Italy in April, Mel Charles told the press that he would 'jump at the chance', whilst Ivor was said to be joining another club in Italy. True to form, the rumour-mongers enlarged on these stories. All the stars were to leave.

Swansea Town FC Season 1952/53 Division 2

#	Date	V	Opponents	Score	Scorers	Att.	King J	Keane TR	Beech G	Williams D	Kiley TJ	Thomas DA	Medwin T	Lucas WH	Turnbull R	Allchurch I	Beech C	Scrine FH	Leavy S	Griffiths H	Groves EG	Palmer D	Dewsbury J	Bellis A	Jones B	Pearson DJ	Allchurch L	Morgan AR	Charles M	Harrop J	Jones CW	Scrine WH	Edwards C
1	Aug-23	H	Sheff. United	1 2	Allchurch	24,103	1	2	3	4	5	6	7	8	9	10	11																
2	Aug-27	A	Doncaster Rovers	3 2	Turnbull, Scrine 2	16,164	1	2	3		5	6	7	4	9	10	11	8															
3	Aug-30	A	Barnsley	1 3	Turnbull	11,797	1	2	3		5	6	7	4	9	10	11	8															
4	Sep-04	H	Doncaster Rovers	2 1	Turnbull 2	19,531	1		3		5	6		4	9	10	11	8	2	7													
5	Sep-06	H	Lincoln City	1 1	Turnbull	21,570	1	2	3		5	6		4	9	10	11	8		7													
6	Sep-10	A	Luton Town	1 3	Beech C	13,218		2	3		5	6	8	4	9	10	11			7	1												
7	Sep-13	A	Hull City	1 1	Griffiths	29,088	1		3		5	6	8	4	9	10	11			7													
8	Sep-18	H	Luton Town	4 2	Medwin 2, Griffiths 2	17,358	1		3		5	6	9	4		10	11		2	7		8											
9	Sep-20	H	Blackburn Rovers	1 1	Lucas	22,237	1		3		5	6	9	4		10	11		2	7		8											
10	Sep-27	A	Nottm. Forest	4 6	Lucas (pen), Beech C, Griffiths, Allchurch	18,035	1		3		5	6	9	4		10	11		2	7		8											
11	Oct-04	H	Everton	2 2	Palmer, Own Goal	22,954	1		3		5	6	9	4		10				7		8	2	11									
12	Oct-11	H	Birmingham City	1 1	Medwin	21,074	1		3		5	6	9	4		10				7		8	2	11									
13	Oct-18	A	Bury	3 1	Griffiths 2, Scrine	17,356			3		5	6	9	4		10				7	1	8	2	11									
14	Oct-25	H	Southampton	1 2	Beech G	20,380			3	4	5	6	9			10				7	1	8	2	11									
15	Nov-01	A	Notts. County	4 3	Medwin 2, Scrine 2	21,171			3		5		4	8		10	11	9		7	1		2			6							
16	Nov-08	H	Leicester City	1 1	Kiley	20,981			3		5		4	8		10	11	9		7	1		2			6							
17	Nov-15	A	West Ham United	0 3		18,600			3		5	6	4	8	9	10	11			7	1		2			6							
18	Nov-22	A	Fulham	1 1	Scrine	20,118			3		5		4	8		10		9		7	1		2			6	7						
19	Nov-29	A	Rotherham United	1 2	Griffiths	12,019					5	6	4	8		10	11	9	3	7	1		2										
20	Dec-06	H	Plymouth Argyle	2 2	Allchurch, Medwin	20,661					5	6	4	8		10	11	9	2	7	1							3					
21	Dec-13	A	Leeds United	1 5	Allchurch	21,065					5	6	4	8		10	11		2	7	1				9			3					
22	Dec-20	A	Sheff. United	1 7	Lucas (pen)	19,842		3		2		6	4	8		10	11	9		7	1								5				
23	Dec-25	A	Huddersfield Town	0 3		28,510		3		4	2	6			9	10	11	8		7									5				1
24	Dec-27	H	Huddersfield Town	3 3	Turnbull, Allchurch, Medwin	24,978		3		4	5	6	7	8	9	10			2	11	1												
25	Jan-03	H	Barnsley	3 0	Allchurch, Medwin, Lucas	19,607				4	5	6	7	8	9	10				11	1							3	2				
26	Jan-17	A	Lincoln City	1 3	Beech C	14,002				4	5	6	7	8		10	9			11	1							3	2				
27	Jan-24	H	Hull City	3 0	Beech C 2, Medwin	18,323				4	5	6	7	8		10	9			11	1							3	2				
28	Feb-07	A	Blackburn Rovers	0 3		21,324				4		6	7	8		10	9		2	11	1							3	5				
29	Feb-14	H	Nottm. Forest	2 1	Thomas, Allchurch	15,946		2		4		6	7	8		10	9			11	1							3	5				
30	Feb-21	A	Everton	0 0		39,618		2				6	7	4		10	9	8		11	1							3	5				
31	Mar-07	H	Bury	2 0	Jones B, Allchurch	17,711		2				6	7			10	9			11	1				8			3	5				
32	Mar-11	A	Birmingham City	4 1	Beech C 2, Medwin 2	7,119		2				6	9	4		10	11			7	1				8			3	5				
33	Mar-14	A	Southampton	4 1	Medwin, Allchurch, Jones B, Griffiths	16,852		2				6	9	4		10	11			7	1				8			3	5				
34	Mar-21	H	Notts. County	5 1	Allchurch 2, Lucas 2, Medwin	20,304		2				6	9	4		10	11			7	1				8			3	5				
35	Mar-28	A	Leicester City	1 2	Allchurch	15,226		2				6	9	4		10	11			7	1				8			3	5				
36	Apr-03	A	Brentford	0 0		17,876		2				6	9	4		10	11			7	1				8			3	5				
37	Apr-04	H	West Ham United	4 1	Lucas 2, Medwin, Griffiths	17,944		2				6	9	4		10	11			7	1				8			3	5				
38	Apr-06	H	Brentford	3 2	Allchurch 3	21,695		2				6	9	4		10	11			7	1				8			3	5				
39	Apr-11	A	Fulham	1 3	Beech C	26,077						6	9	4		10	11			7	1				8			2	5	3			
40	Apr-16	H	Leeds United	3 2	Medwin 2, Jones C	21,262		2				6	9	4		10	11			7	1							3	5		8		
41	Apr-18	H	Rotherham United	0 0		21,116		2				6	9	4		10	11			7	1							3	5		8		
42	Apr-25	A	Plymouth Argyle	2 3	Beech C, Medwin	21,030		2				6	9	4		10	11			7	1							3	5			8	
						Apps	11	21	18	22	27	37	39	38	12	41	34	13	10	39	30	6	9	4	12	4	1	9	20	1	2	1	1
						Gls			1		1	1	17	8	6	15	9	6		9		1			2						1		

#	Date	V	Opponents	Score	Scorers	Att.	King J	Keane TR	Beech G	Williams D	Kiley TJ	Thomas DA	Medwin T	Lucas WH	Turnbull R	Allchurch I	Beech C	Scrine FH	Leavy S	Griffiths H	Groves EG	Palmer D	Dewsbury J	Bellis A	Jones B	Pearson DJ	Allchurch L	Morgan AR	Charles M	Harrop J	Jones CW	Scrine WH	Edwards C
1	Jan-01	H	Kidderminster WC-5	2 0	Lucas, Beech C					4		6		8	9		11			7	1		2					3	5		10		
2	Jan-10	A	Newcastle Utd, FAC-3	0 0	Match abandoned after 7 mins.	63,449																											
3	Jan-14	A	Newcastle Utd, FAC-3	0 3		61,064				4	5	6	7		9	10				11	1	8						3	2				
4	Jan-29	H	Newport Co. WC-6	3 2		5,500				4	5	6	7			10	9		3	11	1				8				2				
5	Mar-05	H	Rhyl WC-S-F	2 3	Scrine, Medwin					4	5	6	7			10		9	3		1	8	2	11								

Swansea Town FC Season 1953/54 Division 2

#	Date	V	Opponents	Score	Scorers	Att.	Groves EG	Keane TR	Thomas DA	Lucas WH	Charles M	Williams D	Griffiths H	Jones B	Medwin T	Allchurch I	Beech C	Pearson DJ	Jones CW	King J	Kiley TJ	Scrine FH	Beech G	Allchurch L	Hole AV	Rowden LA	Palmer D	Leavy S	Harrop J	Price DT	Pressdee J	McIntosh A	Henning RI	Edwards C
1	Aug-19	H	Doncaster Rovers	0 1		20,041	1	2	3	4	5	6	7	8	9	10	11																	
2	Aug-22	A	Birmingham City	0 6		26,817	1	2	3	4	5		7		9	10	11	6	8															
3	Aug-27	H	Leeds United	4 3	Charles, Griffiths, Scrine 2	26,408		2	3		9	4	7			10	11	6		1	5	8												
4	Aug-29	H	Nottm. Forest	2 1	Allchurch I, (2 pens)	11,242	1	2	3		9	4	7			10	11	6			5	8												
5	Sep-02	A	Leeds United	2 3	Allchurch, Beech	20,949		2	3		9	4	7			10	11	6		1	5	8												
6	Sep-05	A	Luton Town	0 2		17,479		2	3			4	7	8		10	11	6		1	5	9												
7	Sep-10	H	West Ham United	1 1	Allchurch	21,015		2				4		8	9	10	11	6		1	5		3	7										
8	Sep-12	H	Plymouth Argyle	0 1		19,676	1	2				4		8	9	10	11	6			5		3	7										
9	Sep-14	A	West Ham United	1 4	Griffiths	22,383		2			8	4	11	7	10	9		6		1	5		3											
10	Sep-19	A	Bury	2 1	Medwin, Beech C	13,753		2				4	6	11	7	10	9		8	1	5				3									
11	Sep-26	A	Rotherham United	1 2	Allchurch	16,280		2				4	6	11	7	10	9		8	1	5				3									
12	Oct-03	A	Leicester City	0 0		21,721		2				4	6	7	10	11			8	1	5				3	9								
13	Oct-10	H	Oldham Athletic	4 0	Charles 2, Jones C(pen), Own Goal	15,910		2		4	9	6	7			10	11		8	1	5				3									
14	Oct-17	A	Everton	2 2	Charles 2,	48,644		2		4	9	6	7			10	11		8	1	5				3									
15	Oct-24	H	Hull City	1 0	Allchurch	18,925		2		4	9	6	7	8		10	11			1	5				3									
16	Oct-31	A	Notts. County	0 3		12,084		2		4	9	6	7			10	11		8	1	5				3									
17	Nov-07	H	Lincoln City	4 2	Beech, Palmer, Allchurch 2	10,074		2	3	4	9	6	7			10	11			1	5						8							
18	Nov-14	A	Bristol Rovers	1 0	Charles	25,692		2	3	4	9	6	11	7		10				1	5						8							
19	Nov-21	H	Brentford	1 0	Griffiths	16,627		2	3	4	9	6	11	7		10				1	5						8							
20	Nov-28	A	Derby County	2 4	Allchurch, Griffiths	17,739			3	4		6		11	9	10				1							7	5	8	2				
21	Dec-05	H	Blackburn Rovers	2 1	Allchurch, Beech C	17,399			3	4		6	7	11		10	9			1	5						8			2				
22	Dec-12	A	Doncaster Rovers	0 1		14,438		2	3	4	9	6	8	7	10	11				1	5													
23	Dec-19	H	Birmingham City	1 3	Medwin	12,493			3		9	6		11	7	10				1					4		5		8	2				
24	Dec-26	H	Stoke City	2 2	Griffiths, Charles	13,117			3		9	4	7		10		11	6		1	5						8			2				
25	Dec-28	A	Stoke City	0 5		17,787			3		9	4	7		10		11	6		1	5						8			2				
26	Jan-02	A	Nottm. Forest	1 2	Allchurch	18,795		2			8	6	11	4	7	10	9			1	5				3									
27	Jan-16	H	Luton Town	1 1	Medwin	16,785		2	3			6		8	9	10	11			1	5						7			4				
28	Jan-23	A	Plymouth Argyle	1 1	Allchurch	18,776		2	3			6		8	9	10	11			1	5						7			4				
29	Feb-06	H	Bury	2 1	Allchurch, Jones C	15,337		2			9	4	7		10	11			6	1	5				3		8							
30	Feb-13	H	Rotherham United	0 2		14,347		2			9		7	8	10		11		6	1	5				4					3				
31	Feb-23	A	Leicester City	1 4	Medwin	14,985		2		4	9	6				10	11			1	5						7			3	8			
32	Feb-27	A	Oldham Athletic	2 2	Allchurch, Price	12,528		2		4	9	6				10	11			1	5						7			3	8			
33	Mar-06	H	Everton	0 2		20,902				4		6				10	11			1	5						7			2	8	3	9	
34	Mar-13	A	Hull City	3 4	Allchurch, Charles 2	16,619				4	9	6		8		10	11			1	5						7			2		3		
35	Mar-20	H	Notts. County	2 2	Medwin, Williams	15,794		2		4	9	6		8		10	11			1							7	5				3		
36	Mar-27	A	Brentford	1 3	Williams	14,023		2		4	5	6			9	10	11			1							7		8			3		
37	Apr-03	H	Derby County	2 1	Medwin, McIntosh	11,972		2	3	4				8	10	6	11			1	5						7					9		
38	Apr-10	H	Lincoln City	1 3	Medwin	12,583		2	3	4	5			8	10	6	11			1							7					9		
39	Apr-16	H	Fulham	2 0	Jones C, Medwin	19,605		2	3	4		6		8	10		11			1	5						7					9		
40	Apr-17	H	Bristol Rovers	3 1	Charles, Palmer, Jones C	21,753		2	3	4		6		8	10		11			1	5						7		9					
41	Apr-19	A	Fulham	3 4	Allchurch 3	17,906		2		4		6		8	10		11			1	5						7		9	3				
42	Apr-24	A	Blackburn Rovers	0 1		31,202		2		4		6		11		10				1	5						7		8			3	9	
	Apps						4	23	35	18	31	36	26	8	29	40	23	14	24	38	20	5	11	17	21	1	11	5	9	4	4	5	0	0
	Gls										10	2	5		8	18	4		4			2					2			1		1		

#	Date	V	Opponents	Score	Scorers	Att.	Thomas DA	Charles M	Williams D	Griffiths H	Jones B	Medwin T	Allchurch I	Beech C	King J	Kiley TJ	Hole AV	Palmer D	Leavy S	McIntosh A	Henning RI	Edwards C
1	Jan-09	A	Barrow FAC-3	2 2	Thomas, Beech C	16,843	3	2	6	7		10	9	11	1	5	4			8		
2	Jan-14	H	Barrow FAC-3Rep	4 2	Kiley, Beech C, Allchurch 2(1 pen)	16,650	3	2	6	7	8	10	9	11	1	5	4					
3	Jan-25	A	Newport County WC-5	2 6	Palmer, Williams	3,971	3		6	7	8	9		11		5		10	2		4	1
4	Jan-30	A	Everton FA Cup-4	0 3		61,609	3	2	6	7	8	10	9	11	1	5	4					

Swansea Town FC Season 1954/55 Division 2

#	Date	V	Opponents	Score	Scorers	Att.	King J	Keane TR	Thomas DA	Burgess WAR	Kiley TJ	Charles M	Griffiths H	Medwin T	Palmer D	Allchurch I	Jones CW	Williams D	Allchurch L	Leavy S	Pearson DJ	Pressdee J	Willis A	Rees W	McIntosh A	Evans KP	Price DT	Jones B
1	Aug-21	H	West Ham United	5 2	Allchurch, Jones C, Palmer 2, Charles	25,329	1	2	3	4	5	6	7	8	9	10	11											
2	Aug-25	A	Doncaster Rovers	1 2	Kiley	15,504	1	2	3	6	5	4	7	8	9	10	11											
3	Aug-28	A	Blackburn Rovers	1 4	Jones C	27,697	1		3	6	5	2	11	9		10			8	4	7							
4	Sep-02	H	Doncaster Rovers	3 0	Allchurch, Griffiths, Charles	20,602	1		3	6	5	4	8	9		10	11		7				2					
5	Sep-04	H	Fulham	2 2	Griffiths, Allchurch	27,620	1		3	6	5	4	8	9		10	11		7				2					
6	Sep-06	A	Port Vale	0 1		18,603	1		3		5	4	8	9		10	11		7		6		2					
7	Sep-11	A	Leeds United	2 5	Jones C, Griffiths	20,040	1		3	6	5	4	8	9		10	11		7				2					
8	Sep-16	H	Port Vale	7 1	Griffiths,Jones C 2,Medwin 2,Allchurch L+Iv	22,265	1	2			5	4	8	9		10	11		7		6		3					
9	Sep-18	A	Notts. County	1 2	Jones C	17,928	1	2			5	4	8	9		10	11		7		6		3					
10	Sep-25	H	Liverpool	3 2	Griffiths 2, Allchurch L	25,836	1		4	6	5		8	9		10	11		7		3		2					
11	Oct-02	A	Bristol Rovers	0 7		28,731	1		3	4	5		8	9		10	11		7		6		2					
12	Oct-09	H	Middlesbrough	2 0	Allchurch, Medwin	24,399	1		3	4	5		8	9		10	11		7		6		2					
13	Oct-16	A	Birmingham City	0 2		19,998	1		3	4	5		8	10	9		11		7		6		2					
14	Oct-23	H	Hull City	1 0	Griffiths	18,067	1		3	6	5	4	8	9		10	11		7				2					
15	Oct-30	A	Luton Town	2 1	Griffiths 2,	15,555	1		3	6	5	4	8	9		10	11		7				2					
16	Nov-06	H	Rotherham United	2 1	Allchurch, Griffiths	21,955	1		3	6	5	4	8	9		10			7				2	11				
17	Nov-13	A	Stoke City	1 4	Allchurch	19,994	1		3	4	5		8			10			7		6		2		9			
18	Nov-20	H	Bury	1 1	Medwin	19,211	1		3	6	5	4	8	9		10	11		7				2					
19	Nov-27	A	Lincoln City	2 2	Medwin, Jones C	11,698	1		3	6	5	4	8	9		10	11		7				2					
20	Dec-04	H	Ipswich Town	6 1	Allchurch 3, Medwin 2, Allchurch L	18,150	1		3	6	5	4	8	9		10	11		7				2					
21	Dec-11	A	Nottm. Forest	0 0		13,112	1		3	6	5	4	8	9		10	11		7				2					
22	Dec-18	A	West Ham United	3 3	Charles, Medwin, Griffiths	15,230	1		3	6	5	4	8	9		10	11		7				2					
23	Dec-25	A	Plymouth Argyle	2 2	Allchurch, Allchurch L	14,416	1		3	6	5	4	8	9		10	11		7				2					
24	Dec-27	H	Plymouth Argyle	4 2	Medwin 2,Charles, Allchurch	27,242	1		3		5	4	8	9		10	11		7		6		2					
25	Jan-01	H	Blackburn Rovers	2 3	Griffiths 2	26,930	1	2	3	6	5	4	8	9		10	11		7									
26	Jan-22	H	Leeds United	2 0	Allchurch, Allchurch L	19,637			3	6	5	4	8	9		10	11		7				2			1		
27	Feb-05	H	Notts. County	3 0	Allchurch, Griffiths, Allchurch L	21,527			3	6	5	4	8	9		10	11		7				2			1		
28	Feb-12	A	Liverpool	1 1	Allchurch L	43,205			3	6	5	4	8	9		10	11		7				2			1		
29	Feb-26	A	Middlesbrough	2 4	Griffiths, Jones C	20,867			3	6	5	4	8	9		10	11		7				2			1		
30	Mar-05	H	Birmingham City	0 3		22,565	1		3	4	5		8			10	11	9	7		6		2					
31	Mar-12	A	Hull City	3 4	Charles 2,Allchurch	12,700	1		3	4	5	9	8			10	11		7		6		2					
32	Mar-19	H	Luton Town	2 1	Charles 2,	19,422			2	4	5	9	8			10	11		7		6		3			1		
33	Mar-31	H	Bristol Rovers	1 1	Allchurch	17,804			2	4	5		8		9	10	11		7		6		3			1		
34	Apr-02	H	Stoke City	3 5	Price 2, Burgess	12,901			2	6	5	4	8			10	11		7				3			1	9	
35	Apr-08	A	Derby County	4 1	Griffiths 2, Jones, Allchurch	14,923	1		2	6	5	4	11	9		10			8				3				7	
36	Apr-09	A	Bury	1 2	Charles	12,284	1		2	6	5	4	11						7			10	3					
37	Apr-11	H	Derby County	3 0	Charles, Price, Jones C(pen)	18,700	1		2	4	5		8	10	9		11				6		3				7	
38	Apr-16	H	Lincoln City	3 1	Jones C, Medwin, Allchurch	17,558	1		2	6	5	4	8	9		10	11		7				3					
39	Apr-20	A	Fulham	1 5	own goal	10,357	1		2	6	5		8	9			11			4			3		10		7	
40	Apr-23	A	Ipswich Town	1 1	Charles	18,514	1		2	4	5	9	8			10	11		7		6		3					
41	Apr-25	A	Rotherham United	0 2		22,033	1		2	6	5	4	8				11		7				3				9	10
42	Apr-30	H	Nottm. Forest	3 2	Allchurch, Thomas, Medwin	14,964	1		2	6		5	8	9		10	11		7				3					4
						Apps	35	4	41	38	37	38	42	33	5	36	41	1	38	4	16	3	32	1	2	7	6	2
						Gls			1	1	1	11	17	12	2	19	11		7								3	

#	Date	V	Opponents	Score	Scorers	Att.	King J	Keane TR	Thomas DA	Burgess WAR	Kiley TJ	Charles M	Griffiths H	Medwin T	Palmer D	Allchurch I	Jones CW	Williams D	Allchurch L	Leavy S	Pearson DJ	Pressdee J	Willis A	Rees W	McIntosh A	Evans KP	Price DT	Jones B
1	Jan-08	A	Blackburn R, FAC-3	2 0	Medwin, Jones C	34,337	1	3	2	6	5	4	8	9		10	11		7									
2	Jan-21	H	Llanelly, WC-5	6 2	Griffiths 2,Charles 3,Medwin																							
3	Jan-29	H	Stoke City FAC-4	3 1	Medwin, Griffiths, Allchurch I	27,892			3	6	5	4	8	9		10	11		7				2			1		
4	Feb-10	H	Wrexham, WC-6	4 4	Allchurch I,Burgess, Griffiths, O/Goal	7,800			3	6	5	4	8	9		10	11		7				2			1		
5	Feb-19	H	Sunderland FAC-5	2 2	Allchurch L, Medwin	28,500			3	6	5	4	8	9		10	11		7				2			1		
6	Feb-23	A	Sunderland, FAC-5 Rep	0 1		39,671			3	6	5	4	8	9		10	11		7				2			1		
7	Mar-09	A	Wrexham, WC-6 Rep	3 4	Griffiths 2, Allchurch I	9,878	1		3	4	5		8	9		10	11		7		6		2					

Swansea Town FC Season 1955/56 Division 2

#	Date	V	Opponents	Score	Scorers	Att.	King J	Willis A	Thomas DA	Charles M	Kiley TJ	Burgess WAR	Allchurch L	Griffiths H	Medwin T	Allchurch I	Jones CW	Jones B	Beech G	Price DT	Henning RI	Palmer D	Pressdee J	Leavy S	Pearson DJ	Nurse M	Peake D	Evans K	Brown T
1	Aug-20	A	Bristol City	1 2	Jones	31,618	1	2	3	4	5	6	7	8	9	10	11												
2	Aug-25	H	Middlesbrough	2 1	Jones(pen),Medwin	21,351	1	2	3	4	5		7	8	9	10	11	6											
3	Aug-27	H	West Ham United	4 2	Griffiths 2, Medwin, Beech	19,960	1	2	3		5		7	8	9	10	11	4	6										
4	Aug-31	A	Middlesbrough	1 4	Allchurch I	22,417	1	2	3		5		7	8	9	10	11	4	6										
5	Sep-03	A	Port Vale	0 3		21,769	1	2	3	4	5		7	8	9	10	11	6											
6	Sep-08	H	Bury	5 3	Allchurch I 2,Jones C,Medwin, Charles	13,870	1	2	3	4	5			8	9	10	11	6		7									
7	Sep-10	H	Rotherham United	4 1	Jones C, Jones B,Charles, Medwin	19,957	1	2	3	4	5			8	9		11	6	10	7									
8	Sep-17	A	Sheff. Wednesday	2 2	Allchurch I, Medwin	28,128	1	2		4	5		7	8	9	10	11	6	3										
9	Sep-19	A	Bury	4 2	Medwin 2,Charles,Beech	10,342	1	2		4	5		7	8	9	10	11	6	3										
10	Sep-24	A	Notts. County	5 1	Allchurch I 3,Medwin 2	16,679	1	2		4	5		7	8	9	10	11	6	3										
11	Oct-01	H	Leeds United	1 1	Griffiths	29,477	1	2		4	5		7	8	9		11	6	3		10								
12	Oct-08	H	Doncaster Rovers	2 0	Allchurch I, Thomas D	20,871	1	2	8	4	5		7		9	10	11	6	3										
13	Oct-15	A	Bristol Rovers	2 1	Charles, Allchurch I	30,042	1	2	8	4	5		7		9	10	11	6	3										
14	Oct-22	H	Hull City	4 1	Palmer,Griffiths,Medwin, O/Goal	16,648	1	2	8		5		7	11	9			6	3			4	10						
15	Oct-29	A	Plymouth Argyle	1 0	Medwin	24,270	1	2		4	5		7	8	9	10	11	6	3										
16	Nov-05	H	Liverpool	2 1	Allchurch L,Medwin	25,139	1	2		4	5		7	8	9	10	11	6	3										
17	Nov-12	A	Leicester City	1 6	Thomas	30,928	1	2	10	4		5	7	8	9		11	6	3										
18	Nov-19	H	Lincoln City	0 2		20,990	1	2	3	4			7	8	9	10	11	6						5					
19	Nov-26	A	Blackburn Rovers	0 3		24,289	1	2	3			5	7	8	9	10	11	6			4								
20	Dec-03	H	Stoke City	0 0		20,449	1	2	3			5	7	8	9	10	11	6			4								
21	Dec-10	A	Nottm. Forest	1 2	Jones C	10,790	1	2	3			5	7	8		10	11	6			4	9							
22	Dec-17	H	Bristol City	2 1	Griffiths, Henning	22,067	1	2	3	5			7	8	9	10	11	6			4								
23	Dec-24	A	West Ham United	1 5	Jones C	15,000	1	2	3	5			7	8	9	10	11	6			4								
24	Dec-26	A	Fulham	1 4	Jones C	18,789	1	2	3	5		4	7	8	9	10	11	6											
25	Dec-27	H	Fulham	2 0	Griffiths, O'Goal	26,059	1	2	3	5		4	7	8	9	10	11	6											
26	Dec-31	H	Port Vale	0 0		24,661	1	2	3	5		4	7	8	9	10	11	6											
27	Jan-21	H	Sheff. Wednesday	2 1	Allchurch I,Charles	14,285	1	2	3	4			7	8	9	10	11	6						5					
28	Feb-04	H	Notts. County	5 1	Jones C,Medwin 2, Griffiths 2	13,114	1	2	3	4			7	9	8	10	11	6						5					
29	Feb-11	A	Leeds United	2 2	Charles, Allchurch I	20,089	1	2	3	9			7	8		10	11	6			4			5					
30	Feb-18	A	Lincoln City	1 3	Allchurch L	7,842	1	2	3	9			7	8			11				4		10	5	6				
31	Feb-25	H	Bristol Rovers	1 2	Charles	23,528	1	2	3	9			7	8		10	11	6			4			5					
32	Mar-03	A	Hull City	4 1	O'Goal,Allchurch I,Medwin,Allchurch L	12,943	1	2	3	4	5		7	9	8	10	11	6											
33	Mar-10	A	Nottm. Forest	0 1		20,945	1	2	3	4	5		7	9	8	10	11	6											
34	Mar-17	A	Liverpool	1 4	Griffiths	48,217	1	2	3	4	5		7	8	9	10	11	6											
35	Mar-24	H	Leicester City	6 1	Medwin 3,Allchurch L,Griffiths 2	16,920	1	2	3	4			7	8	9	10	11		6							5			
36	Mar-31	A	Doncaster Rovers	1 3	Allchurch I	11,864	1	2	3	4			7	8	9	10	11		6							5			
37	Apr-02	A	Barnsley	2 3	Allchurch I,2	12,208	1	2	3	4			11	9	7	10	8	6								5			
38	Apr-07	H	Blackburn Rovers	2 1	Jones C, Medwin	17,493	1	2	3		5		11	9	7	10	8				4	6							
39	Apr-14	A	Stoke City	0 5		12,674	1	2	3		5		11	9	7	10	8				4	6							
40	Apr-21	H	Plymouth Argyle	2 2	Griffiths, Jones C	14,951	1	2	3	4			7	8	9	10	11	6									5		
41	Apr-28	H	Barnsley	3 1	Griffiths 2, Charles	11,502	1	2	3	4	5		7	8		10	11	6				9							
42	May-03	A	Rotherham United	3 2	Griffiths, Palmer, Jones C	5,415			3	4			7	8		10	11	6				9					5	1	2
	Apps						41	41	36	34	22	8	40	40	36	37	41	38	18	3	9	4	1	5	1	3	2	1	1
	Gls								2	8			4	16	18	15	11	1	2		1	2							

#	Date	V	Opponents	Score	Scorers	Att.	King J	Willis A	Thomas DA	Charles M	Kiley TJ	Burgess WAR	Allchurch L	Griffiths H	Medwin T	Allchurch I	Jones CW	Jones B	Beech G	Price DT	Henning RI	Palmer D	Pressdee J	Leavy S	Pearson DJ	Nurse M	Peake D	Evans K	Brown T
1	Jan-07	H	York City FAC-3	1 2	Griffiths	25,636	1	2	3	5		4	11	8	9	10		6		7									
2	Jan-28	A	Newtown WC-5	9 4	Griffiths 3,Allchurch 2,Medwin,Jones C,Allchurch L,Own Goal	5,000	1	2	3	4			7	8	9	10	11	6						5					
3	Feb-30	H	Chester WC-6	1 0	Charles	9,655	1			9	5	6	7	8		10		11		3									2
4	Mar-21	N	Newport Co. WC-S-F	5 2	Allchurch,Griffiths 2,Allchurch L,O/Goal	9,655	1	2	3	4	5		7	8	9	10	11	6											
5	Apr-30	A	Cardiff City WC-Final	2 3	Kiley, Palmer	37,500	1	2	3	4	5		7	8		10	11	6				9							

N – Ninian Park, Cardiff

Swansea Town FC Season 1956/57 Division 2

#	Date	V	Opponents	Score	Scorers	Att.	King J	Willis A	Thomas DA	King D	Peake D	Jones B	Price DT	Charles M	McIntosh A	Allchurch I	Griffiths H	Jones CW	Palmer D	Henning RI	Allchurch L	Kiley TJ	Pearson DJ	Brown T	Evans K	Morris M	Jones D	Beech G	Phillips D	Blackburn D
1	Aug-18	H	Blackburn Rovers	5 1	Allchurch I, Charles 4	20,513	1	2	3	4	5	6	7	8	9	10	11													
2	Aug-22	A	Barnsley	3 2	Charles, Price, Griffiths	13,610	1	2	3	4	5	6	7	8	9	10	11													
3	Aug-25	A	West Ham United	2 1	Peake, Jones C	17,067	1	2	3	4	5	6	7	8		10	9	11												
4	Aug-30	H	Barnsley	2 3	McIntosh, Griffiths	19,342	1	2	3	4	5	6	7	8	10		11		9											
5	Sep-01	H	Nottm. Forest	1 4	Price	24,478	1	2	3			5	6	7	9		10	8			4	11								
6	Sep-08	A	Fulham	3 7	Griffiths 2, O/Goal	25,375	1	2	3	5		6	11	4		10	8		9		7									
7	Sep-13	H	Sheff. United	4 1	Griffiths 2,Palmer, Allchurch I	17,570	1	2	3				11	4		10	8		9		7	5	6							
8	Sep-15	H	Bury	3 0	Griffiths, Palmer, Price	18,544	1		3				11	4	6		8	10	9		7	5	2							
9	Sep-22	H	Lincoln City	1 2	Allchurch I	12,941	1		3			6		4		10	8	11	9		7	5	2							
10	Sep-29	A	Rotherham United	1 6	Allchurch L	13,777	9	2	3			6				10	8	11			7	5	4	1						
11	Oct-06	A	Grimsby Town	0 5		13,507		2	3			6		4		10	8	11	9		7	5			1					
12	Oct-13	H	Doncaster Rovers	4 2	Griffiths 3, Charles	15,790	1		3	4		6		8		10	9	11			7	5	2							
13	Oct-20	A	Leyton Orient	0 3		16,771	1		3	4		6	11	8			9			10	7	5	2							
14	Oct-27	H	Middlesbrough	2 2	Allchurch I, Charles	17,522	1		3	4		6		8		10	9	11			7	5	2							
15	Nov-03	A	Leicester City	1 1	O/Goal	32,745	1		3	4	5	6			9	10	8	11			7		2							
16	Nov-10	H	Bristol Rovers	2 3	Allchurch I, Charles	16,833	1		3	4	5	6			9	10	8	11			7		2							
17	Nov-17	A	Notts. County	4 1	Morris, Jones, Charles, Allchurch L	10,248	1				5	3		4		10	8	11			7	6	2			9				
18	Nov-24	H	Liverpool	1 1	Charles	16,719	1	2			5	3		4		10	8	11	9		7		6							
19	Dec-01	A	Stoke City	1 4	Jones C (pen)	23,416	1	2			5	3				10	8	11	9		7		6	4						
20	Dec-08	H	Huddersfield Town	4 2	Allchurch,Pearson,Palmer, Allchurch L	13,781	1	2			5	3				10	8	11	9		7		6	4						
21	Dec-15	A	Blackburn Rovers	3 5	Allchurch I, Palmer, Jones	19,395		2			5	3		4		10	8	11	9		7		6		1					
22	Dec-22	H	West Ham United	3 1	Jones C(pen),Palmer, Allchurch I	12,091		2			5	3		4		10	8	11	9		7		6		1					
23	Dec-26	H	Bristol City	5 0	Charles 2,Allchurch I,Palmer, Allchurch L	17,954		2			5	3		4		10	8	11	9		7		6		1					
24	Dec-29	A	Nottm. Forest	3 4	Allchurch I, Palmer, Griffiths	18,372		2			5	3		4		10	8	11	9		7		6		1					
25	Jan-01	A	Sheff. United	2 2	Griffiths, Allchurch I	14,049		2			5	3		4		10	8	11			7		6			9	1			
26	Jan-12	H	Fulham	4 5	Griffiths 2,Charles, Allchurch I	17,906		2			5			4		10	8	11	9		7		6				1	3		
27	Jan-19	A	Bury	3 1	Allchurch I, Palmer, Griffiths	11,549	1	2			5			4		10	8	11	9		7		6					3		
28	Feb-02	A	Lincoln City	2 0	Griffiths, Jones C	10,629	1	2			5			4		10	8	11	9		7		6					3		
29	Feb-09	H	Rotherham United	1 0	Palmer	15,611	1	2			5	3		4		10	8	11	9		7		6							
30	Feb-16	H	Grimsby Town	3 1	Jones C 2, Palmer	17,569	1	2			5	3		4		10	8	11	9		7		6							
31	Feb-23	A	Doncaster Rovers	1 0	Jones C (pen)	5,113	1	2			5	3		4	10		8	11	9		7		6							
32	Mar-02	H	Leyton Orient	1 0	Allchurch L	18,446	1	2			5	3		4	10		8	11			7		6			9				
33	Mar-09	A	Middlesbrough	2 6	McIntosh, O/Goal	17,072	1	2			5	3		4	10		8	11	9		7		6							
34	Mar-16	H	Leicester City	2 3	Palmer 2	14,102	1	2			5	3	10	4			11		9		7		6			8				
35	Mar-23	A	Bristol Rovers	1 1	Palmer	21,270	1	2			5	3	10	4			11		9		7		6			8				
36	Mar 30	H	Notts. County	2 1	Palmer 2	13,826	1	2			5	3	10	4			8	11	9		7		6							
37	Apr-06	A	Liverpool	0 2		34,773	1	2			5	3	7	4			8	11	9				6			10				
38	Apr-13	H	Stoke City	1 0	Griffiths	15,090	1	2			5	3		4		10	8	11	9		7		6							
39	Apr-19	A	Port Vale	2 0	Allchurch L, Morris	12,729	1	2			5	3		4		10	11		9		7		6			8				
40	Apr-20	A	Huddersfield Town	2 2	Palmer 2	13,516	1	2			5			4			11		9		7		6			10		3	8	
41	Apr-22	H	Port Vale	2 2	Palmer, Griffiths	11,629	1	2			5	3		4			11		8		7		6			10			9	
42	Apr-27	A	Bristol City	1 3	Peake	19,344	1	2			5	3		4		10	8	11	9		7		6							
						Apps	35	16	39	5	33	36	13	39	7	30	40	32	30	1	37	8	12	26	6	8	2	5	2	
						Gls					2		3	13	2	13	18	9	18		6		1			2				

#	Date	V	Opponents	Score	Scorers	Att.	King J	Willis A	Thomas DA	King D	Peake D	Jones B	Price DT	Charles M	McIntosh A	Allchurch I	Griffiths H	Jones CW	Palmer D	Henning RI	Allchurch L	Kiley TJ	Pearson DJ	Brown T	Evans K	Morris M	Jones D	Beech G	Phillips D	Blackburn D
1	Jan-05	A	Wolves, FAC-3	3 5	Palmer 2, Allchurch I	38,399		2			5	3		4		10	8	11	9		7		6		1					
2	Jan-31	A	Hereford Utd, WC-5	0 0		3,000	1	2			5			4		10	8	11	9		7		6					3		
3	Feb-07	H	Hereford Utd, WC-5Rep	2 0	Allchurch I, Allchurch L	1,500	1	2				3		4		10	8	11			7		6			9				5
4	Feb-28	H	Pwllheli, WC-6	6 0	Price 2, Charles, Jones C(pen),Allchurch I, O/Goal		1	2			5	3	8	4		10		11			7		6			9				
5	Mar-28	N	Newport Co. WC-S-F	1 1	Thomas	12,500	1	2			5	3	10	4			11		9		7		6			8				
6	Apr-01	N	Newport C. WC-S-F. Rep	3 0	Palmer 2, Jones C	7,000	1	2			5	3		4		10	8	11	9		7		6							
7	Apr-15	N	Wrexham, WC-Final	1 2	Jones C	10,000	1	2			5	3		4		10	8	11	9		7			6						

N – Ninian Park, Cardiff

Chapter 13

Exodus and the Barcelona Formation

Mel Charles

When no new players were signed during the summer of 1957, the *Post* printed many letters criticising the inactivity. Manager Burgess, however, told the press that he had players on his books who stood 'as good a chance as any of getting into the First Division'. The paying customers, though, were not impressed: centre-stand season tickets at £16.16s were not selling quickly as the new season approached. As it happened, there were some new faces at the Vetch: two former Schoolboys, Barrie Jones and Mike Johnson joined the groundstaff.

As these young men were setting out on their footballing careers, an executive group representing Divisions Three (North) and (South) of the Football League was meeting to discuss a proposal for a fourth division. To Swans followers at the time, the discussion was purely academic. To those who were still following the fortunes of the club a decade later, the unpleasant realities of the proposed arrangement were to become markedly clear.

1957-58

The season started well enough, with the Swans gaining a point at Cardiff, where there was a 40,000 gate. Five days later, the doubters were astounded when Lincoln City were thrashed 5-1 (and Cliff Jones missed a penalty). Was Burgess right after all? The bush telegraph around Swansea had clearly worked well before the next Vetch match, for 26,542 came to see the Swans play Fulham – 4,000 more than had been at the Lincoln game. What they saw was a typical Fulham/Swans match, a 4-4 draw. As ever, the game was full

Dai Thomas

of excitement but, in defensive terms, the result was far from acceptable. It was true that John King limped at centre-forward for most of the match, but the Swans rearguard looked out-of-sorts. Many commentators blamed young Peake for most of the problems, yet, in fairness, he had little experience of senior football. Circumstances had pitched him from local parks to Second Division football far too quickly.

A few days after the Fulham game, Ray Daniel (then with Sunderland) asked for a transfer. Ron Burgess and the fans wanted him at the Vetch, but the asking price of £20,000 did not appeal to the board. After conceding a further four goals in their next match, and losing the fifth, the team sunk to fifteenth in the table. It was a position hardly in keeping with the talent in the side which, later that year, found itself

providing six men for the Welsh XI to play against East Germany. Whilst only five actually played, they formed the core of a Welsh side which won 4-1. Des Palmer scored a hat-trick to emphasise the point, and he was backed by Dai Thomas, Cliff Jones, Mel Charles and Len Allchurch.

By the end of November, Burgess must have felt that there nothing was going right for him. Mel Charles and John King had asked for transfers, though he persuaded them to stay. Despite the talent in the team, it had gained just twelve points from twenty matches and was firmly entrenched at the bottom of the table. Gate income reflected this situation, which concerned the directors, while the fans were clamouring for new faces.

On 14 December, after six consecutive home defeats, the beleaguered Swans beat Bristol City 5-1. It was a result which amazed the 10,200 supporters who watched the match, as well as those who had not bothered to come. After failing to score in the next fixture, the Swans beat Bristol Rovers 6-4, a result which prompted talk of a revival. Sadly, it was not to be: the handful of wins, encouraging though they were, lifted the club just one position above bottom place.

Burgess was now concerned, and he persuaded the board to allow him to buy a player. He chose George Wright, a West Ham full-back, the fee was set at £6,000, but when a medical check revealed a lump on an ankle, the deal was called off: the directors had learned their lesson about such matters. Meantime, rumours about impending transfers from the Vetch continued to circulate. For example, several clubs were reported as having watched Cliff Jones, but Burgess denied that he was for sale. On 6 January there was a departure: Dudley Price joined Southend for £3,000. Then, on the 25th of the month, Cliff Jones announced: 'Either they let me go or they won't'. Days later, the press reported that Arsenal were to play the Swans in a friendly at the Vetch (both clubs having been knocked out of the FA Cup). At this, Swansea's grapevine broadcasters made two plus two equal five. Renewed denials were of no avail. It had all been said before.

turned him down. Almost in desperation – for the threat of relegation was staring him in the face – Burgess signed Pat Terry from Newport for £5,000 and paid £3,000 for Billy Reed from Ipswich. Unfortunately, the new acquisitions did little to improve matters. By mid-March, even after Ray Daniel had been purchased from Cardiff for £3,000, the side had picked up only six points from the nine matches which it had played since the turn of the year. At that stage of the season the bookmakers were making the Swans favourites for relegation. Yet there was still considerable talent in the side. Burgess did his utmost to remind his charges of that fact and to motivate them to ensure that demotion would be avoided.

Ray Daniel

> **For the match against East Germany on 25 September 1957 six Swans were selected to play for Wales. In the event, only five appeared. They were: Des Palmer (who scored a hat-trick), Len Allchurch, Dai Thomas, Cliff Jones and Mel Charles.**

Throughout this period Burgess strove manfully to find a player to boost his side and, at the end of January, the manager announced that he was about to sign a full-back from Luton. Sadly for Burgess, the player changed his mind at the last minute and joined Aston Villa. As is so often the case, given the chance of joining either a struggling club or a successful one, the thoughtful professional will generally choose the latter.

Five days after its last denial that Cliff Jones was to leave, the board issued a statement to the effect that it had acceded to the player's 'persistent demands for First Division football'. Within an eventful two weeks, during which the tragic Manchester United air disaster occurred in Munich, Jones joined Terry Medwin at Tottenham. The fee was £35,000, a new British record for a winger. Ted Drake, the Chelsea manager, who had been out-bid for the player, declared 'Spurs have signed the best winger in Britain'.

Burgess was now given some money to spend, but Duquemin of Tottenham and Edwards of Charlton

On 22 March the quality of the side chosen to play Doncaster at home was demonstrated by the presence of seven internationals. Another cap, John Charles, home for his brother's wedding, sat in the stand and he and every Swans fan must have felt a sense of foreboding as the game progressed. After twenty minutes the visitors were two goals ahead and little seemed to be going right for the men in white. However, inspired by Harry Griffiths and Ray Daniel the Swans fought back to take both points by the odd goal in five. Those points were to prove invaluable. After each of the next three matches was lost, Derby County came to the Vetch to play the first of four remaining games, each of which was critical with respect to Second Division survival. The pressure was on!

After a clarion call from manager Burgess, almost 16,000 people came to the Vetch to see the Swans play Derby. 'Lift us to a win' was the appeal, and, whether it was such inspiration from the crowd or some new-found self-belief within the side, the Swans rose to the occasion.

Derby were beaten 7-0. The majestic Ivor scored a hat-trick, Mel Charles was described as 'ebullient' and Ray Daniel as 'the master of defence'. By any standards it was an incredible win, and was just the kind of morale booster that the team needed.

After taking three points from the next two games, one of which was won by a memorable Charles hat-trick, the Swans travelled to Bristol City for the final game of the season. It was a vital match! In order to ensure Second Division survival the side had to win. Happily, once again, the team and the fans responded to the challenge. Living up to its name, the Supporters' Club organised special excursions which helped boost the numbers of the several thousand fans who made themselves heard that day. The team responded and ran out the winners by two goals to one. Such was the noise at the end that Burgess and the board must have thought that they had won the FA Cup. Nonetheless, it had been a close-run thing! Burgess was to discover that it had been too close for his comfort.

1958-59

After stating that, in future, it was essential that the drama of the end of the previous season should be avoided, the board announced a savage cut in playing staff. Eleven players were listed and twenty-three retained. There was a ray of hope for the future, however: Swansea

Schoolboys won the Welsh Shield and youngster Barrie Hole was outstanding for them. In the close-season the club undertook a tour of Germany, during which little went right. Then, in June, it was announced that the club was to appoint a general manager. It was a decision which was to result in many changes at the Vetch. Meantime, Brin Jones joined Newport for £3,000, along with Dudley Peake, who cost the Gwent men £2,000. The money which Burgess received was used to bring Norman Lawson from Bury and Wendell Morgan from Gillingham, but it was the appointment at the end of the month which was to have the greatest impact upon things at the Vetch. Trevor Morris joined the club as general manager. The title seemed to indicate that the directors wished to have a man to whom they could delegate the running of the business which was Swansea Town. At first it was assumed that Ron Burgess would retain the title of team manager, but by the end of August the likeable Welsh international had resigned. He was not, he announced, prepared to accept the post of assistant manager.

Meanwhile, in his interviews with the press, Morris made it clear that, 'If the players I have do not come up to standard we will not hesitate to enter the transfer market.' As time passed, Swansea supporters were to understand that 'entering the transfer market' could mean selling as well as buying. As the future was to show, the new man must have had a clear idea as to how he was going to fund his spending.

At the end of August, with just two points from three games, the supporters were concerned. That concern was intensified by more transfer rumours. Newcastle wanted Mel Charles and Ivor, so the story went, while Arsenal were keenly interested in Charles. On the field, with only nine points from ten games, things were almost as bad as they had been during the previous season, though there was one bright spot: Herbie Williams (seventeen years old) made his debut and did well in a fine 5-0 victory over Sunderland. Ivor, however, was the star of the day, scoring four. That feat was the trigger for further rumours about Ivor leaving the Vetch and on 3 October the player

confirmed that he had asked for a transfer. He said that he was twenty-eight and that it was 'now or never'. Presumably after taking the advice of their manager, the directors acceded to Ivor's request. Several clubs responded immediately to the news, but, after just one week, the 'Golden Boy' opted to go to Newcastle. It was a sad day for Swansea fans, many of whom likened the act to selling the crown jewels. None were sadder than Ivor's mentor, Joe Sykes, who had spotted the gangling youngster playing in a Swansea park and had taken the fifteen-year-old to Haydn Green.

The speed with which Trevor Morris now moved indicates that he must have laid his plans some time before Ivor made his request to leave. Within days, Colin Webster was signed from Manchester United for £6,000, while Reg Davies came from Newcastle in part exchange for his international colleague. Overall,

Morris could report a surplus on the three deals of some £19,000 and, what was more, he argued that he had purchased two international players of standing. Unfortunately, the changes did little to improve matters and the side hovered in a lower-middle-table position up to the end of the year.

Herbie Williams, meantime, continued to impress the better judges. Against Middlesbrough, for example, he hammered a superb shot past a helpless Peter Taylor to register his first league goal. He had, wrote Bill Paton, an old head on young shoulders. Herbie, who was to give the club outstanding service, had a marvellous mentor in that tradition. Harry Griffiths, looking after the reserves, picked the youngster at left-half. Williams's response, 'I'll play anywhere for the club', personified the young man's attitude throughout his career at the Vetch.

Two outstanding clubmen enjoy training.

As a result of transactions in the transfer market, particularly the sale of Cliff Jones, the chairman was able to tell the AGM that the club had made a record profit for the year ending 10 June 1958. This enabled the directors to reduce the overdraft from £27,000 to £8,000. Taken together with the money received for Ivor Allchurch (which would be included in the following year's accounts), this provided the board with some comfort. They could argue, too, that the team's results were somewhat better than the previous season. Bill Paton, however, thought this view to be superficial. After analysing the information provided, his conclusion was that the only way the club could survive was to gain promotion to Division One or develop young players and sell them. Nonetheless, both he and the board were heartened when the Supporters' Club, through extensive fund-raising, guaranteed to cover the cost of putting a roof over the main bank. It was a tremendous gesture and one from which generations of Swans supporters have benefitted.

1959 started with the team in mid-table and Reg Davies was beginning to make his mark, scoring a fine hat-trick for example in a 4-4 draw with Derby. In addition, Reg was one of the eleven who created a new club record in the first month of the new year. The team which played at Fulham that day contained eleven Welsh internationals. Eight were full caps, while the other three had played for Wales at youth level. Fulham found the combination to be too hot to handle, and their promotion drive was jolted by a fine Swansea win.

Later in the month, on the day when more successful sides were playing in the FA Cup, the Swans played a friendly against Manchester United. Yet again, the match was hailed by the fans as the harbinger of further Vetch sales and, since Mel Charles had appointed a solicitor to act for him, rumours that he was about to leave reverberated around the town. Trevor Morris, angered by these stories, and by Charles's decision to engage a solicitor, threatened 'appropriate action' if the rumours did not stop. Charles would not comment, which did little to re-assure the Swansea public.

The arrival of Graham Williams from Everton in February helped to distract the fans' attention, for he proved to be an immediate favourite. 'Flicka', as he became known, was received enthusiastically. He 'took players on', he was fast and brave and could cross a ball well, and at £5,000 he was thought to be a genuine bargain. That transaction was not the end of manager Morris's wheeling and dealing, either. In March, Des Palmer went to Liverpool in return for £4,000 and wing-half Roy Saunders. Saunders was reluctant to come to Swansea, but was persuaded by Harry Griffiths with whom he subsequently enjoyed a life-long friendship. However, the positive impact of the purchases had hardly been savoured by the fans when the 'Charles is going' rumour became reality.

The Swans were talking about a record fee, which the player thought to be ridiculous, though the bidding clubs did not. Tottenham headed the queue and found that their bid was accepted by the Vetch club. Charles said later that he did not want to leave the town, but, faced with a clear message from Morris that he could leave, he picked the lowest bidder and joined Arsenal. The fee was £43,000 plus Peter Davies. It was yet another Swansea sale record. In six short months the new manager had netted the club many thousands of pounds. In short-run business terms, to the board he must have seemed like Midas. To the fans, despite his forays into the market as a buyer, he was something less than that. As if in protest, only 6,743 turned up for a match against Brighton in April, while only 7,103 attended the final game of the season.

Nevertheless, the fans were not without hope. Young Mel Nurse was

> **When Mel Charles joined Arsenal for £43,000 the transaction set another 'highest fee received' record.**

Graham 'Flicka' Williams

playing exceptionally well at centre-half, youth cap Barrie Jones, was signed as a professional and the team finished the campaign in eleventh place in the table. Morris pointed to that as an achievement. It was true, he argued, that he had sold several local favourites, but, at least, his team had not had to fight relegation.

Events in the close-season illustrated another aspect of Trevor Morris's approach to his job. He was a respecter of loyalty, and made sure that Harry Griffiths received his £1,000 benefit for ten years service to the club. 'Griffiths,' stated Morris, 'is the acme of loyalty.' No one, then or since, would have disputed that.

Meanwhile, the Supporters' Club were deservedly in the limelight. On 18 August, Walter Bridgeman, president of the club, formerly handed over a cheque for £16,000 to Craven Llewellyn. The director thanked him on behalf of the board, describing the gift as a 'magnificent gesture'. The club had gained a cover for the 'Big Bank', a fact which has been greatly appreciated by many thousands of supporters over the last forty years. The Supporters' Club must have been justifiably proud. Another proud man was Trevor Hoskins, who retired during that same month. Hoskins, who had been an efficient secretary since the days of Haydn Green, left an ordered system for his successor.

Mel Nurse

1959-60

Despite the problems which manager Morris faced as the new season unfolded – there was a spate of injuries to key players – his regime appeared to be making progress. By the end of October the side were fourteenth in the league table and the new men seemed to be settling in. At the end of the previous month, the *Post* had printed a photograph of Mel Charles at the home of his mother-in-law at the time of the birth of his son. For Swans fans of the seventies it was a significant event: the baby's name was Jeremy. During October, another Swansea-born footballer, Mel Nurse, played an outstanding game for Wales against England. His direct opponent was a bustling centre-forward called Clough. At the Vetch, yet another local youngster, Barrie Jones, made his debut. It was as if to reaffirm that the Swansea air was conducive to the development of skilful footballers.

During October, when the Swans won just one match, Morris moved into the transfer market again, bringing Alan Sanders from Everton for a fee of £6,000. The signing was indicative of the manager's patience as a buyer. Several months before, following an enquiry by Morris, the Lancashire club had asked for a far larger fee. Morris withdrew at the time, and only moved when Everton contacted him with a reduced valuation. November ended with the club announcing that it had made a profit of £16,735 on the year's working. Since transfer fees received were £53,000 greater than those paid out, the figures must have been of considerable concern to the board. After all, it is only possible to realise an asset once and Morris had already sold his brightest gems.

After a half season of mediocre results, the Swans stood in a comparable position in the table to that of the previous season. However, there was one result which demonstrated the potential quality of the side: Plymouth were given a 6-1 thrashing, which delighted the crowd, Colin Webster scored a hat-trick. However, this was not the launch-pad for a revival in fortunes. Turn-of-the-year performances in the league reverted to the mundane, but, at least the cup gave Swans fans something to lift their spirits. As the Mumbles train made its final journey, the cup fever about which 'Alarch' had written more than thirty years before, attempted to re-establish itself in Swansea households. After beating Gillingham in the third round, the Swans were drawn to play First Division Burnley

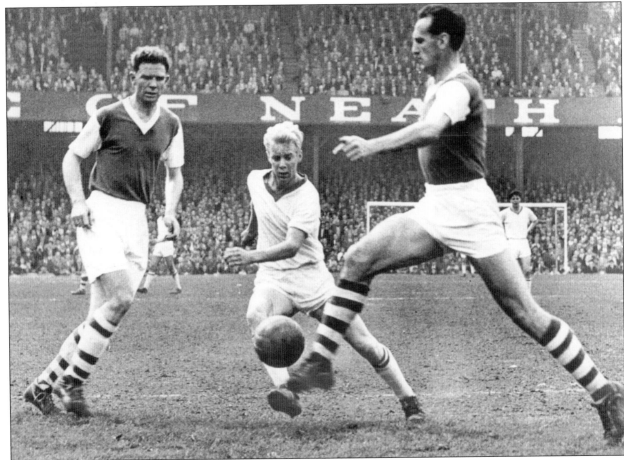

Barrie Jones competes with two Ipswich defenders.

at the Vetch and, in front of 30,000 people gave a good account of themselves. Indeed, Reg Davies had what many believed was a perfectly good goal disallowed. In the replay, at Burnley, Mel Nurse scored with a tremendous thirty-yard drive, but, at the end of the match, it was the Lancashire men who left the field as victors, though the home crowd joined with the Swans supporters in giving the men in white a standing ovation. They could now focus upon the league campaign whilst the board could count the gate income with alacrity.

It was not until February that the Swans won their first match of 1960, beating Charlton convincingly 5-2. Colin Webster scored the first goal of a hat-trick in just thirty seconds and Len Allchurch, who was the star of the game, provided superb crosses throughout the afternoon. The sole disappointment was the size of the crowd. Only 11,000 attended to enjoy the victory, a figure which was indicative of a downward trend in gates which was to continue until the season ended.

On 12 March, a new chapter in the club's history was opened. It involved what the manager called 'the Barcelona formation', in which, it was explained, the team lined up with four full-backs, two half-backs and four forwards. The home supporters, who had been brought up on a more traditional team structure, were somewhat bemused, as were Scunthorpe, who provided the opposition for the first game in which the new formation was used. Unfortunately, though, few other teams seemed at all concerned and only two of the next eight matches were won. Bill Paton, commenting on what he called 'the experiment', felt that the football had lost some of its usual sparkle. The journalist had put his finger upon a problem which, in the eyes of many traditionalists, has reduced the entertainment value of soccer since that time.

Even though the club stood in a respectable mid-table position, as the season progressed, interest in the Swans around the town was at a low ebb. As one correspondent to the *Post* put it, 'We are neither one thing nor the other. Please release that flair, Mr. Morris, before it dies.' Yet, there were several notable events during the last weeks of the season. On 23 April, Dai Thomas played his

300th League match for the club; at the end of March, young Mel Nurse captained the side for the first time; and on 26 April the youngest side ever to represent Swansea Town trounced Bristol City 6-1. It was true that the Swans were flattered by the size of the victory, but, given the youthfulness of the side, it was a remarkable result.

When the retained list was published, it named eleven players who were open to transfer. Only twenty were to stay at the Vetch. In May, Mel Nurse was awarded a well-deserved benefit and Trevor Morris denied that the player was to be transferred. There were other departures, though. Walley Boyes, who had had a heart attack, resigned from the post of trainer, as did one of his staff, Arthur Willis. In July, Walter Robbins joined as the new trainer, while stalwart Joe Sykes was given the title of assistant manager. Then, in July, John Irvine, who had replaced Trevor Hoskins as secretary also resigned. Changes at the Vetch, it seemed, were not confined to playing staff.

1960-61

Sunderland away was the first match of the new campaign. It was a tough start and, although the Swans acquitted themselves well, they lost 2-1. There was a new goalkeeper for the match: Noel Dwyer, purchased from West Ham for £3,500, made his debut in Swansea colours. Several seasons were to pass before he played the game of his life. The club had another new player on its books, too. He was John Haasz, a Hungarian refugee. Whilst he did not make the grade in league football, he was the forerunner of other east European footballers who would wear the white strip.

At the end of September, Dwyer must have wondered whether he had joined the right club. By then, the Swans had played ten games, won only once and were anchored firmly in twenty-second place. When the next match was also lost, Dwyer found himself in the reserves while John King was restored to the side. However, this did not change the trend: the side was rarely off the bottom of the table during that period. Despite the precarious position in which the club found

itself, the fact that it was losing money every week, and Mel Nurse had asked for a transfer, Morris still continued with his policy of rewarding loyalty. Len Allchurch was given a well-deserved benefit of £1,000 to reflect his ten years service. Unfortunately, gate receipts continued to decline and, for the board, the old Swansea standby policy of selling a player became more pressing as each week passed. Even the official opening of the club's new floodlight system did little to lighten the gloom.

Nevertheless, in both September and October, the board rejected Nurse's transfer request and turned down a £30,000 offer for the player from Manchester United. In October, after eighteen-year-old Keith Todd had made his debut, Morris bid £6,000 for Rochdale's Frank Lord. The player came to the Vetch for talks but returned to Lancashire having been unable to agree terms, though not before the wags had milked the potential of 'Lord help us'. During November, the *Post* noted that Billy Ball had died, aged seventy-two at his Swansea home. His passing severed a connection with the origins of the Vetch club and must have provoked many memories for the older Swans fans. Ball had been the first soccer folk hero the town had known.

At the AGM in December the chairman announced a loss on the year's working of £23,169, which, when combined with the club's position in the league, was disconcerting. Trevor Morris, though, no doubt wishing to lift morale, appeared in a confident mood. 'Although we are bottom,' he declared defiantly, 'we will not be relegated.' Few shareholders who were there that evening could share his confidence, but a week later the manager announced that Mel Nurse had agreed to stay. Nurse said that he was determined to help the club climb out of trouble. Was there a light at the end of the tunnel?

As if Mel Nurse's statement was received as a clarion call, the new year started in welcome vein. Port Vale and Preston were both beaten in the FA Cup, as were Norwich in the league. At Charlton, seeking a fourth win in succession, the team succumbed 6-2, though they lost Brian Hughes with a dislocated shoulder early in the game. As a

The Swans v. Pompey at the Vetch, December 1960.
Back row, left to right: Len Allchurch, Peter Davies, John King, Colin Webster, Brian Hughes.
Front: Alan Sanders, Reg Davies, Mel Nurse (Captain), Roy Saunders, Brayley Reynolds, Graham Williams.

result of its new-year victories, by the beginning of February the club had moved off the bottom of the table, while John King had been awarded a £1,000 benefit, and Barrie Jones and Herbie Williams had been capped at under-twenty-three level. At that stage, Morris's confidence appeared to have been well-founded. Even the pessimists were beginning to think that things were going to get better, particularly after the Swans beat Sheffield United (the clear leaders of the division) at the Vetch. Mike Johnson, standing in for the injured Nurse, had done exceptionally well in that game. Meanwhile, Mel Nurse was given the honour of captaining the Welsh Under-23 XI.

The last match in February, a 3-2 victory at Derby, was noteworthy for being the club's first 'double' for two years, and when Orient and Scunthorpe were beaten early in March, Morris could have been forgiven for saying, 'I told you so'. From bottom place at the turn of the year, the club had climbed to a respectable eleventh position and, as

time was to show, they were not finished yet! Nevertheless, there was one cloud on the horizon: Mel Nurse made his fourth request for transfer, declaring: 'I want to play in Division One.' Morris turned him down, but failed to convince the Cwmbwrla boy that his personal target was a possibility at the Vetch.

On 15 March there was a departure from the Vetch. John Harris, a former Swan, then manager of Sheffield United, had the bargain of his lifetime when he paid a modest £14,000 for Len Allchurch. Morris told the press that he did not want to lose the player, but 'we must balance our books'. It was not a popular argument with supporters and, despite the fact that the club had won seven matches in succession, only 13,181 came to see the side extend its run to eight by beating division leaders, Liverpool. Yet, Bill Paton in the *Post* thought that the team looked 'as good as any'. Their collective confidence, it seemed, 'knew no bounds'.

When Ipswich Town, champions

of the Second Division, were beaten on their own ground in the final game of the season, the Swans completed a remarkable sequence of results. From 4 February to the end of the season, they played sixteen league games, winning twelve and drawing four. In the process, they gathered twenty-eight out of a possible thirty-two points. From apparent certainties for relegation they had moved up the table to seventh position – the club's best position in Division Two for thirty-three years. Morris's comments at the AGM now took on a new significance. Had he found a side which could continue to win points as effectively as it had done during the last months of the season? The manager would only say that it was 'encouraging for next season'. There was other encouragement, too. The Swans won the Welsh Cup, beating Bangor City in the final after disposing of Cardiff in the semi-finals, and Ken Morgans, a survivor of the Munich air disaster, joined the club from Manchester United.

Swansea Town FC Season 1957/58 Division 2

#	Date	V	Opponents	Score	Scorers	Att.	King J	Thomas DA	Jones B	Charles M	Peake D	Brown T	Allchurch L	Griffiths H	Palmer D	Allchurch I	Jones CW	Morris M	Jones D	Reid RBA	Beech G	Woods AE	Pearson DJ	Blackburn D	Morris A	Price DT	Pope D	Leavy S	Willis A	Nurse M	Lewis D	Kennedy MSJ	Phillips D	McIntosh A	Rees W	Terry P	Reed WG	Daniel RW
1	Aug-24	A	Cardiff City	0 0		42,482	1	2	3	4	5	6	7	8	9	10	11																					
2	Aug-29	H	Lincoln City	5 1	Palmer,Allchurch,Jones C 2, (1pen), Allchurch L	22,462	1	2	3	4	5	6	7	8	9	10	11																					
3	Aug-31	H	Fulham	4 4	Allchurch L 2,Morris, Griffiths	26,542	1	2	3	4	5	6	7	8		10	11	9																				
4	Sep-04	A	Lincoln City	0 4		10,516		2	3	4	5	6	7	8	9	10	11		1																			
5	Sep-07	A	Barnsley	0 1		15,844		2	3	4	5	6	7	8	9	10	11			1																		
6	Sep-12	A	Notts. County	4 2	Allchurch I 2, Charles 2	11,397		2	3	4	5	6	7	8	9	10	11			1																		
7	Sep-14	H	West Ham United	3 2	Allchurch, Palmer, Allchurch L	19,352		2		4	5	6	7	11	9	10		8		1	3																	
8	Sep-19	H	Notts. County	1 3	Palmer	19,353		2		4	5		7	8	9	10	11			1	3	6																
9	Sep-21	A	Sheff. United	2 2	Griffiths, Palmer	16,725		2		10	5		7	8	9		11			1	3	4	6															
10	Sep-28	H	Blackburn Rovers	0 4		20,767		2	3	4				8	9		11	10		1		6	5	7														
11	Oct-05	A	Ipswich Town	1 0	Jones C	19,861		2	3	4	5		7	8	9	10	11			1		6																
12	Oct-12	A	Liverpool	0 4		37,204		2	3	4	5		7	8		10	9			1		6				11												
13	Oct-19	H	Middlesbrough	1 4	Leavy	8,904			3		5		11	8						1	10	6				7	4	9	2									
14	Oct-26	H	Leyton Orient	1 5	Jones C	16,354			3	4	5		7			10	11			1	8	6						9	2									
15	Nov-02	H	Charlton Athletic	1 3	Jones C	13,839	1				5		7	8		10	11			3	4	6						9	2									
16	Nov-09	A	Doncaster Rovers	0 3		9,256	1			4	5		7	8		10	11				3	6						9	2									
17	Nov-16	H	Rotherham United	1 3	Griffiths	12,984	1		11		5	3	7	8	9	10							6						2	4								
18	Nov-23	A	Huddersfield Town	2 2	Allchurch I 2	12,860			3	4	5		7	8	9	10	11			1									2	6								
19	Nov-30	H	Grimsby Town	0 2		12,573			3	4	5		7	8	9	10	11			1									2	6								
20	Dec-09	A	Stoke City	2 6	Price, Allchurch	23,613	1		3	4	5		7	2		10	11					8				9				6								
21	Dec-14	H	Bristol City	5 1	Jones C 2(1pen),Price,Allchurch L, O/Goal	10,206	1		3	4	5		7	2		10	11									9				6	8							
22	Dec-21	H	Cardiff City	0 1		19,483	1			4	5		7	2		10	11									9				6	8							
23	Dec-25	H	Bristol Rovers	6 4	Jones C 3,Charles 2,Allchurch I	11,340	1			9	5	4	7	2		10	11							3						6	8							
24	Dec-26	A	Bristol Rovers	0 3		22,678	1			9	5	4	7	2		10	11							3						6	8							
25	Dec-28	A	Fulham	0 2		24,784				9	5	4	7	2		10	11			1								3		6	8							
26	Jan-11	H	Barnsley	4 2	Charles, Jones B,Allchurch L 2	9,750	1			9	5	4	7	2		10	11											3		6	8							
27	Jan-18	A	West Ham United	2 6	Jones C 2(1pen)	27,277	1			9	5	4	7	2		10	11											3		6	8							
28	Feb-01	H	Sheff. United	0 2		13,545	1			6	5	4	7	3		10	11											2			8	9						
29	Feb-08	A	Blackburn Rovers	2 2	Morris 2	18,913	1			6	5	4	7	3		10	11											2			8	9						
30	Feb-15	H	Ipswich Town	0 0		10,136	1			6	5	4	7	3		10							9					2			8				11			
31	Feb-22	H	Huddersfield Town	1 1	O/Goal	13,400	1	2		6	5	4	7	3		10															8				11	9		
32	Mar-01	A	Middlesbrough	1 2	Terry	23,312	1	2		6	5	4	7	3												10									11	9	8	
33	Mar-08	H	Leyton Orient	1 2	Lewis	17,445	1	2		4			7	3																6	8				11	9	10	5
34	Mar-15	A	Charlton Athletic	1 1	Allchurch	21,539	1	2	10	4		6	7	3																	8				11	9		5
35	Mar-22	H	Doncaster Rovers	4 3	Allchurch, Allchurch L, Terry 2	13,961	1	2		4		6	7	3		10															8				11	9		5
36	Mar-29	A	Rotherham United	2 5	Allchurch I, Terry	7,064	1	2		4		6	7	3		10															8				11	9		5
37	Apr-05	H	Liverpool	0 2		17,526	1	2	8	4		6	7	3		10																			11	9		5
38	Apr-07	A	Derby County	0 1		14,683	1	2				6	8	3		10														4					11	9	7	5
39	Apr-08	H	Derby County	7 0	Allchurch 3,Charles,Daniel(pen),Allchurch L 2	15,862	1	2		8		6	7	3		10													11	4						9		5
40	Apr-12	A	Grimsby Town	2 2	Charles, Allchurch I	11,550	1	2		8		6	7	3		10													11	4						9		5
41	Apr-19	H	Stoke City	4 1	Charles 3, Allchurch I	20,569	1	2		8		6		3		10													11	4						9	7	5
42	Apr-24	A	Bristol City	2 1	Allchurch L, Terry	18,029	1	2		8		6	7	3		10													11	4						9		5
			Apps				28	24	26	40	22	26	40	42	11	32	27	6	1	13	12	13	5	2	1	8	2	8	9	9	14	4	1	1	5	12	8	10
			Gls						1	10			11	3	4	16	12	3								2		1			1					5		1

#	Date	V	Opponents	Score	Scorers	Att.	King J	Thomas DA	Jones B	Charles M	Peake D	Brown T	Allchurch L	Griffiths H	Palmer D	Allchurch I	Jones CW	Morris M	Jones D	Reid RBA	Beech G	Woods AE	Pearson DJ	Blackburn D	Morris A	Price DT	Pope D	Leavy S	Willis A	Nurse M	Lewis D	Kennedy MSJ	Phillips D	McIntosh A	Rees W	Terry P	Reed WG	Daniel RW
1	Jan-04	A	Burnley FAC-3	2 4	Charles, Lewis	26,593				9	5	4	7	2		10	11			1								3		6	8							
2	Jan-30	A	Newport Co. WC-5	5 2	Allchurch L 2,Lewis,Leavy,Jones	3,500	1			6	5	4	7	3		10	9											2			8				11			
3	Mar-06	A	Chester WC-6	0 2		1,872																																

Swansea Town FC   Season 1958/59   Division 2

#	Date	V	Opponents	Score	Scorers	Att.	King J	Thomas DA	Griffiths H	Woods A	Daniel R	Nurse M	Allchurch L	Charles M	Terry P	Allchurch I	Lawson N	Lewis D	Brown T	Palmer D	Morgan W	Williams H	Reid RBA	Davies Reg	Webster C	John DLJ	Hughes B	Kennedy MSJ	Davies Ron	Williams G	Saunders R	Davies P
1	Aug-23	A	Sheff. Wednesday	1 2	Lawson	23,177	1	2	3	4	5	6	7	8	9	10	11															
2	Aug-28	H	Scunthorpe United	3 0	Terry 2, Charles	21,056	1	2	3	4	5	6	7	8	9	10	11															
3	Aug-30	H	Fulham	1 2	Daniel	25,215	1	2	3	4	5	6	7	8	9	10	11															
4	Sep-04	A	Scunthorpe United	1 3	Terry	13,592	1	2	3		6	5	7	4	9	10	11			8												
5	Sep-06	A	Lincoln City	2 1	Allchurch I, Allchurch L	12,001	1	2	3			5	7	4		10	11		8	6	9											
6	Sep-11	H	Leyton Orient	3 3	Palmer 2, Allchurch L	18,624	1	2	3			5	7	4		10			8	6	9	11										
7	Sep-13	H	Sunderland	5 0	Palmer, Allchurch I, 4	22,696	1	2	3			5	7	4		10				6	9	11		8								
8	Sep-18	A	Leyton Orient	0 0		12,419	1	2	3			5	7	4		10				6	9	11		8								
9	Sep-20	A	Stoke City	0 3		20,196		2	3			5	7	4		10			8	6	9	11	1									
10	Sep-27	H	Charlton Athletic	2 2	Allchurch I, Palmer	19,520	1	2	8			5	7	4		10		3		6	9	11										
11	Oct-04	H	Ipswich Town	4 2	Terry, Charles, Griffiths 2	12,594	1	2	8			5	7	4	10			3		6	9	11										
12	Oct-11	A	Bristol City	0 4		24,309	1	2	8			5	7	4				3		6	9			10	11							
13	Oct-25	A	Huddersfield Town	2 3	Webster 2	15,629	1	2	3			5	7	4						6	9	11		8	10							
14	Nov-01	H	Middlesbrough	5 2	Williams, Lawson, Charles 3	15,741	1	2	3	4	5		7	9			11			6				10	8							
15	Nov-08	A	Rotherham United	3 3	Allchurch L, Davies, Lawson	7,005	1	2	3	4	5		7	9			11			6				10	8							
16	Nov-15	H	Sheff. United	0 2		17,381	1	2	3	6	5		7	4			11							10	8	9						
17	Nov-22	A	Brighton	2 2	Davies 2	18,674	1		3	4	5		7	9			11	10	6					8			2					
18	Nov-29	H	Grimsby Town	1 1	Palmer	14,244	1		3		5		7	9			11			6				10	8		2	4				
19	Dec-06	A	Liverpool	0 4		27,561	1	2	3		5		7	4			11			6	9			8	10							
20	Dec-13	H	Barnsley	2 1	Nurse(pen), Charles	10,038	1	2	3			5	7	9			11							8	10			4			6	
21	Dec-20	H	Sheff. Wednesday	4 0	Palmer, Charles 3	13,721	1	2	3			5	7	9			11							10	8			4			6	
22	Dec-26	A	Derby County	1 3	Charles	23,949	1	2	3			5	7	9			11							10	8			4			6	
23	Dec-27	H	Derby County	4 4	Davies 3, Nurse(pen)	19,942	1	2	3			5	7	9			11			6				10	8			4				
24	Jan-03	A	Fulham	2 1	Palmer, Davies	27,613	1	2	3			5	7	9										10	8	11		4			6	
25	Jan-17	H	Lincoln City	3 1	Palmer 2, Webster	7,809	1		3			5	7				11			9				10	8		2	4			6	
26	Jan-31	A	Sunderland	1 2	Allchurch L	28,595	1		3			5	7	9			11							10	8		2	4			6	
27	Feb-07	H	Stoke City	1 0	Charles	11,568	1		3		5		7	9										10	8		2	4		11	6	
28	Feb-14	A	Charlton Athletic	1 2	Webster	14,376	1		3		5		7								9			10	8		2	4		11	6	
29	Feb-21	A	Ipswich Town	2 3	Davies, Charles	11,024	1		3		5		7	9										10	8		2	4		11	6	
30	Feb-28	H	Rotherham United	3 0	Webster, Griffiths, Charles	11,340	1		3	4	5		7	9										10	8		2			11	6	
31	Mar-07	A	Cardiff City	1 0	Nurse(pen)	24,450	1		3		5		7	9										10	8		2	4		11	6	
32	Mar-14	H	Huddersfield Town	0 1		5,176	1		3	4	5		7	9										10	8		2			11	6	
33	Mar-21	A	Middlesbrough	2 6	Charles, Davies	15,229	1		3		5		7	9										10	8		2	4		11	6	
34	Mar-27	H	Bristol Rovers	2 1	Webster 2	14,921	1			4	5		7											10	8	9	2		3	11	6	
35	Mar-28	H	Bristol City	1 0	Davies	13,336	1		3	4	5		7											10	8	9	2			11	6	
36	Mar-30	H	Bristol Rovers	4 4	Allchurch L, Daniel, Davies, Williams H	15,148	1			4	5		7								9	3		10	8		2			11	6	
37	Apr-04	A	Sheff. United	0 2		16,062	1		3	4	5		7	9										10	8		2			11	6	
38	Apr-11	H	Brighton	4 2	Webster, Allchurch L, Williams H, Williams G	6,743	1		3		5		7									10			8	9	2			11	6	4
39	Apr-15	H	Cardiff City	1 3	Webster	14,893	1		3		5		7									10			8	9	2			11	6	4
40	Apr-18	A	Grimsby Town	1 0	Allchurch L	9,225	1		3	4	5		7									11		10	8	9	2				6	
41	Apr-20	A	Barnsley	1 3	Allchurch L	4,976	1		3	4	5		7									3		10	8		2			11	6	
42	Apr-25	H	Liverpool	3 3	Daniel 2, Allchurch L	7,103	1		3	4	5		7	9										10	8		2			11	6	
						Apps	41	22	41	17	30	25	42	31	5	10	23	5	15	17	7	10	1	31	23	4	23	8	2	15	12	2
						Gls			3		4	3	9	14	4	6	3			9		3		11	9					1		

#	Date	V	Opponents	Score	Scorers	Att.	King J	Thomas DA	Griffiths H	Woods A	Daniel R	Nurse M	Allchurch L	Charles M	Terry P	Allchurch I	Lawson N	Lewis D	Brown T	Palmer D	Morgan W	Williams H	Reid RBA	Davies Reg	Webster C	John DLJ	Hughes B	Kennedy MSJ	Davies Ron	Williams G	Saunders R	Davies P
1	Jan-10	A	Portsmouth FAC-3	1 3	Charles	23,106	1	2	3			5	7	9										10	8	11		4			6	
2	Jan-29	H	Newport Co. WC-5	3 1	O/Goal, Williams H, Daniel(pen)	4,200	1		3		5		7	9								11		10	8		2	4			6	
3	Feb-25	A	Bangor C. WC-6	2 3	Lawson, Nurse(pen)		1			6	4	2	5	7	9		11							10	8						3	

Swansea Town FC Season 1959/60 Division 2

#	Date	V	Opponents	Score	Scorers	Att.	King J	Hughes B	Griffiths H	Davies P	Nurse M	Saunders R	Allchurch L	Davies Reg	Daniel R	Reynolds B	Dodson D	Thomas D	Webster C	Williams G	Jones B	Kennedy MSJ	Lawson N	Reid RBA	Hale D	Sanders A	Williams H	Johnson M	Purcell B	Woods A
1	Aug-22	H	Lincoln City	2 1	Saunders, O/Goal	19,398	1	2	3	4	5	6	7	8	9	10	11													
2	Aug-26	A	Ipswich Town	1 4	Daniel	11,147	1	2	3	4	5	6	7	8	9	10	11													
3	Aug-29	A	Aston Villa	0 1		35,829	1	4	3		5	6	7	8		10	11		2	9										
4	Sep-03	H	Ipswich Town	2 1	Davies, Daniel	16,118	1	4	3		5	6		8	9	10	11		2	7										
5	Sep-05	H	Sunderland	1 2	Dodson	16,001	1	4	3		5	6		8	9		10		2	7	11									
6	Sep-09	A	Huddersfield Town	3 4	Reynolds, Webster, O/Goal	12,369	1	4	3		5	6	7	8		10	11		2	9										
7	Sep-12	A	Portsmouth	3 1	Reynolds, Webster 2	14,755	1	4	3		5	6		8		9	11		2	10	7									
8	Sep-17	H	Huddersfield Town	3 1	Davies 2, Reynolds	15,250	1	4	3		5	6		8		9	11		2	10	7									
9	Sep-19	H	Stoke City	2 2	Webster 2	14,626	1	4	3		5	6			9				2	10	11	7	7							
10	Sep-26	A	Brighton	2 1	Webster, Reynolds	20,960	1	4	3		5	6	7	8		9			2	10	11									
11	Oct-03	H	Liverpool	5 4	Davies, Allchurch, Webster, Reynolds 2	17,187	1	4	3		5		7	8		9	11		2	10		6								
12	Oct-10	A	Charlton Athletic	2 2	Dodson, Webster	13,487	1	4	3		5		7	8		9	11		2	10		6								
13	Oct-24	A	Scunthorpe United	1 3	Reynolds	9,675	1	4	3		5			8		9	11		2	10		6	7							
14	Oct-31	H	Rotherham United	2 2	Allchurch, Nurse(pen)	15,343	1	4	3		5	6	7	8		9			2	10				11						
15	Nov-07	A	Cardiff City	1 2	Webster	34,881		4	3		5		7	8		9	11			10					1	6	2			
16	Nov-14	H	Hull City	0 0		11,866	1	4	3		5		7	8		9				10	11					6	2			
17	Nov-21	A	Sheff. United	3 3	Webster, Allchurch, Nurse(pen)	15,786	1	6	3		5		7	8		9				10	11					4	2			
18	Nov-28	H	Middlesbrough	3 1	Williams H, Williams G, Webster	13,899	1	4	3		5		7			9				10	11					6	2	8		
19	Dec-05	A	Derby County	2 1	O/Goal, Griffiths	13,633	1	4	3		5		7			9			8	11						6	2	10		
20	Dec-12	H	Plymouth Argyle	6 1	Webster 3, Allchurch, Williams H, Williams G	12,355	1	4	3		5		7			9				10	11					6	2	8		
21	Dec-19	A	Lincoln City	0 2		6,112	1	4	3		5		7			9				10	11					6	2	8		
22	Dec-26	A	Bristol Rovers	1 3	Thomas	16,505	1	4	3		5		7			9		10			11					6	2	8		
23	Dec-28	H	Bristol Rovers	3 0	Webster 2, Allchurch	15,270	1	4	3		5		7			9				10	11					6	2	8		
24	Jan-02	A	Aston Villa	1 3	Dodson	24,848	1	4	3		5		7			9				10	11					6	2	8		
25	Jan-16	A	Sunderland	0 4		13,501	1	4	3		5	6	7			9			8		11						2	10		
26	Jan-23	H	Portsmouth	1 1	Nurse(pen)	11,130	1		3		5	6	7			9				10	11					4	2	8		
27	Feb-06	A	Stoke City	2 4	Webster, Davies	11,703	1	4	3		5		7	8		11	9									6	2	10		
28	Feb-13	H	Brighton	2 2	Nurse(pen), Webster	10,163	1	4	3		5	6	7					9		10	11						2	8		
29	Feb-20	A	Liverpool	1 4	Reynolds	31,633	1	4	3		5	6	7	8		9				10	11						2			
30	Feb-27	H	Charlton Athletic	5 2	Webster 3, Allchurch, Reynolds	11,805	1	4	3		5		7	8		9				10	11						2	6		
31	Mar-05	A	Bristol City	2 2	Williams G, Jones	14,368	1		3		5	4		8		9				10	11	7					2	6		
32	Mar-12	H	Scunthorpe United	3 1	Allchurch 2, Webster	11,646	1		3		5	8	7	9				2		10	11						6	4		
33	Mar-19	A	Middlesbrough	0 2		15,479	1		3		5	6	7			9		2		10	11						8	4		
34	Mar-26	H	Cardiff City	3 3	Reynolds 2, Hale	24,004	1		3		5		7			9		2		10	11				6		8	4		
35	Apr-02	A	Hull City	1 3	Reynolds	8,691	1	2			5		7	8		9	3	10			11					4	6			
36	Apr-09	H	Sheff. United	2 1	Reynolds 2	12,404	1				5		7	6		9	3	10	11							4	2	8		
37	Apr-15	A	Leyton Orient	1 2	Reynolds	15,870	1				5		7	6		9	3	10	11							4	2	8		
38	Apr-16	A	Plymouth Argyle	1 3	Dodson	21,969	1				5		7	6		9	10	3	11							4	2	8		
39	Apr-18	H	Leyton Orient	1 0	Dodson	10,447	1	4	3		5					9	10		7		11						2	8	6	
40	Apr-23	H	Derby County	1 3	Dodson	9,594		6	3		5		7			9		2	10	11			1				8	4		
41	Apr-26	H	Bristol City	6 1	Jones 2, O/Goal, Dodson, Allchurch, Williams H	7,920	1	2			5		7			8	9				11					6	10	4	3	
42	Apr-30	A	Rotherham United	1 1	Reynolds	7,029		2	3		5		7	10		8	9				11					1	6	4		
					Apps		39	33	37	2	42	19	34	27	4	37	19	21	37	18	15	3	1	3	19	21	23	7	1	0
					Gls				1		4	1	9	5	2	16	7	1	22	3	3				1		3			

#	Date	V	Opponents	Score	Scorers	Att.	King J	Hughes B	Griffiths H	Davies P	Nurse M	Saunders R	Allchurch L	Davies Reg	Daniel R	Reynolds B	Dodson D	Thomas D	Webster C	Williams G	Jones B	Kennedy MSJ	Lawson N	Reid RBA	Hale D	Sanders A	Williams H	Johnson M	Purcell B	Woods A
1	Jan-09	A	Gillingham FAC-3	4 1	Wiliams H 2, Jones, Hughes	15,301	1	4	3		5	6	7			9				10	11						2	8		
2	Jan-30	H	Burnley, FAC-4 Rep	0 0		30,060	1	4	3		5		7	8		9				10	11					6	2			
3	Feb-02	A	Burnley, FAC-4 Rep	1 2	Nurse	37,038	1	4	3		5		7	8		9				10	11					6	2			
4	Feb-11	H	Merthyr, WC-5	6 1	Williams G, Webster, Allchurch 2, Reynolds, Davies	2,150	1		3		5	4	7	8		9				10	11						2	6		
5	Feb-25	H	Cardiff City, WC-6	1 2	Reynolds	11,000	1		3		5	6				9		10	11	7							2	8		4

Swansea Town FC Season 1960/61 Division 2

#	Date	V	Opponents	Score	Scorers	Att.	Dwyer N	Hughes B	Griffiths H	Johnson M	Nurse M	Hale D	Allchurch L	Reynolds B	Dodson D	Webster C	Jones B	Williams H	Saunders R	Davies Reg	Williams G	Sanders A	King J	Davies P	Todd K	Kennedy MSJ	Morris A	Haasz J	Ward D	Morgans K	Purcell B
1	Aug-20	A	Sunderland	1 2	Allchurch	26,435	1	2	3	4	5	6	7	8	9	10	11														
2	Aug-23	H	Huddersfield Town	2 0	Dodson 2	15,295	1	2	3	4	5	6	7	8	9			11	10												
3	Aug-27	H	Plymouth Argyle	1 2	Webster	14,123	1	2	3	4	5	6	7	8	9	10	11														
4	Aug-31	H	Huddersfield Town	1 3	Williams H	12,913	1	2	3	4	5	6	7	8	9			11	10												
5	Sep-03	A	Norwich City	0 0		26,077	1	2	3		5	6	7	8	9			11	10	4											
6	Sep-06	H	Lincoln City	1 2	Davies R	7,680	1	2	3		5	4			9	7	10	6	8	11											
7	Sep-10	H	Charlton Athletic	3 3	Davies R, Hale, Dodson	9,424	1	2	3		5	4			9	10	7	6	8	11											
8	Sep-14	A	Lincoln City	0 2		7,513	1		3		5	4		8	9	7		11	10	6		2									
9	Sep-17	A	Sheff. United	0 3		14,890	1		3		5	4	7		9	10		11	8	6		2									
10	Sep-24	H	Stoke City	0 0		8,957	1		3		5	4	7		9	10		11	8	6		2									
11	Oct-01	A	Bristol Rovers	2 4	Williams G, Hale	15,132	1	8	3		5	4	7	9		10				6	11	2									
12	Oct-08	H	Derby County	2 1	Todd, Allchurch	8,999		6	3		5		7			10		8			11	2	1	4	9						
13	Oct-15	A	Leyton Orient	2 2	Reynolds, Todd	9,714		6	3		5		7	8		10		11				2	1	4	9						
14	Oct-24	H	Scunthorpe United	2 2	Williams H 2	9,599			3	4	5	6	7	9		10		8			11	2	1								
15	Oct-29	H	Ipswich Town	3 0	O/Goal, Williams H, Williams G	11,178			3	4	5	6	7		9	10		8			11	2	1								
16	Nov-05	H	Brighton	2 3	Williams H, Hughes	11,029			3	4	5	6	7		9	10		8			11	2	1								
17	Nov-12	A	Middlesbrough	1 3	Williams G	17,178			3	4	5	6	7	8	9	10					11	2	1								
18	Nov-19	A	Leeds United	3 2	Morris, Webster, Williams H	11,140	1	2	3		5			8	9	10		11									4	6	7		
19	Nov-26	A	Southampton	0 5		16,077	1	2	3		5		10		9						8	11					4	6	7		
20	Dec-10	A	Liverpool	0 4		25,740		2			5		7	8	9	10					3	1		4			6			11	
21	Dec-17	H	Sunderland	3 3	Webster 2, Allchurch	7,922		2	3		5		7		9	10			6	8	11		1	4							
22	Dec-26	H	Portsmouth	4 0	Davies R 2, Reynolds 2	11,947			3		5		7	9		10			6	8	11	2	1	4							
23	Dec-27	A	Portsmouth	1 1	Williams G	18,859			3		5		7	9		10			6	8	11	2	1	4							
24	Dec-31	A	Plymouth Argyle	0 1		15,617			3		5		7	9		10			6	8	11	2	1	4							
25	Jan-14	H	Norwich City	4 1	Davies R, Webster 3	12,164			3		5			9		10	7		6	8	11	2	1	4							
26	Jan-21	A	Charlton Athletic	2 6	Reynolds, Webster	9,488			3		5		7	9		10			6	8	11	2	1	4							
27	Feb-04	H	Sheff. United	3 0	Davies R, Webster 2	12,621			3	4	5			9		10	7		6	8	11	2	1								
28	Feb-11	A	Stoke City	3 1	Webster 2, Davies R	10,517	1		3		5			9		10	7		6	8	11	2		4							
29	Feb-25	A	Derby County	3 2	Webster, Williams G, Reynolds	8,841	1		3		5			9		10	7		6	8	11	2		4							
30	Feb-28	H	Bristol Rovers	2 1	Davies P, Davies R	12,562	1		3		5			9		10	7		6	8	11	2		4							
31	Mar-04	H	Leyton Orient	1 0	Williams G	12,363	1		3		5			9		10	7		6	8	11	2		4							
32	Mar-11	A	Scunthorpe United	2 1	Todd, Webster	7,926	1		3		5					10	7		6	8	11	2		4	9						
33	Mar-14	H	Rotherham United	2 1	Webster 2	12,594	1		3		5			9		10	7		6	8	11	2		4							
34	Mar-18	H	Liverpool	2 0	Williams G 2	13,181	1		3		5			9		10	7		6	8	11	2		4							
35	Mar-25	A	Brighton	0 0		12,942	1		3		5			9		10	7		6	8	11	2		4							
36	Mar-31	A	Luton Town	2 2	Todd, Hughes	14,286	1	6	3		5					10	7			8	11	2		4	9						
37	Apr-01	H	Southampton	4 1	Jones 2, Webster 2	13,703	1		3		5					10	7		6	8	11	2		4		9					
38	Apr-03	H	Luton Town	3 1	Davies P, O/Goal, Jones	14,884	1		3		5			9		10	7		6	8	11	2		4							
39	Apr-08	A	Leeds United	2 2	Webster, Reynolds	11,862	1				5			9		10			6	8	11	2		4					3	7	
40	Apr-15	H	Middlesbrough	3 2	Saunders, Davies R, Reynolds	15,335	1	2			5			9		10	7		6	8	11			4					3		
41	Apr-22	A	Rotherham United	3 3	Jones 2, Williams G	6,527	1		3		5			9		10	7		6		11	2		4						8	
42	Apr-29	A	Ipswich Town	2 1	Nurse, Reynolds	18,239			3	4	5			9		10	7		6		11	2	1							8	
	Apps						27	25	34	6	41	15	24	29	8	39	27	15	26	24	33	31	15	27	6	3	2	1	2	2	
	Gls							2			1	2	3	8	3	19	5	6	1	9	9			2	4		1				

#	Date	V	Opponents	Score	Scorers	Att.	Dwyer N	Hughes B	Griffiths H	Johnson M	Nurse M	Hale D	Allchurch L	Reynolds B	Dodson D	Webster C	Jones B	Williams H	Saunders R	Davies Reg	Williams G	Sanders A	King J	Davies P	Todd K	Kennedy MSJ	Morris A	Haasz J	Ward D	Morgans K	Purcell B
1	Oct-18	H	Blackburn R, FLC-2	1 2	Williams H	14,340		6	3		5		7		9	10		8			11	2	1	4							
2	Jan-07	H	Port Vale, FAC-3	3 0	Allchurch, Reynolds 2	10,601			3		5	4	7	9		10			6	8	11	2	1								
3	Jan-28	H	Preston, FAC-4	2 1	Davies R, Reynolds	22,352			3		5		7	9		10			6	8	11	2	1	4							
4	Feb-01	A	Barry T, WC-5	3 0	Reynolds, Webster, Jones				3			6		9		10	7	8			11	2	1	4							5
5	Feb-18	A	Burnley, FAC-5	0 4		30,977			3		5		7	9		10			6	8	11	2	1	4							
6	Feb-21	H	Holyhead, WC-6	5 0	Webster 3, Saunders, Reynolds		1		3		5			9		10	7		6	8	11	2		4							
7	Mar-22	N	Cardiff C, WC-S-F	1 1	Reynolds	10,470	1	6	3		5			9		10	7			8	11	2		4							
8	Mar-28	L	Cardiff C, WC-S-F, Rep	2 1	Reynolds 2	11,965	1		3		5			9		10	7		6	8	11	2		4							
9	Apr-26	C	Bangor C, WC-Final	3 1	Reynolds, Jones, Davies R		1		3		5			9		10	7		6	8	11	2		4							

N – Newport
L – Llanelli
C – Cardiff

Chapter 14

Cup Glory and League Misery

1961-62

According to new secretary, Gordon Daniels, there was a brisk demand for season tickets during the close-season. Clearly, the supporters, encouraged by the unbeaten run which the team put together at the end of the previous season, were assuming that the team would be able to recapture that form. Trevor Morris seemed to have no doubt that that would be the case. He heralded the new campaign with the announcement that the players were to be rewarded through an incentive scheme based upon the size of gates.

In July, Dai Thomas was made available for transfer at a nominal fee. Morris said of him, 'Dai has been one of the best club men I have met.' Two others who left at the same time were Dixie Hale, who joined Barrow for £3,000, and Reg Harvey, who was almost eighty when he stood down from an office post. Harvey, who had given the club outstanding service, was the last administrative staff link with pre-war days. Meanwhile, the board extended Trevor Morris's contract for a further three years. The *Post*, in commenting on that news, pointed out that when Morris joined the club 'it had a five figure overdraft, which is no longer the case'. They, also, noted that he had made a net profit of £63,000 on transfers, which, in retrospect, went some way to explaining his financial success. Doubtless there were supporters who read these comments and wondered if the manager was going to add to his transfer profits during the season ahead. However, they did have two other competitions to help distract them. As winners of the Welsh Cup, the Swans were to play in the European Cup Winners' Cup – the first team from Wales to do so. In addition, for the second season, they were engaged in the

Mike Johnson

Football League Cup, meeting Ipswich Town in the first round.

In the event, when these cup matches were played, success eluded the Swans. There were, however, extenuating circumstances which need to be taken into consideration in judging these performances. In the European competition, after a long wrangle, the team was obliged to play both legs of their tie against Motor Jena away from home. After a tiring journey they could only draw their 'home' leg (in Linz, Austria) and subsequently lost at Jena. These games were sandwiched between two exciting games in the Football League Cup, in which the team lost to Ipswich Town 6-5 on aggregate. In addition, January saw the club eliminated from the FA Cup, losing 1-0 to Sheffield Wednesday, although the result, according to most observers, flattered the Yorkshiremen.

Meanwhile, in the league, the hoped-for continuation of the previous season's unbeaten run was

short-lived. After just three matches the side lost at home to Preston. Nonetheless, a record sequence of nineteen games without defeat was set which still stands today. Sadly, results following that defeat were hardly in keeping with the hopes of the supporters. For example, the team was heavily beaten by Southampton and Derby in successive games, while, before 1961 ended, Bristol Rovers scored four, Liverpool five and Sunderland seven, which raised questions about the viability of the defence. Even so, as if to illustrate that support for Swansea soccer was alive and well, there was one large gate: almost 20,000 people came to see the Swans play Stoke City (and Stan Matthews). As it transpired, they saw very little of the veteran winger that day. The man marking him was Harry Griffiths, who had an outstanding match even though he, too, was 'getting on'. Harry had played his 300th game for the Swans two months before.

In November, Malmö, the Swedish club which the Swans had met during their 1927 tour, came to the Vetch for a friendly game which the home side won 5-1. That month also provided a disappointment for the Vetch faithful: the Welsh international side to play Scotland did not contain a single Vetch-based player. It was the first time that this had happened since 1948. November also brought a further denial that Mel Nurse would be allowed to leave, while at the AGM the shareholders were informed that the club had lost £5,000 on the previous season's working. No mention was made of the fact that the loss would have been quadrupled without the benefit of the transfer fee excess. Meantime, Morris continued to wheel and deal, buying Peter Donnelly from Cardiff and selling David Dodson to Portsmouth for a £1,000 less.

In the new year the bush-telegraph in Swansea revived the 'Nurse is leaving' rumour. This time the Vetch authorities did not attempt to deny the stories and, in February, having selected Mike Johnson at centre-half in the place of Nurse, Morris told the press, 'In view of the wealth of centre-half talent we have, Nurse can go.' In the same month, Graham Williams fractured his left leg.

By March, letters to the *Post* were describing the side as the poorest for many seasons. The manager responded tetchily and appealed to fans to stop player-baiting. Unfortunately, the performances of the team did little to allay the fears of supporters: during the windy month, only one point was picked up from six matches – and that in front of the smallest gate since the war (5,425). The form, the flair and the positive results of the previous season were but memories to the fans. With Accrington Stanley having to withdraw from the Football League because of financial difficulties, in the minds of the board and the club's bankers, the viability of the Vetch club must have been called into question.

When March ended, the club was in twentieth place in the table. By mid-April it had sunk to the foot, so, when the Swans faced Plymouth Argyle at Easter, there was genuine concern in the town about the team's ability to avoid relegation. The sole glimmer of hope in the minds of the most ardent supporters concerned the old fable about Argyle and the Swans 'scratching each other's back'. It was a tenuous hope, though the fable gained further credence when the Swans won 5-0, with Reynolds scoring a hat-trick. According to the media (who were not privy to the fable), Houdini had nothing on Trevor Morris, who's men responded positively to his rallying call. When Sunderland, the next visitors to the Vetch, were held to a draw, the single point, hard-earned on the day, ensured safety. In that match, Mel Nurse, still at the club, dealt with Brian Clough with admirable coolness. Thus it was that, when Liverpool, champions of the Second Division, came to the Vetch to play the final game of the season, the team could relax and play to its potential. With English amateur international Mike Pinner, in goal the Swans were outstanding. On the day Hunt, Melia, St. John, Yeats and the like were outplayed by the Swansea men. Indeed, an uninformed spectator attending the game might have been forgiven for thinking that it was the home side which had gained promotion to Division One. For their part, Morris, the Swans board and all Swansea supporters must have wondered how a side which could play so well had been in danger of relegation at the beginning of the previous game?

Reg Davies

1962-63

During the close-season, Reg Davies was transferred to Carlisle for 'a reasonable fee', while Brighton paid £6,000 for Peter Donnelly. Presumably with the proceeds, Morris bought Eddie Thomas from Blackburn for £10,000. It was the second highest fee ever paid by the club. Another recruit was former Swansea Schoolboy, Glyn Davies, who came from Derby County after failing to agree terms with that club. When the team played its first game, Davies was seen to be the captain of the side, which did reasonably well in the early matches. Both newcomers were prominent in these games, with Thomas scoring a brace against Bury. Nevertheless, gates continued to disappoint, only 10,000 coming to each of the first two home matches. When it was reported that twenty managers and scouts had attended the game with Bury, rumours began to circulate, again, about departures from the Vetch. Most stories revolved around Barrie Jones, and Mel Nurse, and letters to the *Post* were at one in pleading with management not to sell any more players. Among them were those who vowed that, were key players to leave, they would not set foot in the Vetch again.

Despite the letters, at the end of September part of the rumour became reality: Mel Nurse joined Middlesbrough for £25,000. At this,

even more letters poured into the *Post* complaining about the constant departures. Trevor Morris, according to one irate supporter, 'was nothing more than a business manager for the board'. Yet, in one sense, he was there for that purpose. As he had said many times, one of his objectives was to balance the books. However, whilst he could claim reasonable success in one season under his patronage, the policies which he was following in order to do so involved an unhealthy syndrome where the future was being mortgaged for short-term survival. What, he might have been asked, was going to happen when the club had no more stars to sell?

In October, one of those stars – Barrie Jones – was awarded his first cap for the game against Scotland. In that month, too, the side was thrashed 6-0 at Newcastle and, in November, the chairman reported a deficit on the season's working of £7,215. Once again, had it not been for transfers out, the loss would have been even greater. The storm cones were hoisted with a vengeance.

At this stage, a local businessman, Denzil Davies, began to make his presence felt. He announced that, he and two colleagues were prepared to make £20,000 available with which to purchase players. There were, however, strings attached to the offer which the directors did not like. Yet something had to be done and that sooner rather than later. Probably as a result of the well-publicized approach from the would-be board members, together with the stark reality of a mid-December gate of just 5,562 which watched the Swans beat Charlton at the Vetch, Morris bid £18,000 for Peter McParland. Whilst the offer was unacceptable to the selling club, at least a gesture had been made. Denzil Davies and his colleagues, though, were unimpressed and, through a variety of channels, they directed what the *Post* described as a 'blistering attack on the board'. The group's main criticism was that the club was selling its major assets for short-term gain. They might have used the analogy of selling Park Lane while playing Monopoly and buying Whitechapel with part of the proceeds. It left cash in hand for a short period, but twice around the board and it was gone. Those who were mounting the 'blistering attack' were of the opinion

Team versus Bury at the Vetch.
Back row, left ro right: Brian Hughes, Roy Saunders, Herbie Williams, Noel Dwyer, Mel Nurse, Harry Griffiths.
Front: Barrie Jones, Eddie Thomas, Glyn Davies (Captain), Colin Webster, Ken Morgans.

that the club was on its second circuit already.

At the end of December, Trevor Morris formally denied that Barrie Jones was about to be transferred. He also pointed to the club's relatively safe mid-table position. Unfortunately, heavy snow which fell as the year ended was to exacerbate the already difficult financial position in which the club found itself.

This, of course, brought greater pressure on Morris's book-balancing objective, for, with just one match played in January, cash flow was adversely affected. One result of this was that what was now called a Swans 'Ginger Group' held a meeting at which Malcolm Struel was reported as saying that the directors had 'promulgated a disastrous policy of running down the club'. In due course, he was to do some promulgation of his own at the Vetch. Perhaps in response to a plea from the directors, Morris sold Alan Sanders to Brighton for £5,000.

> ***Stoke City provided the opposition for the Swans' 1,500th Football League match (away) on 27 March 1963.***

Meantime, the board agreed to meet a deputation from the Ginger Group, a meeting which was to prove to be the bridgehead from which this group eventually secured control of the club.

Paradoxically, despite all the problems and departures from the club, the outcome at the end of the season was fifteenth place in Division Two. On the face of it, this was a comfortable enough result, yet the club had picked up only three more points than it had obtained in the

previous campaign. Nevertheless, there were some encouraging factors to note. The team had taken three points from its two matches with Chelsea, the club which were runners-up in the division that season, they were the first team to score at Stamford Bridge, and their Vetch victory over the Pensioners came after the London team had won eight consecutive away matches. In addition, Keith Todd, Roy Evans and Barrie Jones had all been capped at Under-23 level. Yet, as with the curate's egg, there were also disturbing considerations. Not one of the club's last nine league matches had been won, while just two points were secured and twenty-nine goals conceded. The most worrying factor for the board, however, was the average gate for the season; at 10,362, it was the lowest since the war. The downward trend which this statistic suggested was to continue for many years and would be a key factor in challenging the very

Semi-final squad. Back row, left to right: Trevor Morris, Eddie Thomas, Brian Hughes, Roy Evans, Noel Dwyer, Brian Purcell, Herbie Williams, Walter Robbins. Front: Brayley Reynolds, Barrie Jones, Keith Todd, Mike Johnson (Captain), Derek Draper, Brian Evans, Jimmy McLaughlin.

returned for the Charlton match, absented themselves again and were joined by others. By mid-January, with Scunthorpe as the visitors, the gate was less than half that for the Boxing Day match. At this stage objective analysis might have suggested that the club should budget for an average attendance of around 8,000. Yet, near the end of the season, as they clamoured for FA Cup tickets, three times that number were claiming continuous support.

In January, however, the possibility of the Swans being one match away from Wembley seemed as remote as a Conservative M.P. being elected for Merthyr. Yet, there is always hope in the hearts of football followers. At least the cup gave the fans a different focus away from the drabness of league results. On 4 January this interest was reflected in a gate of 9,488 which came to see the Swans beat Barrow 4-1. That was the game which was a milestone for young Mike Johnson who had established himself at centre-half: it was his first as captain.

When the draw was announced for the fourth round of the cup, the Swans were listed to play Sheffield United in Yorkshire. Sheffield, managed by former Swan, John Harris, and including Len Allchurch in their team, were a successful side and few pundits gave the Vetch men much chance. Yet, as if inspired by

existence of the club. At the time, though, it is doubtful whether the gloomiest pessimist among supporters would have forecast the extent to which that average would fall. Indeed, it is interesting to speculate whether the ardent Ginger Group leaders would have continued with their campaign had they but known. At the time, they were like an opposition party campaigning for change without having seen the books. In due course, what would be revealed was far more disconcerting than they might have expected.

side had won only three of its first ten matches and Vetch attendances were reflecting those results. Further, even though matters on the field improved somewhat, gates continued to diminish throughout October and November. For example, 8,892 saw a game against Swindon in which Keith Todd scored a hat-trick, while 2,000 fewer watched a tremendous 5-1 victory over Preston. There was some encouragement on the field in November, though: the team defeated Northampton to record their first away victory for eighteen matches.

1963–64

To the surprise of most fans, during the close-season, Trevor Morris paid a club-record £16,000 for the Shrewsbury winger Jimmy McLaughlin. Despite that news, season ticket sales were twenty-five per cent less than they had been at the same time the previous season. No doubt, had those who failed to renew known of the excitement which the later stages of the season were to provide, they, too, would have 'signed up'. In the absence of a Delphian oracle, though, they sat on their wallets.

When the season started, the directors must have wondered whether the gate for the first home match of the season was a harbinger for what was to come. Only 10,740 came to see a 1-1 draw with Grimsby. By the end of September the situation was even worse, for the

> *Stanley Matthews scored the opening goal of the game for Stoke City in an FA Cup tie against the Swans on 15 February 1964. He also scored the first goal for the Potteries club against the Swans in another FA Cup game on 12 January 1935. In neither case did he finish on the winning side.*

No doubt encouraged by the better results, one of the largest crowds of the season (15,487) was at the Vetch to see the Boxing Day game with Charlton. Unfortunately, the Swans did not live up to their improved form and lost 2-1. There followed two further defeats, including a 4-0 loss at Leyton Orient, which was the London side's first home victory since September. Inevitably, those lost fans who had

the sudden-death excitement of the competition, the Swans achieved a well-earned draw. Three days later, Bill Paton In the *Post*, wrote, 'Suddenly they are Swans fans again', as 24,109 crowded the Vetch for the replay. Even the 'I'll never set foot in the Vetch again' brigade were there. Encouraged by the vociferous support of the big crowd the Swans overran their famous opponents, scoring four goals in the process.

The defence was outstanding, while Draper, McLaughlin and Thomas were in fine form in front of goal.

Following the victory, league form was forgotten, although, when the next round pairings were announced, there were few Swansea hearts leaping with expectation. It was a tough draw: Stoke City away. Yet, Bill Paton, who covered Swans matters for the *Post*, found the average fan to be full of confidence. Although these were the same players who were struggling in league matches, they were thought of, it appeared, as having some kind of superhuman power in the cup. Amazingly, in the matches in that competition, that belief seemed to transmit itself to the team. At Stoke, despite an early goal from Stan Matthews, the Swans earned a fine draw. Hero of the day was Keith Todd, restored to the side for the match, who led the line with skill and enthusiasm and scored two excellent goals. One interesting statistic from the match concerned Stan Matthews, for his goal turned out to be the veteran's last, prior to his retirement from Football League soccer. As it happened, Matthews had scored the opening goal in an FA Cup tie against the Swans in 1935 and had not finished on the winning side. The few Swans fans who were aware of that fact and who believed in omens, were thus absolutely sure that the Vetch men would win the replay. Nor were they disappointed. Todd and McLaughlin scored the only goals of the match to ensure that the Swans progressed to the quarter-finals of the FA Cup. If the media were astounded by that, they were to be even more incredulous after that stage had been completed.

While the fans awaited the quarter-final (the Swans had been drawn away again, at Liverpool), the side's stumbling form in the league continued to cause dismay. Two away matches in succession were lost, though there were extenuating circumstances for the last defeat: it was the fourth away match which the team had had to play in eight days. By this time there was a feeling among the pessimists in the town that the mighty Liverpool would be a match too far, while the mood was hardly helped by an injury to Eddie Thomas. Nevertheless, despite the awesome reputation of their opponents, the thousands of Swans

Noel Dwyer, Mike Johnson and Roy Evans celebrate the momentous victory at Anfield in the quarter-finals of the FA Cup.

fans who journeyed to fortress Anfield on 29 February 1964, did their best to boost morale en route.

Whatever the fans thought, the 'experts' had no doubt about the outcome of the game. Liverpool, powerfully confident under the management of Bill Shankly, would 'win by a mile'. Just look at the record book, they argued, Swansea have played at Anfield eight times, lost on seven occasions and never won. In all, the Swans had scored a total of three goals, while the Reds had amassed twenty-eight. Then, of course, there was the station of the clubs. Liverpool challenging near the top of Division One, Swansea struggling in the Second. As the Swansea players ran onto the field from the tunnel with its famous daunting sign 'This is Anfield', they could have been forgiven for feeling apprehensive. Yeats, Callaghan, St. John, Hunt and the rest would surely make their task impossible. Yet, when the final whistle was blown, little Swansea Town left the pitch, to the great joy of their

supporters, having beaten the Scouse giants by the odd goal in three.

In retrospect, the unlikely sight, as the teams came out, of Irishman Jimmy McLaughlin carrying a huge leek might have had something to do with the outcome of the match. Whilst we shall never know, perhaps McLaughlin and his countryman, Noel Dwyer gained some magical advantage from the Welsh symbol, for they both played outstanding games. McLaughlin it was who opened the scoring to the disbelief of everyone in the ground. In the thirty-eighth minute, receiving a lovely through-ball from Herbie Williams, he swivelled on his heel and drove a fine shot beyond the hands of the diving Lawrence in the Liverpool goal.

Four minutes later, to the further disbelief of both home and away supporters in the fifty-thousand crowd, the Swans doubled their score. Barrie Jones found McLaughlin with a splendid pass, and the Irishman crossed the ball into the Liverpool goalmouth where

Eddie Thomas pounced to score with a flashing drive. Four-fifths of the huge crowd were silent, the remainder jubilant, though the minority were beginning to be inflicted with doubt as the red hoards bore down on the Swansea goal time and again. Thompson pulled a goal back for Liverpool, but, thereafter, Dwyer in the Swansea goal seemed unbeatable, whilst Evans, Hughes, Johnson and Purcell defended as if their lives depended upon the outcome of the match. But it was Dwyer who excelled. He made countless saves, several from seemingly impossible situations, which might have had something to do with Ronnie Moran's penalty miss later in the game. The full back, who had an excellent reputation as a penalty taker, put the ball on the spot nine minutes from the end of the game and hit his shot high and wide. At that, Noel Dwyer was said to have patted his leprechaun on the head. Afterwards, the football world could hardly believe the result. Bill Shankly summed up this disbelief when he said, 'We should have scored fourteen!' Noel Dwyer did not agree with him – nor did his leprechaun!

The euphoria of the Liverpool result spilled over into the next league match: Southampton were beaten 6-0, but, three days later, Rotherham were the victors by 3-0. Perhaps the adrenalin had stopped flowing and the cold reality of bread-and-butter league fixtures did not suit the players' mood. What was worse, the Rotherham defeat was poor preparation for the semi-final of the FA Cup, a match which was to be played on the following Saturday at Villa Park against Preston North End. At the time, Preston were third in the Second Division whilst the Swans languished in seventeenth place. Nevertheless, on the back of the Liverpool result, the Swansea supporters could point to the fact that Preston had been hammered 5-1 at the Vetch, whilst the Swans had taken a point at Deepdale. Sadly, on the day, the confidence which those results generated in Swansea minds was to evaporate as, before the largest crowd to have watched a

Swans match (68,000), like their 1926 predecessors, the team 'fell at the last fence'. Even though McLaughlin gave the Swans the lead a minute before half-time, Preston equalised with a penalty and won the match with a hopeful 40-yard hoof up field which caught the Swans

Following Noel Dwyer's brilliant performance at Anfield in the quarter-final of the 1964 FA Cup, the Liverpool supporters showered his goal with coins by way of praise. He was reported as having collected 3s.9d. (18p.) from around his net after the game.

goalkeeper off his line. The Anfield hero hung his head in despair.

That defeat effectively signalled the end of the season for the Swans and their supporters. The remaining nine league games produced only two wins and the team finished in nineteenth place in the division. When the dust settled, it was found that the cup run had contributed a valuable £17,000 to club funds – a godsend for the club. Without that money, the club would have been in considerable financial difficulty. In retrospect, though, the windfall simply served to put off the evil day.

Away from the cup euphoria and the concerns of the league, the Vetch said farewell to one of its favourite sons. Harry Griffiths, who had played the last of his 424 league games for the club on 21 September, was given a testimonial match. Twelve thousand of his admirers camed to the Vetch in support of his cause. Many were to return on later occasions to salute the man again for his selfless service to the club in other roles.

1964-65

Notwithstanding the exciting FA Cup run of the previous campaign, having experienced three successive seasons in which their favourites had finished in the lower regions of the league table, Swans fans faced the new term with less than confidence. There were only two new names to bolster the team, whilst Harry

Griffiths, John King, Graham Williams and others had left. The stalwart Griffiths joined Merthyr as player-manager after giving the Vetch outstanding service. He had played for the Swans in a variety of positions, had been worthy of far more caps than his single international appearance suggested, had been a club man *par excellence* and is still one of the club's top ten goal scorers despite playing for most of his career in defence. At thirty-three Harry thought that he still had much to offer. Morris, however, felt otherwise and argued that he wanted to give Griffiths the opportunity to start in management. More than a decade was to pass before the popular Griffiths obtained the only managerial post in which he was really interested. When that came about, the circumstances which he was required to face would be far more critical than those with which Morris had to grapple in what was to be the manager's last term at the Vetch.

John King had been a fixture at the Vetch for fifteen seasons. He started his league career as a seventeen-year-old schoolboy and set a new goalkeeping appearance record for the club which was not surpassed until 1999. When he died in Australia during 1982 the club lost a staunch supporter as well as a stalwart former player. As with Griffiths, the only team that mattered to the burly King played its home matches at the Vetch.

After gaining only three points from the first seven matches of the season, the side found itself, yet again, in the lower regions of the league table. The team appeared to be lacking in confidence and badly needed an 'old head'. Eddie Thomas, who might have provided this quality, had been transferred to Derby County in August, and Roy Saunders had been given a free transfer. Then, on 11 September, inevitably in the eyes of supporters, Barrie Jones left, signing for Plymouth for £45,000. The following day, as if to comment on the sale, the Swans lost 5-2 at home to Leyton Orient, who themselves were to be in danger of relegation as the season moved to its conclusion. The tone of the letters to the *Post* was one of despair. Morris told Bill Paton, 'I will not be stampeded into signing players', yet, within two weeks he recruited Albert Harley from Shrewsbury for £10,000.

As it happened, Harley appeared to be a good omen, for his debut match, against Manchester City, resulted in a fine 3-0 victory, with Keith Todd scoring all the goals. Interestingly, the Manchester game was watched by 10,863 people, which, given the disappointments of the season, suggested that there was still a yearning in the hearts of the town's optimists to follow the Swans. In October, George Kirby joined the club from Coventry City, while two young men made their debuts in a Football League Cup match against Rotherham. They were John Roberts and Georgio Chinaglia, who were both to make their names in other fields far from the Vetch. The club gained a new goalkeeper that month, too: he was Dai Davies, a Welsh-speaker from Ammanford.

The troubles at the club were not only reflected in its station in the league table: its financial position was also of great concern to the directors. At the AGM the chairman addressed a small group of the club's shareholders. He warned, 'Without some abnormal revenue . . . the club cannot meet its wages bill. It was that situation,' he went on, 'coupled with an overdraft of £31,000, which forced the club to part with valuable players. Had it not been for the previous season's FA Cup run,' the chairman continued, 'the situation would have been even more serious.' As it was, the extraordinary meeting which followed gave permission for more money to be borrowed. Had the Ginger Group been present, they might have been tempted to continue the Monopoly analogy: 'Do not pass go, do not collect £200'.

At the turn of the year the team had acquired nineteen points from twenty-four matches and were nineteenth in the division. At that point, the manager announced that four further players were to leave the club before the end of the season. Noel Dwyer, the hero of Anfield, became the first of these, joining Plymouth for £7,500. Even in adversity, it seemed, Trevor Morris

could show a profit on his wheeling and dealing. Plymouth paid £4,000 more than the figure with which the Swans had parted five seasons before.

> *During the Swans' match against Swindon on 8 September 1964 the referee, Mr Spittle, was knocked out by a Herbie Williams clearance.*

In January there was a further departure from the Swansea sporting scene. 'Rolande' (R. M. Jones), who had been writing about the Vetch club since 1930, retired from the *Post*. He was the last of the old breed of journalists, a man whose prose style bridged several generations. In that month, too, the Swans avenged their home defeat by Leyton and in so doing gained their first away victory for fourteen months, but it was of little consequence: only one point was gathered from the next seven games. By mid-March, following a 3-1 defeat at Newcastle, the club languished at the bottom of the table – despite Morris's further excursions into the transfer market: he had signed Humphries from Coventry and McGuigan from Southampton.

The sole bright spot for supporters during the campaign had been the team's performance in the cup, but even that ended in February, when the side lost a replay with Peterborough in the fifth round. As had happened in 1926-7, following the previous season's progression to the semi-final, some FA Cup momentum was retained. This time, though, it was less vibrant, and the 30,000 people who had come to see the match returned home despondent. That was unfortunate for many reasons, not the least of which was that the gate was more than three times the average for league games. At least it helped to boost income and encourage the board with respect to the potential interest which the club generated in the region. As Easter approached,

there was no doubt that the board needed every encouragement which they could muster.

After a run of four consecutive defeats, maximum points were gained from the next three games. Consequently, when the team travelled to Coventry for the final game of the season, there was a reasonable chance that they could avoid relegation. If they could win, while Swindon and Portsmouth lost, they would enhance Trevor Morris's reputation as a latter-day Houdini. Sadly, though, it was not to be. With little to play for, Coventry won 3-0 and the Swans were consigned to Division Three after sixteen consecutive seasons in Division Two. Fourteen difficult years were to pass before the club regained its Second Division status, led by a man who, at this time, was a sixteen-year-old playing his football in a Cardiff park. Immediately after the season ended, Trevor Morris paid the penalty for the team's failure. He resigned after negotiating a terminal sum by way of compensation for the outstanding element of his contract.

Morris had led the club to the semi-final of the FA Cup, but his tenure at the Vetch Field had evoked much controversy. He had been scrupulous about paying loyalty bonuses, even when the club was in financial difficulties, and was respected by his staff. Yet, in the eyes of many supporters, he had destroyed the style and flair which had been the hallmark of Swansea soccer. In addition, he had sold so many talented locally born players with whom the fans could identify and brought in others who tended not to stay long enough to establish such a rapport with the fans. Bill Paton's comment on the side which lost at Newcastle was indicative of this feeling: 'There was not one Welshman in the forward line'. The manager had changed the style of play and, seemingly had altered the footballing ethos of the Vetch club. Many fans saw these as concrete reasons for the club's demotion. Looking back, more than thirty years later, it is difficult not to agree with such feelings. Nonetheless, those who were following the club at the time would point to the FA Cup run to the semi-final as one of the most exciting periods in the club's history. No one can take that away from Trevor Morris.

Swansea Town FC Season 1961/62 Division 2

#	Date	V	Opponents	Score	Scorers	Att.	Dwyer N	Sanders A	Griffiths H	Davies P	Nurse M	Saunders R	Jones B	Davies Reg	Reynolds B	Webster C	Williams G	Johnson M	Hughes B	Todd K	Williams H	Morgans K	Ward D	King J	Dodson D	Donnelly P	Purcell B	Morris A	Pinner M
1	Aug-19	H	Huddersfield Town	1 1	Jones	18,208	1	2	3	4	5	6	7	8	9	10	11												
2	Aug-22	A	Preston North End	1 1	Davies R	14,570	1	2	3	4	5	6	7	8	9	10	11												
3	Aug-26	A	Brighton	2 2	Williams G 2	16,078	1	2	3	4	5	6	7	8	9	10	11												
4	Aug-29	H	Preston North End	1 2	O/Goal	18,499	1	2	3		5		7	8		10	11	4	6	9									
5	Sep-02	A	Southampton	1 5	Webster	12,003	1	2	3		5		7	8	9	10		4			6	11							
6	Sep-06	A	Derby County	3 6	Jones, Williams H, Webster	14,363	1	2	3		5		7	8	9	10	11	4			6								
7	Sep-09	H	Luton Town	3 2	Webster 2, Reynolds	11,813	1	2	3	4			7	8	9	10	11				5	6							
8	Sep-16	A	Newcastle United	2 2	Williams H 2	23,644	1	2	3				7	8	9		11	5	6		10								
9	Sep-19	H	Derby County	3 1	Davies R, O/Goal, Williams G	13,423	1	2	3	4			7	8	9	10	11				5	6							
10	Sep-23	H	Middlesbrough	3 3	Reynolds 2, Williams G	14,730	1	2		4			7	8	9	10	11				5	6	3						
11	Sep-30	A	Walsall	0 0		12,640	1	2	3	6	5		7	8	9		11	4			10								
12	Oct-07	H	Scunthorpe United	2 1	Davies R, Dodson	12,479		2	3	6	5		7	8			11	4			10			1	9				
13	Oct-14	A	Norwich City	1 2	Webster	20,697	1	2	3		5		7	8	9	10		4			6	11							
14	Oct-21	H	Leeds United	2 1	Reynolds, Davies R	11,091	1	2	3		5		7	8	9	10		4			6	11							
15	Oct-28	A	Bristol Rovers	1 4	Webster	12,768		2	3		5		7		9	10	11	4			6	8		1					
16	Nov-04	H	Stoke City	1 0	Reynolds	19,600	1	2	3		5		7	8	9	10	11	4			6								
17	Nov-11	A	Bury	1 1	Reynolds	6,790	1	2	3		5		7	8	9	10	11	4			6								
18	Nov-18	H	Rotherham United	2 2	Reynolds	11,140	1	2	3		5		7	8	9	10	11	4			6								
19	Nov-25	A	Liverpool	0 5		35,724	1	2	3		5		7		9		11	4	6		8					10			
20	Dec-02	H	Charlton Athletic	1 0	O/Goal	10,848	1	2	3	4	5		7		9	8	11				6					10			
21	Dec-09	A	Sunderland	2 7	Reynolds, Williams G	27,560		2	3	6	5		7		9		11	4			8			1		10			
22	Dec-23	H	Brighton	3 0	Jones, Donnelly, Webster	7,937		2	3	4	5		7	8	9		11				6			1		10			
23	Dec-26	A	Leyton Orient	0 1		14,550		2	3	4	5		7	8	9		11				6			1		10			
24	Dec-30	H	Leyton Orient	1 3	Donnelly	9,609	1	2	3	4	5		7	8	9		11				6					10			
25	Jan-13	H	Southampton	0 1		9,681	1	2	3		5		7		9		11	4			6			8		10			
26	Jan-20	A	Luton Town	1 5	O/Goal	8,107	1	2	3	6	5		7			10	11	4			8					9			
27	Feb-02	H	Newcastle United	3 2	Reynolds 2, Jones	16,675	1		3	4			7	8	9	10	11				5	6					2		
28	Feb-10	A	Middlesbrough	3 1	Jones, Webster, Reynolds	11,220	1		3	4			7	8	9	10	11				5	6					2		
29	Feb-17	H	Walsall	1 3	Webster	9,760	1		3	4			7	8	9	10					5	6				11	2		
30	Feb-23	A	Scunthorpe United	0 2		8,437			3	4			11	8	9	10					5	6		1			2	7	
31	Mar-03	H	Norwich City	0 3		6,945			3	4			11	8		10					5	9		1	6		2	7	
32	Mar-10	A	Leeds United	0 2		17,314			3	11	5		7	8	9			4			6			1		10	2		
33	Mar-17	H	Bristol Rovers	1 1	Webster	5,425	1	2	3	4	5		7	8	9	10					6	11							
34	Mar-24	A	Stoke City	0 0		14,777	1	2	3	4	5	6	7			10					8	11				9			
35	Mar-26	A	Huddersfield Town	1 3	Saunders	7,813	1	2	3	4	5	6	7	8	9	10					11								
36	Mar-31	H	Bury	0 1		5,770	1	2	3	4	5	6			9	7					8	11				10			
37	Apr-07	A	Rotherham United	2 1	Webster, Williams H	4,120	1	2	3	4	5	6	7		9	10					8	11							
38	Apr-21	A	Charlton Athletic	2 3	Webster, Reynolds	18,638	1	2	3	4	5	6	7		9	10					8	11							
39	Apr-23	A	Plymouth Argyle	0 0		11,139		2	3	4	5		7		9	10					6	11					8		
40	Apr-24	H	Plymouth Argyle	5 0	Reynolds 3, Donnelly, Morgans	11,697		2	3	4	5		7		9	10					6	11					8		
41	Apr-28	H	Sunderland	1 1	Reynolds	18,071		2	3	4	5		7		9	10					6	11		1			8		
42	May-04	H	Liverpool	4 2	Reynolds, Nurse, Webster 2	12,206		2	3	4	5		7		9	10					6	11					8		1
	Apps						31	36	42	30	33	8	40	29	33	36	25	24	4	2	36	15	1	10	2	16	6	2	1
	Gls										1	1	5	4	18	14	5				4	1			1	3			

#	Date	V	Opponents	Score	Scorers	Att.	Dwyer N	Sanders A	Griffiths H	Davies P	Nurse M	Saunders R	Jones B	Davies Reg	Reynolds B	Webster C	Williams G	Johnson M	Hughes B	Todd K	Williams H	Morgans K	Ward D	King J	Dodson D	Donnelly P	Purcell B	Morris A	Pinner M
1	Oct-03	H	Ipswich T, FLC-2	3 3	O/Goal, O/Goal, Davies R	33,538	1	2	3	6	5		7	8			11	4			10				9				
2	Oct-16	L	Motor Jena, ECWC 1-1	2 2	Reynolds, Nurse(pen)	5,000	1	2	3		5		7	8	9		11	4	6		10								
3	Oct-18	A	Motor Jena, ECWC 1-2	1 5	Reynolds, Nurse(pen)	20,000	1	2	3		5		7		9	10	11	4	6		8								
4	Oct-24	A	Ipswich T, FLC-2 Rep	2 3	Hughes, Reynolds	11,010	1	2	3		5		7		9	10		4	6					8		11			
5	Jan-09	A	Sheff.Wed, FAC-3	0 1		35,000	1	2	3		5		7		9	8	11	4			6					10			
6	Jan-27	A	Haverfordwest, WC-5	7 0	Williams H 2, Donnelly, Jones, Reynolds 3		1		3	4			7	8	9		11				5	6				10	2		
7	Feb-24	H	Holywell, WC-6	2 1	Reynolds, Jones				3	4				8	9		11				5	6		1		10	2	7	
8	Mar-20	C	Wrexham, WC-S-F	2 3	Webster, Donnelly	2,273	1	2	3	4	5		7	8	9	10					6	11							

L – Linz
C – Cardiff

Swansea Town FC Season 1962/63 Division 2

#	Date	V	Opponents	Score	Scorers	Att.	Dwyer N	Hughes B	Griffiths H	Saunders R	Purcell B	Davies G	Jones B	Thomas E	Webster C	Williams H	Morgans K	Nurse M	Davies P	King J	Johnson M	Todd K	Reynolds B	Sanders A	Morris A	Evans R	Draper D	Hayes M	Gilligan M
1	Aug-18	A	Charlton Athletic	2 2	Williams, Morgans	14,995	1	2	3	4	5	6	7	8	9	10	11												
2	Aug-23	H	Bury	3 0	Thomas 2, Williams H	10,326	1	2	3	4			7	8	9	10	11	5	6										
3	Aug-25	H	Stoke City	2 1	Williams H, Webster	16,746	1	2	3	4		6	7	8	9	10	11	5											
4	Aug-30	A	Bury	0 2		10,403		2	3			6	7	8	9	10	11	5	4	1									
5	Sep-01	A	Sunderland	1 3	Morgans	36,922		2	3		5	6	7	8	9	10	11		4	1									
6	Sep-05	H	Cardiff City	2 1	Williams H, Thomas	24,687	1	2	3		5	6	7	8	9	10	11		4										
7	Sep-08	H	Leeds United	0 2		17,696	1	2	3		5	6	7	8	9	10	11		4										
8	Sep-11	A	Scunthorpe United	0 1		10,683	1	2	3		5	6	7	8	9	10	11		4										
9	Sep-15	A	Cardiff City	2 5	Williams H 2	23,454	1	2	3		5	6	7	8	9	10	11		4										
10	Sep-18	H	Scunthorpe United	1 0	Morgans	11,014	1	2	3			6	7	8	9	10	11		4										
11	Sep-22	A	Chelsea	2 2	Thomas, Williams H	22,693	1	2	3				7	8	9	10	11	5	4		6								
12	Sep-29	H	Luton Town	1 0	Thomas	9,441	1	2	3			6	7	8	9	10		5			4	11							
13	Oct-06	H	Huddersfield Town	1 2	Morgans(pen)	11,024	1	2	3			6	7	8	9	10	11				4	5							
14	Oct-13	A	Middlesbrough	2 2	Webster, Thomas	19,718	1	2	3			4	7	8	10	6	11				5	9							
15	Oct-19	H	Derby County	2 0	Todd 2	8,956	1		3			4		8		10	11	6			5	9			2	7			
16	Oct-27	A	Newcastle United	0 6		24,005	1		3			4		8	11	6					5	9	10		2	7			
17	Nov-03	H	Walsall	3 0	Todd 3	7,820	1		3			6	7	8		10	11		4		5	9				2			
18	Nov-10	A	Norwich City	0 5		16,108	1		3			6	7	8		10	11		4		5	9				2			
19	Nov-17	H	Grimsby Town	1 0	Jones	5,606	1		3			6	7	8		10	11		4		5	9				2			
20	Nov-24	A	Plymouth Argyle	0 1		12,526	1		3			6	7	10	8		11		4		5	9				2			
21	Dec-01	H	Preston North End	1 1	Todd	7,085	1		3			6	7	8		10	11		4		5	9				2			
22	Dec-08	A	Portsmouth	0 0		12,410	1		3			6	7	8		10	11		4		5	9				2			
23	Dec-15	H	Charlton Athletic	2 1	Thomas, Todd	5,532	1		3			6	7	8		10	11		4		5	9				2			
24	Dec-26	H	Southampton	1 1	Todd	7,382	1		3			6	7	8		10	11		4		5	9				2			
25	Feb-09	H	Chelsea	2 0	Todd, Thomas	13,359	1		3			6	7	8			11		4		5	9	10			2			
26	Mar-02	H	Middlesbrough	1 1	Thomas	9,686	1		3			6	7	8					4		5	9	10		11	2			
27	Mar-09	A	Derby County	2 0	Todd, Davies G	8,846	1	6	3				7	10			11		4		5	9			8	2			
28	Mar-16	H	Newcastle United	1 0	Draper	7,725	1	6	3				7	10			11		4		5	9				2	8		
29	Mar-23	A	Walsall	1 0	Reynolds	7,609	1	6	3				7	10			11		4		5	9			8	2			
30	Mar-27	A	Stoke City	0 2		26,568	1	6	3				7	10			11		4		5	9			8	2			
31	Apr-06	A	Grimsby Town	0 1		8,670	1	6	3				7	8			10		4		5	9	11			2			
32	Apr-09	H	Norwich City	2 0	Thomas, Reynolds	8,460	1	6	3				7	10					4		5	9	11			2	8		
33	Apr-13	H	Plymouth Argyle	2 1	Thomas, Morgans(pen)	9,804	1		3			6	7	8		10			4		5	9	11	1		2			
34	Apr-15	A	Rotherham United	1 2	Morgans	8,281	1	6	3				7	10			11		4		5	9				2	8		
35	Apr-16	H	Rotherham United	2 2	Todd, Reynolds	10,077	1		3			6	7	8		10			4		5	9	11			2			
36	Apr-20	A	Preston North End	3 6	Morgans, Thomas 2	7,652	1		3			6	7	8		10			4		5	9	11			2			
37	Apr-22	A	Southampton	0 3		14,390	1				6	5	3	7	9	10			4				11			2	8		
38	Apr-27	H	Portsmouth	0 0		6,725	1				5	3	11	8		10					6				9	2		4	7
39	May-01	A	Luton Town	1 3	Todd	7,642	1		3			6	11	8		10					5	9				2		4	7
40	May-06	H	Huddersfield Town	1 4	Thomas	7,964	1		3				11	8		5					6	9	10			2		4	7
41	May-11	H	Sunderland	3 4	Thomas, Davies, Jones	8,567	1	6	3				11	8		10			4		5	9			7	2			
42	May-18	A	Leeds United	0 5		11,314	1	6	3				11	8		10			4		5	9			7	2			
	Apps						39	20	30	29	8	18	39	40	22	22	34	6	36	3	30	26	15	4	7	24	4	3	3
	Gls											1	2	15	2	7	7		1			12	3			1			

#	Date	V	Opponents	Score	Scorers	Att.	Dwyer N	Hughes B	Griffiths H	Saunders R	Purcell B	Davies G	Jones B	Thomas E	Webster C	Williams H	Morgans K	Nurse M	Davies P	King J	Johnson M	Todd K	Reynolds B	Sanders A	Morris A	Evans R	Draper D	Hayes M	Gilligan M
1	Sep-06	A	Coventry City, FLC-2	2 3	Jones, Webster	10,321	1	2	3				7	8	9	10	11	5	4		6								
2	Jan-26	H	QPR, FAC-3	2 0	Thomas, Reynolds	12,500	1		3			6	7	8			11		4		5	9	10			2			
3	Feb-02	H	Caerau, WC-5	6 0	Todd 2, Saunders, Jones 3		1		3			6	7	8			11		4		5	9	10			2			
4	Mar-04	A	West Ham United, FAC-4	0 1		25,924	1	4	3			6	7	8			11				5	9	10			2			
5	Apr-11	H	Cardiff C, WC-6	2 0	Jones, Thomas	11,500	1		3			6	7	10	9				4	1	5		11			2	8		
6	May-09	C	Newport Co. WC-S-F	0 1		5,300	1		3			6	7	9		10			4		5		11			2	8		

C – Cardiff

Swansea Town FC Season 1963/64 Division 2

#	Date	V	Opponents	Score	Scorers	Att.	Dwyer N	Hughes B	Evans R	Davies P	Johnson M	Williams H	Jones B	Thomas E	Todd K	Reynolds B	McLaughlin J	King J	Griffiths H	Morgans K	Evans B	Wilkins A	Draper D	Park C	Purcell B	Ward D	Harries L
1	Aug-24	H	Grimsby Town	1 1	Todd	10,740	1	2	3	4	5	6	7	8	9	10	11										
2	Aug-28	A	Derby County	0 3		15,831		2		4	5	6	7	8	9	10	11	1	3								
3	Aug-31	A	Preston North End	3 3	Todd, Reynolds 2	14,613		2		4	5	6	7	8	9	10		1	3	11							
4	Sep-03	H	Derby County	2 1	Todd, O/Goal	9,919	1	2		4	5	6	11	8	9	10			3		7						
5	Sep-07	H	Leyton Orient	1 0	O/Goal	9,307	1	2		4	5	6	7	8	9				3	11	10						
6	Sep-10	A	Huddersfield Town	0 1		15,846	1	2		4	5	6	11	10	9				3		7		8				
7	Sep-12	A	Scunthorpe United	2 2	Thomas, Jones	8,516		2		4		6	11	10	9				3		7		8	1	5		
8	Sep-17	H	Huddersfield Town	1 2	O/Goal	10,191	1	2			5	6	7	8	9		11		3	4			10				
9	Sep-21	A	Southampton	0 4		15,904	1	2		4	5	6	7	8	9	10	11		3								
10	Sep-28	H	Middlesbrough	2 1	Jones, McLaughlin	10,519	1	3	2	4	5	6	7	10		9	11						8				
11	Oct-05	A	Newcastle United	1 4	Thomas	23,711	1	3	2	4	5	6	7		9	10					11		8				
12	Oct-09	A	Portsmouth	0 0		11,752	1	3	2	4	5	6	7		9	10					11		8				
13	Oct-15	H	Norwich City	3 1	Evans B, Draper, Reynolds	9,127	1	3	2	4	5	6	7		9	10					11		8				
14	Oct-19	A	Cardiff City	1 1	Evans B	21,417	1	3	2	4	5	6	7	10		9					11		8				
15	Oct-26	H	Rotherham United	4 2	Evans R(pen), Todd, Reynolds, Williams	9,160	1	3	2	4	5	6	7		9	10					11		8				
16	Nov-02	A	Man. City	0 1		16,770	1	3	2	4	5	6	7		9	10					11		8				
17	Nov-09	H	Bury	0 2		8,693	1	3	2	4	5	6	7	8	9	10	11										
18	Nov-16	A	Northampton Town	3 2	Williams H, Jones 2	10,985	1	3	2	4		6	7		9	10	11						8		5		
19	Nov-23	H	Sunderland	1 2	Thomas	10,880	1	3	2	4		6	7		9	10	11						8		5		
20	Nov-30	A	Leeds United	1 2	Reynolds	21,870	1	3	2	4		6	7		9	10	11						8		5		
21	Dec-07	H	Swindon Town	3 0	Todd 3	8,892	1	3	2	4		6	7		9	10					11		8		5		
22	Dec-13	A	Grimsby Town	1 1	McLaughlin	6,763	1	3	2			6	7		9	10					11		8		5		
23	Dec-20	H	Preston North End	5 1	Evans, Williams, McLaughlin, Jones, Hughes	6,773	1	3	2			6	7		9	10					11		8		5		
24	Dec-26	H	Charlton Athletic	1 2	Draper	15,497	1	3	2			6			9	10	11				7		8		5		
25	Dec-28	A	Charlton Athletic	1 3	Draper	26,607		3	2			6			10	9	7	11				1	8		5		
26	Jan-11	A	Leyton Orient	0 4		12,570	1	3	2			6			10	9	11				7		8		5		
27	Jan-16	H	Scunthorpe United	4 1	Thomas 2, Evans B, McLaughlin	7,357	1	3	2			6	7	9		8	10				11				5		
28	Feb-08	A	Middlesbrough	1 2	McLaughlin	12,668	1	3	2			6	7	9			10				11		8		5		
29	Feb-22	A	Norwich City	0 3		11,461	1	3	2			6	7	8	9		10				11				5		
30	Mar-03	H	Southampton	6 0	Williams H 3, Evans R(pen), Reynolds, Jones	15,255	1	3	2			6	7			10	9				11		8		5		
31	Mar-07	A	Rotherham United	0 3		7,574	1		2			6	7			10	9				11		8		5	3	
32	Mar-17	H	Newcastle United	0 1		8,712	1	3	2			6	7		9	10					11		8		5		
33	Mar-21	A	Bury	2 3	Thomas, Jones	4,272	1	3	2			4	7		9						11		8		5		6
34	Mar-28	H	Cardiff City	3 0	Draper, Reynolds 2	18,721		3	2			6	7		9	10		1			11		8		5		
35	Mar-30	A	Plymouth Argyle	2 3	Jones, McLaughlin	17,576		2			6	7	8			9	10	1			11				5	3	
36	Mar-31	A	Plymouth Argyle	2 1	McLaughlin, Reynolds	11,929	1	2			6	7			9	10					11		8		5	3	
37	Apr-04	A	Sunderland	0 1		42,505	1	2		4	5	6	7	10		9					11		8			3	
38	Apr-07	H	Northampton Town	1 1	Reynolds	11,898	1	3	2			6	7		9	10					11		8		5		
39	Apr-11	H	Leeds United	0 3		14,321	1	3	2			6	7		9	10					11		8		5		
40	Apr-18	A	Swindon Town	1 2	Reynolds	14,002	1	3	2	6	4	8	7		9	10					11				5		
41	Apr-21	H	Portsmouth	1 1	Reynolds	9,905	1			4	5	6	7		9	10					11		8		2	3	
42	Apr-25	H	Man. City	3 3	Williams, O/Goal, McLaughlin(pen)	13,832	1			4	5	6	7	10	9	11							8		2	3	
	Apps						36	28	40	21	40	41	39	27	25	29	26	5	8	3	29	1	31	1	25	6	1
	Gls							1	2			7	8	6	7	12	8				4		4				

#	Date	V	Opponents	Score	Scorers	Att.	Dwyer N	Hughes B	Evans R	Davies P	Johnson M	Williams H	Jones B	Thomas E	Todd K	Reynolds B	McLaughlin J	King J	Griffiths H	Morgans K	Evans B	Wilkins A	Draper D	Park C	Purcell B	Ward D	Harries L
1	Sep-25	H	Sunderland, FLC-2	3 1	Draper, Todd, Reynolds	8,697	1		2	4	5	6	7		9	10	11		3				8				
2	Oct-22	A	Leeds United, FLC-3	0 2		10,769	1	3	2	4	5	6	7	10		9					11		8				
3	Jan-04	H	Barrow, FAC-3	4 1	Evans B, Evans R (pen), Thomas, Williams	9,488	1	3	2			6			10	9	11				7		8		5		
4	Jan-25	A	Sheff. Utd, FAC-4	1 1	Thomas	25,572	1	3	2			6	7		9	10					11		8		5		
5	Jan-28	H	Sheff. Utd, FAC-4 Rep	4 0	Draper 2, McLaughlin, Thomas	24,109	1	3	2			6	7		9		10				11		8		5		
6	Feb-01	A	Lovells Ath. WC-5	3 1	McLaughlin, O/Goal, Thomas	3,000	1		2			6	7		9		10	11					8		5		3
7	Feb-15	A	Stoke City, FAC-5	2 2	Todd 2	40,444	1	3	2			6	7		9		10				11		8		5		
8	Feb-18	H	Stoke City, FAC-5 Rep	2 0	McLaughlin, Todd	29,582	1	3	2			6	7		9		10				11		8		5		
9	Feb-20	A	Newport Co. WC-6	0 1		5,950		3	2	6	4		7			9		1			11		8		5		
10	Feb-29	A	Liverpool, FAC-6	2 1	McLaughlin, Thomas	52,608	1	3	2			6	7	9		10					11		8		5		
11	Mar-14	N	Preston N E, FAC-S-F	1 2	McLaughlin	68,000	1	3	2			6	7		9	10	11						8		5		

N – Villa Park

Swansea Town FC Season 1964/65 Division 2

#	Date	V	Opponents	Score	Scorers	Att.	Dwyer N	Evans R	Hughes B	Johnson M	Purcell B	Williams H	Jones B	Draper D	Reynolds B	Thomas E	McLaughlin J	Briggs R	Todd K	Evans B	Ward D	Davies P	Wilkins A	Harley A	Rees I	Harries L	Thomas B	Kirby G	Jones A	Pound K	Chinaglia G	Humphries W	McGuigan J	Black J	Roberts J
1	Aug-22	A	Norwich City	1 2	Draper	16,824	1	2	3	4	5	6	7	8	9	10	11																		
2	Aug-25	A	Rotherham United	2 4	Reynolds, Evans B	11,298		2	3	4	5	6	7		9		10	1		8	11														
3	Aug-29	H	Crystal Palace	2 1	McLaughlin, Williams	11,909	1	2	3	4	5	6	7	8	9		10				11														
4	Sep-01	H	Rotherham United	0 3		11,569	1	2	3	4	5	6	7	8	9		10				11														
5	Sep-04	A	Bury	2 2	Evans B, Todd	7,889	1	2	3	4	5	6	7	8			10			9	11														
6	Sep-08	A	Swindon Town	0 3		15,358	1	2	3	4	5	6	7	8			10			9	11														
7	Sep-12	H	Leyton Orient	2 5	Draper 2	8,123	1	2		4	5			8	9		11		10	7	3	6													
8	Sep-15	H	Swindon Town	4 0	Todd 2, Evans, Draper	8,201		2			5	6		8			11	1	9	7	3	4	10												
9	Sep-19	A	Charlton Athletic	0 1		13,580		2			5	6		8			11	1	9	7	3	4	10												
10	Sep-26	H	Man. City	3 0	Todd 3	10,863		2			5	6		8				1	9	7	3			4	10	11									
11	Sep-29	H	Coventry City	1 1	Todd	12,794		2			5	6		8			10	1	9	7	3						11	4							
12	Oct-03	A	Portsmouth	0 1		12,699		2			5	6		8				1		7	3	4	10				11		9						
13	Oct-10	A	Preston North End	2 2	Kirby, Williams	15,336		2			5	6		8			11	1	10		3		7					4	9						
14	Oct-17	H	Ipswich Town	1 1	Kirby	10,508		2			5	6		8			11	1	10		3			4				9							
15	Oct-24	A	Plymouth Argyle	1 2	Draper	16,336		2			5	6		8			11	1	10		3			4				9							
16	Oct-31	H	Bolton Wanderers	2 0	Kirby, Todd	10,651			2			6		8			11	1	10	7	3			4				9	5						
17	Nov-07	A	Middlesbrough	0 4		11,855		2			5	6		8			11	1	10	7	3			4				9							
18	Nov-14	H	Newcastle United	3 1	Kirby, Hughes, Todd	10,457		2			5	6		8				1	10	7	3			4				9				11			
19	Nov-21	A	Northampton Town	1 2	Kirby	13,427	1	2			5	6					11				3			4			8	9							
20	Nov-28	H	Southampton	3 3	Williams, O/Goal, McLaughlin	11,070		2			5	6					8	1	10	7	3			4				9				11			
21	Dec-05	A	Huddersfield Town	0 4		5,533		2			5	6					11	1	10	7	3			4			8	9							
22	Dec-12	H	Norwich City	0 0		9,143		2			5	6		8			10	1		7	3			4				9				11			
23	Dec-19	A	Crystal Palace	3 3	Todd 2, McLaughlin	13,585		2			5	6		8			10	1	9	7	3			4								11			
24	Dec-26	H	Cardiff City	3 2	Todd, Pound, McLaughlin	17,875		2			5	6		8			10	1	9	7	3			4								11			
25	Jan-02	H	Bury	2 2	Todd, McLaughlin	10,353		2			5	6		8			10	1	9	7	3			4								11			
26	Jan-16	A	Leyton Orient	3 2	Pound, Todd, McLaughlin	5,132		2			5	6					8	1	10	7	3			4				9				11			
27	Jan-23	H	Charlton Athletic	1 3	McLaughlin	11,541		2			5	6		8			10	1		7	3			4				9				11			
28	Feb-06	A	Man. City	0 1		11,931		2			5	6					10	1	9	7	3	6		4								11			
29	Feb-13	H	Portsmouth	0 0		9,087		2			5	6		8			10	1		7	3	4		8								11	9		
30	Feb-27	A	Ipswich Town	0 3		12,141		2		5	6						8	1	10	7	3			4				9				11			
31	Mar-06	H	Huddersfield Town	2 2	McLaughlin, Todd	7,574	2			5		6		8			10	1	9	7	3			4								11			
32	Mar-13	A	Bolton Wanderers	1 2	Davies	14,027	2		3	5		6		8			11	1	9					4						10		7			
33	Mar-20	A	Middlesbrough	1 2	Kirby	9,366	2		3	5		6					11	1	9					4						10			7	8	
34	Mar-23	H	Preston North End	4 0	Davies, Todd, McLaughlin, O/Goal	8,686	2		3	5							11		9					4		6				10			7	8	1
35	Mar-27	A	Newcastle United	1 3	Pound	28,634	2		3	5							8							6		4				9		11	7	10	1
36	Apr-03	H	Northampton Town	1 2	Todd	10,516	2		3	5							11	1	8					6		4				9			7	10	
37	Apr-06	A	Cardiff City	0 5		15,896	2		3	5				4			11		8					6						9			7	10	1
38	Apr-10	A	Southampton	1 3	Todd	13,317	2		3		4						11		8					6				9	5				7	10	1
39	Apr-17	H	Plymouth Argyle	3 0	Humphries, Kirby, Todd	8,505	2		3		4								10	11						6		9	5				7	8	1
40	Apr-19	A	Derby County	4 3	Todd, O/Goal, Kirby, McLaughlin	7,457	2		3		4						11		10					6				9	5				7	8	1
41	Apr-20	H	Derby County	2 1	McGuigan, Humphries	11,021	2		3		4						11		10					6				9	5				7	8	1
42	Apr-24	A	Coventry City	0 3		23,717	2		3		4								6									9	5				7	8	1
	Apps						7	22	37	35	13	32	6	23	7	1	38	27	34	30	25	16	4	23	1	3	4	25	6	14	1	10	10	8	
	Gls							1				3		5	1		10		20	3				2				8		3		2	1		

#	Date	V	Opponents	Score	Scorers	Att.	Dwyer N	Evans R	Hughes B	Johnson M	Purcell B	Williams H	Jones B	Draper D	Reynolds B	Thomas E	McLaughlin J	Briggs R	Todd K	Evans B	Ward D	Davies P	Wilkins A	Harley A	Rees I	Harries L	Thomas B	Kirby G	Jones A	Pound K	Chinaglia G	Humphries W	McGuigan J	Black J	Roberts J
1	Sep-23	H	Swindon T, FLC-2	3 1	McLaughlin, Todd, Rees	6,503		2			5		4		8		11	1	9	7	3				10	6									
2	Oct-14	A	Rotherham Utd, FLC-3	2 2	Williams, Johnson	8,993	2			5		6		8			1		10				4							11	7					9
3	Oct-28	H	Rotherham Utd, FLC-3Rep	2 0	Draper, Todd	7,566		2				6		8			11	1	10	7	3			4					5							9
4	Nov-11	A	Chelsea, FLC-4	2 3	Todd, Williams H	5,979		2				6					11	1	10	7	3		8				4	9	5							
5	Jan-09	H	Newcastle Utd. FAC-3	1 0	McLaughlin, Todd, Rees	18,951		2			5	6					8	1	10	7	3			4				9				11			
6	Jan-18	A	Newport Co. WC-5	3 2	McLaughlin, Todd, Evans	5,493	2				5	6					8	1	10	7	3			4				9				11			
7	Jan-30	H	Huddersfield T, FAC-4	1 0	Kirby	22,694		2			5	6					8	1	10	7	3			4				9				11			
8	Feb-11	A	Pwllheli, WC-6	3 1	McLaughlin, Pound, Evans B			2			5	6					8	1	10	7	3			4				9				11			
9	Feb-20	A	Peterborough Utd, FAC-5	0 0		30,096		2		6	5					8	11	1	10	7	3			4				9							
10	Feb-23	H	Peterborough Utd, FAC-5Rep	0 2		29,948		2		6	5					8	11	1	10	7	3			4				9							
11	Mar-10	N	Cardiff C, WC-S-F	0 1	played at Newport	7,500	2			5		6					8		10	7	3	4						9		11					1

Chapter 15

Ivor's Swan Song

1965-66

The club's relegation at the end of the previous season had been disappointing enough, but the outcome of the new campaign in Division Three proved to be doubly so. The Swans finished seventeenth in the table and won just one away match whilst losing fifteen. It was true that performances at the Vetch were better but, when set against the expectations of supporters, overall results left a great deal to be desired.

Brian Purcell

During the close season, a new manager, Glyn Davies, was appointed. A Swansea boy, Glyn had cut his managerial teeth at Yeovil Town, gaining a sound reputation in the process. Soon after his appointment he was joined by Tommy Casey, who was to act as his assistant. The new manager wasted little time in seeking to strengthen his squad. In July he bought the Vetch Field legend, Ivor Allchurch from, Cardiff for £8,000 and George Heyes, a goalkeeper from Leicester. He sold a player, too, transferring Derek Draper to Derby County for £5,000.

Ivor's return was like a shot-in-the-arm to the supporters and there were emotional scenes when he played his first match in the old colours for seven seasons. However, it was not only the presence of the Golden Boy which gave some supporters cause to fancy the chances of the club in its first season in the lower division. As Glyn Davies emphasised to Ivor when negotiating his return, there was a wealth of experience among the playing staff who were on the club's books. Eight of the team which had played in the semi-final of the FA Cup were still at the Vetch, as were Irish international Willie Humphries and experienced Scot, John McGuigan, both of whom had been signed towards the end of the previous campaign. It was not surprising, therefore, that many people felt that the Swans would 'bounce back' at the first time of asking. Even the pessimists found it difficult to be gloomy. Unfortunately, in the event, the team's performances, particularly away from home, shattered the dream. The side suffered several heavy defeats; they lost 5-0 at Shrewsbury early in the season, while Workington Town (the league's new boys) thrashed them 6-1 at the Vetch and 7-0 in Cumbria. Bill Paton described them as 'humiliating defeats' and he was not alone in that judgement.

At the Vetch, Workington apart, things were rather more encouraging. The Swans beat Southend and Bournemouth by the same score (5-0) and York City 7-2. Certainly, no one could complain about the number of goals which the team registered while playing at home, for they set a new club record, finding the net sixty-one times. Their performances on away grounds,

Brian Hughes

however, stood in stark contrast. On their travels the team recorded a total of just twenty goals whilst conceding fifty-nine.

At the beginning of the season, the enthusiastic Davies and his assistant talked about bringing the excitement back to Vetch soccer. Tommy Casey spoke about 'a more open style' and of using something called 'the swivel defence method'. Later, when results were unacceptable, Bill Paton, attempting to put his finger on the reasons for poor performances, claimed that the players were finding it difficult to adapt themselves to the pattern of play which the coaches were demanding. Whatever the reasons, the poor form had its effects on gates, and in November only 4,217 people turned up to watch a match against Bournemouth.

There was some heartening news at the turn of the year, however; Ivor Allchurch was awarded the MBE in the New Year's Honours List with the citation 'for services to football'. The news was received enthusiastically by the football world; Ivor said that he was proud to receive the honour but that it was really for Swansea football. Those who watched the veteran performing week

> *In the New Year's Honours List for 1966 Ivor Allchurch was awarded an MBE for 'services to football'.*

after week in a struggling side would have all agreed that his words reflected the way he played. As Bill Paton put it, 'He gives his all to the side.' Not only had he grafted in every match, at the end of the season, with twelve goals he was second top scorer behind Jimmy McLaughlin (20). Not a bad performance for a thirty-six-year-old whose job was to make as well as take goals.

Despite the disappointment of the league campaign there was some encouragement for manager Davies and the fans: at the end of the season the Swans beat Chester in the final of the Welsh Cup. As a result, once again, the club found itself in the European Cup Winners' Cup. Unfortunately though, the confidence-sapping events of the league season served to have a negative effect on the club and the squad. The painful truth was that the club was poorly equipped for the task of challenging the best in Europe. In the event, after drawing with Slavia Sofia at the Vetch, 1-1, they were beaten 4-0 in the second leg.

Brian Evans

football. No player could complain that he could not understand that.

Joe told the press that he felt that there was the nucleus of a reasonable side on the books. Newcomer Vic Gomersall had joined the club from Manchester City and was forming a

City instead. Neither Gregg nor anyone at the Vetch was to know that he would come to the Vetch in due course, but not as a player. Despite that disappointment, by mid-February the popular Sykes's side had obtained some useful results, which gave his players and the supporters some hope. Reading, Shrewsbury and Workington were all beaten 5-2 and young John Roberts was beginning to get his name on the score sheet. Meantime, the directors continued their search for an experienced manager and on 18 February Billy Lucas returned to the Vetch – this time to manage the club.

Lucas moved into the transfer market immediately and signed Joe Davis from Bristol Rovers for a small fee, but, by the end of March the club, with ten matches to play, was firmly rooted in twenty-third position in the table. By then the team had gathered twenty-five points from thirty-six matches. Prior to the next game, Dilwyn John, a goalkeeper, was signed from Cardiff City and matters began to improve. Colchester and Doncaster were beaten at the Vetch in successive games, with the latter conceding six goals. Subsequently, although the team won three out of its next four matches, it was not enough. To the chagrin of all concerned, Swansea Town were relegated to the basement division. It was a bitter blow for the players, supporters, management team and the board. It also exacerbated the club's dire financial position. At that point, had there been a ready buyer, even Whitechapel Road would have been sold.

1966-67

At a board meeting in July, chairman Philip Holden warned his colleagues of the possibility that the club would not be able to maintain its £30,000 overdraft. By mid-October, that warning appeared to be even more threatening, for the team had been eliminated from the Football League Cup and the Cup Winners' Cup and had been publicly criticised by the vice-chairman for lack of effort. Furthermore, after thirteen league games the Swans had picked up just six points, were bottom of the table, and home gates had averaged less than 7,000. It was a dismal and worrying state of affairs which, in due course, resulted in Davies and Casey being sacked. Meantime, supporters writing to the *Post* were comparing the Swans' predicament with that of Accrington Stanley. When Glyn Davies left, Joe Sykes took over as caretaker manager and, as was his way, did all he could to improve matters. Joe's methods were pure and simple classical

Billy Lucas became the manager at the Vetch in February 1967 and, shortly after, was presented with a white budgie as a good luck charm. Unfortunately, soon after the season ended, the bird escaped. While Billy was extremely sorry that the cage had been left open, he said that he was not superstitious. There were others who were.

useful partnership at full-back with Roy Evans; Herbie Williams was playing well at left half, whilst Willie Humphries, Ivor, Keith Todd and Brian Evans were the pick of the forwards. Yet, these players and others who had much to offer, were ignominiously ejected from the FA Cup in January by non-league Nuneaton. Ten days later, despite Joe's best efforts, they were also eliminated from the Welsh Cup.

In December, Sykes almost made his first signing. Harry Gregg, then thirty-two, was about to sign but changed his mind and joined Stoke

At a shareholders' meeting in April the chairman announced a plan to extend the board. They needed, he argued, 'young blood and up-and-coming workers'. Apparently, however, that description did not fit local solicitor, Malcolm Struel, who offered £1,600 in return for a place on the board. Nonetheless, there was one important reunion: Harry Griffiths was to return as coach and chief scout. It was the beginning of another outstanding period of service which this wholehearted Swansea boy was to give to the club he loved.

Jim Furnell, the Arsenal goalkeeper, pushes an Ivor piledriver over the bar in front of the record crowd for the Vetch.
Arsenal won by the only goal of the game.

1967-68

It is said that the true barometer of interest in a football club is the number of season tickets sold before the campaign starts. If this is the case, at the Vetch in the summer of 1967 there must have been many worried men. Only 800 seasons had been sold, less than fifty per cent of those disposed of only three seasons before. It was another blow to the morale of what was a worried board. There was no money available to try to strengthen the side, so Lucas did his best with the players at his disposal together with John Bird, who had come on a free transfer from Newport. In August an all-white budgie, which had been presented to the club as a good luck charm, escaped from its cage. Lucas was reported as saying that he was not superstitious, yet the hard core of supporters who still followed the club could have done without even the faintest hint of further disaster.

As the season wore on, Lucas began to introduce some of his younger players into league football and transferred one to placate the bank. David Lawrence, son of a pre-war captain, made an impressive

debut in October, as did Billy Screen. In November, John Roberts, who had been the previous season's Player of the Year, was sold to Northampton for £12,000. Two days later, the club announced a deficit of £41,000, and secretary Gordon Daniels pointed out that it was losing money at a rate of £500 per week. Something had to be done, but quite what that was did not seem to be clear at the time – at least to the existing board.

On the playing front, despite some inconsistency, the team was doing reasonably well. At the end of December the club was fifteenth in the league table and in the fourth round of the FA Cup. If ever the Swans needed a good cup run, it was then, and there were some encouraging signs to suggest that there was some hope of that occurring. Earlier in the month, playing in what was to be his last season in league football at thirty-eight-years-of-age, Ivor Allchurch scored six goals in three matches. Three of those, in the game against Doncaster, constituted a memorable hat-trick, which typified the remarkable effort which the player who had graced so many football

pitches around the world put in to his work. Even in his late thirties he was willing to give his all for Swansea Town.

In January, Brighton were beaten in the fourth round of the FA Cup and Doncaster in the fifth. As a result, the club found itself in the sixth round, when it was drawn to play against Arsenal at the Vetch. The question was whether the team good enough to emulate the great 1926 side and beat the Gunners? In the town, Swansea cup fever, which had lain dormant for some time, came to life with a bang. Indeed, such was the interest that, on the day of the game, 32,786 people were crammed into the Vetch. It was (and remains) the largest gate ever at the ground. Sadly though, despite an outstanding performance by the home side, Bobby Gould rose to head home the only goal of the game. It was the end of another cup challenge, but at least it had provided the club with a useful injection of income at a crucial stage in the season. In addition there was the encouragement of a fine performance by the team against First Fivision opponents. Yet, two days later the same side was eliminated from the Welsh Cup and subsequently won only one of its next nine matches. To add to the club's misery, on 2 March a serious fire damaged the centre grandstand and destroyed the treatment centre and its equipment. Then, in the middle of the month, just 3,775 watched the side draw 2-2 with Southend, a match in which Ivor scored his last brace of goals for the club.

Those who searched through the ashes of the season for comfort, the cup run apart, found little to cheer them. Nevertheless, they could reflect on the phenominal service which Ivor Allchurch had given the club. Whilst his team finished in an undistinguished fifteenth place in the lowest division of the Football League, the amazing Ivor finished as top-scorer with twenty-one league and cup goals. In all he had played forty-five matches, which was a tribute to his fitness and skill. In view of this record, it is probable that Allchurch would have signed for a further season, but sadly, in seeking economies, the Vetch management asked him to take a twenty per cent reduction in wages. Given the service which he had given to the club as well as his appearance and goal scoring record during the season which had just finished, it was a penny-pinching decision which probably resulted in the loss of a most gifted player and a regular goal-scorer as well as leaving the man himself feeling disgruntled.

Nevertheless, there was an opportunity to see Ivor in action again, for on 25 May Leeds United came to the Vetch to support his testimonial. His mentor, Joe Sykes, and thousands of his adoring fans paid tribute that day to the blond genius who had given so many Swans fans so much pleasure. Poignantly, D. J. Weaver, who became a director in 1938, died that afternoon and the players wore black arm bands as a mark of their respect for the former board member.

June brought a spate of activity, with Ivor Pursey, Michael Pascoe and Malcolm Struel campaigning to 'stir people out of their apathy'. They made no attempt to hide the fact that the 'people' in this context were the members of the board. On 8 June, however, there was a significant signing: Mel Nurse came back to Swansea in return for a small fee paid to Swindon. Nurse, by then a seasoned professional who had played at the highest level, was an extremely important addition to the staff. He would add steel, discipline and know-how to the Swans defence and lead by example. A week later there was a significant departure from the Vetch; seventy-one-year-old Joe Sykes resigned. Mere words cannot do justice to the superb service which this gentle man gave to the Vetch club. He had been 'the doyen of carpet passers', an admirable and successful player and captain, an excellent coach, scout and a magnificent servant of the club.

The Vetch Field was to be a lesser place without the presence of the man who, in his day, could out-jump men a foot taller than himself, and who, among so many other achievements had discovered the great Ivor. On Joe's departure, Walter Robbins was appointed as assistant manager, while Harry Griffiths became chief trainer. A player was signed, too: Lucas paid Walsall £5,000 for Jimmy McMorrran. That news though, did not deter Malcolm Struel and the Ginger Group from continuing their campaign for the reorganisation of the board.

A petition with four thousand signatures was handed to vice-chairman Trevor Wood in support of the group's appeal. The offer of making money available for better players was also renewed. Wood told the delegates that he and his board colleagues would give the offer careful consideration.

1968-69

Happily, the new season started in fairly encouraging fashion: the side remained unbeaten for the first seven games. Whilst five of these were drawn, it was a distinct improvement on the previous term. The defence was extremely solid, with Mel Nurse outstanding at its heart. By the end of September, only one league match had been lost, with the defence conceding just eight goals in the ten games which had been played. In addition, the side had been 'magnificent in defeat' in losing at Anfield in the Football League Cup and had earned the plaudits of the press, Lucas could have been forgiven for feeling reasonably confident about his side's prospects for the rest of the season. At that stage the team was in fifth place in the table.

Unfortunately, during October that confidence appeared to have been misplaced as the Swans lost three games in a row. One result of this was that Lucas paid his old club, Newport, a small fee to bring Alan Williams to the Vetch. Then, in November, McMorran returned to Walsall and Alfie Biggs came to the Vetch in his stead. However, none of these changes did much to improve the situation and, by the end of January the club was in mid-table and had been eliminated from the FA Cup by Halifax.

When the Swans played Scunthorpe at the Vetch on 11 January 1969 Kevin Keegan was a member of the visiting team.

Nevertheless, there were some encouraging signs. A new lounge was opened for the use of Swansea Town Vice-Presidents' Club. This organisation had thrown its weight behind the parent club and raised funds to assist with the rebuilding of the dressing rooms after the fire. The club's financial results, which were issued at the end of November, showed signs of improvement. With the smallest staff in the club's history, £7,300 had been lost on the previous season's working. Although the total deficit was still a daunting £48,000, the season's loss was £11,000 less than it had been for the previous campaign.

In January another player left the Vetch. Brian Hughes, who had given the club stalwart service, departed to join Atlanta Chiefs in the USA. There was also some tragic news: two of Hughes's contemporaries, Roy Evans and Brian Purcell – who were playing for Hereford at the time – were killed in a car crash. The news was received with great regret, for both players were fine sportsmen and popular individuals.

As the season wore on, Lucas faced many difficulties. He tried every combination which made sense to him, but without a great deal of success. Somehow the excellent form of the early season could not be recaptured, and, in keeping with the poor results which ensued, gates were diminishing and revenue decreasing. On 18 March only 2,539 came to see the team play York, when, although depleted by influenza, the side fought hard to win by the odd goal in three. They also won their next two matches, beating Workington 3-0 and one-time division leaders, Lincoln by 5-0. However, just as things seemed to be improving on the field, Billy Lucas resigned his position to go back into business in Newport. Trevor Wood, now the club's chairman, stated that they were sorry to lose the hard-working Lucas, while Lucas himself emphasised that it was his own decision: no pressure had been brought to bear on him.

When Lucas left, the club was in tenth position in the league table. Walter Robbins became caretaker manager, a position he held until the curtain came down on the season. Under Robbins the team won five of its nine matches and lost a two-

legged Welsh Cup Final to Cardiff. The scorer of three of the five goals which were netted by the Taffsiders was a young man called Toshack. That name was to make a bigger impact on the Vetch Field in the not too distant future. In general, despite some excellent performances by the team, particularly Nurse, Gomersall, Herbie Williams and Lawrence, the season's outcome was far from cheering for the board. The average attendance for the twenty-three home league games was 5,666, the lowest in the history of the club. There was another new unwanted record, too. On 12 April, with an England-Wales rugby match being shown on television, only 1,984 people came to the Vetch Field. It was hardly surprising that the board was worried.

1969-70

In May 1969 a consortium of local businessmen, headed by the persistent Malcom Struel, deposited £35,000 with a bank in Swansea. The money, the group announced was 'to be held to the order of Swansea Town AFC Ltd. provided that the existing board resign'. This

action prompted discussions between the board and the Ginger Group and, in due course, a compromise was agreed. Trevor Wood remained as chairman and his colleague, Peter Walters, stayed as a member of the new board. Walters also matched the individual commitment of the members of the incoming group by putting £5,000 of his own money into the club. Philip Holden did the same on behalf of Trevor Wood, and the remainder of the old board resigned. The men who formed the new board with Wood and Walters, were Malcom Struel, Richard Englert, Terry Francis, David Goldstone, Ivor Pursey and Trevor Wignall. Like an opposition party which had been swept into power after years in the wilderness, they were to find that it is difficult to arrest a downward trend.

Nonetheless, their enthusiasm and personal cash commitment gave the club immediate fresh momentum. Len Allchurch was back to add guile to the forward line and in July, Welsh international Tony Millington was signed from Peterborough for a small fee; he was to have a fruitful career at the Vetch and became a great favourite with supporters. Then, as if to demonstrate their intention not to sell good, young players, the board rejected a bid of £8,000 from Bristol Rovers for David Gwyther. Gwyther, who had finished second to Herbie Williams in the club's goalscoring list for the previous campaign, was thought to have considerable potential.

Meantime, Malcolm Struel had undertaken what the *Post* called 'a two-thousand-mile fact-finding mission'. His conclusion was that 'time is against us. We must get money if Swansea is going to make an impact this season.' Two weeks later John Burgum, who was now covering Swans matters for the *Post*, wrote what, at this distance, can be regarded as a prophetic paragraph. Commenting on the news that the new board intended to pay a salary of £5,000 to attract a manager of calibre, he declared: 'All that remains is for Swansea to find the right man and the "revolution" which has taken Swansea football by storm can develop its new image . . . as a city.' While the man who was appointed early the following month had some initial success, he was not to be the new messiah.

Tony Millington

Swansea City FC Season 1971/72 Division 3

#	Date	V	Opponents	Score	Scorers	Att.	Millington T	Jones P	Screen T	Evans W	Williams H	Hole B	Slattery C	Thomas G	Davies G	Gwyther D	Evans B	Screen W	Williams A	Holme P	Sullivan A	Beer A	Evans K	Rees R	Payne D	Ingram G	Morgan D	Fury P	Thomas B
1	Aug-14	A	Bradford City	2 0	Davies, Thomas	5,183	1	2	3	4	5	6	7	8	9	10	11												
2	Aug-21	H	Port Vale	0 1		6,457	1	2	3	4	5	6	7	8	9	10	11*	12											
3	Aug-27	A	Tranmere Rovers	0 0		3,724	1	2	3	4	5	6	7	8	9	10	11												
4	Aug-31	H	Bristol Rovers	2 0	Evans B, Screen W	6,801	1	2	3	4	5	6		8	9	10	11	7											
5	Sep-04	H	Barnsley	2 0	Thomas(pen), Davies	6,068	1	2	3	4	5	6		8	9	10	11	7											
6	Sep-11	A	Mansfield Town	2 0	Davies 2	3,547	1	2	3	4	5	6		8	9	10	11	7											
7	Sep-18	H	Torquay United	0 0		7,396	1	2		4	5	6		8	9	10	11	7	3										
8	Sep-25	A	Blackburn Rovers	2 1	Evans B, O/Goal	6,695	1	2		4	5	6		8	9	10	11	7	3										
9	Sep-28	A	Rotherham United	0 4		5,282	1	2		4	5	6	12	8	9*	10	11	7	3										
10	Oct-02	H	Notts. County	1 1	Davies	9,703	1	2		4	5	6		8	9	10	11	7	3										
11	Oct-09	A	Bournemouth	1 2	O/Goal	12,057	1	2		4	5	6		8	9	10	11*	7	3	12									
12	Oct-16	A	Bradford City	2 0	Thomas(pen), Evans B	6,539	1	2	3	4	5	6		8	9	10	11	7											
13	Oct-19	H	Brighton	2 1	Gwyther, O/Goal	6,206	1	2	3	4	5	6		8	9	10	11	7											
14	Oct-23	A	Bolton Wanderers	0 0		11,242	1	2	3	4		6		8	9	10	11	7	5										
15	Oct-30	H	Rochdale	1 0	Gwyther	7,743	1	2	3	4	5	6	11	8	9	10		7											
16	Nov-05	A	Shrewsbury Town	0 3		5,417	1	2	3	4	5	6		8	9	10	11	7											
17	Nov-13	H	Walsall	2 0	Thomas(pen), Davies	6,407	1	2	3	4	5	6		8	9	10		7			11								
18	Nov-27	H	Halifax Town	3 0	Davies G, Gwyther 2	5,285	1	2	3		5	6		8	9	10				4	7	11							
19	Dec-04	A	Chesterfield	2 1	Gwyther, Sullivan	8,108	1	2	3		5	6		8	9	10	11			4	7								
20	Dec-18	A	Barnsley	1 0	O/Goal	4,032	1	2	3		5	6		8	9	10				4	7		11						
21	Dec-27	H	Aston Villa	1 2	Williams H	24,419	1	2	3		5	6		8	9	10				4	7		11						
22	Jan-01	A	Torquay United	4 1	Holme 3, Beer	3,572	1	2	3		5	6		8	9	10				4	7		11						
23	Jan-08	H	Tranmere Rovers	1 1	O/Goal	5,824	1	2	3		5			8	9*	10	11		6	4	7		12						
24	Jan-22	H	Rotherham United	0 2		8,717	1	2	3			6	12	8	9		11			4	7		5	10*					
25	Jan-24	A	York Ciy	1 1	Holme	4,795	1	2	3			6				10	11		8	4	9		7	5					
26	Jan-29	A	Brighton	0 1		13,083	1	2	3			6				10		7	8	4	9		5	11					
27	Feb-12	H	Bolton Wanderers	3 2	Slattery, Thomas 2(2 pens)	4,962		2	3			6	5	9		10		7	8			4	11	1					
28	Feb-19	A	Rochdale	1 1	Slattery	3,097	1	2	3	4		6	5	9		10		7	8				11						
29	Feb-26	H	Shrewsbury Town	1 0	Gwyther	5,068	1	2	3	4		8	6	5		9		7	10				11						
30	Mar-04	A	Walsall	0 4		3,808		2	3	4		8	6	5		9		7	10				11	1					
31	Mar-11	H	Bournemouth	1 2	Slattery	7,718	1	2	4*	3		8	6	5		10		7	9	12			11						
32	Mar-14	H	York City	2 1	Gwyther, Screen W	3,749	1	2		3		8	6	4		10		7	9	5			11						
33	Mar-18	A	Port Vale	0 3		3,257		2				6	7	4		10	11		8	5	9				1	3			
34	Mar-24	H	Mansfield Town	1 1	Screen W	3,494		2			5	8	4	7*	9	10			6	12			11		1	3			
35	Mar-28	A	Oldham Athletic	0 1		6,243		2				6	5	7		10	8			4	9		11		1		3		
36	Apr-01	A	Aston Villa	0 2		33,394		2*		12		6	5	7		10	8			4			11		1	9	3		
37	Apr-03	A	Notts. County	0 5		14,019		2				6	5	9		10	7			4*	12		11		1	8	3		
38	Apr-04	H	Blackburn Rovers	0 1		3,367					9	6	4			10							11	7	1	8	3	2	5
39	Apr-08	H	Plymouth Argyle	1 1	Evans B	2,974						6		9		10			12	7			11		1	8	3	2	5*
40	Apr-11	H	Wrexham	0 2		2,826						9	5			10	11			4	12	7*	8		1	6	3	2	
41	Apr-15	A	Halifax Town	1 0	Gwyther	2,620	1						5	7		10	11			4	9		8		6	3	2		
42	Apr-18	H	Oldham Athletic	0 0		2,541	1						5	7		10	11			4	9		8		6	3	2		
43	Apr-22	H	Chesterfield	1 3	Evans B	2,887	1				9*		5	7		10	11			12		4	8		6	3	2		
44	Apr-25	A	Bristol Rovers	1 2	Gwyther	6,881							7	5	9	10				8		4	11		1	6	3	2	
45	Apr-29	A	Wrexham	0 2		3,805	1						7	5	9	10				12		8	4	11	6	3		2*	
46	May-02	A	Plymouth Argyle	1 4	Thomas G	8,321	1						12	5	3	10	7	8		9*		4	11		6			2	
			Apps				35	36	26	24	22	36	17	43	35	46	37	26	23	16	4	5	8	21	11	13	11	9	2
			Subs						1				3						2	2	4	2							
			Gls								1		3	7	7	9	5	3		4	1	1							

#	Date	V	Opponents	Score	Scorers	Att.	Millington T	Jones P	Screen T	Evans W	Williams H	Hole B	Slattery C	Thomas G	Davies G	Gwyther D	Evans B	Screen W	Williams A	Holme P	Sullivan A	Beer A	Evans K	Rees R	Payne D	Ingram G	Morgan D	Fury P	Thomas B
1	Aug-17	H	Brighton, FLC-1	0 1		5,680	1	2	3	4	5	6	7	8	9	10	11												
2	Nov-20	H	Brentford, FAC-1	1 1	Davies	7,915	1	2	3		5	6		8	9	10	7*	12	4		11								
3	Nov-22	A	Brentford, FAC-1Rep	3 2	Williams A, Thomas, Gwyther	15,000	1	2	3		5	6		8	9	10		12	4	7	11*								
4	Dec-11	H	Exeter C, FAC-2	0 0		8,397	1	2	3	4		6		8	9	10				5	7		11						
5	Dec-15	A	Exeter C, FAC-2Rep	1 0	Holme	6,858	1	2	3		5	6		8	9	10				4	7		11						
6	Jan-03	H	Cardiff C, WC-5	0 2		14,319	1	2	3		5	6		8	9	10				4	7		11						
7	Jan-15	H	Gillingham, FAC-3	1 0	Gwyther	5,099	1	2	3			6	9	8		10	11			4	7		5						
8	Feb-05	A	Portsmouth, FAC-4	0 2		19,782	1	2	3	12		6		8*	9	10				7	4		5	11					

Swansea City FC Season 1972/73 Division 3

#	Date	V	Opponents	Score	Scorers	Att.	Millington T	Screen T	Ingram G	Thomas G	Williams H	Harvey K	Johnson J	Henson P	Davies G	Gwyther D	Evans B	Rees R	Fury P	Curtis A	Lenihan M	Evans W	Jones P	Davies L	Evans K	McLaughlin J	Evans M	Carver D	Moore J	Allan S	Davies D L	James R
1	Aug-12	A	Scunthorpe United	0 1		5,455	1	2	3	4	5	6	7	8	9	10	11															
2	Aug-19	H	Walsall	2 1	Thomas(pen), Williams	4,211	1	2	3	4	5	6		8	9	10	11	7														
3	Aug-25	A	Southend United	1 3	Gwyther	10,985	1		3	4	5	6	7		9	12				2	8*	10	11									
4	Aug-29	A	Charlton Athletic	0 6		4,262	1		3	4	5	6	7		9	10				2		11	8									
5	Sep-02	H	Rochdale	2 3	Williams, Evans B	2,475	1		3	4	5	6	7		12	10	11	8			9*		2									
6	Sep-09	A	Brentford	2 0	Gwyther, Ingram	9,980	1	2	6	5	10			8		9	11	7				4	3									
7	Sep-16	H	Rotherham United	0 1		3,465	1	3	6	5	9			8		10	11	7				4	2									
8	Sep-19	H	Tranmere Rovers	1 1	Williams	2,617	1	3	8	4	10	6				9	11	7				5	2									
9	Sep-23	A	Shrewsbury Town	1 2	Johnson	2,415	1	3	8	4	10	6				9	11	7				5	2									
10	Sep-27	A	Notts. County	0 2		6,118			6	4	10			8	3	9	11	7				5	2	1								
11	Sep-30	H	Bristol Rovers	0 2		3,711			6	4	10			8	3	9	11	7				5		1	2							
12	Oct-07	H	Grimsby Town	6 2	Evans B, Rees, Thomas 3, Gwyther	3,071	1		12	8	5	6			3	10	11	7		9*		4	2									
13	Oct-11	A	Bolton Wanderers	0 3		6,112	1		6	8	5	9			3	10	11	7				4	2									
14	Oct-14	A	Plymouth Argyle	1 3	Thomas	5,034	1			9	8	5	6		3	10	11	7				4	2									
15	Oct-21	H	Blackburn Rovers	2 2	Evans B, Williams	3,060	1		6		9	5			3	10	11	7		8		4	2									
16	Oct-24	H	Chesterfield	2 1	Evans B, Gwyther	2,630	1	2	7	4	9	5	8		3	10	11			6												
17	Oct-28	A	Oldham Athletic	0 2		5,890	1	2	7	4	9	5*		8	10		11			6		3	12									
18	Nov-04	H	Notts. County	3 0	Williams 2, Gwyther	3,508	1	3	6	4	9				2	10	11			8		5	7									
19	Nov-10	A	Tranmere Rovers	1 1	Evans B	6,051	1	3		4	9				2	10	11			8		5	7			6						
20	Nov-25	A	Halifax Town	1 1	Williams	1,815	1	3		4	9				2	10	11	7		8		6	5									
21	Dec-01	H	Wrexham	3 1	Gwyther 2, Jones	2,206	1	3		4	9				2	10	11	7		8		6	5									
22	Dec-23	A	York City	0 3		2,218	1	2	3	5	9					10	11	7	8*			4	6				12					
23	Dec-26	H	Shrewsbury Town	0 2		4,460	1			5	9				2	10	11	8	7*			4	6				12	3				
24	Jan-06	H	Southend United	1 1	Evans W	2,466	1		6	5	9				2	10	7	8			11*	4	12				3					
25	Jan-13	A	Chesterfield	0 1		4,934	1			5	11				2	10	7	8		9		4	6				3					
26	Jan-26	H	Brentford	2 1	Evans B, Evans W	2,119	1			5	9					10	11	8		7		4	6				3	2				
27	Jan-29	A	York City	1 3	Johnson	3,269	1			12	9					10	11	8		7*		4	6				3	2	5			
28	Feb-03	H	Scunthorpe United	2 1	Williams, Thomas(pen)	1,607	1			8	9		12			10*		7			11	4	6				3	2	5			
29	Feb-10	A	Rotherham United	2 0	Evans W, Gwyther	3,042	1	2		8	9		7			10	11					4	6				3		5			
30	Feb-14	A	Walsall	1 1	Rees	4,262	1	2		8	9		7			10	11					4	6				3		5			
31	Feb-24	A	Watford	1 0	Evans M	6,051	1	2		8	5		7			9	11					10	6				3		4			
32	Feb-27	H	Watford	2 1	Evans W, Thomas(pen)	3,439	1	2		8	9		7			10	11					5	6				3		4			
33	Mar-03	A	Grimsby Town	0 2		11,701	1	2*		8	9		7			10	11					5	6				12	3	4			
34	Mar-06	H	Bournemouth	1 0	Evans W	5,390	1	2		8	9		7			10	11					5	6				3		4			
35	Mar-09	H	Plymouth Argyle	1 1	Gwyther	4,584	1	2		8	9		7			10	11					5	6				3		4			
36	Mar-12	A	Rochdale	1 1	Gwyther	2,037	1	2		8	9		7			10	11					5	6				3		4			
37	Mar-17	A	Blackburn Rovers	0 3		8,388	1	2*		8	9		7			10	11					5	6				3		4		12	
38	Mar-19	A	Port Vale	1 3	Johnson	5,104	1			8	5*		7			10	12	11				3	2			6			4	9		
39	Mar-24	H	Oldham Athletic	0 0		3,062	1			8	5		7		2		11					9	6				3		4	10		
40	Mar-31	H	Halifax Town	2 0	Johnson, Allan	2,499	1			8	5		7		2		11					9	6				3		4	10		
41	Apr-04	H	Bolton Wanderers	2 3	Thomas, O/Goal	3,096	1			8	5		7		2	10	11						6				3		4	9		
42	Apr-07	A	Wrexham	0 1		3,364	1			8	5		7		2	10	11			12			6				3		4	9		
43	Apr-14	A	Port Vale	0 1		2,549	1			8	5		7		2		11					10	6				3		4	9		
44	Apr-20	A	Bristol Rovers	1 3	O/Goal	8,348	1			8	5		7		2*	12	11					10	6			9	3		4			
45	Apr-21	H	Bournemouth	0 2		8,579	1		4	8*	5		7		6	9	11	10					2				3				12	
46	Apr-28	H	Charlton Athletic	2 1	Thomas(pen), Johnson	1,880		9	6*	5	10		4								11	12	2	1	8		3					7
					Apps		43	23	18	45	40	11	37	1	28	39	31	34	2	13	6	38	38	3	2	8	18	3	18	6	0	1
					Subs				1	1			1		1	2	1	1			1		1				4				1	1
					Gls				1	9	8		5			10	6	2				5	1				1			1		

#	Date	V	Opponents	Score	Scorers	Att.	Millington T	Screen T	Ingram G	Thomas G	Williams H	Harvey K	Johnson J	Henson P	Davies G	Gwyther D	Evans B	Rees R	Fury P	Curtis A	Lenihan M	Evans W	Jones P	Davies L	Evans K	McLaughlin J	Evans M	Carver D	Moore J	Allan S	Davies D L	James R
1	Aug-15	H	Newport Co. FLC-1	1 1	Thomas	3,998	1	2	3	4	8	5	6	7*	9	10	11	12														
2	Aug-22	A	Newport Co. FLC-1Rep	0 3		5,230	1	2*	3	4	5	6	7	12	9	10	11	8														
3	Nov-18	A	Margate, FAC-1	0 1		3,014	1	3		5	9				2	10	11	12		8		4	7			6*						
4	Jan-09	H	Newport C, WC-5	0 0		2,990	1	3		5	9				2	10	7	8			11	4	6									
5	Jan-16	A	Newport Co. WC-5Rep	0 3		4,042	1	3		5	9				2	10	11	8		7		4	6									

Swansea City FC Season 1973/74 Division 4

#	Date	V	Opponents	Score	Scorers	Att.	Millington T	Bevan P	Evans M	Bruton D	Moore J	Williams H	Lally P	James R	Screen T	McLaughlin J	Bartley D	Evans W	Curtis A	Lenihan M	Jones P	Rees R	Davies G	Thomas G	Bala'c P	Davies DJ	Rimmer J	Thomas S	Abbott P	Davies Dai
1	Aug-25	H	Chester	2 0	McLaughlin, Screen	2,500	1	2	3	4	5	6	7	8	9	10	11													
2	Sep-01	A	Rotherham United	0 1		2,993	1	2	3	4	5	12	6	7*	9	10	11	8												
3	Sep-08	H	Gillingham	0 3		2,144	1	2	3	4	5	6*	8					12	11		9	7	10							
4	Sep-12	A	Crewe Alex	0 0		1,889	1	2	3	4	5		8	7	10	12		9			6*	11								
5	Sep-15	A	Mansfield Town	1 2	Evans M	3,249	1	2	3	4	5		8	7*		12		9			6	11	10							
6	Sep-18	H	Northampton Town	1 1	McLaughlin	1,301	1	2	3	4	5		8			10	7	9			6*	11		12						
7	Sep-22	H	Colchester United	2 0	Screen, Thomas	1,981	1	2	3	4	5		8			10	9	11			7		6							
8	Sep-29	A	Torquay United	1 3	Curtis	3,003	1	2	3	4	5	12	8			10	9	11*			7		6							
9	Oct-02	A	Northampton Town	0 2		5,257	1	2		4	5	10	8			3	9	11*	12		7		6							
10	Oct-06	H	Scunthorpe United	1 2	Thomas(pen)	1,743	1	2		4	5		8			10	3	9*	7	12	6		11							
11	Oct-13	A	Stockport County	1 0	Curtis	3,100		2	3	4	5		8			9	10				7	6	11		1					
12	Oct-20	A	Peterborough Utd	0 3		6,686		8	3	4	5		7			9	10	12	11		2		6*		1					
13	Oct-23	H	Crewe Alex	2 0	Bruton(pen), Evans W	1,908		6	3	4	5		8			10	11	2	7				9		1					
14	Oct-27	H	Barnsley	2 0	Bruton(pen), Davies G	2,669		6	3	5			8			10	11*	2	7	12			9		1	4				
15	Nov-03	A	Doncaster Rovers	1 3	Davies G	1,523		6	3	5*			8			10	11	2	7				9			4	1			
16	Nov-10	H	Lincoln City	3 0	Lally, Curtis, Davies G	1,855		6	3	5			8			10		2	7			11	9			4	1			
17	Nov-12	A	Darlington	1 1	Williams H	1,822		6	3	5		12	8			10		2	7			11	9*			4	1			
18	Nov-17	H	Hartlepool	0 0		2,389		6	3	5			8			10		2	7			11	9*	12		4	1			
19	Dec-01	H	Exeter City	2 0	Evans M, Lally	2,046		6	3	5			8			10		2	7	9		11				4	1			
20	Dec-08	A	Bury	2 0	Rees, Screen	3,220		6	3	5				8	10			2	7	9		11				4	1			
21	Dec-22	H	Torquay United	0 1		1,889		6	3	5		12	8	9	10*			2	7			11				4	1			
22	Dec-26	A	Reading	2 1	Screen 2	5,679		6	3	5			8	9	10			2	7			11				4	1			
23	Dec-29	A	Gillingham	1 1	Screen	9,979		6	3	5		12	8	9	10			2	7			11*				4	1			
24	Jan-01	H	Rotherham United	4 2	James, Bruton (2pens), Screen	4,962		6	3	5			8	9	10			2	7			11				4	1			
25	Jan-05	A	Brentford	2 0	Rees, Bevan	3,500		6	3	5			8	9	10			2	7			11				4	1			
26	Jan-12	H	Mansfield Town	2 0	Bruton(pen), Rees	4,196		6		5		12	8	9	10			2	7			11				4	1	3*		
27	Jan-19	A	Chester	0 1		2,407		6		5		12	8	9	10*			2	7			11	3			4	1			
28	Jan-27	H	Workington	1 0	Bevan	6,712		6	3	5			8	9	10			2	7			11				4	1			
29	Feb-03	H	Bradford City	0 1		6,377		6	3	5		12	8	9				2	7			11	10*			4	1			
30	Feb-08	A	Colchester United	0 2		5,040		6	3	5		12	8	9	10		11	2								4*	1			
31	Feb-17	H	Stockport County	3 0	Evans W, Lally, James	3,414		6	3	5			8	9	10		11*	2				7				4	1	12		
32	Feb-23	A	Scunthorpe United	0 0		2,238			3	5		8	6	9				2	7*			11	12			4		10		1
33	Mar-03	H	Reading	2 1	Abbott 2	3,353			3	5		8	6	9				2	7			11				4		10		1
34	Mar-10	A	Barnsley	0 1		4,540			3	5		8	6	9				2	7			11				4		10		1
35	Mar-16	H	Peterborough Utd	0 2		2,536			3	5		12	6	9	8			2	7			11				4*		10		1
36	Mar-20	H	Bradford City	1 3	Davies G	2,271			3	5		4	6	8			11		7				10	12				2	9*	1
37	Mar-23	A	Lincoln City	2 2	Curtis, Lally	2,353		12	3	5		4	6	8			11*		7				10					2	9	1
38	Mar-26	H	Brentford	0 0		2,148	1	12	3	5		4	6	9			11	2	7*				8						10	
39	Mar-30	H	Doncaster Rovers	0 0		1,855	1	6	3	5		4	7*	8			11	2	12				10						9	
40	Apr-03	A	Workington	0 1		1,009	1	6	3	5		4	7	8			11*	2	12				10						9	
41	Apr-06	H	Darlington	0 0		1,527	1	6	3	5		12	8				11	2	7*				10	9		4				
42	Apr-13	A	Hartlepool	1 0	Bruton	2,657	1	6	3	4		5	8				11	2					9	7					10	
43	Apr-15	H	Newport County	1 1	Davies	2,303	1	6		4		5	7				11	2					9	8		3			10	
44	Apr-16	A	Newport County	1 2	Bevan	3,103	1	6		4		5	8	11	9			2	7*					12		3			10	
45	Apr-20	H	Bury	0 1		1,821	1	6	3			12	8	9*					7			11		4		5			2	10
46	Apr-27	A	Exeter City	0 2		2,515	1	6		4		5	8	9				2	7			11*	12						3	10
	Apps						19	39	39	45	13	15	45	28	29	12	17	37	36	3	6	24	16	11	4	24	17	7	14	6
	Subs							2				12				3		2	2	2			2	4					1	
	Gls							3	2	6		1	4	2	7	2		2	4				3	5	2				2	

#	Date	V	Opponents	Score	Scorers	Att.	Millington T	Bevan P	Evans M	Bruton D	Moore J	Williams H	Lally P	James R	Screen T	McLaughlin J	Bartley D	Evans W	Curtis A	Lenihan M	Jones P	Rees R	Davies G	Thomas G	Bala'c P	Davies DJ	Rimmer J	Thomas S	Abbott P	Davies Dai
1	Aug-28	H	Exeter C, FLC-1	1 1	Screen	3,036	1	2	3	5	4	6*	8	7	10	9	11	12												
2	Sep-05	A	Exeter C, FLC-1Rep	1 2	Lally	3,023	1	2	3	5	4	6	10		8	9	11*	12	7											
3	Nov-24	A	Walsall, FAC-1	0 1		3,975		6	3	4		12	8			10		2	7			11	9*		1	5				
4	Dec-15	H	Stourbridge, WC-5	1 2	Screen	1,385		6	3	4			8*			10		2	7	9		11		12		5	1			

Swansea City FC Season 1974/75 Division 4

#	Date	V	Opponents	Score	Scorers	Att.	Bellotti D	Evans W	Thomas S	Bruton D	Davies DJ	Bevan P	Roberts D	Lally P	Thomas G	Abbott P	Rees R	Williams H	Evans M	James R	Screen T	Curtis A	Potter S	Tones J	Davies G	Murray D	Bartley D	Dalling N	Bekker J
1	Aug-17	A	Darlington	2 3	Abbott, Bruton	2,367	1	2	3	4	5	6	7	8	9	10	11*	12											
2	Aug-24	H	Barnsley	0 3		2,421	1	5		4		2	7	8	10	9	11		3	6*	12								
3	Aug-27	H	Darlington	1 0	Evans W	1,820	1	2		4		6	7	8	10	9			5	3		11							
4	Aug-31	A	Brentford	0 1		4,910	1	2		5		6	7	8	9*	10			4	3		11							
5	Sep-03	A	Newport County	0 3		3,150	1	2		4		6	7	8	12	10			5	3	9*	11							
6	Sep-07	H	Doncaster Rovers	3 3	Thomas 3	1,532		2		5		6	7	12	9	10*			4	3	8	11	1						
7	Sep-14	A	Shrewsbury Town	0 2		2,880		2		4		6	7	8	9	12			5*	3	10	11	1						
8	Sep-18	A	Workington Town	0 2		1,393		2		4		6*		10		7				3	8	12	11	1	5	9			
9	Sep-21	H	Bradford City	1 1	Thomas	1,729	1	2		4		6	7		9			10	3	8		11			5				
10	Sep-24	H	Lincoln City	2 1	Evans W, Lally	1,801	1	2		4		6	7*	12	9			10	3	8		11			5				
11	Sep-28	A	Hartlepool United	2 0	Williams H 2	2,791	1	2		4		6	7*	12	9			10	3	8		11			5				
12	Oct-01	H	Mansfield Town	1 2	James	2,273	1	2		4		6	7	12	9			10*	3	8		11			5				
13	Oct-05	H	Crewe Alex	2 1	Thomas, James	2,183	1	2		4		6	7	10	9				3	8		11			5				
14	Oct-07	A	Mansfield Town	0 3		3,672	1	2		4		6	7		9				3	8*	10	11			5	12			
15	Oct-12	A	Exeter City	2 1	Evans M, O/Goal	3,867	1	2		4		6		12	9	10	7*		3	8		11			5				
16	Oct-15	H	Newport County	2 0	Evans M, Thomas	3,372	1	2		4		6	7		9	10			3	8		11			5				
17	Oct-18	H	Rochdale	3 3	Bruton(pen), Evans W, Bevan	2,767	1	2	3	4		6	7		9	10				8		11			5				
18	Oct-26	A	Northampton Town	1 5	James	5,096	1	2		4		6*	7	12	9			10	3	8		11			5				
19	Nov-01	A	Stockport County	1 2	Thomas	2,086				4		6	7		9	10			3	8		11	1	2	5				
20	Nov-08	H	Rotherham United	0 2		2,414		2		4		6	7	12	9	10				8*		11	1	3	5				
21	Nov-16	A	Chester	0 3		4,641			3	5		6	7	8	9				4	12	10		1		2	11*			
22	Nov-30	A	Scunthorpe United	2 1	James 2	1,037	1			4		6	7	11					9	3	10	2*	8		5				
23	Dec-06	H	Southport	2 2	Evans W, Evans M	1,708	1	9				6	7	11					4	3	8	2*	10		5				12
24	Dec-21	A	Reading	2 1	Bevan, James	3,693	1	9				6	7	11					4	3	8	2	10		5				
25	Dec-26	H	Shrewsbury Town	1 4	Williams	3,501	1	9				6*	7	11					4	3	8	2	10		5				12
26	Dec-28	A	Torquay United	0 0		2,589		9		12		6	7	11					4*	3	8	2	10	1	5				
27	Jan-04	H	Workington Town	0 1		1,887		9		4		6			10	7				3	8	2	11*	1	5				12
28	Jan-10	A	Southport	0 3		1,508		2		4		6	7	11	9	10*		12	3	8			1		5				
29	Jan-18	H	Scunthorpe United	1 0	Roberts	1,428		2		4		6	7*	11	12	9			3	8	10		1		5				
30	Feb-01	A	Rotherham United	0 1		4,123		2		4			12	7	6			11	3	9	10	8*	1		5				
31	Feb-08	H	Stockport County	1 0	Screen	1,673		2		4			12	7	6			11	3	9	10	8*	1		5				
32	Feb-15	A	Cambridge United	0 2		3,004				4	2	7	12		6			11*	3	9	10	8	1		5				
33	Feb-22	H	Chester	0 1		2,174		5		4	12	2			6			11	3	7	10	8	1						9*
34	Feb-28	H	Brentford	0 1		1,706		2		4	5	6*	7		8			11		10	12		1				3		9
35	Mar-04	H	Cambridge United	2 1	Thomas, Bruton(pen)	1,520		2		4		8	12		6			11*		7	10		1		5		3		9
36	Mar-08	A	Lincoln City	3 1	Bekker, Screen, James	6,200		2		4		11			6	8				7	10		1		5		3		9
37	Mar-15	H	Hartlepool United	1 0	Bekker	2,303		2		4		11			6	8				7	10		1		5		3		9
38	Mar-21	A	Doncaster Rovers	2 3	Evans W 2	5,011		2		4		11			6	8				7	10		1		5		3		9
39	Mar-28	H	Torquay United	0 1		1,959		2		4		11			6	8				7	10*	12	1		5		3		9*
40	Mar-29	H	Reading	1 2	Evans W	1,833		2		4		11			6	8				7	10	12	1		5		3		9*
41	Mar-31	A	Bradford City	2 1	James, Bruton	2,523		2		4		12	7*		6	9				3	10	8	1		5	11			
42	Apr-05	H	Northampton Town	1 0	O/Goal	1,591		2		4			7		6					3	10	8	1		5	11			9
43	Apr-12	A	Crewe Alex	2 2	Bekker, Bruton(pen)	2,206		2		4			7		6	12				3	10	8	1		5	11			9*
44	Apr-19	H	Exeter City	0 2		2,000		2		4			7*		6	12				3	9	8	1		5	11			10
45	Apr-22	A	Barnsley	0 1		2,839		2		4			7	5	9*					3	6	8	1			11			10
46	Apr-26	A	Rochdale	0 1		1,548		2		4			7	5	9					3	6*	8	1		10	11			12
	Apps						19	42	3	42	3	38	31	21	38	21	9	17	35	41	19	35	27	7	27	5	14	0	12
	Subs							1	1	1	5	6	2	3		2			1	3	2		1					3	1
	Gls							7		5		2	1	1	8	1		3	3	8	2								3

#	Date	V	Opponents	Score	Scorers	Att.	Bellotti D	Evans W	Thomas S	Bruton D	Davies DJ	Bevan P	Roberts D	Lally P	Thomas G	Abbott P	Rees R	Williams H	Evans M	James R	Screen T	Curtis A	Potter S	Tones J	Davies G	Murray D	Bartley D	Dalling N	Bekker J
1	Aug-21	A	Exeter City, FLC-1	1 3	Abbott	3,472	1	2	3	5	4*	6	7	8	9	10	11	12											
2	Nov-26	H	Kettering T, FAC-1	1 1	Lally	3,175	1			5	4	6	7	8	9*			10	3	12		11			2				
3	Dec-02	A	Kettering T, FAC-1Rep	1 3	Evans W	5,973	1	12		5	4	6	7*	8					9	3	10	2	11						
4	Jan-06	A	Kidderminster, WC-5	0 0		1,887																							
5	Jan-20	H	Kidderminster, WC-5Rep	3 0	Williams H 3	1,026		2		4		6	7	11				9	3	8	10		1		5				
6	Feb-12	A	Newport Co. WC-6	1 1	James	2,368		2		4			7	6				11	3	9	10	8	1		5				
7	Feb-17	H	Newport Co. WC-6Rep	1 2	Bruton(pen)	2,087		2		4	5	8			6			11	3	9	10	7	1						

Chapter 17

Harry Builds the Foundations

1975-76

Although there had been a considerable improvement on the previous year's working, the loss on the 1974-5 season still amounted to £40,000. Despite all the economies which had been in force, the average gate – a little over two thousand – was completely inadequate as a means of sustaining the club as a going concern. Now that the ground had been sold, it became even clearer that somehow, the revenue flow of the business had to be increased. Harry Griffiths knew that he needed to strengthen his side, but he was also aware that the lack of money meant that very little would be available to him for that purpose. Nevertheless, the manager and his chairman were sustained by two factors. They had a fundamental belief that the club could be viable and the crowds would return – if the team played attractive, winning football. That they were able to retain those beliefs, when season-ticket sales for the new campaign, 503, were even lower than for the previous season, says much for their tenacity.

During the close-season, Griffiths had spent a total of £1,250. That was the fee which he paid to obtain the permanent transfer of goalkeeper Stephen Potter, who had been on loan at the Vetch during the previous campaign. Potter was joined by

Geoff Bray, a striker from Oxford United, Paul Harris, who was 6'4" and came from Leyton Orient, and Andy Leitch, who joined the club on trial from Western League football. The most significant signing, however, was George Smith, who came to the Vetch on a free transfer from Cardiff. Smith, who was very experienced, was thirty. As the next two seasons were to show, he was the ideal player, a mid-field general, to lead the side in restoring some dignity to Swansea football.

By the end of September, the influence of the Smith-Griffiths axis could be seen on the field. Although no one wished to claim that the side was playing outstanding football, it was, certainly an improvement on the previous campaign. Furthermore, the Swans were sixth in the league table and there was a little encouragement with regard to gates. While they were still a long way short of what was necessary, at around three thousand they were twenty per cent better than those of the previous season. Modest as they were, the statistics did indicate a move in the right direction.

Throughout this period, manager Griffiths continued with his quest to

The Swans' squad, 1975-76 season.
Standing, left to right: Roy Saunders (Coach), Nigel Stevenson, Jeremy Charles, Gary Moore, Eddie May, Steve Potter, Keith Barber, Dave Bruton, Neil Davids, Robbie James, Jeff Griffiths, Stephen Morris, Harry Griffiths (Manager).
In front: Micky Conway, Les Chappell, Pat Lally, Alan Curtis, George Smith (Captain), Wyndham Evans, Danny Bartley, Nigel Dalling, Kevin Moore.

*George Smith being welcomed by Harry Griffiths. George went on to make
a significant contribution to the revival of the club.*

promote and provide the brand of football in which he believed. George Smith, an immaculate passer of the ball, was his willing ally in all this and their philosophy was rubbing off on the younger players in particular. One benefit of this greater success was that the manager was able to field a far more settled side than hitherto; Potter, Smith, Harris, Thomas, Bray, Curtis and James were virtually, ever-present during this period. In turn, that stability enabled the side as a whole to evince greater understanding and confidence than it had previously done.

At the end of November, 9,420 people watched the Swans play in an away match, though the majority had not come to see them. The attraction was a certain George Best, who had agreed to play for Stockport on a match basis.

Wyndham Evans had the task of marking the Irishman and, while he did well, the former Manchester star led his side to victory. On Boxing Day, the Swans had a reasonable crowd of their own, for 4,091 people turned up to see them beat Watford 4-2. It was the largest gate for two seasons and provided further encouragement for the Vetch management that things were moving in the right direction. Among the Swans scorers that day was Alan Curtis, who drove home a

marvellous goal from thirty yards. It was a goal which inspired Griffiths to use the youngster in a different role later in the season.

The victory over Watford was a fine Christmas present for Harry Griffiths, which was augmented by another received on Christmas Eve: the signature of winger, Micky Conway from Brighton for a fee of £2,000. The young man made his debut in the first match of the new year and was to carve out a special place in the hearts of Swansea folk during a brief but exciting career.

At about the same time as Conway joined the Swans an event occurred which, at this distance, can only be described as remarkable. The brief description here outlines the key factors in a story which has been verified by several people. It is re-told simply because the story is extraordinary. From a scientific point of view, one event is not 'proof' of anything, but the story is worth telling for all that. Linda Pomford, who was one of the club's catering ladies, visited a Swansea fortune teller, a Mrs. Plunchart. Part of their conversation went along the following lines:

Mrs. P.: 'You are associated with a business by the sea.'
Linda: 'Yes, we have a kiosk near the beach.'
Mrs. P.: 'No, it's not that. I can see

crowds of people in a big space. There are not many at the moment but there will be more.'
Linda: 'Well, I do help at the Vetch.'
Mrs. P.: 'That will be it. They aren't doing very well at the moment, are they? But they will, you'll see.'
Linda: 'What do you mean?'
Mrs. P.: 'In 1981 or 82 they'll be promoted to the First Division, but it will go right to the last game before they'll know.'

At the Vetch, the story was greeted with wry smiles. Everyone would have like to believe it, but despite the encouraging developments at the club, real life was not like Roy of the Rovers. In any event, argued the superior men, fortune-tellers were for the ladies. Secretly, though, more than one of them kept his fingers crossed, just in case.

After beating Crewe on 3 January, the side was twelfth in the league table and was unbeaten at home. Up to that point, though, the Swans had not won an away match. The chairman and manager, in assessing the club's position, believed that considerable progress had been made and promised themselves, for their New Year's resolution, more of the same. Harry Griffiths thought that it was only a matter of time before the club could mount a serious promotion challenge. He said that he felt a sense of pride when he considered what they had achieved within six months. Considering the position in which he had started his managerial career, no one could be found who would argue with that assessment.

By the end of January, Griffiths was intensifying his search for new men, though the results of his efforts were disappointing. On no fewer than five occasions he agreed terms with other clubs, but failed to persuade the players concerned to come to the Vetch. Griffiths's interim response was to look to his younger players. He thought that three of the lads who were on the groundstaff at that time had a distinct chance of making the grade. The trio were, seventeen-year-old Nigel Stevenson, eighteen–year-old Stephen Morris, and Jeremy Charles, who was sixteen. Time would show that he was a pretty good judge.

February brought with it further encouragement for the Vetch management. The first home match of the month saw promotion challengers Reading being beaten 5-1. It was the club's biggest victory for four years and was achieved in fine style. In that match, Smith marshalled his men admirably, while Curtis, James and Conway were scintillating in attack. Conway, with his swift raiding down either flank, was becoming a firm favourite with supporters, while Curtis and James were attracting much wider attention. In the next match, it was Torquay's turn to be beaten. In itself that win was noteworthy, for it was the first away victory of the campaign, but it was also Robbie James's one hundredth league match: a truly remarkable statistic.

During March, progress was maintained on the field: of the six games played in the windy month three were won and another drawn. The biggest victory was a 5-0 thrashing of Stockport at the Vetch, though only 2,692 were there to enjoy it. In April, for the game against Southport, Harry Griffiths gave Nigel Stevenson and Stephen Morris their league debuts. Both youngsters did well and finished on the winning side. The manager had other encouragement, too. Later that month Alan Curtis was chosen to represent Wales against England. It was a considerable compliment for the youngster to be taken from the obscurity of the Fourth Division and matched with the best in the land. From the club's point of view, Curtis's selection broke a sequence of five years during which no player from the Vetch had been capped. After the previous season's events it was a welcome signal. Furthermore, it gave the Vetch management another opportunity to demonstrate their resolve. Alan Curtis was not for sale!

At the end of the season, the club was in eleventh place in the division. In some ways it was a disappointing outcome, yet, when measured against the events of the previous season, it represented a considerable improvement. There was encouragement, too, in that the reserves won the Welsh League championship for the first time for eleven years. Notwithstanding the improvement in the style of play as well as results which was achieved,

the biggest disappointment for management was the size of the average gate. It was true that it was an increase of fifty per cent over the previous campaign, but to ensure financial viability, there was still a long way to go.

1976-77

During the close-season, John Charles, who had been acting as youth team manager, resigned and was replaced by Roy Saunders. It was the second time that Harry Griffiths had persuaded the rugged Saunders to come to the Vetch. Another event during that period was a European Championship international between Wales and Yugoslavia, when, according to the crowd, one of the visiting full-backs, a player called Hadziabdic, 'dived' in order to claim a free kick. The crowd let him know that they were not impressed. However, there was one man playing that day, a certain John Toshack, who was taken with the silky skills of the back. The Yugoslav, for his part, was, also impressed by the Welshman, and consequently, when the two were to meet again several years later, it was that mutual respect which underwrote the contract.

At the Vetch, as one Charles left another arrived. Jeremy Charles, who had been associated with the club as an amateur, signed as an apprentice professional. Charles's signing was another indication of the improvement in the club's image. It was also a mark of the respect with which Harry Griffiths was held by all who knew him. Other newcomers to the Vetch at that time were thirty-three-year-old Eddie May and Les Chappell from Doncaster Rovers. Both men were to make effective contributions to the Swansea cause in the months which lay ahead.

The first game of the new season at the Vetch was a Football League Cup clash with Newport County. It was significant in that during the match, sixteen-year-old Jeremy Charles, who had replaced Robbie James, scored twice. In fact, the latest 'Charlo' put the ball in the net within two minutes of being on the pitch. The supporters were delighted. Was this another piece in the ever-developing jigsaw which the Swans manager was building? Could

this be the basis of a team of local boys of quality enough to emulate that of the fifties in which Harry Griffiths himself played? It was all exciting stuff.

After the match, the Harry Griffiths and his chairman did not try to hide their delight. The manager was able to point out that the Swans were among the best-paid sides in the lower divisions. He said that the treatment which they were receiving from the board should make them feel 'part of a going concern'. Chairman Struel agreed with this assessment and pointed out that, if the club was to improve its position, everyone at the Vetch and the supporters had to believe in themselves.

By the end of September the team had won its way through to the fourth round of the Football League Cup, beating Chester and Torquay in the process. During this run, Charles, Curtis and James were names which frequently appeared among the scorers. In league matches, however, the same young men were rather less in evidence. Indeed, the team as a whole scored only ten goals in its first seven matches, only two of which were won. Nine points were gained in the process and the club lay in twelfth place in the league table.

Meantime, the Home Office had delivered a blow to Swansea's soccer pride. It did not include the Vetch among thirty-nine grounds which were required to obtain safety certificates as potential international venues. For the Vetch authorities, the small print in the relevant bill was a further reminder of the precariousness of their situation. Although they no longer owned the ground, they were responsible for its upkeep and development. The intentions declared in the Safety of Grounds Act meant that that responsibility was going to prove to be extremely expensive. Being aware of this and wishing to contribute, the Vice Presidents' Club provided the money to help improve the club's floodlights. It was a welcome gesture, which was warmly received.

In mid-October, an exciting 5-3 victory over Brentford was seen as an encouraging prelude to the fourth-round Football League Cup tie with First Division Bolton Wanderers. The crowd at the Brentford match saw Charles score twice in a game in which the Swans were a goal behind on two occasions. The enthusiasm of the team on the field in that game was more than matched by that of the supporters. It was, according to the late Tom Phillips, the point in the revival of Swansea City when the spirit of Swansea soccer began to flicker again. Certainly, there was a considerable degree of confidence around the Vetch. It was almost as if the team was saying, 'Bring on Bolton'.

On the evening of the Bolton match, that spirit was evident in the cauldron which was the Vetch Field. The largest Vetch gate for many years was treated to a tremendously exciting display of attacking football. Wave after wave of Swansea attacks threatened the Bolton goal. In the end, though, a sturdy Wanderers defence and a thoroughly professional performance denied the Swans a victory. As a result, the team had to travel to Bolton to replay the tie. In the afterglow of the Vetch game, Ian Greaves, the Bolton manager, praised Harry Griffiths's team as the best he had seen in the lower divisions. He was equally complimentary after the replay, for although the Swans were beaten by 5-1, crucial goalkeeping errors were the root cause of the defeat.

As ever, football has the habit of kicking the unwary in the teeth. Unfortunately, in the aftermath of the Bolton ties there was a slump in league form. By late November, not only had the side slipped to eighteenth in the table, it had also been beaten at home in the FA Cup. To make matters worse, the victorious opponents in that competition were non-league Minehead, and their winning goal had been scored by former Swan, Andy Leitch.

Harry Griffiths reacted sharply to this slump in form, criticizing his men for lack of effort. 'Buck up or get out,' he was reported as saying. 'You are not professional enough.' Whatever the rights and wrongs of this situation, it illustrated for the first time a problem which the likeable Griffiths had in motivating some players. Unfortunately, not every professional footballer is as wholehearted as Griffiths was throughout his career. The manager expected people to give their all as a matter of principle. When they did not, Harry felt cheated. As a result,

people with lower standards than his own were to be the cause of continuing concern to the Swansea manager. In the end, his unwillingness to accept anything less than his own impeccable loyalty, enthusiasm and dedication to the Swans was a major reason for his future resignation. An inability to see that such standards are uncommon among men might be taken as a weakness in Griffiths's managerial armoury. Yet, it was his own outstanding qualities, which he imbued in others around him, which were to result in a reversal of the negative trend manifest at the time.

If the results which followed are anything to go by, then the manager's outburst had the desired effect. Following the Minehead FA Cup defeat, four of the six games played were won. Including a fine 3-1 victory over Cambridge and a 4-0 defeat of Workington. At that stage, Jeremy Charles and Robbie James had each scored seven goals. There was further encouragement for the management, too, in that for the final game of the year, 5,666 people were at the Vetch. That gate was the club's largest in Division Four for seven seasons.

In January, with the Swans in sixth position, Griffiths attempted to buy a full-back, but the player declined, saying that he did not wish to drop down into the Fourth Division. If he could have seen into the future, there is little doubt that he would have made a different decision. During this month, too, Harry Griffiths was encouraged by the views of several knowledgeable football figures. Geoff Twentyman, the Liverpool chief scout, for example, said that he had tremendous admiration for the Swans. In addition, rarely did the team play a match without there being several visiting managers or scouts in the stand. Then, to put the icing on the cake, that soccer legend, John Charles, was convinced that the team would gain promotion. However, the Swans fans, although they enjoyed the fact that other clubs were watching their favourite players, were apprehensive, because they believed that money would talk and the best players would be sold. This was not surprising, for this had long been the policy at the Vetch. It was to be some time before the supporters could come to accept the

statement that 'No promising younger players will be sold!'

Later in January, Newport County were beaten 4-1 in a Welsh Cup match in which Alan Curtis scored his first senior hat-trick. There followed a fine 4-0 win at Darlington – the club's biggest away victory for twenty-two years. By the end of the month, with twenty-one games to play, the team was seventh in the league table. February, though, was a disappointment; despite having Mike Stead on loan from Tottenham, two league matches and a Welsh Cup tie were lost in succession. Then, on what should have been something of a gala occasion, the St. David's Day match with Bradford City was also lost by the odd goal in five. That game was chosen to inaugurate the club's new floodlights, which had cost the Vice-Presidents' Club £2,500. The only saving grace that night was that, after being two goals down, the Swans showed spirit in fighting back to level matters. Unfortunately, the visitors stole the match with a goal four minutes from the end. It was the first home defeat of the season. The after-match criticism fell heavily upon the shoulders of goalkeeper Potter; yet, given the very small of amount of money which was available to him, Griffiths had been unable to recruit a replacement.

In Swansea, the general consensus of opinion was that new blood was needed to reinvigorate the team's drive for promotion, but as it transpired, as March progressed, the form of the team improved to the extent that, of the next five matches, four were won and the fifth drawn. Only in the fifth match, against Stockport, was there any cause for alarm. Then, in front of the club's largest gate of the season, home supporters were stunned to silence when, shortly after half-time, the visitors increased their lead to four goals to nil. With only twenty-five minutes of the game left, that was still the score. Then, in a fourteen-minute period of excellence, the Swans fought back with goals from Smith, Chappell, May and Curtis. At the end, following ten minutes during which either side might have snatched victory, the teams left the field to warm applause. For Vetch supporters, though, that applause was tinged with relief. Their team was exciting but hardly consistent!

For the management team at the Vetch that inconsistency was frustrating.

There followed an unexpectedly heavy defeat at Brentford and, some days later, the news that popular winger Micky Conway was 'very ill' in Singleton Hospital after being involved in a car accident. Quite apart from the genuine concern of everyone associated with the club for the young player, Harry Griffiths could ill afford to lose Conway's pace and enthusiasm. Necessity being the mother of invention, he had to evolve a slightly different way of playing.

One consequence of this was that Les Chappell, a mid-fielder, was handed Conway's shirt, and the new system paid off. April's results were outstandingly successful for the Vetch men. Seven of the nine matches played were won, while the other two were drawn on away grounds. From the beginning of the month, when 3,577 watched Newport being beaten, to the end, when 9,613 saw the match with Huddersfield, there was a steady growth in gate income. There were those at the time who noted that the size of the Huddersfield gate was in sharp contrast to the 972 people who came to see the Vetch men play at Southport, which was the lowest recorded league crowd to watch a Swans league game.

One effect of the April surge was to place the team on the fringe of the promotion race, for on 3 May, after 10,689 had seen the Swans beat Rochdale at the Vetch, the side was fourth in the table. During the following week, letters from former Swans Tom Kiley and Joe Payne were printed in the *Post*, congratulating Harry Griffiths and his team and urging supporters to 'get behind the players and lift them to promotion!' With just two games to play, achieving that goal was a distinct possibility.

Prior to the penultimate match with Watford on 7 May, Harry Griffiths was presented with a 'Manager of the Month' award for April. The ten thousand people who were present that day, including

Wyndham Evans – tireless stalwart in the Swans defence.

injured captain George Smith, rose as one to salute the popular Griffiths. All that remained was to defeat the visitors. Unfortunately, the inconsistency bug struck again. Without their influential captain, the Swans lost control of the match early in the first half and Watford took every advantage of the situation to lead the men in white 4-0 at the interval. The Swans scored once in the second half, but found it to be impossible to claw back a four-goal lead. As a consequence of this unexpected set-back, instead of going to Cambridge on the final day of the season wanting only a draw, now they had to win there. And even if they were able to do that, the Swans had to rely on Colchester losing at home. It was asking too much of the gods. Despite a fine win at Cambridge, who were division champions, Colchester took the points in their match. The Vetch men were confined to the Fourth Division for another season.

Tremendous enthusiasm had been generated in the city by the challenge which the Swans had mounted in the final quarter of the season. Naturally, supporters were disappointed that promotion had not been achieved, yet despite that feeling there was much to be delighted about. The side had scored ninety-two goals – a

new club record. Furthermore, this total was the highest registered by any club in the Football League. At 5,204, the average gate was the best for four seasons and more than eighty per cent greater than for the previous campaign. Young Jeremy Charles had scored on twenty-three occasions and was top scorer in the club, while Alan Curtis and Robbie James (fourteen goals each) demonstrated that the future was in good hands. When Harry Griffiths reviewed the season, after mentioning the three young strikers, he praised other members of his side, too. The captain, George Smith, had been outstanding; Bartley and Wyndham Evans had formed an effective partnership at full-back; May and Bruton had done well at the centre of the defence, while Lally and Chappell had made fine contributions in mid-field. The manager did not forget Micky Conway either, and was pleased to report that he was making good progress following his accident.

Chairman Malcolm Struel was also upbeat in his comments. Contrasting the season with the two or three which had preceded it, he said that he and his board colleagues were delighted with the progress which had been made. After praising the efforts of his manager he declared: 'It's little use crying over spilt milk. Naturally, we are disappointed that we came so near to promotion and didn't make it, but we've learnt a lot. Our target is the Second Division in two years.' Whatever his listeners felt about that, there was no denying their delight at his continuing resolve: 'We shall not sell any of our promising youngsters. Our funds are limited, but it is our intention to buy rather than sell.'

All this euphoria seemed to confirm Tom Phillips's comment about the renewed spirit at the Vetch Field. The board, the players, the management team and the fans could not wait for the new season to come. 'Swansea football' was being played again. No one, however, could have had any idea at that time of the drama, controversy, tragedy and joy which the 1977-8 campaign was to bring.

Swansea City FC Season 1975/76 Division 4

#	Date	V	Opponents	Score	Scorers	Att.	Potter S	Evans W	Bartley D	Smith G	Bruton D	Harris P	James R	Curtis A	Thomas G	Bray G	Lally P	Bekker J	Davies G	Leitch A	Dalling N	Tynan T	Evans P	Conway M	Abbott P	Williams S	Morris S	Stevenson N	Griffiths J	Harvey L
1	Aug-16	H	Tranmere Rovers	1 1	Evans W	2,866	1	2	3	4	5	6	7	8	9	10*	11	12												
2	Aug-23	A	Rochdale	1 2	Leitch	1,169	1	2	11	4	5	6	12	8				7*	9	3	10									
3	Aug-30	H	Cambridge United	1 0	Bekker	2,082	1	2	3	6	4	5	10	7				8		9	11*									
4	Sep-05	A	Southport	1 1	Curtis	1,017	1	2	3	4	5	6	10	7			11*	8	12	9										
5	Sep-13	H	Workington Town	1 0	James	2,126	1	2	11	4	5	6	7	8		12		10	3	9*										
6	Sep-19	A	Northampton Town	0 0		5,428	1	2	11	4	5	6	7	8	9	10			3											
7	Sep-23	H	Newport County	2 2	Thomas, Bruton(pen)	4,500	1	2	11*	4	5	6	9	8	7	10			3	12										
8	Sep-27	H	Scunthorpe United	2 0	Thomas, Bray	3,098	1	2	11	4	5	6	9	8	7	10			3											
9	Oct-04	A	Lincoln City	0 4		5,323	1	2	11	4	5	6	9	8*	7	10			12	3										
10	Oct-11	H	Huddersfield Town	1 1	Bray	3,230	1	2	3	4	5	6	11*	8	7	10		12		9										
11	Oct-18	A	Doncaster Rovers	1 2	Tynan	6,640	1	2		4	5	6	11*	8	7	10	3		12			9								
12	Oct-21	H	Darlington	2 0	Bray, Bruton	2,200	1	2		4	5	6	11	8	7	10			3			9								
13	Oct-25	H	Bradford City	3 1	Tynan, Bray 2	3,380	1	2		4	5	6	11	8	7	10			3			9								
14	Nov-01	A	Barnsley	0 0		2,709	1	2		4	5	6	7	8	11	10			3			9								
15	Nov-05	A	Reading	0 1		5,499	1	2	12	4	5	6	7	8	11*	10			3			9								
16	Nov-08	H	Torquay United	3 0	James 2, Bray	3,170	1	2		4	5	6	7	8	11	10			3			9								
17	Nov-14	A	Exeter City	0 3		2,967	1	2	11	4	5	6	9	8	7	10			3											
18	Nov-28	A	Stockport County	2 3	Curtis, Bruton	9,220	1	2		4	12	6	9	8		10	7		3	11*				5						
19	Dec-06	H	Hartlepool United	3 1	Bray(pen), Leitch 2	2,253	1	2		4		6	9	8		10	7		3	11				5						
20	Dec-20	A	Crewe Alex	1 2	Bray(pen)	2,088	1	2		4	12	6	9	8		10*	7		3	11				5						
21	Dec-26	H	Watford	4 2	2 O/Goal, Leitch, Curtis	4,091	1	2	11	4		6	7	8		10			3	9				5						
22	Dec-27	A	AFC Bournemouth	0 2		6,714	1	2	11	4		6	7	8		10			3	9				5						
23	Jan-03	H	Crewe Alex	4 0	Leitch 2, Bray 2	2,513	1	2		4		6	11	8		10			3	9				5	7					
24	Jan-10	A	Cambridge United	1 3	James	2,534	1	2		4	12	6	11	8		10			3	9				5*	7					
25	Jan-16	H	Northampton Town	1 1	Bray	3,656	1	2		4	5	6		8	7	10			3	9						11				
26	Jan-24	A	Workington Town	1 1	Davies	1,270	1	2	12	4	5	6		8	7	10			3	9*						11				
27	Feb-06	H	Reading	5 1	Bray, Conway, James, Curtis 2	2,750	1	2	11	4	5	6	9	8*		10			3					7	12					
28	Feb-14	A	Torquay United	2 0	Curtis 2	2,670	1	2	11	4	5	6	9	8	3	10								7						
29	Feb-20	H	Exeter City	0 3		4,252	1	2	11		5	6		8	3	10			4	9				7						
30	Feb-23	A	Newport County	2 1	Bruton, Bray	2,040	1	2	11	4	5	6	9	8	3	10								7						
31	Feb-28	A	Bradford City	0 0		6,672	1	2	11	4	5	6	9	8	3	10								7						
32	Mar-05	H	Barnsley	3 1	Bray, Thomas, James	2,510	1	2	11	4	5	6	9	8	3	10								7						
33	Mar-09	H	Lincoln City	2 2	Thomas, Curtis	4,000	1	2	11	4	5	6	9	8	3	10								7*	12					
34	Mar-13	A	Huddersfield Town	0 2		6,393	1	2	11	4	5	6	9	8	3	10								7						
35	Mar-16	H	Doncaster Rovers	2 1	Bray, O/Goal	3,128	1	2	3	4	5	6	9	8	7	10										11				
36	Mar-19	H	Stockport County	5 0	Bray, Bartley, Curtis, Harris, Williams S	2,692	1	2	11		5	6	9	8	4	10								7		3				
37	Mar-27	A	Hartlepool United	0 1		1,708	1	2	3	4	5	6	9	8		10					7					11				
38	Apr-02	A	Tranmere Rovers	0 3		3,475	1	2	3	4	5	6	9	8	7	10										11				
39	Apr-06	A	Scunthorpe United	1 1	Lally	3,015	1	2	11	4	5	6		8	3	10	7		9											
40	Apr-10	H	Southport	2 0	Evans W, James	2,147	1	2	3	4			9	8			7							11		10	5	6		
41	Apr-16	A	Brentford	0 1		4,360	1	2	3	4	5	6	9	8	7	10								11						
42	Apr-17	A	Watford	1 2	James	4,536	1		3	2	8	6	9	11	4	10						5		7*		12				
43	Apr-20	H	AFC Bournemouth	1 1	Bray	2,354	1	2	3	4	9	6*	7	8		12						5		11		10				
44	Apr-23	A	Rochdale	1 1	Bruton	1,604	1	8	3	4	9		7		2	10						5				11		6		
45	Apr-26	A	Brentford	2 2	Bray 2 (1pen)	1,311	1	2	3		6			8	4	10			5					7*		11	12		9	
46	Apr-28	A	Darlington	1 1	Evans W	4,295	1	2		4		6*	9	8		10			3							11	5		7	12
	Apps						46	45	32	43	37	43	44	41	31	40	9	4	26	15	1	6	10	20	0	7	2	2	2	0
	Subs							2		3		1						2		3	2	1			1	1	2			1
	Gls							3	1		5	1	8	9	4	19	1	1	1	6		2		1		1				

#	Date	V	Opponents	Score	Scorers	Att.	Potter S	Evans W	Bartley D	Smith G	Bruton D	Harris P	James R	Curtis A	Thomas G	Bray G	Lally P	Bekker J	Davies G	Leitch A	Dalling N	Tynan T	Evans P	Conway M	Abbott P	Williams S	Morris S	Stevenson N	Griffiths J	Harvey L
1	Aug-09	H	Torquay Utd, FLC 1-1	1 2	Bekker	2,143	1	2	11	4	5	6		8*		10	7		9	3	12									
2	Aug-22	A	Torquay Utd. FLC 1-2	3 5	Leitch 2, Bruton(pen)	3,197	1	2	11	4	5	6		8				10	3	9	7									
3	Nov-21	A	Southend Utd. FAC-1	0 2		5,383	1	2		4	5	6	11		7	10			9	3	8									
4	Dec-13	H	Cardiff Corries, WC-5	6 0	Bray 2, Leitch 2, James, ?		1	2		4		6	9	8		10	7		3	11				5						
5	Feb-17	A	Cardiff City, WC-6	1 1	Bruton	5,812	1	2	11		5	6	9	8	3	10	4							7						
6	Feb-27	H	Cardiff City, WC-6Rep	0 3		10,075	1	2		4	5	6	9	8	3	10	4		12					7*						

Swansea City FC Season 1976/77 Division 4

#	Date	V	Opponents	Score	Scorers	Att.	Potter S	Evans W	Bartley D	Smith G	May E	Bruton D	Conway M	Curtis A	James R	Bray G	Lally P	Charles J	Moore G	Schroeder N	Reece G	Chappell L	Harris P	Griffiths J	Brown G	Stead M	Harvey L
1	Aug-21	H	Darlington	2 1	Conway, Bray(pen)	3,830	1	2	3	4*	5	6	7	8	9	10	11	12									
2	Aug-25	A	Bradford City	1 4	Conway	2,720	1	2	3*	4	5	6	7	8	9	10	11		12								
3	Aug-27	A	Stockport County	0 3		4,730			3	2	5	4	7	8	6	10*	11	12	9		1						
4	Sep-04	H	Barnsley	2 1	Moore, James	3,132	1	2	3	4	5	6		9	8		7	10	11								
5	Sep-11	A	Huddersfield Town	2 2	Smith(pen), James	4,048	1	2	3	4	5	6		10	8		7	9	11								
6	Sep-18	H	Doncaster Rovers	1 1	Moore	3,504	1	2	3	4	5	6		9	7		8	11*	10			12					
7	Sep-25	A	Aldershot	2 2	Charles, James	5,120	1	2	3	4	5	6		11	9		7	8*	10			12					
8	Oct-02	H	Southport	2 1	James 2	3,778	1	2	3	4	5	6	12	9	8		7		10			11*					
9	Oct-09	A	Torquay United	1 2	May	2,800	1	2	3	4	5	6		9	8*		7	12	10			11					
10	Oct-15	H	Brentford	5 3	James 2, Charles 2, Smith	3,656	1	2	3	4	5	6		9	8		7	11				10					
11	Oct-22	A	Newport County	2 0	Charles 2	3,416	1	2	3		5	4		9	8		7	11				10	6				
12	Oct-30	A	Crewe Alex	1 3	Curtis	2,538	1	2	3		5	6	11*	9	8		7					10	4	12			
13	Nov-06	H	Exeter City	0 0		3,848		2	3	12	5	6		9	8		7*	10				11	4	1			
14	Nov-09	A	Halifax Town	0 1		2,228		2	3	12	5	4*		9	8		7	10				11	6	1			
15	Nov-27	H	Workington Town	4 0	Chappell, May, Moore, Curtis	2,442		6	3	2	5		11	9	8		4		10			7		1			
16	Dec-04	A	Watford	0 2		4,595		2	3	4	5		12	9	8		6	11*	10			7		1			
17	Dec-11	H	Scunthorpe United	2 0	Conway, May	2,392	1	2	3	4	5		11	9*	8		6	12	10			7					
18	Dec-18	H	Cambridge United	3 1	Charles, Chappell, Conway	3,280	1	2	3	4	5		11	9	8		6	12	10*			7					
19	Dec-27	A	AFC Bournemouth	1 1	James	6,329	1	2	3	4	5		11	9	8		6	10				7					
20	Dec-29	H	Colchester United	2 1	May, Charles	5,666	1	2	3	4	5		11	9	8		6	10				7					
21	Jan-01	A	Exeter City	0 2		3,596	1	2	3	4	5		11	9	8		6	10*				7	12				
22	Jan-04	H	Crewe Alex	3 0	James, Charles, Chappell	5,066	1	2	3	4	5		11	9	8		6	10				7					
23	Jan-08	A	Rochdale	0 1		1,436	1	2	3	4	5		11*	9	8		6	10			12	7					
24	Jan-22	A	Darlington	4 0	Charles, Smith, Conway, James	3,436	1	2	3	4	5		11	9	8		6	10				7					
25	Jan-29	H	Hartlepool United	4 2	Curtis 2, Smith, Conway	5,034	1	2	3	4	5		11	9	8		6	10				7					
26	Feb-12	A	Barnsley	0 1		6,598	1	2*	3	4	5	12	11	9	8		6	10				7					
27	Feb-26	A	Doncaster Rovers	1 2	Charles	4,369	1		3	4	5		11	9	8		6	10				7			2		
28	Mar-01	H	Bradford City	2 3	Charles, Smith	4,987	1		3	4	5		11	9	7*		6	10				8	12		2		
29	Mar-05	H	Aldershot	4 2	Charles 2, James, Conway	3,170	1		3		5		7	9	8		6	10				4				2	11
30	Mar-11	A	Southport	3 1	Curtis, Conway, Harris	972	1	2		4	5		11	9	8		6	10*				7	12		3		
31	Mar-15	A	Southend United	2 1	Curtis, Chappell	3,762	1	2		4	5		11	9	8		6	10				7			3		
32	Mar-18	H	Torquay United	4 1	O/Goal, James, Curtis, Charles	4,780	1	2	3	4	5		11	9	8		6	10*				7	12				
33	Mar-23	H	Stockport County	4 4	Smith, Chappell, May, Curtis	6,383	1	2	3	4	5		11	9	8		6	10				7					
34	Mar-26	A	Brentford	0 4		6,200	1	2	3	4	5	12	11	9	8*		6	10				7					
35	Apr-02	H	Newport County	3 1	Charles 2, O/Goal	3,577	1	2	3	4	5	6		9	8		11	10*	12			7					
36	Apr-08	A	Colchester United	1 1	O/Goal	5,184	1	2	3	4	5	6		9	8		7	10				11					
37	Apr-11	H	AFC Bournemouth	3 0	Charles, Curtis, James	6,920	1	2	3	4	5	6		9	8		7	10*				11	12				
38	Apr-12	H	Southend United	2 0	Bartley, Moore	8,155	1	2	3	4	5	6		9	8		11		10			7					
39	Apr-16	A	Scunthorpe United	3 0	Smith 2, James	2,079	1	2	3	4	5	6		9	8		7	10				11					
40	Apr-18	A	Hartlepool United	2 2	Charles 2	1,063	1	2	3	4	5	6		9	8		7	10	12			11*					
41	Apr-23	H	Halifax Town	2 1	James 2	7,344	1	2	3	4	5	6		9	8		7	10				11					
42	Apr-26	H	Huddersfield Town	2 1	May, Charles	9,613	1	2	3	4*	5	6		9	8		7	10	12			11					
43	Apr-30	A	Workington Town	3 1	Moore 2, Curtis	1,249	1	2	3		5	6		9	8		4	10	11			7					
44	May-03	H	Rochdale	3 2	Curtis 2, Charles	10,689	1	2	3		5	6		9	8		7	10	11			4					
45	May-07	H	Watford	1 4	Charles	11,000	1	2	3		5	6		9	8		4	10	11			7					
46	May-14	A	Cambridge United	3 2	Curtis 2, Charles	7,795	1	2	3		5	6		9	8		7	10	11			4					
						Apps	41	43	45	35	46	26	23	46	46	3	46	36	16	1	0	39	4	0	4	5	1
						Subs				2			2	2					5	4		2	1	2	4		
						Gls			1	8	6		8	14	16	1		23	6			5	1				

#	Date	V	Opponents	Score	Scorers	Att.	Potter S	Evans W	Bartley D	Smith G	May E	Bruton D	Conway M	Curtis A	James R	Bray G	Lally P	Charles J	Moore G	Schroeder N	Reece G	Chappell L	Harris P	Griffiths J	Brown G	Stead M	Harvey L
1	Aug-14	H	Newport Co. FLC 1-1	4 1	Chappell, Charles 2, Bray(pen)	3,300	1		3	2	5	6	7	9	8*	10	11	12				4					
2	Aug-18	A	Newport Co. FLC 1-2	0 1		2,720	1		3	2	5	6	7*	8	12	10	11	9				4					
3	Aug-31	A	Chester, FLC 2	3 2	Curtis, Bartley, Charles	3,372	1	2	3	4	5	6		8	9		7	11	10			4					
4	Sep-22	A	Torquay Utd. FLC-3	2 1	James, Curtis	4,430	1	2	3	4	5	6		9	8		7	11	10			4					
5	Oct-26	H	Bolton W, FLC-4	1 1	Curtis	13,600	1	2	3	12	5	6		9	8		7	10*				11	4				
6	Nov-02	A	Bolton W, FLC-4 Rep	1 5	James	14,955	1	2	3		5	4	12	9	8		7	10*				11	6				
7	Nov-20	H	Minehead, FAC-1	0 1		3,435		2	3	4		6	12	9	8		7	11*	10			5		1			
8	Jan-18	H	Newport Co. WC-5	4 1	Curtis 3, May	3,755	1	2	3		5		11	9	8		7	10				4	11				
9	Feb-21	A	Wrexham, WC-6	1 4	May	5,400	1		3	2	5		11	9	8		7	10*	12			4					6

Chapter 18

Toshack Arrives

1977-78

In contrast to previous seasons, Swansea City started the new campaign as the bookmakers' favourites to win the championship of the Fourth Division. Although this opinion on the part of the betting fraternity was extremely gratifying, for Harry Griffiths, it also had its drawbacks. Apart from anything else, it created an expectation which was to put pressure on the manager and his squad and, in due course, would result in his resignation.

Nevertheless, in the August before the season began, Griffiths was quietly confident in the quality of his group of players. During the summer he had strengthened the squad by buying goalkeeper Keith Barber from Luton, Kevin Moore, a winger from Blackpool, and Neil Davids from Norwich. The supporters, meanwhile, had shown their feelings through season-ticket sales. The 1,354 which had been sold represented the highest total for seven seasons. Overall, there was an air of confidence about the Vetch and, for that matter, about the city.

Whilst that feeling was hardly reinforced by the club's dismissal from the first round of the Football League Cup, the Vetch management was not too concerned, for early league results served to justify their optimism. By 16 September the side had lost only one of its seven league matches. The team was playing well as a unit, while Curtis, relishing his newly established role as a striker, had converted half the goals which had been scored. Goalkeeper Barber and winger Moore had also settled in well and home gates were more than double those at the same stage of the previous campaign.

Although Swans supporters were beginning to get used to the idea that none of the club's young players would be sold, there was still concern about the persistence of certain First Division clubs in tracking the team. When they played at Darlington, for example, the London papers carried

> **On 1 April 1978 a new club record was set at the Vetch when Hartlepool were beaten 8-0.**

reports that representatives of ten clubs from the senior division watched the game. The targets, they said, were Alan Curtis (who had been named the best player in the Fourth Division at the end of the previous season) and Jeremy Charles. The now-familiar denials were issued from the Vetch, but it does not take a psychologist to understand that established patterns of expectation take time to eradicate. The resident Swansea pessimists still found it difficult to believe that the transformation in Vetch Field policies was inviolate.

After what had been an encouraging start, there followed a dismal spell during which the Swans won only one match in seven. By the end of October the side had slipped to mid-table, while gates had been reduced by twenty per cent. Part of the problem could be traced to an unfortunate spate of injuries, but Griffiths also complained about lack of fight. The sole positive news at that time was the announcement that the club had made a profit on its previous season's workings. Gate income had doubled, as had that from commercial activities. Indeed, the latter virtually coincided with the reported surplus of £12,221. The growing importance of non-gate income as an element in the club's strategy was clear for all to see, and chairman Struel congratulated commercial manager Geoff Ford for his efforts.

During that dismal October spell, it was announced that money would be made available for the manager to strengthen the team. With George Smith being released to join

Hartlepool, the manager signed Pat Morrissey on loan from Aldershot and made Eddie May captain. By the end of the month, Morrissey had not impressed and rumours were circulating in Swansea that Harry Griffiths had been fired.

On 29 October it was confirmed that the manager had resigned and immediately a groundswell of public opinion rallied in his support. The popular view was that the manager had done a better job than any of his immediate predecessors and justified being retained. Such was the pressure from the pro-Griffiths lobby that, had there been a referendum in Swansea at the time the result would surely have been in his favour.

However, there was little understanding of the pressures under which the respected Griffiths had been working, nor of his honest personal concern at what he felt was his inability to motivate certain members of his squad. It is undeniable that part of his concern stemmed from his own impeccable standards, from his modest disposition, and the fact that the resulting pressures which enveloped him were intensified by the expectations of those around him. Yet the board, like that of any other business, had the task of meeting the club's objectives. A key aspect of those objectives was promotion.

In the event, following a period during which Griffiths carried on in an acting capacity and several candidates who had been approached refused the Vetch post, the local man was reinstated. By the year-end that decision seemed well-justified. The team had won its way to the third round of the FA Cup, Crewe had been beaten 5-0 at the Vetch, the side had registered its first away victory of the season by beating Brentford, and Harry Griffiths had received the 'Manager of the Month' award for November. Griffiths had also undertaken an extensive search for new players. Unfortunately, those he saw were either too expensive, did not come up to expectation, or refused to come to Swansea.

Apart from an FA Cup defeat at Walsall and a home league game lost to Darlington, the side's improved form continued into January. At the end of that month the team was fourth in its division and, by then, the board had demonstrated its resolve. Chairman Struel announced that a bid of £165,000 from Sunderland for Alan Curtis had been rejected, and that bids for Robbie James and Jeremy Charles had been dealt with in the same way.

After a spell of poor weather during which the Pools Panel sat, the Swans beat Newport County 4-0 at the Vetch on the day a new lottery was launched. The proceeds from the lottery were to be used for ground development and team building. On 25 February, after losing a two-goal lead at Aldershot during the last five minutes of the match, the Swans were fifth in the league table. That draw followed a week during which Harry Griffiths resigned for the second time. The circumstances surrounding this ongoing drama were brought into the open during the game against Newport. In the stand for that match was Eddie McCreadie, who had been manager at Chelsea. McCreadie told the press that he was considering several offers, including one from Swansea. Chairman Struel made it clear at the same time that all developments were taking place with the complete knowledge and agreement of Harry Griffiths. The chairman disclosed that Harry, on his reappointment, had advised him that the club should seek to appoint a young, track-suited manager, and that McCreadie should be approached. For his part, Harry Griffiths emphasised that he was not opting out: he had to face the fact that he was not getting any younger, and he wished to concentrate on the club's youth activities.

On 23 February, Eddie McCreadie became the third manager to refuse Swansea City's job offer. Instead, he flew to America to manage Memphis Rogues. Despite the confusion and disappointment in Swansea, his was a momentous decision as far as Swansea City was concerned. It opened the door for chairman Struel to approach a fourth candidate. This time he was to be successful.

Negotiations started between the Liverpool chairman, John Smith, and Malcolm Struel regarding John Toshack. Toshack himself was to join the chairmen on the following day and, if agreement was reached, would watch his new charges at Rochdale that evening. 'Tosh', as he was known in football circles, had turned down projected transfers to Norwich, Newcastle and Anderlecht, as well as a player-manager post at Hereford. He wanted, he said, to return to Wales. The Swansea post seemed to satisfy his desires admirably and when Liverpool waived the £80,000 transfer fee for the player as a mark of appreciation

> *Not long before the kick-off in a Vetch match against Scunthorpe on 25 April 1978, Harry Griffiths died whilst working in the treatment room. After the magnificent service which he had given to the club, it was a cruel irony that he should die just before the penultimate game of a season which saw his beloved Swans promoted.*

for his services, agreement was reached. John Toshack was to be player-manager at the Vetch with Harry Griffiths as his assistant. Despite the fact that his new charges stumbled to an ignominious defeat that evening at Rochdale, Toshack declared his intentions boldly: 'The potential at Swansea is immense,' he said, 'I believe that I have come to the right place at the right time . . . When I went to Anfield the place was a shed, now the club has a cabinet of trophies.'

The Swans supporters who heard the statement or read about it only wished to put one interpretation upon it. The youngest manager in the league was going to transform Swansea in the same way. Whilst hope is different from belief, most recognised that, at the very least, the tall Cardiffian would make a major contribution as a player in the fifteen games which remained.

Furthermore, despite the Rochdale result, the young manager was adding his football skills and know-how to the Swansea cause which was already well-placed for a promotion drive. Surely, argued the optimists, we shall do it this time!

In Swansea, the excitement generated by the news of Toshack's appointment knew no bounds. Fifteen thousand people packed into the Vetch to watch the new manager's first home game. In an electric atmosphere, which one commentator referred to as a 'response to a second-coming', the Swans drew with eventual champions Watford, Although the draw was gained through an Alan Curtis goal late in the game after the Swans had surrendered a two-goal lead, there was nothing but optimism in the air. Toshack's presence had given the team and the supporters new impetus. Wait until he's had time to work with the lads! The optimists' battalion had reinforced itself exponentially.

On 17 March, after drawing at home with Southend and losing at York, the club gained its first win under the new manager. By then the side had slipped to eighth in the table. However, as if to demonstrate that Tosh had had time 'to work with the lads', there followed five successive victories, including a new club record (8-0) defeat of Hartlepool, when both Robbie James and Alan Curtis scored hat-tricks. By then the Swans had regained fourth position in the league table. Once again, promotion was a possibility and remained so despite defeats at Crewe, Grimsby and Northampton. With two matches to be played, both needed to be won if the Swans were to gain third place at the expense of Brentford.

The first of these matches took place on 25 April and was watched by 13,228 people. They came in good spirits, determined to cheer their side to victory. In the event, they saw a match played in an atmosphere of muted respect. Harry Griffiths had died that evening whilst working in the treatment room prior to the kick-off. As the teams came out, the shock of the highly respected man's sudden death seemed to envelop the ground. For John Toshack and his team the poignancy of the moment presented a very special challenge. Harry was gone

The Swans' squad for 1978-79.
Back row, left to right: P. Lloyd, C. Marustik, I. McCarthy, I. Edwards, M. Baker, D. White, W. Phillips, P. Reeves.
Middle: D. Williams (Physiotherapist), R. James, A. James, K. Moore, K. Barber, G. Crudgington, P. Langley, S. Morris,
N. Stevenson, P. Lally. Front: A. Waddle, W. Evans, A. Curtis, T. Medwin (Assistant Manager), J. Toshack (Manager),
L. Chappell (Coach), J. Charles, D. Bartley, D. Bruton.

but his spirit lived on. The team would win the match for him. They did not let him down: Scunthorpe were beaten 3-1.

Many hundreds of words have been written about Harry Griffiths' all have stressed his dedication to every aspect of Swansea soccer and there is no doubt that he was one of the most popular men in the annals of the Vetch club's history. Everyone who knew him formed the same impression of honesty, integrity, dedication and loyalty. He brought these qualities to every one of the many roles which he filled for the club. No one can explain the sad irony of his death during the week in which his beloved Swans gained the promotion for which he had worked so hard. Even in death, though, his spirit played an integral part in the life of the club which he loved. As Robbie James put it, 'When the whistle went for full-time I found myself looking to the bench for Harry's smiling face.' His body might not have been there, but for players and supporters alike, his spirit was. John Toshack concurred. When promotion was assured he vowed: 'We shall leave no stone unturned to do him proud.'

In the final match of the campaign the team began that process. Visitors Halifax held out against determined Swansea attacks until the sixty-eighth minute. At that point the Swans were awarded a free kick ten yards outside the Halifax penalty area. To the delight of the crowd, Toshack took the kick himself and bent his shot around the Halifax wall to give the Vetch men the lead. Four minutes from time, Alan Curtis scored the second goal of the game to ensure promotion. The joy of the Swansea supporters among the 16,130 who were there that day knew no bounds. The march had begun but few, if any, could have conceived of the speed with which it was to develop.

1978-79

Some pointers to the pace of development at the Vetch began to be evident as John Toshack's close-season plans took shape. The manager's first task was to persuade Alan Curtis to stay at the Vetch after the player had asked for a transfer. Within a week, not only had Toshack been successful in that respect, he had also signed Leicester striker Alan Waddle for £24,000 and had agreed terms with Terry Medwin to bring him back as assistant manager. On top of that, just in case anyone doubted his intentions, Liverpool stalwart Tommy Smith had joined

the club, as had goalkeeper Geoff Crudgington, whom the manager had bought from Crewe for £30,000. The whole of Swansea seemed to reverberate with the news of these transactions. Even the cynics were lost for words. There were departures, too. In August, Pat Lally, who had made a sound contribution whilst he was at the Vetch, joined Doncaster for £10,000. Then, before the end of the year, Dave Bruton, another player who had given stalwart service, was transferred to Newport County.

In early August, Everton came to the Vetch to play in a pre-season friendly, as a result of which some £3,000 was raised for Harry Griffiths's widow, Gwen. It was another token of appreciation of Harry's services to Swansea sport. Given the event, the quality of young Chris Marustic's performance that evening was particularly pertinent. The former manager had signed the youngster, who was to become a full-time professional under John Toshack two weeks later.

On the business front, Malcolm Struel was delighted to announce that season-ticket sales had increased to 2,360, the highest figure for more than twenty years. The new lottery and other commercial activities had also raised record sums during the previous campaign. As a result, apart from allowing the manager to strengthen his squad, it enabled the club to invest £150,000 in ground developments.

As had become the norm, competitive football began with the Football League Cup. After losing to Newport County in the first leg of the first round, the Swans made amends at the Vetch by winning 5-0. This took them into the second round where they drew Tottenham Hotspur. For Swansea folk, this was something of a fairy tale. On the evening, 24,375 packed into the Vetch to see the Swans play the First Division side which included two much-publicized Argentinians, Ardiles and Villa. In the fashion which was to become his hallmark, Toshack boldly fielded two inexperienced youngsters, Stephen Morris and Nigel Stevenson, to serve at the heart of his defence. Tommy Smith was deployed in front of them. At the end of the evening, following a thrillling, hard-fought match, the score was 2-2. Most commentators felt that the Swans had done enough to win, but to do so at Tottenham in the second leg was another matter. In the event, with John Toshack playing at centre-half, the Spurs were outplayed and the Swans won 3-1. The Fleet Street press was loud in its praise, as was Ricardo Villa, who likened Toshack to his Argentinian team-mate Kempes. Tosh enjoyed that, but said that he was very proud of his team, who had played 'out of their skins'.

In the league, after winning its fourth match on 2 September, the newly promoted club sat at the top of the Third Division table. That victory was important in that it impressed Ian Callaghan, who watched the game from the stand. It was said that he was contemplating whether to join the Swans or go to Queens Park Rangers. Whilst Callaghan pondered, Toshack moved again. This time he paid a new club record fee of £35,000 to Luton for Phil Boersma. The Swansea fans could hardly believe their eyes. Not only were the club's best young players not being transferred, but £81,000 had already been spent on new men.

During the remainder of September, Toshack continued to fuel the club's early season momentum. With ITV's 'Big Match' cameras at Watford to record the

Swans' match with the home club, his team won with something to spare. This was a game in which he made one of those eyebrow-lifting decisions for the press to ponder. At the beginning of the second half, he substituted Nigel Stevenson for himself. No one, he seemed to be saying, would be exempt from being replaced, not even the manager. In the next game, Boersma's debut, the team drew 4-4 with Rotherham.

Ian Callaghan, a true professional, who covered more ground in a match than men half his age.

In the meantime, Ian Callaghan had agreed to join his former Liverpool colleague and he made his debut in the following match. After seven games the club was top and had not been beaten, and even though the next two matches were lost, when September ended, John Toshack received the 'Manager of the Month' award. By then the club was third in the table. It had been an encouraging start, but one which was marred somewhat by an injury to Alan Curtis which was to keep the player out of the side until December.

There was defeat, too, in the next round of the Football League Cup against Queen's Park Rangers. Despite an excellent performance by Robbie James, in which he outshone the much publicised Bowles and Francis, goalkeeping errors led to victory for the home side. In the league, though, results throughout October gave every Vetch fan considerable encouragement.

In these matches, Callaghan, James, Waddle, Toshack and Smith often caught the eye. In the match against Hull, Crudgington, who had had an unhappy early season, saved a penalty. After the final home game of the month, the side extended its unbeaten home run to nineteen and, after fifteen matches, the Swans were third in the divisional table, just one point behind leaders Watford and Shrewsbury.

As if inspired by his previous feat, during November Geoff Crudgington again saved a penalty in a 1-0 victory over Bury. It was an extremely important save, for it kept the Swans in touch with the top teams. That match was noteworthy in another respect: it marked the debut of yet another Toshack purchase. Leighton Phillips had cost the Swans £70,000, a fee which set a 'highest purchase' record for the second time that season. In that game, Phillips was one of seven new players in the side who had not been with the club during the previous season. By then, if the Swansea fans had anything left to be surprised about, it was that Toshack's new team had settled down as a unit so well and so quickly.

When the year ended, John Toshack was able to look back on an encouraging half season. Despite some problems in disposing of non-league Woking in the FA Cup, and two successive league defeats at the end of December, the side was third in the division and in the fifth round of the cup. In addition, Alan Curtis had returned from injury and was weaving his magic to such a degree that he scored seven goals in the first three games following his comeback. In freezing conditions, the only games which were played in January were two cup matches. In the first, Bristol Rovers surprised the Swans by scoring the only goal of the game to earn a fourth round place in the FA Cup. The second proved to be an easy 6-1 victory over Kidderminster in the Welsh Cup, during which Robbie James scored a hat-trick.

Meantime, Fleet Street, seizing on the fact that the Swans had five former Anfield men in the team, had labelled the Vetch men 'Liverpool Reserves'. In addition, when any player was about to leave Anfield, he was connected with the Swans. Toshack reacted philosophically to the first charge, but hotly denied that

Emlyn Hughes was about to move to south Wales. In addition, he took the Swansea public to task. 'They keep asking me to get the Swans back in the Second Division,' he snapped, 'What's wrong with Division One?' Those who listened began to believe that he meant it, while the chairman's target, set eighteen months before – the Second Division – seemed then to be a distinct possibility.

establish himself in the side after a series of injuries, was tackled heavily by the home centre-back, Aizelwood. As a result of this he was carried from the field. It was to prove to be his last appearance in the Football League. The win, however, pushed the Swans into second place in the table, with six to play. Two matches later, the side was top of the division. In addition, four Swans – Toshack, James, Curtis and Phillips – were

match at Plymouth (making their 'Match of the Day' debut in the process), Swansea City faced Chesterfield at the Vetch for their final game. Coincidentally, Chesterfield had been the club's opponents for the final match of a previous successful season. That, according to the Swans supporters, was an omen of gigantic proportion, though, when the visitors had the audacity to score after fifteen minutes, the atmosphere at the Vetch was somewhat tense. Even when Waddle scored the equaliser, the matter was not resolved. The teams battled on until, twenty minutes from the end, John Toshack brought himself on to replace Attley. Ten minutes later, Bartley placed a perfectly judged free kick near the far post and there was manager Toshack, hanging in the air to head home a fine goal. The Swans were back in the Second Division! After fourteen years in the wilderness, the young manager had led his men to a significant promotion. Moses could not have done a better job! For twenty-four hours the Swans sat proudly at the top of their division but, subsequently, Watford and Shrewsbury gained extra points to push the Swans to third. No one at the Vetch worried about that, though. A dream had become reality.

'Tosh' scores a vital promotion goal v. Chesterfield.

Unfortunately, during February, results were so poor, only two points were gathered from five matches, that by the end of the month, the side had dropped to sixth in the table. No longer was the possibility of promotion distinct. March, however, proved far more beneficial for the Swans. Inspired by goals from Tommy Smith and the manager, they soundly beat Hull, and that win started an encouraging sequence of results. Rotherham, Gillingham, Colchester and Plymouth were beaten to take the Swans back to second place. Smith, Wyndham Evans, Phillips, James and Callaghan were all outstanding during this period. Ian Callaghan expressed himself delighted with his first season in Division Three. He was determined, he said, to help the Swans to promotion and was encouraged by the quality of the players around him. With ten games to be played, the supporters were talking about promotion again.

In mid-April the side gained a fine victory at Swindon, who were also challenging for promotion. They did so, though, at considerable cost. Phil Boersma, who was beginning to re-

selected for the Wales squad. At the time, chairman Struel, the board, the players and the fans were all confident that Second Division football was now a certainty for the next season. Fate, however, had a few more tricks to play yet.

On 28 April Southend came to the Vetch to play the first of the Swans' last three matches. The visitors had been in contention for promotion and came to deny the Swans victory. A point seemed to be their target, but, after the men in white had taken the lead, Southend struck back and, in the space of eight minutes were in the lead. The tension at the Vetch was audible. As the minutes hurtled by and the fans were becoming restless, Toshack brought himself on to replace a mid-fielder. Even so, it was not until the seventy-sixth minute that Waddle scored the second goal to equalise. Was a point sufficient? It was a question which was to prove superfluous, for in the final minute, Alan Waddle rose to head home his third goal of the match. The exhalation of Swansea breath could have blown out a thousand candles.

Having drawn their penultimate

In his first full season in football management John Toshack had achieved a great deal, though he was not finished yet. Eight days after scoring the Swans promotion goal he registered a hat-trick playing for Wales against Scotland. Little wonder that he relished the challenge which lay ahead. Was there anything he could not achieve?

1979-80

After so much joy at the Vetch, came genuine disappointment. At the end of May, after he had requested a move to a First Division club, Alan Curtis joined Leeds United for a fee of £350,000. The fact that that fee constituted a record for both clubs, for the Third Division, and for any Welsh club, was of little consolation to the Vetch authorities and the supporters. Nevertheless, John Toshack was able to use the bulk of the money to strengthen his side for the Second Division challenge. David Rushbury was signed from

The Swans' squad, 1979-80.
Back row, left to right: P. Reeves, B. Attley, C. Medwin, M. Baker, C. Marustik, A. James.
Middle: L. Chappell, P. Boersma, P. McQuillan, G. Crudgington, A. Waddle, N. Stevenson, J. Charles,
S. Morris, R. James, T. Medwin (Assistant Manager).
Front: W. Evans, T. Craig, T. Smith, J. Toshack (Player-Manager), L. Phillips (Captain), D. Rushbury, J. Mahoney, D. Bartley.

Sheffield Wednesday and made soccer history in the process. The fee for his transfer was set at the first meeting of the newly formed Transfer Appeals Commission. Professor John Woods and his panel ruled that the Swans should pay Wednesday £60,000. Then, in quick succession, Tommy Craig joined the club from Aston Villa for another new Swans record fee of £150,000, while John Mahoney arrived from Middlesborough for £100,000. Thereafter, before the season ended, the manager added five other players to his squad. In mid-September, Glan Letheran came from Chesterfield in exchange for £50,000; Neil Robinson from Everton (£70,000) arrived in October, and David Giles, for the same figure, from Wrexham in November; in February, David Stewart from West Bromwhich added £58,000 to the bill while, during the last week of the season, Leighton James came from Burnley, £130,000 being the fee. While Alan Curtis would be missed, clearly Toshack was intent on building a team which could make a genuine challenge for promotion to Division One.

Not surprisingly, there were departures, too. As a result of persistent problems with his knee, Tommy Smith's contract was terminated by mutual consent. In the following month, Danny Bartley, who had given stalwart service to the club in its darkest days and through the lower divisions was given a free transfer to join Hereford. Another

> **On 5 May 1979 the Swans were featured on 'Match of the Day' for the first time. By gaining a point from that match (versus Plymouth away) and winning the next they gained promotion for the second season in succession.**

departure was Stephen Morris who, together with Geoff Crudgington, joined Plymouth Argyle, the latter recouping the fee which the Swans had paid for him.

At the end of the 1979-80 season the club was in twelfth position in the Second Division. After the euphoria of the two previous campaigns, the outcome was slightly disappointing in the eyes of some. However, clubs in this division were better organised and had better players than those in the lower leagues. One result of this was that manager Toshack had to adapt his style of play to suit, which affected the team's scoring rate negatively. After three seasons of plenty, this looked to some like a retrograde step, but those who held that opinion took little account of the potential of the squad of players who were then at the Vetch.

On the business front, the average league gate for the season was 14,391, the highest figure recorded for fifteen seasons. Non-gate income had also improved tremendously, with the commercial department contributing £170,000 as a result of its efforts. Both these figures represented trends which encouraged the directors to proceed with the next stage of the development of the Vetch. A new stand was to be erected at the small-bank end of the ground as the first stage in a visionary reconstruction of the old stadium. The plans involved were indicative of the determination of the board to continue with the transformation of the club as a whole – despite the recession in which the British economy and football in particular were embroiled. In the special programme which was issued to commemorate the opening of the new stand, former manager Trevor Morris referred to the 'resolution and spirit of adventure' of the directors in undertaking such a scheme. Certainly, they were demonstrating the implementation of the fundamental business principles, the basis of which had underscored their campaign as the Ginger Group a decade before. Had they been a political party no one could other than agree that they had lived up to the promise of their manifesto.

Although 1979-80 had not been an outstanding season on the field, it had provided some exciting incidents. The height of that excitement, without doubt, was an FA Cup tie with Crystal Palace which necessitated three matches to produce a result. On New Year's Day, Cardiff City provided the opposition for a Vetch match in which the home goals were scored by two former Bluebirds – John Toshack and David Giles. Giles scored his in the last minute of injury time. Later in January, Ian Callaghan equalled Stanley Matthews's record by appearing in his eighty-fifth FA Cup game at the age of thirty-seven. Three weeks later, he set a new record when he appeared in a Swans defeat at West Ham. Since Ian retired at the end of the season he was not able to add to that total. Nonetheless, the statistic is indicative of the professionalism of a player who gave his 'everything' on the field to the Swansea City cause. In many matches he covered more ground than players half his age. Naturally, age had blunted his powers by the time he came to the Vetch, but there were few occasions when he failed to measure up to the best players on the field.

Of the new men, Stewart performed soundly, Leighton Phillips and Giles made major contributions,

Alan Waddle outjumps Peter Nicholas of Crystal Palace only to be foiled by goalkeeper Burridge.

as did Rushbury. After an unfortunate pre-season injury, Robinson came back to play fourteen games. Tommy Craig showed his class and composure in many matches, while John Mahoney, despite a series of injuries, also made his mark. There was encouragement, too, in the development of young players. Nigel Stevenson played on thirty-one occasions and grew in confidence, while Chris Marustic

looked as though he was going to develop into a useful footballer. The question was whether the particular blend of players which the manager had at his disposal was good enough to challenge for promotion in the season ahead. By the time the new campaign was about to start, John Toshack appeared to suggest that it was. No new players had been signed during the close-season.

Swansea City FC Season 1977/78 Division 4

#	Date	V	Opponents	Score	Scorers	Att.	Barber K	Evans W	Bartley D	Bruton D	May E	Davids N	Moore K	Chappell L	Curtis A	Moore G	Charles J	James R	Smith G	Lally P	Dalling N	Conway M	Potter S	Morrissey P	Grey M	Griffiths J	James A	Morris S	Kennerley K	Toshack J	McCarthy I
1	Aug-21	A	Huddersfield Town	0 0		4,435	1	2	3	4	5	6	7	8	9	10	11														
2	Aug-23	H	Doncaster Rovers	3 0	Bruton, Moore G, Curtis	6,284	1	2	3	4*	5	6	10	7	9	8	11	12													
3	Aug-27	H	Barnsley	2 1	Curtis 2	6,739	1	2	3	4	5	6	8	7	9	10*	12	11													
4	Sep-03	A	Darlington	1 1	Curtis	1,778	1	2	3	4	5	6	12	7	9	10	11*	8													
5	Sep-10	H	Rochdale	3 0	May, Charles, Curtis	4,348	1	2	3	6	5		8	11	9	10*	12	7	4												
6	Sep-12	A	Southend United	1 2	Curtis	6,174	1	2	3		5	6	11	7	9	10	8		4*	12											
7	Sep-16	H	Grimsby Town	2 0	Evans, James(pen)	7,402	1	2	3		5	6	10*	7	9			8	4	11	12										
8	Sep-24	A	Newport County	0 1		5,115	1	2	3		5	6	10	7	9		11	8*	4		12										
9	Sep-27	A	Scunthorpe United	0 1		2,654	1	2	3		5	6	10	8	9			11*	4	7	12										
10	Oct-01	H	Aldershot	1 0	Curtis(pen)	5,721	1	2	3		5		11	8	9		10		4		6	7									
11	Oct-04	H	Southport	1 1	Evans W	6,346	1	2	3		5			7	9	10	8		4		6	11									
12	Oct-08	A	Watford	1 2	Curtis	10,252	1	2	3		5			7	9	10	8		4		6	11									
13	Oct-15	H	York City	1 1	Charles	5,346		2	3		5		8		9	10	7		4		6	11*	1	12							
14	Oct-22	A	Stockport County	0 2		4,028		2	3	4	5			7	9	10		8*				11	1	6	12						
15	Oct-29	H	Reading	2 1	Griffiths, Curtis	4,755		2	3	4	5		11		9	10*	8	12					1	6		7					
16	Nov-05	A	Wimbledon	1 1	Lally	2,701		2	3	4	5		11		9	12	8			7			1	6		10*					
17	Nov-12	H	Crewe Alex	5 0	Lally, Bartley, Curtis 3	4,253	1	2	3	4	5				9	6	8			7		11				10					
18	Nov-19	A	Brentford	2 0	Curtis, Conway	6,340	1	2	3	4*	5		12		9	6	8			7		11				10					
19	Dec-03	H	Northampton Town	2 4	Curtis, Lally	5,500	1	2	3		5	4*			9	6	8			7		11				10	12				
20	Dec-10	A	Halifax Town	1 3	James	1,722	1	2	3	4	5		7		9	10	8					11				6*	12				
21	Dec-26	H	Torquay United	1 1	James R (pen)	7,300	1	2		6	5		11		9*	10	8		4	7		12						3			
22	Dec-27	A	AFC Bournemouth	1 0	Moore G	5,552	1	2		6	5		11	7	9	10	8		4									3			
23	Dec-31	A	Hartlepool	4 0	Curtis 2, Moore K 2	3,196	1	2		6	5		11	7	9		8		4									3			
24	Jan-02	H	Wimbledon	3 0	O/Goal, James(pen), Charles	9,700	1	2		6	5		11	7	9	10*	12	8	4									3			
25	Jan-10	A	Doncaster Rovers	1 1	Moore K	2,509	1	2		6	5		11	7	9*	10	12	8	4									3			
26	Jan-14	H	Huddersfield Town	1 0	Moore G	5,906	1	2		6	5		11	7	9	10	8											3			
27	Jan-28	H	Darlington	1 2	James(pen)	5,402	1	2		6	5		11*	7	9	10	8		4			12						3			
28	Feb-17	H	Newport County	4 0	Conway, Evans, James 2	6,056	1	2		6	5				9	10	8		4			11						3	7		
29	Feb-28	A	Aldershot	2 2	Bartley 2	3,806	1	2	10	6	5				9		8		4			11						3	7		
30	Feb-27	A	Rochdale	1 2	Curtis	1,057	1	2		6	5		12	7	9	10	8		4			11*						3			
31	Mar-03	H	Watford	3 3	Moore K, Toshack, Curtis	15,500	1	2		6			11	7	9			8*	4									3	5	10	
32	Mar-07	H	Southend United	0 0		11,316	1	2		6	5			7	9	10	8		4			11						3			
33	Mar-11	A	York City	1 2	Curtis	1,962	1	2		6	5		12		9		8		4			11				7*		3		10	
34	Mar-17	H	Stockport County	3 1	Toshack, Curtis, James(pen)	7,400	1	2		6	5		11	7	9		8		4									3		10*	12
35	Mar-24	A	Reading	4 1	James R(2 pens), Curtis, Morris	6,046	1	2		6	5			7	9		8		4			11						3		10	
36	Mar-25	A	AFC Bournemouth	1 0	Moore K	7,500	1	2		6*	5		11	7	9		8		4			12						3		10	
37	Mar-27	H	Torquay United	4 2	Bruton, Toshack, Curtis 2	5,252	1	2		6	5		11	7	9		8		4									3		10	
38	Apr-01	H	Hartlepool	8 0	Curtis 3, James R 3, Toshack, Lally	6,961	1	2	3	6	5		11	7	9		8			4*		12								10	
39	Apr-04	A	Southport	3 0	James A, Curtis, Toshack	2,750	1	2	3		5		11	7	9		8		4								6			10	
40	Apr-08	A	Crewe Alex	1 2	May	2,941	1	2	3	6	5		11	7	9		8		4									12		10*	
41	Apr-11	A	Barnsley	2 0	James R 2	8,634	1	2	4	6	5		11	7	9		8					10*					12	3			
42	Apr-15	H	Brentford	2 1	Curtis 2	16,140	1	2	4	6	5		11*	7	9	12	8											3		10	
43	Apr-18	A	Grimsby Town	1 2	James R	5,692	1	2	4	6	5			7	9	10*	8					11					12	3			
44	Apr-22	A	Northampton Town	1 3	Bartley	4,584	1	2	11	6	5		7		9		8		4								12	3		10	
45	Apr-25	H	Scunthorpe United	3 1	Bruton, Curtis 2	13,228	1	2	4	6	5			7	9		8					11						3		10	
46	Apr-29	H	Halifax Town	2 0	Toshack, Curtis	16,130	1	2	4	6	5			7	9		8					11						3		10	
			Apps				42	46	43	28	44	9	37	26	39	14	27	41	8	31	1	13	4	3	1	5	5	24	2	13	0
			Subs										3	1			6		1		2	3	3		1	1	3	3	2		1
			Gls					3	4	3	2		5		32	3	3	16		4		2				1	1	1		6	

#	Date	V	Opponents	Score	Scorers	Att.	Barber K	Evans W	Bartley D	Bruton D	May E	Davids N	Moore K	Chappell L	Curtis A	Moore G	Charles J	James R	Smith G	Lally P	Dalling N	Conway M	Potter S	Morrissey P	Grey M	Griffiths J	James A	Morris S	Kennerley K	Toshack J	McCarthy I
1	Aug-13	H	Swindon T, FLC 1-1	1 3	Moore G	5,878		2	3		5	6	8*	11	9	10	12	7	4						1						
2	Aug-16	A	Swindon T.FLC 1-2	1 2	Charles	5,500	1	2	3		5	6	7		9	10	11	8	4*			12									
3	Nov-27	A	Leatherhead, FAC-1	0 0		3,000	1		3		5	4			9	6	8			7		11				10	2				
4	Nov-29	H	Leatherhead, FAC-1R	2 1	Charles, Curtis	7,235	1	2	3		5	4			9	6	8			7		11				10					
5	Dec-17	A	Portsmouth, FAC-2	2 2	Curtis, Moore K	11,863	1	2		6	5		11		9	10	8		4								7	3			
6	Dec-20	H	Portsmouth, FAC-2Rep	2 1	O/Goal, Moore G	8,844	1	2		6	5		11		9	10	8		4								7	3			
7	Jan-07	A	Walsall, FAC-3	1 4	James	7,057	1	2		6	5		11*	7	9	10	12	8										3			
8	Jan-17	H	Newport Co. WC-5	0 0		7,500	1	2		6	5		10		9		8					11				7		3			
9	Jan-24	A	Newport Co. WC-5Rep	0 1		6,100	1	2		6	5	4*	11	8	9	10						12				7		3			

Swansea City FC Season 1978/79 Division 3

#	Date	V	Opponents	Score	Scorers	Att.	Crudgington G	Evans W	Bartley D	Toshack J	Bruton D	Reeves P	Lally P	James R	Curtis A	Waddle A	Moore K	Smith T	Charles J	James A	Stevenson N	Morris S	Boersma P	Marustik C	Callaghan I	Baker M	Phillips L	Attley B
1	Aug-19	A	Colchester United	2 2	James 2	2,918	1	2	3	4	5	6	7	8	9	10	11											
2	Aug-22	H	Lincoln City	3 0	Charles, Curtis, Waddle	17,000	1	2	3	7	5			8	9	10	11	4	6*	12								
3	Aug-26	A	Oxford United	2 0	James 2	4,957	1	2	3	5*				8		9	11	6	10				7	4	12			
4	Sep-02	H	Bury	2 0	James, Charles	10,500	1	2	3			12		8	9*	10	11	4	7		5	6						
5	Sep-09	A	Watford	2 0	Waddle, Moore	17,345	1	2	3	7*	5			8	9	10	11	4	6		12							
6	Sep-12	H	Rotherham United	4 4	Charles 2, Curtis 2	17,065	1	2	3		5			8*	9	10	11	4	6				7	12				
7	Sep-16	H	Tranmere Rovers	4 3	Charles, Waddle, Bartley, Curtis	16,132	1	2	3	6	5				9	10	12	4	7*				8		11			
8	Sep-23	A	Chester	0 2		8,583	1	2	3					8	9*	10		4	6		5		11	12	7			
9	Sep-25	A	Carlisle United	0 2		8,489	1	2	3						10	8			6		5	4	7	9	11			
10	Sep-30	H	Brentford	2 1	Charles, James	11,470	1	2	3	5				8	9	7		4	6*		12	10	11					
11	Oct-07	A	Chesterfield	1 2	Charles	7,033	1	2	3	5				8	9	7*		4	6			10	11	12				
12	Oct-14	H	Exeter City	1 0	Toshack	10,957	1	2	3	6				8		10	7	4	9		5		11					
13	Oct-17	H	Mansfield Town	3 2	James(pen), Baker 2	10,985	1	2		10				8	9	7		4	6		5		12		11	3*		
14	Oct-21	A	Hull City	2 2	Toshack, Waddle	6,152	1	2	12	5				8	9	7*		4	6		3		10		11			
15	Oct-28	H	Peterborough United	4 1	Waddle 2, Toshack, Charles	11,302	1	2	3	10		12		8		11		4	6		5		7					
16	Nov-04	A	Gillingham	0 2		11,329	1	2	3	10				8	9			4	6		5		11	7				
17	Nov-11	A	Bury	1 0	James	5,186	1	2					6	8		9		4			5	3	11		7		10	
18	Nov-18	H	Oxford United	1 1	Waddle	11,491	1	2	11	10				8		9		4	6			3	7				5	
19	Dec-02	H	Sheff. Wednesday	4 2	Boersma, Toshack 2, Charles	10,000	1	2	3	5				8	9	11*			6		12		10	7			4	
20	Dec-08	A	Southend United	2 0	Curtis 2	8,935	1		3					8	9	10		2	6		5		7		11		4	
21	Dec-23	A	Shrewsbury Town	0 3		8,567	1		3					8	9	10		2	6		5	7*			11	12	4	
22	Dec-26	H	Swindon Town	1 2	Toshack	16,770	1	2	12	7				8	9	10*		3	6		5				11		4	
23	Dec-30	H	Blackpool	1 0	Charles	12,549	1	2		7				8	9			3	6		5		10*		11	12	4	
24	Feb-02	H	Carlisle United	0 0		10,821	1	2						8	9	10	7	4	6		5				11		3	
25	Feb-10	A	Brentford	0 1		7,250	1	2	3	5				8	9	10		4	7*		12				11		6	
26	Feb-20	A	Walsall	1 1	Bartley	4,338	1	2	3	10				8	9			4	6		5				11		7	
27	Feb-24	A	Exeter City	1 2	Curtis	7,897	1	2	3	10				8*	9			4	6		5				11		7	12
28	Feb-27	H	Chester	2 2	Toshack, Stevenson	7,983	1	2	3	8					9	10		4	12		5				11*		6	7
29	Mar-02	H	Hull City	5 3	Toshack 2, Smith 2, Charles	8,849	1		3	10				8	9			4	6		5				11		2	7
30	Mar-06	A	Rotherham United	1 0	Waddle	8,947	1		3	10*				8	9	12		4	6		5	2			11			7
31	Mar-10	A	Peterborough United	0 2		5,550	1	2	3			12		8	9	10					5	4	6*		11			7
32	Mar-16	H	Gillingham	3 1	Curtis, Waddle, O/Goal	10,832	1	2	3	10*				8	9	12			6		5				11		4	7
33	Mar-20	H	Watford	3 2	Curtis 2, James	19,850	1	2	3					8	9	10		12	6		5				11		4	7*
34	Mar-24	A	Lincoln City	1 2	James	3,568	1	2*	3					8	9	10		12	6		5				11		4	7
35	Mar-27	H	Colchester United	4 1	Waddle 2, James, Attley	11,645	1		3					8	9	10		4	6*		5		12		11		2	7
36	May-31	H	Plymouth Argyle	2 1	Stevenson, Waddle	11,412	1		3					8	9	10		2	6*		5		12		11			7
37	Apr-03	A	Tranmere Rovers	2 1	James, Waddle	3,499	1		3					8	9	10		4			5		6		11		2	7
38	Apr-07	A	Sheff. Wednesday	0 0		12,101	1		3					8	9	10		2			5		6		11			7
39	Apr-10	H	Shrewsbury Town	1 1	James	19,566	1		3	12				8	9	10		4	6*		5				11		2	7
40	Apr-14	A	Swindon Town	1 0	James	16,971	1		3					8	9	10		4	12		5		6*		11		2	7
41	Apr-17	H	Walsall	2 2	Toshack, Waddle	18,096	1		3	12				8	9*	10		4	6		5				11		2	7
42	Apr-21	A	Blackpool	3 1	Curtis, Toshack, Charles	5,977	1	2	3	6*				8	9	10			12		5				11		4	7
43	Apr-23	A	Mansfield Town	2 2	James(pen), Waddle	6,420	1	4	3	6				8	9	10					5				11		2	7
44	Apr-28	H	Southend United	3 2	Waddle 3	15,941	1	2	3	12				8	9	10			6		5				11		4	7*
45	May-05	A	Plymouth Argyle	2 2	Curtis, Toshack	13,406	1	2	3	6				8	9	10			12		5				11		4	7*
46	May-11	H	Chesterfield	2 1	Waddle, Toshack	22,341	1	2	3	12				8	9	10			6		5				11		4	7*
	Apps						46	35	40	24	7	2	1	43	34	40	14	34	36	1	36	7	15	2	40	2	28	19
	Subs							2	4	1		2					1	2	4	1	3	2	3	2		3		1
	Gls								2	13				15	12	19	1	2	12		2		1			2		1

#	Date	V	Opponents	Score	Scorers	Att.	Crudgington G	Evans W	Bartley D	Toshack J	Bruton D	Reeves P	Lally P	James R	Curtis A	Waddle A	Moore K	Smith T	Charles J	James A	Stevenson N	Morris S	Boersma P	Marustik C	Callaghan I	Baker M	Phillips L	Attley B
1	Aug-12	A	Newport Co. FLC 1-1	1 2	Waddle	5,500	1	2	3	5	6		4	8	9	10	7		11*		12							
2	Aug-15	H	Newport Co. FLC 1-2	5 0	James 3, Curtis 2	8,734	1	2	3	4	5	6	7	8	9	10	11											
3	Aug-29	H	Tottenham, FLC 2	2 2	James, Charles	24,335	1	2	3					8	9	10	11*	4	6		5	7		12				
4	Sep-06	A	Tottenham, FLC 2 Rep	3 1	Toshack, Charles, Curtis	33,672	1	2	3	10	5			8	9	11		4	7		6							
5	Oct-03	A	QPR, FLC 3	0 2		18,513	1	2	3	10	5			8		9		4			6	12	7*		11			
6	Nov-25	H	Hillingdon Boro, FAC-1	4 1	James, Charles 2, Waddle	7,824	1	2			3			8	9	11		5	10				6	7		4		
7	Dec-16	H	Woking, FAC-2	2 2	Curtis 2	7,172	1	2	12					8	9	10		3	6		5		7*		11	4		
8	Dec-19	A	Woking, FAC 2 Rep	5 3	Curtis 3, Toshack, James	4,800	1		3	7				8	9	10		2			5	6			11	4		
9	Jan-08	H	Bristol Rovers, FAC-3	0 1		16,500	1	2	3	7				8	9	10		4	6		5				11		5	
10	Jan-29	H	Kidderminster, WC-4	6 1	James R 3, Curtis 2, Charles	4,100	1	2						8	9	10*		3	6		5		12		11	4		
11	Mar-12	A	Wrexham, WC-5	2 3	James, Curtis	9,946	1		3					8	9	10		2	12		5	4	7*		11			6

Swansea City FC Season 1979/80 Division 2

#	Date	V	Opponents	Score	Scorers	Att.	Crudgington G	Attley B	Bartley D	Charles J	Phillips L	Rushbury D	Craig T	Mahoney J	James R	Waddle A	Toshack J	Callaghan I	Marustik C	Baker M	Stevenson N	Letheran G	Evans W	Giles D	Loveridge J	Robinson N	Stewart D	James A	James L	Sander C
1	Aug-18	H	Shrewsbury Town	2 0	James, Waddle	17,400	1	2	3	4	5	6	7	8	9	10	11													
2	Aug-21	A	Watford	0 0		15,208	1	2	3	4	5	6	7	8	9	10			11											
3	Aug-25	A	Preston N E	1 1	Waddle	12,116	1	2	3	4	5	6	7	8		10	9	11												
4	Sep-01	H	Burnley	2 1	Toshack, Craig(pen)	16,660	1	2		4	5	6	7	8		10	9	11	3*	12										
5	Sep-08	A	Luton Town	0 5		10,004	1	2		4	5	6	7	8		10*		11	3	9	12									
6	Sep-15	H	QPR	1 2	Charles	16,000	1	2	3	10	4	6	7	8*	9			11		12	5									
7	Sep-22	A	Notts. County	0 0		8,139		2		4	5	3	7	8	9*	10		11	12		6	1								
8	Sep-29	H	Leicester City	0 2		15,104		12		4	5	3	7		8*	10	9	11			6	1	2							
9	Oct-06	A	Cambridge United	1 0	Charles	5,182		7		6	4	3	10	8	9			11			5	1	2							
10	Oct-09	H	Watford	1 0	Waddle	15,185		7		4	5	3	8*	9	10	12		11			6	1	2							
11	Oct-13	H	Fulham	4 1	Stevenson, O/Goal, James, Attley	12,906		7		4	5	3		8	9	10		11			6	1	2							
12	Oct-20	A	Birmingham City	0 2		18,624		2		4	5	3	7	8	9	10		11			6	1								
13	Oct-27	H	Oldham Athletic	2 0	James 2	12,654		7		6	5	3	10	8*	9			11	12		4	1	2							
14	Nov-03	A	Shrewsbury Town	2 2	O/Goal, Craig	9,815		7*		6	4	3	10	8	9	12		11			5	1	2							
15	Nov-10	H	Sunderland	3 1	Attley, Stevenson, James	15,826		8		4	5	3	7	10*	9	12		11			6	1	2							
16	Nov-17	A	West Ham United	0 2		21,210		8		4	5	3	7	10*	9	12		11			6	1	2							
17	Nov-24	H	Newcastle United	2 3	Charles, James	15,442		8		4	5	3	7	10	9	12		11*			6	1	2							
18	Dec-01	A	Wrexham	0 1		10,651		8		6	4	3			9	10		11			5	1	2	7						
19	Dec-08	H	Charlton Athletic	1 0	Callaghan	11,861		8		4	5	3	7*	6	9	10		11			12	1	2							
20	Dec-15	A	Chelsea	0 3		18,065		8		4	5	3		7	9	10		11			6*	1	2	12						
21	Dec-21	H	Orient	0 1		10,352		8*		4	5	3		6	9			11			12	1	2	7	10					
22	Dec-26	A	Bristol Rovers	1 4	Waddle	9,352		8		4	5	3	7	11	9	10						1	2	6						
23	Dec-29	H	Preston N E	1 0	Waddle	11,401		12		4	2	3	7	8	9	10*		11			5	1		6						
24	Jan-01	H	Cardiff City	2 1	Toshack, Giles	21,400				4	2	3	7	8	9	10		11			5	1		6						
25	Jan-12	A	Burnley	0 0		8,806				10	4	3	7	8	9	10		11		2	5	1		6						
26	Feb-02	A	QPR	2 3	O/Goal, Toshack	11,153				4	5	3	7	8	9	10		11*		2		1		6		12				
27	Feb-09	H	Notts. County	0 1		13,213				6		3	7	8	9	10		11			5	1		4		2				
28	Feb-20	A	Leicester City	1 1	Toshack	17,597				9	4	3	7	8		10		11			5			6		2		1		
29	Feb-23	A	Fulham	2 1	Toshack, Craig(pen)	6,145				9	4	3	7	8		10		11			5			6		2		1		
30	Feb-29	H	Birmingham City	0 1		16,363				9	4	3	7	8		10		11			5			6		2		1		
31	Mar-04	H	Luton Town	2 0	Giles 2	12,785				9	4	3	7	8		10		11	5					6		2		1		
32	Mar-08	A	Oldham Athletic	1 4	Giles	8,445		12		5	4	3	7	9		10		11	8					6		2*		1		
33	Mar-14	H	Cambridge United	2 4	Charles, Craig	11,224		11		4		3	7	8*	9			10			5			6		2		1	12	
34	Mar-22	A	Sunderland	1 1	Giles	25,175		8		4	9	3	7	10				11			5			6		2		1		
35	Mar-29	H	West Ham United	2 1	Craig 2	13,275		8		4*	5		7	11	9								12	6	3	10	2	1		
36	Apr-05	H	Bristol Rovers	2 0	Waddle, Attley	11,730		8		5		3			9			11	7		12			6	4	10	2*	1		
37	Apr-07	A	Cardiff City	0 1		14,667		8		4			7	11	9		10*				12			5	2	6	3	1		
38	Apr-12	H	Wrexham	1 0	Waddle	11,825		8		12	5	3	7*	11	9					2				6	4	10		1		
39	Apr-19	A	Newcastle United	3 1	Giles 2, Stevenson	14,349		8		4	5	3		10*	9			11						6	2	7	12	1		
40	Apr-26	H	Chelsea	1 1	Charles	18,016				4	5	3		10	9			11	8					6		7	2	1		
41	Apr-30	A	Orient	0 0		3,779		8		4	6	3	7	9				11			5			10		2		1		
42	May-03	A	Charlton Athletic	2 1	James L, Giles	3,672		8		4	6	3		10	9*			11			5			7		2		1	12	
						Apps	6	30	4	39	40	40	33	26	29	30	15	36	10	1	31	21	16	25	1	14	15	0	0	
						Subs		3		1							4	1		2	5	1			1	2		1	1	
						Gls		3		5			6		6	7	5	1			3			8					1	

#	Date	V	Opponents	Score	Scorers	Att.	Crudgington G	Attley B	Bartley D	Charles J	Phillips L	Rushbury D	Craig T	Mahoney J	James R	Waddle A	Toshack J	Callaghan I	Marustik C	Baker M	Stevenson N	Letheran G	Evans W	Giles D	Loveridge J	Robinson N	Stewart D	James A	James L	Sander C
1	Aug-11	H	AFC Bournemouth, FLC 1-1	4 1	Waddle 3, Toshack	13,500	1	7	3	6	5	2	11	4	8	9	10*											12		
2	Aug-14	A	AFC Bournemouth, FLC 1-2	0 0		5,834	1	7	3	6	5	2	10	4	8	9														
3	Aug-29	A	Stoke C, FLC 2-1	1 1	Mahoney	18,004	1	2		4*	5	6	7	8		10	9	11	3	12										
4	Sep-04	H	Stoke C, FLC 2-2	1 3	Craig(pen)	20,039	1	2	3*	4	5	6	7	8		10	9	11		12										
5	Jan-05	H	C. Palace, FAC-3	2 2	Toshack 2	17,970				4		3	7	11	8	9	10			2	5	1		6						
6	Jan-08	A	C. Palace, FAC 3 Rep	3 3	Waddle, Giles, Toshack	27,006				4		3	7	11	8	9	10			2	5	1		6						
7	Jan-14	N	C. Palace, FAC 3, Rep 2	2 1	Toshack, Giles (at Ninian Park)	21,400				4	5	3	7			8	9	10	11	2		1		6						
8	Jan-22	H	Pontllanfraith, WC-4	4 0	Charles 2, Craig, James	4,202	10			4	5	3	7	11	8	9								6		2				1
9	Jan-26	H	Reading, FAC-4	4 1	Giles 2, Waddle, James	18,752				4	5	3	7			8	9	10	11	2		1		6						
10	Feb-16	A	West Ham Utd, FAC-5	0 2		30,497				9	4	3	7			8	10	11			5	1		6		2				
11	Feb-29	H	Kidderminster H, WC-5	2 0	Toshack 2	4,029		11		9	4		7			8	10		3		5			6		2				1
12	Mar-25	H	Shrewsbury T, WC S F	2 2	Toshack, Waddle	10,000		8		5	4	3	7			9	10	11						6		2			1	
13	Apr-15	A	Shrewsbury T, WC S F Rep	2 2	Giles, Charles, lost 4 3 on pens	6,698		8		10	4	3	7			9		11			5			6		2			1	

Chapter 19

The Ultimate Promotion

1980-81

During the club's pre-season tour of Scotland, John Toshack was approached regarding a Yugoslavian full-back called Hadziabdic. Toshack remembered the player from a Cardiff international some years before and expressed his interest. In due course the manager arranged for the Yugoslav to play in a pre-season friendly match against Spurs at the Vetch and, in forty-five minutes of football, the player won the hearts of Swansea supporters. Early in the second half of the match Hadziabdic, who was suffering from a heavy cold, was replaced. The player, who was on the far side of the pitch when called off, left the field at that point and ran around the perimeter to the bench. As he did, the spectators, seemingly ignoring the play which was proceeding, rose as one to applaud as if the player was on a lap of honour. The Vetch management had seen enough to recognise that Hadziabdic was a skilful player, but they were delighted to hear the home supporters endorse their judgement. As John Toshack said at the time, 'He's box-office.'

Since it was necessary to obtain a work permit for him, the Yugoslav was not available for the early-season games. Indeed, it was not until 2 September that he made his debut in a Football League Cup tie at Highbury. In the meantime, the Swansea players found it to be difficult to pronounce the Yugoslav's first name (Dzemel) and settled on 'Jimmy' as the nearest approximation. It was a name which was to generate feelings of warm appreciation among his colleagues and the Vetch Field fans.

The club's initial games in their Second Division programme produced what can only be described as average results. After seven league games, however, the club had

Promotion squad, 1980-81.
Back row, left to right: N. Henson, W. Evans, D. Giles, M. Hughes, C. Sander, G. Letheran, D. Stewart, D. Gale, T. Guard, H.Lake. Middle: L. Chappell, L. James, A. James, J. Mahoney, M. Powell, C. Marustic, A. Waddle, P. McQuillan, N. Stevenson, C. Medwin, M. Baker, J. Loveridge, D. Lewis. Front: T. Medwin, N. Robinson, I. Callaghan, T. Craig, L. Phillips, J. Toshack, J. Charles, R. James, D. Rushbury, B. Attley, P. Boersma. Seated: H. Morgan, A. Rees, D. Saunders, S. Maloney, G. Richards, B. Cokley.

climbed to fourth position in the table. Leighton James, who scored a fine goal against Bristol City, Giles, Hadziabdic, Phillips and Mahoney all caught the eye during these early matches. However, what pleased most observers was the sound understanding which the whole team was beginning to demonstrate.

One result of this was that Toshack was able to retain the same side for six consecutive matches during October and early November. Four of those games were won, while the others were drawn. By that time, nineteen points had been won from fourteen games and the side had consolidated its fourth position. From the business point of view, the average gate for the club's matches at the Vetch was as good as that of the previous season. However, it was the growth in non-gate income which gave the Vetch management greatest comfort. For the previous year there had been a record contribution from this source of £240,000; there was every indication that this figure would be improved upon during current season. It was income which was absolutely essential for the club. Large sums had been spent on players (Hadziabdic's fee amounted to £160,000 to add to that total) and there was the necessity to fund the extensive ground development work being undertaken. Despite the club's improved fortune on the field, those who directed Swansea City needed to be constantly aware that the club's expenditure should not exceed its income. As the future was to show, when the converse is true it proves to be a recipe for disaster.

On the field, November began in less than encouraging fashion, and only two points were picked up from four matches. By the twenty-second of the month this series of results had taken the club to sixth in the table. At that stage the Swans were seven points behind the leaders and they had six fewer than the teams which occupied second and third places. However, although the team did not play well, the next match was won and some confidence restored. That confidence was boosted on 13 December when, before the game against Newcastle at the Vetch, Alan

Victory dance at Preston: Swans promoted to Division One.

Curtis came onto the field to wave to the crowd. Curtis, who had never settled at Leeds, had been transferred back for £170,000. It was good business for the Swans in that the player had been sold to the Yorkshire club for twice that amount only eighteen months before. Nonetheless, it was a bold purchase even if John Toshack had acquired an experienced international and a popular local icon. The fans, not having to worry about the financial implications of the deal, gave a warm welcome home to the Rhondda-born striker, and whether the transaction was financially prudent or not, the player's return was a marvellous psychological boost for all at the Vetch. 'Curt' was back!

As it happened, the game with Newcastle was recorded by BBC's 'Match of the Day' cameras and viewers were able to see highlights of a match which was won by the Swans by four clear goals. The two Jameses and Jeremy Charles scintillated in that match, in which the silky runs of Hadziabdic also caught the eye. Three days after that game, Alan Curtis made his second debut in a match against Watford. He had touched the ball twice when Robbie James was fouled in the penalty area. Curtis took the kick to win the game and move the Swans up to third place in Division Two.

At this, the positive thinkers among the club's followers began to talk about the possibility of achieving

> **Promotion to the First Division was ensured when the Swans beat Preston at Deepdale on 2 May 1981.**

the ultimate promotion. To them, the First Division was now reachable. However, whatever he thought in private, John Toshack refused to be drawn on the subject. 'There's a long way to go,' he said, 'Ask me again in the middle of May.' But, with the club in second position in the table and twenty-five matches played, even the gloom merchants were beginning to think that there was a chance. The success of the club in December led to expectations that that form

would be carried through into 1981, but the result of an FA Cup tie at the Vetch on 3 January severely dented that confidence. Middlesbrough, after dealing with early pressure from a Swans side which played flowing football, broke away twice to give themselves a 2-0 lead at half time. When three further goals were added in the second half the Vetch was steeped in disappointment.

The optimists shrugged off the defeat with the old rationale that the team could now concentrate upon their league campaign. Unfortunately, even that canvas was soon tinged with grey as five league matches were lost in succession. To add to the club's chagrin, the first of these defeats came on an otherwise gala day when the new stand was opened. Following the fifth, the Swans had slipped to ninth position in the league table. With thirty-two points from thirty games the club had fifteen fewer than the leaders, West Ham. A comment from the *Guardian* following the fifth match (against Sheffield Wednesday) put the matter into perspective: 'Swansea are a team riddled with self-doubt'. The fluent, successful football played in the previous month was but a memory.

Having sold Alan Waddle to Newport County for £80,000, John Toshack moved into the transfer market again, bringing another Yugoslav, Anto Rajkovic, to the Vetch for £100,000. Rajkovic came with a reputation as a strong defender. Unfortunately, because the player was not fully fit, it transpired that he would only play two matches before the season ended. This and injury problems with other players forced the manager into making several bold decisions. He restored the club's longest serving player, Wyndham Evans, to the first team

'Speedy' (alias Nigel Stevenson) outjumps the Preston defence during the Swans' 3-1 victory.

and gave teenager Dudley Lewis, his second game as sweeper. He also brought back Tommy Craig, who had been out of favour for some time. Toshack stressed the need for his players to believe that they could win the next home match, against Bolton, which they did by the margin of 3-0. The hero of the day was Leighton James, who converted two penalties and scored a third goal with a twenty-five yard drive.

Despite losing at Grimsby and drawing their next two games, by 18 April Swansea City were once again in contention for promotion. With four games to play they were fourth in the division, two points behind third-placed Blackburn with a match in hand. In addition, having beaten Wrexham in the semi-final of the Welsh Cup, and knowing that their opponents in the final were to be Hereford, an English club, they were guaranteed a place in the European Cup Winners' Cup for the 1981-2 season. The season's finale promised much in the way of drama. Could the team overtake Blackburn? After the Swans won the first two of their remaining matches, promotion appeared to most supporters as probable rather than possible. Two days after the second of these victories, against Chelsea, fifth-placed Luton came to the Vetch for a crucial game. The Swans needed to win to increase their chances of promotion. If they were to lose . . . The very thought was unbearable to the majority of the 21,354 people who crowded the Vetch that evening. Within thirty minutes Leighton James and Tommy Craig had given the Swans a two-goal lead, but, in a tense, electric atmosphere, Luton fought back to equalise. The Swans had to be satisfied with a point. The next morning, thousands of fans and everyone at the Vetch poured over the league tables. With one game to be played by both the Swans and Blackburn the Swans lay in third place (on account of a superior goal difference). This meant that to ensure promotion the team had to win at Preston. Aside from a freak result, even if Blackburn won at Bristol, the goal difference advantage would suffice. As it happened,

Preston were not attending the Deepdale match to make up the party. They had an important objective of their own: they needed to win to avoid relegation, though had they known of the fortune-tellers prediction, they might have approached the game with stoic acceptance: 'They will be promoted to Division One. It will go right to the last game.'

During the 1981-82 season the Swans met the Arsenal in the league for the first time and won both matches – a notable double for newcomers to the top flight.

For Swansea folk who were there, the magic of that moment at Deepdale when the referee blew the final whistle will be cherished forever. The hard-fought victory had been gained in a supercharged atmosphere, and the glittering prize which it brought would have been inconceivable half a decade before. It was the ultimate promotion, the impossible dream which had eluded generations of Swans followers, the passport which meant that the giants of the game would be playing at the Vetch Field within three short months. For the Swansea board the victory was the culmination of ten years of dedicated effort. The worry, the problems, the pleading for support from other clubs to ensure re-election, were engulfed by the glow of victory on that fateful May afternoon.

For John Toshack, as he embraced his youngest player and did a celebratory war-dance in front of his massed supporters, it was a moment of immense pride. His was the achievement which was to result in his mentor, Bill Shankly, paying him the compliment which Tosh most appreciated: 'Manager of the season? More like manager of the century!' The Swansea manager, who had packed so much into his short carer at the helm, now had a new pinnacle on which to stand.

That historic game at Preston was not won in comfort. The home side belied their lowly position in the league and fought hard to ensure their survival. After Leighton James gave the Swans an early lead with a

superbly struck shot, and Tommy Craig added a second from a Robinson cross, Bruce scored for Preston. From that moment until Jeremy Charles hammered home Swansea's third after a fine run by Curtis, Preston exerted tremendous pressure on the Swans' defence. Happily for all associated with the Vetch, the men in blue (the Swans wore a change strip) had made history. Swansea City was to be a First Division side.

Despite an indifferent period at the beginning of 1981, the Swans who won promotion set many new club records in the process. Among other things, relating to their Division Two history they:

(i) Achieved the club's highest position (3rd).
(ii) Conceded the fewest goals per league game (1.05).
(iii) Gained most points (50).
(iv) Won most points away (21).

And equalled the previous:

(v) Best goal difference (+20).
(vi) Longest sequence of games without defeat (8); and
(vii) Most 'clean sheets' (16).

Nevertheless. as the 1981-2 season was about to start, the London bookmakers were unimpressed. Swansea City's chances of winning the First Division championship were quoted as 200-1. To put it another way, they were considered to be favourites for relegation back to Division Two.

1981-82

There was little in the way of a close-season break for the Vetch management.The tremendous interest which the approaching First Division campaign engendered resulted in a high level of activity at the ground. During that period, John Toshack's forays into the transfer market were indicative of his intention to strengthen his squad for the challenge ahead. In July he signed the English international Bob Latchford from Everton for £125,000, and in the same month, Dai Davies from Wrexham for a fee

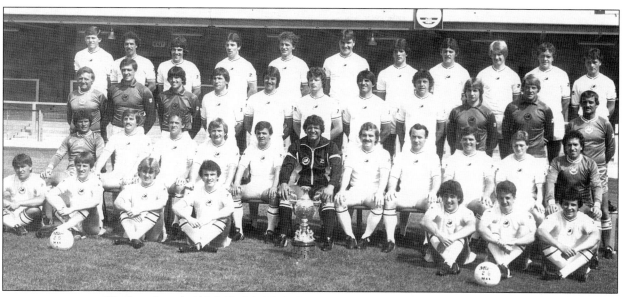

The Swans' squad which finished sixth in its first season in Division One and won the Welsh Cup.

of £45,000. One player to leave the Vetch was Leighton Phillips, who joined Charlton Athletic for £25,000. The size of the fee reflected the excellent service which Phillips had given the club during his time at the Vetch. In August the manager paid a club record fee of £350,000 to Liverpool for central-defender Colin Irwin. It was the boldest decision which Toshack had taken in his short career in management – at least in financial terms. Irwin was the first non-international for whom the manager paid a six-figure fee. The transfer of Dave Rushbury to Carlisle for £40,000 recouped some of that money but, later that month, half that figure was spent on Max Thompson, who had been with Blackpool. Clearly, the board at the Vetch were backing their young manager to the hilt.

On Saturday 29 August 1981, they must have felt that their trust in Toshack's judgement was justified, for 23,489 people came to see the most historic match in the club's history. Leeds United were the opponents and, as play began in bright sunshine, the ghosts of Jock Weir, W. Y. Brown, Billy Ball and the rest must have looked down approvingly. This was their dream come true. Whatever the founding fathers felt, the crowd could not have had an inkling of what was going to happen. At half time the score stood at 1-1, then, forty-five seconds after the restart, Bob Latchford put the Swans ahead. Within ten minutes he had scored two more to register the

first hat-trick for the club in Division One. Alan Curtis, playing against his former club, added a superb fifth goal before the end and the BBC teleprinter chattered out: Swansea City 5 Leeds United 1. It was an incredible start to the club's initial season in the premier division of the Football League. Yet, on the following day, at least one commentator remained unimpressed. Swansea should remember Norwich City, he wrote: 'They won their first game 5-1 last season and look where they are now!' That writer was to be one of several who would be forced to modify their views before the season ended.

The management team which took Swansea City into the Leeds game differed from that which had done duty during the previous term. Terry

Medwin, who had been unwell for much of the previous season, moved to become chief scout. His role was in keeping with the importance to the club of its youth policy. Medwin, well-known and respected in the city, brought with him to his new task friendliness and perception and a thorough knowledge of football. In his place as assistant manager, Toshack appointed Phil Boersma and added the Welsh international team trainer Doug Livermore to his staff. At board level, Douglas Sharpe, who became a director in March 1981, began his first full season with the club. Together with Winston Rees, who joined the board in April 1978, he represented an extension of the managerial resource available to the chairman. Sharpe's appointment was to have a longevity and

Bob Latchford scores the first of his three goals in the 5-1 victory over Leeds United on the opening day of the season.

Peter Shilton dives despairingly trying to reach a Robbie James rocket.

importance in the history of Swansea City which no one at the Vetch foresaw at that time of joy.

For the Swansea board the club's entry into the First Division represented a new challenge, far different from that which they had faced six short years before. This was a challenge which they were prepared to relish. One statistic which gave them considerable encouragement was the volume of season-ticket sales which preceded the start of the new campaign. Secretary Gordon Daniels was able to announce that 3,350 stand seasons had been sold, a figure which almost equalled that of the halcyon days after the war. However, on this occasion 5,000 field tickets had also been taken up. At a time when the recession was still biting hard in Swansea and its hinterland these were remarkable statistics.

When Brighton were beaten on their own ground in the season's second game, Swansea fans found themselves supporting the leading team in the land: the Swans had maximum points and the best goal-difference. It might not have meant much, but it was a statement. The Vetch men had arrived! Nonetheless, despite this success and all that of preceding seasons, there remained, in some, a lingering doubt that Toshack's long march could continue. On 5 September those doubts were reinforced: the Swans were beaten 4-1 at West Bromwich. Toshack declared the defeat 'a one off'. Happily, during the week which followed, the Vetch club received a timely boost to its morale. Six Swansea City players were selected to play for their country. It was a new record for Wales and for the club and was indicative of the

importance of Swansea soccer at the time. As the season developed, a further three Swans were capped, and David Giles appeared as a substitute. Whilst this record was regarded with considerable pride by all at the Vetch, it represented a significant commitment by a single club. In retrospect, having in mind Toshack's relatively small squad, it is reasonable to argue that it could have been a detrimental factor which adversely affected the team's ability to stay the course at the very top. On the other hand, playing international football helped to mature at least two of the nine men who, as the manager pointed out, had no previous experience of football in Division One.

By the end of September every one at the Vetch could look back with considerable pride on the club's first month in the top flight. After seven matches had been played the Swans were third in the table. Whilst they had lost at Old Trafford by the only goal of the game, Notts County, Tottenham and Sunderland had all been defeated at the Vetch. It was true that Lokomotiv Leipzig had eliminated the club from the European Cup Winners' Cup; however, the Vetch management accepted that beating philosophically. The implication was, 'We shall be back'. On 28 September, John Toshack bought yet another player. He was Gary Stanley from Everton, who came in exchange for £130,000.

October started with an emotional game at Anfield. During the week prior to the match John Toshack's mentor, Bill Shankly, died. The effect of the death of this legend on the football world as a whole was

immense. To Liverpool supporters, staff and management and to the Swansea manager the sense of loss was even greater. It was as though some loved one in the family had died. In the supercharged moments before the game began it was said that strong men were moved to tears. In those moments John Toshack stood with his team wearing the red shirt of Liverpool as his own special tribute to his football father-figure. Through the ironies of fate, the young man's team was to take part in what was effectively a memorial match. The television cameras and the largest crowd which Anfield had seen that season were there to witness it. As if inspired by their respect for Shankly, the teams provided a match which one commentator described as 'an extravaganza of excitement, incident and movement'. It was a match worthy of the Scot, a man whose principles, ideas and enthusiasm had been guidelines for those who managed both clubs. The result was a 2-2 draw, after the Swans had taken a two-goal lead. There was still much to do, but Swansea City had come through a stringent examination, visited the cauldron of football passion and left in the belief that they should have won.

During the rest of October there was the disappointment of defeat at Coventry, ejection from the Football League Cup and a dull draw with Wolves. Nonetheless, on the evening of 17 October, following the defeat of Stoke, there was a moment of glory for Swansea City. The club was top of the First Division. It was the first time a Welsh club had achieved such distinction for almost sixty years. Four weeks later, the club was still in contention, lying in second place after a thrilling victory at Portman Road. Following the match, the respected Ipswich manager, Bobby Robson, admitted that, over the previous five years, no club had so dominated a game there as Swansea had done. Ipswich, to quote one journalist, were 'out-fought and out-thought'. Not all, however, was sweetness and light. November proved to be a difficult month in which Jeremy Charles suffered a knee injury which necessitated a cartilage operation and he did not play for several months. Jimmy Hadziabdic was finding it difficult to adapt to the stresses of the First Division and was, also carrying a leg injury, while Dai Davies was suffering a loss of confidence, though, in due course, he worked his way out of this indifferent period to make a significant contribution during the remainder of the season. The one player who consistently attracted much positive comment was Anto Rajkovic. Indeed, the general opinion of the media was that he was one of the best defenders in the Football League.

During December, Swansea City led the First Division table for the second time, on this occasion following a fine victory over Aston Villa. Both Swansea goals were scored by Robbie James who, five years before, had played in the match at Rochdale following which the Vetch club was obliged to seek re-election. Ironically, the Villa goalkeeper whom James beat to score his goals had also sampled difficult times at the Vetch. He was Jimmy Rimmer, then the proud possessor of a League Championship medal from the previous season. Unfortunately, the players did not respond positively to life at the top of the table and, following a week during which it was announced that John Toshack had been awarded the MBE, his team stumbled to three consecutive defeats.

A report of one of these matches carried the headline 'Toshack's honourable week lies in ruins'. That, however, was not how the young manager saw the situation. Nonetheless, he realised that something needed to be done. His answer was to buy Ray Kennedy, a seasoned campaigner, from Liverpool for £160,000. Kennedy's presence had the desired effect. In front of a crowd of 23,900, the Vetch's largest gate of the season, Manchester United were defeated by 2-0, Alan Curtis and Leighton James scoring for the Swans. There followed a sequence of nine matches during which the team conceded just one goal. Among the club's victims during this heady period was Liverpool, also beaten 2-0. After that match John Toshack, for once, was lost for words. 'I can't describe how I feel. Our first season in Division One and we beat Liverpool.' Few teams were to equal that feat before the season ended.

The outcome of that Liverpool match began a sequence during

Anto Rajkovic

which a further club record was set. Dai Davies remained unbeaten for six consecutive games, beating the previous record which had been held jointly by Jack Parry and Tony Millington. At the end of that sequence of nine matches, Swansea City was top of the First Division for the third time in its first season in the top echelon of the Football League. It was a remarkable achievement, which, sadly, as the final period of the season unfolded, the team was not able to sustain. Nevertheless, when the season ended the Swans were in sixth position in the table, yet they had started the campaign as the bookmakers' favourites for relegation. As had been the case on previous occasions, they finished higher in the league than the clubs with whom they had been promoted and, throughout the season they were never out of the top six places in the table. In addition, the club had beaten four clubs away and at home to register a very respectable initial record for Division One. Then, to add to what had been achieved during a remarkable season, Cardiff City were defeated in the Welsh Cup final tie, even though the Swans had ten men for most of the second half. This meant, of course, that the club would enter the European Cup Winners' Cup for the second year in succession. Coincidentally, the club had also qualified for entry to the

UEFA Cup by virtue of being in the top six positions of the First Division – the first Welsh club to have done so. There were arguments as to their eligibility, but, in the circumstances all that was academic.

In the midst of the joy at the achievements of the Swans, there was genuine sadness. Both the other Welsh clubs in the Football League, Cardiff and Wrexham, were relegated to Division Three. For Welsh football it was a sad day reminiscent of the late 1920s when the Vetch club stood alone as a viable entity. As they had on previous occasions, everyone at the Vetch wished their Welsh colleagues a speedy return to a higher grade of football.

In looking back on what had been a very successful first season in soccer's top flight, the club's management did so with pride. The whole squad had achieved a great deal, though, as always happens, some were outstanding. Robbie James was nominated 'Player of the Year'; Anto Rajkovic won the applause of opponents as well as friends and supporters, with performances of the highest quality; Alan Curtis had tormented the best defences, while Nigel Stevenson stuck doggedly to his task, to show every young player that hard work can bring its own reward. What was most significant though, was that these players did not see themselves as stars. The success of Swansea City was founded upon the fact that they constituted an integrated squad. The sole blot on the horizon was the fact that the Swans lost five of their last six games.

The respite of the close-season at the end of the club's initial campaign in the First Division was extremely welcome to all at the Vetch. The experiences of that first season, like those of the father of a first-born son, could never be repeated. However, the summer break gave everyone a chance to digest those experiences and see what could be learned from them. Within a matter of weeks the management would need to plan for the coming season, this time stripped of some of the benefit of surprise from which a new team in a competition can benefit. The task was to build upon the foundations which had been laid down. It would be a task which demanded continuing attention and professionalism.

Swansea City FC Season 1980/81 Division 2

#	Date	V	Opponents	Score	Scorers	Att	Stewart D	Marustik C	Rushbury D	Attley B	Stevenson N	Phillips L	Giles D	James R	James L	Charles J	Robinson N	Mahoney J	Craig T	Toshack J	Evans W	Hadziabdic D	Waddle A	Loveridge J	Curtis A	Lewis D	Rajkovic A	Letheran G
1	Aug-16	A	Watford	1-2	James R (pen)	11,316	1	2	3	4	5	6	7*	8	9	10	11	12										
2	Aug-19	H	Shrewsbury Town	2-1	Attley, Giles	12,754	1	2	3	4	5	6	7	8	9	10*	11		12									
3	Aug-23	A	QPR	0-0		10,854	1		3	4	5	6	7	8	9		2		11	10								
4	Aug-30	H	Cambridge United	1-1	O/Goal	11,112	1		3	4	5	6	7	8	9		11	12		10*	2							
5	Sep-06	A	Bristol City	1-0	James L	9,528	1			2	5	6	7	8	9	10	11*	4				3	12					
6	Sep-13	H	Notts. County	1-1	Stevenson	10,921	1			2	5	6	7		9	10	11	4				3						
7	Sep-20	A	Bolton Wanderers	4-1	Waddle 2, James L, Robinson	9,419	1			2	5	6	7		9	10	11	4	12			3	8*					
8	Sep-27	H	Sheff. Wednesday	2-3	Giles, Charles	9,764	1	4*		2	5	6	7		9	10	11	12				3	8					
9	Oct-04	A	Wrexham	1-1	Giles	8,544	1			2	5	6	7	12	9	10	11	4				3	8*					
10	Oct-07	H	Oldham Athletic	3-0	Giles 2, Waddle	8,645	1			2	5	6	7		9	10	11	4				3	8					
11	Oct-11	H	Derby County	3-1	James L 3 (1 pen)	13,323	1			2	5	6	7*	12	9	10	11	4				3	8					
12	Oct-18	A	Newcastle United	2-1	Attley, Waddle	16,392	1			2	5	6	7		9	10	11	4				3	8					
13	Oct-21	A	Luton Town	2-2	Waddle 2	8,402	1			2	5	6	7*	12	9	10	11	4				3	8					
14	Oct-24	H	Grimsby Town	1-0	Charles	12,928	1			2*	5	6	7	12	9	10	11	4				3	8					
15	Nov-01	A	Blackburn Rovers	0-0		10,846	1		5	2		6	7*	12	9	10	11	4				3	8					
16	Nov-08	H	Orient	0-2		10,922	1			2	5	6	7		9	10	11*	4	12			3	8					
17	Nov-11	A	Shrewsbury Town	0-0		5,843	1		8	2	5	6	7		9*	10	11	4	12			3						
18	Nov-22	A	West Ham United	0-2		27,376	1		4	2		6		9		5	11		10	7		3*	8	12				
19	Nov-28	H	Preston N E	3-0	Robinson 2, Waddle	9,115	1			2	5	6		7	9	10	11	4				3	8					
20	Dec-06	A	Chelsea	0-0		20,067	1			2	5	6		7	9	10	11	4				3	8					
21	Dec-13	H	Newcastle United	4-0	James L, James R 2, Charles	11,672	1		4	2	5	6		8	9*	10	11		7	12		3						
22	Dec-16	H	Watford	1-0	Curtis (pen)	13,305	1		4	2	5	6		8	9*	10	11		7			3			12			
23	Dec-20	A	Oldham Athletic	2-2	James R, Curtis	5,486	1			2	5	6		8	9	10	11	4				3			7			
24	Dec-26	H	Bristol Rovers	2-1	Stevenson, James R	15,135	1		4	2	5	6		8	9*	10	11		7			3			12			
25	Dec-27	A	Cardiff City	3-3	Robinson, Curtis, James L	21,239	1			2	5	6		8	9	10	11		7			3			7			
26	Jan-10	H	West Ham United	1-3	Curtis	22,110	1			2	5	6	12	7	9*	10	11	4				3			8			
27	Jan-17	A	Cambridge United	1-3	Curtis	5,121	1		12	2	5	6	7	8		10	11*	4				3			9			
28	Jan-31	H	QPR	1-2	Stevenson	12,518	1			2		6	7*	8	11	5	12	4				3		10	9			
29	Feb-07	A	Notts. County	1-2	Robinson	8,628	1			2	5	6	12		10*		11		8	7		3			9	4		
30	Feb-21	A	Sheff. Wednesday	0-2		17,887	1	4			12	6	7*	8	10	5	2		11			3			9			
31	Feb-28	H	Bolton Wanderers	3-0	James L 3 (2pens)	9,468	1					6		8	10	5			11	7	2	3			9			
32	Mar-06	H	Wrexham	3-1	James R, James L (pen), Stevenson	12,103	1					6		8	10	5		12	11	7	2	3			9*	4		
33	Mar-17	H	Bristol City	0-0		10,832	1					6		8	10	5		12	11	7	2	3			9*		4	
34	Mar-28	A	Grimsby Town	0-1		12,166	1					5		12	7	9		4	11*	10	2	3			8	6		
35	Mar-31	A	Derby County	1-0	Charles	16,210	1		4			5		7	8	9	10				2	3*	11		12	6		
36	Apr-04	H	Blackburn Rovers	2-0	Stevenson, James L	12,011	1		4			5		7	8	9	10				2	3	11			6		
37	Apr-11	A	Orient	1-1	Craig	4,984	1		4			5		7*	8	9	10				2	3	11		12	6		
38	Apr-18	H	Cardiff City	1-1	James L	19,038	1					5		8	9	10					2	3	11		7	6	4	
39	Apr-21	A	Bristol Rovers	2-1	James R, Curtis	8,250	1					5	4	8	9	10*		12			2	3	11		7	6		
40	Apr-25	H	Chelsea	3-0	Robinson, Hadziabdic, James R	16,063	1					5		8	9		10	4			2	3	11*		7	6		
41	Apr-27	H	Luton Town	2-2	Craig, James L	21,354	1					5		8	9	12		4	10		2	3	11*		7	6		
42	May-02	A	Preston N E	3-1	James L, Craig, Charles	18,970	1					5		8	9	10		4			2	3	11		7	6		
					Apps		42	3	11	32	39	29	24	30	40	37	33	31	14	3	13	38	13	0	16	12	2	
					Subs			1		1			3	5				1	3	4	5			1	1	4		
					Gls					2	5		5	8	15	5	6		3			1	7		6			

#	Date	V	Opponents	Score	Scorers	Att	Stewart D	Marustik C	Rushbury D	Attley B	Stevenson N	Phillips L	Giles D	James R	James L	Charles J	Robinson N	Mahoney J	Craig T	Toshack J	Evans W	Hadziabdic D	Waddle A	Loveridge J	Curtis A	Lewis D	Rajkovic A	Letheran G
1	Aug-26	H	Arsenal, FLC 1-1	1-1	James L	17,036	1	2*	3		5	6	7	8	9		11	4	10	12								
2	Sep-02	A	Arsenal, FLC 1-2	1-3	Charles	26,399	1		4	2	5	6	7	8	9	10			11			3						
3	Nov-25	H	Caerleon, WC-4	5-1	Toshack, Craig, Robinson 2, James R	1,778			3	6	7	5		8	9			4	11	10	2							1
4	Jan-03	H	Middlesbrough, FAC-3	0-5		18,015	1		4	2	5	6	12	8		10*	11		7			3			9			
5	Jan-24	A	Merthyr, WC-5	2-0	Rushbury, Curtis	4,600	1		3		5	6	7	8	9			4			2		11		10			
6	Feb-18	H	Maesteg Park, WC-6	4-1	O/Goal, Attley 2, James L (pen)	1,819	1		8	2	5	6			10			4		7		3	11		9		6	
7	Apr-07	H	Wrexham, WCSF 1-1	2-2	Charles 2	4,182	1		3		5	4	7	8	9	10					2		11				6	
8	Apr-14	H	Wrexham, WCSF 1-2	1-2	Curtis	10,761	1			7	5			8	9	10		4			2	3	11				6	
9	May-04	H	Hereford Utd, WC F 1-1	1-0	James R	12,500	1							8	9	5		4	7		2	3	11		10		6	
10	May-11	A	Hereford Utd, WCF 1-2	1-1	James R	7,038	1		3				10	8	9	5		4	7		2		11				6	

Swansea City FC Season 1981/82 Division 1

#	Date	V	Opponents	Score	Scorers	Att	Davies D	Robinson Neil	Hadziabdic D	Rajkovic A	Irwin C	Mahoney J	Curtis A	James R	James L	Charles J	Latchford B	Attley B	Thompson M	Giles D	Stanley G	Marustik C	Stevenson N	Kennedy R	Walsh I	Evans W	Sander C	Richards G	Lewis D	Gale D	Loveridge J
1	Aug-29	H	Leeds United	5-1	Latchford 3, Charles, Curtis	23,500	1	2	3	4	5	6	7	8	9	10	11														
2	Sep-01	A	Brighton	2-1	James L, Latchford	19,885	1	2	3	4	5	6	7	8	9*	10	11	12													
3	Sep-05	A	WBA	1-4	Robinson	18,063	1	2	3	4	5	6	7	8	9	10*	11	12													
4	Sep-12	H	Notts. County	3-2	Curtis, James L, Latchford	14,391	1	2	3	4	5	6	7	8	9		11		10												
5	Sep-19	A	Manchester United	0-1		47,309	1	2	3	4	5	6	7	8			11*	9	10	12											
6	Sep-22	H	Tottenham Hotspur	2-1	James R, Curtis	22,026	1	2	3*	4	5	6	7	8	9	12	11		10												
7	Sep-26	H	Sunderland	2-0	Curtis, James L (pen)	17,876	1	2	3	4	5	6	7	8	9	10*	11		12												
8	Oct-03	A	Liverpool	2-2	James L (pen), Latchford	48,645	1	2	3*	4	5	6	7	8	9	12	11		10												
9	Oct-10	H	Arsenal	2-0	James L, Thompson	20,600	1	2	3	4	5	6	7	8	9	12	11*		10												
10	Oct-17	A	Stoke City	2-1	Stanley, Latchford	14,665	1	2	3	4	5	6	7	8	9*		11		10		12										
11	Oct-24	A	Coventry City	1-3	Curtis	14,050	1	2		4	5	6	7	8	9		11		10*		3	12									
12	Oct-31	H	Wolverhampton W	0-0		17,750	1			4	5	6	7	8	9		11		3		2		10								
13	Nov-07	A	Ipswich Town	3-2	Curtis, Latchford, Stanley	24,190	1	2		4	5	10	7	8	9		11				3		6								
14	Nov-21	A	Manchester City	0-4		34,744	1		2*	4	5	10	7	8	9		11			12	3		6								
15	Nov-24	H	Brighton	0-0		14,459	1			3	4*	5	7	8	9	12	11				10	2									
16	Nov-28	H	Birmingham City	1-0	James R	15,097	1	2	12		5	4	7	8	9		11				10	3*	6								
17	Dec-05	A	Everton	1-3	Latchford	23,860	1	2	3	4	5	6	7	8	9		11				10*	12									
18	Dec-12	A	Nottm. Forest	1-2	James R	17,550	1	2		4	5	6	7	8	9		11				10		3								
19	Dec-15	H	Aston Villa	2-1	James R 2	15,191	1			4		6	7	8	9		11				10	2	3	5							
20	Dec-28	A	Southampton	1-3	Rajkovic	22,703	1		3*	4	5	6	7	8	9		11				10	2	12								
21	Jan-16	A	Leeds United	0-2		18,732	1	9		4	5	6	7	8	12		11				10*	2	3								
22	Jan-30	H	Manchester United	2-0	Curtis, James R	24,115	1	11*					7	8	12		9				10	2	3	5							
23	Feb-06	A	Notts. County	1-0	James L (pen)	10,070	1	11		6	4		7	8	9						10	2	3	5							
24	Feb-13	A	Middlesbrough	1-1	Kennedy	11,209	1	12	3	6*	4		7	8	9	11					10	2		5							
25	Feb-16	H	Liverpool	2-0	James L, Curtis	22,644	1			6	4		7	8	9	11					10	2	3	5							
26	Feb-20	A	Sunderland	1-0	James L	13,163	1			6	4		7	8	9	11					2	3	10	5							
27	Feb-27	A	Arsenal	2-0	Kennedy, James R (pen)	29,724	1	11		6	4		7	8	9*						2	3	10	5	12						
28	Mar-06	H	Stoke City	3-0	James R 2, Charles	11,811	1	2		6	4		7	8	9	11					10	3		5							
29	Mar-13	H	Coventry City	1-0		16,425	1	2		6	4		7	8	9	11*					10	12	3	5							
30	Mar-20	A	Wolverhampton W	1-0	Walsh	14,158	1	11	3	6	4		7	8							2		10	5	9						
31	Mar-27	H	Ipswich Town	1-2	James R (pen)	20,450	1				4	11	7	8	9				10		2	3	6	5							
32	Mar-30	H	West Ham United	0-1		20,252	1	2	3*	6	4		7	8	9		11				12		10	5							
33	Apr-06	H	WBA	3-1	Marustik, Curtis, Latchford	15,744	1		3	6	4		7	8	12		11				9*	2	10	5							
34	Apr-10	A	West Ham United	1-1	James R	26,566	1	12	3	6	4		7	8			11				9	2*	10	5							
35	Apr-13	H	Southampton	1-0	Curtis	23,771	1	2	3	6	4		7	8	9		11*				12		10	5							
36	Apr-17	H	Manchester City	2-0	Stanley, Latchford	19,212	1		2	6			7	8	9		11				4	3	10	5							
37	Apr-24	A	Birmingham City	1-2	Walsh	14,973	1		3	6	4*		7	8	9		11				2		10	5	12						
38	May-01	H	Everton	1-3	James R	16,243	1		3	6	4		7	8	12		11				9	2	10	5*							
39	May-05	A	Tottenham Hotspur	1-2	James L	26,358	1	2		6		5	7	8	9						12	3	10		11	4*					
40	May-08	A	Nottm. Forest	2-0	James R 2	15,037	1	2	3	6		5	7	8	9		11*		4		12		10								
41	May-15	H	Middlesbrough	1-2	Latchford	12,961	1		3	6				8	9		11		4		12	2	10	5	7*						
42	May-21	A	Aston Villa	0-3		18,294		2		6	5*	9		8			11						10				1	3	4	12	7
					Apps		41	27	25	40	37	25	40	42	34	9	31	2	22	0	22	19	20	18	3	1	1	1	1	0	1
					Subs			2	1							4	4	2	1	2	7	3			2					1	
					Gls			1		1			10	14	9	2	12		1		3	1		2	2						

#	Date	V	Opponents	Score	Scorers	Att	Davies D	Robinson Neil	Hadziabdic D	Rajkovic A	Irwin C	Mahoney J	Curtis A	James R	James L	Charles J	Latchford B	Attley B	Thompson M	Giles D	Stanley G	Marustik C	Stevenson N	Kennedy R	Walsh I	Evans W	Sander C	Richards G	Lewis D	Gale D	Loveridge J
1	Sep-16	H	Loko Leipzig, ECWC 1-1	0-1		10,295	1	2	3	6				10	7	8	9		11	4				5							
2	Sep-30	A	Loko Leipzig, ECWC 1-2	1-2	Charles	22,500	1	2	3	6		4	7	8	9	10	11							5							
3	Oct-06	A	Barnsley, FLC 2-1	0-2		12,793	1	2			5		7		9*	6	11	12	10		8	4							3		
4	Oct-27	H	Barnsley, FLC 2-2	3-2	James L (pen), Irwin, Curtis	9,897	1	2		4	5	6	7	8	9		11*				10	3	12								
5	Dec-02	A	Stafford R, WC-3	4-0	Curtis, Thompson, O/Goal, Latchford	3,077	1	2	3		4	6	7	8	9		11		10				5								
6	Dec-22	H	Worcester C, WC-4	6-0	James R 3, James L, Stanley, Attley	4,848	1		3	6		4	7	8	9			10			11	2	5								
7	Jan-02	H	Liverpool, FAC-3	0-4		24,179	1			4	5	10	7	8	9		11				12	2	3*	6							
8	Feb-09	H	Colwyn Bay, WC-5	2-2	Stanley, Irwin	3,385		2	3	6	5			8	9	10					11	4	7				1				
9	Mar-02	H	Colwyn Bay, WC-5 Rep	3-0	Curtis, James R 2	4,922	1	2	3	6	5	4	9	8			11				10		7								
10	Mar-16	A	Bangor C, WCSF 1-1	2-1	James L, Curtis	7,500	1			4	6		7	8	9		11				3	2	10	5							
11	Apr-20	H	Bangor C, WCSF 1-2	0-0		5,700	1		3	6			7	8	9		11				4	2	10	5							
12	May-11	A	Cardiff C, WCF 1-1	0-0		11,960	1		3	6			7	8	9		11		10			2	4	5							
13	May-19	H	Cardiff C, WCF 1-2	2-1	Latchford 2	15,858	1	2	3	6			7	8	9		11				10		4	5							

Chapter 20

Receivership and Rapid Demotion

1982-83

The first Portuguese side to visit the Vetch – Sporting Braga – provided the opposition for the opening match of the new campaign. The game was played before the English season started, being the first leg of a European Cup Winners' Cup-tie. As such, it provided an ideal opportunity for the players to take part in a competitive match prior to the start of the domestic season. In addition, should they progress, it afforded them the chance of playing against major European club sides.

Before the game, having been unbeaten in the club's four pre-season matches, manager Toshack told the press that 'the squad was in good heart' and that 'we are looking to build upon the good work that we did last season'. And 'build' they did, for the Iberian side was defeated 3-1 (on aggregate) over the two legs. That 'building' continued in the next round, when the Swans set a new club record by beating the Maltese side Sliema Wanderers 12-0 at the

'Curt' on the cover.

Vetch and 5-0 in Malta. It was impressive stuff! However, matters in the league were less encouraging.

The second leg of the Sliema tie took place at the end of September, by which time the Swans had played seven league matches. They started well enough, defeating Coventry and Norwich at the Vetch and drawing at Notts County. The Norwich victory (4-0), with Latchford scoring a hat trick, was a particularly fine performance. It was one, which gave supporters every hope that the previous season's form had been recaptured. However, the next three games all ended in defeat, with Liverpool, for example, winning 3-0 at the Vetch with something in hand. After the Norwich match, the side was second in the table, whereas, when they travelled to Villa Park on 25 September, they were in sixteenth position. Toshack shuffled his pack as he attempted to improve matters and, speaking to the press, the manager made the valid point that good players do not become poor from one season to the next. He said that he was confident that the Swans could 'play their way out of this bad patch', and given the manager's track

record, it would have been a brave man who would have sought to contradict him.

The Villa match was the first to be played after Toshack made that statement, and those Swansea supporters who travelled to Birmingham that day were hoping to see evidence that their manager had not lost his golden touch. Sadly, they saw Colin Irwin being badly injured and the Swans losing 2-0, making it the fourth match in succession in

A typical Robbie James charge.

which the side had been beaten. For Toshack, the loss of Irwin was a savage blow, for the manager had paid a club record £340,000 for the central defender. Now he would have to manage without the player and use others to try to fill the gap. Before the end of the campaign, six others had been used in the role but somehow, the chemistry of the side was never again in balance.

By the turn of the year the side was still struggling. Of the twenty matches played up until that time, only six had been won and four drawn. Not only was this a worrying situation on the field: the financial implications were considerable. Ideally, Toshack would have liked to sign two or three new players to strengthen his squad, but that would have been asking the impossible of the board. During the previous eighteen months, they had authorised transfers-in to the extent of £1,250,000. Some of this was being paid in three or four installments, a number of which were due in December 1982. In addition, in keeping with their station in the first division, the club had enhanced the contracts of key

The Swans' squad, 1982-83.
Back row, left to right: Chris Marustic, Bob Latchford, Jeremy Charles, Max Thompson, Nigel Stevenson, Colin Irwin, Neil Robinson.
Centre: Phil Boersma (Assistant Manager), Alan Curtis, Ian Walsh, Dai Davies, Leighton James, John Mahoney, Doug Livermore (Coach).
Front: Robbie James, Dzemal Hadziabdic, Ante Rajkovic, John Toshack (Manager), Ray Kennedy, Gary Stanley, Wyndham Evans.

players. Taken together, these factors were significant. Like any other businessmen, in planning ahead to meet these costs, the board had made assumptions regarding the income they could expect to receive. For example, during the club's first season in Division One, home gates had averaged 19,191. Since the team had been so successful during that campaign, the board felt it to be reasonable to budget for an average of 18,500. At the turn of the year, the actual average was just over 13,000 and, by the time the season had ended that had fallen to 11,304. All in all, this represented a significant financial shortfall, particularly in the face of large outgoing phased payments which had to be made. In the not too distant future this was to have an extremely damaging impact on the Vetch club.

John Toshack had another problem, too. In January 1982 he had agreed to pay Liverpool £160,000 for the services of Ray Kennedy. Kennedy had an impressive playing record with Arsenal, Liverpool and England, and was believed to have been a valuable acquisition. Unfortunately, particularly during the rather fraught 1982-3 season, the player did not

> **The Swans beat Sliema Wanderers 12-0 in the European Cup Winners' Cup to create a new club scoring record.**

perform at the expected level; he was not the influential mid-fielder which his reputation suggested, whilst his play was strangely lethargic. Toshack tried everything to motivate him, but in due course, faced with little or no improvement, the relationship between player and manager began to deteriorate. Unfortunately, as the future was to show, at the time, unbeknown to anyone, Kennedy was suffering from the early stages of Parkinson's Disease. In due course, this resulted in the club having to buy him out of his contract. To John Toshack's chagrin he had lost another key player.

Not having money to spend, the manager was obliged to blood his most promising youngsters earlier than he had intended. During this period, Colin Pascoe, Darren Gale,

and Huw Lake were all given their chance, following Jimmy Loveridge, Gary Richards and Chris Sander, all of whom had made their debuts during the previous campaign. Unfortunately, at the time, these young men were not what was necessary to 'steady the ship'; the situation demanded experienced professionals.

In October and November the club was eliminated from the European Cup Winners' Cup by Paris St. Germain, and from the Milk Cup by Brentford (after drawing in London), whilst, in January, the side fell at the first fence in the FA Cup, losing to Norwich City at Carrow Road by the odd goal in three. Although, to use an old adage, this allowed Toshack and his men to concentrate on the league, from the financial point of view, this meant that there was no hope of exceptional income to make up for the considerable shortfall which the club faced. As importantly, it did not present the manager and his staff with opportunities to restore confidence.

The second half of the season turned out to be much like the first; eleven matches were lost and six drawn out of the twenty-one which were played. It was true that several defeats were by a single goal, but the realities of the points system in football take little account of such matters. It was following a 2-1 defeat at Old Trafford in the season's penultimate match that the Swans found themselves destined to return to Division Two.

In retrospect, the season's statistics hardly made pleasant reading for those who followed Swansea City. Nevertheless, mention must be made of the contribution of Robbie James, who played 40 league matches and scored 9 times, and Bob Latchford, who registered 20 goals in 38 matches in which he appeared. One other consolation for the club's management and supporters was the team's victory over Wrexham in the final of the Welsh Cup. At least, in the season ahead, everyone at the Vetch could look forward to entering the European competition once again.

After the curtain had fallen on what had been a most disappointing season, it would not have been surprising if the board, management and supporters had looked to the future with some concern. Yet, still, there were optimists among them who felt that the squad which the club had that time was better than that which had won the ultimate promotion. And, taking that line of thinking to its conclusion, that they would 'bounce back' at the first attempt. John Toshack, although somewhat bruised by the experiences of the previous season, remained confident in his ability to turn things around. For the board, though, one matter which remained unresolved was the reason for the significant reduction in gate receipts when compared with the previous season.

In attempting to find answers to this question several ideas were put forward. An obvious one was the fact that football supporters like to follow successful teams, and since they had seen so little of that at the Vetch that season, some had stopped coming. Others, so the rumour had it, had been disappointed with the general

quality of football in Division One and had 'cherry picked' the matches they wished to watch (20,322, for example came to watch the Liverpool game). Another reason which was suggested, concerned the economic situation in south-west Wales at the

Dai Davies

time. Then, unemployment levels were extremely high and ordinary fans had little in the way of disposable income. Finally, there was the perennial problem that, after the surfeit of the previous campaign, no new faces appeared to whet the appetites of supporters. Whatever the reason(s), it was clear that the outcome of the 1983-4 campaign would be of considerable importance to the future of Swansea City. As far as the directors were concerned, they could not contemplate a relaxing close-season. Rather, they were obliged to face the harsh realities of the club's financial predicament and make appropriate decisions in the interest of securing the very future of the club.

1983-84

During the close–season the members of the board spent many hours in discussion and debate, some of it acrimonious, but found that the options open to them were extremely

limited. Strenuous efforts had been made to find an interested investor who might provide the necessary capital to alleviate the pressing financial problems, but no knight in shining armour appeared. As a consequence, in order to be able to meet the demands being made upon them by creditors, the directors were forced to dispose of saleable assets. At the Vetch Field at that time, that could only mean selling the better and more experienced players who were still on the club's books.

Whilst that was difficult enough to contemplate, they also found that market conditions were not in their favour. Whereas, two seasons before, it had been a sellers' market, now it favoured the buyers. One reason for this change was the recession which was biting deeply at the time throughout the United Kingdom; another was a new Football League regulation which required all transfer fees to be paid in a maximum of two instalments. Coupled with the recession, this ruling had a severely dampening effect upon the transfer market. There were fewer buyers because only a handful of clubs had the wherewithal to be able to pay fifty per cent of the fee on signing a player, whereas when the initial percentage had been thirty, or even twenty-five per cent, there were many more. As a result of this the Vetch men found that players whom they had valued quite reasonably at, say £300,000, were only attracting half that amount. Then, when buying clubs realised that the Swans *had* to sell (and quickly), fees of even smaller proportion were attracted and, given that the football world in Britain is close-knit, it was not long before that began to happen.

The exodus started in June 1983 when Robbie James was sold to Stoke City for £130,000 (his estimated value had been £350,000). Whilst the reduced size of the fee received for the player provided the board with one financial problem, it also signalled another. The fans,

Chris Sander leaps to save.

already dazed by events on the field, saw the sale as a reversion to past Vetch policies. James, along with Alan Curtis, was something of an icon, a local boy who had been a key member of the club's teams which had surged from the fourth to the first division. Robbie was not the only James to leave, either; Leighton, who had joined the club in time to contribute to the ultimate promotion campaign, also left to join Sunderland on a free transfer. The disillusionment of the fans was evident in letters to the *Post* and to the club. However, to the informed financial observer, these sales would have appeared to be symbolic of the harsh realities of the multi-stage purchasing system which had been in vogue, when coupled with a significant drop in income.

Nevertheless, in the August sun, before the new season started, John Toshack and his charges were reported as being in fine fettle. Once again they started their campaign with an European Cup Winnners' Cup-tie with IFC Magdeburg at the Vetch; this time, though, the club's finances and the team's confidence were not boosted. After drawing at the Vetch the Swans lost the away leg 1-0 and were eliminated from the competition at the first stage.

The first league match of the season did little to bring comfort to the Vetch management and supporters, either; Sheffield Wednesday were far faster to the ball and they defeated the Swans by the only goal of the game. The gate of 10,900, whilst only marginally down on that of the opening match of the

> *During the 1983-4 season the Swans created two unwanted records. They won only seven games whilst losing twenty-seven.*

previous season, was still significantly lower than the 'break-even' figure which was necessary to keep the club afloat. The result of the match was disappointing for all concerned and prompted the usual Swansea analysis by optimists and pessimists among the club's supporters. The gloom merchants argued that the side would struggle, although it is very unlikely that even the gloomiest among them could have foreseen the extent of the disaster ahead. The optimists, on the other hand, argued that the team had to find its feet again in the Second Division environment. For their part, objective statisticians would have sided with the pessimists; their reasoning would have been straightforward, At the end of the 1981-2 season the club had lost five of its last seven matches; and in 1982-3 they had been beaten in four of the last seven, winning only once. In each case, the trend from the end of the previous season had been carried forward into the next. On that basis, and having lost key men, it was not unreasonable to argue that

a similar pattern was likely to emerge in 1983-4.

Unfortunately, time was to show that the statisticians were right. It was not until 24 September that the team won a match in the league; they beat Cambridge at home. By then, the desperate Toshack had called his former team-mate, Emlyn Hughes out of retirement to help the Swans cause. At that stage in the season, the Swans had played six games, lost four and won only once. There followed a 0-5 thrashing at Fulham and further defeats by Manchester City and Newcastle. Whilst a point was earned in the next match, Blackburn's win in the eleventh match of the season was followed by changes at board level. According to the minute book, at that point, Malcom Struel and Tom Phillips resigned in response to a proposal from Doug Sharpe which involved him injecting £300,000 into the club whilst he became chairman. Two days later, John Toshack also resigned, Emlyn Hughes left the club and Doug Livermore assumed the role of acting manager. Doug Sharpe took the chair at this time as an interim measure, with Bobby Jones as his assistant. Six weeks later, after Jeremy Charles had been sold to Queens Park Rangers for £100,000, Livermore also left the club, at which point Les Chappell became acting manager. As these events indicate, there was little in the way of stability or hope at the Vetch at that time, but then, out of the blue came some good news.

Doug Sharpe had gone to London to negotiate the deal with Queens Park Rangers regarding Jeremy Charles, and it was whilst he was there that a remarkable gesture was made. During the time Sharpe was at Loftus Road, he received a telephone message requesting him to meet with the Liverpool director, Sir John Smith at his London hotel. Since the Swansea man knew that the Vetch club owed Liverpool some £300,000, he was rather apprehensive as he travelled across London. However, when he met the Liverpool man and a colleague, his concern evaporated in an instant, to be replaced by what Doug Sharpe could only describe as 'a warm glow'. Sir John, after welcoming him, opened a bottle of champagne to toast the Swansea club and told the amazed Swans chairman that Liverpool was going to write-off the Swansea debt. Given the unhappy circumstances in which the Vetch club found itself at that time, Sir John's gesture was truly magnificent. Doug Sharpe could not find enough words to express his and the club's gratitude. Within nine months, the action of the Liverpool knight would be seen to be of even greater importance to Swansea City football club.

Sadly, there was no such fairy tale being enacted on the pitch. After a 6-1 thumping at Chelsea, the side had a run of eight matches during which it won only once whilst six were lost. In addition, there had been an unfortunate injury; senior goalkeeper Jimmy Rimmer split open his hand in making a save. It was an injury which was to take a long time to heal. Meantime, Vetch Field morale suffered a further blow when Alan Curtis, the last of the trio of Swansea gems, was sold to Southampton for a miserly £80,000.

With the Swans in twenty-second place in the table, the board, without the funds to strengthen the squad, and the club managerless, there came a surprise announcement; John Toshack was to return as manager. Les Chappell was to be his assistant and Wyndham Evans assumed the role of player-coach. Toshack said at the time that the club had been 'an important part of his life' and that he felt 'honour-bound to do all that he could to turn things around'. Not that John Toshack was blindly optimistic. By this time there were many youngsters in the team and precious little in the way of experience. Players like Chris Sander, Dean Holtham, Chris Marustic, Huw Lake, Jimmy Loveridge, Huw Morgan and Dean Saunders, were having to learn their trade in the difficult environment of a strong Second Division. In itself this was hard enough, but when that had to be done whilst playing in an unsuccessful side, the scope of the task was even greater.

In the January of 1984, the weather was foul enough to cause mass cancellations, and there followed a period of eighteen days during which no football was played. Immediately before the start of this period, young Mike Hughes took over as goalkeeper and was unfortunate enough to have to pick the ball out of his net six times in a humiliating defeat at Sheffield

Jimmy Rimmer

Wednesday. However, the young man was not put off by the experience and developed into a fine goalkeeper.

During the eighteen-day 'holiday', Toshack worked hard with his young charges and with the relatively few senior men who remained. Given the raw talent with whom he was working, it was asking a great deal of the manager to make any impact, but no one could accuse him of not trying. Meantime, the board, when challenged by the fans or by the media to explain the situation at the Vetch, could only point to the precarious financial position in which the club found itself. Football debts had to be paid and with far less money coming in than was scheduled to go out, the storm warnings were hoisted with a vengeance. Not surprisingly, creditors began to get impatient. It was true that the Swansea board had had to face similar problems before; this time, however, they had few saleable assets and there seemed to be a shortage of white knights standing in the wings with the offer of a cash injection in

return for a place on the board.

When football recommenced, despite his best endeavours, John Toshack was not able to alter the situation for the better. Indeed, it could have been argued that his task was impossible. In any event, on 5 March, a date very close to the anniversary of his coming to the Vetch, Toshack was sacked. It was a tough decision for the board which had come so far with the young manager, but they felt that he had done all that he could. After all the exciting days of Toshack's reign at the Vetch, it was a sad event when he left the ground for the last time.

Les Chappell took over as manager on an acting basis, but he, too, found the task of changing the club's fortunes beyond him. On 24 April, after being beaten at Shrewsbury, the Swans were relegated for the second consecutive season. It was a bitter pill for all concerned and was in stark contrast to the hope and glory of the years when the club had climbed from the Fourth to the First in such rapid time. The members of the board as well as the club's loyal fans were stunned by the state of affairs. Sadly, as time was to show, they were all to be challenged to an even greater degree before many moons had passed across the heavens.

For those who concerned themselves with such matters, subsequent analysis of the season's statistics made unhappy reading. Two unwanted new records had been established. The club had won just seven matches during the campaign whilst losing on twenty-seven occasions. It was a cheerless time!

1984-85

On 16 May a new manager, Colin Appleton, formerly with Hull City, was appointed to the Vetch post. Appleton had been successful with the Humberside club and Doug

Sharpe was hoping that the new man would transfer that success to the Vetch. As agreed with the Swansea chairman, Appleton appointed Colin Meldrum as his assistant and the pair set out to try to strengthen their squad before the season began. Meantime, at board level, there was further acrimony relating to the funds which had been promised on Malcolm Struel's resignation and, in due course, Doug Sharpe stood down as chairman and was replaced by Bobby Jones. Malcolm Struel was reinstated as chief executive and a new financial package was put in place. Three new directors were added to the board: Mel Nurse, former club captain, Harry Hyde, and Dave Savage. Between them they invested some £200,000 which was matched by the club's bankers and augmented by shirt sponsorship money provided by Harry Hyde's company, DP Products.

Meanwhile, without money to spend, Colin Appleton scoured the close-season market for players who were being released on a free transfer basis, while the exodus from the Vetch continued. Neil Robinson joined Grimsby in exchange for £20,000, Ian Walsh went to Burnley 'free', while, after a brave fight to regain match fitness, Colin Irwin was forced to retire as a player. Consequently, leaving aside the men Appleton was planning to bring in, the Swans squad consisted of youngsters plus a fit-again Jimmy Rimmer, Nigel Stevenson and Wyndham Evans. The optimism

Alan Waddle is rather pleased with himself after scoring against Bury.

which the new financial package had stimulated was severely blunted and matters were hardly helped when Bobby Jones was faced with a crisis in his own business which forced him to resign to concentrate on saving it. At that stage, even the optimists were finding it to be difficult to see a silver lining in the cloud which hung over the Vetch. On Jones's departure, Doug Sharpe and Winston Rees took control, with the latter initially acting as chairman.

Given these developments, it was hardly surprising that, when the season started, early results reflected the club's difficult position. The first two league games were lost and the club was knocked out of the Milk Cup at the first hurdle. By the end of

September, only one match had been won out of the nine which had been played and the team's position in the table (23rd) was indicative of those statistics. Appleton had tried various combinations in seeking to turn the tide, including fielding several trialists, but nothing came of them. There was, it is true, a week at the beginning of October when the side won two matches in succession, but there followed three consecutive defeats. It was at that point that the new manager announced a major signing; the English international, Gerry Francis, joined the club 'until the end of the season'. Given his footballing pedigree, persuading Francis to come to the Vetch was something of a coup for the Swans'

This was the squad at the start of the 1984-85 campaign.
Standing, left to right: Colin Meldrum (Coach), Chris Marustic, Wyndham Evans, Gary Richards, Roger Mullen, Michael Hughes, Jimmy Rimmer, Chris Sander, Pat McQuillan, Darren Gale, David Hough, Dudley Lewis, Les Chappell (Coach).
Front: Tony Cottey, Dean Saunders, Neil Robinson, Colin Pascoe, Mark Hughes, Colin Appleton, Nigel Stevenson, Jimmy Loveridge, Steve Mardenborough, Phil Williams.

manager. Apart from anything else, the player should have made an ideal captain. Unfortunately, the longer term effects of that were never tested. Within a matter of weeks, Francis left to join Portsmouth.

In November, things went from bad to worse; the Swans lost all their league matches in the month and also suffered the ignominy of being ejected from the FA Cup by non-league Bognor Town. Colin Appleton's best efforts with the material which he had had come to nought. He was never able to field a settled side, he had introduced trialists frequently in an endeavour to find the right chemistry, and his teams failed to replicate training ground cohesion in actual matches. By then, completely dissatisfied with what was happening, chairman Doug Sharpe called a halt. On 6 December Appleton and Meldrum were sacked. Afterwards, Appleton said that he had not had enough time to make an impact. That seemed a reasonable enough statement, but Doug Sharpe felt that he had to make a change to try to halt the club's decline.During this barren period, gates had been falling in the face of continuing defeats and a complete lack of pattern in the play of the team. On 1 December only 3,124 people were in the ground to see Plymouth beat the Swans.

For almost two weeks, Les Chappell, who had, once again, been appointed acting-manager on Appleton's departure, ran the club. Then, on 12 December it was rumoured in the media that John Bond was to be the new Swans manager. Chairman Sharpe had decided that a well-known 'name' was needed, and Bond, who seemed to meet the bill in many respects, was willing to come and was given the task. Unfortunately, when the appointment was announced, a disappointed Les Chappell vented his feelings in public, the consequence of which was that he left the club when Bond arrived.

On arrival, Bond lost little time in scouring his football network for suitable players with experience. Almost immediately, Paul Price, who had cost Tottenham £200,000, joined after returning from the United States; Ray McHale, a competent mid-fielder, came from Sheffield United, Derek Parlane from Manchester City, and Gary Williams

joined them from Bristol City. Several other Bond signings were to be made before the curtain came down on the season. One result of this activity, coupled with Appleton's efforts with trialists, was that a new record was set for the number of men used in the Swans first team during a season. In all, thirty-eight players appeared during the campaign, several of them for little more than a handful of matches. Unfortunately, though, in the main it was a question of quantity rather than quality.

Despite the contribution of the new men whom Bond had brought to the club, the manager found it to be difficult to improve the side's position in the league table. However, there were odd matches in which the team repaid the patient loyalty of Swansea's corps of fans. After failing to win a match in the first twenty-seven days of March, the team delighted a small crowd (2,380) by beating Preston North End 4-1 in an exciting game. There followed an impressive run during which the team was unbeaten in five successive matches, four of which were victories. This took the Swans up to twentieth in the table and gave the Vetch faithful cause to believe that Bond had found the formula for success. Sadly, only one point was picked up over the next three games and the side slipped back into the relegation zone. At that point, Bond urged his charges to make one more effort, and in an emotion filled match, the Swans beat Bristol Rovers in the penultimate game of the campaign, the winning goal being scored two minutes from the end.

It was the next match, however, which really caught the imagination of the Swansea public. Since it was the final game of the campaign, the Swans approached it knowing exactly what they had to do. In order to save themselves from relegation, at least one point had to be gained from the match. The atmosphere that night at the Vetch was electric. Three other clubs had the same number of points as the Swans, but had played all their matches. No doubt, the supporters of these sides would have been willing the visitors, Bristol City, to win, but, if they were, they would have been disappointed. The *hwyl* generated by a passionate crowd of 10,702 which packed the Vetch that memorable night, was powerfully

effective. It was as though the fans were watching a cup final, the only element missing being goals. Such was the atmosphere that both teams were lifted. Whilst it ended 0-0, a truly thrilling match ensued and the Swans had avoided relegation by a single point. The euphoria generated in the ground was such that when the final whistle was blown it was as though the Swans had won promotion.

Not surprisingly, there were many among those who streamed away from the Vetch in the glow of that balmy evening who spoke about success in the season ahead. All the trials and tribulations of the past season were forgotten; next season would be different, John Bond would get them playing!

Given the joy of the evening, even to those who habitually tended to look on the dark side found their judgement tinged with positive thoughts. As John Bond drew on his celebration cigar, he could have been forgiven for feeling rather pleased with himself and with his players. It had been an evening of relative glory and, after so much misery, it was there to be enjoyed. Yet, in the morning, those who had the task of managing the club's finances, whilst encouraged by the evening and the size of the gate, were obliged to contemplate yet another close season when there was far less money in the club's coffers than was needed to service its debts.

1985-86

There were three new players at the Vetch to welcome what was to prove to be a traumatic season: Colin Randell from Blackburn, Gary Emmanuel (son of a former Swan) and Tommy Hutchison. Two other players were to come to the Vetch later in the campaign. One of those who left at the same time was a certain Dean Saunders. Manager Bond had signalled his intention to give the lad a chance to start again with another club during the previous season. Then, Saunders went to Cardiff on loan, but the Ninian Park men were not impressed, either. As a consequence, the young man was given a free transfer and joined Brighton.

Given the club's parlous financial position, chairman Sharpe and his colleagues were hoping that the large gate which had been attracted to the final game of the previous season would result in a 'healthy' crowd for the first of the new campaign. Unfortunately, they were disappointed, only 4,700 turned up to see the 'opener', and when that match and the following three were lost, there were a thousand fewer to watch the fifth – against Rotherham. Prior to the game with the Yorkshiremen, the Swans were twenty-third in the table, but, after winning that contest, they moved up one place. As if buoyed by that success, on 14 September the Swans travelled to Molyneux to play Wolverhampton Wanderers. It was a match which football pool enthusiasts would have marked down as a 'home banker'. Yet, on the day, the Swans played like champions and thrashed the home side 5-1. It was an amazing result and one which encouraged the Swansea optimists to believe that the corner had been turned. Unfortunately, it was not the right turning.

After drawing the next game only one further win was recorded in the next thirteen matches, whilst three of the defeats (1-5 at Derby, 1-5 at Gillingham and 0-6 at Darlington) could only be described as comprehensive. Morale was low, as was the team's position in the league table. The press, who had been bemused by the club's win at Wolverhampton, were equally confused by these defeats. One journalist described the team's football in the game at Darlington as 'diabolical'. Yet, two weeks later, in a match watched by only 2,779 people, the Swans played with some style to beat York City – who were then in second place in the division – by the only goal of the game. After that match, rumours were circulating in Swansea regarding an American millionaire who had been seen at the Vetch during the game. It was said that the man was interested in buying the club. It was not known whether the American knew anything about football. However, there is little doubt, assuming that he existed, that his financial judgement was sound. Six days later the club was put into the hands of the receiver.

That news was like a bombshell! Swansea City was finished. The media said so. John Bond was sacked and there was talk of the players

Harold Woolacott locks up at the Vetch for what many believed to be the last time.

John Bond drives away 'at the end'.

becoming the property of the League. The *Western Mail* chose to run the story on its front page under the headline 'Swansea City Wound Up', whilst television and radio bulletins seemed to confirm that fact, as ex-players, journalists and fans spoke in hushed tones of the great days at the Vetch. The *Post* carried a poignant photograph of stadium manager Harold Woolacott padlocking the main gates at the ground, which seemed as a metaphor for 'this is the end'.

In the first edition of this book, the club's need to apply for re-election to the Football League was described as the nadir of its history. Friday, 20 December 1985 proved that statement to have been based upon a false assumption. On that grey

December day, the shock of the news seemed to have numbed the whole of the old borough, whereas on the previous occasion there was vision and hope. Many people swore life-long allegiance to the Vetch club, but, said the pessimists, it's too late to do anything now. Thankfully, there were those who took the opposite view. Their position was, not *if* the club could be saved, but, rather *how* it could be saved?

The first hurdle to overcome for these men was that concerned with obtaining permission to continue trading whilst being in the hands of the receiver. This was an urgent task for, according to Football League rules, if the Swans did not play their scheduled match at Ninian Park on 26 December, the club would be expelled from the league. Happily, on 23 December this permission was received and the former board members arranged for Tommy Hutchison to act as manager with Ron Walton as his assistant. It had looked like being a bleak Christmas for all who loved the Swans. Now, the festival could be celebrated along with this temporary reprieve. Some saw it more dramatically. It was Christmas, not Easter, and yet, was not this a resurrection?

On that special Boxing Day, Hutchison lead his players out onto the Ninian Park pitch to a thunderous reception from almost 2,000 Swansea fans, and in an emotional match, the Scot's patchwork side battled as well as they

A Swans side of the period.

knew. Unfortunately, there was no fairy-tale ending, for Cardiff spoiled the party by scoring in the last two minutes of the game. Whilst, for the Swansea contingent, the result of the match was disappointing, the club had fulfilled the Football League obligation. It was clear that there was a long way to go, but at least the club was alive again – if not, yet, out of the financial wood.

Following the Cardiff game, there were two groups intent on saving the Swans. Doug Sharpe and Glyn Hammond, his financial adviser, lead one, while Peter Howard and his colleagues formed the other. Both parties had attended the High Court, where it was made clear that the best chance for the club was to have a single focussed group working on the project. In the meantime, the Howard group launched a public appeal to allow the club to continue trading. This attracted more than £60,000. There was also a major fund-raising event involving the visit of Manchester United to the Vetch. This was organised by Bobby Jones and Tommy Hutchison, each using Old Trafford connections and, in due course, Ron Atkinson brought a side to the Vetch which attracted a gate income in excess of £45,000. Later, however, Peter Howard's party withdrew, giving the Sharpe/ Hammond group a clear field in the important task of saving the Swans. Thus it was that Doug Sharpe began the process.

On the field, matters hardly went Tommy Hutchison's way. Of the remaining twenty-four matches in the league campaign, only six were won and seven drawn. After a 0-3 defeat by Derby County at the Vetch in the final match of the season, the

Tommy Hutchinson and Ron Walton: the new management team.

Swans found themselves at the bottom of Division Three and were relegated.

While supporters were downcast about this demotion, their sadness was tinged with relief. At least, Swansea City Football Club still existed and with it hope beat eternal in the hearts of loyal fans. The objective among them might have pondered on the club's lack of funds, which would inhibit the board in attempting to do anything about strengthening the team; and about the possibility of relegation from the Football League itself (which was possible now that the club was a member of Division Four), but even they could be swayed. Had not Manchester United come to play a game at the Vetch at Tommy Hutchison's behest. Did not that show that the Scot had friends in high places, and there were promising youngsters coming through. Whatever their conclusions, they must have been heartened by

the news that Doug Sharpe and his colleagues were making sound progress with their mission objectives.

Throughout the months which followed, Sharpe's group worked very hard to satisfy the requirements of the High Court. Several deadlines were set and met during this time and, on each occasion there was greater hope that there would be a positive outcome to the affair. Many people contributed in someway during this process; some gave up their shares in support of the High Court appeal. Debenture holders waived their rights in order to assist the cause, and many people, young, old, rich and poor, sent in sums of money. Later, after the club had been reprieved, Sharpe emphasised the importance of this assistance, without which his mission would have been impossible. That being said, it is right and proper to stress that, without Doug Sharpe's dedicated effort, Swansea City might not exist today. On 20 July 1986 when Mr Justice Hoffman lifted the order on Swansea City, he congratulated Doug Sharpe on his persistence. All who cared about the Vetch would have supported that statement, and that day, when that persistence was rewarded will live long in their memory.

In closing this chapter, it is pertinent to comment on the effects of the club going into receivership as it related to the men who were its directors at the time. Every one of them lost all the money which they had put into the club and, since those figures varied from £30,000 to £100,000, they were not insignificant. In addition these men had to meet certain guarantees which they had given to the bank, and in at least two cases this resulted in the individuals having to sell their homes. Quite properly, people who direct businesses have to accept the responsibilities which go with their office. In the commercial world they receive salaries and other benefits as compensation; in football, only executive directors are paid. It follows that the often much maligned football club director must either be a fanatical supporter of his club or a rather naive businessman. Given these facts, if the average fan was reluctant to take on such responsibility, could he or she be blamed?

Swansea City FC Season 1982/83 — Division 1

#	Date	V	Opponents	Score	Scorers	Att	Davies D	Marustik C	Hadziabdic D	Irwin C	Mahoney J	Stanley G	James L	James R	Charles J	Stevenson N	Latchford B	Curtis A	Rajkovic A	Kennedy R	Loveridge J	Lewis D	Thompson M	Gale D	Walsh I	Evans W	Robinson N	Richards G	Pascoe C	Sander C	Lake H	Toshack J
1	Aug-28	A	Notts. County	0 0		8,061	1	2	3	4	5	6	7	8	9	10	11															
2	Aug-31	H	Coventry City	2 1	James R (pen), Latchford	11,712	1	2*	3	4	5		7	8	9	10	11	12	6													
3	Sep-04	H	Norwich City	4 0	Latchford 3, James R	11,694	1	2	3	4		12	9	8*	10	5	11	7	6													
4	Sep-07	A	Watford	1 2	Stevenson	15,535	1	2	3	4			7	8	9	10	11*	12	6	5												
5	Sep-11	A	Stoke City	1 4	Latchford	14,058	1	2*	3	4			9	8	12	10	11	7	6	5												
6	Sep-18	H	Liverpool	0 3		20,322	1	2*	3	4			12	8	9	10	11	7	6	5												
7	Sep-25	A	Aston Villa	0 2		21,246	1	12	3	4*	6	2	8	9	10	11				5	7											
8	Oct-02	H	Tottenham Hotspur	2 0	Thompson, Latchford	16,381	1	2			6		9	8	4		11	7		5			3	10								
9	Oct-09	A	Brighton	1 1	Lewis	11,050	1		3		11*		9	8	4	6		7		5		2	10	12								
10	Oct-16	H	Everton	0 3		11,183	1		3				9	8	4	10*	11	7		5		2	6		12							
11	Oct-23	H	Southampton	3 2	O/Goal, James R, Latchford	10,694	1		3		11*	10	8			9	7	6	5	12	2					4						
12	Oct-30	A	Manchester City	1 2	Latchford	25,021	1		3		5	2	9*	8	4	10	11	12	6					7								
13	Nov-06	H	Sunderland	3 0	Curtis 2, James R	10,035	1	3*			5	11	12	8	4	10	9	7	6					2								
14	Nov-13	A	WBA	3 3	James L, Charles, James R	12,432	1		3		9	7	8		4	10	11		6	5*								12				
15	Nov-20	H	Arsenal	1 2	Latchford	12,389	1		3		9	2		8	4	10	11		6		7	5										
16	Nov-28	A	Ipswich Town	1 3	James L	17,849	1		3		5	2	9	8	5	10	11		4		7											
17	Dec-04	H	Luton Town	2 0	Latchford, Curtis	9,556	1		3		9	2	12	8	4	10	11	7*	6	5												
18	Dec-11	A	Nottm. Forest	1 2	James R	14,585	1		3		9	2	12	8		10	11	7	6	5*							4					
19	Dec-18	A	Manchester United	0 0		15,748	1		3		9	2	12	8		10	11	7*	6								5	4				
20	Dec-27	A	West Ham United	2 3	Latchford 2	23,843	1		3		9	2	7	8		10	11		6								5	4				
21	Dec-29	H	Birmingham City	0 0		11,840	1		3		4		9	8	10*	12	11	7	6			2					5	2				
22	Jan-01	A	Arsenal	1 2	Curtis	25,237	1		3		5	12	9			10	11	7*	6		8						4	2				
23	Jan-03	A	Norwich City	0 1		16,236	1		3		9	12		8		10	11	7	6		4						5	2*				
24	Jan-15	H	Notts. County	2 0	Gale, Latchford	8,992	1		3		9	10*	8	4	5	11	7	6					12				2					
25	Jan-22	A	Coventry City	0 0		9,964	1		3		9	10	8	4	5	11	7						2				2					
26	Feb-06	H	Watford	1 3	Latchford	14,461	1		3		12		8	4*	5	11	7	6	10				9				2					
27	Feb-12	A	Tottenham Hotspur	0 1		24,632	1		3		9	10	8		11	7	6*	5				12					2					
28	Feb-26	A	Everton	2 2	James R, Gale	17,112	1		3		10		8		11			5	7	4	9			2	6							
29	Mar-01	H	Brighton	1 2	Latchford	8,825	1		3		7*		8		11		5	10	4	9			2	6	12							
30	Mar-05	A	Southampton	1 2	Loveridge	16,842	1	2	12		9	4		10	5*	7	6	11		8	3											
31	Mar-12	H	Manchester City	4 1	Latchford, Walsh 2, James R (pen)	9,884		2			10		8	4	11	6	7	5	12	9*		3							1			
32	Mar-19	A	Sunderland	1 1	Marustik	17,850		2			10		8	11	6	7	5	9		4	3								1			
33	Mar-26	H	WBA	2 1	James R, Latchford	11,222		2			10	4	11	12	6	7	5	9*		3								1				
34	Apr-02	A	Birmingham City	1 1	Latchford	13,591		2			10	4	11	6	7	5	9	3										1				
35	Apr-05	H	West Ham United	1 5	Walsh	13,303		2			10	4	11	6	7	5	12	9*	3									1				
36	Apr-09	A	Liverpool	0 3		30,010		2			10	8	12	9	5	7	6	4	3	11*	1											
37	Apr-16	H	Stoke City	1 1	Charles	10,100		2			8	4	12	11	6	7	5	9*	10	3	1											
38	Apr-23	A	Luton Town	1 3	Latchford	11,561		2			8	4	11	6	10	7	5	9*	3	12	1											
39	Apr-30	H	Ipswich Town	1 1	Rajkovic	8,568		2			8	4	11	6	10	7*	5	9	3	12	1											
40	May-02	H	Aston Villa	2 1	Pascoe, Gale	9,175		2			10	8	4	11	5	6	9	3	7	1												
41	May-07	A	Manchester United	1 2	Latchford	35,724		2			10	8	4	11	5	6	9	3	7	1												
42	May-14	H	Nottm. Forest	0 3		9,226				4	6	8			5	10	7	2		9	3	11*	1	12								
					Apps		30	22	24	8	24	24	14	40	30	24	38	17	33	21	16	23	3	10	7	6	17	15	4	12	0	0
					Subs			1	1			4	5			2	2		4		1				5	1		1		3		1
					Gls			1					2	9	2	1	20	4	1		1	1	1	3	3				1			

#	Date	V	Opponents	Score	Scorers	Att	Davies D	Marustik C	Hadziabdic D	Irwin C	Mahoney J	Stanley G	James L	James R	Charles J	Stevenson N	Latchford B	Curtis A	Rajkovic A	Kennedy R	Loveridge J	Lewis D	Thompson M	Gale D	Walsh I	Evans W	Robinson N	Richards G	Pascoe C	Sander C	Lake H	Toshack J
1	Aug-17	H	S Braga, ECWC Prelim	3 0	Charles 2, O/Goal	10,614	1	2	3	4			8	7	9	10*	11"		6	5		12		13								
2	Aug-25	A	S Braga, ECWC Prelim	0 1		17,000	1	2	3	4	5	10	7	8	9		11		6													
3	Sep-15	H	Sliema W, ECWC 1-1	12 0	Walsh 3, Loveridge 2, Irwin, Charles, Rajkovic 2, Stevenson, Latchford, Hadziabdic	5,130	1	2	3	4		12	8	9	10	11"		6	5	7*				13								
4	Sep-29	A	Sliema W, ECWC 1-2	5 0	Curtis 2, Gale 2, Toshack	2,000		10	3		8				4		7*	5	11	2	6	9							1		12	
5	Oct-05	A	Bristol Rovers, MC 2-1	0 1		9,279	1	2			6		8	4	11	7	5	9	3	10												
6	Oct-20	H	P St. Germain, ECWC 2-1	0 1		9,505	1	5*	2		7	11	12	8	4	10*	9		3		6			13								
7	Oct-26	H	Bristol Rovers, MC 2-2	3 0	Latchford 3	9,755	1		3		10	9	8	4	11	7	6	5							2							
8	Nov-03	A	P St. Germain, ECWC 2-2	0 2		50,000	1		2*		8	5	9	6	7	3	10*	11	4		12			13								
9	Nov-09	A	Brentford, MC 3	1 1	Latchford	15,258	1		3		9	2		8	4	10	11	7	6	5												
10	Nov-17	H	Brentford, MC 3 Rep	1 2	Loveridge	6,676	1		3		9	2	7	8	4	10	11		6		12						5*					
11	Dec-08	A	Spencer Works, WC-3	3 0	James R 2, Latchford	1,711	1	2			9	6	7	8	4		11		5	10	3											
12	Jan-08	A	Norwich C, FAC-3	1 2	Gale	13,222	1	10	3		12		8*	5		11	7	4		6		9					2					
13	Jan-18	H	Shrewsbury T, WC-4	2 1	Latchford, Gale	4,511	1	2	3		7		8	9	5	11	10	4		6												
14	Feb-09	H	Hereford Utd, WC-5	3 1	Latchford 2, James R	2,688	1	2		3			8	9	10	11	7	6	5								4					
15	Mar-08	A	Colwyn Bay, WCSF 1-1	1 0	Latchford	3,500		2			8	5	11	6	10	4	9											3	7	1		
16	Mar-22	H	Colwyn Bay, WCSF 1-2	3 0	Stevenson, Curtis, Latchford	2,932		2			4	8	5	11		10	6	9									3	7	1		
17	May-10	A	Wrexham, WCF 1-1	2 1	Gale, Latchford	2,395			4		8	9*	10	11	6	5	2			7							3	12	1		
18	May-17	H	Wrexham, WCF 1-2	2 0	Latchford 2	5,630		2			4	8	9	12	11	5	6	10								3	7*	1		

Swansea City FC Season 1983/84 — Division 2

Player columns (left to right): Rimmer J, Robinson N, Marustik C, Charles J, Stevenson N, Lewis D, Curtis A, Stanley G, Pascoe C, Kennedy R, Latchford B, Lake H, Richards G, Walsh I, Maddy P, Gale D, Chivers G, Hughes E, Loveridge J, Saunders D, Guard T, Morgan H, Sander C, Irwin C, Holtham D, Evans W, Toshack J, Hughes M, McQuillan P, Rajkovic A, Mullen R, Hough D, Williams P

Match results

#	Date	V	Opponents	Score	Scorers	Att
1	Aug-27	H	Sheff. Wednesday	0 1		10,900
2	Sep-03	A	Derby County	1 2	Latchford	9,711
3	Sep-06	H	Oldham Athletic	0 0		7,244
4	Sep-10	H	Brighton	1 3	Lake	7,643
5	Sep-17	A	Huddersfield Town	0 1		10,224
6	Sep-24	H	Cambridge United	2 1	Curtis, Latchford	7,197
7	Oct-01	A	Fulham	0 5		7,253
8	Oct-08	A	Manchester City	1 2	Latchford	23,571
9	Oct-16	A	Newcastle United	1 2	Marustik	9,807
10	Oct-22	A	Charlton Athletic	2 2	Stevenson, Loveridge	5,737
11	Oct-29	H	Blackburn Rovers	0 1		10,588
12	Nov-05	H	Carlisle United	0 0		6,958
13	Nov-12	A	Barnsley	2 3	Lake, Gale	8,161
14	Nov-19	H	Grimsby Town	0 1		6,178
15	Nov-22	H	Chelsea	1 3	Pascoe	7,848
16	Nov-26	A	Middlesbrough	0 1		6,084
17	Dec-03	H	Crystal Palace	1 0	Gale	6,304
18	Dec-06	A	Chelsea	1 6	Walsh	21,389
19	Dec-17	H	Portsmouth	1 2	Maddy	6,404
20	Dec-26	A	Cardiff City	2 3	Stanley(pen), Toshack	14,580
21	Dec-27	H	Shrewsbury Town	0 2		7,706
22	Dec-31	H	Derby County	2 0	Stevenson 2	6,578
23	Jan-02	A	Cambridge United	1 1	Richards	3,406
24	Jan-14	A	Sheff. Wednesday	1 6	Marustik	13,787
25	Jan-18	H	Huddersfield Town	2 2	Walsh 2	4,944
26	Feb-05	H	Fulham	0 3		7,350
27	Feb-11	A	Brighton	1 1	Gale	11,979
28	Feb-15	A	Leeds United	0 1		10,031
29	Feb-25	H	Charlton Athletic	1 0	Pascoe	5,222
30	Mar-03	A	Carlisle United	0 2		4,280
31	Mar-07	A	Blackburn Rovers	1 4	Maddy	5,554
32	Mar-10	H	Barnsley	0 2		4,864
33	Mar-17	A	Oldham Athletic	3 3	Saunders, O/Goal, Maddy	3,597
34	Mar-31	A	Newcastle United	0 2		27,306
35	Apr-07	H	Manchester City	0 2		6,261
36	Apr-14	A	Grimsby Town	0 3		5,851
37	Apr-21	H	Cardiff City	3 2	Saunders 2, Walsh	10,275
38	Apr-24	A	Shrewsbury Town	0 2		3,060
39	Apr-27	H	Middlesbrough	2 1	Walsh 2	3,648
40	May-05	A	Crystal Palace	0 2		5,318
41	May-07	H	Leeds United	2 2	Marustik (pen), Loveridge	5,485
42	May-12	A	Portsmouth	0 5		7,359

Season totals

	Rimmer J	Robinson N	Marustik C	Charles J	Stevenson N	Lewis D	Curtis A	Stanley G	Pascoe C	Kennedy R	Latchford B	Lake H	Richards G	Walsh I	Maddy P	Gale D	Chivers G	Hughes E	Loveridge J	Saunders D	Guard T	Morgan H	Sander C	Irwin C	Holtham D	Evans W	Toshack J	Hughes M	McQuillan P	Rajkovic A	Mullen R	Hough D	Williams P
Apps	14	18	38	10	37	37	9	14	29	3	18	14	32	22	18	16	10	7	16	14	1	5	7	3	6	17	3	21	19	3	0	1	0
Subs	1									1	3			4	2	2	2	4		2	5	2									1	1	1
Gls			4		3		1	1	2		3	2	1	6	3	3			2	3						1							

Cup matches

#	Date	V	Opponents	Score	Scorers	Att
1	Aug-24	H	Magdeburg, ECWC Pre	1 1	Walsh	6,476
2	Aug-31	A	Magdeburg, ECWC Pre	0 1		25,000
3	Oct-04	H	Colchester Utd, MC 2-1	1 1	Gale	3,758
4	Oct-25	A	Colchester Utd, MC 2-2	0 1		5,204
5	Nov-29	H	Abercynon, WC-3	5 2	Lake 2(1 pen), Holtham, Pascoe, Walsh	1,397
6	Jan-07	A	Brighton, FAC-3	0 2		11,330
7	Jan-10	H	Bangor C, WC-4	4 2	Gale 2, Latchford, Maddy	3,100
8	Feb-08	H	Barry T, WC-5	1 1	Pascoe	3,139
9	Feb-21	H	Barry T, WC-5 Rep	2 1	Saunders, Toshack, (after extra time)	3,139
10	Mar-20	A	Shrewsbury Town, WCSF 1-1	0 2		950
11	Apr-03	H	Shrewsbury Town, WCSF 1-2	1 0	Richards	2,659

Swansea City FC Season 1984/85 — Division 3

#	Date	V	Opponents	Score	Scorers	Att
1	Aug-25	A	Millwall	0 2		4,616
2	Sep-01	H	York City	1 3	Mardenborough	4,211
3	Sep-08	A	Bristol City	2 2	Mardenborough, Saunders	8,464
4	Sep-15	H	Bradford City	1 2	Saunders	4,196
5	Sep-18	H	Bolton Wanderers	2 1	Pascoe, Mardenborough	3,636
6	Sep-22	A	Brentford	0 3		4,298
7	Sep-29	H	Gillingham	0 1		3,784
8	Oct-03	A	AFC Bournemouth	2 1	Wellings, Mardenborough	2,847
9	Oct-06	H	Orient	3 1	Wellings 2, Marustik	4,109
10	Oct-13	A	Newport County	0 2		5,006
11	Oct-20-	H	Walsall	1 2	Marustik	4,124
12	Oct-23	A	Hull City	1 4	Saunders	6,706
13	Oct-27	A	Cambridge United	2 0	Mardenborough, Loveridge	2,087
14	Nov-03	H	Wigan Athletic	2 2	Stevenson, Mardenborough	3,883
15	Nov-06	A	Preston N E	2 3	Saunders (pen), O/Goal	3,200
16	Nov-10	H	Reading	1 2	Saunders	3,630
17	Nov-24	A	Doncaster Rovers	1 4	Lewis	3,575
18	Dec-01	H	Plymouth Argyle	0 2		3,124
19	Dec-15	A	Burnley	1 1	McQuillan	3,772
20	Dec-22	A	Bristol Rovers	2 4	Saunders, Mardenborough	5,546
21	Dec-27	H	Rotherham United	1 0	Saunders (pen)	3,814
22	Dec-29	H	Derby County	1 5	Saunders (pen)	5,187
23	Jan-01	A	Lincoln City	0 1		2,517
24	Jan-12	A	York City	0 1		5,544
25	Jan-26	A	Bradford City	1 1	Parlane	6,001
26	Feb-02	A	Gillingham	1 1	Hough	4,821
27	Feb-09	H	Brentford	3 2	Saunders, Pascoe, Hough	4,440
28	Feb-12	H	AFC Bournemouth	0 0		4,121
29	Feb-16	A	Bolton Wanderers	0 0		5,448
30	Mar-01	H	Cambridge United	2 2	Pascoe 2 (1 pen)	4,372
31	Mar-05	A	Hull City	0 2		4,104
32	Mar-09	A	Walsall	0 3		4,756
33	Mar-17	H	Newport County	0 3		5,160
34	Mar-23	A	Orient	2 4	Pascoe 2 (1 pen)	2,423
35	Mar-26	H	Millwall	1 2	Marustik	3,606
36	Mar-30	H	Preston N E	4 1	Turner 2, Waddle, Pascoe	2,380
37	Apr-06	A	Rotherham United	1 0	Waddle	3,145
38	Apr-09	H	Lincoln City	2 2	Waddle, Turner	4,506
39	Apr-13	A	Reading	1 0	Turner	3,175
40	Apr-19	H	Doncaster Rovers	3 1	Waddle 2, Marustik	3,707
41	Apr-27	A	Plymouth Argyle	2 1	Parlane, Marustik	4,994
42	Apr-30	A	Wigan Athletic	0 2		2,406
43	May-04	H	Burnley	0 1		5,221
44	May-06	A	Derby County	1 1	Pascoe	10,117
45	May-11	A	Bristol Rovers	3 2	Turner, Pascoe, Parlane (pen)	5,155
46	May-17	H	Bristol City	0 0		11,709

Cup Competitions

#	Date	V	Opponents	Score	Scorers	Att
1	Aug-28	H	Walsall, MC 1-1	0 2		3,633
2	Sep-04	A	Walsall, MC 1-2	1 3	Pascoe	4,305
3	Nov-17	H	Bognor Regis, FAC 1	1 1	Richards	2,434
4	Nov-21	A	Bognor Regis, FAC 1Rep	1 3	Marustik	3,600
5	Dec-04	H	Spencer Works, WC-3	1 1	Cole	792
6	Dec-12	H	Spencer Works, WC-3 Rep	5 0	Saunders, Cole, Stevenson, Pascoe, Mardenborough	880
7	Jan-22	H	Bristol Rovers, FRT 1-1	2 0	O/Goal, Saunders (pen)	2,648
8	Jan-29	H	Sully, WC-4	7 1	Pascoe 2,Hough, Marustik,Stevenson,Mardenborough, Saunders	1,057
9	Feb-27	H	Hereford Utd, WC-5	2 0	Pascoe (pen), Hough	2,235
10	Mar-19	A	Bristol Rovers, FRT 1-2	2 0		2,223
11	Apr-02	H	Shrewsbury T, WCSF 1-1	2 2	Mardenborough 2	2,074
12	Apr-04	A	Newport Co. FRT 2	0 0	after extra time, Swans won 4-3 on pens	2,016
13	Apr-11	H	Brentford, FRT 3	0 2		1,653
14	Apr-16	A	Shrewsbury T, WCSF 1-2	1 2	Mardenborough	1,491

Apps: Rimmer J 33, Evans W 18, Lewis D 43, Rajkovic A 1, Stevenson N 34, Hughes M 12, Saunders D 28, Robinson N 5, Loveridge J 5, Mardenborough S 32, Pascoe C 41, Marustik C 41, Hough D 24, McQuillan P 6, Williams P 6, Cottey A 2, Richardson P 12, Richards G 15, Cole D 7, Wellings B 5, Gardner P 4, Kellow T 0, Francis G 3, Wassell K 1, Webber A 0, Mullen R 2, Hughes M 13, Price P 21, McHale R 19, Parlane D 21, Williams G 6, Powell B 8, Fisher P 2, Gale D 0, Waddle A 12, Sullivan C 12, Turner R 11, Andrews K 1

Subs: Evans W 2, Stevenson N 1, Saunders D 2, Robinson N 3, Loveridge J 4, McQuillan P 1, Williams P 1, Cottey A 5, Richardson P 1, Richards G 1, Kellow T 1, Webber A 1, Mullen R 1, Sullivan C 1

Gls: Evans W 1, Stevenson N 1, Mardenborough S 9, Marustik C 1, Hough D 7, McQuillan P 9, Williams P 5, Cottey A 2, Richardson P 1, Wellings B 3, Parlane D 3, Turner R 5, Andrews K 5

Swansea City FC Season 1985-86   Division 3

#	Date	V	Opponents	Score	Scorers	Att	Rimmer J	Lewis D	Sullivan C	Price P	Stevenson N	Marustik C	Hutchison T	Turner R	Waddle A	McHale R	Pascoe C	French N	Andrews K	Emmanuel G	Randall C	Burrows P	Williams P	Harrison C	Sharp J	Hughes M	Gibbins R	Hough D	McCarthy S	Price N	Budd K	Melville A	Davies I	Foley W
1	Aug-17	H	Wigan Athletic	0 1		4,700	1	2	3	4	5	6	7	8	9	10	11*	12																
2	Aug-24	A	Walsall	1 3	McHale	3,722	1	2	3	4	5	6	7	8	9	10	11																	
3	Aug-26	H	Plymouth Argyle	0 2		3,906	1	2	3	4	5	6	7	8	9		11				10													
4	Aug-31	A	Blackpool	0 2		3,085	1	2	3	4	5	6	7		9		11			8	10													
5	Sep-07	H	Rotherham United	1 0	Hutchison	3,697	1	2	3	4	5	6	7		9*	10	11			12	8													
6	Sep-14	A	Wolverhampton W	5 1	Emmanuel, Randall, Turner 2, Hutchison	4,064	1	2	3	4	5	6*	7		9	10				11	8	12												
7	Sep-17	H	Newport County	1 1	Turner	5,534	1	2	3	4	5	6	7		9	10*				11	8			12										
8	Sep-21	A	Reading	0 2		5,126	1	2	3	4	5	6*	7		9	10				11	8			12										
9	Sep-28	H	Bristol Rovers	0 1		4,008	1	2	3	4	5		7		9	12	10			11	8			6*										
10	Oct-02	A	Derby County	1 5	Emmanuel	9,169	1	2	3	4	5*		7		9	12	11			10	8			6										
11	Oct-05	A	Brentford	0 1		3,508	1		3	4			7		9	5	11			10	8			6	2									
12	Oct-11	H	Lincoln City	3 1	Pascoe, Waddle, Emmanuel	3,600			3	4*			7		9	6	11			12	8			5	2	1	10							
13	Oct-19	A	Bolton Wanderers	1 1	Pascoe	3,558	1		3				7		10	6	11			4	8			5	2	9								
14	Oct-22	H	Doncaster Rovers	0 2		3,827	1	12	3				7	8*	11	10	6			4				5	2	9								
15	Oct-26	A	Gillingham	1 5	French	3,082	1	12	3				7		10	6				4	8			5	2*	9								
16	Nov-02	H	Bury	1 0	Waddle	3,530	1	2	3	4*			7		10		11				8			5		9	6	12						
17	Nov-05	H	Chesterfield	1 1	Pascoe (pen)	3,424	1		3				7		10*		11	12					4	5		9	6	8	2					
18	Nov-09	A	Darlington	0 6		2,600	1		3	4*					10		11	8		6			7	5		9	2						12	
19	Nov-23	H	Bristol City	1 3	Harrison	4,414	1		3						10	7				6	8			5	4	2	9		11*	12				
20	Nov-30	A	Notts County	0 3		3,912			3		5				10	7				6	8			3	1	9	2	12					5	11
21	Dec-14	H	York City	1 0	Waddle	2,779			3	4			7		10					6	8			3	1	9	2						5	11
22	Dec-26	H	Cardiff City	0 1		9,375			3*	4			8		10	7				6				1	9	2	12						5	11
23	Dec-28	A	Plymouth Argyle	0 2		8,622			3	4			10			7				6				5	1	8	2	9						11
24	Jan-01	H	AFC Bournemouth	1 1	McCarthy	6,989				4			11*		7		8			6	12			5	1	9	2	10				3		
25	Jan-07	H	Walsall	2 1	Gibbins 2	4,250			3	4			12		7	8*				6				5	1	9	2	10						11
26	Jan-11	H	Blackpool	2 0	Gibbins, Harrison (pen)	5,705			3	4			7		8					6				5	1	9	2	10						11
27	Jan-18	A	Wigan Athletic	0 5		3,308			3	4			12		7		8			6*				5	1	9	2	10						11
28	Jan-25	H	Wolverhampton W	0 2		4,966			3	4			12		7*		8			6				5	1	9	2	10						11
29	Feb-01	A	Rotherham United	1 4	Gibbins	2,932				4	5*		7		10		8			6				11	1	9	2						3*	12
30	Feb-04	A	Doncaster Rovers	0 0		2,029		2		4			7		10		12			6				5	1	9	11						3*	8
31	Feb-08	H	Bolton Wanderers	3 1	Foley 2, Hough	4,242		2	3	4			7		10					6				5	1	9	11	12						8*
32	Feb-16	A	Newport County	0 2		2,805		2*	3	4			7		10					6				5	1	9	11	12						8
33	Feb-22	H	Reading	2 3	Harrison (pen), Hutchison	4,965		2	3	4			7		10*					6				5	1	9	11	12						8
34	Mar-01	A	Bristol Rovers	0 0		3,098			3*	4			8							6	7		11	5	1	9	2	10					12	
35	Mar-08	H	Brentford	2 0	McCarthy, Gibbins	3,683				4			7			11				6	8		3	5	1	9	2	10						
36	Mar-16	A	Lincoln City	1 4	McCarthy	2,846			3	4			7			8	11*			6				5	1	9	2	10					12	
37	Mar-22	H	Gillingham	2 2	Williams, Gibbins	3,364		2	3	4			7							6			11	5	1	9	8	10						
38	Mar-25	A	Bury	2 2	Williams, Harrison	2,049		2	3	4			7							6	12		11	5	1	9	8*	10						
39	Mar-29	A	AFC Bournemouth	0 4		3,328		2	3*	4			7							6	8		11	5	1	9	12	10						
40	Mar-31	H	Cardiff City	2 0	Hough, Williams	6,643			3	4			7		12					6	8		11	5	1	9*	2	10						
41	Apr-05	A	Chesterfield	1 4	Hough	2,100			3	4			7		12	10				6*	8		11	5	1	9	2							
42	Apr-12	H	Darlington	2 2	Harrison (pen), Waddle	3,357			3	4			7		10	8				6			11	5	1	9	2							
43	Apr-19	A	Bristol City	1 0	Price	6,013		2	3	4			7		10	9	8			6				5	1	11								
44	Apr-26	H	Notts County	0 0		3,869	1	2	3	4			7		10	9*	8			6				5	1	11	12							
45	May-03	A	York City	1 3	Waddle	3,132		2	3	4			7*		10	9	8			6				12	1	5	11							
46	May-06	H	Derby County	0 3		3,974		2	3				7		10	9	8			6				4	1	5	11							
			Apps				19	22	41	40	12	8	38	9	27	26	18	11	1	38	18	1	11	34	5	27	35	30	16	1	1	2	11	4
			Subs					2												3		2	1	3		2	1	2	1	2			1	6	2	3	1
			Gls							1			3	3	5	1	3	1		3	1		3	5			6	3	3					2

#	Date	V	Opponents	Score	Scorers	Att	Rimmer J	Lewis D	Sullivan C	Price P	Stevenson N	Marustik C	Hutchison T	Turner R	Waddle A	McHale R	Pascoe C	French N	Andrews K	Emmanuel G	Randall C	Burrows P	Williams P	Harrison C	Sharp J	Hughes M	Gibbins R	Hough D	McCarthy S	Price N	Budd K	Melville A	Davies I	Foley W
1	Aug-20	A	Cardiff C, M C 1-1	1 2	Marustik	4,218	1	2	3	4	5	6	7	8*	9	10	11	12			8													
2	Sep-03	H	Cardiff C, M C 1-2	3 1	Randell 2, Pascoe	4,621	1	2	3	4	5	6	7		9	10	11				8													
3	Sep-24	A	West Ham Utd, M C 2-1	0 3		9,282	1	2	3	4	5	6	7		9		11				8		10											
4	Oct-08	H	West Ham Utd, M C 2-2	2 3	Waddle, Randell	3,584			3	4	12		7		9	10*	5	11			8	6		2	1									
5	Nov-16	H	Leyton Wingate, FAC-1	2 0	Waddle, Williams	3,295	1		3						10	6	11*			9	8		7	5		4	2						12	
6	Nov-27	A	Haverfordwest, WC-3	6 2	McHale 3, Emmanuel, McCarthy, Price	900			3	4					10	6				9			7	5*	1	8	2	11					12	
7	Dec-07	H	Bristol Rovers, FAC-2	1 2	Burrows	4,302				4					10	7	12			6	8		3		1	10	2	9		9*			11	
8	Jan-15	A	Sully, WC-4	2 1	French, Gibbins	500			3	4			8		7					6				5	1	10	2	9					11	
9	Jan-20	A	Newport Co. FRT-1	1 1	French	2,863	1		3	4			7			8				6				5		9	2	10					11	
10	Jan-28	A	Cardiff City, FRT-2	2 0	McCarthy 2	1,006		2*		4*			7		12		8			6				5	1	9	11	10				3	13	
11	Feb-13	H	Kidderminster, WC-5	1 1	Foley	1,796		2	3	4			7		10					6				5	1	9	11							8
12	Feb-19	H	Torquay Utd, FRT Q F	1 0	O/Goal	2,200		2	3	4			7		10					6				5	1	9	11							8
13	Feb-26	A	Kidderminster, WC 5 R	0 4		1,809		2	3	4			7							6	8		12	5	1	9	11*	10						
14	Apr-02	A	Hereford Utd, FRT S-F	0 0	aet, lost 5-4 on pens	3,729			3	4			6		10					5	8		11	7	1	9	2							

Chapter 21

Sharpe's Victory

1986-87

Terry Yorath, the manager, together with the Swans board, Doug Sharpe, Glyn Hammond and Mal Griffiths.

With such a short close-season within which to work, Doug Sharpe had to make plans based on the assumption that his plea at the High Court was going to be successful. Clearly, he was not in a position to make anyone job offers, but that did not preclude him talking with interested parties. At least, by this means, he could sound out prospective staff. As a consequence, as soon as Mr. Justice Hoffman had handed down his verdict, Sharpe was able to recruit his preferred manager. Within days it was announced that Terry Yorath was coming to the Vetch, ostensibly as player-manager. However, the new man made it clear that he would only play in emergencies. In Swansea the appointment was well-received, for Yorath had a fine reputation as a player for Leeds and Wales, and as a person. The new man commenced his duties immediately, for he had very little time in which to get to know his charges and to shape them into the team he sought.

Since Jimmy Rimmer had left the club during the close season, together with Sullivan, Turner, Waddle and Gibbins, the manager inherited a very young side, for which Harrison, Hutchison and Nigel Stevenson provided the experience. Yorath himself made a single signing, bringing a young full-back, Terry Phelan, from Leeds. The new manager believed that the youngster would do well, and in that regard he was to be proved absolutely right. Dudley Lewis was given the captaincy and he was to be partnered at the heart of the defence by eighteen-year-old Andrew

Melville, one of the products of the club's youth scheme. Tommy Hutchison provided the experience in mid-field, while two further youth-scheme men, Sean McCarthy and Colin Pascoe made up the strike force.

With newcomer Phelan showing up well, the Swans won the first match of the new season in some style, beating Stockport County 3-0 at the Vetch. The 4,774 people who enjoyed that experience must have spread the word about the form of the team, for, when Northampton came to the ground on 20 September, the gate was 6,902.

The Swans' squad for 1986-87.
Back row, left to right: Ron Walton, Andrew Melville, Nigel French, Phil Williams, Mike Hughes, Chris Harrison, Sean McCarthy, Colin Pascoe, David Hough, Graham Davies. Front: Keri Andrews, Colin Randell, Dudley Lewis, Tommy Hutchinson, Terry Yorath (Manager), Gary Emmanuel, Terry Phelan, Paul Burrows.

Following that match, a 2-1 victory, the men in white sat proudly at the top of the league table, and, in the eyes of the fans, after three seasons of almost unremitting gloom, Yorath's efforts put him in the messiah category. Furthermore, the side was playing attractive football. That special buzz of success was re-emerging in the city. Even the incredulous, who had pinched themselves black and blue, were beginning to believe that they had not been dreaming.

Whilst the side lost its top place following a 1-1 draw at Crewe, it was well into the first month of 1987 before the Swans dropped out of the first three places in the league table. *En route*, Terry Yorath had been manager of the month (in November) and his teams were playing bright attractive football. Yorath, well pleased with the progress which had been made, nonetheless, knew that his side needed strengthening. As a result, in October, he borrowed Lyndon Symmons from Leeds to add to his strike force and fuel his promotion push.

The side did reasonably well, too, in cup competitions. In the Littlewoods Cup it had reached the second round only to be beaten over the two legs by Leicester City. In the FA Cup, after winning through two rounds, the Swans were drawn at home against West Bromwich Albion and surprised the pundits by winning a typical cup match 3-2 at the Vetch. It was after that game that commentators in the media and on Swansea's streets began mentioning the greater strength of purpose of the side. No one needed to look far for the inspiration for that change. Manager Yorath had not exactly played the game like a fairy. Apart from the win over WBA, it was encouraging for all concerned that the gate (8,792) was as large as it was. When that number was added to the 9,590 which had watched the match with Leicester City, the directors must have interpreted it as an indication that the crowd-pulling potential of successful football at the Vetch remained undiminished.

Off the field, chairman Sharpe had laid down the dictum: 'It [the insolvency] must never happen again.' That remained the basis of his philosophy throughout his years at the Vetch. Sharpe formed a small

Terry Phelan

board, consisting of himself, Glyn Hammond and dyed-in-the-wool Swans supporter, local businessman, Mal Griffiths. Harry Hyde, another Swansea businessman, whose company was to sponsor the Swans, joined them after a short while. However, it is fair to say that the chairman's dedication to his dictum (and to the club), coupled with his natural style of management, meant that he dealt with all key issues in his own inimitable way. Rightly or wrongly he was nothing but consistent in his approach. Bank managers dealing with newly resurrected business are not known for their liberal loan policies, and like Trevor Morris before him, Doug Sharpe was determined to balance the books.

In January, a controversy arose which concerned the chairman and his colleagues as much as it did the now-buoyant fans. After he had earned his second 'Manager of the Month' award in the first month of 1987, Bradford City tried to entice Terry Yorath from the Vetch. With the side in second place in the table and home gates beginning to build, losing a successful manager was the last thing which the Swansea board wished to happen. In the event, after a long talk with his manager, the chairman announced that Terry Yorath was staying at the Vetch. At that, everyone who followed the club was relieved, particularly when the manager went out of his way to say that he was determined to gain

promotion for the club. In due course, he was to fulfill that promise, but not at that time. Meanwhile, Bradford City withdrew from the scene to bide their time, but as time would tell, the predators would come again.

In an end-of-the-season interview, Terry Yorath, discussing his disappointment at not having gained promotion, cited his captain's knee injury as a major factor. Dudley Lewis sustained the injury early in February and, without him in the side, the defensive unit did not function as well and the whole side lost confidence. It was a 1-4 defeat at Aldershot during Lewis's absence which brought everyone at the Vetch back to earth. After this match, which took place on the last day of February, the Swans slipped to fourth place in the table. By then, Terry Yorath had used the loan market on two further occasions. One consequence of this was that, after the heavy defeat in Hampshire, Yorath selected himself for an away game with Wolves at Molyneux. There, after a hard-fought first half, the home side led by the only goal of the game, but, sadly, the Wolves scored three more in the last fifteen minutes. Eight goals conceded in just two matches was hardly promotion form. Then, after the next three matches were lost, the side slipped to eleventh. Somehow, the confidence and fluidity of the first half of the season had evaporated.

A problem which the management had to face in March did not help matters either. The Swans were due to play Rochdale away, but during the week before the match, a virus swept the Vetch and affected several players. When this was coupled with an unusually large injury list, Yorath found himself with just ten players including himself. Because of this, the Swans asked for the game to be postponed but the league refused. Consequently, when the Swans felt unable to travel to Lancashire and postponed the fixture themselves, they were fined three points and dropped five places in the table. Later in the season, chairman Sharpe and the manager successfully appealed against the decision and the points were restored. By then, though, coupled with the team's loss of form at the time of the fine, the original judgement proved to be psychologically damaging.

The Swans' squad for 1987-88.
Back row, left to right: Joe Allon, Phil Williams, Chris Harrison, Keri Andrews, Alan Davies.
Middle: Paul Raynor, David Hough, Alan Knill, Michael Hughes, Andrew Melville,
Jason Ball, Ian Love, Ron Walton (Coach). Seated: Sean McCarthy,
Terry Yorath (Manager), Dudley Lewis, Tommy Hutchinson, Colin Pascoe.

Although the side's failure to gain promotion after such a fine start disappointed the fans in Swansea, they, Yorath and the Swans board could look back on a season in which there had been some success. The side had been in the top three for the bulk of the campaign and had finished a respectable twelfth. Even the latter was a significant improvement on the previous four seasons, when the Swans ended their campaigns in the bottom four places in the table. Several youngsters had established themselves in the side, not the least of whom were McCarthy and Pascoe, who led the scoring with 14 and 11 goals respectively. Both were thought to have good futures. The club had done reasonably well in the FA Cup, losing by the only goal of the game at Hull in the fourth round, but only, it was reported, because of the brilliance of the home goalkeeper. Then, as importantly, chairman Sharpe had kept a tight rein on costs, which was necessary to satisfy the bank, for despite his efforts there was still a shortfall.

Nonetheless, the chairman had sanctioned the signing of Paul Raynor (£30,000 from Huddersfield) on the eve of the transfer deadline. By then, though, he was aware that Wimbledon were going to sign Terry Phelan for £100,000 during the close-season. Strangely, when that news was made public, it was received with relative equanimity by the long-suffering supporters. Perhaps, the publicity which was given to the demotion of Lincoln City from the Football League (after being beaten at the Vetch in the final game of the season) had made the fans more aware of the blessings they should be counting. There but for the grace of God . . .

1987-88

Terry Yorath spent a busy six weeks between seasons. He trawled his football network for talent and made some signings which were to prove to be significant. He paid Halifax £15,000 for centre-back Alan Knill, took Alan Davies and Joe Allon from Newcastle, and brought home Swansea boy Chris Coleman, who had been on the books of Manchester City. In addition, the manager announced that Lyn 'the leap' Davies was to assist in fitness training. The wags made much of 'leaping up the table' and 'jumping to conclusions', whilst Yorath expressed himself quietly confident about the season ahead.

That confidence appeared to be well-placed when the side won a comfortable victory in the first match of the new season away to Stockport. Was this, mused the optimists among the fans, the start of another promotion campaign? Unfortunately,

after what had been an encouraging start, the form of the side deteriorated and, by the end of September, the team was in twenty-first position in the league table. After the riches of the early part of the previous campaign, this was depressing for the team, management and fans. Not surprisingly, the size of the gates at the Vetch began to reflect that fact. In addition, during this period, the team was ejected from the Littlewoods Cup at the first time of asking, and in due course were to lose at an early stage in the FA Cup. During this depressing period, Yorath shuffled his pack in an endeavour to find a winning blend, and following a fine victory at Tranmere, it appeared that he was working in the right direction.

By the turn of the year, the improved form of the side had resulted in an upward movement to thirteenth place in the table. Such were the encouraging signs that chairman Sharpe felt able to sanction the purchase of Robbie James from Leicester City for £35,000 to help bolster the team's mid-field. No one was surprised when James's 're-debut' was greeted with great enthusiasm by the Vetch crowd and was marked by a fine 3-0 victory over Scarborough. That win took the side to tenth in the table and gave the Swans fans encouragement enough to start talking about reaching a play-off spot.

Spirits were high at the Vetch at that time but, at the end of February came the news which stunned the club and its supporters. Young goalkeeper Mike Hughes had been suffering from headaches and had been referred for a brain scan. This was thought at the time to be merely a cautionary routine but, sadly, the procedure resulted in the young man having to give up the game immediately. It was a body-blow for the popular Hughes who stood at the threshold of what was generally regarded as a very promising career which had been terminated almost before it had begun. Apart from the human tragedy so evident in the situation, without a suitable deputy in reserve, Yorath was faced with the task of finding a new goalkeeper at short notice. His solution to the problem was to sign Peter Guthrie on loan from Tottenham until the end of the season. The young man was to find himself taking part in several nail-biting matches before returning to London.

March ended for the Swans with an away win at Torquay. It was a result which lifted the team to fifth place in the table, and which provoked much discussion in Swansea about the possibility of going up automatically. That was asking a great deal but, after the relatively poor start which had been made by the team, the situation was ready fodder for the optimists. Immediately prior to that match at Torquay, just before the transfer deadline, manager Yorath agreed to sell Colin Pascoe to Sunderland for £70,000 and brought in Peter Bodak from Crewe for £5,000. Whilst there was disappointment among the fans at losing yet another young star, there seemed by then to be an almost resigned acceptance of the fact that better players had to be sold in order to keep the club in a financially secure position. There were those who suggested that this was because the trauma of the club's insolvency was still fresh in the minds of those who supported the Swans. What was never in doubt was that that was certainly the case with the chairman!

At that stage of the season, the departed Pascoe was the club's leading scorer with 13 goals and Joe Allon was second with 11, Robbie James was running the midfield and Alan Davies was in fine form just behind the front two. All in all, despite the loss of Pascoe, up to Easter the team was playing well and results were going their way. Inexplicably, from the match which followed that of Easter Monday the side seemed to lose its ability to score enough goals. As a result, the Swans lost the next three games and drew the fourth. In a very congested league table, this sequence resulted in the Swans sinking to tenth. Happily, with Tommy Hutchison back to lend the side valuable experience, the last two matches in the league schedule were both won: the Swans were in the play-offs.

At that time, both the semi-final and the final of the play-off competition were organised on a two-leg basis, each side playing away and at home. The Swans opponents in the semi-final were Rotherham United and two hard-fought games

Sean McCarthy celebrates after scoring against Torquay in the play-offs.

ensued, with the Vetch men progressing to the final on the back of an aggregate score of 2-1. The other finalists proved to be Torquay United, and after a fine 2-1 victory at the Vetch, the Swans travelled to Plainmoor for the second leg. There, in torrential rain, a nerve tingling match was played out. With Torquay throwing everything at the Swans defence and clawing back an early two goal lead, the outcome was uncertain right up until the last minute. Indeed, such was the tension that, fifteen minutes from the end, Vetch Field stadium manager, Harold Woolacott, left his seat and went into the Torquay guest room in order to settle his nerves. Many more might have wished they could have

Swans captain, Robbie James, holding the front page of the 'Evening Post' announcing the club's promotion.

joined him, but stayed to suffer as the home side strove to pull back the Swansea lead. Happily for the visiting supporters, the Swans held out and the final whistle was received with ecstatic relief by the handful of their fans who had been allowed to see the match. (The local police had insisted on no more than 1,000 Swansea supporters being in attendance.) Promotion had replaced relegation, joy had succeeded gloom and the whole of city could hold its head up high. Perhaps it was then that many Swanseaites first realised what saving the club had meant to the very soul of the city.

Not surprisingly, this time, Terry Yorath's end-of-the-season interview with the *Post* was extremely positive. The manager said that he intended to build upon the success of the previous season and he praised his players and supporters for their efforts throughout the campaign. Alan Knill, as Yorath pointed out, had done sterling work and had been ever-present; Alan Davies had played 42 games and had been selected for the Division Four side by his fellow professionals; and Sean McCarthy had scored important goals, particularly during the play-offs. Unfortunately, Plymouth Argyle were impressed by McCarthy's form and in July, they paid the Swans £50,000 for his services.

Another development in the month before the season ended involved Terry Yorath being appointed as part-time manager of Wales. The appointment covered three friendly matches and the

The Swans' squad for 1988-89.

Back row, left to right: R. Walton, J. Allon, D. Hough, I. Love, A. Melville, Lee Jones, A. Knill, C. Coleman, D. Lewis, D. D'Auria, K. Davey.
Front: A. Davies, B. Wade, S. Thornber, T. Hutchison, R. James, T. Yorath, P. Bodak, P. Raynor, I. Marsh.

Swansea man felt that he could handle this extra work and wanted to try. For his part, Doug Sharpe was reluctant to have his manager distracted by doing another job, but did not wish to stand in his way. Unfortunately, Sharpe was to be proved right. The arrangement was unworkable and, in due course was to result in acrimony.

1988-89

This last full season of the decade was to provide the Vetch board with an unwanted problem. During this season they were to find that they could add 'football administration' to the adage: 'all is fair in love and war'. In February 1989, Terry Yorath walked out of the Vetch Field to join Bradford City as their manager. Since, at the time, Yorath had six months of his Swansea contract to run, the Swansea men arranged for an appropriate injunction to be served on the Yorkshire club. However, two weeks later, after much discussion and professional advice, the board concluded that further legal action could be counterproductive. As a consequence of this, the injunction was lifted and it was accepted that Terry Yorath was *de facto* a Bradford City employee. Given the improvements which the

Welsh international had brought about at the Vetch, this insight was as sobering as the circumstances surrounding his defection. For his part, Yorath told the media that 'This is not about money, I want to be near my family.'

> **In February 1989 Bradford City enticed Terry Yorath away from the Vetch with six months of his contract there still to run.**

In July, when both Yorath and Sharpe believed they were about to embark upon another season together, the manager worked hard to strengthen the squad. Still without a goalkeeper, he arranged for Rhys Wilmot to come to the Vetch on loan from Arsenal and for Dean Holdsworth to join from Crystal Palace on the same basis. Fees were paid for Brian Wade, a forward from Swindon (£10,000 plus a further £5,000 after a given number of matches), and Steve Thornber, a £10,000 purchase from Halifax. At the time, Yorath believed that his

squad was good enough to challenge for promotion and, indeed, when he left the Vetch in unhappy circumstances, the side was in fifth position in the table.

In the early part of the season, youngsters Melville and Coleman were benefiting from the presence of goalkeeper Wilmot as well as solid centre-back Alan Knill, and their performances improved game by game. Robbie James was providing the experience in mid-field, while Alan Davies inspired the front men. Such was the quality of their play at this time that, in September, Knill and Davies were selected by Wales while, at the end of the season, young Coleman was given the accolade of being selected by his peers for the Third Division XI.

Results to the turn of the year, at least in the league, reflected this quality, the Swans winning nine and drawing eight of the twenty-one matches played. Only Wolves, Bristol City and Chester beat them. If there was a problem it was that the side was not scoring enough goals. The defence, apart from a 5-2 hammering at the Vetch by Wolverhampton, performed effectively. So much so indeed, that, during October, goalkeeper Wilmot claimed four consecutive 'clean sheets'. Although things did not go quite so well in November, the team, inspired by

Indian Summer performances from veteran Tommy Hutchison, took Wigan's unbeaten home record. In that same month, Rhys Wilmot had to return to Arsenal and twenty-year-old Lee Bracey took over in goal.

In February, once he knew that Terry Yorath was leaving, Doug Sharpe scoured his football network to find a successor and, within three weeks had appointed Ian Evans. The new man, who had been assistant to Steve Coppell at Crystal Palace, did not have any experience as manager of a Football League club, but was well thought of in the game. Tommy Hutchison, who had filled the gap until Evans arrived, reverted to player-coach with warm words of praise from his chairman. On his arrival, one of the first tasks which faced the new man was to agree with his chairman that a bid of £200,000 by Reading for Chris Coleman should be rejected. Both men believed that the player was worth more. They were to be proved to be right.

Despite the best efforts of the new manager, the second half of the season proved to be much like the first, except that fewer goals were scored by the Swans, and more matches were lost (many by a single goal). Despite Lee Bracey's lack of experience in goal, the defence continued to do well. During this period, the letters in the *Post* from supporters pleaded for the management to buy 'someone who can put the ball into the net'. The *crie de coeur* did not go unnoticed, but, like previous and subsequent managements, Ian Evans and Doug Sharpe were not in possession of a divining fork to point them to such a gem.

However, it was not for the want of trying. During the season, the management brought in several men to try to sharpen the side's strike power. David Puckett came from Bournemouth on a month's loan, and Colin W. West from Chelsea for a similar period. Then, in January, the Swans paid £30,000 for Stewart Phillips from West Bromwich Albion. Unfortunately, none of these men made an impact, and the lack of the side's ability to score enough goals affected confidence and results. The most worrying aspect of this was that the Swans did not register a win in any of their last twelve matches. At that, those who recalled the wisdom

Ian Evans

Tommy Hutchison

of the statisticians, remembered that a winning or losing trend tends to be carried forward from one season to the next. If that were to be the case, then the Swans were destined to struggle during the 1989-90 campaign. There was, however, one more cheerful omen: the Swans beat Kidderminster Harriers 5-0 in the final of the Welsh Cup. This meant that the success-starved supporters at the Vetch could at least look forward to European cup football once again. It was something which they could happily contemplate during the close-season, for they had been without the stimulus of that competition for six long years.

1989-90

With Alan Knill refusing to re-sign, during the close-season manager Evans brought Terry Boyle from Cardiff City to take his place. In addition he arranged for John Solako, a player he knew well, to come to the Vetch on loan from Crystal Palace. Unfortunately, these reinforcements proved to insufficient to meet the needs which were pressing on the young manager. After a run of five matches during which only one game was won, Evans paid Crystal Palace £25,000 for centre-back Mark Harris. The manager believed that the player would 'stiffen his defence'. Unfortunately, on his debut, the converse was true; the side succumbed at home to a rampant Reading team in which Senior, the visitors centre-forward, scored a hat-trick. Harris, who happened to have been born in Reading, was mortified, but promised that it would not occur again. Eight days later, clearly concerned about his defence, Evans went back into the market to take the young, Newport-born player, Roger Freestone on loan from Chelsea. Freestone's stay at the Vetch during that fraught period taught him a great deal. Later, he was to say that he had gained greater confidence from his experiences at the Vetch as well as a warm feeling towards the club. Given the service he was to give to the Swans, Ian Evans's decision to recruit him can be seen to have been extremely valuable.

During the period Freestone was with the club, Ian Evans recruited three players from Scotland, one of whom, like the Chelsea goalkeeper, was to go on to give lengthy service to the Swans. It was at the end of November that Evans made his purchases, spending some £264,000 on Keith Walker and Paul Chalmers from St. Mirren, and John Hughes from Berwick. Chalmers and Hughes were strikers, whilst Walker was a mid-fielder. Since, six weeks earlier, the manager had paid Cardiff £8,000 to bring Alan Curtis back to the Vetch, the supporters were amazed at the extent of this expense. True to form, the cynical amongst them, having in mind chairman Sharpe's 'book-balancing' policy, steeled themselves for news of departures, but no one left the Vetch.

Swans v. Bristol Rovers, April 1989.
Back row, left to right: I. Evans, D. Hough, D. Lewis, C. Coleman, A. Knill, L. Bracey, A. Melville, A. Davies, S. Phillips, K. Davey.
Front: P. Raynor, S. Thornber, R. James, T. Hutchison, C. West.

Although subsequent progress in league football did not reflect this expensive activity, the form of the team in two cup competitions gave supporters something to shout about. At the very least, apart from enriching the club's exchequer, these performances were a happy diversion from the grind of a less-than-successful league schedule (where the team won just once in its first seven matches). In the process, once again, this sequence confirmed the theory of the statisticians that trends tend to get carried from one season to the next. There was, it was true, an improvement in the club's fortunes in October, when five matches out of the seven played were won, but that proved to be a false dawn. In November and December the side won just two of its seven games.

As the season wore on and the situation deteriorated, Evans began to look like a man under pressure. Later, when he was sacked, Doug Sharpe was to say that Ian had 'worked very hard, but nothing he did came right'. Certainly, Evans and the players lost confidence when matters failed to improve, with the season's nadir coming when non-league Merthyr scored three goals without reply to eject the previous season's cup winners from the Welsh

Cup at the first hurdle. 'Dreadful': the single-word headline said it all.

Two months earlier, that scenario would have appeared as unlikely as snow in August. Then, the Swans travelled to Greece to play the country's cup-winners Panathinaikos. On the night, in front of a hostile crowd of 53,500, they found themselves three goals down after only eight minutes of the second half had been played. At that stage it looked like a rout, but the side showed tremendous character in fighting back. Raynor and then Salako scored for the men in white to reduce the deficit to a single goal. The media was full of praise for the side and there was pride in the old borough again.

Prior to the Vetch leg, the received wisdom was that the Greeks would not relish paying at the compact ground. Nor did they, but sadly, neither did the referee. After building up a two-goal lead, the Swans found themselves on the receiving end of at least three dreadful refereeing decisions. In effect, the official gave the Greeks two illicit goals, including an obvious hand ball. The result was that, whilst the Swans scored a third goal in the sixty-fourth minute, the visitors registered their third seven minutes from the end. With the aggregate score 6-5 in their favour,

the Greeks, unjustly, progressed to the next round.

Despite still struggling in the league, the Swans also made reasonable progress in the FA Cup. After beating Kidderminster and Peterborough, Ian Evans's men drew the plum tie of the fourth round of the competition. They were drawn at home against the mighty Liverpool. Grobbelaar, Nicol, Hansen, Beardsley, Rush *et al.* were to visit the Vetch. When they did, the atmosphere generated by a voiciferous crowd of 16,038 (the largest at the Vetch for eight years), saw the Swans hold the Reds to a 0-0 draw. Indeed, had Keith Walker's 'screamer' in the second half been six inches lower, the men from Merseyside would have had to lick their wounds as they made their way home. Every Swan was a hero. Lee Bracey had an outstanding game, and there was much talk about him emulating Noel Dwyer when the sides met again in the replay. Sadly, that was not to be the case: history did not repeat itself and the Swans suffered a humiliating 8-0 defeat.

In the league, after failing to win in January, Ian Evans had a rare moment to relish when the Swans beat Fulham, winning in style 4-2. The hero that day was Paul Chalmers, who scored a hat-trick.

Unfortunately the Scot never matched that performance again, and in the next five matches, the side managed to win just once more. It was following the last of the defeats registered during this period that chairman Sharpe acted. During that game there had been some disturbing scenes as supporters vented their feelings about the form of the team. That was the final straw for the board and, on 13 March, Ian Evans was sacked. The chairman told the media that he had been forced to act because 'if I waited until the end of the season we could be back in the Fourth Division.' Ian Evans departed from the Vetch with dignity. A thoroughly nice man, he had found the transition from assistant to manager too great a barrier to climb, although, as everyone at the Vetch would have agreed, it was not for the want of trying.

Once again, Doug Sharpe found himself in need of a manager, though, this time the fates appeared to have smoothed his path. Three days after Evans had left, it was announced that Terry Yorath was returning to the Vetch. Things had not worked out for him at Bradford and he was available immediately to come back to manage the Swans. Having 'walked out on them', the returning manager said that he was hoping that he could 'win-over the unforgiving faithful'. The truth was that, whilst there was some animosity towards the returning Yorath as a result of his defection, most supporters were simply anxious for success. If Terry Yorath could achieve that goal for a second time they would forgive him almost anything.

Unfortunately, the returning manager did not come back with a magic wand. Money was not available to be spent on strengthening the side, gates and other income streams had

deteriorated and Yorath was obliged to do the best he could with the players who were available to him. Unfortunately, his search for the right blend proved to be elusive and from 17 March, when he was in charge for the first time, until 3 April, his sides failed to win a single game. During that period, despite the number of strikers who were said to be on the Swans' books,

Alan Davies in a Swans away shirt beats an Orient defender.

for the second time that season the team failed to score in four successive matches. By that time, the threat of relegation hung over the Vetch like a Damoclesian sword.

At the start of April, though, the beleaguered manager achieved some success. Walsall, Cardiff City and Wigan were all beaten with something to spare, but the team could not maintain that momentum. Only one point was picked up from the next three games. Once again, the Swans were in the relegation zone. In the final analysis, in order to avoid demotion, the team needed at least one point from a home match with Bolton. Since Bolton also needed a point to achieve a play-off place, those who were at the Vetch that day came in expectation of a challenging game. Was this to be another Bristol City match with tingling nerves stretched to the limit? Unfortunately, the council's safety committee had seen fit to limit the gate to under six thousand, which was a blow to the club's supporters and to its finances. Nevertheless, depleted as they were, the home

fans gave the Swans every encouragement, which was reflected in the volume and intensity of their support. The roar which greeted the sound of the final whistle said it all. With honours having been even at the end of the match, both sides had achieved their goal. For the Swans this meant that they were still members of the Third Division.

Many supporters that day seemed almost reluctant to leave the ground. Clearly, they were delighted that their club had avoided relegation, but there were those who reflected upon the fact that they had seen Alan Curtis play his last match. 'Curt', who had been a veritable icon at the Vetch had finally hung up his boots. There was another farewell, too. Harold Woolacott, that prince of groundsmen, also announced his retirement. Happily, ten years on, both are still connected with the club, 'Curt' as assistant manager to John Hollins, and Harold, who is always there on match days.

When the dust settled, there was much for the management at the Vetch to consider. There were several problems to be addressed, not the least of which concerned scoring goals. The leading goal scorer at the end of the campaign was Paul Raynor with just six. Together with 1983-4 and 1985-6 it was the lowest leading total ever recorded. Similarly, the team's total score (45) was one of the lowest in the club's history. On the financial front, gates had been badly affected and were fifteen per cent lower than for the previous campaign. Then, of Ian Evans's expensive signings, only Keith Walker looked as if he would fulfil the promise of his fee. The situation in which the club found itself did not augur well for the future.

Swansea City FC Season 1986/87 Division 4

#	Date	V	Opponents	Score	Scorers	Att	Hughes M	Harrison C	Phelan T	Lewis D	Melville A	Emmanuel G	Hutchison T	Randall C	Love I	Pascoe C	Andrews K	Hough D	McCarthy S	French N	Williams P	Stevenson N	Simmonds L	Atkinson P	Lovell S	Kean S	Yorath T	Raynor P	Davey S
1	Aug-23	H	Stockport County	3 0	Pascoe 2, Love	4,774	1	2	3	4	5	6	7	8	9	10	11												
2	Aug-30	A	Preston N E	1 2	McCarthy	4,362	1	2	3	4	5	6		8*	9	10	11	7	12										
3	Sep-06	H	Orient	4 1	Harrison 2(2 pens), Melville, Love	4,935	1	2	3	4	5	6	12		9	10	11*	7	8										
4	Sep-12	A	Southend United	2 1	Harrison(pen), McCarthy	3,444	1	2	3	4	5	6	11		9	10		7	8										
5	Sep-16	A	Burnley	1 1	McCarthy	2,266	1	2	3	4	5	6	11	12	9	10		7	8*										
6	Sep-20	H	Northampton Town	2 1	McCarthy, Love	6,902	1	2	3	4	5	6	11		9	10		7	8										
7	Sep-27	A	Crewe Alex	1 1	Pascoe	1,941	1	2	3	4	5	6	11		9	10		7	8										
8	Sep-30	H	Aldershot	2 1	Hough, French	6,404	1	2	3	4	5	6	11		9	10		7	8*	12									
9	Oct-04	A	Halifax Town	0 1		1,003	1	2	3	4	5	6	11		9			7	8						10*	12			
10	Oct-11	H	Scunthorpe United	1 2	Harrison (pen)	5,412	1	2	3	4	5	6	11		9	10		7	8*	12									
11	Oct-18	H	Wolverhampton W	1 0	Emmanuel	5,795	1	2	3	4	5	6	11			10*		7	8		12			9					
12	Oct-22	A	Peterborough Utd	1 1	Harrison (pen)	2,301	1	2	3	4	5	6	11			10		7	8					9					
13	Oct-25	A	Torquay United	5 3	Harrison(pen), Melville, Hough, McCarthy 2	1,774	1	2	3	4	5	6	11			10		7	8					9					
14	Nov-01	H	Rochdale	1 0	Simmonds	5,612	1	2	3	4	5	6	11			10		7*	8				12	9					
15	Nov-04	H	Cambridge United	2 0	Harrison, Pascoe	5,688	1	2	3	4		6	11			10		7	8			5		9					
16	Nov-08	A	Tranmere Rovers	1 1	French	1,800	1	2	3	4			11					10	7*	8	12	6	5	9					
17	Nov-22	H	Hartlepool United	1 0	McCarthy	4,420	1	2	3	4	5	6	11		9				8			10		7					
18	Nov-29	A	Wrexham	0 0		4,909	1	2	3	4	5	6	11		9*			7	8			10		12					
19	Dec-13	A	Lincoln City	0 4		1,988	1	8	3	4	5	6	11		9	10		7*				2		12					
20	Dec-20	H	Colchester United	1 2	McCarthy (pen)	4,515	1	2	3	4	5	6			9	10		11*	8		12			7					
21	Dec-26	A	Cardiff City	0 0		11,505	1	2	3	4	5	6	11		9*	10			8		12			7					
22	Dec-27	A	Hereford United	1 3	Pascoe	6,274	1	2	3	4	5	6*	11			10			8		12	9		7					
23	Jan-01	H	Exeter City	1 0	Andrews	6,057	1	2	3	4	5	6	11			10	9*		8		12			7					
24	Jan-03	A	Hartlepool United	1 1	Atkinson	1,814	1	2	3	4	5	6	11			10	9		8					7					
25	Jan-17	H	Preston N E	1 1	Pascoe	7,677	1	2	3	4	5	6	11			10			8			9		7					
26	Jan-24	A	Orient	4 1	Pascoe, McCarthy 2, Emmanuel	2,605	1	2	3	4	5	6	11			10			8			9		7					
27	Jan-31	H	Southend United	1 0	Melville	6,968	1	2	3	4	5	6	7			10	11		8			9							
28	Feb-06	H	Burnley	2 2	Pascoe, Lovell	6,015	1	2	3		5	6	7			10	12	4	8		11*				9				
29	Feb-14	A	Northampton Town	1 0	Pascoe	8,288	1	2	3		5	6	11			10	12	4	8		7				9*				
30	Feb-21	H	Crewe Alex	1 1	McCarthy (pen)	5,050	1	2	3		5	6	11		9*	10		4	8		7							12	
31	Feb-28	A	Aldershot	0 1	Pascoe	2,592	1	2	3		5	6	11		9*	10		4	8			12						7	
32	Mar-14	A	Wolverhampton W	0 4		7,695	1	2	3			6	11			10		4	8		12	5				9*		7	
33	Mar-17	H	Peterborough Utd	0 1		4,168	1	2	3	4*	5	6	11			10		12	7			8		9					
34	Mar-21	A	Scunthorpe United	2 3	McCarthy 2	1,590	1	2	3		5	6	11		9*	10		7	8		12			4					
35	Mar-29	H	Halifax Town	0 2		3,962	1	2	3		5	6	11			10		12	8					4	7			9*	
36	Apr-03	H	Tranmere Rovers	2 0	Hough, Andrews	3,001	1	2	3		5					10		11	7	8	12			4	6*			9	
37	Apr-07	H	Torquay United	0 1		3,259	1	2			5							3	7	8	10			4	6	11*		9	12
38	Apr-11	A	Cambridge United	0 1		2,552	1	2	3		5	6				10		11*	12		8			4	7			9	
39	Apr-18	A	Exeter City	2 2	Pascoe, Raynor	2,330	1	2	3		5	7	11			10			8					4	6			9	
40	Apr-20	H	Cardiff City	2 0	Atkinson, O/Goal	6,653	1	2	3	4		7	11			10			8			5		6				9	
41	Apr-24	A	Colchester United	1 2	Atkinson	3,323	1	2	3	4		7	11		10*	12			8			5		6				9	
42	Apr-27	A	Stockport County	1 3	McCarthy	2,216	1	2	3	4		7	11		10	12			8			5		6*				9	
43	Apr-29	A	Rochdale	0 2		2,203	1	2	3	4	5	7	11		10				8			12		6*				9	
44	May-02	A	Wrexham	0 3		3,134	1	2	3	4	5	7	11		10				8					6				9	
45	May-04	A	Hereford United	0 2		2,474	1	2	3	4	5	7	11		10				8					6				9	
46	May-09	H	Lincoln City	2 0	Hutchison, Williams	2,544	1	2	3	4	5	7	11		10				8*		12			6				9	
	Apps						46	46	45	32	42	44	40	2	15	41	14	27	43	2	12	12	7	18	2	3	1	12	0
	Subs													1	1		3	4		1	10	4	3	1		1			1
	Gls							7			3	2	1		3	11	2	3	14	2	1	1		3	1			1	

#	Date	V	Opponents	Score	Scorers	Att	Hughes M	Harrison C	Phelan T	Lewis D	Melville A	Emmanuel G	Hutchison T	Randall C	Love I	Pascoe C	Andrews K	Hough D	McCarthy S	French N	Williams P	Stevenson N	Simmonds L	Atkinson P	Lovell S	Kean S	Yorath T	Raynor P	Davey S
1	Aug-27	A	Hereford Utd, L C 1-1	3 3	Andrews, French, Harrison (pen)	2,604	1	2	3	4	5	6	7*	8	9	10	11				12								
2	Sep-02	H	Hereford Utd, L C 1-2	5 1	McCarthy 2, Hough, Pascoe, Harrison	3,870	1	2	3	4	5	6			9	10	11	7	8										
3	Sep-23	H	Leicester City, L C 2-1	0 2		9,500	1	2	3	4	5	6	11		9	10*		7	8		12								
4	Oct-08	A	Leicester City, L C 2-2	2 4	Harrison, McCarthy	5,884	1	2	3	4	5	6	11		9			7	8		12			10*					
5	Nov-11	H	Newport County WC-3	1 3	Stevenson	4,756	1	2	3	4	5		11					7*	8		12	10	6	9					
6	Nov-15	A	Wealdstone, FAC-1	1 1	Williams	2,576	1	2	3	4		6	11					12	7	8	9*	10	5						
7	Nov-24	H	Wealdstone, FAC-1 Rep	4 1	Williams, Hough, McCarthy, Hutchison	3,031	1	2	3	4	5	6	11		9			7	8			10							
8	Dec-02	A	Torquay United, FRT 1	0 0		601	1	2	3	4	5	6	11		9"			7*			12			10	13	8			
9	Dec-06	H	Slough, FAC 2	3 0	Pascoe, McCarthy (pen), Hutchison	4,819	1	2	3	4	5	6	11		9	10			8		7								
10	Dec-09	H	Walsall, FRT 1	3 0	Love, Emmanuel, Pascoe	2,909	1	2	3	4	5	6	11		9	10		7	8		12								
11	Jan-10	H	WBA, FAC 3	3 2	McCarthy 2, Melville	8,792	1	2	3	4	5	6	11		9	10			8		7								
12	Jan-26	A	Aldershot, FRT 2	0 2		1,198	1	2	3	4	5	6	7			8	11*		9		12	10							
13	Feb-03	H	Hull City, FAC 4	0 1		8,853	1	2	3	4*	5	6	7			10	11	12	8		9								

Swansea City FC Season 1987/88   Division 4

#	Date	V	Opponents	Score	Scorers	Att	Hughes M	Harrison C	Coleman C	Melville A	Knill A	Davies A	Williams P	McCarthy S	Raynor P	Pascoe C	Hutchison T	Hough D	Allon J	Andrews K	D'Auria D	Emmanuel G	Lewis D	Marsh I	Lewis J	James R	Davey S	Love I	Guthrie P	Bodak P
1	Aug-18	A	Stockport County	2 0	Raynor, McCarthy	2,482	1	2*	3	4	5	6	7	8	9	10	11"	12	14											
2	Aug-22	H	Exeter City	0 2		5,557	1		3	4	5	6	7	8	9	10		2	11*	12										
3	Aug-29	A	Cardiff City	0 1		6,010	1		3*	4	5	6	7	12	9	10		2	8	11										
4	Aug-31	H	Hartlepool United	2 1	Pascoe, McCarthy	3,569	1		3	4	5	6	7"	12	9	10		2	8*	11	14									
5	Sep-05	A	Burnley	0 1		4,778	1	2	3	4	5	6	7	8	9	10		12		11*										
6	Sep-12	H	Hereford United	3 0	McCarthy, Pascoe 2	3,794	1	2	3	4	5	6	7	8	9	10							11							
7	Sep-16	A	Halifax Town	1 3	Raynor	1,236	1	2	3*	4	5	6	7	8	9	10		12		14		11"								
8	Sep-19	A	Scarborough	0 2		3,033	1	2		4	5	7	3	8	9"	10		12	14	11*		6								
9	Sep-26	H	Crewe Alexandra	2 4	Williams, Pascoe	3,832	1	2		4	5		7	12	8	10				9*		6			3	11				
10	Sep-29	A	Colchester United	1 2	Raynor(pen)	1,140	1	2	3	4	5		7	8"	9	10		12		14		6	11*							
11	Oct-03	H	Cambridge United	1 1	Melville	3,378	1	2	3	4	5	6	7		9	10			8*	12	11	6								
12	Oct-10	A	Wrexham	2 1	Harrison(pen), Allon	3,741	1	2	3	4	5		7			10			8	9	11	6								
13	Oct-17	H	Newport County	1 2	Allon	3,739	1	2"	3	4	5		8			10	7	12	9	11*	14	6								
14	Oct-20	A	Tranmere Rovers	2 1	Raynor, Allon	2,210	1		3	4	5	7		8*	10	11		2	9		12	6								
15	Oct-24	H	Leyton Orient	3 0	Allon, Pascoe, Davies	3,895	1		3	4	5	7		8	10			2	9	11*	12	6								
16	Oct-31	A	Bolton Wanderers	1 1	Allon	4,607	1		3	4	5	7	12	8	10			2	9*			6			11					
17	Nov-03	H	Wolverhampton W	1 2	Allon	5,293	1		3	4	5	7	12	8*	10			2	9			6			11					
18	Nov-07	A	Rochdale	3 2	Pascoe 2, McCarthy	1,243	1		3	4	5	7		12	8	10		2	9			6*			11					
19	Nov-21	H	Peterborough Utd.	2 1	Melville, Pascoe	4,033	1		3	4	5	7	12	8	10			2	9			6			11*					
20	Nov-28	A	Scunthorpe United	2 1	Raynor, Allon	2,309	1		3	4	5	7		8	10			2	9			6			11					
21	Dec-12	H	Carlisle United	3 1	Melville, Allon 2	3,876	1		3	4	5	7		8	10			2	9	11		6								
22	Dec-19	A	Darlington	0 2		1,726	1	12	3*	4	5	7		8	10			2	9			6			11					
23	Dec-26	A	Crewe Alexandra	2 2	Melville, Pascoe	2,976	1	2	3	4	5	7		8*	10				9	12		6			11					
24	Dec-28	H	Torquay United	1 1	Pascoe	6,108	1	2	3	4	5	7				12			9	8		6			11*					
25	Jan-01	H	Cardiff City	2 2	Allon, Raynor	10,360	1	2	12	4	5	7		8	10				9	11		6				3*				
26	Jan-02	A	Hereford United	0 0		3,504	1	2	3	4	5	7		8	10				9	11		6								
27	Jan-09	A	Exeter City	1 3	Allon	2,225	1	2	3	4	5	7	12	8	10				9	11*		6								
28	Jan-16	H	Scarborough	3 0	Raynor, Pascoe, Andrews	4,366	1	2			5	7		8	10					11			4		3	6		9		
29	Jan-23	H	Halifax Town	1 1	Pascoe	5,064	1	2			5	7*		8	10			12		11			4		3	6		9		
30	Jan-30	A	Hartlepool United	2 0	James, Love	2,092	1	2	11		5	7		8						12			4		3	6		9*	10	
31	Feb-06	H	Burnley	0 0		3,498	1	2	11		5	7		8						10			4		3*	6		9	12	
32	Feb-19	H	Stockport County	1 1	Melville	4,405	1	2		14	5	7	12	10	8				9*				4	11"	3	6				
33	Feb-27	A	Cambridge United	3 0	Harrison, Love, Lewis J	2,080		2			5	7		12	8	10			9"			12	4		3	6*		11	1	
34	Mar-01	H	Colchester United	1 2	Love	4,011		2			5	7		9*	8	10						12	4		3	6		11	1	
35	Mar-05	A	Newport County	2 1	McCarthy(pen), Pascoe	2,235		2		14	5"	7		12	8	10					9		4		3	6		11*	1	
36	Mar-12	A	Wrexham	2 1	Love, James	1,916		2			5	7		9	8	10							4		3	6		11	1	
37	Mar-18	H	Bolton Wanderers	1 0	Love	3,980		2		12	5	7		9*	8	10							4		3	6		11	1	
38	Mar-26	A	Leyton Orient	0 3		3,390		2		12	5	7		9*	8						14		4		3	6		11"	1	10
39	Mar-29	A	Torquay United	1 0	Davies	3,037		2			5	7		9	8								4		3	6		11	1	10
40	Apr-02	H	Rochdale	0 3		5,367		2		12	5	7		9"	8*						14		4		3	6		11	1	10
41	Apr-04	A	Peterborough Utd.	1 0	Allon	3,360		2			5	7		8					9			12	4		3	6		11	1	10*
42	Apr-09	H	Tranmere Rovers	1 2	James(pen)	4,104		2		14	5	7		12	8				9				4		3"	6		11*	1	10
43	Apr-23	A	Wolverhampton W	0 2		12,344			3	4	5	7		12	8			14	9*				2		10"	6			1	11
44	Apr-30	H	Scunthorpe United	1 1	McCarthy	3,482		2	3	4	5	6		9	8		11					12				10			1	7*
45	May-02	A	Carlisle United	1 0	Knill	1,854		2	3	4	5	7		9*	8		11					12				6			1	10
46	May-07	H	Darlington	3 0	Davies, McCarthy 2 (1 pen)	4,071		2	3	4	5	7		9	10*		8					12				6			1	11
					Apps		32	34	29	31	46	42	13	17	43	34	6	14	26	16	0	22	18	1	25	19	4	11	14	9
					Subs			1	1	6				5	8	1		1		6	6	6	4	5				1		
					Gls			2		5	1	3	1	8	7	13			12	1					1	3		5		

#	Date	V	Opponents	Score	Scorers	Att	Hughes M	Harrison C	Coleman C	Melville A	Knill A	Davies A	Williams P	McCarthy S	Raynor P	Pascoe C	Hutchison T	Hough D	Allon J	Andrews K	D'Auria D	Emmanuel G	Lewis D	Marsh I	Lewis J	James R	Davey S	Love I	Guthrie P	Bodak P
1	Aug-18	A	Torquay Utd, LWC 1-1	1 2	Raynor	1,964	1		3	4	5	6	7	8	9	10		2	11											
2	Aug-25	H	Torquay Utd, LWC 1-2	1 1	Raynor	3,803	1		3*	4	5	6	7	14	9	10"	11	2	8	12										
3	Oct-27	H	Wolverhampton W, FRT Pre	1 1	Allon	2,886	1		3	4	5	7		8	10			2	9	11		6								
4	Nov-10	A	Bristol City, FRT Pre	0 2		5,037	1	12	3	4	5	7	14	11	8	10		2*	9			6"								
5	Nov-14	A	Hayes, FAC-1	1 0	Pascoe	2,682	1	12	3*	4	5	7		14	8	10"		2	9			6			11					
6	Nov-25	A	Cwmbrân T, WC-3	4 0	Pascoe, Knill, Raynor, McCarthy	1,098	1		3*	4	5	7	14	12	8	10		2	9			6			11"					
7	Dec-05	A	Leyton Orient, FAC-2	0 2		4,668	1		3	4	5	7		12	8"	10			9	14		6	2*		11					
8	Jan-12	H	Merthyr T, WC-4	0 2		3,604	1	2		4	5	6	3"	8		10			9	7*				14	11		12			
9	May-15	H	Rotherham Utd, P/Off SF 1 leg	1 1	McCarthy	9,148		2	3	4	5	7		9	10		8									6		12	1	11*
10	May-18	A	Rotherham Utd, P/Off SF 2 leg	1 1	McCarthy	5,568		2	3	4	5	7		9	10		8*									6			1	11
11	May-25	H	Torquay Utd, P/Off Final 1 leg	2 1	McCarthy, Love	10,825		2	3	4	5	7		9	10		8									6		12	1	11*
12	May-28	A	Torquay Utd, P/Off Final 2 leg	3 3	Raynor, McCarthy (pen), Davies	4,990		2	3	4	5	7		9	10		11*									6		12		8

Swansea City FC Season 1988/89   Division 3

	Date	V	Opponents	Score	Scorers	Att	Wilmot R	Hough D	Coleman C	Melville A	Knill A	James R	Thornber S	Wade B	Love I	Davies A	Raynor P	Holdsworth D	Hutchison T	Allon J	D'Auria D	Legg A	Bodak P	Lewis D	Davey S	Bracey L	Puckett D	Phillips S	West C	Trick D	Marsh I
1	Aug-27	A	Gillingham	3 2	Knill, James 2 (1pen)	4,437	1	2	3	4	5	6	7	8*	9	10	11	12													
2	Sep-03	H	Bury	1 1	James R	5,141	1	2	3	4	5	6	7		9	10	11*	8	12												
3	Sep-09	A	Southend United	2 0	Raynor, Melville	4,357	1	2	3	4	5	6	7			10	11	8	9												
4	Sep-17	H	Brentford	1 1	Melville	5,015	1	2	3	4	5	6	7*			10	8	9	11"	12	14										
5	Sep-24	H	Wolverhampton W	2 5	Holdsworth, Melville	5,240	1	2	3	4	5	6	7	10	8*		9	12			11										
6	Oct-01	A	Bristol City	0 2		7,786	1	2		4"	5	6	7		12	8					9*	14	3	10	11						
7	Oct-04	H	Bolton Wanderers	1 0	James R	3,253	1	2	3		5	6		12	8						9		4	10	11	7*					
8	Oct-09	A	Aldershot	1 0		2,809	1	2	3	12	5	6			8						9		4	10*	11	7					
9	Oct-15	H	Northampton Town	1 0	D'Auria	4,583	1		3	2	5	6		12	8						9		4	10	11	7*					
10	Oct-22	H	Fulham	2 0	Davies, Hutchison	4,737	1		3	2	5	6	7			8					9		4	10	11						
11	Oct-25	A	Huddersfield Town	1 1	Davies	5,711	1	12	3	2	5	6	7	14		8					9		4*	10*	11						
12	Oct-29	H	Preston NE	1 1	Melville	5,370	1	12	3	2	5		7	10	8*	6					9		4"	14	11						
13	Nov-01	A	Wigan Athletic	2 1	Melville, Hutchison	2,432	1	4	3	2	5	8	7	10		6					9			11							
14	Nov-05	A	Chester City	1 3	Melville	2,263	1	4"	3	2	5	6	7*	8	12	10					9		14	11							
15	Nov-08	H	Mansfield Town	3 1	Wade, Bodak, Davies	3,526	1	4*	3	2	5	6		8	12	10					9		7	11							
16	Nov-12	A	Port Vale	1 2	Melville	6,248	1	4*	3	2	5	8		14	10	12	6				9		7"	11							
17	Nov-26	A	Blackpool	0 0		3,443		4	3	2		8	7	10*	12	6					9			11		1	5				
18	Dec-03	H	Sheff. United	2 2	Wade, Melville	5,676		4	3	2		8	7	10		6					9			11		1	5				
19	Dec-17	H	Chesterfield	2 0	Davies, Bodak	3,656		4	3	2	5	8	7		12	6*					9		10	11		1					
20	Dec-26	A	Cardiff City	2 2	Puckett, Davies	10,675		4	3	2	5	8	7			6					9			11		1	10				
21	Jan-31	A	Bristol Rovers	1 1	Puckett	4,803		4	3	2	5	8	7			6					9			11		1	10				
22	Jan-02	H	Reading	2 0	Wade, James	6,772		4	3	2	5	8	7*	12		6					9			11		1	10				
23	Jan-07	H	Notts. County	2 0	James, Wade	5,808		4		2	5	8	12	3		6			10					11		1	7*	9			
24	Jan-14	A	Bury	0 1		2,608		4		2	5	8	7"	3*		6			10		14			11		1	12	9			
25	Jan-21	H	Southend United	2 0	Puckett, Raynor	3,388		4	3	2	5	6			11	8	12		10		14		7"			1	9*				
26	Feb-03	H	Bristol City	1 1	James(pen)	6,523	14*	3	4	5	6	7"	10		8	12			11				2			1		9			
27	Feb-11	A	Bolton Wanderers	0 1		4,178	2*	3	9	5	6			10	8	12			11	7"			4			1		14			
28	Feb-17	H	Aldershot	1 0	Bodak	4,922	2	3	5		6		10		8				11				7	4		1		9			
29	Feb-25	A	Northampton Town	0 1		3,900	2	3	10	5	6			12	8	9			11	7*				4		1					
30	Mar-04	A	Fulham	0 1		4,710	2	3	10	5	6		7"		8	9			11*	14			12	4		1					
31	Mar-11	H	Chester City	1 1	Melville	4,311		3	2	5	6		10		8	9			11				7	4		1					
32	Mar-14	A	Preston NE	1 1	Knill	8,975		3	2	5	6		7		8	9			11				10	4		1					
33	Mar-19	H	Gillingham	3 2	West, Bodak, Raynor	4,252	12	3	2	5	6				8	9	11*						7	4		1			10		
34	Mar-22	H	Huddersfield Town	1 0	James (pen)	4,075	12	3	2	5	6				8	9	11						7*	4		1			10		
35	Mar-25	A	Reading	0 2		4,367	12	3	2	5	6				8	9	11"						7*	4		1			10		
36	Mar-27	A	Cardiff City	1 1	Raynor	9,201	7	3*	2	5	6	12	14		8	9	11							4		1			10"		
37	Apr-01	A	Chesterfield	0 2		3,349	7*	3	2	5	6	12	14		8"	9	11							4		1			10		
38	Apr-04	A	Notts. County	0 1		3,940	7	3	2	5		6	12		8	9	11							4		1			10*		
39	Apr-08	H	Bristol Rovers	1 2	Melville	5,645	12	3	2	5	7	6			8	9*	11							4		1			14	10"	
40	Apr-14	H	Wigan Athletic	1 2	West	3,719	7	3	2	5	6				8	9	11						12	4		1			10*		
41	Apr-22	A	Wolverhampton W	1 1	West	13,921	7*	3	2	5		6			8	9	11						12	4		1			10		
42	Apr-29	H	Port Vale	0 0		4,229		3	2	5		6			8	9	11						7	4		1			10		
43	May-02	A	Mansfield Town	0 0		2,550		3	2	5		6			8	9	11						7	12	4	1			10*		
44	May-06	A	Sheff. United	1 5	James (pen)	15,383	14	3	2	5	12	6			8	9"	11						7*	4		1			10		
45	May-09	A	Brentford	1 1	Hutchison	4,415	14	3"	2	5	12	6			8	9	11						7*	4		1			10		
46	May-13	H	Blackpool	1 2	Raynor	3,494	14	3"	2	5	12	6			8	9	11*						7	4		1			10		
						Apps	16	30	43	44	43	38	27	17	7	42	23	4	42	1	9	6	16	40	3	30	7	4	14	0	0
						Subs		10	1			3	4	8	7		3	1	2	1	5		6				1	2			
						Gls				10	2	9		4		5	5	1	3		2		4				3		3		

	Date	V	Opponents	Score	Scorers	Att	Wilmot R	Hough D	Coleman C	Melville A	Knill A	James R	Thornber S	Wade B	Love I	Davies A	Raynor P	Holdsworth D	Hutchison T	Allon J	D'Auria D	Legg A	Bodak P	Lewis D	Davey S	Bracey L	Puckett D	Phillips S	West C	Trick D	Marsh I
1	Aug-30	A	Cardiff C, LWC 1-1	1 0	Thornber	6,241		2	3	4	5	10	7	8*	9	6	11		12							1					
2	Sep-20	H	Cardiff C, LWC 1-2	0 2		6,987		2	3	4	5	6	7		9	10	11		8*		12					1					
3	Nov-19	H	Northampton T, FAC-1	3 1	Melville, Hutchison, Wade	4,521		2	3	4	5	6	7	8		10			9				11			1					
4	Nov-23	A	Merthyr T, WC-3	3 0	Melville, Wade, Coleman	3,546		2	3	4	5	6	7	8*		10	12		9				11			1					
5	Nov-29	H	Torquay Utd, FRT Pre	1 0	Wade	1,409		4	3			6*	7	14	8	10			9"		12		2			1	11			5	
6	Dec-06	A	Cardiff C, FRT Pre	0 2		2,986		4			5	6	7	8*	12	10			9"				14	2		1	11				3
7	Dec-10	A	Colchester Utd, FAC-2	2 2	Coleman, Melville	2,697		2	3	4	5	8	7	10		6			9*				12	11		1					
8	Dec-13	H	Colchester Utd, FAC-2 Rep	1 3	Wade	4,045		2	3	4	5	8	7"	10"		6			9				12	11		1	14				
9	Jan-17	H	Caersws, WC-4	0 0		2,055		2		5	8	3"	14	10	6				9		4*					1	7	11		12	
10	Jan-31	A	Caersws, WC-4 Rep	2 0	James, Melville	2,000		2	3	4	5	6		8		10"	7		9*		14		11	12		1					
11	Feb-14	A	Wrexham, WC-5	4 1	Bodak 2, Wade, Phillips	2,548		2	3	4	5*	6		9		8			7				10	11		1		12			
12	Apr-11	A	Barry T, WCSF 1-1	1 0	West	1,865		2	3	4	5	6			8	9			7				11			1			10		
13	Apr-18	H	Barry T, WCSF 1-2	3 1	Raynor 3	2,338		12	3	4	5	6	7*	12	8	2			9				11			1			10		
14	May-21	H	Kidderminster H, WCF	5 0	Wade, James, Raynor, Hutchison, Thornber	5,100		3	4	5	6	7	10*		8	2			9				12	11		1					

Swansea City FC Season 1989/90 Division 3

#	Date	V	Opponents	Score	Scorers	Att	Bracey L	Hough D	Coleman C	Melville A	Boyle T	James R	Cobb G	D'Auria D	Raynor P	Salako J	Hutchison T	Phillips S	Trick D	Legg A	Davey S	Harris M	Freestone R	Wade B	Curtis A	Thornber S	Bowen J	Hughes J	Chalmers P	Walker K	Heeps J
1	Aug-19	A	Huddersfield T	0 1		5,775	1	2	3	4	5	6	7	8	9*	10	11	12													
2	Aug-26	H	Northampton T	1 1	Melville	3,495	1	2	3	4	5	6	7		12	10	11*	9		8											
3	Sep-02	A	Birmingham C	0 2		8,071	1	2	3	4	5	6	7	11	12	10		9		8*											
4	Sep-09	H	Chester	2 1	Raynor 2	2,738	1	2	3	4	5	6	7*	8	11	10	9			12											
5	Sep-16	A	Fulham	0 2		4,520	1	2	3	4	5		7	6	11	10	9			8	12										
6	Sep-23	H	Reading	1 6	Phillips	3,511	1		3	4*	5	6			11	10	7	9	12	8		2									
7	Sep-30	A	Notts. County	0 0		3,075		2	3*	4	5	6			11*	10	9			8	12	7	1	14							
8	Oct-07	H	Crewe Alex	3 2	Melville 2, Hutchison	3,847		2	3	4	5	6			11*	10	9					7	1	12	8						
9	Oct-14	A	Bristol C	3 1	Salako 2, Raynor	8,794		2	3	4	5	6			11	10	9	12				7	1		8						
10	Oct-17	A	Bury	2 3	Curtis, Salako	3,336		2	3	4	5	6			11*	10	9	12				7	1		8						
11	Oct-20	H	Tranmere Rovers	1 0	Curtis	3,669		2	3	4	5	6			11	10	9*	12				7	1		8						
12	Oct-25	A	Mansfield T	0 4		2,643		2	3	4	5	6			11*	10	9	12				7	1		8						
13	Oct-28	A	Walsall	1 0	James R	3,469		2	3	4	5	6*				10	9				12	7	1		8	11					
14	Oct-31	H	Rotherham Utd	1 0	Curtis	4,077		2	3	4	5		12				9				11	7	1	10	8	6					
15	Nov-04	A	Bolton W	0 0		6,618		2"	3	4	5						9	12	14		11	7	1	10*	8	6					
16	Nov-11	H	Preston N E	2 1	Melville, Boyle	3,843		2	3	4	5				10		9				11*	7	1	12	8	6					
17	Nov-25	A	Bristol Rovers	0 2		5,623		2	3	4	5				10		11	12		9*		7	1		8"	6		14			
18	Dec-02	H	Blackpool	0 0		4,020		2	3	4					10		11*		5	12		7	1			6		9	8		
19	Dec-16	A	Wigan Ath	0 2		2,034			3	4	5*				10			12	2	11		7	1		8	6		14	9"		
20	Dec-26	H	Cardiff City	0 1		12,244			3	4					10			12	14	2	11*	7	1		8"	6		9		5	
21	Dec-30	H	Brentford	2 1	Coleman, Hughes	4,537	1		3	4					10*					2	11	7			8	6		9	12	5	
22	Jan-01	A	Shrewsbury T	1 1	Chalmers	3,515	1		3	4					10					2	11	7			8	6		9	10	5	
23	Jan-13	A	Northampton T	1 1	Melville	3,799	1		3	4	12									2	11	7			8*	6		9	10	5	
24	Jan-21	H	Huddersfield T	1 3	James R(pen)	4,488	1		3*	4		8			10				14	2	11	7		12		6		9		5"	
25	Jan-26	A	Chester	0 1		2,150		2	3	4	5				10*		11				8	7				6		12	9"	14	1
26	Feb-10	H	Fulham	4 2	Chalmers 3, Hutchison	3,433	1	2"	3	4	5	12			10		11"				8	7				6		14	9		
27	Feb-14	H	Birmingham C	1 1	Harris	3,603	1	2	3	4	5*	12			10		11"				8	7				6		14	9		
28	Feb-17	A	Rotherham Utd	2 3	Davey, Raynor	5,062	1	2	3	4	5	12			10		11				8	7				6			9		
29	Feb-20	A	Reading	1 1	Coleman	4,064	1	2	3	4	5				10		11				8	7			12	6			9		
30	Feb-24	H	Bristol Rovers	0 0		5,664	1	2	3	4	5*				10		11				8	7			12	6			9		
31	Mar-03	A	Leyton Orient	2 0	Hough, Davey	3,628	1	2	3	4	5				10*		11			12	8	7				6		14	9"		
32	Mar-06	A	Notts. County	1 2	Hughes	4,862	1	2	3	4	5				10*		11			12	8	7				6		14	9"		
33	Mar-10	H	Mansfield T	1 0	Legg	3,304	1	2*	3	4	5				10		11			12	8	7				6			9	14	
34	Mar-17	A	Crewe Alex	1 1	Harris	3,898	1		3		5	2			10		11			12	8	7			4*	6			9"	14	
35	Mar-21	H	Bristol C	0 5		6,867	1		3	4	5			12	10*		11	13	2		8"	7				6		9			
36	Mar-23	H	Bury	0 1		3,042	1		3	4	5				10		11	9	2		8*	7				6		12			
37	Mar-30	A	Tranmere Rovers	0 3		8,111	1		3	4	12				10		11*	9	2			7			14	6		8		5"	
38	Apr-03	H	Leyton Orient	0 1		2,582	1		3	4		8					11	9	2	12	7*	5				6		14		10"	
39	Apr-07	H	Walsall	2 0	Raynor, Hughes	2,474	1		3	4		8	2	7				12			11	5				6		9		10	
40	Apr-14	H	Shrewsbury T	0 1		3,386	1		3	2	6		7*	8							11	5			14	12	10	9"		4	
41	Apr-16	A	Cardiff City	2 0	Hughes, Wade	8,350	1	2	3	4		8		7*				12			11	5		14	10	6		9"			
42	Apr-21	H	Wigan Ath	3 0	James R 2(1 pen), Legg	3,141	1	2	3	4		8		7							11	5		12	10*	6		9			
43	Apr-28	A	Preston N E	0 2		6,695	1	2	3	4		8			7						11*	5		12	10*	6		9	14		
44	Apr-30	H	Blackpool	2 2	Raynor, Legg	1842	1	2	3	4		8			7						11*	5		12	14	6		9		10"	
45	May-02	A	Brentford	1 2	Thornber	4950	1	2	3	4		8			7					12	11*			14		6		9		10"	
46	May-05	H	Bolton W	0 0		5,623	1	2	3	4		8			7						11	5			10	6		9			
				Apps			31	32	46	46	27	25	5	6	38	13	31	6	11	20	16	41	14	2	21	34	0	16	13	11	1
				Subs								4		1	2		5	7	3	5	2				9	5		6	3	2	
				Gls				1	2	5	1	4			6	3	2	1		3	2	2			1	3	1	4	4		

#	Date	V	Opponents	Score	Scorers	Att	Bracey L	Hough D	Coleman C	Melville A	Boyle T	James R	Cobb G	D'Auria D	Raynor P	Salako J	Hutchison T	Phillips S	Trick D	Legg A	Davey S	Harris M	Freestone R	Wade B	Curtis A	Thornber S	Bowen J	Hughes J	Chalmers P	Walker K	Heeps J
1	Aug-23	A	Exeter City, LWC 1-1	0 3		2,777	1	2*	3	4	5	6	7	8"	10		11	9	13	12											
2	Aug-29	H	Exeter City, LWC 1-2	1 1	Raynor	1,987	1	2	3	4	5	6	7	8	10			9			11										
3	Sep-13	A	Panathinaikos ECWC 1-1	2 3	Salako, Raynor	53,500	1	2	3	4	5	6	7	8	11	10	9														
4	Sep-27	H	Panathinaikos ECWC 1-2	3 3	Melville 2, James (pen)	8,276	1	2	3	4	5	6			11	10	7	9		8											
5	Nov-07	H	Merthyr, WC-3	0 3		4,153		2	3	4	5						11				9	7	1	10	8	6					
6	Nov-18	A	Kidderminster, FAC-1	3 2	Melville 2, Davey	3,248	1	2	3	4	5				10						9	11		7	8	6					
11	Dec-05	A	Bristol C, L Daf Prelim	1 2	Raynor	3,488		2	3	4					10*		11		5	13		7	1		12	6"		9	8		
7	Dec-09	A	Peterborough, FAC-2	3 1	Chalmers 2, Raynor(pen)	4,175		2	3	4	5				10					2	11	7			8	6		9			
8	Jan-06	H	Liverpool, FAC-3	0 0		16,098	1		3	4										2	11	7			8	6		9	10	5	
9	Jan-09	A	Liverpool, FAC-3Rep	0 8		29,194	1		3	4	12						13			2*	11	7			8"	6		9	10	5	
10	Jan-17	H	Reading, L Daf Prelim	1 2	Trick	1,829	1		3	4		8						12		2	11	7				6		9	10*	5	

Chapter 22

A Scot in Charge

1990-91

In May 1991, at the end of an undistinguished campaign, the Swans were in twentieth position in the league table. By then, Frank Burrows had replaced Terry Yorath as manager and a new chapter in the club's history had begun. Yet, prior to the start of the season, Yorath's position had seemed secure, particularly since he had spent a great deal of money on new men: Jimmy Gilligan (£175,000), Terry Connor (£150,000), and Andy Watson (£45,000). In addition, Alan Davies had been exchanged for Robbie James. Those who left the Vetch included John Hughes, bought by Falkirk for £70,000, and Chris Coleman who, much to Doug Sharpe's annoyance, had been snapped up by Crystal Palace with the fee having to be settled by the arbitration panel. Whilst Sharpe believed that the player was worth £500,000, a figure of £275,000 (plus two tranches of £50,000 after a stated number of games had been played) was handed down. While the chairman was far from happy about the Coleman deal, overall, the supporter in the Swansea street was encouraged by the spate of signings. At least, the board had shown itself willing to back the manager's judgement. Major Reg Pike, who, for several decades, has kept a careful finger on the pulse of Swans followers, told Yorath that 'the town was buzzing', and his terminology for the old borough said something about the warmth of that reaction. Whilst Swansea was a city, 'town', somehow, got to the heart of matter.

There was also a structural change at the Vetch which involved a prominent feature having its roots in the days when Swansea was a town. Because it had been declared unsafe, the old double-decker was being demolished. It was a sad day for many people who had enjoyed watching Swans games from an elevated position which was unique in Wales. In September, the *Sporting*

Jimmy Gilligan

league left much to be desired. The expectations which the transfer activity had promised had not been satisfied and, as often happens in such circumstances, this resulted in greater dissatisfaction among supporters than might have been the case had little money been spent. After five of the club's first ten matches had been lost, the Swans were in seventeenth place in the table. At that point, manager Yorath bought another player, Russell Coughlin from Blackpool, for £30,000, whose arrival coincided with the return of Terry Connor, who had been out for six weeks with a broken arm. Happily, the presence of the duo appeared to make a difference, for, of the next ten matches, only three were lost. Then, at the turn of the year, the team won three games in succession in some style. During this spell, they beat Wigan 4-2 on their own ground and Rotherham 5-0 at the Vetch, gathered ten points from four matches and scored fourteen goals. With the Swans moving up to a mid-table position as a result of these wins, supporters were beginning to believe that Yorath had found the

> *During the close-season the 'double-decker' stand at the Richardson Street end of the Vetch was demolished. It had been the only one of its type in Wales. In its place, the terrace which had been underneath the seated part of the old stand was roofed over.*

Post, in commenting on what many saw as the loss of a popular amenity, and on the reduction in ground capacity which new legislation had forced upon the club, asked the question: 'How long will they [the Swans] stay at the Vetch Field? . . . A possible move to the Morfa Stadium has been on the cards for a while'. At the time of writing, ten years later, that question can be answered at last. Plans for the construction of a new stadium have been drawn up and the processes involved in building it are taking their course. All concerned are determined to ensure that it will have been worth waiting for.

Despite the heavy expenditure on new players, early results in the

right blend. There were some, even, who began talking about getting to a play-off position.

Unfortunately, the revival in form proved to be short-lived. Between 26 January and 15 March the team created a new and unwanted record when it lost nine matches in succession. It was a disastrous series of results which triggered a spate of rumours in Swansea regarding the imminent departure of Terry Yorath. Although, at the beginning of March, Doug Sharpe stated that there was no truth in the stories, he could hardly deny that he had given the matter of replacing his manager some thought. Eventually things came to a head. In the middle of the month, a *Post* headline captured the mood of

The Swans' squad, 1990-91 season.
Back row, left to right: Stephen Jenkins, Des Trick, Keith Walker, James Heeps, Paul Raynor, Lee Bracey, David Hough, Chris Coleman,
Jimmy Gilligan. Middle row: Clive Freeman, Phil Evans, Simon Davey, Mark Kendall, Paul Chalmers, Jason Bowen, Tommy Hutchinson.
Front row: Alan Davies, Steve Thornber, Andy Watson, Mark Harris, Terry Connor, David D'Auria, Andrew Legg.

the time: 'Yorath on the ropes', which was an apt metaphor to describe the situation, for manager and chairman were locked in disagreement. Yorath said that he had been sacked, Sharpe denied it, and the dispute became public. The official announcement from the Vetch was that Yorath had been sent home for a few days rest. To most this was a euphemism for the manager being sacked, but, whatever the truth, it was clear that the partnership had come to an end. Within days Terry Yorath and Tommy Hutchison had departed, and Frank Burrows had been installed as manager. Doug Sharpe had wasted little time in finding a successor.

On his arrival, Frank Burrows was well aware that his job was hardly a sinecure. When he joined, the team was in nineteenth position in the league table and had failed to win one of its last ten matches. Consequently, when the Swans beat Stoke 2-1 at the Vetch and then held Reading to a draw in Berkshire, he and the supporters must have felt that the side had begun to regain a semblance of form.

But then, Wigan came to the Vetch for the next fixture and scored six goals whilst the Swans could manage only one. It was a humiliating defeat and, it was said that, following the

game, the walls of the home dressing-room resounded with scolding Scottish vernacular. Whatever was said had the desired effect for, in the next match, at Rotherham, the team, playing scintillating soccer, beat the home side 3-2. Clearly, at that stage in the season, and having started from a poor position, the manager's key objective was to ensure that Third Division football was played at the Vetch in the 1991-2 season. That he achieved this with three matches to play, allowed him the luxury of giving some of his youngsters an opportunity to show him what they could do. For the last game of the season, Burrows included Stephen Jenkins at full-back, which, for the young Merthyr boy was of particular significance. Jenkins had been told by Terry Yorath that he was surplus to requirements, but Frank Burrows had come to a different conclusion and time was to prove him right. Another youngster on show was Jason Bowen.

The league campaign ended with a run of indifferent results, but the final match of the season lifted everyone's spirits. At the National Stadium in Cardiff, the Swans beat Wrexham to win the Welsh Cup. The silverware was a morale booster for everyone associated with the club. On-loan David Penney was

outstanding that day, and Coleman, Legg and Connor did well. After the match, manager Burrows, in answering questions from the press, made a particular point of praising the absent Jimmy Gilligan, the club's leading scorer, for playing so often during the season when less than fully fit. It was a salute of one old-fashioned professional to another.

1991-92

Having lost Andy Melville before the start of the previous season, Doug Sharpe was disgusted when Crystal Palace 'played the arbitration system' in signing Chris Coleman. Following the pattern of the Melville case, Palace had agreed terms with the player and then offered the Swans a fee less than half their valuation. The chairman's argument was that, by doing this, Palace had, in fact, set a sale figure which greatly favoured them. The Swans had asked for £500,000, Palace had offered £175,000, so the panel, according to Doug Sharpe, would pick a figure somewhere in between. In the event, a fee of £275,000 was agreed with a further £100,000 being paid after the player had appeared a given number of times. Since both Coleman and Melville were subsequently each sold for seven-figure fees, the chairman had a point. In Coleman's case, there was another drawback for the Swans: they were obliged to pay a percentage of the fee to Manchester City, the club from which he came to the Vetch.

Given the extent of the incoming funds, Frank Burrows was allowed some money to spend, and, as the future was to show, he used it well. He bought John Cornforth from Sunderland for £25,000 (with a similar amount being paid after a number of appearances); John Williams and John Ford from non-league Cradley Heath for £5,000 each and, soon after the season started, made Roger Freestone's loan into a transfer, paying Chelsea £45,000 in the process. Each of these players was to give the Vetch club an excellent return on its investment on and off the field. Despite the loss of Coleman, these signings created considerable interest in the city and, as the new season approached there was an air of quiet confidence around the Vetch. Not that the bookmakers agreed; one of them made the Swans favourites for relegation.

Unfortunately, early results appeared to confirm the opinions of the betting fraternity. After five games the Swans had gained just one point and, following the last of these, the side was bottom of the table. This prompted urgent action; the

manager brought Derek Brazil from Manchester United to the Vetch on loan.

He also sold Terry Connor to Bristol City for £175,000 and, in October, let Andy Watson join Carlisle for £45,000. Soon after he added to his loan squad by taking Joey Beauchamp from Oxford United, while Reuben Agboola signed on a free transfer from Sunderland. As before, Frank Burrows had made room for new blood on his terms. In a relatively short while he had transformed his squad.

> **The Swans were the only club in their division not to have a man sent off.**

Two weeks before, supporters had the opportunity to take their minds off problems in the league. In the European Cup Winners' Cup, the Swans were drawn to play Monaco with the first leg taking place at the Vetch. While the Swans were defeated on the night by two goals to nil, they did not disgrace themselves against a side which had considerable European experience and wealthy

backers. Among those who were at the Vetch to support the visitors was Prince Rainier, who made a piece of Vetch Field history by being the first royal head of state to visit the old ground.

As it transpired, the experience gained in the European Cup proved to be invaluable during the following week, when Tottenham Hotspur were beaten at the Vetch in the first leg of the Rumbellows League Cup. Furthermore, the team played fine football, with Gilligan scoring a superb goal two minutes from time. That night was appreciated, too, by deputy chairman Glyn Hammond, who also served as finance director. The gate of 11,406 was about three times that attracted to a league game. Although the Swans were heavily beaten in the away legs of both competitions, Burrows could, at least point to the potential of the side which he was building.

Not that there was much sign of that in league matches. With only three wins from the first fifteen games of the season and with the team languishing near the foot of the table, the result of the next match confounded the critics as well as Swans supporters. The Swans travelled to Bradford and beat the home side 6-4, with John Williams scoring a fine hat-trick. It was an unbelievable result and one which caused the BBC announcer to repeat

Swans' squad, 1991-92.
Back row, standing, left to right: Ron Walton (Youth Team Manager), David Hough, Paul Chalmers, Des Trick, Mark Harris, James Heeps, Lee Bracey, Mark Kendall, Chris Coleman, Keith Walker, Paul Raynor, Paul Williams, Bobby Smith (Assistant Manager), Ken Davey (Physiotherapist). Middle row, sitting: Simon Davey, Steve Thornber, Philip Evans, Russell Coughlin, Frank Burrows (Manager), Clive Freeman, Terry Connor (Captain), Andrew Legg, David Penney. Seated, front: Alan Davies, Jason Bowen, Andy Watson, Stephen Jenkins, David D'Auria.

The Swans' squad, 1992-93.
Back row, left to right: Tony Cullen, Reuben Agboola, Colin Pascoe, Des Lyttle, Russell Coughlin.
Middle: Stephen Jenkins, John Ford, Andy McFarlane, Steve McMahon, Mark Harris, Colin West, Keith Walker.
Front row: Paul Wimbleton, Shaun Chapple, Roger Freestone, John Cornforth, James Heeps, Jason Bowen, Andrew Legg.

the score twice as it clattered through on the teleprinter. Since that victory came a week after the Swans had knocked Cardiff City out of the FA Cup, it did a great deal for morale at the Vetch. Nevertheless, the win did not herald a revival in the league and, at the end of the campaign the Swans were nineteenth in the table. Although this was disappointing, most observers believed that Frank Burrows had made great progress in assembling a side which was devoted to playing attractive football; three players had scored hat-tricks, which demonstrated the potential of the team as an attacking unit, and that despite the fact that Jimmy Gilligan had been absent for almost half the season following a second back operation. Frank Burrows could also point to the best disciplinary record in the Third Division; the Swans were the only club not to have a man sent off.

Overall, those who looked back on what had been an eventful season must have seen it rather like the curate's egg. The final position was disappointing: without Gilligan, very few goals were scored in the last ten matches; the team did not win a single game during this sequence;

and Andy Legg, who had been ever-present, asked for a transfer. Yet, as John Cornforth put it, 'We have been playing some good football and we can build on that next season.' Roger Freestone had had an excellent campaign, John Ford and John Williams had established themselves very quickly in league football, Mark Harris and Keith Walker had developed a fine understanding at the heart of the defence, and young Steve Jenkins had repaid his manager's faith by playing well in over thirty matches in his first season in the Football League. Frank Burrows had reduced the wage bill significantly and had also sold players to a gross value of £650,000 whilst spending less than twenty per cent of that. Although it was revealing to consider the problems and opportunities which lay behind these positive and negative outcomes, they were put into context by a tragic incident which shocked everyone associated with the club. Alan Davies, a popular figure at the Vetch, was found dead in his car. The sobering effect of this inexplicable news served to make whatever problems the club was facing seem trivial. A capable player

and a thoroughly nice man, Davies was to be missed.

1992-93

When the fixture list for the new season was published, the Swans found that they were playing the first match of the campaign away for the sixth time in succession. Clearly, someone had programmed the Football League computer in a way which was hardly equitable. Meantime, Frank Burrows was reaping the reward for the thousands of miles of motorway which he had covered in search of new talent. He signed Des Lyttle from Worcester City for £12,500 and, around the same time, sold John Williams to Coventry for £250,000 – a remarkable profit on the £5,000 which had been paid for the ex-postman just twelve months earlier. A week later, frugal as ever with the club's money, Burrows brought Colin Pascoe back from Sunderland for a three-months loan and signed Colin West from West Bromwich Albion and Andy McFarlane from Portsmouth. West was a free transfer and McFarlane cost £20,000. The club had a new sponsor, too: Action Petroleum was the new name on Swansea shirts.

In August, the *Post* printed an interview with Frank Burrows in which he said, 'The modern supporter wants results rather than good football, but we'll endeavour to supply both.' After the side lost the first game by the only goal of the match, results thereafter appeared to show that the manager was fulfilling his promise. Mansfield Town were the first visitors to the Vetch Field and, after a cautious first half, the flowing football and the victory were sealed, the Swans scoring four without reply. The sole problem for the club was the size of the gate: only 2,792 people saw the match. Next they won a fine match at Wigan and, after thirteen games had been played, the Swans sat at the top of the table. Up to that point they had gained twenty-five points and lost only twice. Frank Burrows had achieved the kind of start which he had wanted. The task now was to build upon that beginning.

Unfortunately, results from then until the end of January were not as good, though no one could complain about the defence. Freestone, Jenkins, Ford, Harris and Walker were a very effective unit at the back; the problem was that the team was not scoring enough goals. One result of this was that, after drawing 0-0 with Bradford City in the middle of January, the Swans had dropped to twelfth in the table with thirty points. To put it another way, they had gained just nine points from twelve matches since they were top. There was some consolation for the board, however: a crowd of 7,220 watched the Vetch fixture with Bolton on 28 December more than double the average for the season.

During the month of January, Frank Burrows moved again to strengthen his strike-force. Former Arsenal man Martin Hayes was signed from Celtic on a free transfer. Since the player had cost the Scottish club £650,000, much was expected of him and, early in his time at the club he endeared himself to supporters by scoring the winning goal in an Autoglas Trophy tie at Ninian Park. A week earlier, the team had won a famous victory in the FA Cup at Oxford. After extra-time in the replay (the teams had drawn at the Vetch) the score stood

at 2-2 and the tie had to be decided on penalties. After Roger Freestone had saved brilliantly from Chris Allen, Keith Walker strode forward to convert the winning kick. Given the less than exciting form of the team in the league, it was a very welcome fillip to all at the Vetch.

In March, after a run of four matches without defeat, the team beat Chester 4-2, with Jason Bowen getting a hat-trick. Since Bowen had given an outstanding performance on Preston's plastic pitch the week before, much was being made of the young man on television, radio and in the newspapers. Answering media questions after the Chester match, manager Burrows said that, if he believed in himself and worked hard, Bowen could 'go all the way'. Although this was encouraging for the Vetch Field faithful, the supporters soon hoisted the 'another one to go' flag on the Vetch Field yardarm. Team performances were also improving, and when Stoke City (the division's leaders) came to Swansea, the best Vetch gate of the season was registered – 8,346. In that game, another Swans starlet, Andy Legg, scored a superb goal to give the Swans the lead, only for the visitors to take control in the second half and snatch the points. Despite this setback, the table was developing in such a way that, if the Swans could put together a sequence of wins, there was a reasonable chance that they might get into the play-offs. After the disappointment of the previous two seasons, all concerned with Vetch Field matters viewed this prospect with some relish.

With eight matches to play and the Swans in eleventh place, the team travelled to Bolton, a club already in contention for a play-off place. Whilst the purists argue that the play-off system is unfair, and that the fourth team in the table should be promoted automatically, there is little doubt that the excitement which the process generates is welcomed by many. Apart from the prospect of promotion for the side which wins the competition, the revenue which is generated for the participating clubs is extremely welcome. There is also the opportunity to play at Wembley Stadium in the final. Particularly for lower-league players, that in itself is justification for the system, for, in most cases, they

would be highly unlikely to appear there on major occasions. Certainly, the squad at the Vetch was extremely motivated by the prospect and, whilst they failed at Bolton, they went on to win their next four matches, scoring ten goals without reply and moving up to fifth. The Swans manager was also relishing the prospect, although he kept his 'We'll take each match as it comes' philosophy for public viewing. As John Burgum put it in the *Post*: 'Frank Burrows may be keeping his own counsel, but his players are doing plenty of talking on the pitch and answering all questions about character and commitment.' The words spoke volumes about the motivating ability of the Swansea manager and, when talking to the press, he took every opportunity to praise the efforts of his players. Unfortunately, one of the bright lights of the side, Jason Bowen, was carried-off in the season's penultimate game and could not take part in the play-off fixtures.

The Swans' opponents in the semi-final were West Bromwich Albion, a side which had beaten the Vetch men 3-0 earlier in the season. Despite that fact, the manager expressed himself confident that his team was good enough to win the tie and the competition. Whilst many felt that to be a bold statement, with 13,917 people at the Vetch for the first leg, the Swans played extremely well to take a two-goal lead. Had they been able to take that advantage to Birmingham for the second leg, Burrows's confidence might have been justified. Unfortunately, in the late stages of the game, West Brom snatched a goal which was to prove crucial. Andy McFarlane, back trying to help the defence, was on the home goal line when a speculative shot hit him on the head and flashed past Roger Freestone in goal. Consequently, the Swans travelled to the Hawthorns with just a single goal lead. It was not enough, although the Swans' cause was hardly helped by the sending off of Colin West, who, after coming on as substitute stamped on an opponent in retaliation and was dismissed from the field. Already two down at that point, the task was too great for the men in white and the home team won the tie 3-2 on aggregate.

At least, the Swans had offered their fans some encouragement and shown them that Frank Burrows's objective of playing winning and attractive football was not a pipe dream. It was natural that all at the Vetch should be disappointed after getting so far, yet there were encouraging points to be drawn from the experiences of the season. Three men had been ever-present: Roger Freestone, Andy Legg and Des Lyttle (the latter in his first season in league football); the club had finished the season in its highest position for several years; and the team was beginning to blend into a fine combination. Sadly, though, one man would not be attempting to break into that side again. Jimmy Gilligan had been forced to give up playing because of his back condition. A fine footballer and a dedicated professional, he was to be missed. When asked about the disappointment of not getting to Wembley, manager Burrows was as philosophical as ever. 'Sometimes football slaps you in the face. We've just got to go out and do better next time.' And they did, though in another context.

1993-94

The Football League computer, once again, sent the Swans on their travels for the first match of the season, this time to York City, where they lost narrowly. There followed three wins in succession which pushed the side into third place in the table. It was the kind of start for which everyone concerned with the Vetch had hoped. The question now was, could the side build upon that promise? Following the team's performance at the end of the previous campaign, for the optimists at least, it seemed very likely that they would.

Before the season started, Frank Burrows had been wheeling and dealing, much to the financial benefit of the club. After Andrew Legg had insisted upon leaving, Notts County signed him, with the fee (£275,000) being agreed by the ubiquitous panel, and Des Lyttle, bought by Burrows for £12,500 only twelve months before, was sold to Nottingham Forest for a record £375,000. In addition, there was a windfall profit from the sale of Andrew Melville for a seven-figure sum – the Swans received £275,000 as the agreed proportion of Oxford's

profit. Russell Coughlin was exchanged for John Hodge, with the Swans paying Exeter £20,000, and another player from the Devon club, Andy Cook, came to the Vetch for a fee of £125,000. There were two other signings by the Swans: Stephen Torpey (another tribunal deal) cost £110,000, with a 'sell-on' clause and Colin Pascoe came back from Sunderland for £120,000.

It is a well-recognised fact in football that, when players leave and others come in their place, it takes time for a team to blend. Consequently, to have made such a good start despite all the changes which had been made was greatly encouraging. Unfortunately, as far as the league was concerned, as the season progressed, the early successes were not reflected in results. By the end of December, the club was in eighteenth place in the division, having won just six of its twenty-one matches and lost nine. Meantime, results in three cup competitions were mixed. In the Coca Cola Cup, after disposing of Bristol City over two legs, in the next round the Swans beat Oldham 2-1 at the Vetch, only to lose 0-2 in Lancashire. However, such was the quality of their football, the Swans were given a standing ovation at the end of the game by the home crowd. Yet, in the following month, a non-league side, Nuneaton Borough, held the Swans to a draw at the Vetch (albeit in dreadful conditions) and had the audacity to win the replay. The Vetch men were more successsful, however, in the Autoglass Trophy. By the end of December the side had progressed to the quarter final of that competition, though, at that stage, most supporters saw it simply as a diversion from the rigours of the league.

An analysis of the results in league and cup for the first half of the campaign showed that the perennial problem of under-achieving football teams – not scoring enough goals – was at the heart of the team's lack-lustre league performance. The Swans had scored twenty-four goals and conceded thirty-two. It was true that Burrows had not been lucky with injuries; for example, both Keith Walker and John Ford had been sidelined for periods of six week. Nevertheless, it was the shortage of goals which was of

greater concern. Steve Torpey, who had announced that he had set himself a target of twenty-five goals, did not score in a league match until the end of November, by which time McFarlane had netted three. Given that strikers thrive on confidence this relatively barren period did little to help matters. Not that the side did not play well on occasions: a superb team effort resulted in the Swans beating Burnley on a cold, damp Tuesday; in a match at Brentford, John Cornforth scored with a twenty-five-yard free kick which would have had the TV pundits drooling had they been there; and, in October, Hull City were well beaten at the Vetch with Andy McFarlane scoring for the second match in succession.

During the first half of the season, Frank Burrows had used his connections to bring several players to the Vetch on loan. Warren Aspinall and Chris Burns came from Portsmouth and, in January, Matthew Rush (West Ham) came to stay for three months and endear himself to the fans. Meantime, Jason Bowen, who finished the previous season as top scorer, was still attracting the attention of other clubs, and as Swans fans gritted their teeth, the player went to Newcastle to train with United. Nothing came of that, but for the supporters, it was an indication that the club's better players were still for sale. From the board's point of view, they could, justifiably, explain that the poor gate income which they were receiving made such sales necessary. Not that there was a great deal of financial information available for the fans since the old annual meetings had been dispensed with. Not surprisingly, the fans did their own sums and, erroneous as they might have been, drew their own conclusions.

With the club in mid-table position for the remainder of the campaign, the focal point of attention began to be the Autoglass Trophy. This competition, which many managers refer to as 'Mickey Mouse', takes on a different aura as the final stages approach. This was certainly the case at the Vetch, where supporters began to dream of a visit to Wembley when the Swans beat Leyton Orient 2-0 on their own ground in February. That victory put the Swans into the regional final which, if the side could win the tie (over two legs), would

The winners celebrate.

mean that they would appear in the final proper. Wembley beckoned, and the supporters, management and team basked in the excitement of that possibility. Wycombe Wanderers were the opponents and, for the home leg, many stay-away fans augmented the gate for the game. They were not disappointed! Playing superb football, the men in white won the match 3-1, which gave them a healthy lead to take to Wycombe for the second leg. There, despite windy conditions and the home side's long-ball game, they were in control for the bulk of the match. Whilst they lost 1-0, the aggregate score was in their favour. Swansea City were to play in the final at Wembley. The joyous Swans fans made themselves heard: 'We're going to Wem-ber-ley, Wem-ber-ley'. Huddersfield Town, the winners of the northern semi-final, were to be their opponents.

On Sunday 24 April 1994, Frank Burrows and John Cornforth led the side out onto the famous turf. The bookmakers were undecided as to which side would win, but, looking for omens, Swans fans noted that, in league competition, the team had beaten the Yorkshire side at the Vetch and drawn in Huddersfield.

The older heads among them, though, would have reminded the others about 1964, when the Swans met Preston in the semi-final of the FA Cup. That season, too, the Vetch men had taken three points of the four which were, then, available from two league matches. The cup, they might have stated wisely, is a different kettle of fish. There was also the problem that Keith Walker had been injured and would be unable to play in the final, Burrows had to draft in Michael Basham into the heart of the defence. The manager also made an unexpected change in the team's forward line. He started the game with Andy McFarlane as principal striker. Later, explaining this decision, the wily Scot claimed that the lanky forward's athleticism was better suited to Wembley's wide-open spaces. Within eight minutes, McFarlane had shown the manager's judgement to be sound, scoring a fine goal to give the Swans the lead. That advantage was retained until a quarter-of-an-hour into the second half when Logan netted for the Yorkshire men. Thereafter, both sides became extremely cautious with the almost inevitable consequence that, after extra-time had been played, the score

still stood at 1-1. Since a result had to be achieved that day, a penalty shoot-out had to take place. The tension in the air as John Cornforth ran in to take the first Swansea penalty was almost audible. Happily for the Swans, Cornforth, Pat Ampadu and Steve Torpey converted effectively, whilst one Huddersfield man hit the bar and Roger Freestone saved the shot from another. Swansea City were the Autoglass Trophy winners for 1994. The team, the fans, the management and the board were delighted and, those who were there will remember the occasion for the rest of their lives. If nothing else, it put Swansea soccer on the map again. The result and the reaction of the whole city of Swansea to the success of its heroes that day, demonstrated the importance of a successful football team to the morale of a town or city. Sociologists have argued that production in a town's factories always improves when the local football team is doing well. Although that research was undertaken when matches were played on Saturdays and there was a day to recover in between, at least there was a joyful air about the city when the Monday dawned.

Swansea City FC Season 1990/91   Division 3

#	Date	V	Opponents	Score	Scorers	Att	Bracey L	Raynor P	Coleman C	Hough D	Harris M	Walker K	Thornber S	Davies A	Gilligan J	Connor T	Legg A	Watson A	Trick D	Chalmers P	D'Auria D	Hutchison T	Freeman C	Davey S	Coughlin R	Honor C	Miller P	Bowen J	Kendall M	Williams P	Penney D	Jenkins S	Chappell S
1	Aug-25	A	Leyton Orient	0 3		4,206	1	2	3	4	5	6*	7	8	9	10	11	12															
2	Sep-01	H	Huddersfield Town	1 0	Gilligan	4,787	1	2	3		5	6	7	8	9	10	11			4													
3	Sep-08	A	Exeter City	0 2		4,719	1	2	3		5	6*	7	8*	9		11	10		4	12	14											
4	Sep-15	H	Brentford	2 2	Davies, Legg	4,127	1	2	3	12	5	6	7	8	9		11		4*	10													
5	Sep-18	H	Bury	1 2	Davies	3,505	1	2	3		5	12	7	8	9		11	6	4	10*													
6	Sep-22	A	Bradford City	1 0	D'Auria	7,724	1	2		3	5	12		8	9			7	4		6	10*	11										
7	Sep-28	H	Tranmere Rovers	1 1	Raynor(pen)	4,884	1	2		3	5			8	9			7	4	10*	6		11	12									
8	Oct-02	A	Southend United	1 4	Gilligan	3,635	1	2		3	5	11		8	9			7*	4	12	6	10"			14								
9	Oct-06	A	Grimsby Town	0 1		5,974	1	2	3		5			8	9			11	7	4	10	6											
10	Oct-13	H	Crewe Alex	3 1	Davies, D'Auria, Raynor(pen)	3,888	1	2	3	4	5			8	9	10*	11	7		12	6												
11	Oct-20	H	Fulham	2 2	Chalmers, Gilligan	4,500	1	2	3	5				8	9		11	7	4	10						6							
12	Oct-24	A	Shrewsbury Town	2 1	Gilligan, Watson	2,859	1	2	3	4	5			8	9		11	12		10*	6					7							
13	Oct-27	A	Bolton Wanderers	0 1		4,158	1	2	3	4		5	14	8	9		11	12		10*	6"					7							
14	Nov-03	H	Cambridge United	0 0		3,902	1	2	3	14	5	4"		8	9	10	11			12	6*					7							
15	Nov-10	A	Mansfield Town	0 2		2,200	1	7"	3	2	5		8	6	9*	10	11		4	12	14												
16	Nov-24	H	Chester City	1 0	Raynor	3,361	1	12	3	2	5	4		6		10	11	7"				14			9*	8							
17	Dec-01	H	Birmingham City	2 0	Connor 2	4,896	1	7	3	2	5	4	14	6	9*	10	11								12	8"							
18	Dec-14	A	AFC Bournemouth	0 1		5,031	1	7	3	2	5	4	9	6	12	10	11*									8							
19	Dec-22	H	Reading	3 1	Gilligan 2, Connor	3,778	1	7	3	2	5	4	12	6	9"	10	11*				14					8							
20	Dec-26	A	Stoke City	2 2	Gilligan 2(1 pen)	12,534	1	7"	3	2	5	4		6	9	10	11*				14	12				8							
21	Dec-29	A	Wigan Athletic	4 2	Gilligan 3, Raynor	2,525	1	7	3	2	5	4	11*	6	9	10	12									8							
22	Jan-01	H	Rotherham United	5 0	Legg 2, Gilligan, Connor, D'Auria	5,938	1	7	3	2	5	4	12	6	9*	10	11				14					8*							
23	Jan-12	A	Huddersfield Town	2 1	O/Goal, D'Auria	4,052	1	7*	3	2	5	4	12	6	9	10	11"				14					8							
24	Jan-26	A	Brentford	0 2		5,373	1	12		3	5	4"		6	9	10	11*			7						8	2	14					
25	Feb-02	A	Bury	0 1		2,135	1	10		3	5	4	7*	6	9		12			14						8	2	11"					
26	Feb-23	H	Mansfield Town	1 2	Gilligan	3,354	1	7"	3		5			9	10	11*	2			6	12				14	8		4					
27	Feb-26	H	Exeter City	0 3		2,385	1	12	3	2	5			9	10					6	11				8			4	7*				
28	Mar-02	A	Birmingham City	0 2		6,903	1	12	3	2	5			8	9					11	14	6	10*		7			4"					
29	Mar-09	H	AFC Bournemouth	1 2	Gilligan	3,086	1		3	2	5			4	9	10	11			12		7*			8	6							
30	Mar-12	H	Southend United	1 4	Gilligan	2,712	1		3	2	5"			4*	9	10	11		14	12		7			8	6							
31	Mar-15	A	Tranmere Rovers	1 2	Chalmers	5,412			3	2				4	9	10			5	11					7	8		6	1				
32	Mar-19	A	Crewe Alex	0 3		2,622	1	12	3	2				4	9	10"			5*	11	14				7	8		6	1				
33	Mar-23	H	Grimsby Town	0 0		3,203	1	7	3	4	5			8	9	10	6			11					2								
34	Mar-26	A	Preston NE	0 2		3,491	1	7	3	4	5			8	9		6			11*					2	10			12				
35	Mar-30	A	Stoke City	2 1	Legg, Harris	4,418	1	7	3	4	5			8	9		6								10					2	11		
36	Apr-11	A	Reading	0 0		3,597		12	3	4	5			8	9*	10	6								7					1	2	11	
37	Apr-06	H	Wigan Athletic	1 6	Gilligan	2,869		12	3*	4	5			8"	9	10	6	14							7					1	2	11	
38	Apr-13	A	Rotherham United	3 2	Penney, Davey 2	3,510		9	3	4	5					10	6								8	7*		12		1	2	11	
39	Apr-16	A	Preston NE	3 1	O/Goal, Penney, Connor	2,507		7	3	4	5			8*	9	10	6								12					1	2	11	
40	Apr-20	A	Fulham	1 1	Legg	4,208	8		3	4	5	7*	12			10	6								9"			14		1	2	11	
41	Apr-23	A	Chester City	1 2	Raynor	852	8		3	4	5	7	12			10	6*								9"			14		1	2	11	
42	Apr-27	H	Shrewsbury Town	0 1		3,152	8		3	4	5"	14	12			10	6								7*	9				1	2	11	
43	Apr-30	H	Leyton Orient	0 0		2,132	8		3	4	5	7				10	6								9					1	2	11	
44	May-04	H	Bolton Wanderers	1 2	Penney(pen)	4,713	8		3	4	5		7			10	6*	14			12				9					1	2"	11	
45	May-09	H	Bradford City	0 2		2,126	1	8	3	4	5		7"			10	6								12	9*			14		2	11	
46	May-11	A	Cambridge United	0 2		9,023	1	8*	3	4	5					10	6					7"			12	9					2	11	14
						Apps	35	36	41	39	41	21	11	35	36	33	37	9	14	12	12	6	2	11	29	2	8	1	11	12	12	0	
						Subs	7		2		3	8		1			2	5	1	9	8	3		7			4	2				1	
						Gls	5		1				3	16	5	5	1		2	4			2							3			

#	Date	V	Opponents	Score	Scorers	Att	Bracey L	Raynor P	Coleman C	Hough D	Harris M	Walker K	Thornber S	Davies A	Gilligan J	Connor T	Legg A	Watson A	Trick D	Chalmers P	D'Auria D	Hutchison T	Freeman C	Davey S	Coughlin R	Honor C	Miller P	Bowen J	Kendall M	Williams P	Penney D	Jenkins S	Chappell S
1	Aug-29	A	Stoke City, RC 1-1	0 0		7,806	1	2	3	4	5	6	7	8	9	10	11																
2	Sep-04	H	Stoke City, RC 1-2	0 1		4,464	1	2	3		5	6*	7	8	9	10"	11	14	14	4		12											
3	Oct-30	H	Llanelli, ABWC-3	8 1	Gilligan 3, Chalmers 3, Harris, Davies	1,663	1	2*	3	12	5	6	7	8	9					10	4												
4	Nov-06	A	Torquay Utd, LDC Pre	1 1	Harris	2,095	1	7	3	2	5			12	6	9	10	11		4					8*								
5	Nov-17	H	Welling Utd, FAC-1	5 2	Legg 2, Gilligan(pen), Connor, Thornber	3,156	1	7*	3	2	5		4	8	6	9"	10	11							14								12
6	Nov-27	H	Shrewsbury T, LDC Pre	1 1	Davies	1,540	1	9	3	2	5	4		6		10	11	7*							12	8							
7	Dec-08	A	Walsall, FAC-2	2 1	Connor, Gilligan(pen)	3,744	1	7*	3	2	5	4	12	6	9	10	11								8								
8	Jan-01	H	Rotherham Utd, FAC-3	0 0		6,478	1	7	3	2*	5	4		6	9	10	11								8	12							
9	Jan-21	A	Rotherham Utd, FAC-3 Rep	0 4		4,233	1	7	3	2	5	4	14	6	9"	10	11				12					8*							
10	Jan-23	H	Shrewsbury T, LDC Pre Rep	4 2	Gilligan 2(1 pen), Legg 2	1,385	1	2	3	4	5			12	6	9	10	11"			7				14	8*							
11	Jan-28	A	Torquay Utd, LDC Pre Rep	0 2		1,664	1	12		2	5	4	11"	6*	9	10	14				7				8	3							
12	Jan-30	H	Merthyr, ABWC-4	2 1	Coleman, Thornber	2,794	1	7*	3	2	5	4	11	6"	9	10	12				14				8								
13	Feb-18	A	Birmingham C, LDC-1	0 0	aet, lost 2-4 on pens.	3,555	1	9	3		5			14	6	10	11"	12	4		7*				8	2							
14	Feb-20	H	Colwyn Bay, ABWC-5	1 1	Connor	1,000	1		3		5			11	6*	9	10	12		4					7	8					2		
15	Mar-05	H	Colwyn Bay, ABWC-5Rep	2 1	Connor 2	1,308	1		3	4	5			8	6	9	10	11							12	7*					2		
16	Apr-03	A	Barry T, ABWCSF 1-1	2 2	Harris, Davies	1,977		9	3	4	5			6		10	11	12		14					7*	8"				2	1		
17	Apr-18	H	Barry T, ABWCSF 1-2	1 0	Gilligan	2,169	1	6	3*	4	5	8		9		10	11					12			7				2	1		
18	May-19	N	Wrexham, ABWC Final	2 0	Penney(pen), Raynor	5,250		9	3	4						10	11	7*	5	12					8					1	2	6	

at National Stadium, Cardiff

Swansea City FC Season 1991/92   Division 3

#	Date	V	Opponents	Score	Scorers	Att	Bracey L	Jenkins S	Thornber S	Coughlin R	Harris M	Hough D	Raynor P	Comforth J	Davies A	Connor T	Legg A	Chalmers P	McClean C	Williams J	Ford J	Kendall M	Freestone R	Chapple S	Brazil D	Gilligan J	Davey S	Freeman C	Bowen J	Beauchamp J	Walker K	Agboola R	Purnell P	Wallace R	Hodgson D	Davies M	Barnhouse D	Trick D	Watson A
1	Aug-17	A	Stockport County	0 5		4,241	1	2	3	4*	5	6	7	8	9	10	11	12																					
2	Aug-24	H	Bolton Wanderers	1 1	Connor	3,578	1	2	3		5	6	9"	8		10	11	12	4	7"	14																		
3	Aug-31	A	Chester City	0 2		1,162	1	2	3		5	6	14	8*		10	11	12	9"	7	4																		
4	Sep-03	H	Reading	1 2	Williams	3,206		2	3*	8	5	6				10	11	12	9	7	4	1																	
5	Sep-07	A	Fulham	0 3		3,426		2	3	4	5	6	12			10	11"		9*	7	8	1	14																
6	Sep-14	H	Preston NE	2 2	O/Goal, Raynor	3,170		2	3*	4	5				9	14	10	11		7"	8	1		6	12														
7	Sep-20	A	Shrewsbury Town	0 0		3,427		2	3	4*	5				10	12	11				8	1		6	9	7													
8	Sep-28	H	Peterborough Utd.	1 0	Legg	2,685		2	3	4	5				10		11			7*	8	1		6	9	12													
9	Oct-05	A	Huddersfield Town	0 1		5,578		2		4	5				10	8	11			12	3	1		6	9*	7													
10	Oct-11	H	Hull City	0 0		2,725		2		4*	5				10	8	11			3			1	12	6	9	7"	14											
11	Oct-19	H	Stoke City	2 1	Harris, Davies	3,363		2		4	5				10	8	11			3			1		6	9		7											
12	Oct-26	A	Torquay United	0 1		1,908		2		4	5				10	8*	11			3			1	9	6		7	12											
13	Nov-01	A	Wigan Athletic	0 1		2,092		2	14	4	5				12		11			3			1	8"	6	9	7*		10										
14	Nov-05	H	Leyton Orient	2 2	Coughlin, Beauchamp	2,081		2	8	4	5						11			7	3		1		6	9			10										
15	Nov-08	H	AFC Bournemouth	3 1	Brazil, Walker, Williams	2,698		2	8	4	5						11			7	3*		1		6	9			10	12									
16	Nov-23	A	Bradford City	6 4	Williams J 3, Beauchamp, Legg, Gilligan	5,728			4*	8	5						11	14		7"	2		1		6	9			10	12	3									
17	Nov-30	A	Brentford	2 3	Williams, Legg	6,669			12	8*	5						11	14		7	2		1		6	9			10*	4	3									
18	Dec-14	H	Exeter City	1 0	Williams	2,848				8	5				12		11			7	2		1	6		9				4	3	10*								
19	Dec-26	H	Chester City	3 0	Gilligan 3	4,098		14		8	5				12		11			7*	2		1	6"		9				4	3	10								
20	Dec-28	H	Stockport County	2 1	Purnell, Gilligan	4,353				8	5						11			7	2		1	6		9				4	3	10								
21	Jan-01	A	Reading	0 1		5,083		14		8"	5				12		11			7*	2		1	6		9				4	3	10								
22	Jan-11	A	Bury	0 1		2,161		2	12	8	5						11			7	3		1	6*		9			14	4		10"								
23	Jan-18	H	Birmingham City	0 2		4,147		2		8	5				12		11			7	3		1	6		9			10*	4										
24	Jan-25	A	WBA	3 2	Thornber 3	10,395		2	12		5				10"		11	14		7	3		1	6		9				4										
25	Jan-28	H	Darlington	4 2	Williams 2, Legg, Chapple	2,743		2		8	5				10		11			7	3		1	6		9				4										
26	Feb-01	A	Stoke City	1 2	Gilligan	11,299			12	8	5				10		11			7	3		1	6*		9				4	2									
27	Feb-08	A	Torquay United	1 0	Gilligan	3,418		2	6	8	5				10		11			7	3		1			9				4										
28	Feb-11	H	Brentford	1 1	Legg	3,582			6	8	5				10		11			7	3		1			9				4	2									
29	Feb-15	A	Exeter City	1 2	Harris	2,360		14	6	8	5				10*		11				3		1	12		9			7	4	2"									
30	Feb-22	H	Bury	2 1	Raynor, Legg	2,787				8	5				10		11			7	3		1	6		9				4	2									
31	Feb-29	A	Hartlepool United	1 0	Thornber	2,669		7	6	8	5				10*		11			12	3		1			9				4	2									
32	Mar-03	A	Birmingham City	1 1	Williams	9,475		6	8		5				10	9	11			7	3		1						12	4	2*									
33	Mar-06	H	WBA	0 0		5,629		2	8		5				12	6	11	9*		7	3		1						10	4										
34	Mar-10	A	Leyton Orient	2 1	Chalmers, Legg	3,328		2	8	6					9		11"	10		7	3		1						5	12	4									
35	Mar-14	H	Wigan Athletic	3 0	Legg, O/Goal, Chalmers	3,726		2	8	6					9		11	10		7	3		1						5		4									
36	Mar-20	A	AFC Bournemouth	0 3		4,385		2*	12	6	5				9		11	10		7	3		1						8"	14	4									
37	Mar-28	H	Bradford City	2 2	Chalmers 2	3,748			12	6	5						11	10		7	3*		1	8					9"		4			2	14				
38	Mar-31	A	Preston NE	1 1	Chalmers	3,637					5				9		11"	10		12			1	8						4	6			2	7					
39	Apr-04	H	Fulham	2 2	Chalmers 2	3,307		2	3	12	5				9		11	10		7	14		1	8*						4	6"									
40	Apr-07	A	Bolton Wanderers	0 0		3,535		2	3*		5				9		11	10		7	8		1			12				4	6									
41	Apr-11	A	Darlington	1 1	Williams	1,507		2	3		5				9"		11	10		7	8		1	14					12	4	6*								✓	
42	Apr-17	H	Shrewsbury Town	1 2	Harris	3,429		2	3		5				9		11	10		7	8		1							4	6									
43	Apr-21	A	Peterborough Utd.	1 3	Legg	5,526		2	3		5				9		11	10		7	8*		1				14			4	6"				12					
44	Apr-25	H	Huddersfield Town	0 1		3,964			3"		5				9*		11	10		7	8		1			14	6			4	12					2				
45	Apr-28	H	Hartlepool United	1 1	Chapple	2,167					5				9		11	10		7	3		1	8			2			4	6									
46	May-02	A	Hull City	0 3		4,070					5				9		11	10		7	3		1	8"			2*	12		4	6							14		
	Apps						3	31	26	32	44	5	18	17	6	6	46	14	4	36	42	1	42	17	12	24	3	8	5	5	30	20	5	2	1	1	0	0	0
	Subs							3	7	1			8		2			7		3	2		4		1	2	4	6		2	1		2		1				
	Gls								4	1	3		2		1	1	9	7		11				2	1	7			2	1		1						

#	Date	V	Opponents	Score	Scorers	Att	Bracey L	Jenkins S	Thornber S	Coughlin R	Harris M	Hough D	Raynor P	Comforth J	Davies A	Connor T	Legg A	Chalmers P	McClean C	Williams J	Ford J	Kendall M	Freestone R	Chapple S	Brazil D	Gilligan J	Davey S	Freeman C	Bowen J	Beauchamp J	Walker K	Agboola R	Purnell P	Wallace R	Hodgson D	Davies M	Barnhouse D	Trick D	Watson A
1	Aug-20	H	Walsall, RC 1-1	2 2	Thornber, Chalmers	2,029	1	2	3	14	5	6	9"	8	7*	10	11	12	4																					
2	Aug-27	A	Walsall, RC 1-2	1 0	Thornber	2,812	1	2	3		5	6	12	8		10	11		9	7*	4																			
3	Sep-17	H	Monaco, ECWC 1-1	1 2	Legg	6,208		2	3	4	5				8	10	11		9			1				7						6								
4	Sep-25	H	Tottenham H, RC 2-1	1 0	Gilligan	11,416		2	3	4	5				10		11			7	8		1		6	9														
5	Oct-01	A	Monaco, ECWC 1-2	0 8		5,000		2	3	4	5*				10	8	11					1		14		9	7"					6		12						
6	Oct-09	A	Tottenham H, RC 2-2	1 5	Chapple	20,198		2	3	4*	5				10	8	11			14			1	12	6	9	7*													
7	Oct-22	A	AFC Bournemouth, AGT Pre	0 3		1,814		2			5				10	8	11				3		1	4	6	9		7*	12											
8	Oct-29	A	Merthyr, ABWC-3	2 0	Watson, Chapple	1,098		2		4	5						11				3		1	8	6	9	7													10
9	Nov-16	H	Cardiff City, FAC-1	2 1	Gilligan, Harris	9,315		2	8	4	5						11			7			1			9				10		6	3							
10	Nov-19	H	Cardiff City, AGT-Pre	0 0		2,955		2	4		5				12		11			7			1	8	6	9					10		3*							
11	Dec-07	A	Exeter City, FAC-2	0 0		4,186				8	5						11			7	2		1	6		9				10		4	3							
12	Dec-17	H	Exeter City, FAC-2 Re	1 2	Walker	3,159		12		8	5*				14		11			7	2		1	6		9				10"		4	3							
13	Jan-06	A	Kidderminster H, ABWC-4	3 1	Chapple, Legg, Williaams	1,815		2	12	4*	5				14		11			7	3		1	6		9				10"		4								
14	Feb-18	H	Cardiff City, ABWC-5	0 1		7,303			3	8	5				10*		11			7	6		1			9				12		4	2							

Swansea City FC Season 1992/93   Division 2(3)

#	Date	V	Opponents	Score	Scorers	Att	Freestone R	Lyttle D	Jenkins S	Walker K	Harris M	Coughlin R	Cullen T	Pascoe C	McFarlane A	Cornforth J	Legg A	Bowen J	Ford J	Agboola R	West C	Connor T	Wimbleton P	Chapple S	Hayes M	McMahon S
1	Aug-15	A	Burnley	0 1		10,913	1	2	3"	4	5	6*	7	8	9	10	11	12	14							
2	Aug-22	H	Mansfield Town	4 0	Pascoe, Cornforth, Legg, O/Goal	3,082	1	2			5	6	7	8	9	10	11		3	4						
3	Aug-29	A	Wigan Athletic	3 2	Harris, Ford, Cornforth	1,565	1	2		8	5	6*	7		9"	10	11	12	3	4	14					
4	Sep-01	A	Hull City	0 1		4,408	1	2			5	6	7	8	9	10	11*		3	4	12					
5	Sep-05	H	Port Vale	2 0	West 2 (1 pen)	3,868	1	2		4	5	6	7*	8		10	11	12"	3	14	9					
6	Sep-12	H	Blackpool	3 0	West, Pascoe, Legg	3,861	1	2		4	5	6	7*	8		10	11	12	3		9					
7	Sep-15	A	Fulham	1 1	Cornforth	4,268	1	2		4	5	6	12	8		10	11	7*	3		9					
8	Sep-18	A	Huddersfield Town	2 1	West, Legg	4,839	1	2		4	5	6	12	8		10	11	7*	3		9					
9	Sep-26	H	Bradford City	1 1	West (pen)	4,781	1	2		4	5	6	12	8		10	11	7*	3		9					
10	Oct-03	A	Stockport County	1 1	Cullen	4,943	1	2		4	5	6*	7	8		10	11	12	3		9					
11	Oct-10	H	Exeter City	0 0		4,439	1	2		4	5	6	7	8		10	11		3		9					
12	Oct-17	A	Hartlepool United	1 0	Harris	4,175	1	2		4	5	6	7*	8		10	11	12	3		9					
13	Oct-24	H	Reading	2 1	Cornforth, Harris	5,317	1	2		4	5	6	7	8		10	11		3		9					
14	Oct-31	A	Leyton Orient	2 4	Pascoe, Cullen	5,683	1	2	14	4	5	6*	7	8		10	11	12	3"		9					
15	Nov-03	H	Plymouth Argyle	0 0		5,430	1	2	12	4*	5	6	7	8		10	11		3		9					
16	Nov-07	A	Chester City	2 3	Pascoe, Legg	2,861	1	2	14		5	6*	7	8		10	11	12	3"	4	9					
17	Nov-20	H	Brighton	0 1		4,645	1	2	3			8		12	7*	11	6	5	4	10	9					
18	Nov-28	A	Stoke City	1 2	Cullen	13,867	1	2	3		5		7		12	10	11	6	14	4	9*	8"				
19	Dec-12	H	WBA	0 0		5,763	1	2								10	11	12	3		9	8*				
20	Dec-18	A	Rotherham United	0 0		4,600	1	2	3	4	5	6			7*	10	11	12			9		8			
21	Dec-26	A	AFC Bournemouth	2 0	West, Legg	4,995	1	2	3	4	5				7*	10	11	12	6		9		8			
22	Dec-28	H	Bolton Wanderers	1 2	West	7,220	1	2	3	4	5			7"	14	10	11	12	6*		9		8			
23	Jan-05	A	Blackpool	0 0		3,417	1	2	3	4	5	6			7*		11	12			9		8	10		
24	Jan-09	H	Fulham	2 2	Wimbleton, West	5,048	1	2	3	4	5	6				10"	11	12	14		9		8			7*
25	Jan-16	A	Bradford City	0 0		5,551	1	2	3	4	5					10	11	12			9		8		6	7*
26	Jan-30	A	Mansfield Town	3 3	West, McFarlane, Ford	2,641	1	2	3	4	5				14	10"	11	12			9		8"		6	7
27	Feb-05	H	Burnley	1 1	Bowen	4,973	1	2	3	4	5					10	11	8	12		9				6*	7
28	Feb-13	A	Port Vale	0 2		7,191	1	2	3	4	5				12	10	11	14	6		9		8"			7*
29	Feb-20	H	Hull City	1 0	McFarlane	2,656	1	2	12	4	5	6	7			10*	11	8	3		9					
30	Feb-27	A	Exeter City	2 0	Lyttle, West	3,146	1	2	3	4	5			8	12	10	11	7*	6		9					
31	Mar-05	H	Stockport County	2 2	Bowen, West (pen)	4,755	1	2	3	4	5			8	12	10	11	7*	6		9					
32	Mar-09	A	Preston N E	3 1	West (pen), Bowen 2	4,396	1	2	3	4	5			8	12	10	11*	7	6		9					
33	Mar-13	H	Chester City	4 2	Bowen 3, Legg	4,056	1	2	3	4				8		10	11	7	6		9					5
34	Mar-20	A	Plymouth Argyle	1 0	Bowen	6,233	1	2	3	4				8		10	11	7	6		12		9			5
35	Mar-23	H	Stoke City	1 2	Legg	8,366	1	2	3	4	5			8	9	10"	11	7	6*		14		12			
36	Mar-27	A	Brighton	2 0	Legg, Bowen	7,558	1	2	3	4	5			8	9		11	7	6				10			
37	Apr-07	A	WBA	0 3		13,401	1	2	3	4	5			8*	9	10	11	7	6				12			
38	Apr-10	H	AFC Bournemouth	2 1	Legg, Bowen	5,101	1	2	3	4	5			8	9*	10	11	7"	6		14		12			
39	Apr-12	A	Bolton Wanderers	1 2	Ford	10,854	1	2	3	4	5	14			10	6"	11	8			9		7*			12
40	Apr-17	H	Rotherham United	2 0	McFarlane, Cornforth	4,658	1	2	3	4	5			8	9	10	11	7	8*				12			
41	Apr-20	H	Huddersfield Town	3 0	Legg, Harris, Walker	5,190	1	2	3	4	5			8	9	10*	11	7	6				12			
42	Apr-24	H	Hartlepool United	3 0	Legg, Walker, McFarlane	5,310	1	2	3	4	5		14	8	9	10*	11	7	6"				12			
43	Apr-27	H	Preston N E	2 0	Harris, McFarlane	6,933	1	2	3	4	5		7		9	6	11	10	8							
44	May-01	A	Reading	0 2		6,922	1	2	3	4	5		14	8	9	10*	11	7	6*				12			
45	May-04	H	Wigan Athletic	2 1	Coughlin, Legg	7,361	1	2	3	4	5		12	8	9"	10	11	7*			14				6	
46	May-08	H	Leyton Orient	0 1		6,543	1	2	3	4	5		7*	8	9	10"	11		14				12		6	
	Apps						46	46	29	42	42	38	20	15	17	44	46	23	36	6	29	3	10	4	8	2
	Subs								4		1	7		7				15	7	1	4		4		7	
	Gls							1		2	5	1	3	4	5	5	12	10	3		12				1	

#	Date	V	Opponents	Score	Scorers	Att	Freestone R	Lyttle D	Jenkins S	Walker K	Harris M	Coughlin R	Cullen T	Pascoe C	McFarlane A	Cornforth J	Legg A	Bowen J	Ford J	Agboola R	West C	Connor T	Wimbleton P	Chapple S	Hayes M	McMahon S
1	Aug-18	A	Oxford Utd, C C Cup 1-1	0 3		3,582	1	2			5	6	7	8	9	10	11		3	4						
2	Aug-25	H	Oxford Utd, C C Cup 1-2	1 0	McFarlane	2,256	1	2	14		5	6	7"	8	9*	10	11		3	4	12					
3	Oct-27	A	Merthyr, ABWC-3	0 2		2,516	1	2	12	4	5	6*	7"	8		10	11	14	3		9					
4	Dec-05	A	Exeter City, FAC-2	5 2	West. Legg, Wimbleton, Cullen, Bowen	2,914	1	2	3	4	5	6			7"	10	11	14	12		9		8			
5	Jan-02	H	Oxford Utd, FAC-3	1 1	Bowen	6,985	1	2	3	4	5	6	7			10"	11	14			9		8			
6	Jan-12	A	Oxford Utd, FAC-3 Rep	2 2	Cornforth, Coughlin, aet, won 5-4 on pens.	4,707	1	2	3	4	5	6*			14	10	11	7	12		9		8"			
7	Jan-19	A	Cardiff C, AGT-1	2 1	Legg, Hayes, aet	13,516	1	2	3*	4	5				14	10	11		12		9		8"		6	7
8	Feb-02	H	Grimsby T, FAC-4	0 0		8,307	1	2	3	4	5				12	10	11		14		9		8"		6*	7
9	Feb-09	A	Grimsby T, FAC-4 Rep	0 2		8,452	1	2	3	4	5					10	11"	8	6		9		12	14		7*
10	Feb-16	H	Leyton Orient, AGT-2	1 0	West (pen)	3,339	1	2	3*	4	5	12	7			10	11	8	6		9*					
11	Feb-23	H	Exeter C, AGT South S-F	2 3	O/Goal, Legg, aet	4,971	1	2	3	4	5		7		12	10	11	8	6"		9*				14	
12	May-16	H	WBA, Play Off S-F 1-1	2 1	McFarlane, Harris	13,917	1	2	3	4	5		7"	8	9	10"	11	12			14				6	
13	May-19	A	WBA, Play Off S-F 1-2	0 2		26,045	1	2	3	4	5		7	8	9	10"	11	12			14					6"

Swansea City FC Season 1993/94   Division 2(3)

#	Date	V	Opponents	Score	Scorers	Att	Freestone R	Clode M	Cook A	Walker K	Harris M	Pascoe C	Hodge J	Bowen J	Torpey S	Cornforth J	Hayes M	Chapple S	Ford J	Jenkins S	Jones R	McFarlane A	Barnhouse D	Perrett D	Aspinall W	Coates J	Burns C	Rush M	Ampadu K	Penney D	Moore M	Basham M
1	Aug-14	A	York City	1 2	Hodge	4,596	1	2"	3	4	5	6	7*	8	9	10	11	12	14													
2	Aug-21	H	Wrexham	3 1	Harris, Pascoe, Cornforth (pen)	5,383	1	2	3"	4	5	6	7*	8	9	10	11	12	14													
3	Aug-27	A	Barnet	1 0	Bowen	1,996	1	2		4	5	6*	12	8	9	10	11	7	3													
4	Aug-31	H	Huddersfield Town	1 0	Hayes	4,318	1		14	4	5		12	8	9*	10	11	7"	3	2	6											
5	Sep-04	H	Plymouth Argyle	0 1		4,616	1		14	4	5		12	8	9	10*	11	7"	3	2	6											
6	Sep-11	A	Brentford	1 1	Cornforth	5,042	1			4	5			8*	9	10	11	7	3	2	6	12										
7	Sep-14	A	Cambridge United	0 2		3,338	1		3					8	9	10	11	7*		2	6	12				4						
8	Sep-18	H	Bradford City	2 0	Hayes, Walker	3,373	1			4	5	6		8	9	10	11	7*	3	2		12										
9	Sep-25	A	Exeter City	0 1		3,655	1		14	4	5	6		8*	9	10	11	7*	3	2		12										
10	Oct-01	H	Reading	1 1	McFarlane	4,245	1		8	4	5	6		7		9*	10		3	2		11		12								
11	Oct-09	H	Blackpool	4 4	Pascoe, Cornforth, Hayes, Walker	3,775	1		8	4	5	6	12		14	10*	11		3	2		9		7"								
12	Oct-16	A	Rotherham United	1 1	McFarlane	3,178	1		3	4	5	6	12			10	11			2		9		7*	8							
13	Oct-23	H	Hull City	1 0	McFarlane	3,774	1	2	3	4	5	6	12	7*		10	11					9			8							
14	Oct-30	A	Stockport County	0 4		4,641	1	2	3*	4	5	6	7			10	11"			12	14	9			8							
15	Nov-02	H	Burnley	3 1	Hayes, Pascoe, Bowen	3,358	1	3		4	5	6	14	7	12	10	11			2		9*			8"							
16	Nov-06	A	Port Vale	0 3		7,854	1	2"	3	4	5	6	12	7		10	11			14		9*			8							
17	Nov-20	H	Leyton Orient	1 1	Torpey	3,160	1	2"	3	4	5	6	7		9		11	8	12						10							
18	Nov-27	A	Fulham	1 3	Chapple	3,282	1	2	3	4	5	6	7		9	10		8							11"	14						
19	Dec-11	A	Wrexham	2 3	Torpey 2	2,726	1	2"	3		5	6	7		9			12	10	8		14	4"		11							
20	Dec-18	H	York City	1 2	Chapple	2,749	1		3	4*		5			7	9		8	12	10"		11			14	6						
21	Dec-22	A	Cardiff City	0 1		9,815	1		14	3		5			9	10	7	8*	4	2		12			11"		6					
22	Jan-01	A	Bristol Rovers	2 1	Coates, Harris	6,285	1		14	3		5	6	7*		10*			4	2		11				12	8					
23	Jan-14	H	Rotherham United	0 0		3,271	1		3			5	6	7	9				4	2		11*				12	10	8				
24	Jan-22	A	Blackpool	1 1	Torpey	7,080	1		3			5	6	14	7	9		11"	10	4	2							8				
25	Jan-29	H	Hartlepool United	1 1	Jenkins	2,573	1		3			5	6		7	9*	10	11	4	2						12		8				
26	Feb-05	H	Hull City	1 0	Chapple	4,668	1	3*	12		5		7	9	10	11		6	4	2								8				
27	Feb-12	H	AFC Bournemouth	1 1	Bowen	3,255	1		4	3		5		12	7	9*	10	11	6*		2	14						8				
28	Feb-18	H	Barnet	2 0	Bowen 2	3,278	1	3		4	5	14		7	9	10	11"	6		2								8"		12		
29	Feb-22	A	Huddersfield Town	1 1	Cornforth	3,854	1	3		4	5	14	12	7	9	10		6"		2								8		11*		
30	Feb-26	A	Plymouth Argyle	1 2	Torpey	8,930	1		3	4	5	6	7*		9	10		14		2"		12						8		11		
31	Mar-05	H	Brentford	1 1	Bowen	3,187	1		3	4	5	6		7	9*	10				2		12						8		11		
32	Mar-08	H	Brighton	3 0	Pascoe, Torpey 2	2,893	1		3	4	5	6	14	7	9	10				2								8		11"		
33	Mar-12	A	Bradford City	1 2	Cornforth	8,200	1		3	4	5	6	14	7*	9	10				2		12						8		11"		
34	Mar-15	H	Cambridge United	4 2	Bowen 2, Torpey, Pascoe	2,699	1		3	4	5	6	11	7	9	10		12		2								8*				
35	Mar-19	H	Exeter City	2 0	Bowen, Clode	2,512	1	3		4	5	6	11	7	9*	10				2		12						8				
36	Mar-25	A	Reading	1 2	Bowen	6,464	1		3	4	5	6	11	7		10"		12		2		9								8*	14	
37	Mar-29	A	Hartlepool United	0 1		1,354	1		3"		5	6	11	7	9*	10		14	4	2		12								8		
38	Apr-02	H	Cardiff City	1 0	Penney (pen)	3,711	1		3		5	6	11	7	9	10		12	4	2										8*		
39	Apr-06	A	Brighton	1 4	Penney	9,303	1		3		5	6*	11	7	9	10		12	4	2		14							11"	8		
40	Apr-09	H	Bristol Rovers	2 0	Ford, O/Goal	3,961	1		3		5			7"	9	10		6	4	2	12	12							11"	8		
41	Apr-12	H	Stockport County	1 2	Hodge	2,483	1		3		5		7	11	9*	10			4	2		6								12		
42	Apr-15	A	Burnley	1 1	Harris	10,694	1		3*		5	6		11	9					2	10	12							7	8		4
43	Apr-19	A	AFC Bournemouth	1 0	Torpey	2,465	1		3		5	6	11		9			14	12	2*		7							10	8"		4
44	Apr-26	H	Port Vale	0 1		4,252	1				5		11*	12	9	14		6"	3	2	8	10							7			4
45	Apr-30	A	Leyton Orient	1 2	Cornforth	3,529	1		3		5		11	7		14	10			2		9							6"	8		4
46	May-07	H	Fulham	2 1	Bowen, Perrett	4,355	1		3*		5		11	7"	14	10				2		9		12					6	8		4
			Apps				46	26	23	27	46	31	15	39	36	37	22	19	21	38	6	15	2	8	5	0	4	13	11	11	0	5
			Subs					2	4			2	12	2	4	1		10	6	2	1	13	1	3	4			2		1		
			Gls					1		2	3	5	2	11	9	6	4	3	1	1		3		1		1				2		

#	Date	V	Opponents	Score	Scorers	Att	Freestone R	Clode M	Cook A	Walker K	Harris M	Pascoe C	Hodge J	Bowen J	Torpey S	Cornforth J	Hayes M	Chapple S	Ford J	Jenkins S	Jones R	McFarlane A	Barnhouse D	Perrett D	Aspinall W	Coates J	Burns C	Rush M	Ampadu K	Penney D	Moore M	Basham M
1	Aug-17	H	Bristol City, CCCup 1-1	0 1		3,746	1	2	3*	4	5	6	7	8	9	10	11			12												
2	Aug-24	A	Bristol City, CCCup 1-2	2 0	Bowen 2	4,633	1	2		4	5	6		8	9	10	11	7	3													
3	Sep-21	H	Oldham Ath, CCCup 2-1	2 1	Torpey, Pascoe	5,056	1	2		4	5	6		8	9	10	11	7	3	2												
4	Sep-28	A	Plymouth A, AGT-1	3 1	McFarlane, Cook, Perrett	2,664	1		8	4	5	6	12			10	11		3	2		9*		7								
5	Oct-06	A	Oldham Ath, CCCup 2-2	0 0		6,433	1		8	4	5	6	12		14	10	11		3*	2		9"		7								
6	Oct-19	H	Exeter C, AGT-1	2 0	Bowen, Harris	2,071	1	2	3	4	5	6		7	12	10	11					9*			8							
7	Nov-09	H	Merthyr, ABWC-3	0 0		2,431	1		14	3	4*		6	7	9	10	11			12	2"				8							
8	Nov-13	H	Nuneaton, FAC-1	1 1	Torpey	3,532	1	2	3	4	5*	6	7"	9		11	8	12		14					10							
9	Nov-23	A	Nuneaton, FAC-1Rep	1 2	Torpey, aet	4,443	1	2"	3	4	5	6	7	9	10	11"	8	12		14												
10	Dec-02	A	Merthyr, ABWC-3 Rep	2 1	Perrett, Bowen	2,108	1	2	3	4	5	6"	7	9	10		8*		12	14				11								
11	Dec-04	A	Rhyl, ABWC-4	2 0	Perrett 2	700	1	2	3	4	5		7	9	10			8	6"	14				11								
12	Dec-07	H	Exeter C, AGT-2	2 1	Cook, Bowen	1,560	1	2	3		5	6	7	9*	10*			12	8		14	4		11								
13	Jan-11	H	Port Vale, AGT QF	1 0	Burns	2,630	1		3		5	6	7	9					4	2		11					10	8				
14	Jan-25	H	Hereford Utd, ABWC-5	1 0	Pascoe	1,726	1		3		5	6	7	9	10	11			4	2								8				
15	Feb-08	A	L Orient, AGT SF	2 0	Chapple, Torpey	7,010	1		3		5	12	7	9	10	11		6	4	2								8*				
16	Mar-01	H	Wycombe AGT Sth F-1	3 1	Pascoe 2, Bowen	6,335	1		3	4	5	6	12	7	9	10				2								8		11*		
17	Mar-22	A	Wycombe AGT Sth F-2	0 1		6,710	1		3"	14	4	5	6	11	7	9*	10			2		12						8				
18	Apr-14	H	Cardiff C, ABWC SF 1-1	1 2	Cornforth	3,286	1		3		5	6	11	7		10"		8*	4	2		9	14						12			
19	Apr-24	N	Huddersfield T, AGT F	1 1	McFarlane, won 3-1 on pens	47,733	1		3"		5	6	11*	7	12	10		14		2		9						8				4
20	Apr-28	A	Cardiff C, ABWC SF 1-2	1 4	McFarlane	5,606	1		3		5	6	11*	7	14	10"			4	2		9		12				8				

Chapter 23

Resignation, Farce and Relegation

1994-95

After the excitement and success of the club's Wembley experience, there was an expectation among Swans supporters that the team would do well in the new campaign. The reality, at least as far as league football was concerned, proved to be rather different, and the fans quickly became disillusioned. The clearest indicator of this was the size of Vetch gates for the early matches of the season, which were less than encouraging from the start. For the first home match there were just 4,600 people in the ground to see the Swans draw with Brighton, and by the end of November two thousand fewer came to see them play Rotherham. By then there was what appeared to be an orchestrated 'Sharpe out' campaign, with which the chairman dealt stoically. Whilst managers pay for lack of success with their jobs, chairmen in the same situation are villified. In both cases, though, whatever good has been done in the past is forgotten; such is the fickle nature of some football fans.

Nevertheless, it was understandable that the supporters should have felt frustrated. During the close-season, several pundits had suggested that what the Vetch club needed were another two or three effective players to turn the squad into a promotion-chasing outfit. Yet, Frank Burrows had only been able to buy one player – David Penney, from Oxford for £20,000. He had also recruited Michael Basham a free transfer from West Ham. As it happened, both men had been at the Vetch on loan during previous seasons. Given Frank Burrows' success with buying inexpensive players, the fans had been expecting more new faces. Presumably, though, the chairman, having in mind the poor gates which had been attracted to the Vetch, and his own determination that the club should not find itself in financial difficulties again, had held the purse-strings tightly. Manager Burrows' reaction was to bring in another 'loan' player, striker John Hendry from Spurs, who spent two months at the club.

Whilst early results in the league were disappointing, there were some encouraging performances. In September the side beat Hull City and Cambridge on their own grounds, and played an exciting 3-3 draw with Shrewsbury at Gay

Swans' squad, 1994-95.
Back row, left to right: David Barnhouse, Martin Hayes, Roger Freestone, Andy McFarlane, Lee Jones, David Penney, Darren Perrett.
Middle: Jimmy Rimmer (Youth Coach), Bobby Smith (Assistant Manager), Mike Basham, Mark Harris, John Ford, Steve Torpey,
Steve Jenkins, Shaun Chapple, Ron Walton (Youth Coach). Front: Mark Clode, Kwame 'Pat' Ampadu, John Hodge,
Frank Burrows (Manager), John Cornforth (Captain), Colin Pascoe, Jason Bowen.

Meadow. After that match, Frank Burrows was reported as saying, 'That's what the public want to see and we've got to serve up matches like that to bring the crowds back.' Unfortunately for the Swans, they were not coming back to the Vetch. Whilst the club's away form was encouraging, home results were giving cause for concern. By the end of September the side had played five matches at home, had drawn four times, and lost the other. Furthermore, they had scored just one goal in those games and no fewer than three games had ended 0-0. It was obvious that these results did not match the criteria of which the manager had spoken at Shrewsbury.

Happily, the team had been more successful in the cup competitions, which, at least, gave the supporters something to cheer about. In the Coca Cola Cup, after disposing of Exeter in the first round, the side was drawn against Premiership club, Norwich City, and, despite losing the tie 3-1 on aggregate, the team gave a fine account of itself. This was particularly true at the Vetch, where the game was won by an outstanding goal by Colin Pascoe. In the FA Cup they did even better. After two non-league sides had been beaten, the Swans were drawn to play Middlesbrough at the Vetch. Given the pedigree of the Ayresome Park side, this caught the imagination of the public and many stay-away fans returned to boost the gate to 8,400. Frank Burrows, the board and chief executive Robin Sharpe must have wished that the team could attract crowds of that size to every home match. From the manager's point of view there was also an important psychological advantage which stemmed from the vocal support of the larger crowd. As the football cliché has it, vociferous support of the right kind is worth a goal start; the problem is that supporters need to be reminded of this fact on an ongoing basis.

As Burrows was to say after the game, the Swans supporters did an outstanding job in 'lifting' their heroes to match their more highly stationed opponents. Indeed, such was the Vetch team's form then, that they took the lead through a John Ford goal after thirty-five minutes. The visitors equalised halfway through the second period, and when the final whistle was blown, neither side had been able to score again. With that result, Middlesbrough, the press and the realists among Swans fans settled for a scenario where the headlines following the replay in Cleveland would be about 'brave Swansea's fight'. There was no doubt which team was the favourite in the eyes of the bookmakers to move into the next round: after all, the Ayresome Park club was leading the First Division whilst the Swans were struggling in the Second. Encouraged by their performance at the Vetch, however, the Swans had other ideas. With little to lose, they could relax and play attractive football; and they did. After twenty minutes of the game, the men in white had the audacity to take the lead, Steve Torpey scoring. Then, to the chagrin of the home supporters, David Penney added another ten minutes into the second half. At that, Midddlesbrough were stung into frantic action; the Swans goal was under siege for long periods, but the defence played superbly; Jenkins, Ford, Basham, Walker and Freestone, aided by the majority of their team mates, defended as if their lives depended on the result. Although the home side did manage to break down the Swans' defence once, the game ended as a famous victory for Swansea City. Frank Burrows was delighted! It had been an outstanding performance by the underdogs.

The draw for the next round provided the Swans with another mountain to climb. Newcastle at St. James's Park were the opponents and that proved to be a bastion too far for the Swansea men. Kitson scored a hat-trick for the Geordies, though, if the Swans had taken a golden opportunity in the first minute, things might have turned out differently. As it was, the quality of the football played by the Welshmen that day was a fine advertisement for the Second Division. The team received a great deal of praise, which is best summed up by quoting the Newcastle manager, Kevin Keegan: 'Swansea surprised me by the quality of their play. I find it difficult to believe they are only a mid-table team in the Second Division.' A delighted Frank Burrows might have owned to the fact that he was equally as puzzled. At least, though, he had the satisfaction of seeing the return of Keith Walker to the heart of his defence. The Scot had been absent for six months and his sterling qualities and experience had been missed. It was no coincidence that, following his return, the chemistry and balance of the side's defensive group improved considerably. In turn, that allowed players like Cornforth and Penney to pay more attention to supporting the side's attacking endeavours. In the weeks ahead, league results reflected these facts.

After taking three points off Stockport on their own ground, the team played nine consecutive matches without defeat, scoring sixteen goals in the process and conceding just five. That sequence resulted in the team moving into sixth position in the league table, and caused the optimists to begin talking about possible promotion. Unfortunately, a spate of injuries disrupted progress and, at the beginning of April, the team lost three successive matches – albeit all

> *During a match against Oxford United at the Manor Ground in April 1995, the Swans were awarded a penalty. It was the identity of the penalty-taker which intrigued the crowd, for it was goalkeeper Roger Freestone who took the kick. Thereafter, Roger took the penalties for the Swans until the arrival of Jan Molby.*

Swans' squad, 1995-96.
Back row, left to right: Denis Spiteri, Darren Perrett, Lee Jones, Roger Freestone, Ben Miles, David Barnhouse, Jamie Rickard.
Middle: Mark Clode, David Thomas, Michael Basham, Christian Edwards, Steve Torpey, Carl Heggs, Keith Walker,
Jason Price, Shaun Chapple. Front: David Beresford, Jonathan Coates, John Hodge, Colin Pascoe, John Cornforth,
David Penney, Andy Cook, Kwame Ampadu, Steve Jenkins.

away from home. There followed a workmanlike victory over Leyton Orient, which revived the hope of a play-off position but, sadly, subsequent results did not go the way of the Swans. Naturally, there was a great deal of disappointment at the Vetch, though John Cornforth, summing up the season in discussion with John Burgum, wanted to look at the positives: 'We tried hard to give the fans something to shout about . . . Middlesbrough have won the First Division championship and we knocked them out of the cup . . . We'll do better next season, you'll see.' Mark Aizelwood, who had seen many of the Swans' games, offered a suggestion as to the reason why the Swans had missed-out: 'Swansea are the best passing side in the Second Division, but they are not consistent. They need to be more effective in and around the penalty box – they do not put the ball into the box often enough to pressurise defenders.' Such comments are rarely welcomed by hard-working, experienced managers, even if there is more than an element of truth in what is said. What the BBC man might have added, was that the inconsistency at various times during the campaign could be traced in part to the absence of key players and the lack of suitable cover; no fewer than eight

senior men had been injured at crucial times during the campaign. Had Frank Burrows been luckier with the fitness of his squad, it is highly likely that the Swans would have been in contention for promotion.

1995-96

There were further departures of senior players from from the Vetch during the close season. John Ford joined Bradford City for a fee (arranged by the tribunal) of £210,000 (£57,000 of which went to the player's former club); Jason Bowen signed for Birmingham City in exchange for a fee of £275,000 plus a further £75,000 after a given number of appearances; Andy McFarlane was sold to Scunthorpe for £15,000; and Mark Harris left for Gillingham on a free transfer. The only incoming players were Carl Heggs, bought by Burrows from West Bromwich for £60,000, and David Beresford, who came on loan from Oldham. To say that the fans were disappointed is severely to understate their mood. They wanted to see the side being reinforced by acquisitions rather than weakened by further selling. Although no one at the Vetch had said as much, the

general consensus of the supporters' opinion was that, despite the huge sums which had been generated by selling key men, the manager had not been given the money to make the purchases which he believed to be necessary. As if to underline the point, only 3,500 turned up for the opening game – against Shrewsbury – a thousand fewer than had attended the first match of the previous campaign.

Paradoxically, those who came saw the Swans make a fine start by beating the visitors 3-1; furthermore, after three matches the side remained unbeaten and the optimists were in the ascendancy. During this period, too, Peterborough had been beaten comprehensively(4-1) in the first leg of a Coca-Cola Cup tie. Consequently, in the final week of August, things looked extremely promising, until the team seemed to lose its way, playing six league games without a win. There was disappointment in the Coca Cola competition, too. Having done so well at the Vetch, virtually the same side succumbed to the 'Posh' by three goals to nil in the second leg at Peterborough. At that stage the club was in nineteenth place in the table, having been second after three matches had been played. Frank Burrows, whose cause had not been helped by an inopportune injury to John Cornforth, tried all he knew to get his team to recover its early-season form.

Unfortunately, after a 3-0 defeat at Burnley and two days to consider his position, the Scot resigned his post at the Vetch. Unlike some managers who succeeded him, Burrows behaved with great dignity and said very little to the press as to his reasons for leaving. He had, he stated, done as much as he could, and he wished the club well. Doug Sharpe said that he was very sorry to see Frank go, and thanked him for his efforts.

Whatever might be said about Frank Burrows, no one can deny the contribution which he made to Swansea City AFC whilst he was in charge. His record speaks for itself, not least in financial terms, where he made a massive contribution to club funds as a result of his dealings in the transfer market. A manager of the old school, he set standards of honesty, integrity and dedication to the task, which converted the job of manager into a calling.

Gloomy as the Vetch Field was at the time, it is doubtful whether even the most dyed-in-the-wool pessimist could have foreseen the train of events which would stem from the Scot's resignation. On Burrows' departure, Bobby Smith took on the task of manager on a temporary basis. His first match in charge produced a 2-0 victory for the Swans, with new loan-players, Frank Lampard, Jr., and Robbie Dennison playing a part, but the mini-revival ended abruptly following another transfer from the Vetch. Steve Jenkins, whose career Frank Burrows had resurrected, joined Huddersfield Town for £275,000 plus a sell-on clause. It was another body-blow to the dwindling band of supporters and the chairman suffered again as the chants were aimed at him.

In the meantime, the side was humiliated at Fulham, losing 7-0 in an FA Cup tie. That defeat was a huge psychological blow for all who cared about the Swans and marked the beginning of the end of manager Smith's brief reign at the Vetch. After the Fulham debacle, though, there was a signing: Steve Jones, a defender, was purchased from Cheltenham Town for £25,000. The new man's presence seemed to make an immediate difference to the side's defensive performance, but, after two successive clean sheets, the Swans lost 5-1 at Oxford and then were beaten 4-2 by Burnley at the Vetch. A significant statistic relating to the Burnley match was the size of the crowd: only 2,078 turned up. Four days earlier, it had been announced that Chris Coleman had been transferred to Blackburn from Crystal Palace. The relevance of that transaction for the Swans was that, as a result of a sell-on clause, the Vetch club would receive a wind-fall percentage of the fee paid by the Lancashire men. After Manchester City's proportion had been deducted, the Swans received £612,000.

Not surprisingly, the supporters expected some new faces to help reinvigorate the side; instead, Doug Sharpe and Bobby Smith had something of a confrontation. While the press suggested that the set-to concerned a consignment of boots which Smith had purchased without clearance from the chairman, at the heart of the matter was Doug Sharpe's lack of confidence in his temporary manager. The validity of arguments on both sides might be questioned, but, as ever, it is results that count in the cutthroat environment of football. During his time in charge, Bobby Smith's sides had won just two of the twelve league matches which had been played. Smith departed and Jimmy Rimmer was appointed in his place.

> *In December 1995, Chris Coleman was transferred from Crystal Palace to Blackburn. The significance of this for the Swans was that they received a 'sell-on' windfall of £800,000 from the transaction, although £188,000 of the fee had to be paid to the player's former club, Manchester City. When the gross figure is added to that received from Crystal Palace when the player left the Vetch (£375,000), it will be seen that Coleman's sale price totalled £1,175,000.*

What was subsequently made clear, was that Rimmer had accepted the 'acting' job with the knowledge that the chairman was negotiating with a third party. Immediately after the Burnley defeat at the Vetch, Sharpe had announced that he was open to offers for his shares in the club. He had come to the end of his tether. It was the culmination of a series of occasions when, under considerable, sometimes vindictive, pressure from some supporters he had hinted that he would go. Indeed, at one point he even stated that he would not set foot in the Vetch again. On 27 January 1996, with the club in twenty-second place in the league table, it was announced that the new owner of the club was Michael Thompson – said to be a millionaire friend of the family of Blackburn's stakeholder, Jack Walker. The *Post* published a photograph of the new owner shaking hands with Robin Sharpe. At the time, Doug Sharpe was in Spain, having stood down as chairman to facilitate the processes concerned with transferring ownership. With the Swans' match off because of a frozen ground, Thompson took the opportunity to announce his intentions. He was, he said, going to recruit a top management team, and his objective was to get the club into the Premier League by 2000. In addition, as soon as possible, he was going to reopen talks with the council about the Morfa Stadium. To the Swans fans Thompson's words seemed like those of a knight in shining armour who had ridden to rescue them from the slough of despond. What happened next, though, was to shatter that image and lead to great consternation among Swans followers, provoke ridicule and disbelief in the football world, and, in due course, to the take-over being aborted.

After hinting at the recruitment of a 'big-name' management team, when Michael Thompson called a press conference to introduce his new manager, he amazed his audience by saying that the new team would be Kevin Cullis and Paul Molesworth. 'Kevin who?,' asked the press, 'What are his credentials?' The answer to the second question brought cries of derision from the media men: Cullis, it seemed, had been youth coach at Cradley Town, had not played football at full-time professional level and had no experience of managing a senior football team let alone a Football League side. Subsequently, the club and its supporters had to suffer days of ridicule, as Swansea City Football Club became the laughing stock of the day. All this was made worse on the only occasion when Cullis was in charge for a Vetch league game (versus Swindon). So much out of his depth was the man that he was unable to give the usual half-time talk. Instead it was given by senior player, David Penney.

When Doug Sharpe heard about the appointment of the new manager, he booked a seat on the first available flight home. As the vendor, he was aware that, until the end of the twenty-one day period during which either party can withdraw, a contract for the sale of a business is not validated. A self-confessed Swans fanatic, Sharpe was coming home to nip the trouble in the bud. Not wasting any time at all, he did that. Thompson and his lieutenants left the Vetch, the former chairman took charge again and Jimmy Rimmer was reinstated as temporary manager. Not that that arrangement lasted very long; within days the chairman had moved to sign the man who had been touted by Michael Thompson as a possible player-coach, Jan Molby.

To the Swansea chairman, as well as to the fans, the idea of Molby as player-manager was appealing. A seasoned international, personable and well-respected as a footballer, the Dane projected the right kind of image for the task in hand. There was also the fact that he would join

from Liverpool, from whence came John Toshack, the most successful player-manager in the history of the Vetch. There was considerable difference between the two situations, however. When 'Tosh' came to Swansea, Harry Griffiths's side was already pushing for promotion. When Molby made his Vetch debut, the team was bottom-but-one in the Second Division and had not scored a single goal in its previous five matches. To put it mildly, Molby's order was considerably taller than that which faced John Toshack on his arrival.

In his first interview, the new manager made it clear that his initial focus would be on his contribution on the field, where he could do more for the club in the shorter term. He also commented on the playing staff, saying that he had been pleasantly surprised by the quality of some of his players. At the end of March, though, Molby's squad lost one of its better footballers, when John Cornforth joined Birmingham City for £350,000. The Dane moved immediately to bring in two new men: centre-back Shaun Garnett was recruited from Tranmere (£150,000) and Linton Brown joined from Hull (£60,000). Then, in March, the Swans received another windfall payment, Falkirk paying £62,000 in respect of the Swans' share of the profit the Scottish club had made on selling John Hughes to Celtic.

Unfortunately, despite Jan Molby's presence and that of the newcomers, results for the remainder of the season continued to disappoint. Following a run of four matches without defeat in early March, the Swans did not record a win in their next six games. By that time relegation appeared to be inevitable, and, despite a late flurry of victories, when the side lost 4-0 at Notts County, Swansea City were destined for Division Three. Paradoxically, amidst the gloom there was a feeling of relief around the Vetch. The positive thinkers among the supporters were talking about Jan Molby leading the club back to the Second Division at the first time of asking. The manager's presence on the field was seen to be a key factor in the equation, a point not lost on Doug Sharpe, who, despite the Dane's expensive contract, agreed to bring in Billy Ayre as assistant manager, to allow Jan to concentrate

on playing whilst he increased his management knowledge.

As they left for the short summer break, Molby said that he and his team were looking forward to recharging their batteries and that they would come back refreshed for the next campaign. Among those refreshed would be Alan Curtis, who returned as youth coach, while Jimmy Rimmer left. In May an AGM had been held during which the chairman announced that the club had lost £176,000 in the season during which they went to Wembley, and that, despite an excellent cup run, that figure had increased to £473,000 in 1995. Nonetheless, Doug Sharpe declared himself optimistic about the future, 'At least,' he said, 'we are solvent; how many clubs can say that?'

1996-97

There were many eyebrows raised in Swansea when it was announced that Jan Molby had signed a player from Benfica. The man concerned was Joao Moreira who, at six foot three and fifteen stone, looked every inch the athlete. Another summer signing was Richard Appleby, an English youth international. The management team had agreed new roles, with Billy Ayre being responsible for the many detailed administrative and organisational tasks involved in running a football team. This enabled the manager to concentrate on the playing side and on relationships with the media. Molby made no secret of the fact that he did not enjoy what he called 'office work' and several observers felt that he was finding the transition from player to manager to be something of a challenge because of the scope of the job. As it transpired, leaving aside the office tasks, as the season unfolded the Dane had enough on his mind to occupy him. In the first match of the campaign he missed a penalty and was sent off for two bookable offences. Whilst that match was won 2-1, the next four were lost, at which point the manager said that to lose four matches in a row was 'a major disaster as far as I am concerned'. During this period there was little doubt that he was extremely frustrated: those whom he thought not to be performing were treated to Molby tongue-lashings

The Swans' squad, 1996-97.
Back row, left to right: Joao Moreira, Christian Edwards, Shaun Garnett, Roger Freestone, Ben Miles, Lee Jones, Steve Torpey, Jason Price.
Middle: Mike Davenport (Physiotherapist), Alan Curtis (Youth Team Coach), Linton Brown, David Thomas, Steve Jones, Jonny Grey,
Kristian O'Leary, Carl Heggs, Paul Morgan (Kit Man), Ron Walton (Youth Development Officer).
Front: Kwame Ampadu, Colin McDonald, Robert King, Damian Lacey, Billy Ayre (Assistant Manager), Jan Molby (Player-Manager),
David Penney, Mark Clode, Richard Appleby, Shaun Chapple.

which were formidable. Speaking after his departure, one senior professional believed that the Dane 'expected us to be Premiership players'. Whether that was true or not, he demanded high standards and, when they were not forthcoming, he often responded angrily. On the other hand, the majority of the players were inspired by the Dane's style, his natural charm off the pitch and by his skills and vision on it. Yet, as results disappointed, without previous experience of managing a small group of men in the tight-knit environment of professional football, Molby was handicapped. He tended to blow hot and cold, whereas motivating individuals and groups requires leadership which has consistency. Individuals may well be motivated by different things, but, for the best results each man needs to know the parameters within which he is working. Jan Molby's problem was that he had to try to learn these things 'on the hoof'. Fortunately, Billy Ayre was at his side to assist, but learning when you appear to be sliding down a slippery slope is far from easy.

It was not surprising, therefore, that all concerned would have liked to see Jan doing what he was best at: playing football while he was learning the 'trade' as a manager. When he

did play, his silky skills, physical strength and football vision set him apart from the players around him. Deft short balls, long searching passes and powerful drives with scarcely a backlift, lit up many matches. The problem was that ageing muscles and weight increase tended to make him more prone to injury than had formerly been the case. All in all, the player-manager was passing through a difficult phase in his apprenticeship. On 7 September there was further pressure brought to bear on the Dane. Doug Sharpe, faced with further abuse, said that he was 'putting the club up for sale'. Then, despite the fact that the next match was won comfortably by 4-0, with only 2,419 people in the ground to see the victory, the chairman remained unmoved: 'It's the end of the road for me!' he announced. There followed some sparring in print between manager and chairman, when Molby complained to the press about lack of support, to which Sharpe's response was that, including the manager, the club had signed six new players since February. At that point the chairman left for Spain and, in his absence, chief executive Robin Sharpe read a resignation letter to the press which had been signed by his father.

On 6 October, every player on the

club's books was offered for sale which, Molby said, was a 'body blow,' adding, 'This demonstrates the kind of help I've had.' The manager's frustration was further aggravated by the knowledge that, because of a Football League ban, had any player left, he would not have been able to buy replacements. By 26 October, the net result of these difficulties was that the club was twenty-second in the league table having gained just fourteen points from fifteen matches. By that time, too, Shaun Garnett, Jan Molby's most expensive signing, had left the Vetch for Oldham in exchange for £150,000. Garnett had never settled in the side, nor shown the form which had recommended him to the Swansea manager. Since he could not bring in new players, the Dane gave youth its head. Damian Lacey, Dai Thomas, Lee Jenkins, Kris O'Leary, Chris Edwards, Jonathan Coates and Ryan Casey were all given a chance. Jenkins, in particular took full advantage of the opportunity and, with all the confidence of youth, made remarkable progress. Meanwhile, Steve Jones was an ever-present rock at the heart of the defence having made a seamless entry to the Football League, while Roger Freestone, David Penney, Steve Torpey and Keith Walker provided the senior experience.

Having been dismissed at the first time of asking from the Coca-Cola Cup and from the FA Cup, Molby and his squad could, at least, concentrate upon improving their league position. They were to do that in remarkable style. After losing at Torquay on 26 October, they lay in twenty-second position in the table. With the manager back in the side for the next game, the Swans won at the Vetch to start a run of thirteen games, of which they won ten and drew one. That form was sufficient to take the side to fourth in the table – a remarkable change in fortunes. Not only was the team winning, but, particularly when Molby was playing, they were doing so with some style. Such was the revival in interest in the city that, for a Christmas time match at the Vetch with Carlisle there were more than 7,000 people in the ground – double the season's average up to that point.

The team's good form continued into the new year, with the manager playing outstandingly in a match against Leyton. The *Post* caught the mood of that day with the headline 'Molby Magic'. Those who looked beyond the particular match being reported might have thought that, after such a poor start, it could be argued that there was something magical about the conversion of the team from strugglers to promotion hopefuls. Not that the revival was without its casualties. Late in January, in a match against Bristol City, young Lee Jenkins leaped to head a ball in competition with a big visiting defender and crashed to the ground concussed. It transpired that the youngster had fractured his cheekbone and, together with complications he would be sidelined for some time. Sadly, this was only the first of two incidents which were to affect young footballers at the Vetch during that campaign, which illustrates something of the vagaries of being a professional footballer.

Whilst the team's form was mixed for the rest of the season, it was able to maintain its place among the play-off group and, when the season proper had ended, they found themselves paired with Chester City in a two-leg semi-final. After holding Chester to a draw on their own pitch, the Swans, with 10,000 people in the Vetch to support them, worked well to win the match and the tie 3-0. The game, though, was won at the

Kwame Ampadu in action against Rochdale.

cost of Steve Jones's broken leg. It was cruel luck for the young man that the accident occurred in the semi-final of a competition which was to culminate at Wembley. It was particularly disappointing since Jones had made a significant contribution to the achievement of a play-off position. Typical of the man, he vowed that he would be back and wished his team-mates good luck. The pathos of the situation was not lost on two men who had had the experience of missing a Wembley final themselves. Keith Walker and David Penney had not been involved in the previous Swans match at the famous stadium, but were to play on this occasion. Consequently, they had had experience of the disappointment felt by those who are not involved. It was small comfort to Steve Jones, but the young man greatly appreciated the concern of the two senior professionals.

Almost 47,000 people were in Wembley to see the play-off final between the Swans and Northampton, with the Welsh contingent being outnumbered almost two to one. Nevertheless, they made themselves heard. Jan Molby has spoken about his own problems on that day, including the difficulty of telling some players that they would not be involved, and of feeling drained physically and mentally himself. The tensions involved with building up to the final, coupled with emotional stress stemming from the team's poor start to the season, seemed to have taken their toll. As a result, the big Dane was not the influential figure which the day

demanded. Nonetheless, the Swans almost took the lead in the first five minutes of the match. Carl Heggs crashed a superb volley goalwards only to see the opposing goalkeeper make a brilliant save. After that, although the teams worked hard, neither side seemed to be able to take control until, with five minutes remaining of the normal time, Northampton were awarded a free kick on the edge of the Swans' penalty area, although there were doubts about the validity of the decision. As usual, a 'wall' was formed in front of the kicker. Then, as the Northampton man ran in to shoot, a Swansea player broke from the wall to charge down the shot. The referee ruled that the Swan had moved too early and said that the kick should be taken again. At the time, no one noticed, but subsequently, in watching the television footage, it could be seen that the Northampton player had moved the ball two feet or so to the left of the original position. This gave him a better angle and a clear path for his shot. He took advantage of this to crash the ball beyond Roger Freestone. With hardly time to kick off again, the match was won and lost. The 'Cobblers' were promoted, while the Swans remained in the Third Division. A day which began with a great deal of hope for the Swansea contingent had turned into one of disappointment. Nevertheless, the optimists took the view that what had been achieved in getting to the final could be built upon. And Doug Sharpe had talked about new owners. There was hope there surely?

Swansea City FC Season 1994/95 — Division 2(3)

#	Date	V	Opponents	Score	Scorers	Att	Freestone R	Jenkins S	Clode M	Ford J	Harris M	Ampadu K	Penney D	Bowen J	Hayes M	Cornforth J	Hodge J	Pascoe C	Torpey S	Perrett D	Hendry J	Jones L	Basham M	Chapple S	Walker K	Burns C	Barnhouse D	McFarlane A	Williams J	Edwards C	Coates J	Cook A	Thomas D
1	Aug-13	H	Brighton	1-1	Penney (pen)	4,640	1	2	3	4	5	6	7	8	9	10	11*	12															
2	Aug-20	A	Hull City	2-0	Cornforth, Ampadu	3,797	1	2	3	4	5	6	8	7	9"	10	11			14													
3	Aug-27	H	Birmingham City	0-2		5,797	1	2	3	4	5	6"	7		9*	10	11	12	8	14													
4	Sep-03	A	Cardiff City	1-1	Hayes	5,523	1	2	3	4	5	6*	7		9"	10	11	12	8	14													
5	Sep-06	A	Shrewsbury Town	3-3	Hodge, Pascoe, Ford	3,534	1	2	3	4	5		8	7		10	11"	6	9	14													
6	Sep-10	H	Bradford City	0-0		3,448	1	2	3	4	5	14		8	12	7*	10	11"	6	9													
7	Sep-13	H	Bristol Rovers	0-0		3,226	1	2	3	4	5	14		8	12		10	11	6*	9	7"												
8	Sep-17	A	Cambridge United	3-1	Penney 2, Torpey	2,795	1	2	3	4	5	14		8	7"		10		6	9	11												
9	Sep-24	H	York City	0-0		2,875	1	2	3	4	5	12		8*	7		10	11"	6	9	14												
10	Oct-01	A	Wycombe W	0-1		4,150	1	2	3	4	5	12		8*	7		10	11	6"	9	14												
11	Oct-08	A	Chester City	2-2	Ampadu, Ford	2,186	1	2	3	4	5		7	8"	12		10	14	6	9*		11											
12	Oct-15	H	Oxford United	1-3	Hendry	3,724	1	2	3	4	5		7	8*	12	14		11	6	9"		10											
13	Oct-22	A	Blackpool	1-2	Ampadu	4,911	15	2		3	5	10		8	7			11"	6		9	1"	4	12									
14	Oct-29	H	Peterborough Utd.	2-0	Hendry, Bowen	2,733	1	2		3	5*	14		8	7	12	10	11"	6		9		4										
15	Nov-01	H	Rotherham United	1-0	Pascoe	2,511	1	2	3	5		12		8*	7	14	10	11"	6		9		4										
16	Nov-05	A	Crewe Alex	2-1	Bowen 2	3,242	1	2	3	5		6		8*	7	14	10	11"			9		4	12									
17	Nov-19	H	Stockport County	2-0	Ampadu, Cornforth	3,019	1	2	3	5		6		8		7"	10	11*	14	12	9		4										
18	Nov-26	A	Wrexham	1-4	Ford	3,598	1	2	3	5		6		8"	12	7*	10	11	14		9		4										
19	Dec-10	H	Hull City	2-0	Torpey 2	2,903	1	2		5				10	8*	7	11				9		4	6	3	12							
20	Dec-17	A	Brighton	1-1	Torpey	6,817	1	2*		5				10	8	7"	11			14	9		4	6	3	12							
21	Dec-26	H	Plymouth Argyle	3-0	Hodge, Hayes 2	4,859	1			5				10	12	7	11"				9		4	6	3	8*	2						
22	Dec-27	A	Leyton Orient	1-0	Hayes	3,259	1			5				10	8	7	6	11"		12	9		4		3		2						
23	Dec-31	H	Huddersfield Town	1-1	Torpey	5,438	1			5				8	14	7*	10	11		12	9		4		3	6"	2						
24	Jan-02	A	AFC Bournemouth	2-3	Hodge, Penney	3,816	1			5				8	12	7	10*	11		14	9		4		3	6"	2						
25	Jan-14	A	Brentford	0-0		7,211	1	2		5				6	8	7	10	11*			9		4		3				12				
26	Feb-04	H	Wrexham	0-0		4,588	1	2		5		3		8	12	7*	10	11			9				4				11				
27	Feb-11	A	Rotherham United	3-3	Williams, Pascoe, Hodge	2,858	1	2		5		3		8		7*	10	12	6	9"					4				14	11			
28	Feb-17	H	Brentford	0-2		3,935	1	2	3	5					8	7"	10	14	6	12					4				9*	11			
29	Feb-21	A	Stockport County	1-0	Torpey	3,088	1	2	3	5		10		7*				12	6	9					4					11	8		
30	Feb-25	H	Wycombe W	1-1	Torpey	3,699	1	2	3"	5		10		7			12	11	6	9			14		4				11*	8			
31	Feb-28	A	Blackpool	1-0	Torpey	2,308	1	2	3	5		10		8	7		11		6	9					4								
32	Mar-04	A	York City	4-2	Bowen 2, Torpey, Hodge (pen)	2,920	1	2	3	5		10"		14	7*		11		6	9					4					12	8		
33	Mar-07	H	Cardiff City	4-1	Williams, Penney, Pascoe, Chapple	3,942	1	2	3	5		10		8			11		6	9				12	4				7*				
34	Mar-11	A	Birmingham City	1-0	Hodge (pen)	16,191	1	2	3	5		10		12	7"		11"		6	9					4						8	14	
35	Mar-17	H	Shrewsbury Town	0-0		4,130	1	2	3	5		10		8*	7"	12	11		6	9					4						14		
36	Mar-21	A	Bradford City	3-1	Cornforth, Ampadu 2	4,417	1	2	3	5		7		12			10	11"	6	9					4					8			
37	Mar-24	A	Cambridge United	1-0	Torpey	4,007	1	2	3	5		7		8			10	11"	6	9					4						14		
38	Apr-01	A	Bristol Rovers	0-1		7,062	1	2		5		7					10	11	6*	9	8		14		4					3"	14		
39	Apr-04	A	Peterborough Utd.	0-1		3,764	1	2	3*	5		7					10	11	6	9	12				4					8			
40	Apr-08	A	Huddersfield Town	0-2		10,105	1	2		5		7*			12	14	10	11"	6	9					4					8		3	
41	Apr-15	H	Leyton Orient	2-0	Torpey, Pascoe	3,277	1	2*	3	5		8			12	7	10	11	6	9					4								
42	Apr-17	A	Plymouth Argyle	1-2	Hodge	5,890	1	2	3	5		8*			14	7	10	11	6	9					4								12
43	Apr-22	H	AFC Bournemouth	1-0	Clode	2,664	1	2	3	5		8			12	7	11	6	9						4								10*
44	Apr-25	H	Crewe Alex	0-1		2,600		2	3	5		10			12	7	11"	6	9		1				4					8*			14
45	Apr-30	A	Oxford United	2-1	Freestone (pen), Chapple	5,244	1	2	3	5		10				7	11	6	9					8	4								
46	May-06	H	Chester City	0-1		2,065	1	2	3	5		14				7	10	11"	6	9*					4							12	8
			Apps				44	42	33	46	14	36	29	25	14	32	38	32	37	3	8	2	13	4	28	3	4	1	6	9	0	1	2
			Subs				1					8	6	6	10	1	5	3	4	12				5		2		2	1		5		2
			Gls				1			1	3		6	5	5	4	3	7	11			2			2				2				

#	Date	V	Opponents	Score	Scorers	Att	Freestone R	Jenkins S	Clode M	Ford J	Harris M	Ampadu K	Penney D	Bowen J	Hayes M	Cornforth J	Hodge J	Pascoe C	Torpey S	Perrett D	Hendry J	Jones L	Basham M	Chapple S	Walker K	Burns C	Barnhouse D	McFarlane A	Williams J	Edwards C	Coates J	Cook A	Thomas D
1	Aug-17	A	Exeter C, CC Cup 1-1	2-2	Harris, Hodge	2,050	1	2	3	4	5	6	8*	7	9	10	11	12															
2	Aug-23	H	Exeter C, CC Cup 1-2	2-0	Penney 2(1pen)	2,523	1	2	3	4	5	6	12	7"	14	10*	11	8	9														
3	Sep-21	A	Norwich C, CC Cup 2-1	0-3		8,053	1	2	3	4	5	12		8	7		10	14	6*	9	11"												
4	Oct-04	H	Norwich C, CC Cup 2-2	1-0	Pascoe	3,568	1	2	3	4	5	7		8	12		10*	11	6	9													
5	Oct-18	A	Torquay Utd, AWS-1	3-1	Hendry 2, Bowen	885		2	3		5			8	7	12		11"	6		9	1	4	10									
6	Oct-26	H	Taffs Well, ABWC-3	7-0	Bowen 3, Hendry 2, Ampadu, Hayes	620	1	2	3	5*		10		8	7	12		11"	6		9		4										14
7	Nov-08	H	Hereford Utd, AWS-1	1-1	Torpey	1,215	1	2	3*	5		6		8"	7	14	10	11		12	9		4										
8	Nov-21	A	Walton&Hersham, FAC-1	2-0	Penney, Ampadu	2,230	1	2	3	5		6		8	7	12	10	11*			9		4										
9	Nov-29	A	Northampton T, AWS-2	1-0	Hendry	2,706	1	2		5				8	7	12	10	11*			9		4	6			3						
10	Dec-04	A	Bashley, FAC-2	1-0	Torpey	2,047	1	2		5				8	7"		10	11		14	9		4	6*	3	12							
11	Dec-07	H	Rhyl, ABWC-4	5-1	O/Goal, Perrett 3, Torpey	491	1			5		10	8			2	11*	9	7				4"	6	3					14			12
12	Jan-07	H	Middlesbrough, FAC-3	1-1	Ford	8,407	1			5		6		8		7*	10	11	9				4		3	2	12						
13	Jan-10	A	Oxford Utd, AWS-QF	2-1	Torpey, Hayes	2,321	1	2"		5		6		8	7		10	11	9				4	14	3								
14	Jan-17	A	Middlesbrough, FAC-3 Rep	2-1	Torpey, Penney	13,940	1	2		5		6		8		7	10	11"	9				4	14	3								
15	Jan-28	A	Newcastle Utd, FAC-4	0-3		34,372	1	2		5				8		7*	10	11	9				4	6	3					12			
16	Jan-31	A	Birmingham C, AWS SF	2-3	Pascoe, O/Goal, aet	20,326	1	2		5				8	14	7	10	11"	6*		9		4	3						12			
17	Feb-14	H	Porthmadog, ABWC-5	8-0	McFarlane 2, Hayes 3, Bowen, Cornforth, Thomas	716	1	2	3					7	6	12	9*	8"	11				4					10	5				14
18	Apr-11	H	Cardiff C, ABWC SF 1-1	0-1		2,654	1	2		5		8			7	12	10	11"	6	9	14		4									3*	
19	May-02	A	Cardiff C, ABWC SF 1-2	0-0		4,227	1	2	3*	5			11		7	12	10		6	9				8	4								

Swansea City FC Season 1995/96   Division 2(3)

Player columns (left to right): Freestone R, Jenkins S, Barnhouse D, Walker K, Edwards C, Pascoe C, Coates J, Heggs C, Torpey S, Cornforth J, Hodge J, Beresford D, Ampadu K, Basham M, Cook A, Clode M, Thomas D, Perrett D, Lampard F, Dennison R, Chapple S, Jones S, Penney D, Mardenborough S, Hurst G, B Edinboro J, Molby J, Garnett S, McDonald C, Brown L, Chapman L, O'Leary K, Jones L

#	Date	V	Opponents	Score	Scorers	Att
1	Aug-12	H	Shrewsbury Town	3 1	Heggs, Cornforth, Freestone (pen)	3,588
2	Aug-19	A	Bristol Rovers	2 2	Torpey, Basham	6,689
3	Aug-26	H	Chesterfield	3 2	Freestone (pen), Torpey, Edwards	3,492
4	Aug-29	A	Stockport County	0 2		4,433
5	Sep-01	H	Carlisle United	1 1	Heggs	3,345
6	Sep-09	A	Walsall	1 4	O/Goal	3,788
7	Sep-12	A	Hull City	0 0		3,519
8	Sep-16	H	York City	0 1		2,422
9	Sep-23	A	Oxford United	1 1	Heggs	2,505
10	Sep-29	A	Burnley	0 3		8,068
11	Oct-07	H	Bradford City	2 0	Torpey 2	2,207
12	Oct-14	A	Peterborough Utd	1 1	Ampadu	3,834
13	Oct-21	H	AFC Bournemouth	1 1	Heggs	1,988
14	Oct-28	A	Wrexham	0 1		4,002
15	Oct-31	A	Brighton	2 0	Torpey, Lampard	4,230
16	Nov-04	H	Wycombe W	1 2	Torpey	2,809
17	Nov-17	A	Crewe Alex	1 4	Pascoe	3,608
18	Nov-25	H	Notts. County	0 0		2,327
19	Dec-02	H	Rotherham United	0 0		1,788
20	Dec-09	A	Oxford United	1 5	Torpey	4,674
21	Dec-16	H	Burnley	2 4	Hurst, Torpey	2,078
22	Dec-26	A	Bristol City	0 1		6,845
23	Jan-10	A	Swindon Town	0 3		6,555
24	Jan-13	H	Bristol Rovers	2 2	Torpey, Edwards	2,956
25	Jan-20	H	Shrewsbury Town	2 1	Heggs, Cornforth	6,532
26	Feb-03	A	Chesterfield	2 3	Torpey 2	4,050
27	Feb-06	A	Stockport County	0 3		1,938
28	Feb-10	H	Swindon Town	0 1		4,452
29	Feb-13	A	Blackpool	0 4		3,992
30	Feb-17	H	Hull City	0 0		1,909
31	Feb-20	A	Carlisle United	0 3		4,645
32	Feb-24	A	York City	0 0		2,786
33	Feb-27	H	Walsall	2 1	Torpey, Hodge	3,546
34	Mar-02	A	Bristol City	2 1	Chapple, Molby	4,109
35	Mar-09	A	Rotherham United	1 1	Torpey	2,714
36	Mar-12	H	Brentford	2 1	Chapple, Molby (pen)	3,538
37	Mar-16	H	Blackpool	0 2		4,478
38	Mar-23	A	Brentford	0 0		4,378
39	Mar-30	A	Bradford City	1 5	Chapman	4,183
40	Apr-02	H	Peterborough Utd	0 0		3,805
41	Apr-06	H	Wrexham	1 3	Torpey	4,256
42	Apr-09	A	AFC Bournemouth	1 3	Chapman	4,049
43	Apr-13	H	Brighton	2 1	Ampadu, Chapman	2,373
44	Apr-20	A	Wycombe W	1 0	Chapman	3,672
45	Apr-27	A	Notts. County	0 4		5,051
46	May-04	H	Crewe Alex	2 1	Torpey, Thomas	2,604

Apps: 45 15 12 32 36 9 7 28 41 17 34 4 40 9 30 25 3 2 8 9 15 16 28 1 2 2 12 9 3 3 7 1 1

Subs: 3 1 2 4 11 4 1 7 2 3 2 3 5 13 2 1 7 1 1 2 5 1

Gls: 2   2 1   5 15 2 1   2 1   1   1   2   1 2   4

#	Date	V	Opponents	Score	Scorers	Att
1	Aug-15	H	Peterborough CCC 1-1	4 1	Hodge 2, Ampadu, Torpey	1,862
2	Aug-22	A	Peterborough, CCC 1-2	0 3	aet, lost on away goals	1,871
3	Sep-26	H	Shrewsbury T, AWS-1	1 1	Torpey	943
4	Oct-17	H	L Orient, AWS-1	0 0		798
5	Nov-11	A	Fulham, FAC-1	0 7		4,798
6	Nov-28	A	Peterborough, AWS-2	0 1	aet, lost on golden goal	1,952

Swansea City FC Season 1996/97 Division 3(4)

#	Date	V	Opponents	Score	Scorers	Att	Freestone R	Appleby R	Clode M	Molby J	Garnett S	Jones S	Penney D	Lacey D	Torpey S	Ampadu K	Thomas D	Chapple S *	Brown L "	McDonald C ^	O'Leary K	Heggs C	Coates J	Edwards C	Walker K	Jenkins L	McGibbon P	Casey R	King R	Phillips G	Moreira J	Price J	Hills J	Brayson P	Willer T	Jones L
1	Aug-17	H	Rochdale	2 1	Thomas, Penney	4,272	1	2	3	4	5	6	7	8	9*	10	11"	12	13																		
2	Aug-24	A	Darlington	1 4	Brown	2,752	1	2*	3"	4	5	6	7	8	9	10	11^	12	13	14																	
3	Aug-27	A	Chester City	0 2		1,946	1	2*	3	4	5	6	7	8"	9	10^	11	12	13	14																	
4	Aug-30	H	Lincoln City	1 2	Penney (pen)	3,111	1			4	5	6	8	14	12	10	11	2	7"	9*	3^	13														
5	Sep-07	A	Carlisle United	1 4	Thomas	5,114	1	7				6	8	4	13	5	11"	2		12	3	9*	10													
6	Sep-10	H	Hereford United	4 0	Thomas, Torpey, Penney(pen), Jenkins	2,479	1	12			5"	6	8		9		11	2		13		14	10	3*	4	7^										
7	Sep-14	H	Fulham	1 2	Thomas	3,791	1	12			5	6	8		9		11	2*		13			10	3	4	7"										
8	Sep-21	A	Doncaster Rovers	1 0	Penney (pen)	1,391	1				6	8			2	11			9*			12	10	3	4	7	5									
9	Sep-28	H	Hull City	0 0		2,961	1			12	5	8			2*	11				4	9	10	6	3	7										
10	Oct-01	A	Leyton Orient	0 1		3,536	1	13^		10	6	8	3		11"	2		12	5	9			4	7"	14										
11	Oct-04	H	Colchester United	1 1	Torpey	2,531	1			10	6	8	3	9	11			5				4	7	2											
12	Oct-12	H	Mansfield Town	0 0		2,003	1		7		6	8	3	9	11"	2				12	10"	5	4		13										
13	Oct-15	A	Hartlepool United	1 1	Torpey	1,310	1		7		6	8	3	9		2*	13		12		10"	5	4		11										
14	Oct-19	H	Scunthorpe United	1 1	Torpey	2,373	1	2"		10	6	8	3	9			13		12		7	5*	4		11										
15	Oct-26	A	Torquay United	0 2		2,755	1	2"	3		6	8		9	13			12	11*		10	5	4	7											
16	Oct-29	H	Wigan Athletic	2 1	Clode, Torpey	2,227	1		3	10	6	8		9		12	2*			11	5	4	7												
17	Nov-02	H	Northampton Town	1 0	Torpey	3,335	1		3	10"	6	8		9			2*		13	12	11	5	4	7											
18	Nov-09	A	Cambridge United	1 2	Coates	3,178	1		3		6	8		9			2		5	13	11	4*	7			10	12"								
19	Nov-19	H	Brighton	1 0	Penney	2,692	1		3		6	8	9	10			2			11	5		7			4									
20	Nov-23	A	Scarborough	1 0	Jenkins	2,005	1		3		6	8	9	10			2			11	5		7			4									
21	Nov-30	H	Torquay United	2 0	O'Leary, Torpey	2,889	1		12		6	8		9	13				2	10"	11	5	4	7			3*								
22	Dec-03	A	Cardiff City	3 1	Ampadu, Jones, Thomas	3,721	1		3		6	8		9	2	12				10*	11	5	4	7											
23	Dec-21	A	Exeter City	2 1	Penney 2(1pen)	2,801	1		3	10	6	8		9	2					11	5	4	7												
24	Dec-26	A	Hereford United	1 0	Penney	4,202	1		3	10	6	8		9	2					11	5	4	7												
25	Dec-28	A	Carlisle United	0 1		7,340	1			10	6	8		9	2					11	5	4	7					3							
26	Jan-11	A	Hull City	1 1	Brown	2,810	1			10	6			9	2		8			11	5	4	7					3							
27	Jan-14	H	Barnet	3 0	Brown, Ampadu, Penney (pen)	3,570	1		12	10*	6	8		9	11"	2	7"			13	5	4	14					3							
28	Jan-18	H	Leyton Orient	1 0	Molby	3,435	1			10	6	8		9	11*	2	7			12	5	4						3							
29	Jan-25	A	Wigan Athletic	2 3	Torpey, O/Goal	4,058	1		3	10	6	8		9	12	2	7			11	5	4						3							
30	Jan-28	H	Doncaster Rovers	2 0	Ampadu, Coates	3,464	1		3*		6	8		9	10		12	7^	13	11"		4			5			2	14						
31	Jan-31	H	Cambridge United	3 1	Penney 2, Brayson	5,772	1			10	6	8		9	2				12	11*	5	4										3	7		
32	Feb-08	A	Northampton Town	2 1	Brayson, Penney (pen)	6,178	1			10*	6	8			2		12	9		11	5	4		13								3	7"		
33	Feb-11	A	Fulham	1 2	Coates	4,836	1				6	8			2	10*	9			11	5	4		12								3	7		
34	Feb-15	A	Scarborough	1 2	Penney (pen)	3,312	1				6	8			2	10	9*	12		11	5	4										3	7		
35	Feb-22	A	Brighton	2 3	Brayson, Walker	6,645	1				6	8		9		10*	2			11	5	4		12								3	7		
36	Mar-02	H	Cardiff City	0 1		4,443	1	10"		12	6	8		9		13	2*			11	5^	4		14								3	7		
37	Mar-08	H	Exeter City	3 1	Brayson, Thomas 2	3,115	1				6	8		9	2	10*	12		4	11"	5			13								3	7		
38	Mar-15	A	Barnet	1 0	Ampadu	1,881	1				6	8		9	2	10*	12			11	5											3	7	4	
39	Mar-22	H	Darlington	1 1	Molby (pen)	4,176	1			10	6			9	2	8				11	5											3	7	4	
40	Mar-29	A	Rochdale	3 2	Molby 2(1pen), Brayson	1,884	1			10	6	8		9	12	2*				11	5											3	7	4	
41	Mar-31	H	Chester City	2 1	Molby (pen), Torpey	6,284	1			10	6	8		9	12	2				11	5											3	7	4*	
42	Apr-05	A	Lincoln City	0 4		3,348	1			10	6	8		9	2				4*	11	5		12						3	9					
43	Apr-11	A	Colchester United	1 3	Molby	3,162	1			10	6	8		9	3	2				12	11	5		7*										4	
44	Apr-19	H	Mansfield Town	3 2	Thomas, Heggs 2	4,868	1			10	6	8		9	3	2*		12		13	11	5		7										4"	
45	Apr-26	A	Scunthorpe United	0 1		3,130	1			10*	6	8		9	3	2				12	11	5	4	7											
46	May-03	H	Hartlepool United	2 2	Thomas, Appleby	5,423	1	7*			6	8		9	12	2					11	4								3					5	1
	Apps						45	8	16	26	6	46	44	9	37	25	31	10	13	3	9	5	38	36	31	21	1	3	2	0	10	1	11	11	7	1
	Subs							3	2	2			1	2	4	5	7	9	7	3	9	2		2		7		1		1						
	Gls							1	1	6		1	13		9	4	9		3		1	2	3		1	2							5		

#	Date	V	Opponents	Score	Scorers	Att	Freestone R	Appleby R	Clode M	Molby J	Garnett S	Jones S	Penney D	Lacey D	Torpey S	Ampadu K	Thomas D	Chapple S *	Brown L "	McDonald C ^	O'Leary K	Heggs C	Coates J	Edwards C	Walker K	Jenkins L	McGibbon P	Casey R	King R	Phillips G	Moreira J	Price J	Hills J	Brayson P	Willer T	Jones L
1	Aug-20	H	Gillingham, CCC 1-1	0 1		2,711	1	2	3	4	5	6	8	7*	9	10	11"	12	13																	
2	Sep-03	A	Gillingham, CCC 1-2	0 2		3,633	1	9			5	6	8		13		11	2	7"		3*		10	4							12					
3	Nov-16	H	Bristol City, FAC-1	1 1	Torpey	5,629	1		3		6	8		9	10			2*		12	11"	5		7			13			4						
4	Nov-26	A	Bristol City, FAC-2 Rep	0 1		8,017	1		3*		6	8		9	10	12				2	7	11	5							4						
5	Jan-08	H	Wycombe, AWS-1	1 1	Thomas, aet, Swans won 6-5 on pens	1,638	1		13	12	6	8		9	10	2			7*		11"	5	4							3						
6	Jan-21	H	Bristol City, AWS-2	0 1		5,360	1		13		6	8		9		2	10				11	5	4	7"				12		3*						
7	May-10	A	Chester C, P/Off SF-1	0 0		5,104	1	7			6	8		9	10	2*				12	11	5	4							3						
8	May-14	H	Chester C, P/Off SF-2	3 0	Thomas, Torpey, Heggs	10,027	1				6*	8		9"	10	2	12	13		7	11	5	4							3						
9	May-24	N	Northampton T, P/Off F	0 1	at Wembley	46,804	1			10		8		9	6	2*		12		7	11	5	4							3						

Chapter 24

Enter Silver Shield plc

1997-98

When Doug Sharpe announced that the new owners of the Swans were the Silver Shield Group plc, the analogy of the knight in shining armour riding to the rescue of the club was easily evoked. The knight, or more properly the knights, said that they were determined to develop a viable club at the Vetch and, in the near future, a purpose-built stadium at Morfa. The vision and the determination which they evinced caught the public imagination, though inevitably there were those who were cynical about the motives of the new owners.

The men who were charged with ensuring that the objectives were met were Neil McClure, the chairman of the plc and Steve Hamer, a native of Neath and a long-standing Swans fan, who was to take on the chairmanship of the Vetch club. The pair had been introduced to Doug Sharpe by former Swans director Terry Francis in May 1997, but it was not until the middle of July of that year that agreement was finally reached. The plan, the new directors announced, was to build the new stadium in conjunction with the council of the City and County of Swansea and Swansea Rugby Club and have it ready for the start of the 1999-2000 season. It was clear that McClure's staff had done their homework in relation to the potential of Swansea to sustain a professional club in both sports. As he said, 'Swansea is larger than Newcastle, I can't see any reason why it could not support a Premier League club.' There was a caveat, though, for he added, 'There's no point in going straight up to division one unless we have built a club which is on a sound business footing so as to sustain development.' That, he said, was their intention.

On the playing side, when they arrived, the new board found that several senior players had not signed the contracts which they had been offered because they considered the terms to be inadequate. Hamer and McClure urged them all to give the new board a chance to think over the issues. Unfortunately, David Penney had already agreed to join Cardiff City, Dai Thomas had been sold to Watford for £100,000 and Carl Heggs was determined to leave. Keith Walker and Roger Freestone were 'considering their position', but, after urgent talks, both men signed for the club again. The takeover had not been completed in time to retain the others.

Early discussions with Jan Molby resulted in an offer being accepted from Bristol City for Steve Torpey (£400,000, of which a third had to be passed to the player's former club), while Tony Bird and Dave O'Gorman came to the Vetch from Barry Town for a combined fee of £60,000. In August, the manager brought John Hills back to Swansea for a further loan period, signed Gary Jones from Caernarfon and, in September, paid Wrexham £108,000 for Steve Watkin. Molby also made changes in his support structure, promoting Alan Curtis to first-team coach and long-serving Ron Walton

The Swans' squad, 1997-98.
Back row, left to right: Jamie Harris, Christian Edwards, Jason Jones, Roger Freestone, Lee Jones, Aidan Newhouse, Jason Price.
Middle: Paul Morgan (Kit Man), Joao Moreira, Jonathan Coates, Mark Clode, Kwame Ampadu, Steve Watkin, Richard Appleby,
Tony Bird, Kristian O'Leary, Nick Cusack, Alan Curtis (Coach), Ron Walton (Coach).
Front: Ryan Casey, Steve Jones, Damian Lacey, David O'Gorman, Keith Walker, Alan Cork (Manager),
Gary Jones, Lee Jenkins, Linton Brown, Robert King.

Tony Bird – airborne v. Cardiff.

to youth team manager. The Dane expressed himself quietly confident about the season ahead and believed that the team would do well again. No Swans supporter could be found who did not cherish the same hope.

After two matches had been played, the manager's forecast appeared to have been soundly based. Brighton and Scunthorpe were both beaten without either club registering a goal against the Swans. At that point, the talk in the pre-season period about the club needing new defenders appeared to lack substance. Unfortunately, that myth was exploded in the next match, when, after having seventy per cent of the play, the team lost 7-4, at Hull. That defeat pushed the Swans down to twelfth in the table and, by the end of December they were in eighteenth place. Throughout this period the manager had been unable to play, which was unfortunate, for, as had been demonstrated during the previous campaign, his presence made a significant difference to the

performance of the side. Chairman Steve Hamer, urged the Dane to play, but Molby was reluctant, saying that he was not fit. He appeared to have put on weight and some believed that his experience at Wembley, when he was unable to satisfy his own demanding standards,

had convinced him that his playing days were over. Yet, ostensibly, he was a player-manager, and, in the eyes of the Swansea chairman, given the unfavourable results, it was vital that Jan Molby was back in the side as soon as possible. Molby's reaction to the chairman's enthusiastic, involved style was also less than

wholehearted. As a consequence of these and several other matters, relationships deteriorated and following a 3-1 defeat at Peterborough, the sixth in the first ten league matches, and defeat in the Coca Cola Cup, the Dane and his assistant, Billy Ayre, were dismissed. It was hardly the outcome desired by the new board. Yet, in striving to develop an effective organisation, if key figures cannot work together, for whatever reason, then changes have to be made, even though unpopular.

Meantime, at Fulham, the new owner had dismissed the club's management team of Micky Adams and Alan Cork, even though the duo had taken the club to promotion. Being London-based, and seeking a new manager for the Swans, Steve Hamer and Neil McClure took the opportunity to talk to the two men about the possibility of their coming to the Vetch. Their response was positive, and they were appointed on 8 October, Adams as manager and Cork as first-team coach. On arriving, Micky Adams said that he was going to take time to 'look at things', leaving training for the next league match in the hands of Alan Curtis. When that match was lost and was followed by two further defeats, on 23 October the manager announced that he had resigned. He told the press that replacing Jan Molby had been part of the challenge but that Swansea needed quality Third Division footballers and 'At the moment I do not see many there.' He also complained about not being given the money to buy new men, although, on his arrival, when told that cash would be available in eight weeks, he replied, 'That's fine. I need time to assess the squad.' Ten days before his resignation, there was a strong rumour in footballing circles

> *An unhappy series of events resulted in the club having eight managers from the resignation of Frank Burrows until the appointment of John Hollins. Burrows resigned on 2 October 1995; Bobby Smith was installed on 3 October and sacked on 22 December, at which point Jimmy Rimmer was appointed in an acting role. On 7 February, Michael Thompson appointed Kevin Cullis as manager and Cullis was relieved of his duties by Doug Sharpe a week later. Jimmy Rimmer returned as acting manager on that date and remained until Jan Molby was appointed on 22 February 1996. Molby was sacked on 8 October 1997 and was replaced by Micky Adams on the following day. When Adams resigned on 22 October, Alan Cork was given the opportunity to manage the club and did so until he was replaced by John Hollins on 1 July 1998.*

The Swans' squad, 1998-99.
Back row, left to right: Jonathan Coates, Aidan Newhouse, Jason Smith, Mathew Bound, Karl Munroe, Jamie Harris, Jason Price.
Middle: Malcolm Elias (Youth Development Officer), Ron Walton (Youth Coach), Nick Cusack, Ryan Casey, Julian Alsop, Lee Jenkins,
Steve Watkin, Roger Freestone, Jason Jones, Tony Bird, Kristian O'Leary, Carl Mainwaring, Charlie Hartfield,
Mike Davenport (Physiotherapist), Jeremy Charles (Youth Coach), Paul Morgan (Kit Manager).
Front: Alan Curtis (Assistant Manager), Martin Thomas, Michael Howard, Gareth Phillips, Richard Appleby, Damian Lacey, Keith Walker,
Stuart Roberts, Dave O'Gorman, Steve Jones, Jamie Davies, Mark Clode, John Hollins (Manager).

that Micky Adams was going to join a London club and that, for a variety of reasons, he favoured that location. As it happened, within days of leaving the Vetch he joined Brentford as their manager, confirming statements made during the previous week by Eddie May and Barry Fry, among others, that it was well-known in London that he had been in discussions with the Griffin Park club. Unfortunately, whatever the truth, his resignation was hardly helpful to the Swansea cause. The journalists had a field day as they listed the number of managers the Swans had had over a three-year period. Clearly, the new board had to respond to Micky Adams's change of mind and, when Alan Cork said that he would like to stay, it was agreed that he should be given the chance to be manager. Even though, during the Adams-Cork partnership, the record had been: played three lost three, the new manager saw more in the club's squad than did his former boss. Alan Cork was appointed on 23 October and took Alan Curtis as his assistant. In addition, Ian Brandfoot, an experienced Football League manager in his own right, was to continue to act as adviser and chief scout.

Happily, the next match (away at Doncaster) was won 3-0, with goals from Tony Bird, Dave O'Gorman and Damian Lacey, and that was followed by a fine win at Ninian Park, where a Keith Walker

'screamer' beat the home side. In addition, there was a new man in the Swans team for the next match, Cork brought Nick Cusack to the Vetch from Fulham (£15,000) and, days later, recruited Aidan Newhouse from the same club (£30,000). Unfortunately, there followed a sequence of four matches during which only one point was picked up. Cork's next move was to take advantage of Ian Brandfoot's advice and sign Matthew Bound, a big, left-sided defender, from Stockport County (£55,000), who was followed by Charlie Hartfield, who had been on Sheffield United's books. As is always the case, new men took time to settle in and the Swans could not get away from the bottom quarter of Division Three. There were some fine performances, though, which encouraged the team, management and supporters. Interestingly, one followed an experiment with positive thinking. After Darlington had been beaten 4-0 at the Vetch, the manager, in his weekly *Post* column, told his readers that he had called in a local hypnotist, Ron Cole, to help boost the squad's confidence. 'It's not a gimmick,' he wrote, 'but a serious attempt to help the players.' Perhaps the manager should have continued with the experiment, for, as the season wore on, results were still largely unfavourable, and this despite the presence of 6'5" striker, Julian Alsop, who had been signed for

£25,000 after a loan period. There was concern, too, about the club's disciplinary record and the worrying financial considerations. For example, in November, a Sky televised match from the Vetch attracted less than three thousand people and, a lack-lustre performance from the Swans hardly helped promote the club among those who might have attended. At the end of the campaign the Swans were twentieth in the league table and there was a general feeling among supporters, despite the number of signings, that little progress had been made. Certainly, the board was frustrated, as were the management team and the players. These were among the anxieties which festered during the close season.

1998-99

On 24 June, two new men were signed by Alan Cork: Martin Thomas, a mid-fielder, came from Fulham, and Jason Smith, a central defender, joined from Tiverton Town. Thomas came out of contract, whilst Smith cost £10,000. Smith had been recommended by Phil Chant and, subsequently by chief executive Peter Day, who had seen the player in an FA Vase final at Wembley. They were to prove to be sound signings, although Cork was not to have the opportunity of working with them. On the last day of June, the former Wimbledon striker departed from the Vetch to be replaced by John Hollins, MBE, the former Chelsea, Arsenal and England player. The general consensus of opinion at board level was that Alan Cork had done as much as he could, and that, despite a series of difficulties which he'd had to face, he had worked hard. In addition, several of his signings were to prove to be of considerable importance to the Vetch club. However, given the board's ambitious plans, it was felt that an experienced manager should be appointed to take the club through its next stage of development. Hollins, they believed, was the man for that job.

The timing of the new manager's appointment surprised many people, but the major reason was to give John Hollins the opportunity to get to know his squad and work with them in good time before the start of the new season. A pre-season programme had already been put in place, involving a week at an Army assault course complex and friendly matches in Ireland. Hollins adopted this schedule and made his presence felt during this period whilst he assessed his squad and laid down the footballing approach which he wanted to follow. On returning from Ireland, he told the press that he had been impressed by the quality of some of the players, picking out some of the younger men in the process and speaking warmly about the work which had been done by Alan Curtis and Ron Walton in bringing them through the club's youth scheme.

Unfortunately, the 'feel-good factor' which the manager had hoped for was not promoted by early results. The first five league matches of the season included one win, one draw and three defeats, though the supporters were heartened by the kind of football which Hollins was trying to get his team to play. In the Coca Cola Cup, for example, Norwich City were held to a draw at the Vetch and only won the second leg at Carrow Road after extra time. Furthermore, the quality of the football played by the Swans matched that of the Canaries. In the Vetch leg, Roger Freestone had saved a penalty and young Stuart Roberts was a revelation on the right wing. Nonetheless, in the league, by

Stuart Roberts skips past West Ham's Julian Dicks.

the end of October, results still left much to be desired. Despite the style of football, the side had won just four of the fifteen matches which had been played and lost six, but then the team was given a bigger stage on which to perform; they were drawn to play Millwall at the Vetch in the FA Cup. Nearly six thousand people were at the match which was won in style 3-0, with Alsop, Price and Thomas scoring the goals. It was a victory which gave the Swansea faithful something to purr about. They had outplayed the London side in both skill and tenacity and were widely acclaimed by the press. In the next round, for another home tie, Stoke City, then top of Division Two, were the opponents. Prior to the match, the Potteries side were made favourites, but, with an eight thousand gate to cheer them on, the Swans won again, this time courtesy of a Richard Appleby goal. The relatively poor league form was forgotten, as cup fever, once more, swept the city.

Importantly, the performances of the team in the cup had a positive effect on league form and by the turn of the year, the side had improved its position in the table. After half the matches of the season had been played the Swans were eleventh. Whilst manager Hollins invoked the 'one-game-at-a-time' gospel which was reflected in these improved results, it was the cup which continued to attract the attention of the Swansea public, indeed, the football world. By then, Cyril the Swan had become a firm favourite with fans and the media and, when it

Cyril the Swan.

was announced that the Swans were to play West Ham United on their own pitch, the mascot and a small army of supporters wended their way to Upton Park in good spirits. Once again, it was the home side which the experts expected to win, the Swans being thought to have little chance against a Premier League team on their own turf. Indeed, had the Swansea supporters who travelled to Upton Park believed all they read in the papers, they would not have bothered to go. As it was, not only did they go but, even though heavily outnumbered, the vocal support which they provided for the under-dogs was of remarkable benefit to the Swansea players. Bouyed up by this support, the Vetch men 'played out of their skins', taking the lead through a Jason Smith goal and only conceding a rather fortuituous equaliser minutes from the end. As a result, a replay was necessary. At the Vetch, a capacity crowd (at least those supporting the team in white) came to see another piece of giant-killing; and they did. In the twenty-ninth minute of the match an ebulient Martin Thomas crashed home a fine goal to give the Swans the lead, which they held until the final whistle, though Roger Freestone did make a fine save during the last quarter of the match. John Hollins was delighted with his men, most of whom had been written off only months before as not good enough for the Third Division. They had beaten an expensively assembled Premiership side whilst playing good football and had been an outstanding team, with every man supporting the others. Once again, the city had a team about which it could feel proud.

Because of cup commitments, the Swans did not play a league match in January until they visited Exeter City on the ninth of the month and then were not involved until a visit to Barnet on the thirtieth. After their amazing exploits in the cup, the result of the Exeter match was something of a surprise, the Devon club winning 4-0. Yet the fans were unmoved. The boys, they reasoned, must have had the next round of the cup on their minds. Whilst manager Hollins might have had little sympathy with that reasoning, the reality of the situation was that the confidence of the players was unaffected. The team, the management and the supporters were savouring the thought of a visit from another Premier League side, Derby County. Whilst, this time, the fairytale writer was absent, during an exciting, hard-fought match the Swans gave a fine account of themselves and, for much of the game it looked as though there would need to be a replay at Derby. Unfortunately for the Swans, with just nine minutes left to play, the visitors scored to give them a lead which was held until the end. The Swans were out of the cup, but they had made their mark and shown many qualities individually and as a team of which they could feel proud.

Between the cup defeat and the end of March the Swans won six and drew three of their league matches. This surge took the team to sixth

position in the table and, even though Plymouth spoiled the party by winning at the Vetch and Brentford won on their own ground, three victories in the last four matches of the season saw the Swans finish in seventh position. One again, the team were in the play-offs. Given their slow start to the season as well as heavy cup commitments, John Hollins and Alan Curtis must have felt pleased with the outcome. Unfortunately, a fresher, physical, direct Scunthorpe side won the semi-

> *During the 1998-99 season Ron Walton's youth squad won all four of the competitions in which they were involved.*

final of the competition over two legs, though Lady Luck had a great deal to say in the process. The Scunthorpe woodwork was rattled on several occasions during both legs, while the final match was only won in extra time. Disappointment notwithstanding, there was resolve at the Vetch: we'll do it . . . next season! The spirit in the camp boded well. However, the management team, the board, the players and the fans must have secretly muttered, but, please, this time, let's finish in the first three!

Looking back over the season the management team could take great satisfaction from the performances of club's youth squad. Ron Walton's youngsters had the satisfaction of winning all four competitions in which they were involved, and Malcolm Elias and Jeremy Charles made great headway in developing the broader youth organisation which focused particularly upon recruiting and developing younger footballers. Several of the young players associated with the scheme have caught the eye of knowledgeable observers and much is expected of them. At first team level, Michael Howard and Jason Smith could look back on a successful first full season in the Football League, Matthew Bound played more matches than anyone else and was a dominant figure in defence, and Nick Cusack, who played almost as many, led by

example. Of the youngsters, Stuart Roberts promised much for the future, while Lee Jenkins began to remind everyone of his rich talent.

On the financial front, however, at the summer annual meeting the chairman announced a deficit of £480,000 for the season 1997-8. As he said, it was clear that the club could not continue to endure such losses and that it was vital that it was managed as astutely as possible so as to ensure its viability in the short, medium and long term.

1999-2000

Whoever in the Great Hall of Sporting Fates was responsible for writing the script for Division Three's turn-of-the-century season, he must have had a dark sense of humour. Particularly during the later stages of the campaign, several sides who had been in contention for most of the season, the Swans among them, stumbled and stuttered as, seemingly easy points went a-begging. Of course, given that mere mortals have little insight into the complexities of scriptwriting in the Great Hall, those who manage football clubs have to make do with their own projections and assumptions and are not to know when or if these tension-building episodes will occur.

At the Vetch, as the new season approached, the thinking of the fans and management alike was influenced by several factors. For example, after having reached the play-off stage at the end of the previous season, there was an expectation that the club would be running for promotion this time. Indeed, one bookmaker made the Swans joint-favourites to achieve that goal. The fans, of course, also harboured such hope, though the man in the Swansea street was of the opinion that the squad needed to be strengthened in order to ensure that promotion was achieved. Yet, when the players reported back after their summer break, there was just one 'new' face. Former Vetch favourite, John Cornforth, announced that he was to join the Swans in their pre-season activities with a view to signing a contract, if all went well. In the event, manager Hollins decided not to take up the option and 'Corny' moved on to Cardiff City. The manager's conclusion

The Swans' squad, 1999-2000 – The Champions.
Back row, left to right: A. Bird, J. Smith, J. Jones, R. Freestone, C. Thomas, M. Bound, S. Jones, K. O'Leary.
Middle: M. Howard, M. Thomas, J. Price, D. Lacey, J. Davies, J. Alsop, J. Coates, R. Appleby, T. Mutton, M. Keegan, B. Morgan.
Front: S. Roberts, L. De Vulgt, G. Phillips, A. Curtis, N. Cusack, J. Hollins, R. Casey, L. Jenkins, D. Barwood.
Absent: Steve Watkin and Walter Boyd.

disappointed many fans, but was indicative of his objective decision-making. Hollins was certainly not seeking popular acclaim; he was doing what he believed to be right. In response to a continual stream of questions on the topic of new faces from the media at large, he repeated his mantra, 'I believe that I have the players in my squad to do the job!' It was a message which he was to restate time and again as the season developed.

The opening match of the new campaign took place at York, where the newly relegated side beat the Swans by the only goal of the game. John Holllins, however, was not fazed, for the side had played well, and his confidence was shown to be soundly based when his team won four victories in succession. In one of those, against Carlisle, Roger Freestone made three crucial saves. When being interviewed after the game, the goalkeeper, interestingly, felt it necessary to say, 'There are a lot of doubting Thomases in Swansea and we mean to prove them wrong. Whatever eleven players are on the pitch will give their blood for the club.' The victories propelled the team into joint-third position in the table, and by then, the side's defensive unit was proving to be extremely effective, with Matthew

Bound and Jason Smith dominant at its heart. Others did well, too, with Jason Price scoring three of the seven goals registered. With such momentum generated, it was unfortunate, then, that the club took the opportunity to postpone the next fixture (with Cheltenham) on the grounds that it had several players in the Welsh squad. Without a match on the Saturday, when they played again, the team seemed to have lost momentum. There followed a sequence of seven matches during which only one was won. That win, however proved to be important for it was a fine 2-0 victory over Rotherham, who were to be runners-up to the Swans. New signing Walter Boyd, a Jamaican international, endeared himself to the Vetch faithful by scoring both goals.

Nonetheless, with the Swans having slipped down to thirteenth in the table, supporters began to let their feelings be known. After a dismal draw with Cheltenham, there were even calls for the manager's head. At that, chairman Steve Hamer stated quite clearly, that he and the board were confident in John Hollins's management skills and that they were fully behind their manager. Given that 'the chairman's full backing' can sometimes be a precursor to a sacking, there were

some rueful comments around the Vetch at that time. John Hollins, however, answered his critics with positive results. As it transpired, the 0-0 draw with Cheltenham began a remarkable sequence of eight matches during which the opposition failed to score. Roger Freestone, Steve Jones, Michael Howard and the club's two centre-backs, seemed impregnable. In addition, by beating Chester City 1-0 on their own ground on 27 November, the 'clean sheet' sequence merged with another. In succession, York, Hartlepool, Brighton, Leyton, Plymouth, Peterborough, Hartlepool and Macclesfield were all defeated, and, in the process another club record was established. During that run, apart from the meanness of the defence, excellent performances from Nick Cusack, Jonathan Coates, Steve Watkin and others, demonstrated the strength of the side. Primarily, though, it was a team effort. They worked for each other, they were determined, confident in their collective ability and, as demonstrated by an excellent win at Peterborough after being two goals down, they never gave up. Cusack proved to be an inspirational leader as well as a scorer of crucial goals. Unfortunately, Damian Lacey, who had established himself in the side,

Steve Watkin wrestling for the ball.

suffered a leg injury, which was to keep him out of football for the remainder of the season. Such are the frustrations of the professional footballer. When the winning run ended with a 2-1 defeat at Southend, the Swans had climbed briefly into first position in the table, but subsequently fell back to third. Talk among the fans was about automatic promotion. Yet there were many contenders still in with a chance. When pressed about the team's chances, the Hollins/Curtis axis kept its powder dry. The old message was, we're taking one game at a time. Cliché it might have been, but the management team's focused philosophy was to stand them in good stead as the season unravelled.

At the beginning of February the team had established itself in second place in the table and the Vetch crowds were there in numbers to reinforce the promotion drive. They came to expect victory, albeit by narrow margins, and were overjoyed when, in a Sky-televised match, promotion contenders Northampton Town were beaten 4-1. The atmosphere in the ground that day was superb and with a dozen matches to play and the Swans firmly placed in second spot, to the fans, promotion seemed assured. That was also the view of bookmaker Jack Brown, for he paid out on bets which had been placed at the beginning of the season that the Swans would be promoted. John Hollins, though, would have none of it: 'We haven't won anything yet,' was his telling remark.

As it happened, these were very

wise words, for, in the next eight matches, the Swans won just once. Importantly, though, they picked up five points from draws. Those points were to prove to be invaluable, for, as the Swans were stumbling, so were those around them. Thus it was that, prior to the match against Torquay on 22 April, the Swans still held second spot in the table. Then, when the Devon club was defeated 2-1 and rival teams did not do well, the Vetch men moved into first place. Happily, the next two matches were also won, as was automatic promotion – as a result of a fine victory over Exeter. So it turned out that, with second-placed Rotherham away as the final match of the season, the stage was set for a dramatic ending to a remarkable campaign. By then, management and fans were focused on winning the championship, for the Swans needed only to draw to achieve that goal.

The whole squad set off for Yorkshire, although three of the regulars were sidelined. Jason Smith had a knee injury, as did Julian Alsop while, and for the second season in succession, key forward Steve Watkin was unavailable, this time due to a facial injury. It was bad luck for these players, all of whom had made a fine contribution during the season, and it meant that John Hollins had to bring in others from his squad. Typically, Hollins shrugged off the problem: 'We've got the men to do the job!' The manager switched the dependable Steve Jones to partner Matthew Bound, moved Jason Price to right back and brought Kris O'Leary into central mid-field. Against a rawboned set of attackers, after ten minutes of settling down, the new combination did very well, containing Rotherham and probing on the attack. It was a hard-fought contest which, with the home side adopting a no-nonsense approach, called for a resolute performance from each man in the team. They were not found wanting. Walter Boyd weaved a bit of magic only for the ball to bobble as he shot; Martin Thomas, anticipating beautifully, ran onto a through ball only to be thwarted by the home keeper; and, with minutes to go, Jason Price, legs a-whirling, dribbled into the home penalty area only to be brought down. Matthew Bound took the penalty which was awarded and the Swans were in the lead with minutes to go. There followed a pitch invasion with, strangely, the home supporters refusing to leave, which necessitated the referee taking the players off the field. By then the tension in the ground was audible.

J.J. clattered to the ground, Walter Boyd looks on as Martin Thomas shoots.

When the the players returned, Rotherham were also awarded a penalty. Although Roger Freestone got his hand to the ball, he could not prevent it going into the net. Two minutes later, the Swans were champions, for the game ended 1-1. The Swansea contingent in the ground were ecstatic. For the first time since 1949, Swansea City had won the championship of their division.

Medals and a substantial trophy were presented and, after the ceremony, the players and management returned to the coach which was to transport them back to the Vetch. It was then that the whole party were stunned by the news that a loyal supporter, Terry Coles, had lost his life that afternoon, having apparently been crushed by a police horse as he queued to get into Millmoor. As the enormity of the news hit everyone, the triumph of the day was pushed into the background and celebrations cancelled. It was a sad irony that a loyal, level-headed supporter, having travelled many miles to see his favourites play, would not be coming home.

On the Tuesday following the clinching of the championship, a match with Premiership Aston Villa had been arranged as part of the benefit celebrations for Keith Walker. After careful consideration, the Vetch management decided to go ahead with the game and to combine the event, sensitively, with a memorial for Terry Coles. That a poignant prelude to the game was achieved with great dignity said much for all concerned. Wreaths were laid on the centre circle, the championship trophy, dressed in black ribbon, set among them and a touching prayer said by Kevin Johns. The fans responded appropriately and, after the game, as the supporters streamed away from the Vetch, one could sense an air of thoughtfulness. The

Nick Cusack by Rhys

Swans were champions; Terry Coles would have been delighted with that.

P.S.
You can't do better than first! That was the achievement of John Hollins and his management team, who might be forgiven for singing Sinatra's 'My Way'. Yet, despite the fact that 'the tables do not lie' and the silverware is in the Vetch trophy cabinet, after the dust had settled, there were still the doubters to whom Roger Freestone had referred early in the season. One man said that many people did not believe that the new stadium would be built at Morfa; another that 'at last we have admitted that we have no cash', and another that 'unless we strengthen our midfield and attack, we'll come straight back, like Cardiff City'. Given that the club's owners have reported losses over the last three years in excess of £1,250,000 and are said to be having to face a further

Matthew Bound and Nick Cusack were selected for the Division Three XI by their peers. John Hollins was voted Nationwide 'Manager of the Season' for Division Three and Roger Freestone was capped by Wales against Brazil. Roger's achievement in becoming an international from a Third Division base equals that of Alan Curtis, who in 1976 was picked by Wales whilst playing in the old Fourth Division. Freestone also walked away with the Sky Sports 'Third Division Goalkeeper of the Year' award, polling more than double the number of votes obtained by the runner-up.

deficit of around £650,000 in the promotion season, it does not take a genius to see that running a club like the Swans is financially demanding. When you make a loss in business it is obvious that you are spending more than you are receiving. So, without the continuing commitment of Ninth Floor (successors to Sliver Shield plc), the football club could not trade. Even so, early in the season, a six-figure sum was provided to bring Walter Boyd to the Vetch, while the company has continued to support football at the Vetch at considerable cost to itself. In addition, significant sums have been spent on the planning process for the Morfa and, as reported, in conjunction with the rugby club and the council the stadium will be built. Certainly, as far as the Swans are concerned, the new stadium is a vital factor in the development of the club and its board will do everything possible to ensure, with its partners, that it does happen. As regards new players, chairman Steve Hamer is on record as saying that the board will back the manager's judgement. That remains the key. In two seasons in charge, the manager has reached the play-offs and won the championship. It's the kind of record which suggests that he knows what he's about.

As the Second Division beckons, every Swans fan will be hoping that the Hollins/Curtis team can keep the momentum going. Onwards and upwards is the objective, though the club must ensure that it becomes and remains viable as a business entity. The manager and the key players are of the opinion that they will do well in their new competition. Time will tell, but if that confidence is justified, there is no reason why some future writer will not be arguing that the 2000-2001 season was the springboard for further promotion for Swansea City.

Up the Swans!

Swansea City FC Season 1997/98 Division 3(4)

#	Date	V	Opponents	Score	Scorers	Att	Freestone R	Price J	Moreira J	Walker K	Edwards C	Coates J	Lacey D	O'Gorman D	Bird T	Ampadu K	Puttnam D	Hills G	Jones G	Chapple S	Appleby R	O'Leary K	Harris J	Jenkins L	Jones L	Agnew P	Watkin S	Molby J	Casey R	Phillips G	Clode M	Cusack N	Newhouse A	Bound M	Mainwaring C	Hartfield C	Trevitt S	Brown L	Barwood D	Alsop J	Howard M	Munroe K	Jones J
																		12*	13*	14^																				
1	Aug-09	H	Brighton	1 0	Bird	6,640	1	2	3	4	5	6	7	8	9	10	11																										
2	Aug-23	H	Scunthorpe United	2 0	O/Goal, Bird (pen)	4,895	1	2		4	5	6		8"	9	10	11	3	7*	12	13																						
3	Aug-30	A	Hull City	4 7	Coates, Bird, Price, O/Goal	5,198	1	2		4	5	6		8	9	10	11	3			7																						
4	Sep-02	A	Barnet	0 2		1,946	1	2				6		8	9	10	11*	3			7	5	12																				
5	Sep-05	H	Torquay United	2 0	O'Gorman, Bird	4,135	1	2		4		6		8	9	10		3	12	11*	7	5																					
6	Sep-09	A	Darlington	2 3	Bird, O'Gorman	2,150	1	2		4		6		8	9	10		3			7	5		11																			
7	Sep-13	A	Macclesfield Town	0 3		2,479		2		4	5	12		8"	9	10		3*			7		13	11	1	6																	
8	Sep-20	H	Colchester United	0 1		3,414	1	2*		4	5	6		8	9	10*		11"	12		7		13			3																	
9	Sep-27	H	Leyton Orient	1 1	Bird	3,494	1	2	3	4	5	6		8"	9		11		7*		12	13				10																	
10	Oct-04	A	Peterborough Utd.	1 3	Bird	5,849	1	2			5	11			9			8*	6	7	4		3			10	12																
11	Oct-11	A	Exeter City	0 1		3,909	1	2		4	5	6*	7"		9			13	8	12		14		3	10		11																
12	Oct-18	H	Notts. County	1 2	Edwards	3,668	1	2	6	4	5	7		12	9			10*	11"	13			3	8*			14																
13	Oct-21	H	Mansfield Town	0 1		2,589	1	2^	6	4	5	7"		12	9			13	10*	11			3	8			14																
14	Oct-24	H	Doncaster Rovers	3 0	Bird, O'Gorman, Lacey	1,170	1	2	6*	4	5	7	13	11"	9			10*	2				3	8			14																
15	Nov-02	A	Cardiff City	1 0	Walker	6,459	1	2		4	5	6		9*				10	11				8							3	7	12											
16	Nov-04	H	Hartlepool United	0 2		2,949	1	2		4	5	6	12	9				10*	11				13							3	7	8"											
17	Nov-08	H	Lincoln City	0 0		2,871	1	2*		4	5	6		9"			12	10	11				13							3	7	8											
18	Nov-18	A	Scarborough	2 3	Bird 2 (1 pen)	1,408		2		4	5	3	12	9	7*			10	11"				1			14					13	6	8^										
19	Nov-26	A	Chester City	0 2		1,510	1			4	5	11		9	7			8												3	6		2	10									
20	Nov-29	A	Shrewsbury Town	1 0	Coates	2,697	1	2		4	5	11		12	9	10										8*					7		6		3								
21	Dec-02	H	Rotherham United	1 1	Coates	2,463	1	2		4	5	11		12	9*	10										8					7		6		3								
22	Dec-13	A	Rochdale	0 3		1,482	1	12		4	5	11"		13	9	10				14						8					7		6		3^	2*							
23	Dec-20	H	Cambridge United	1 1	Watkin	2,605	1	2		4	5	11		12	13	10				9						8*					7		6		3"								
24	Dec-26	A	Torquay United	0 2		2,998	1	2		4	5	11		12	13	10				9				14		8*					7		6		3"								
25	Dec-28	H	Barnet	0 2		3,987	1			4			2	12	9			10	5		8					13					11"	7	6		3*								
26	Jan-10	A	Brighton	1 0	Bird	2,997	1				8	3	11*	7	12			5		9						13					10	6	4		2*								
27	Jan-17	H	Hull City	2 0	Bird, Coates	2,899	1			5		3	2	12	9^			4		8						10"					11"	7								13	14		
28	Jan-24	A	Scunthorpe United	0 1		2,123	1			4	5	3	2	12	9*			11*		8						13					7	6								10			
29	Jan-27	H	Darlington	4 0	Edwards, Alsop, Appleby, O'Gorman	2,128	1	8		4	5	3		12	9*			11								13					7	6	2							10"			
30	Jan-31	H	Macclesfield Town	1 1	Alsop	3,293	1	8		4	5	3		12	9*			11					13								7	6	2*							10			
31	Feb-06	A	Colchester United	2 1	Coates, Price	2,789	1	8		4	5	3		12	9*			11^		14						13					7	6	2							10*			
32	Feb-14	H	Peterborough Utd.	0 1		3,737	1	8"			4	3		12	13				5							9	11*				7	6	2							10			
33	Feb-21	A	Leyton Orient	2 2	Coates, O'Gorman	4,261	1	8		4	3*	12	13	9	14			11*		5						10					7	6	2^										
34	Feb-24	H	Notts. County	1 2	Hartfield	4,484	1	8*			4"	11	12		9	3				5						10					7	6	2^								14		
35	Feb-28	H	Exeter City	2 1	Hartfield, Bird	3,323	1	12		5	4	11	8*		9					13						10"					7	6	2		14	3^							
36	Mar-03	A	Lincoln City	1 1	Price	2,281	1	8		4	5	11	2*		9					12	10										7	6			13	3"							
37	Mar-08	A	Cardiff City	1 1	Coates	5,621	1	8		4	5	11	3^	12	9				10*	13	14										7	6	2"										
38	Mar-14	A	Hartlepool United	2 4	Watkin, Walker	1,727	1	8*		4	5	11^	12						10	13	3"					2					7	6	14						9				
39	Mar-21	H	Scarborough	0 0		2,797	1			5		3	2	12					10	4						8*					7	6	11						9				
40	Mar-28	H	Chester City	2 0	Barwood, Watkin	2,500	1				3	2	12						10*	4	8^					9	13	14		5		6	7				11"						
41	Apr-04	H	Shrewsbury Town	0 1		2,623	1				3	2*	12	13				11	4^	8						10"					5	14	6	7					9				
42	Apr-11	A	Rotherham United	1 1	Alsop	2,942	1			5	3^	2	12	13				10*	4	14						8					7	6	11						9*				
43	Apr-13	A	Rochdale	3 0	Appleby 2, Walker	2,854	1			5		2	12	13				10	4	3*						8					7	14	6	11					9^				
44	Apr-18	A	Cambridge United	1 4	Bird	2,336	1			5		12	2	13	9			10*	4	3						8*					7	14	6	11^									
45	Apr-25	H	Doncaster Rovers	0 0		3,661	1	2*		5		11	3^	12					4		8"					10		14			7	13	6						9				
46	May-02	A	Mansfield Town	0 1		2,867	1			5^		3						11	4	2						12	13			7		6	10*	8					9*		14	1
	Apps						43	31	5	39	32	41	16	12	34	17	4	7	3	33	25	0	14	2	7	24	1	2	0	7	32	3	28	2	22	1	0	1	12	2	0	1
	Subs							3			2	6	22	7	2			5	1	2	4	6	7		8		4	6	1		5		1			2	2			1	1	
	Gls							3		3	2	7	1	5	14				3								3							2			1	3			

#	Date	V	Opponents	Score	Scorers	Att	Freestone R	Price J	Moreira J	Walker K	Edwards C	Coates J	Lacey D	O'Gorman D	Bird T	Ampadu K	Puttnam D	Hills G	Jones G	Chapple S	Appleby R	O'Leary K	Harris J	Jenkins L	Jones L	Agnew P	Watkin S	Molby J	Casey R	Phillips G	Clode M	Cusack N	Newhouse A	Bound M	Mainwaring C	Hartfield C	Trevitt S	Brown L	Barwood D	Alsop J	Howard M	Munroe K	Jones J
1	Aug-12	A	Reading CC Cup 1-1	0 2		4,829	1	2	3	4	5	6	7	8*	9	10	11"	13		12																							
2	Aug-26	H	Reading CC Cup 1-2	1 1	Coates	3,333	1	2	3*	4	5	6		8	9	10	11	7		12																							
3	Nov-14	H	Peterborough FAC-1	1 4	Appleby	2,821	1	2		4	5	7		9^	12			10	11				13							3*	6	8"		14										
4	Jan-06	H	Peterborough AWS-2	1 2	Bound	1,179	1				12	2	10*	9					4		8					5					11	7		6		3								

Swansea City FC Season 1998/99 Division 3(4)

#	Date	V	Opponents	Score	Scorers	Att	Freestone R	Price J	Howard M	Cusack N	Smith J	Bound M	Appleby R	Thomas M	Newhouse A	Watkin S	Coates J	O'Gorman D	Alsop J	Casey R	Roberts S	Walker K	Jenkins L	Bird T	Jones S	O'Leary K	Clode M	Jones J	Lacey D	Davies J	Gregg M	Phillips G
1	Aug-08	H	Exeter City	2 0	Thomas, Watkin	5,089	1	2	3	4	5	6	7*	8	9"	10	11	12	13													
2	Aug-15	A	Cambridge United	1 2	Casey	3,074	1	2	3	4	5	6		8		10	11		9	7*	12											
3	Aug-22	H	Leyton Orient	1 1	Bird	4,629	1	2	3"	4		6	7	8		10	11*		9		12	5		13								
4	Aug-29	A	Mansfield Town	0 1		2,421	1	2	3"	4	5	6	11	8*		10		12	9^			13	7	14								
5	Aug-31	H	Scunthorpe United	1 2	Alsop	4,024	1	2	3	4	5	6	11	12			8"		9			13	7	10*								
6	Sep-05	A	Brighton	0 1		2,931	1		3	4^	5	6	11	8		10		12	13	7"			14	9*	2							
7	Sep-08	A	Carlisle United	2 1	Howard, Watkin	2,816	1	7	3	4	5	6	11	8		10			9						2							
8	Sep-12	H	Scarborough	2 0	Watkin (pen), Price	3,360	1	7	3	4	5	6	11	8		10			9						2							
9	Sep-19	A	Torquay United	1 1	Smith	2,527	1	7	3	4	5	6	11	8*		10"			9				13	12	2							
10	Sep-26	H	Southend United	3 1	Alsop, Watkin, Bird	3,890	1	7	3	4	5	6	11	8^		10"		12	9				14	13	2*							
11	Oct-03	A	Darlington	2 2	Watkin, Price	3,046	1	7	3	4	5	6	11*	8		10		12	9						2							
12	Oct-09	H	Rotherham United	1 1	Thomas	5,180	1		3	4	5	6	11	8		10		12	9	7*					2							
13	Oct-17	A	Chester City	1 1	Alsop	3,926	1	7	3	4	5	6				10	11*	12	9					8	2							
14	Oct-20	A	Shrewsbury Town	0 1		2,328	1	7^	3*	4	5	6			13	10	11		9			4	14	8"	12	2						
15	Oct-31	A	Halifax Town	0 2		2,383	1	7"	3			6	11	8		10			9			4	13	12	2	5*						
16	Nov-07	H	Peterborough Utd.	0 0		3,771	1	7"	3	4	5	6	11	8	12	10							13	9*	2							
17	Nov-10	A	Plymouth Argyle	2 1	Watkin, Alsop	4,517	1	7"	3	4	5	6	11	8	9*	10		12						13	2							
18	Nov-22	H	Cardiff City	2 1	Thomas, Bound	7,757	1	7	3	4	5	6	11	8	9*	10		12							2							
19	Nov-28	A	Hartlepool United	2 1	Alsop 2	2,051	1	7*	3	4	5	6	11	8		10"			9					13	12	2						
20	Dec-12	H	Rochdale	1 1	Alsop	4,010	1	7"	3	4	5	6	11	8		10*		12	9					13	2							
21	Dec-19	A	Hull City	2 0	Appleby, Watkin	4,280	1		3	4	5	6	11*	8		10	7		9					12	2							
22	Dec-26	A	Leyton Orient	1 1	Alsop	5,343	1	12	3"	4	5	6	11	8		10	7*		9					13	2							
23	Dec-28	H	Barnet	2 1	Smith, Watkin	6,514	1	12	3	4	5	6		8		10"	7		9		11*			13	2							
24	Jan-09	A	Exeter City	0 4		3,213	1	12		4	5	6		8^		10"	11		9*		7		14	13	2	3						
25	Jan-30	A	Barnet	1 0	Appleby	2,259			3	4		6			12	10"	11		9		7*			13	2	5	1	8				
26	Feb-05	H	Brighton	2 2	Jones S, Watkin	6,563			3	4	5	6			12	10"	11		9		7*			13	2		1	8				
27	Feb-13	H	Carlisle United	1 1	Roberts	4,753			3		5	6		10			9^		11	12	7	4*		13	2"		1	8	14			
28	Feb-16	H	Brentford	2 1	Appleby, Watkin	5,109		2	3	4	5	6	8			10	11*		9		13			7"						12	1	
29	Feb-20	A	Scarborough	1 2	Smith	1,512		2	3	4	5"	6	8			10		12		7*				9					13	11	1	
30	Feb-23	H	Mansfield Town	1 0	Alsop	4,361		2	3	4		6	8			10	11	12	9	7*						5					1	
31	Feb-27	H	Torquay United	0 0		5,594		2^	3	4		6	8			10*	11		9	7"	13			12		5			14		1	
32	Mar-06	A	Southend United	0 2		3,713	1		3	4	9	6	8			10	11			7*				12		5		2"			1	13
33	Mar-09	H	Darlington	2 0	O'Leary, Watkin	4,078	1		3	4	5	6	8			10	11		9*		7			12	2							
34	Mar-13	A	Peterborough Utd.	1 0	Roberts	4,182	1		3	4	5	6	8			10	11		9		7				2							
35	Mar-20	H	Halifax Town	1 2	Cusack	4,974	1		3	4	5	6				10"	11		9	8"	7			12	2				13			
36	Mar-23	A	Scunthorpe United	2 1	Watkin 2	3,631	1	7*	3	4	5	6	8			10	11		9					12	2							
37	Apr-03	H	Chester City	1 1	Roberts	5,994	1			4	5	6	8			10"	11		9		7*		13	12	2	3						
38	Apr-05	A	Rotherham United	0 1		4,257	1		3"	4	5	6	8			10"	11		9		13			12	2	7						
39	Apr-09	H	Shrewsbury Town	1 1	Bound	5,113	1			4	5	6	8		13	10	3		9*		11"			12	2	7						
40	Apr-13	H	Hartlepool United	1 0	Smith	4,429	1	12			5	6	7	8*		10	3							9	2	4			11			
41	Apr-18	A	Cardiff City	0 0		10,809	1	11			5	6	7	8*		10"	3				9			12	2	4			13			
42	Apr-24	H	Plymouth Argyle	2 3	O'Leary, Jones S	5,660	1				5	6	7"	8		12	3		9		14	13		10*	2	4		11^				
43	May-01	A	Rochdale	3 0	Price 2, Alsop	1,654	1	8"		11	5	6	7*	13		10^	3		9			14		12	2	4						
44	May-04	A	Brentford	1 4	Bird	7,156	1	8*	12	11	5	6	7		13		3		9"			14		10	2	4^						
45	May-06	A	Cambridge United	2 0	Watkin 2 (1 pen)	6,086	1		3	4	5	6	8			10	11		9		7				2							
46	May-08	H	Hull City	2 0	Watkin 2	9,226	1		3	4	5^	6	12	8		10	11		9"		7*			13	2				14			
					Apps		38	25	38	42	42	45	36	26	5	40	30	2	37	5	15	1	6	8	31	17	2	3	7	0	5	0
					Subs			3	1	1		3	4	1	3		3	3		4	5	17	6	20	1	2			5	1		1
					Gls			4	1	1	1	4	2	3		17			10		3			3	2	2						

#	Date	V	Opponents	Score	Scorers	Att	Freestone R	Price J	Howard M	Cusack N	Smith J	Bound M	Appleby R	Thomas M	Newhouse A	Watkin S	Coates J	O'Gorman D	Alsop J	Casey R	Roberts S	Walker K	Jenkins L	Bird T	Jones S	O'Leary K	Clode M	Jones J	Lacey D	Davies J	Gregg M	Phillips G
1	Aug-11	H	Norwich C, CC Cup 1-1	1 1	Cusack	3,803	1	2	3	4	5	6		8		10	11"		9	7*		12	13									
2	Aug-18	A	Norwich C, CC Cup 1-2	0 1 aet		13,146	1	2	3	4	5	6		8"		10^			9	7*	14	12	13									
3	Nov-13	H	Millwall, FAC-1	3 0	Price, Thomas, Alsop	5,728	1	7	3	4	5	6	11	8	9*	10		12							2							
4	Dec-05	H	Stoke City, FAC-2	1 0	Appleby	7,460	1	7	3	4	5	6	11	8					9				12	10*	2							
5	Dec-08	H	Barnet, AWS-1	4 1	Appleby, Smith, Bird 2	1,017	1	2*	3	4	5	6	11		14			13	9^	7"				8	10	12						
6	Jan-02	A	West Ham Utd, FAC-3	1 1	Smith	26,039	1		3	4	5	6		8		10	7		9		11				2							
7	Jan-05	H	Gillingham, AWS-2	0 1		5,126	1	11"				6				10	7		9*		13			8	12	2		5	3	4		
8	Jan-13	H	West Ham Utd, FAC-3 Rep	1 0	Thomas	10,116	1		3	4	5	6		8		10	7		9		11				2							
9	Jan-23	H	Derby County, FAC-4	0 1		11,383	1		3	4		6	13			10	11"		9		7			12	2	5*		8				
10	May-16	H	Scunthorpe Utd, P/O SF-1	1 0	Bound	7,828	1		3	4	5	6	12	8		10"	11		9		7*			13	2							
11	May-19	A	Scunthorpe Utd, P/O SF-2	1 3	Bird, aet	7,089	1	13	3	4	5	6	14	8		10	11^				7"			9	2*	12						

Swansea City FC Season 1999/2000 Division 3(4)

No	Date	V	Opponents	Score	Scorers	Att	Freestone Roger	Jones Steve	Howard Michael	Cusack Nick	Smith Jason	Bound Matthew	Appleby Richie	Thomas Martin	Alsop Julian	Watkin Steve	Coates Jonathan	Price Jason	Bird Tony	O'Leary Kristian	Lacey Damian	Jones Jason	Roberts Stuart	Barwood Danny	Casey Ryan	Phillips Gareth	Jenkins Lee	Mutton Tommy	Boyd Walter	Keegan Michael	DeVulght Lee	Morgan Bari	Evans Kevin
1	Aug-07	A	York City	0 1		3,036	1	2	3	4*	5	6	7	8	9"	10	11^	12	13	14													
2	Aug-14	H	Carlisle United	1 0	Price	5,452	1		3	4	5	6	13	8*	12	10		2	9"	7			11										
3	Aug-21	A	Macclesfield Town	2 1	Appleby 2	2,121	1		3	4	5	6	13	8	12	10*		2	9	11^	14	16	7"										
4	Aug-28	H	Southend United	3 1	Roberts, Watkin(pen), Price	4,757	1	12	3	4*	5	6	7			9	10^	13	2	14			8						11*				
5	Aug-30	A	Lincoln City	1 0	Price	2,893	1	2	3		4	5	9	12	10	11	8*	6		7													
6	Sep-11	H	Barnet	1 2	Thomas	5,173	1	12	3		4	5	6*	7	10	11^		2	14	8	13		9"										
7	Sep-18	A	Hull City	0 2		5,871	1	13	3		4	5		7	11^	10*	9	2	12	8			6"								14		
8	Sep-25	A	Rochdale	0 0		2,975	1	2	3	11	4	5		7	10		9	6		8													
9	Oct-02	H	Mansfield Town	0 1		4,322	1	2	3*		4	5	6	14	7	13		8	10^	9							12	11"					
10	Oct-12	H	Rotherham United	2 0	Boyd 2	5,287	1	12	10	4	5		7					3*	2	8			9				6		11				
11	Oct-16	A	Torquay United	0 1		2,488	1			10	4	5	12	7				13	3	2	8		9*					6"	11				
12	Oct-19	A	Exeter City	1 1	Boyd	2,692	1	12	3	8	4	5		7				10	9	2			6*						11				
13	Oct-22	H	Rochdale	1 0	Cusack	4,843	1	2	3	8	4	5		7^	12	10	9			14			6*						11*	13			
14	Nov-02	A	Northampton Town	1 2	Appleby	4,495	1		3	8	4	5	6"	7	10	11	9*	2								12			13				
15	Nov-05	H	Halifax Town	3 1	Appleby, Coates 2	3,375	1		3	8	4	5	6		10	11	9	2		7									14				
16	Nov-12	A	Shrewsbury Town	1 1	Bound(pen)	2,531	1		3	7	4	5	6*	11	10^	9		2		8						13	12		14				
17	Nov-16	H	Cheltenham Town	0 0		4,299	1		3	7	4	5	6^	14	13	10	9*	2		8						12			11"				
18	Nov-23	H	Darlington	0 0		3,748	1	2	3"	7	4	5	6^	14	11	10	9*			8						13			12				
19	Nov-27	A	Chester City	1 0	Cusack	2,713	1	2	3*	8	4	5		13	11	10	6	9"		7						12							
20	Dec-04	H	York City	1 0	Price	3,812	1	2	3	7	4	5		12	11	10	9	6		8*													
21	Dec-11	A	Hartlepool United	1 0	Price	2,397	1	2	3	7	4	5		12	10	11"	9	6*		8							13						
22	Dec-18	H	Brighton & H A	2 0	Cusack, Coates	4,555	1	2	3	7	5	4			10	11	9*	6		8						12							
23	Dec-26	A	Leyton Orient	1 0	Boyd	4,447	1	2	3	7	4	5			10								8				9*		11	6	12		
24	Dec-28	H	Plymouth Argyle	1 0	Boyd	9,075	1	2	3	7	4	5		12	10*	13	9	14					8*						11	6^			
25	Jan-03	A	Peterborough Utd	3 2	Thomas, Alsop, Cusack	6,439	1	2	3*	7	4	5		13	12	10	9^						8				14		11	6"			
26	Jan-08	H	Hartlepool United	2 1	Watkin, Smith	7,163	1	2		6	4	5		8	11	9	3						7				12		10*				
27	Jan-22	H	Macclesfield Town	1 0	Boyd	6,913	1	2*		7	4	5		6	11	10	3								12	8			9				
28	Jan-29	A	Southend United	1 2	Cusack(pen)	3,860	1	4		7	5			8*	11	9	3					12		13	6^	2			10"		14		
29	Feb-04	H	Lincoln City	2 1	Alsop, Coates	6,846	1	5		7	4*			8	9	11	3	2								6			10				12
30	Feb-13	A	Cheltenham Town	0 0		4,220	1	5		7			12		11	10	3	2						13	8*	6"			9				4
31	Feb-18	A	Chester City	2 1	O/Goal. Watkin	6,336	1	2	3	7		5	8	12^	10	9*	6	14	4*		13								11				
32	Feb-26	H	Hull City	0 0		6,147	1	2	3	7	4	5	6	10^	9	8"	12	14			13								11*				
33	Mar-04	A	Barnet	1 0	Watkin	2,911	1	2	3	7	4	5	8*	10	11	9	6"		13							12							
34	Mar-07	A	Halifax Town	1 0	Watkin	1,657	1	2	3	7	4	5		8	11	10"	9	6*	13							12							
35	Mar-10	H	Northampton Town	4 1	Watkin, Coates, Thomas, Bird	7,430	1	2	3	7	4	5		8"	12	10*	9	6	11	13													
36	Mar-18	A	Darlington	1 1	Cusack	6,632	1	2	3	8	4	5		7	10*		9	6	11	12													
37	Mar-21	A	Shrewsbury Town	1 1	Boyd	6,612	1	2	3	7	4	5	12	8		9*	6"	10			13								11				
38	Mar-25	H	Leyton Orient	0 0		6,330	1	2	3"	4	5	6	14	7		8	9*	10^	13							12			11				
39	Mar-28	A	Carlisle United	0 2		2,748	1	2	3"	7	4	5	12	8		11	9*	6^	10	14									13				
40	Apr-01	A	Brighton & H A	1 1	Alsop	5,718	1	2	3	7	4	5		8	10	11	9*	6"								12			13				
41	Apr-08	H	Peterborough Utd	0 0		6,572	1	2	3	8	4	5	12	7"	11	10	9^	6"											13				
42	Apr-15	A	Plymouth Argyle	0 1		5,881	1	2	3	7^	4	5	6	8	10	11"	9*	13			14								12				
43	Apr-22	H	Torquay United	2 1	Watkin, Price	6,396	1	2	3	8	4	5		7	10*	12	9	6	13										11"				
44	Apr-24	A	Mansfield Town	1 0	Cusack	2,162	1	2	3	8	4	5		7		10	9	6											11				
45	Apr-29	H	Exeter City	3 0	Thomas, Coates, O/Goal	10,743	1	2	3	8	4	5	13	7		11"	9	6"	12										10				
46	May-06	A	Rotherham United	1 1	Bound(pen)	11,500	1	2	3	4		5		6		7	10	8	9								12		11*				
			Apps				46	34	39	43	43	43	10	32	29	36	41	35	8	9	14	0	9	0	0	2	7	1	21	3	0	0	1
			Subs					4	1				10	8	8	3	1	4	8	11	2		2		11	1	9	1	6	1	2		1
			Gls							7	1	2	4	4	3	7	6	6		1			1						7				

No	Date	V	Opponents	Score	Scorers	Att	Freestone Roger	Jones Steve	Howard Michael	Cusack Nick	Smith Jason	Bound Matthew	Appleby Richie	Thomas Martin	Alsop Julian	Watkin Steve	Coates Jonathan	Price Jason	Bird Tony	O'Leary Kristian	Lacey Damian	Jones Jason	Roberts Stuart	Barwood Danny	Casey Ryan	Phillips Gareth	Jenkins Lee	Mutton Tommy	Boyd Walter	Keegan Michael	DeVulght Lee	Morgan Bari	Evans Kevin
1	Aug-11	H	Millwall WC 1-1	2 0	Watkin, Price	3,793	1		3^	6	4	5	13	8	12	10*	14	2	11	9			7"										
2	Aug-24	A	Millwall WC 1-2	1 1	Bird(pen)	4,242	1	12		6	4	5	9	7*	11	10*	3	2	13		8												
3	Sep-14	H	Derby County WC 2-1	0 0		6,260	1		3		4	5		7	12	10	9	2	11"	8			6										
4	Sep-22	A	Derby County WC 2-2	1 3	Bound(pen)	19,152	1		3		4	5	13	7^	10		9	2	11*	8			6"				14		12				
5	Oct-30	H	Colchester Utd, FAC-1	2 1	Cusack, Watkin	3,622	1		3	8	4	5	6		10	13		2		7^	14				12				11"	9*			
6	Nov-20	A	Oldham Athletic, FAC-2	0 1		4,332	1	2	3	7	4	5	6*		11	10	9						8						12				
7	Dec-07	H	Colchester Utd, AWS-1	3 1	Mutton, Thomas, Watkin	1,220	1	2			4	5	6	8	10	13	12				14		3			7*	11"		9^				
8	Jan-11	A	Exeter City, AWS-2	0 2		964	1				4	5	12	7*					13				6			2	9^	11	10*	8	3	14	

Records and Statistics

Chairmen at the Vetch

J. W. Thorpe	1912-13		Trevor Wood	1969-70
Frank Newcombe	1913-15		David Goldstone	1970-71
B. Watts-Jones	1915-22		Malcolm Struel	1972-83
J. W. Thorpe	1922-23		Bobby Jones	1983
Owen Evans	1923-27		Winston Rees	1983
Tom Martin	1927-29		Doug Sharpe	1985-97
J. Barclay Owen	1929-35		Steve Hamer	1997-
Owen Evans	1935-38			
Abe Freedman	1938-52		Harry Hyde also served	
Philip Holden	1952-69		for a short period.	

Managers at the Vetch

Walter Whittaker	1912-14		John Toshack MBE	1978-Oct 83
William Bartlett	1914-15		John Toshack MBE	Dec 1983-84
War			Colin Appleton	1984
Joe Bradshaw	1919-26		John Bond	1984-85
No Manager			Terry Yorath	1986-88
James Thomson	1927-31		Ian Evans	1988-89
No Manager			Terry Yorath	1989-91
Neil Harris	1934-39		Frank Burrows	1991-95
Haydn Green	1939-47		Jan Molby	1996-97
Billy McCandless	1947-55		Alan Cork	1997-98
Ron Burgess	1955-58		John Hollins MBE	1998-
Trevor Morris	1958-65			
Glyn Davies	1965-66			
Billy Lucas	1967-69			
Roy Bentley	1969-72			
Harry Gregg	1972-75			
Harry Griffiths	1975-78			

Also: Joe Sykes, Walter Robbins, Doug Livermore, Les Chappel, Bobby Smith, Tommy Hutchison and Jimmy Rimmer acted as 'caretaker', while Kevin Cullis was manager for one week and Micky Adams for three weeks.

Secretaries at the Vetch

S. B. Williams	1912-47
Trevor Hoskins	1947-59
Gordon Daniels	1960-73
Ken Sweet	1973-74
Geoff Ford	1973-74
Gordon Daniels	1975-84
David Morris	1984
George Taylor	1984-95
Robin Sharpe	1995-97
Vicki Townsend	1997-2000

Southern League Appearances and Goals

Appearances and goals scored in Southern League 1912-20. The years indicate the first and last played.

Name		Appearances	Goals	Name		Appearances	Goals
Allman, A.	1913-14	21	–	Jepp, S. R.	1912-13	17	1
Anderson, D.	1913-15	33	14	Johnson, B.	1914-15	5	–
Ball, Billy	1912-20	57	27	Jones, Ivor ★	1919-20	20	7
Bassett, S.	1913-14	21	2	King	1919	1	–
Beynon, Ben ★	1914-20	26	12	Lloyd, Amos	1914-20	28	9
Brazell, Thos.	1912	1	–	Lock, Charlie	1914-15	5	–
Brown, Ivor	1914-20	36	8	Mayo, Billy	1913-14	9	3
Brown, W. Y. ★	1919-20	26	10	Messer, Bryn	1920	2	–
Buck, F.	1914-15	6	1	Messer, Willie	1912-14	30	6
Bulcock, Joe	1914-15	20	–	Mitchell, Ted	1913-14	8	1
Burch F.	1919	4	–	Morris, Llew	1914	1	–
Cartwright	1919	2	–	Mortimer	1914	2	1
Cleverley, A.	1912-14	20	–	Nicholas, Jack	1912-20	45	1
Coleman, J.	1912-14	31	9	Ogley, W. ★	1919-20	26	–
Collins, Jimmy ★	1919-20	32	1	Pinch, C	1919-20	2	–
Crumley, Jas ★	1919-20	20	–	Prideaux	1912-13	6	–
Cubberley	1913-14	21	1	Read, W. H.	1914-15	16	1
Denoon, Jock ★	1919-20	15	–	Robson, Fred ★	1919-20	38	–
Duffy, Jack	1912-15	51	–	Sheldon, F.	1919-20	13	2
Durnin, J. ★	1919-20	32	1	Soady	1913	2	–
East	1915	1	–	Spottiswoode, Joe ★	1920	14	3
Evans	1919	1	–	Storey	1913-14	14	–
Evans, D. J. (Tich)	1919	16	3	Sutherland, A.	1912-13	10	–
Fisher, Ernie	1913-15	28	–	Swarbrick, Jimmy	1912-13	23	1
Fyfe, George	1913	8	–	Thomas, Harry	1919	1	–
Gilboy, Bert	1914	6	–	Walton	1919-20	6	–
Greer, Robert	1913-14	20	3	Weir, Jock	1913-19	34	13
Grierson, R. T.	1912-13	17	8	Whittaker, Walter	1912	7	–
Hamilton, Jock	1912-14	21	1	Williams, Jack ★	1913-20	29	–
Harris, Fred	1919	14	–				
Heath, Clem.	1915-19	9	–				
Hewitt, T. J.	1914-19	25	–				
Heyward	1919	1	–				
Hirst	1919	1	–				
Hole, Billy ★	1919-20	19	3				
Houston	1919	1	–				
Hurst, Ben	1914-15	12	–				

These statstics have been compiled using all available information. Some players who appeared may not be listed, and some of those that are may have played more games than shown.

Those players marked with an asterisk also played for the Swans in the Football League.

An important job in the summer of 1913 was to build a stand as proposed by this sketch. It was the centre section of the present main stand, which still contains the gable shown in this illustration.

Football League Appearances
(1920-21 to 1999-2000)

Player	Apps.	Gls.	Years Played
Abbott, Peter	40	3	1974-1976
Agboola, Reuben	28		1991-1993
Agnew, Paul	7		1997
Allan, Sandy	7	1	1973 (loan)
Allchurch, Ivor	445	164	1949-1958, 1965-1968
Allchurch, Len	347	60	1950-1961, 1969-1971
Allon, Joe	34	12	1987-1989
Alsop, Julian	90	16	1998-2000
Ampadu, Kwame	148	12	1994-1998
Andrew, Matt	4		1948-1951
Andrews, Keri	41	3	1984-1988
Anstiss, Henry	28	6	1931-1933
Appleby, Richie	105	11	1996-2000
Armand, Jack	54	10	1929-1931
Aspinall, Warren	5		1993 (loan)
Atkinson, Paul	18	3	1986 (loan), 1987 (loan)
Attley, Brian	89	6	1979-1982
Baker, Mark	11	2	1978-1980
Bal'ac, P.	4		1973 (loan)
Bamford, Tommy	36	14	1938-1939
Barber, J.	4		1950-1951
Barber, Keith	42		1977-1978
Barnhouse, David	23		1993-1996
Barnwell, E. Jamie	4		1995 (loan)
Bartley, Danny	199	8	1973-1980
Barwood, Danny	3	1	1998-2000
Basham, Michael	29	1	1994-1995
Beauchamp, Joey	5	2	1991 (loan)
Beech, Cyril	136	29	1949-1954
Beech, Gilbert	157	3	1949-1957
Beer, Alan	15	2	1971-1972
Bekker, Jan	20	4	1975-1976
Bell, Gordon C.	19	6	1930-1931
Bellamy, Herbert	90	2	1923-1926
Bellis, Alf	41	11	1951-1953
Bellotti, Derek	19		1974-1975
Bennett, E.	11		1923-1925
Beresford, David	6		1995 (loan)
Beresford, Joe	13	1	1937-1938
Bevan, Paul	80	5	1973-1975
Beynon, B.	25	11	1920-1922
Biggs, Alf	16	4	1968-1969
Bird, John	8		1967-1968
Bird, Tony	87	18	1997-2000
Black, John	15		1964-1966
Black, William	11	1	1928-1929
Blackburn, Derek	2		1957
Blair, H.	62	11	1932-1935
Bodak, Peter	31	4	1988-1989
Boersma, Phil	18	1	1978-1979
Booth, L.	1		1934-1935
Booth, Robert	36	3	1923-1924
Boston, H. J.	19		1931-1933
Bound, Matthew	116	4	1997-2000
Bowen, Jason	124	26	1990-1995
Boyd, Walter	27	7	1999-2000
Boyle, Terry	27	1	1989-1990
Bracey, Lee	99		1988-1992
Brain, Joe	49	26	1934-1937
Brazil, Derek	12	1	1991 (loan)
Bray, Geoff	45	20	1975-1976
Brayson, Paul	11	5	1997 (loan)
Briddon, Samuel	18		1939-1946
Briggs, Ronnie	27		1964-1965

Player	Apps.	Gls.	Years Played
Brookes, G. H.	37		1923-1924
Brown, Graham	4		1976
Brown, Linton	28	3	1996-1998
Brown, T. H.	68		1955-1959
Brown, W. Y.	65	16	1920-1922
Bruce, Walter	13	1	1938-1939
Bruton, Dave	194	19	1973-1978
Budd, Kevin	1		1985
Burgess, Ron	46	1	1954-1958
Burns, Chris	9		1993 (loan), 1994 (loan)
Burns, Frank	171	8	1946-1952
Burrows, Paul	3		1984-1986
Bussey, Walter	72	18	1934-1936
Bye, Leslie	3		1938
Caldwell, Tommy	55		1928-1937
Callaghan, Ian	76	1	1978-1981
Campbell, A. F.	7	2	1922-1923
Canning, Danny	47		1949-1951
Carr, J. E. C.	7	1	1926-1927
Carver, David	3		1973 (loan)
Casey, Ryan	37	1	1996-2000
Catlow, T.	1		1920-1921
Chalmers, Paul	55	13	1989-1992
Chapman, Lee	7	4	1996
Chapple, Les	67	5	1976-1978
Chapple, Shaun	106	9	1991-1997
Charles, Jeremy	247	52	1977-1983
Charles, Mel	233	66	1952-1959
Chedgzoy, S.	18	2	1938-1939
Cheetham, John	25	11	1929-1930
Chinaglia, Georgio	5	1	1965-1966
Chivers, Gary	10		1983-1984
Clarke, Kevin	10		1948-1952
Clode, Mark	119	3	1993-1999
Coates, Jonathan	185	17	1993-2000
Cobb, Gary	5		1987 (loan)
Cole, David	8		1984-1985
Coleman, Chris	160	2	1987-1991
Collins, Jimmy	275	9	1919-1930
Collins, Terry	2		1967-1968
Comley, Len	28	7	1946-1948
Connor, John	12	1	1938-1939
Connor, Terry	42	6	1990-1991, 1992 (loan)
Conway, Micky	61	11	1975-1978
Cook, A. F.	17		1922-1923
Cook, Andy	61		1993-1997
Corkingdale, W. J.	18	2	1923-1926
Cornforth, John	149	16	1991-1996
Cottey, P. A.	4		1984-1985
Cotton, Terry	12	1	1969-1971
Coughlin, Denis	40	10	1966-1968
Coughlin, Russell	101	2	1990-1993
Craig, Arthur	3		1929-1932
Craig, Tommy	52	9	1979-1982
Crapper, J.	3		1923-1924
Craven, Joe	49		1931-1934
Crotty, Colin	2	1	1968
Crowe, Edward	1		1936-1937
Crudgington, G.	52		1978-1979
Crumley, J. B.	28		1919-1923
Cullen, Tony	27	3	1992-1993
Cunliffe, Reg	2		1946-1947
Curtis, Alan	359	95	1972-79, 80-83, 89-90
Cusack, Nick	118	8	1997-2000

Player	Apps.	Gls.	Years Played
Dackins, H. V.	2		1935
Dalling, Nigel	8		1975-1978
Daniel, Ray	44	7	1958-1959
D'Auria, David	44	6	1987-1991
Davey, Simon	47	4	1987-1992
Davids, Neil	9		1977-1978
Davies, Alan	127	12	1987-1989, 1990-1992
Davies, D. J.	28		1973-1975
Davies, D. L.	1		1973-1975
Davies, Dai	86		1969-70, 73 (L), 81-83
Davies, Glen	145	13	1970-1976
Davies, Glyn	18	1	1962-1963
Davies, Glyn L.	3		1929-1931
Davies, Ian	11		1985-1986
Davies, Jack	5		1928-1929
Davies, Jamie	1		1998-2000
Davies, Lyn	3		1972-1973
Davies, Mark	1		1991-1992
Davies, Peter	134	5	1959-1965
Davies, Ron G.	2		1958-1959
Davies, E. R. (Reg)	111	29	1958-1962
Davies, R. Gordon	57		1933-1947
Davies, Willie	129	22	1922-1924, 1933-1936
Davis, Joe	36		1967-1968
Deacon, Harry	319	86	1922-1931
De Vulgt, Lee	2		1999-2000
Dennison, Robbie	9		1995 (loan)
Denoon, Jock	173		1919-1927
Dewsbury, John	9		1950-1955
Dodds, T. B.	11	2	1947
Dodson, D. A.	29	11	1959-1961
Donnelly, Peter	16	3	1961-1962
Donovan, Frank	15	2	1950
Draper, Derek	63	10	1962-1966
Durnin, John	24		1919-1922
Dwyer, Noel	140		1960-1965
Eastham, George	15		1947-1948
Easton, W. C.	56	18	1930-1931
Edmundson, Jimmy	60	33	1920-1923
Edwards, Christian	115	4	1995-1998
Edwards, Cliff	1		1951
Edwards, E. J.	11	1	1925-1926
Edwards, George	2		1939
Elwell, Terry	62		1948-1952
Emmanuel, Gary	111	5	1985-1988
Emmanuel, Len	49	1	1937-1947
Emmanuel, Tom	46	1	1936-1938
Evans, Brian	343	57	1963-1973
Evans, Fred	1		1920-1921
Evans, J. H.	7		1925-1927
Evans, Keith	12		1970-1973
Evans, Ken P.	14		1950-1957
Evans, Kevin	2		2000
Evans, Micky	92	6	1972-1975
Evans, Phil	10		1975-1976
Evans, Roy	214	7	1960-1968
Evans, Wyndham	390	20	1971-1983, 1983-1985
Feeney, Jim	88		1946-1950
Ferguson, Alex	280		1927-1935
Firth, Jack	102	16	1933-1936
Fisher, C. K.	65		1946-1948
Fisher, Phil	2		1985
Foley, Will	5	2	1986
Ford, John	160	7	1991-1995
Ford, Trevor	16	9	1946-1947
Foreman, John J.	14	2	1937-1938
Foster, Thomas C.	14	3	1936-1937

Player	Apps.	Gls.	Years Played
Fowler, Jack	167	102	1924-1929
Francis, Gerry	3		1984
Freeman, Albert	23		1929-1930
Freeman, Clive	14		1990-1992
Freestone, Roger	410	3	1989 (loan), 1991-2000
French, Nigel	26	3	1985-1987
Fury, Paul	11		1971-1973
Gale, Darren	37	6	1981-1985
Gardner, Paul	4		1984
Garnett, Shaun	15		1996
Gibbins, Roger	35	6	1985-1986
Giles, David	54	13	1979-1982
Gilligan, Jimmy	62	23	1990-1993
Gilligan, Malcolm	3		1962
Gomersall, Vic	178	6	1966-1971
Gooderidge, A. E.	1		1950-1952
Gough, C. W. M.	12	4	1922-1923
Gray, G. R.	39	2	1920-1922
Gray, Mark	2		1977
Greaves, E.	1		1922-1923
Green, R. C. G.	8	4	1937-1938
Greene, Chris	4		1936-1937
Gregg, Matt	5		1999 (loan)
Grey, W. Brian	30	9	1966-1970
Griffiths, Harry	422	72	1949-1964
Griffiths, Jeff	14	1	1976-1978
Groves, E. Gwyn	34		1952-1954
Guard, Tony	1		1983-1984
Gunn, Ken	95	36	1928-1933
Guthrie, Peter	14		1988 (loan)
Gwyther, David	216	60	1967-1973
Haasz, John	1		1960-1961
Hadziabdic, Dzemal	89	1	1980-1983
Haines, J. T. W.	30	6	1946-1947
Hale, R. J.	34	3	1959-1961
Handley, C. H. J.	19	4	1929-1931
Hanford, Harry	201		1927-1936
Hanvey, Keith	11		1972-1973 (loan)
Harley, Albert	26		1964-1965
Harris, Jamie	6		1997-1998
Harris, John	29	4	1935-1939
Harris, Les	4		1963-1965
Harris, Mark	228	14	1989-1995
Harris, Paul	49	2	1975-1977
Harrison, Chris	117	14	1985-1988
Harrop, Jack	10		1952-1956
Hartfield, Charlie	22	2	1997-1999
Harvey, Leighton	2		1975-1977
Harwood, John	45	3	1922-1924
Hayes, Martin	61	8	1993-1995
Hayes, Michael	3		1961-1962
Heeps, James	1		1989-1993
Heggs, Carl	46	7	1995-1997
Hendry, John	8	2	1994 (loan)
Henning, R. I.	10	1	1955-1957
Henson, G. H.	23	5	1936-1937
Henson, Phil	1		1972 (loan)
Heyes, George	99		1965-1969
Hiles, J. (Billy)	7	2	1927-1928
Hill, Len	12	1	1970-1972
Hills, J. J.	8		1926-1927
Hills, John	18		1997 (Jan. loan), (Sept. loan)
Hindley, Robert A.	3		1929-1931
Hodge, John	111	10	1993-1996
Hodges, L. H.	3		1950-1951
Hodgson, David	3		1991

Player	Apps.	Gls.	Years Played
Holdsworth, Dean	5	1	1988 (loan)
Holdsworth, Edward	7		1920-1921
Hole, A. V.	21		1953-1954
Hole, Barrie	78	3	1970-1972
Hole, Billy	341	36	1919-1931
Holland, Jack	21	2	1923-1925
Holmes, Phil	23	5	1971-1972
Holtham, Dean	6		1983-1984
Honor, Chris	2		1991 (loan)
Hooper, P. G.	12		1947-1948
Hopkins, G. G.	2		1946-1947
Hough, David	188	9	1983-1992
Howard, Michael	82	1	1998-2000
Howarth, Syd	41	7	1950-1952
Howells, R. G.	9		1946-1948
Hoyland, Fred	9		1921-1922
Hughes, Alan	1		1968-1969
Hughes, Brian	231	7	1956-1966, 1969
Hughes, Emlyn	7		1983
Hughes, John	16	4	1989-1990
Hughes, Mark	12		1984
Hughes, Michael	139		1983-1988
Humphries, Brinley	11	1	1923-1927
Humphries, Willie	143	21	1965-1968
Huntley, K. S. M.	2		1951-1952
Hurst, Glyn	2	1	1995 (loan)
Hutchison, Tommy	173	9	1985-1991
Illingworth, J.	1		1935-1936
Imrie, J. W. N.	27	1	1938-1939
Ingram, Gerry	38	1	1970-1973
Irwin, Colin	48		1981-1984
Jackson, Sam	6	1	1921-1922
James, Anthony	11	1	1977-1980
James, Dai	12	7	1947-1948
James, George	4	1	1934
James, Leighton	98	27	1980-1983
James, Robbie	478	118	1973-1983, 1988-1990
James, W. G.	4		1949-1950
Jenkins, Lee	71	2	1996-2000
Jenkins, Stephen	165	1	1990-1995
Jennings, Walter	3		1921-1922
John, D. L. J.	4		1958-1959
John, Dilwyn	80		1967-1970
John, W. R.	40		1937-1939
Johnson, G. H.	1		1922-1924
Johnson, Jeff D.	38	5	1972-1973 (loan)
Johnson, Mike G.	165		1958-1966
Jones, Alan	61	6	1963-1968
Jones, Barrie S.	166	23	1959-1964
Jones, Brin R.	122	4	1951-1958
Jones, Cliff W.	167	48	1952-1958
Jones, David	3		1955-1958
Jones, Fred	6		1932-1933
Jones, Gary	8		1997-1998
Jones, Idwal G.	4		1946-1947
Jones, Ivor	65	14	1920-1922
Jones, Jason	4		1998-2000
Jones, John Lewis	34	5	1931-1934
Jones, Lee	6		1994-1998
Jones, Les J.	2		1946-1947
Jones, Peter A.	81	1	1971-1974
Jones, Richard	7		1993-1994
Jones, Steve	133	3	1995-2000
Jones, W. E. A.	37	3	1946-1947
Keane, Steve	4		1987
Keane, T. R.	164		1947-1954
Kellow, Tony	1		1984
Kendall, Mark	12		1990-1992
Kennedy, M. S. J.	17		1957-1961
Kennedy, Ray	42	2	1982-1983
Kennerley, Kevin	2		1978 (loan)
Kiley, Tom J.	129	2	1947-1957
King, Derek	5		1956-1957
King, John	363		1951-1963
King, Robert	2		1996-1998
Kirby, George	25	8	1964-1965
Knill, Alan	89	3	1987-1989
Keegan, Michael	4		1999-2000
Lacey, Damian	60	1	1996-2000
Lake, Huw	19	2	1981-1984
Lally, Pat	161	10	1973-1978
Lamb, W. C.	3		1924-1925
Lamie, R.	2		1951
Lampard, Frank	9	1	1995 (loan)
Lang, W.	1		1930-1931
Lang, Thomas	33	1	1937-1938
Langford, A. E.	78		1923-1928
Latchford, Bob	87	35	1981-1984
Lawrence, D. W.	97	2	1967-1971
Lawrence, S. J.	312	11	1930-1939
Lawson, Norman	24	3	1958-1960
Leavy, Steve	37	1	1950-1958
Legg, Andrew	157	29	1988-1993
Leitch, Andy	16	6	1975-1976
Lenihan, Michael	12		1972-1974
Letheran, Glan	21		1979-1980
Lewis, D. Jenkin	127	5	1930-1936
Lewis, David S.	19	1	1957-1960
Lewis, Dudley	232	2	1979-1989
Lewis, Harry	36	12	1937-1939
Lewis, Idris	60	5	1935-1938
Lewis, John	25	1	1987-1988
Lewis, Wilf L.	65	43	1926-1928
Leyland, Peter	25		1936-1939
Lindsay, John	16	2	1930-1931
Lloyd, Clifford	39		1926-1930
Lloyd, Joseph M.	211	1	1932-1939
Lockhart, N. H.	47	13	1946-1947
Logie, James	2	1	1925-1926
Love, Ian	41	8	1986-1989
Lovell, Steve	2	1	1987 (loan)
Loveridge, Jimmy	47	4	1979-1985
Lowrie, Geo.	19	3	1936-1938
Lowry, S. H.	60	21	1932-1935
Lucas, W. H.	205	35	1948-1954
Lyttle, Des	46	1	1992-1993
McCullum, Donald	60	2	1920-1923
McCarthy, Ian	1		1978
McCarthy, Sean	91	25	1985-1988
McClean, Christian	4		1991
McCrory, Sam	104	47	1946-1950
McDevitt, William	5		1921-1923
McDonald, Colin	18		1996-1997
McFarlane, Andy	55	8	1992-1995
McGibbon, Pat	1		1996 (loan)
McGuigan, John	28	4	1965-1966
McHale, Ray	47	1	1985-1986
McIntosh, Albert	15	3	1954-1958
Mackay, William	19	3	1936-1937
McLaughlin, Jimmy	163	47	1963-1967, 1972-1974
McMahon, Steve	2		1991-1993
McMillan, W. H.	8		1930-1931
McMorran, Jimmy	14	1	1968

Player	Apps.	Gls.	Years Played
McPherson, Lachlan	199	28	1924-1929
McQuillan, Pat	26	1	1983-1985
Maddy, Paul	20	1	1983-1984
Mahoney, John	110		1979-1983
Mainwaring, Carl	3		1997-1999
Mardenborough, Steve	37	7	1984-1985, 1995
Marlow, Owen	2		1926-1927
Marsh, Ian	1		1987-1989
Marson, Fred	14	4	1928-1929
Martin, T. J.	117	46	1932-1936
Marustic, Chris	152	11	1978-1985
May, Eddie	90	8	1976-1978
Medwin, Terry	147	57	1948-1956
Meek, Joe	16	5	1939
Melville, Andrew	175	23	1985-1990
Messer, Bryn	1		1920-1921
Middleton, Jack	1		1930
Miller, James	135	2	1930-1934
Miller, Jimmy	25	1	1924-1925
Miller, Paul	12		1991
Millington, Joseph	44	7	1937-1939
Millington, Tony	178		1969-1974
Milne, W. E.	586	7	1920-1937
Molby, Jan	41	8	1996-1997
Molloy, William	11	2	1932-1933
Moore, Gary	34	9	1976-1978
Moore, John	31		1973-1974
Moore, Kevin	55	6	1977-1979
Moore, Michael	1		1993-1994
Moore, Stan	123		1935-1939
Moore, Thomas	4		1936-1937
Moreira, Joao	15		1996-1998
Morgan, A. R.	12		1948-1953
Morgan, Denley	14		1969-1972
Morgan, Huw	7		1982-1984
Morgan, M. M.	3		1933-1934
Morgan, Wendall	7		1958-1959
Morgans, K. G.	54	8	1961-1964
Morley, E. J.	123		1920-1928
Morris, Alan	12	1	1958-1963
Morris, D. H.	9	5	1925-1926
Morris, M. J. G.	14	5	1956-1958
Morris, Stephen	39	1	1975-1979
Morris, W. H.	16	1	1947-1949
Morrissey, Pat	4		1977 (loan)
Mullen, Roger	3		1983-1985
Munroe, Karl	1		1999
Murray, Don	5		1974 (loan)
Mutton, Tommy	2		1999-2000
Newell, E.	22		1946-1951
Newhouse, Aidan	14		1997-1999
Nicholas, D. S.	151	14	1924-1930
Nurse, Mel T. G.	257	12	1955-1962, 1968-1971
O'Driscoll, J. F.	118	24	1947-1952
Ogley, William	6	3	1919-1921
O'Gorman, Dave	39	5	1997-1999
O'Leary, Kristian	81	3	1996-2000
Olsen, T. B.	188	50	1930-1939
O'Sullivan, John	2		1948
Owen, Robert	6	1	1970 (loan)
Palmer, Des	84	38	1950-1959
Park, Colin	1		1963-1964
Parlane, Derek	21	3	1985
Parry, B. J.	96		1946-1951

Player	Apps.	Gls.	Years Played
Pascoe, Colin	270	54	1983-1988, 1992 (loan), 1993-1996
Passmore, E.	6	2	1946-1947
Paton, T. G.	6		1938-1939
Pattimore, H.	2		1928
Paul, Roy	159	11	1946-1950
Payne, Don	11		1970-1972
Payne, I. E. H.	52	14	1938-1949
Peake, D. J.	57	2	1956-1958
Pearce, Cyril	55	43	1931-1932, 1937-1938
Pears, Jack	50	10	1935-1937
Pearson, D. J.	52	1	1950-1958
Penney, David	131	23	1991 (loan), 1993-1997
Perrett, Darren	30	1	1993-1995
Phelan, Terry	45		1986-1987
Phillips, Don	3		1956-1958
Phillips, Gareth	11		1996-2000
Phillips, Leighton	97		1978-1981
Phillips, Stewart	12	1	1989-1990
Pinner, M. J.	1		1962
Pope, David	2		1956-1957
Potter, Steve	118		1974-1978
Pound, Ken	26	4	1964-1966
Powell, Barry	8		1985
Powell, Ray	18	5	1947-1951
Prentice, J. H.	3		1920-1921
Pressdee, Jim	8		1951-1955
Price, D. T.	34	9	1950-1958
Price, Jason	103	13	1995-2000
Price, Neil	3		1985-1986
Price, Paul	61	1	1985-1986
Puckett, David	8	3	1988 (loan)
Purcell, Brian	165	1	1958-1968
Purnell, Phil	5	1	1991 (loan)
Puttnam, David	4		1997
Rajkovic, Anto	80	2	1978-1983, 1984
Randell, Colin	22	1	1985-1986
Ranson, J. G.	2		1931
Rawcliffe, Frank	25	17	1947-1948
Raybould, Phil	6	4	1968-1969
Raynor, Paul	189	26	1987-1992
Reece, Gil	2		1976-1977
Reed, W. G.	8		1958
Rees, E. G.	9		1930-1933
Rees, Ioan	3		1964-1965, 1968-1969
Rees, Ronnie	89	5	1972-1975
Rees, William	6		1954-1959
Reeves, Peter	4		1978-1979
Reid, E. J.	1		1932-1933
Reid, R. B. A.	17		1957-1959
Reynolds, Brayley	150	58	1959-1964
Rhodes, R. A.	25	1	1938-1939
Richards, Gary	66	1	1981-1985
Richards, S. V.	62	35	1948-1950
Richardson, E. W.	18	2	1938-1939
Richardson, Paul	12		1984
Rigsby, Herbert	10		1920-1921
Rimmer, Jimmy	83		1973-1974 (loan), 1983-1986
Roberts, Albert	16		1938-1939
Roberts, Dave	36	1	1974-1975
Roberts, J. H.	16	1	1950-1951
Roberts, John	37	16	1964-1967
Roberts, O. J.	24		1946-1948
Roberts, Stuart	43	4	1998-2000
Robinson, Neil	123	7	1979-1984
Robson, E. R.	29		1924-1926
Robson, F. E.	76		1919-1922

Player	Apps.	Gls.	Years Played
Rosser, Doug	29	1	1967-1971
Roulson, Joseph	49	2	1922-1924
Rouse, V. A.	4		1925-1926
Rowden, L. A.	1		1953-1954
Rush, Matthew	13		1994 (loan)
Rushbury, Dave	52		1979-1981
Salako, John	13	3	1989 (loan)
Sampy, W. E.	41		1927-1930
Sander, Chris	20		1981-1985
Sanders, Alan	92		1959-1963
Saunders, Dean	49	12	1983-1985
Saunders, Roy	95	3	1959-1963
Schroder, Nico	1		1976-1977
Scott, Harry	40	7	1932-1933
Screen, Anthony	128	9	1970-1975
Screen, Willie	142	15	1967-1972
Scrine, Frank	142	45	1947-1953
Scrine, W. H.	1		1951-1954
Sharpe, John	5		1985
Simms, J. L.	4	2	1931-1932
Simons, Reuben	107		1931-1939
Slater, John	10	3	1920-1922
Slattery, Clive	70	10	1969-1972
Slee, Carl	119		1966-1971
Smith, Frank	1		1920-1921
Smith, George	88	10	1975-1977
Smith, J. W.	66	33	1922-1924
Smith, Jason	85	5	1998-2000
Smith, Tommy	36		1978-1979
Sneddon, W. C.	2		1946-1946
Spottiswoode, Joseph	159	9	1920-1925
Squires, Frank	36	5	1946-1947
Stanley, Gary	72	4	1981-1984
Stapleton, William	7		1920-1922
Stead, Michael	5		1977 (loan)
Steele, Alex	2		1927
Stevenson, Nigel	257	15	1975-1987
Stewart, Dave	57		1980-1981
Sullivan, Alan	7	1	1971-1972
Sullivan, Colin	53		1985-1986
Sykes, Joe	314	7	1924-1935
Symmonds, Lyndon	8	1	1986 (loan)
Symmons, Iorie	16		1948-1954
Tabram, Phil	11	1	1939
Tabram, W. D.	20		1930-1933
Terry, Pat	17	9	1958
Thomas, Barry	2		1971-1972
Thomas, Brian	4		1964-1965
Thomas, D. A.	296	14	1948-1961
Thomas, David	56	10	1994-1997
Thomas, Eddie	68	21	1962-1964
Thomas, Geoff	357	52	1965-1976
Thomas, George	64	10	1924-1931
Thomas, Martin	70	7	1998-2000
Thomas, Steve	10		1973-1975
Thompson, Albert	4		1937-1938
Thompson, Len	188	89	1922-1928
Thompson, Max	26	2	1981-1983
Thornber, Steve	117	5	1988-1992
Todd, Keith	198	78	1959-1968
Tones, John	7		1974
Torpey, Steve	164	44	1993-1997
Toshack, John	63	25	1978-1984
Trevitt, Simon	1		1997

Player	Apps.	Gls.	Years Played
Trick, Des	29		1988-1992
Turnbull, R. W.	67	37	1951-1953
Turner, Charlie	2		1948-1949
Turner, Robin	20	8	1985-1986
Tynan, Tommy	6	2	1975 (loan)
Vernon, J. L.	7		1937-1938
Waddle, Alan	127	43	1978-1980, 1985-1986
Wade, Brian	27	5	1988-1990
Walker, Keith	268	9	1989-2000
Wallace, Ray	2		1992 (loan)
Walsh, Ian	37	11	1982-1984
Walton, J. W.	64		1933-1935
Ward, D. A.	44		1959-1966
Ward, Joseph	1		1922-1923
Warner, Jack	135	9	1934-1938
Wassell, Kim	2		1984-1985
Watkin, Steve	114	27	1997-2000
Watson, Andy	14	1	1990-1991
Webber, Andrew	1		1986
Webster, Colin	157	66	1958-1963
Wellings, Barry	5	3	1984
West, Colin	33	12	1992-1993
West, Colin W.	14	3	1989 (loan)
Weston, Reg	229	1	1946-1952
Whitehead, W. T.	4	1	1923-1925
Whitehouse, J. F.	2		1928-1929
Wilkie, L. H.	5		1932-1933
Wilkins, A. J.	5		1963-1965
Willer, Thomas	7		1997
Williams, Alan	143	7	1968-1972
Williams, Albert	3		1936-1937
Williams, B. D.	101		1926-1929
Williams, Darwell	130	4	1946-1954
Williams, G. G.	91	17	1959-1964
Williams, Gary	6		1985
Williams, H. J.	489	103	1958-1975
Williams, J. L.	85	4	1913-1924
Williams, John	46	13	1991-1992, 1995 (loan)
Williams, Len H.	42		1930-1931
Williams, Paul	12		1991 (loan)
Williams, Phil	58	5	1983-1988
Williams, Ron	10	1	1968-1969
Williams, Ronnie	185	51	1929-1935, 1936-1939
Williams, Steve	8	1	1976
Willis, Arthur	98		1954-1957
Wilmot, Rhys	16		1988 (loan)
Wilson, Ambrose	1		1950-1951
Wimbleton, Paul	14	1	1992-1993
Woods, A. E.	30		1956-1960
Woodward, T.	59		1926-1929
Wookey, K. W.	12		1948-1950
Wright, James	4		1937-1938
Yorath, Terry	1		1987

League Matches only. Play-off matches not included.

Substitute appearances included in above matches.

There were three men who played for the Swans first team who are not included in this listing. This is because the 1939-40 season was aborted after just three matches because of the outbreak of war. Strictly speaking, these games should not be included in this record. However, Messrs. Rogers, Gallon and Coulter did play in all three matches.

Football League Hat-tricks

Player	Goals	Opponents	Home/Away	Date	Season
Beynon, B.	3	Norwich C.	H	16.09.20	1920-1
Brown, W. Y.	3	Bristol Rovers	H	15.04.22	1921-2
Collins, J.	3	Bristol Rovers	H	15.04.22	1921-2
Gough, C.	3	Swindon T.	H	02.10.22	1922-3
Smith, J.	3	Portsmouth	A	18.11.22	1922-3
Smith, J.	3	Merthyr T.	H	10.11.23	1923-4
Fowler, J.	3	Brentford	H	19.04.24	1923-4
Fowler, J.	5	Charlton Ath.	H	27.09.24	1924-5
Deacon, H.	3	Brentford	H	08.11.24	1924-5
Thompson, L.	4	Brentford	H	08.11.24	1924-5
Fowler, J.	3	Luton Town	H	22.11.24	1924-5
Fowler, J.	3	Darlington	A	19.12.25	1925-6
Fowler, J.	3	Preston N.E.	H	16.01.26	1925-6
Thompson, L.	3	Blackpool	H	25.02.26	1925-6
Fowler, J.	3	Southampton	H	29.03.26	1925-6
Fowler, J.	3	Barnsley	H	18.09.26	1926-7
Fowler, J.	3	Darlington	H	02.10.26	1926-7
Lewis, W.	3	Oldham Ath.	H	27.12.26	1926-7
McPherson, L.	3	Man. City	H	05.09.27	1927-8
McPherson, L.	3	Wolves	H	17.09.27	1927-8
Fowler, J.	3	Wolves	H	17.09.27	1927-8
Lewis, W.	3	South Shields	H	01.10.27	1927-8
Deacon, H.	4	Blackpool	H	27.08.28	1928-9
Gunn, K.	3	Preston N.E.	H	02.03.29	1928-9
Williams, R.	3	Notts County	H	25.12.29	1929-30
Easton, W.	3	Bury	H	13.09.30	1930-31
Williams, R.	3	Nottm. Forest	H	22.04.30	1931-31
Pearce, C.	4	Notts County	H	19.09.31	1931-2
Pearce, C.	3	Port Vale	A	21.09.31	1931-2
Gunn, K.	3	Burnley	H	28.11.31	1931-2
Martin, T.	3	Fulham	H	07.01.33	1932-3
Martin, T.	3	West Ham Utd.	H	02.03.35	1934-5
Martin, T.	4	Bury	H	05.10.35	1935-6
Bussey, W.	4	Bradford C.	H	22.02.36	1935-6
Olsen, T.	3	Hull C.	H	18.04.36	1935-6
McCrory, S.	3	Northampton Town	H	22.11.47	1947-8
Rawcliffe, F.	3	Norwich	H	06.12.47	1947-8
Richards, S.	4	Swindon T.	H	30.09.48	1948-9
Scrine, F.	3	Bristol Rovers	H	02.10.48	1948-9
McCrory, S.	3	Torquay	H	19.02.49	1948-9
Turnbull, R.	3	Blackburn Rovers	H	08.09.51	1951-2
Allchurch, I.	3	Brentford	H	06.04.53	1952-3
Allchurch, I.	3	Fulham	A	19.04.54	1953-4
Allchurch, I.	3	Ipswich T.	H	04.12.54	1954-5
Allchurch, I.	3	Notts C.	A	24.09.55	1955-6
Medwin, T.	3	Leicester C.	H	24.03.56	1955-6
Charles, M.	4	Blackburn Rovers	H	18.08.56	1956-7
Griffiths, H.	3	Doncaster Rovers	H	13.10.56	1956-7
Jones, C.	3	Bristol Rovers	H	25.12.57	1957-8
Allchurch, I.	3	Derby Co.	H	08.04.58	1957-8
Charles, M.	3	Stoke C.	H	19.04.58	1957-8
Allchurch, I.	4	Sunderland	H	13.09.58	1958-9
Charles, M.	3	Middlesborough	H	01.11.58	1958-9
Charles, M.	3	Sheffield W.	H	20.12.58	1958-9
Davies, R.	3	Derby Co.	H	27.12.58	1958-9
Webster, C.	3	Plymouth Argyle	H	12.12.59	1959-60
Webster, C.	3	Charlton	H	27.02.60	1959-60
Webster, C.	3	Norwich C.	H	14.01.61	1960-1
Reynolds, B.	3	Plymouth Argyle	H	24.04.62	1961-2
Todd, K.	3	Walsall	H	03.11.62	1962-3
Todd, K.	3	Swindon T.	H	07.12.63	1963-4
Williams, H.	3	Southampton	H	03.03.64	1963-4
Todd, K.	3	Man. City	H	26.09.64	1964-5

Player	Goals	Opponents	Home/Away	Date	Season
McLoughlin, J.	3	Bournemouth	H	23.11.65	1965-6
Williams, H.	4	York City	H	25.03.66	1965-6
Allchurch, I.	3	Doncaster	H	23.12.67	1967-8
Williams, H.	3	Bradford (PA)	H	07.03.70	1969-70
Gwyther, D.	3	Reading	H	27.03.71	1970-1
Holme, P.	3	Torquay	A	01.01.72	1971-2
Thomas, G.	3	Grimsby T.	H	07.10.72	1972-3
Thomas, G.	3	Doncaster Rovers	H	07.09.74	1974-5
Curtis, A.	3	Crewe Alex.	H	10.11.77	1977-8
James, R.	3	Hartlepool Utd.	H	01.04.78	1977-8
Curtis, A.	3	Hartlepool Utd.	H	01.04.78	1977-8
Waddle, A.	3	Southend Utd.	H	28.04.78	1977-8
James, L.	3	Derby Co.	H	11.10.80	1980-1
James, L.	3	Bolton W.	H	28.02.81	1980-1
Latchford, R.	3	Leeds Utd.	H	29.08.81	1981-2
Latchford, R.	3	Norwich C.	H	04.09.82	1982-3
Chalmers, P.	3	Fulham	H	26.01.90	1989-90
Gilligan, J.	3	Wigan Ath.	A	29.12.90	1990-1
Williams, J.	3	Bradford C.	A	23.11.91	1991-2
Gilligan, J.	3	Chester C	H	27.12.91	1991-2
Thornber, S.	3	W.B.A.	A	25.01.92	1991-2
Bowen, J.	3	Chester C.	H	13.03.93	1992-3

Major Cup Hat-tricks

Player	Goals	Opponents	Home/Away	Date	Season	Competition
Fowler, J.	4	Stoke C.	H	30.01.26	1925-6	FA Cup
Thompson, L.	3	Bury	H	08.01.27	1926-7	FA Cup
McLaughlin, J.	3	Folkstone	H	29.11.66	1966-7	FA Cup
Gwyther, D.	4	Oxford C.	A	06.12.69	1969-70	FA Cup
Gwyther, D.	3	Telford Utd.	H	12.12.70	1970-71	FA Cup
Gwyther, D.	3	Rhyl	H	02.01.71	1970-71	FA Cup
Curtis, A.	3	Woking	A	13.12.78	1978-9	FA Cup
James, R.	3	Newport Co.	H	15.08.78	1978-9	Football League Cup
Walsh, I.	3	Sliema Wdrs.	H	15.09.82	1982-3	European Cup Winners Cup

The changing face of the Vetch field. How the skyline altered when Swansea built the east stand.

Internationals – Players capped whilst at the Vetch

Note: The first date listed is that of the year in which the player won his initial cap with the Swans.

1920-29

Jones, Ivor	1920-2	(6)
Hole, Billy	1921-9	(9)
Davies, Willie	1924	(3)
Fowler, Jack	1925-9	(6)
Morley, Ernie	1925	(1)
Lewis, Wilf	1927-30	(3)
Nicholas, Dai	1927	(2)
Williams, Ben	1928-30	(4)

1930-39

Lewis, Dai	1933	(2)
Lawrence, Sid	1932-6	(7)
Hanford, Harry	1934-6	(3)
*Blair, Hugh	1935	(1)
Warner, Jack	1937	(1)
John, Roy	1939	(2)

1946-49

Ford, Trevor	1947	(1)
Jones, Ernie	1947	(2)
* Keane, Rory	1949-50	(5)
* O'Driscoll, Jack	1949-50	(6)
Lucas, Billy	1949-51	(7)
Paul, Roy	1949-50	(9)

1950-59

Scrine, Frank	1950	(2)
* Feeney, Jim	1950	(1)
Allchurch, Ivor	1951-66	(42)+
Parry, Jack	1951	(1)
Medwin, Terry	1953	(3)
Griffiths, Harry	1953	(1)
Jones, Cliff	1954-7	(11)
King, John	1955	(1)
Allchurch, Len	1955-64	(8)+
Charles, Mel	1953-9	(21)
Palmer, Des	1957-8	(3)
Thomas, Dai	1957-8	(2)

1960-69

Nurse, Mel	1961-71	(9)+
* Dwyer, Noel	1961-5	(10)
Williams, Graham	1961-2	(5)
Jones, Barrie	1963-5	(7)
Johnson, Mike	1964	(1)
Evans, Roy	1964	(1)
* McLaughlin, Jimmy	1965-6	(7)
* Humphries, Willie	1965	(3)
* Briggs, Ronnie	1965	(2)
Williams, Herbie	1965-72	(6)

1970-79

Millington, Tony	1970-2	(8)
Hole, Barry	1971	(1)
Evans, Brian	1972-3	(6)
Curtis, Alan	1976-84	(23)+
James, Robbie	1979-83	(18)+
Phillips, Leighton	1980-1	(7)
Toshack, John	1979-80	(6)
Mahoney, John	1980-83	(7)

1980-89

Giles, David	1980-2	(9)

James, Leighton	1980-2	(16)
Charles, Jeremy	1981-4	(12)
Davies, Dai	1982-3	(8)
Marustic, Chris	1982-3	(6)
Walsh, Ian	1982-4	(4)
Stevenson, Nigel	1982-3	(4)
Lewis, Dudley	1983	(1)
Pascoe, Colin	1984	(2)
Davies, Alan	1988-9	(3)
Knill, Alan	1989	(1)

1990-99

Melville, Andy	1990	(4)
*Agboola, Reuben	1992	(1)
Bowen, Jason	1994	(1)
Cornforth, John	1995	(2)
Edwards, Chris	1996	(1)
Jenkins, Steve	1996	(1)

2000

Roger Freestone	2000	(1)

Notes

The players with a + against their name also played with other clubs during the period shown in the listing.

The figures in brackets are the number of caps which were awarded to the player whilst on the books at the Vetch. Apart from the players marked with an asterisk, all were capped by Wales.

Seven of these marked with an asterisk were capped by Irish international teams; both Rory Keane and Jack O'Driscoll had caps for 'Ireland' and Eire; Dwyer for the Republic of Ireland; Feeney, McLaughlin, Humphries and Briggs for Northern Ireland. Reuben Agboola was capped by Nigeria.

Footnote: Not only can the club be proud of such an extensive list of internationals, it can also point out that it includes:

* Thirty-two players who were born in Swansea.
* Three fathers and sons (Mel & Jeremy Charles; Billy & Barry Hole; Ivor and Cliff Jones).
* An uncle and nephew (Roy Paul & Alan Curtis).

Relations

* Overall, seven fathers and sons have played first team football at the Vetch;
* Three are included in the international list, the others are : Sid & David Lawrence; Tom & Gary Emmanuel; Roy & Dean Saunders and Alan & Gary Williams.
* Including those listed in the international section, there have been four sets of uncles and nephews. The other two are: Frank Squires & Dudley Lewis; Wyndham Evans & Stuart Roberts and Len & Gary Emmanuel.
* Eight sets of brothers have also worn the first team strip:
* Ivor & Len Allchurch, Gilbert & Cyril Beech, Len & Tom Emmanuel, Barry & Alan Hole, Cliff & Brin Jones, Billy & Tony Screen, Frank & Billy Scrine and Phil & Bill Tabram.

Final League Results – Season by Season

Southern League

Season	Competition	Final Position	P	W	D	L	F	A	Pts
1912-13	Division 2	3rd	24	12	7	5	29	23	31
1913-14	Division 2	4th	30	20	4	6	66	23	44
1914-15	Division 2	4th	24	16	1	7	48	21	33
1919-20	Division 1	9th	42	16	11	15	53	45	43

Football League

Season	Competition	Final Position	P	W	D	L	F	A	Pts
1920-1	Division 3	5th	42	18	15	9	56	45	51
1921-2	Division 3 (South)	10th	42	13	15	14	50	47	41
1922-3	Division 3 (South)	3rd	42	22	9	11	78	45	53
1923-4	Division 3 (South)	4th	42	22	8	12	60	48	52
1924-5	Division 3 (South)	1st (Champions)	42	23	11	8	68	35	57
1925-6	Division 2	5th	42	19	11	12	77	57	49
1926-7	Division 2	12th	42	16	11	15	68	72	43
1927-8	Division 2	6th	42	18	12	12	75	63	48
1928-9	Division 2	19th	42	13	10	19	62	75	36
1929-30	Division 2	15th	42	14	9	19	57	61	37
1930-1	Division 2	20th	42	12	10	20	51	74	34
1931-2	Division 2	15th	42	16	7	19	73	75	39
1932-3	Division 2	10th	42	19	4	19	50	54	42
1933-4	Division 2	19th	42	10	15	17	51	60	35
1934-5	Division 2	17th	42	14	8	20	56	67	36
1935-6	Division 2	13th	42	15	9	18	67	76	39
1936-7	Division 2	16th	42	15	7	20	50	65	37
1937-8	Division 2	18th	42	13	12	17	45	73	38
1938-9	Division 2	19th	42	11	12	19	50	83	34
1946-7	Division 2	21st	42	11	7	24	55	83	29
1947-8	Division 3 (South)	5th	42	18	12	12	70	52	48
1948-9	Division 3 (South)	1st (Champions)	42	27	8	7	87	34	62
1949-50	Division 2	8th	42	17	9	16	53	49	43
1950-1	Division 2	18th	42	16	4	22	54	77	36
1951-2	Division 2	19th	42	12	12	18	72	76	36
1952-3	Division 2	11th	42	15	12	15	78	81	42
1953-4	Division 2	20th	42	13	8	21	58	82	34
1954-5	Division 2	10th	42	17	9	16	86	83	43
1955-6	Division 2	10th	42	20	6	16	83	81	46
1956-7	Division 2	10th	42	19	7	16	90	90	45
1957-8	Division 2	19th	42	11	9	22	72	99	31
1958-9	Division 2	11th	42	16	9	17	79	81	41
1959-60	Division 2	12th	42	15	10	17	82	84	40
1960-1	Division 2	7th	42	18	11	13	77	73	47
1961-2	Division 2	20th	42	12	12	18	61	83	36
1962-3	Division 2	15th	42	15	9	18	51	72	39
1963-4	Division 2	19th	42	12	9	21	63	74	33
1964-5	Division 2	22nd	42	11	10	21	62	84	32
1965-6	Division 3	17th	46	15	11	20	81	96	41
1966-7	Division 3	21st	46	12	15	19	85	89	39
1967-8	Division 4	15th	46	16	10	20	63	77	42
1968-9	Division 4	10th	46	19	11	16	58	54	49
1969-70	Division 4	3rd	46	21	18	7	66	45	60
1970-1	Division 3	11th	46	15	16	15	59	56	46

Season	Competition	Final Position	P	W	D	L	F	A	Pts
1971-2	Division 3	14th	46	17	10	19	46	59	44
1972-3	Division 3	23rd	46	14	9	23	51	73	37
1973-4	Division 4	14th	46	16	11	19	45	46	43
1974-5	Division 4	22nd	46	15	6	25	46	73	36
1975-6	Division 4	11th	46	16	15	15	66	57	47
1976-7	Division 4	5th	46	25	8	13	92	68	58
1977-8	Division 4	3rd	46	23	10	13	87	47	56
1978-9	Division 3	3rd	46	24	12	10	83	61	60
1979-80	Division 2	12th	42	17	9	16	48	53	43
1980-1	Division 2	3rd	42	18	14	10	64	44	50
1981-2	Division 1	6th	42	21	6	15	58	51	69

3pts for a win

1982-3	Division 1	21st	42	10	11	21	51	69	41
1983-4	Division 2	21st	42	7	8	27	36	85	29
1984-5	Division 3	20th	46	12	11	23	53	80	47
1985-6	Division 3	24th	46	11	10	25	43	87	43
1986-7	Division 4	12th	46	17	11	18	56	61	62
1987-8	Division 4	6th*	46	20	10	16	62	56	70
1988-9	Division 3	12th	46	15	16	15	51	53	61
1989-90	Division 3	17th	46	14	12	20	45	63	54
1990-1	Division 3	20th	46	13	9	24	49	72	48
1991-2	Division 3	19th	46	14	14	18	55	65	56

Premier League set up

1992-3	N2	5th	46	20	13	13	65	47	73
1993-4	N2	13th	46	16	12	18	56	58	60
1994-5	N2	10th	46	19	14	13	57	45	71
1995-6	N2	22nd	46	11	14	21	43	79	47
1996-7	N3	5th*	46	21	8	17	62	58	71
1997-8	N3	20th	46	13	11	22	49	62	50
1998-9	N3	7th*	46	19	14	13	56	48	71
1999-2000	N3	1st (Champions)	46	24	13	9	51	30	85

* = Play-offs

N = New, following reorganisation when 2 became 1, 3 became 2 and 4 became 3.

Steve Hamer, Chairman.

Club Records

(Other than where denoted, all the following data relate to Football League matches only)

IN A SEASON

A. GOALS

(i) **(Total) Scored & Conceded**

	No.	Season	Games	Ave.	No.	Season	Games	Ave.
Most Scored	90	1956-7	42	2.14	92	1976-7	46	2.00
Least Scored	36	1983-4	42	0.86	43	1995-6	46	0.93
Most Conceded	99	1957-8	42	2.36	96	1965-6	46	2.09
Least Conceded	34	1948-9	42	0.81	30	1999-2000	46	0.65

(Home) Scored & Conceded

	No.	Season	Games	Ave.	No.	Season	Games	Ave.
Most Scored	60	1948-9	21	2.86	61	1965-6	23	2.65
Least Scored	31	1937-8	21	1.48	20	1983-4	23	0.87
Most Conceded	45	1957-8	21	2.14	39	1984-5	23	1.70
Least Conceded	10	1923-4	21	0.48	14	1969-70	23	0.61

(Away) Scored & Conceded

	No.	Season	Games	Ave.	No.	Season	Games	Ave.
Most Scored	37	1956-7	21	1.76	38	1966-7	23	1.65
Least Scored	10	{ 1921-2 1936-7	21	0.48	14	1972-3	23	0.61
Most Conceded	58	1955-6	21	2.76	59	{ 1965-6 1966-7	23	2.57
Least Conceded	23	{ 1924-5 1948-9	21	0.91	29 19	1978-9 1999-2000	23 23	1.26 0.83

(ii) **Goal Difference**

Best + 53 1948-9   Worst – 49 1983-4

(iii) **Clean Sheets & Failure to Score**

Most Clean Sheets	21	1924-5	42	22	1999-2000	46
Fewest Clean Sheets	4	{ 1951-2 1957-8	42	5	1967-8	46
Most Failing to Score	19	1973-4 1974-5, 1975-6, 1989-90				
Least Failing to Score	3	1956-7				

(iv) **Highest Aggregate Goals in a Game**

Win	6-4	v.	Bristol Rovers (Home)	25.12.57
Draw	5-5	v.	Blackpool (Home)	27.08.28
Defeat	4-7	v.	Manchester City (Away)	29.08.27

(v) **Biggest Wins and Defeats**

Wins	8-0	v.	Hartlepool	01.04.78
	8-1	v.	Bristol Rovers	15.04.22
	8-1	v.	Bradford City	22.02.36
Defeat	1-8	v.	Fulham	22.01.38

(vi) **Cup Matches**

Wins	12-1	Sliema Wanderers (H)	E.C.W. Cup	15.09.82
Defeat	0-8	Liverpool (A)	FA Cup	01.10.91

Scorers

(i) **All-Time Leading Scorers**

Rank by Average per Game	Player	Games	Goals	Goals/Game	Rank by no of goals
1	Jack Fowler	167	100	.60	4
2	Len Thompson	187	86	.46	7
3	Keith Todd	199	76	.38	8
4	Ivor Allchurch	446	166	.37	1
5	Mel Charles	233	69	.30	10
6	Harry Deacon	319	88	.28	6
7	Alan Curtis	365	95	.26	5
8	Robbie James	468	116	.25	2
9	Herbie Williams	515	102	.20	3
10	Harry Griffiths	424	72	.17	9

To put the above data into context it should be noted that Harry Griffiths, Herbie Williams, Mel Charles and Robbie James each played a significant number of games in mid-field or defensive positions.

(ii) **Individual Record Holders – Goals Scored**

Most in a match:	5	Jack Fowler v. Charlton 27.9.24
Most in a season:	35	Cyril Pearce 1931-32 season
Most in a Vetch Career	166	Ivor Allchurch 1949-58; 1965-68

B.　POINTS

		No.	Season	Games	No.	Season	Games
(i)	Most gained	69	1981-2	42*	85	1999-2000	46*
		62	1948-9	42			
	Least gained	29	1983-4	42	31	1974-5	46*
		29	1946-7	42			

* 3 points for a win

C.　RESULTS

(i) **Wins, Draws & Defeats – Most & Least**

			No.	Season	Games	No.	Season	Games
	Wins	Most (Total)	27	1958-9	42	25	1976-7	46
		Fewest (Total)	7	1983-4	42	11	1985-6	46
						11	1995-6	46
		Most (Home)	20	1948-9	21	18	1976-7	23
		Fewest (Home)	7	1983-4	21	7	1984-5	23
		Most (Away)	9	1920-1	21	11	1987-8	23
				1922-3				
		Fewest (Away)	0	1933-4	21	1	1965-6	23
				1983-4	21			
(ii)	**Draws**	Most (Total)	15	1920-1	42	18	1969-70	46
				1921-2	42			
				1933-4	42			
		Most (Home)	10	1920-1	21	9	1966-7	23
		Fewest (Home)	0	1932-3	21	3	1976-7	23
		Most (Away)	8	1951-2	21	11	1970-1	23
		Fewest (Away)	1	1964-5	21	2	1967-8	23
(iii)	**Defeats**	Most (Total)	27	1983-4	42	25	1974-5	46
							1985-6	46
		Fewest (Total)	7	1948-9	42	7	1969-70	46
		Most (Home)	11	1946-7	21	11	1984-5	23
		Fewest (Home)	0	1924-5	21	1	1969-70	23
			0	1948-9	21	1	1975-6	23
						1	1978-9	23

D. SEQUENCES

(i) **Wins, Draws, Defeats**

Wins (Total)	9	1999-2000
Wins (Home)	17	1948-9
Wins (Away)	4	1955-6, 1987-8, 1992-3, 1999-2000
Draws (Total)	5	1933-4, 1970-1, 1991-2, 1992-3
Draws (Home)	4	1938-9, 1952-3, 1968-9, 1973-4
Draws (Away)	5	1954-5 or 6 1960-1 & 2
Defeats (Total)	9	1990-1
Defeats (Home)	6	1957-8
Defeats (Away)	11	1963-4 also into 1964-5

(ii)

'Clean Sheets' (Total)	8	1999-2000
'Clean Sheets' (Home)	5	1948-9, 1923-4, 1981-2, 1994-5, 1999-2000
'Clean Sheets' (Away)	4	1969-70, 1999-2000

(iii)

Games without defeat (Total)	19	1960-2, 1970-1
Games without defeat (Home)	27	1947-8, 1948-9 and into 1949-50
Games without defeat (Away)	12	1970-1
Games without a win (Total)	12	1931-8
Games without a win (Home)	9	1938-9, 1997-8
Games without a win (Away)	43	1932-3 and into 1934-5

(iv)

Games failing to score (Total)	6	1995-6
Games failing to score (Home)	4	1973-4
Games failing to score (Away)	7	1991-2

(v) **Individual Scoring sequences**

Cyril Pearce: 16 goals in 8 consecutive League games (1931-2)

Ivor Allchurch: 9 goals in 9 consecutive games (including an FA Cup tie)

E. FINAL LEAGUE POSITION BY DIVISION

	BEST		WORST	
Division	*Position*	*Season*	*Position*	*Season*
1st	6th	1981-2	21st	1982-3
2nd	3rd	1980-1	22nd	1964-5
3rd (South)	1st	1924-5	10th	1921-2
	1st	1948-9		
3rd	3rd	1978-9	24th	1985-6
4th	3rd	1969-70	22nd	1974-5
	3rd	1977-8		
New 2nd	5th	1992-3	22nd	1995-6
New 3rd	1st	1999-2000	20th	1997-8

F. FINAL RECORDS – BEST & WORST

Best (Total) Record	1948-9	P42	W27	D8	L7	F87-A34
Worst (Total) Record	1983-4	P42	W7	D8	L27	F36-A85
Best (Home) Record	1948-9	P21	W20	D1	L0	F60-A11
Worst (Home) Record	1983-4	P21	W7	D4	L10	F20-A28
Best (Away) Record	1987-8	P23	W11	D3	L9	F27-A28
Worst (Away) Record	1983-4	P23	W0	D4	L17	F16-A51

G. OTHER RECORDS

(i) **Players used in a season**
Most	37	1984-5 and 1997-8
Least	18	1966-7 and 1969-70

(ii) **Youngest and Oldest to appear for first Team**
Youngest	Nigel Dalling	15 yrs 10 months
Oldest	Tommy Hutchison	43 yrs 5 months

(iii) **Attendance Records**
Highest (Vetch)	v.	Leeds Utd	29,477 (League)	1.10.55
	v.	Arsenal	32,786 (FA Cup)	17.2.68
Lowest (Vetch)	v.	Northampton T.	1,301 (League)	18.9.73
Highest (Away)	v.	Newcastle Utd.	54,966 (League)	7.8.46
(Neutral)	v.	P.N.E. (Villa Park)	68,000 (FA Cup Semi-final)	14.3.64
Lowest (Away)	v.	Southport	972 (League)	11.4.77

(iv) **Most Games Played**
In a season by the Club:	66:	1993-4
In a season by an individual:	66:	Mark Harris, Roger Freestone
In a career by an Individual	587:	(League) & 44 (FA Cup), Wilfie Milne

(v) **Most consecutive games played by an individual**
League	Roger Freestone	186	1991-1994
FA Cup	Wilfie Milne	44	1920-1937

Ivor and young fans at his Testimonial Match, 1968.

FA Cup Record

1913/14					
PR	27.09.13	H	Port Talbot	4-0	
1Q	11.10.13	H	Caerleon A.	8-1	
2Q	13.11.13	H	Mid-Rhondda	1-0	
3Q	15.11.13	H	Aberdare A.	4-0	
4Q	29.11.13	H	Cardiff C.	2-0	
5Q	13.12.13	H	Wellington T.	3-0	
1	10.01.14	H	Merthyr T.	2-0	
2	31.01.14	H	Q.P.R.	1-2	

1919/20					
6Q	20.12.19	H	Gillingham	1-1	
R	23.12.19	A	Gillingham	1-1	
R	31.12.19	C	Gillingham	0-0	
R	05.01.20	Ch	Gillingham	1-3	

C = Cardiff   Ch = Chelsea

1921-22					
5Q	03.12.21	H	Bournemouth	4-0	
6Q	17.12.21	H	Bristol R.	2-0	
1	07.01.22	H	West Ham Utd.	0-0	
R	11.01.22	A	West Ham Utd.	1-1	
R	16.01.22	B	West Ham Utd.	1-0	
2	28.01.22	A	Southend Utd.	1-0	
3	18.02.22	A	Millwall	0-4	

B = Bristol City

1923-24					
1	12.01.24	H	Clapton O.	1-1	
R	17.01.24	A	Clapton O.	0-0	
R	21.01.24	T	Clapton O.	2-1	
2	02.02.24	H	Aston Villa	0-2	

T = Tottenham

1925-26					
1	28.11.25	A	Exeter C.	3-1	
2	12.12.25	H	Watford	3-2	
3	09.01.26	A	Blackpool	2-0	
4	30.01.26	H	Stoke C.	6-3	
5	20.02.26	A	Millwall	1-0	
6	06.03.26	H	Arsenal	2-1	
S/F	27.03.26	T	Bolton W.	0-3	

T = Tottenham

1927-28					
3	14.01.28	A	Wrexham	1-2	

1929-30					
3	11.01.30	A	Walsall	0-2	

1931-32					
3	09.01.32	A	Bury	1-2	

1933-34					
3	13.01.34	H	Notts Co.	1-0	
4	27.01.34	A	Bury	1-1	
R	01.02.34	H	Bury	3-0	
5	17.02.34	H	Portsmouth	0-1	

1914/15					
4Q	21.11.14	H	Newport Co.	1-0	
5Q	05.12.14	H	Port Vale	1-0	
6Q	19.12.14	H	Leicester C.	1-0	
1	09.01.15	H	Blackburn R.	1-0	
2	30.01.15	A	Newcastle Utd	1-1	
R	06.02.15	H	Newcastle Utd	0-2	

1920/21					
6Q	18.12.20	H	Hartlepool Utd.	3-0	
1	08.01.21	H	Bury	3-0	
2	29.01.21	H	Plymouth A	1-2	

1922-23					
5Q	02.12.23	A	Merthyr T.	0-0	
R	07.12.23	H	Merthyr T.	0-1	

1924-25					
1	10.01.25	H	Plymouth A.	3-0	
2	31.01.25	A	Aston Villa	1-3	

1926-27					
3	08.01.27	H	Bury	4-1	
4	29.01.27	A	Barnsley	3-1	
5	19.02.27	A	Sth. Shields	2-2	
R	24.02.27	H	Sth. Shields	2-1	
6	05.03.27	H	Reading	1-3	

1928-29					
3	12.01.29	A	Nottm F.	2-1	
4	26.01.29	A	Leicester C.	0-1	

1930-31					
3	10.01.31	A	Notts C.	1-3	

1932-33					
3	14.01.33	H	Sheff. Utd.	2-3	

1934-35					
3	12.01.35	H	Stoke C.	4-1	
4	26.-1.35	A	Derby Co.	0-3	

1935-36

3	11.01.36	A	Liverpool	0-1

1937-38

3	08.01.38	H	Wolves	0-4

1945-46

3	05.01.46	A	Bristol C.	1-5

1947-48

3	10.01.48	A	Bristol R	0-3

1949-50

3	07.01.50	H	Birmingham C.	3-0
4	28.01.50	A	Arsenal	1-2

1951-52

3	12.01.52	A	Reading	3-0
4	02.02.52	H	Rotherham Utd.	3-0
5	23.02.52	H	Newcastle Utd.	0-1

1953-54

3	09.01.54	A	Barrow	2-2
R	14.01.54	H	Barrow	4-2
4	30.01.54	A	Everton	0-3

1955-56

3	07.01.56	H	York C.	1-2

1957-58

3	04.01.58	A	Burnley	2-4

1959-60

3	09.01.60	A	Gillingham	4-1
4	30.01.60	H	Burnley	0-0
R	02.02.60	A	Burnley	1-2

1961-62

3	09.01.62	A	Sheff. Wed.	0-1 4

1963-64

3	04.01.64	H	Barrow	4-1
4	25.01.64	A	Sheff. U.	1-1
R	28.01.64	H	Sheff.U.	4-0
5	15.02.64	A	Stoke C.	2-2
R	18.02.64	H	Stoke C.	2-0
6	27.02.64	A	Liverpool	2-1
S/F	14.03.64	V	Preston N.E.	1-2

V = Villa Park

1965-66

1	13.11.65	A	Walsall	3-6

1936-37

3	16.01.37	H	Carlisle U.	1-0
4	30.01.37	H	York C.	0-0
R	03.02.37	A	York C.	3-1
5	20.02.37	A	Sunderland	0-3

1938-39

3	07.07.39	A	Blackburn R.	0-2

1946-47

3	11.01.47	H	Gillingham	4-1
4	25.01.47	A	Luton Town	0-2

1948-49

1	04.12.48	A	Southend Utd.	2-1
2	11.12.48	A	Bristol C.	1-3

1950-51

3	06.01.51	A	Mansfield	0-2

1952-53

3	10.01.53	A	Newcastle Utd. (Fog. Abandoned)	0-0
R	14.01.53	A	Newcastle Utd.	0-3

1954-55

3	08.01.55	A	Blackburn R.	2-0
4	29.01.55	H	Stoke C.	3-1
5	19.02.55	H	Sunderland	2-2
R	23.02.55	A	Sunderland	0-1

1956-57

3	05.01.57	A	Wolves	3-5

1958-59

3	10.01.59	A	Portsmouth	1-3

1960-61

3	07.01.61	H	Port Vale	3-0
4	28.01.61	H	Preston N.E.	2-1
5	18.02.61	A	Burnley	4-0

1962-63

3	26.01.63	H	Q.P.R.	2-0
	04.03.63	A	W. Ham Utd.	0-1

1964-65

3	09.01.65	H	Newcastle Utd.	1-0
4	30.01.65	H	Huddersfield T.	1-0
5	20.02.65	A	Peterborough Utd.	0-0
R	23.02.65	H	Peterborough Utd.	0-2

1966-67

1	26.11.66	A	Folkstone	2-2
R	29.11.66	H	Folkstone	7-2
2	07.01.67	A	Nuneaton B.	0-2

1967-68

1	18.12.67	H	Enfield	2-0
2	06.01.68	H	Brighton	2-1
3	27.01.68	A	Doncaster R.	2-0
4	17.02.68	H	Arsenal	0-1

1969-70

1	15.11.69	A	Kettering	2-0
2	06.12.69	A	Oxford C.	5-1
3	03.01.70	A	Leeds Utd.	1-2

1971-72

1	20.11.71	H	Brentford	1-1
R	22.11.71	A	Brentford	3-2
2	11.12.71	H	Exeter C.	0-0
R	15.12.71	A	Exeter C.	1-0
3	15.01.72	H	Gillingham	1-0
4	05.02.72	A	Portsmouth	0-2

1973-74

1	24.11.73	A	Walsall	0-1

1975-76

1	22.11.75	A	Southend Utd.	0-2

1977-78

1	26.11.77	A	Leatherhead	0-0
R	29.11.77	H	Leatherhead	2-1
2	17.12.77	A	Portsmouth	2-2
R	20.12.77	H	Portsmouth	2-1
3	07.01.78	A	Walsall	1-4

1979-80

3	05.01.80	H	Crystal Palace	2-2
R	08.01.80	A	Crystal Palace	3-3
			(After extra time)	
R	14.01.80	C	Crystal Palace	2-1
4	26.01.80	H	Reading	4-1
5	16.02.80	A	West Ham Utd.	0-2

C = Cardiff

1981-82

3	02.01.82	H	Liverpool	0-4

1983-84

3	07.01.84	A	Brighton	0-2

1985-86

1	16.11.85	H	Leyton Wingate	2-0
2	07.12.85	H	Bristol R.	1-2

1987-88

1	14.11.87	A	Hayes	1-0
2	05.12.87	A	Leyton O.	0-2

1968-69

1	16.11.68	A	Oxford C.	3-2
2	07.12.68	A	Weymouth	1-1
R	10.12.68	H	Weymouth	2-0
3	04.01.69	H	Halifax T.	0-1

1970-71

1	21.11.70	H	Exeter C.	4-1
2	12.12.70	H	Telford Utd.	6-2
3	02.01.71	H	Rhyl	6-1
4	23.01.70	A	Liverpool	0-3

1972-73

1	18.11.72	A	Margate	0-1

1974-75

1	26.11.74	H	Kettering	1-1
R	02.12.74	A	Kettering	1-3

1976-77

1	20.11.76	H	Minehead	0-1

1978-79

1	25.11.78	H	Hillingdon Bor.	4-1
2	16.12.78	H	Woking	2-2
R	19.12.78	A	Woking	5-3
3	08.01.79	H	Bristol R.	0-1

1980-81

3	03.01.81	H	Middlesbrough	0-5

1982-83

3	08.01.83	A	Norwich	1-2

1984-85

1	17.11.84	H	Bognor Regis	1-1
R	21.11.84	A	Bognor Regis	1-3

1986-87

1	15.11.86	A	Wealdstone	1-1
R	24.11.86	H	Wealdstone	4-1
2	06.12.86	H	Slough T.	3-0
3	10.01.87	H	W.B.A.	3-2
4	03.02.87	H	Hull City	0-1

1988-89

1	19.11.88	H	Northampton T.	3-1
2	10.12.88	A	Colchester Utd.	2-2
R	13.12.88	H	Colchester Utd.	1-3

1989-90

1	18.11.89	A	Kidderminster H.	3-2
2	09.12.89	H	Peterborough	3-1
3	06.01.90	H	Liverpool	0-0
R	09.01.90	A	Liverpool	0-8

1991-92

1	16.11.91	H	Cardiff C.	2-1
2	07.12.91	A	Exeter C	0-0
R	18.12.91	H	Exeter C	1-2

1993-94

| 1 | 13.11.93 | H | Nuneaton Bor. | 1-1 |
| R | 23.11.93 | A | Nuneaton Bor. | 1-2 |

1995-96

| 1 | 11.11.95 | A | Fulham | 0-7 |

1997-98

| 1 | 14.11.97 | H | Peterborough Utd. | 1-4 |

1999-2000

| 1 | 30.10.99 | H | Colchester Utd. | 2-1 |
| 2 | 20.11.99 | A | Oldham Ath. | 0-1 |

1990-91

1	17.11.90	H	Welling Utd.	5-2
2	08.12.90	H	Walsall	2-1
3	05.01.91	H	Rotherham Utd.	0-0
R	21.01.91	A	Rotherham Utd.	0-4

1992-93

1	BYE			
2	15.12.92	A	Exeter C.	5-2★
3	02.01.93	H	Oxford Utd.	1-1
R	12.01.93	A	Oxford Utd.	2-2°
4	02.02.93	H	Grimsby T.	0-0
R	09.02.93	A	Grimsby T.	0-2

★ = Replay of abandoned match (5.12)

° = won 5-4 on penalties

1994-95

1	21.11.94	A	Walton & Hersham	2-0
2	04.12.94	A	Bashley	1-0
3	07.01.95	H	Middlesbrough	1-1
R	17.01.95	A	Middlesbrough	2-1
4	28.01.95	A	Newcastle Utd.	0-3

1996-97

| 1 | 16.11.96 | H | Bristol C. | 1-1 |
| R | 26.11.96 | A | Bristol C. | 0-1 |

1998-99

1	13.11.98	H	Millwall	3-0
2	05.12.98	H	Stoke C.	1-0
3	02.01.99	A	West Ham Utd.	1-1
R	13.01.99	H	West Ham Utd.	1-0
4	23.01.99	H	Derby Co.	0-1

*Mrs. Pauline Lewis, a life-long supporter of
Swansea City F.C., hugs the Autoglass Trophy
Cup after the Swans' victory at Wembley
Stadium on 24th April, 1994.*

Football League Cup Record

Season	Date	H/A	Opponents	Score
1961-62	03.10.61	H	Ipswich Town	3-3
	24.10.61	A	Ipswich Town	2-3
1962-63	26.09.62	A	Coventry	2-3
1963-64	25.09.63	H	Sunderland	3-1
	22.10.63	A	Leeds United	0-2
1964-65	23.09.64	H	Swindon Town	3-1
	14.10.64	A	Rotherham United	2-2
	28.10.64	H	Rotherham United	2-0
	11.11.64	A	Chelsea	2-3
1965-66	21.09.65	H	Aston Villa	2-3
1966-67	24.08.66	A	Newport County	2-0
	13.09.66	A	Bristol City	1-1
	19.09.66	H	Bristol City	3-1
	12.10.66	A	Queens Park Rangers	1-2
1967-68	23.08.67	A	Oxford United	1-3
1968-69	13.08.68	A	Bristol Rovers	2-0
	03.09.68	A	Walsall	1-1
	10.09.68	H	Walsall	3-2
	25.09.68	A	Liverpool	0-2
1969-70	12.08.69	A	Newport County	3-2
	02.09.69	H	Swindon Town	1-3
1970-71	18.08.70	A	Exeter City	0-0
	25.08.70	H	Exeter City	4-2
			(After extra time)	
	09.09.70	A	Tottenham H.	0-3
1971-72	17.08.71	H	Brighton	0-1
1972-73	15.08.72	H	Newport County	1-1
	22.08.72	A	Newport County	0-3
1973-74	28.08.73	H	Exeter City	1-1
	05.09.73	A	Exeter City	1-2
1974-75	21.08.74	A	Exeter City	1-3
1975-76	19.08.75	H	Torquay United	1-2
	27.08.75	A	Torquay United	3-5
1976-77	14.08.76	H	Newport County	4-1
	17.08.76	A	Newport County	0-1
	31.08.76	A	Chester	3-2
	22.09.76	A	Torquay United	2-1
	26.10.76	H	Bolton W.	1-1
	02.11.76	A	Bolton W.	1-5
1977-78	13.08.77	H	Swindon Town	1-3
	16.08.77	A	Swindon Town	1-2
1978-79	12.08.78	A	Newport County	1-2
	15.08.78	H	Newport County	5-0
	29.08.78	H	Tottenham H.	2-2
	06.09.78	A	Tottenham H.	3-1
	03.10.78	A	Queens Park Rangers	0-2
1979-80	11.08.79	H	Bournemouth	4-1
	14.08.79	A	Bournemouth	0-0
	28.08.79	A	Stoke City	1-1
	04.09.79	H	Stoke City	1-3
			(After extra time)	
1980-81	26.08.80	H	Arsenal	1-1
	02.09.80	A	Arsenal	1-3
1981-82	06.10.81	A	Barnsley	0-2
	27.10.81	H	Barnsley	3-2

Season	Date	H/A	Opponents	Score
1982-83	04.10.82	A	Bristol Rovers	0-1
Now Milk				
Cup	26.10.82	H	Bristol Rovers	3-0
	09.11.82	A	Brentford	1-1
	16.11.82	H	Brentford	1-2
1983-84	04.10.83	H	Colchester United	1-1
	25.10.83	A	Colchester United	0-1
1984-85	28.08.84	H	Walsall	0-2
	04.09.84	A	Walsall	1-3
1985-86	20.08.85	A	Cardiff City	1-2
	03.09.85	H	Cardiff City	3-1
	24.09.85	A	West Ham United	0-3
	09.10.85	H	West Ham United	2-3
1986-87	27.08.86	A	Hereford United	3-3
Now	02.09.86	H	Hereford United	5-1
Littlewoods	23.09.86	H	Leicester City	0-2
Cup	08.10.86	A	Leicester City	2-4
1987-88	18.08.87	A	Torquay United	1-2
	25 08.87	H	Torquay United	1-1
1988-89	30.08.88	A	Cardiff City	1-0
	20.09.88	H	Cardiff City	0-2
1989-90	23.08.89	A	Exeter City	0-3
	29.08.89	H	Exeter City	1-1
1990-91	29.08.90	A	Stoke City	0-0
Now				
Rumbellows	04.09.90	H	Stoke City	0-1
Cup				
1991-92	20.08.91	H	Walsall	2-2
	27.08.91	A	Walsall	1-0
	25.09.91	H	Tottenham H.	1-0
	09.10.91	A	Tottenham H.	1-5
1992-93	18.08.92	A	Oxford United	0-3
	25.08.92	H	Oxford United	1-0
1993-94	17.08.93	H	Bristol City	0-1
Now				
Coca Cola	24.08.93	A	Bristol City	2-0
Cup	21.09.93	H	Oldham Ath.	2-1
	06.10.93	A	Oldham Ath.	0-2
1994-95	17.08.94	A	Exeter City	2-2
	23.08.94	H	Exeter City	2-0
	21.09.94	A	Norwich City	0-3
	05.10.94	H	Norwich City	1-0
1995-96	15.08.95	H	Peterborough United	4-1
	22.08.95	A	Peterborough United	0-3
			(After extra time, lost on away goals)	
1996-97	20.08.96	H	Gillingham	0-1
	03.09.96	A	Gillingham	0-2
1997-98	12.08.96	A	Reading	0-2
	27.08.96	H	Reading	1-1
1998-99	11.08.98	H	Norwich City	1-1
Now	18.08.98	A	Norwich City	0-1
Worthington			(After extra time)	
Cup				
1999-2000	11.08.99	H	Millwall	2-0
	25.08.99	A	Millwall	1-1
	14.09.99	H	Derby County	0-0
	22.09.99	A	Derby County	1-3

European Cup Winners' Record

1961-62

16.10.61	H*	Motor Jenna	2-2	* Played at Linz in Austria
18.10.61	A	Motor Jenna	1-5	

1966-67

21.09.66	H	Slavia	1-1
05.10.66	A	Slavia	0-4

1981-82

16.09.81	H	Lokomotiv Leipzig	0-1
30.09.81	A	Lokomotiv Liepzig	1-2

1982-83

17.08.82	H	Sporting Braga	3-0
25.08.82	A	Sporting Braga	0-1
15.09.82	H	Sliema Wdrs.	12-0
29.09.82	A	Sliema Wdrs.	5-0
20.10.82	H	Paris St. Germain	0-1
03.11.82	A	Paris St. Germain	0-2

1983-84

23.08.83	H	IFC Magdeburg	1-1
31.08.83	A	IFC Magdeburg	0-1

1989-90

13.09.89	A	Panathinaikos	2-3
27.09.89	H	Panathinaikos	3-3

1991-92

17.09.91	H	Monaco	1-2
01.10.91	A	Monaco	0-8

From the 1995-96 season, as a result of a reorganisation of Welsh football, the Swans, along with Cardiff and Wrexham, were no longer allowed to enter the Welsh Cup competition which was their best route into Europe.

Welsh Cup Record

Season	Round	Date	H/A	Opponents	Score
1912-13	Prelim.	31.10.12	H	Milford	3-1
Winners	1st	02.11.12	H	Mond Nickel	2-2
	Replay	07.11.12	A	Mond Nickel	5-0
	2nd	07.12.12	H	Llanelli	2-1
	3rd	04.01.13	A	Wrexham	3-1
	4th	25.01.13	A	Merthyr T.	3-0
	S.-Final	15.02.13	C	Cardiff City	4-2
	Final	19.04.13	C	Pontypridd	0-0
	Replay	24.04.13	T	Pontypridd	1-0

C = Cardiff   T = Tonypandy

Season	Round	Date	H/A	Opponents	Score
1913-14	3rd	03.01.14	H	Chester	1-0
	4th	24.01.14	H	Oswestry Utd.	1-1
	Replay	29.01.14	A	Oswestry Utd.	2-1
	S.-Final	07.03.14	P	Llanelli	1-2

P = Pontypridd

Season	Round	Date	H/A	Opponents	Score
1914-15	In the 3rd round the opponents				
Runners-	scratched (Milford)				
up	4th	23.01.15	H	Pontypridd	2-1
	S.-Final	13.02.15	H	Llanelli	1-0
	Final	10.04.15	A	Wrexham	1-1
	Replay	25.04.15	C	Wrexham	0-1

C = Cardiff

Season	Round	Date	H/A	Opponents	Score
1919-20	3rd	17.01.19	H	Mid-Rhondda	3-2
	4th	07.02.20	A	Barry Town	1-0
	S.-Final	24.03.20	A	Cardiff C.	1-2
1920-21	3rd	15.01.21	A	Mid-Rhondda	0-1
1921-22	3rd	23.01.22	A	Aberdare Ath.	3-2
	4th	27.02.22	A	Tonpentre	0-1
1922-23	6th	12.03.23	H	Llanelli	2-1
	7th	19.03.23	H	Newport Co.	4-2
	S.-Final	11.04.23	A	Cardiff City	2-3
1923-24	4th	14.02.24	H	Ebbw Vale	1-0
	5th	05.03.24	H	Wrexham	0-0
	Replay	19.03.24	A	Wrexham	0-1
					(AET)
1924-25	5th	02.03.25	H	Cardiff City	4-0
	6th	23.03.25	H	Aberdare Ath.	1-0
	S.-Final	20.04.25	H	Wrexham	1-3
1925-26	4th	24.02.26	A	Colwyn Bay	1-1
Runners-	Replay	04.03.26	H	Colwyn Bay	8-2
up	5th	08.04.26	A	Wrexham	1-0
	S.-Final	22.04.26	W	Rhyl	3-1
	Final	29.04.26	A	Ebbw Vale	2-3

W = Wrexham

Season	Round	Date	H/A	Opponents	Score
1926-27	5th	28.03.27	A	Aberdare Ath.	1-3
1927-28	5th	28.02.28	A	Holyhead	8-1
	6th	02.04.28	A	Cardiff City	0-1
1928-29	5th	28.02.29	A	Newport Co.	1-5

Season	Round	Date	H/A	Opponents	Score
1929-30	5th	13.03.30	H	Merthyr T.	4-2
	6th	02.04.30	A	Cardiff City	0-4
1930-31	5th	26.02.31	H	Llanelli	2-0
	6th	06.03.31	A	Oswestry	2-0
	S.-Final	15.04.31	Ch	Wrexham	2-5

Ch = Chester

Season	Round	Date	H/A	Opponents	Score
1931-32	5th	12.02.32	A	Merthyr T.	2-2
	Replay	18.02.32	H	Merthyr T.	2-1
	6th	17.03.32	A	Newport Co.	0-0
	Replay	04.04.32	H	Newport Co.	2-0
	S.-Final	13.04.32	A	Chester	2-0
	Final	05.05.32	A	Wrexham	1-1
	Replay	06.05.32	H	Wrexham	2-0
1932-3	7th	08.02.33	A	Bristol Rovers	3-0
	8th	09.03.33	H	Cardiff City	1-1
	Replay	15.03.33	A	Cardiff City	1-2
1933-34	6th	07.02.34	A	Chester	1-2
1934-35	6th	21.02.35	A	Milford Utd.	4-1
	7th	18.03.35	H	Wrexham	6-0
	S.-Final	24.04.35	W	Chester	0-5

W = Wrexham

Season	Round	Date	H/A	Opponents	Score
1935-36	6th	06.02.36	H	Newport Co.	1-0
	7th	11.03.36	A	Chester	1-4
1936-37	6th	03.03.37	A	Bristol City	2-1
	7th	15.03.37	A	Newport Co.	0-7
1937-38	6th	10.02.38	H	Llanelli	8-0
Runners-	7th	31.03.38	H	Worcester City	1-0
up	S.-Final	27.04.38	Ch	Rhyl	7-2
	Final	04.05.38	A	Shrewsbury T.	2-2
	Replay	19.09.38	A	Shrewsbury T.	1-2

Ch = Chester

Season	Round	Date	H/A	Opponents	Score
1938-39	5th	08.02.39	A	Cardiff City	2-2
	Replay	23.02.39	H	Cardiff City	1-4
1939-40	5th	20.01.40	H	Gwynfi	7-2
Runners-	6th	09.03.40	H	Aberystwyth Town	2-0
up	S.-Final	13.04.40	H	Newport Co.	1-0
	Final	01.06.40	S	Wellington	0-4

S = Shrewsbury

Season	Round	Date	H/A	Opponents	Score
1946-47	6th	17.02.47	H	Chester	1-3
1947-48	5th	14.01.48	A	Barry Town	0-2
1948-49	5th	12.01.49	A	Barry Town	7-1
Runners-	7th	12.02.49	H	South Liverpool	9-1
up	S.-Final	07.04.49	W	Rhyl	3-0
	Final	05.05.49	C	Merthyr T.	0-2

Bye 6th Round   W = Wrexham   C = Cardiff

Season	Round	Date	H/A	Opponents	Score
1949-50	5th	11.01.50	H	Caerau	4-1
Winners	7th	23.02.50	H	Cardiff City	3-0
	S.-Final	30.03.50	C	Merthyr T.	5-1
	Final	27.04.50	C	Wrexham	4-1

Bye 6th Round C = Cardiff

Season	Round	Date	H/A	Opponents	Score
1950-51	5th	10.02.51	H	Pembroke Bor.	5-0
	6th	01.03.51	A	Newport Co.	1-2
1951-52	5th	03.01.52	A	Merthyr T.	1-2
1952-53	5th	01.01.53	H	Kidderminster	2-0
	6th	29.01.53	H	Newport Co.	3-2
	7th	05.03.53	H	Rhyl	2-3
1953-54	5th	25.01.54	A	Newport Co.	2-6
1954-55	5th	21.01.55	H	Llanelli	6-2
	6th	10.02.55	H	Wrexham	4-4
	Replay	09.03.55	A	Wrexham	3-4
					(AET)
1955-56	5th	28.01.56	A	Newtown	9-4
Runners-	6th	01.03.56	H	Chester	1-0
up	S.-Final	21.09.56	C	Newport Co.	5-2
	Final	30.04.56	A	Cardiff City	2-3

C = Cardiff

Season	Round	Date	H/A	Opponents	Score
1956-57	5th	31.01.57	A	Hereford Utd.	0-0
Runners-	Replay	07.02.57	H	Hereford Utd.	2-0
up	6th	28.02.57	H	Pwllheli	6-0
	S.-Final	28.03.57	C	Newport Co.	1-1
	Replay	01.04.57	C	Newport Co.	3-0
	Final	15.04.57	C	Wrexham	1-2

C = Cardiff

Season	Round	Date	H/A	Opponents	Score
1957-58	5th	03.01.58	A	Newport Co.	5-2
	6th	06.03.58	A	Chester	0-2
1958-59	5th	29.01.59	H	Newport Co.	3-1
	6th	25.02.59	A	Bangor City	2-3
1959-60	5th	11.02.60	H	Merthyr T.	6-1
	6th	25.02.60	H	Cardiff City	1-2
1960-61	5th	01.02.61	A	Barry Town	3-0
Winners	6th	21.02.61	H	Holyhead	5-0
	S.-Final	22.03.61	N	Cardiff City	1-1
	Replay	28.03.61	L	Cardiff City	2-1
	Final	26.04.61	C	Bangor City	3-1

N = Newport, L = Llanelli, C = Cardiff

Season	Round	Date	H/A	Opponents	Score
1961-62	5th	27.01.62	A	Haverfordwest	7-0
	6th	24.02.62	A	Holywell	2-1
	S.-Final	20.03.62	C	Wrexham	2-3

C = Cardiff

Season	Round	Date	H/A	Opponents	Score
1962-63	5th	02.02.63	H	Caerau	6-0
	6th	11.04.63	H	Cardiff City	2-0
	S.-Final	09.05.63	C	Newport Co.	0-1

C = Cardiff

Season	Round	Date	H/A	Opponents	Score
1963-64	5th	01.02.64	A	Lovells Athletic	3-1
	6th	20.02.64	A	Newport Co.	0-1

Season	Round	Date	H/A	Opponents	Score
1964-65	5th	18.01.65	A	Newport Co.	3-2
	6th	11.02.65	A	Pwllheli	3-1
	S.-Final	10.03.65	N	Cardiff City	0-1

N = Newport

Season	Round	Date	H/A	Opponents	Score
1965-66	5th	04.01.66	H	Cardiff City	2-2
Winners	Replay	08.02.66	A	Cardiff City	5-3
	6th	16.02.66	A	Porthmadoc	1-1
	Replay	22.02.66	H	Porthmadoc	5-0
	S.-Final	16.03.66	H	Merthyr T.	3-1
	Final	18.04.66	H	Chester	3-0
	Final	25.04.66	A	Chester	0-1
	Final	02.05.66	A	Chester	2-1
1966-67	5th	12.01.67	H	Cardiff City	0-4
1967-68	5th	15.01.68	H	Ammanford	5-0
	6th	19.02.68	A	Newport Co.	1-3
1968-69	5th	14.01.69	H	Newport Co.	0-0
Runners-	Replay	21.01.69	A	Newport Co.	0-0
up	2nd Replay	28.01.69	H	Newport Co.	2-1
	6th	05.02.69	A	Wrexham	1-1
	Replay	26.02.69	H	Wrexham	2-1
	S.-Final	12.03.69	H	Hereford Utd.	1-0
	Final	22.04.69	H	Cardiff City	1-3
	Final	29.04.68	A	Cardiff	0-2
1969-70	5th	10.01.70	H	Barry Town	4-0
	6th	27.01.70	H	Oswestry T.	8-0
	S.-Final	11.03.70	A	Cardiff City	2-2
	Replay	25.03.70	H	Cardiff City	0-2
1970-71	5th	07.01.71	A	Llanidloes	4-2
	6th	17.02.71	A	Chester	1-2
1971-72	5th	03.01.72	H	Cardiff City	0-2
1972-73	4th	09.01.73	H	Newport Co.	0-0
	Replay	16.01.73	A	Newport Co.	0-3
1973-74	4th	15.12.73	H	Stourbridge	1-2
1974-75	4th	06.01.75	A	Kidderminster	0-0
	Replay	20.01.75	H	Kidderminster	3-0
	5th	12.02.75	A	Newport Co.	1-1
	Replay	17.02.75	H	Newport Co.	1-2
1975-76	4th	13.12.75	H	Cardiff Corries	6-0
	5th	17.02.75	A	Cardiff City	1-1
	Replay	02.03.75	H	Cardiff City	0-3
1976-77	4th	18.01.77	H	Newport Co.	4-1
	5th	07.02.77	A	Wrexham	1-4
1977-78	4th	17.01.78	H	Newport Co.	0-0
	Replay	24.01.78	A	Newport Co.	0-1
1978-79	4th	29.01.79	H	Kidderminster	6-1
	5th	12.03.79	A	Wrexham	2-3
1979-80	4th	22.01.80	H	Pontllanfraith	4-0
	5th	25.02.80	H	Kidderminster	2-0
	S.-Final	25.03.80	H	Shrewsbury T.	2-2
	Replay	15.04.80	H	Shrewsbury T.	2-2
	(Lost on penalties)				5-6

Season	Round	Date	H/A	Opponents	Score	Season	Round	Date	H/A	Opponents	Score
1980-81 *Winners*	3rd	25.11.80	H	Caerleon	5-1	**1985-86**	3rd	27.11.85	A	Haverfordwest	6-2
	4th	24.01.81	A	Merthyr T.	2-0		4th	15.01.86	A	Sully	2-1
	5th	18.02.81	H	Maesteg Park	4-1		5th	13.02.86	H	Kidderminster	1-1
	S.-Final	07.04.81	A	Wrexham	2-2		Replay	26.02.86	A	Kidderminster	0-4
	S.-Final	14.04.81	H	Wrexham	1-1						
				(won on away goals)		**1986-87**	3rd	11.11.86	H	Newport Co.	1-3
	Final	04.05.81	H	Hereford Utd.	1-0	**1987-88**	3rd	25.11.87	A	Cwmbrân	4-0
	Final	11.05.81	A	Hereford Utd.	1-1		4th	12.01.88	H	Merthyr T.	0-2
1981-82 *Winners*	3rd	01.12.81	A	Stafford Rangers	4-0	**1988-89** *Winners*	3rd	23.11.88	A	Merthyr T.	3-0
	4th	22.12.81	H	Worcester City	6-0		4th	17.01.89	H	Caersws	0-0
	5th	09.02.82	H	Colwyn Bay	2-2		Replay	31.01.89	A	Caersws	2-0
	Replay	02.03.82	H	Colwyn Bay	3-0		5th	14.02.89	A	Wrexham	4-1
				(Colwyn elected to come to Vetch)			S.-Final	11.04.87	C	Barry Town	1-0
	S.-Final	16.03.82	A	Bangor City	2-1		S.-Final	18.04.89	H	Barry Town	3-1
	S.-Final	20.04.82	H	Bangor City	0-0		Final	21.04.89	H	Kidderminster	5-0
	Final	11.05.82	A	Cardiff City	0-0				C = Cardiff			
	Final	12.05.82	H	Cardiff City	2-1	**1989-90**	3rd	07.11.89	H	Merthyr T.	0-3
1982-83 *Winners*	3rd	08.12.82	A	Spencer Works	3-0	**1990-91** *Winners*	3rd	30.10.90	H	Llanelli	8-1
	4th	18.01.83	H	Shrewsbury T.	2-1		4th	30.01.91	A	Merthyr T.	2-1
	5th	09.02.83	H	Hereford Utd.	3-1		5th	20.02.91	A	Colwyn Bay	1-1
	S.-Final	08.03.86	A	Colwyn Bay	1-0		Replay	05.03.91	H	Colwyn Bay	2-1
	S.-Final	22.03.83	H	Colwyn Bay	3-0		S.-Final	03.04.91	A	Barry Town	2-2
	Final	10.05.83	A	Wrexham	2-1		S.-Final	18.04.91	H	Barry Town	1-0
	Final	17.05.83	H	Wrexham	2-0		Final	19.04.91	C	Wrexham	2-0
1983-84	3rd	30.11.83	H	Abercynon	5-2			C = National Stadium, Cardiff				
	4th	10.01.84	H	Bangor City	4-2	**1991-92**	3rd	29.10.91	A	Merthyr T.	2-0
	5th	08.02.84	A	Barry Town	1-1		4th	06.01.92	A	Kidderminster	3-1
	Replay	21.02.84	H	Barry Town	2-1		5th	05.02.92	H	Cardiff City	0-1
	S.-Final	20.03.84	A	Shrewsbury T.	0-2						
	S.-Final	03.04.84	H	Shrewsbury T.	1-0	**1992-93**	3rd	27.10.92	A	Merthyr T.	0-2
1984-85	3rd	04.12.84	H	Spencer Works	1-1	**1993-94**	3rd	09.11.93	H	Merthyr T.	0-0
	Replay	12.12.84	A	Spencer Works	5-0		Replay	02.12.93	A	Merthyr T.	2-1
	4th	29.01.85	H	Sully	7-1		4th	04.12.93	A	Rhyl	2-0
	5th	27.02.85	H	Hereford Utd.	2-0		5th	25.01.94	H	Hereford Utd.	1-0
	S.-Final	02.04.85	H	Shrewsbury T.	2-2		S.-Final	14.04.94	H	Cardiff City	1-2
	S.-Final	16.04.85	A	Shrewsbury T.	1-2		S.-Final	28.04.94	A	Cardiff City	1-4

Rory Keane thinks he's a goalkeeper v. Arsenal.

Index